Managing Behavior in Organizations

FIFTH EDITION

MANAGING BEHAVIOR IN ORGANIZATIONS

Jerald Greenberg

Prentice Hall

Boston   Columbus   Indianapolis   New York   San Francisco   Upper Saddle River
Amsterdam   Cape Town   Dubai   London   Madrid   Milan   Munich   Paris
Montreal   Toronto   Delhi   Mexico City   Sao Paulo   Sydney   Hong Kong
Seoul   Singapore   Taipei   Tokyo

Editorial Director: Sally Yagan
Acquisitions Editor: Jennifer M. Collins
Editorial Project Manager: Claudia Fernandes
Product Development Manager:
Ashley Santora
Director of Marketing: Patrice Lumumba
Jones
Marketing Manager: Nikki Jones
Marketing Assistant: Ian Gold
Senior Managing Editor: Judy Leale
Project Manager: Kelly Warsak
Senior Operations Supervisor: Arnold Vila
Operations Specialist: Diane Peirano
Manager, Rights and Permissions:
Charles Morris

Associate Director Central Design: Jayne Conte
Cover Designer: Margaret Kenselaar
Manager, Cover Visual Research &
Permissions: Karen Sanatar
Cover Art: Painting by Julie Karabenick
www.karabenick-art.net
Media Project Manager, Production:
Lisa Rinaldi
Media Project Manager: Denise Vaughn
Full-Service Project Management: Thistle Hill
Publishing Services, LLC
Composition: Integra Software Services
Printer/Binder: Edwards Brothers
Cover Printer: Lehigh-Phoenix Color
Text Font: 10/12 New Baskerville

Library of Congress Cataloging-in-Publication Data

Greenberg, Jerald.
    Managing behavior in organizations / Jerald Greenberg.—5th ed.
        p. cm.
    Includes bibliographical references and index.
    ISBN-13: 978-0-13-199238-2 (pbk.)
    ISBN-10: 0-13-199238-4 (pbk.)
    1. Organizational behavior.   I. Title.
HD58.7.G7176 2009
658.3—dc22

                                                    2009007228

10 9 8 7 6 5 4 3 2 1

Prentice Hall
is an imprint of

www.pearsonhighered.com

ISBN 13: 978-0-13-199238-2
ISBN 10:   0-13-199238-4

To Carolyn, for being my world.
—Jerald Greenberg

Brief Contents

Contents

Preface

NEW TO THE FIFTH EDITION

Specific details regarding updates to the fifth edition can be found later in the Preface. However, highlights of changes include:

➤ New chapter-opening cases for all 14 chapters.

➤ Brand new feature—Back to the Case—which shows students how the chapter material relates to the opening case.

➤ Updated organizational examples in the Winning Practices sections throughout the text.

➤ Updated corporate examples of concepts throughout the text.

➤ Additional coverage of personality in Chapter 3.

➤ Additional coverage of emotions in Chapter 4.

As this book goes to press, the world is struggling to cope with fallout from a "perfect storm" of human frailties that has led it to the brink of financial disaster. Although economists surely would offer a more statistically sophisticated analysis, to me, the financial crisis reflects the inherent irrationality and imperfect nature of individuals, groups, and the organizations in which they work. Here, I speak of the arrogance and greed of some corporate executives (of several venerable brokerage firms), investors' seemingly blind faith in individuals trusted as experts (securities analysts), and the collective belief that ostensibly risky investments (financial instruments backed by subprime mortgages) would be safe. History has revealed otherwise.

Although I am shaken by this crisis as a citizen of the planet, the scientist within me cannot help but marvel at what it reveals about the stunning complexity of human behavior in the workplace. It showcases precisely why, in the final analysis, it is people more than anything else that make the ultimate difference in organizations. As such, it reinforces our ongoing investment in developing the rich tapestry of *organizational behavior* (or *OB*, as it's commonly called) as a field to study and to apply. And of course, it also illustrates precisely what makes grappling with these complexities so worthwhile.

ABOUT THIS BOOK

The fifth edition of *Managing Behavior in Organizations* does not promise to shed light on the world's financial state, or even to address finances at all. However, it will leave readers with a good understanding of the factors that lead us to make seemingly irrational decisions, that promote our trust in others, and that make us greedy (or, at least, willing to try to get away with greedy behavior). These dynamics, and scores of others covered in this book, are useful not only for understanding financially motivated behavior but for shedding light on a myriad of situations people are likely to face on a daily basis in their work lives. To say, then, that its approach is broad would be an understatement. The book covers vast, and vitally important, territory because so too does the field on which it reports.

This, together with the brevity of this book (relative to traditional, hardcover books that are twice as long), makes it apparent that it's not intended to provide an in-depth account of the field of OB. Instead of covering every surface of the field's terrain, this book simply offers a tour of the scientific and practical highlights of OB housed in a succinct package. It gets "right to the point" by focusing on essential concepts and practices that students *really* must know. Fortunately, the thousands of students to whom I have taught this material over the years have done a fine job (albeit sometimes with painful bluntness) of letting me know precisely what is wheat and what is chaff. It was with an eye toward answering their proverbial question, "What's the most important stuff?" that I wrote this book.

For Whom Is This Book Intended?

This book is aimed squarely at readers who have no special background or training in the social sciences. It is designed to be read by students taking their first class in organizational behavior, organizational psychology, or management. Specifically, these readers include:

➤ Undergraduate students (in both two-year and four-year colleges)

➤ MBA students, and those in related masters-level programs

➤ Practicing managers and executives in corporate training programs

Readers who know nothing about this topic needn't be afraid of using this book. Instead, they should welcome the fact that it is aimed at them and that it promises to keep them from making such a proclamation of ignorance by the time they finish it. Everybody has to start learning a topic somewhere, and this book is designed to provide this foundation for the field of OB. Indeed, it is a designed to be a stand-alone guide to the essentials of OB.

Still, some professors who've assigned previous editions of this book to their classes have chosen to supplement it with additional materials such as cases, exercises, and readings that reflect their own particular approach to teaching OB. That is completely understandable. In fact, rather than attempting to be an all-inclusive package that dictates precisely what and how to teach, this book offers instructors the ultimate in flexibility. Whether an instructor is teaching OB using the case method, an experiential approach, a seminar format, distance learning, or a traditional series of lectures, students must recognize, understand, and appreciate the essentials of OB as a practical and scientific field. Regardless of the mode of delivery, it is necessary for students to understand the basics of the field. In a nutshell, this book is designed to provide that understanding.

A Balanced Approach to Research, Theory, and Practice

Many textbooks take a particularly narrow approach to whatever field they are describing. In the field of OB, some texts focus primarily on research and theory whereas others focus primarily on managerial practice. Some promise "strategic" approaches and still others offer "international" orientations. In my opinion, these skewed orientations are misleading and do readers a disservice insofar as they fail to reflect the true nature of the field of OB.

By its very nature, OB is a deliberate blend of all these things—an applied science in the truest sense. And, this carefully balanced orientation is reflected in this book. Accordingly, I have prepared this book such that readers will come away with a firm understanding of *what* should be done—and what currently *is* being done—to improve the functioning of organizations and the satisfaction of people who work in them, as well as the research and theory that accounts for *why* these practices are effective.

This balanced orientation is reflected on each page of the book, but let me offer a few examples to make it clear what I mean. Take Chapter 6, on motivation. Here, my treatment of the various classic theories of motivation is framed in terms of the central practical question: How do you motivate employees? The same may be said for Chapter 12 on culture, creativity and innovation. Here, readers come away with not only a basic understanding of the concepts of culture and creativity, but also the very practical matter of how to promote a culture in which creativity abounds. Virtually every chapter captures this dual allegiance to theory and practice.

Because OB is a field predicated on sound scientific research, I used the occasion of revising this book as an opportunity to highlight specific examples of the research that OB scholars conduct. This edition of the book contains several accounts of OB research to help students understand the nature of this craft. In each such instance, I describe the question the researchers were attempting to answer, how they went about finding the answer, and what the findings reveal about the question they raised. A graph (the "talking graphics" to which I refer below) highlights and explains the findings in a manner that ties them back to the question of interest. By stripping away all the technical details, my descriptions of contemporary OB research are designed to be not only informative, but importantly, interesting as well.

These accounts of OB research are designed to give students a good idea of *how* scientists come to understand behavior in organizations. I believe that it is important to describe some scientific studies not only as an end in themselves, but to emphasize the key point that there is a sound scientific basis for the useful advice offered by OB practitioners; it is not a field predicated simply on what appears to be common sense. "Some" is the operative word here. Rather than making the book too laborious by explaining research support behind every point, I have sprinkled a few well-chosen examples of OB research throughout this book selectively, wherever they appeared to offer the greatest value.

KEEPING ABREAST OF THE SHIFTING LANDSCAPE

Keeping up with the ever-changing world of organizations is a full-time job. I know, because it's mine. As a researcher, consultant, educator, and author, I spend my working hours probing into the world of organizational behavior, which at cocktail parties I have been known to define as the field that explains "what makes people tick" on the job (I've already learned better than to say that I'm an OB doctor!). In the almost four decades I have studied, taught, and written in this field, my standard cocktail party line has not changed (much to the chagrin of my wife), although the field surely has.

Several of the topics we regarded as central while I watched the Watergate hearings have faded into the background as others have gained prominence. Research findings I took for granted when my hair covered my ears like headphones are seen in a new light today, when I consider myself fortunate to have hair at all. And, those organizations in which I applied my knowledge while wearing my best double-knit polyester slacks have undergone dramatic transformations—if, like those pants, they still even exist. Such core issues as what people do, how and why they do it, and even where they do it, are more important than ever today, but they cannot be understood from the lava lamp mentality of the 1970s.

New Topics Covered

Importantly, to understand truly the world of organizations today, we must seriously consider changes in organizational theory and practice that were made since the previous edition of this book was published. Taken together, sweeping changes in the economy, technology, and the world's new political realities have revolutionized the functioning of organizations and the ways people work within them. Any reasonable effort to characterize the world of OB must reflect these rapid advances. Indeed, keeping abreast of such changes is both the challenge and the joy of writing textbooks in this field. Finding a sufficiently stable terrain about which to write amidst an ever-shifting landscape is my ongoing mission in revising this book. It was with an eye toward chronicling the most current thinking about the state of the field of OB that I prepared this book. As a result, it contains topics that are completely new to this edition as well as material that was presented in different contexts or with different emphases in earlier editions. Specifically, here is just a sampling of topics that are new or greatly expanded in the fifth edition of this book: multifoci approach to justice (Chapter 2), emotional intelligence (Chapter 4), preferential and nonpreferential affirmative action (Chapter 5), executive compensation (Chapter 6), ideals (Chapter 7), battling rumors at Coca-Cola (Chapter 8), person sensitivity bias (Chapter 10), perspectives on management innovation (Chapter 12), strong vs. weak organizational cultures (Chapter 12), and the Sarbanes-Oxley Act as a force for organizational change (Chapter 14).

These additions, and many others, reflect growing interest in these topics in recent years. They were guided by informal feedback from professors and students using the previous edition of this book, formal feedback by reviewers, as well as my own assessment of what's happening in the field of OB. I resisted the temptation to include the latest fads. To have done otherwise would have triggered a departure from my mission of focusing on the essentials—in addition to dating the book prematurely and diminishing its usefulness for readers. As such, changes in content were made only where warranted.

Newly Organized Chapters

In the time since the fourth edition of this book was published, the field has witnessed vast growth in the field of emotions. I have added coverage to this topic by devoting half of Chapter 4 to it and now blending it with coverage of stress, with which it is connected conceptually and empirically. In so doing, I also was able to add more new material to the discussion of personality in Chapter 3, which also has seen a great deal of growth in recent years.

All New Chapter-Opening Cases: "Making the Case for . . ."

Unlike most other brief OB texts, this book includes a chapter-opening case that introduces and leads into the material. Entitled *Making the Case for . . .* , it is designed to do precisely what the name implies—to describe a real organizational case that foreshadows and suggests the importance of the material in each chapter. Although such cases are more commonly found in full-featured OB texts than in brief ones, I included them here because they play the vital pedagogical function of establishing the relevance of the topic. And, insofar as the true importance of OB may be found in the insight it provides into real organizational situations, these cases play a critical role in conveying the nature of the field.

In my quest to keep the book as current as possible, *each of these 14 cases is brand-new to this edition.* These reflect a broad range of organizations, including giant corporations (American Express, Chapter 3), startup firms (Better Place, Chapter 9), retail organizations (Costco, Chapter 6), wholesale organizations (AmerisourceBergen, Chapter 12), government organizations (NASA, Chapter 13), and even professional athletics organizations (National Basketball Association, Chapter 4; NASCAR, Chapter 7).

New Feature: "Back to the Case"

Just as each chapter begins with a brand new case, it also ends with an opportunity for students to apply the material in the chapter to analyzing that case. These sections, entitled ***Back to the Case,*** consist of questions that call for identifying concepts, applying theories, recommending practices, suggesting ways of overcoming limitations, and/or otherwise attempting to draw connections between the opening case and the chapter material. In short, this new feature encourages students to think about the text in ways that bring it to life. With the bread of these chapter-closing exercises and chapter-opening cases, each chapter's meaty contents is now filling in a tempting but still good-for-you sandwich.

COMMITMENT TO PEDAGOGICAL FEATURES

It would be a mistake to take this book's diminutive size as an indication that it is short on pedagogical features. This could not be farther from the truth. In fact, its package of pedagogical features is stronger than ever.

Enhanced and Thoroughly Updated Company Examples

In this book, it is not only the chapter-opening cases, but organizational examples sprinkled throughout that reflect the varied nature of OB in today's organizations. Within each chapter, readers will find many examples of organizational practices that illustrate the substantive points being made. This represents my deliberate attempt to bring OB to life by showing how it is used in organizations.

This is particularly apparent in the special boxed section entitled ***Winning Practices*** that appears in each chapter. These sections call readers' attention to current organizational practices that illustrate one or more key OB concepts from each chapter. They provide close-up examples of specific ways in which organizations have been using OB principles to improve a wide variety of different aspects of organizational functioning.

Of course, it is neither practical nor appropriate to devote such close attention to all organizational practices. In many cases, I illustrate the connections between OB concepts and organizational practices in the form of separate tables (e.g., Table 10.1 listing examples of successful strategic examples in organizations, and Table 9.3, offering team success stories). These tables supplement many examples of company practices presented as brief mentions or descriptions within the text or in bullet points. Importantly, to illustrate that OB is applicable to a broad array of organizations, the examples range from references to giant companies well known for their sensitivity to OB principles (e.g., General Electric) to tiny startups that are struggling to gain traction.

I also should note that I have gone out of my way to ensure that the company examples I give in this book are accurate and applicable to the points being made, at least at press time. Given how rapidly today's companies change names due to mergers or simply go out of business, researching these updates has been a time-consuming and sometimes eye-opening exercise when considering that we're talking about the comings and goings of once venerable organizations. CellularOne became Cingular, but is now AT&T; Barclays purchased (for now, at least) the bankrupt Lehman Brothers; and DaimlerChrysler is now back to being the separate companies Daimler and Chrysler, as they were only 10 years earlier. And although the once competing satellite radio giants Sirius and XM have merged, they now face a more formidable enemy—a rocky economy that has kept people from buying new cars (where the vast majority of satellite radios are installed), thereby shrinking the pool of potential new subscribers.

And as if this scorecard isn't enough of a mess, I shudder to think of the number of once-aspiring startups whose names I had to delete because they no longer exist. I suspect that by the time you read this some of these changes will be history as well. This is unfortunate, but inevitable, of course; but if nothing else, it underscores my point about the ever-changing nature of organizations (as chronicled in Chapter 14).

Enhanced Tables and Illustrations

This book is more richly illustrated and full of descriptive tables than its predecessors—and most other brief books in this field. I have incorporated these features into this edition because I am convinced that charts and diagrams help students understand and remember ideas that otherwise get camouflaged in the body of the text. I don't take tables and figures lightly. Over the years, my students have always expressed their appreciation for exhibits that capture the essence of ideas and key points, leading me to ensure that the ones in this book are as useful as possible.

New tables have been added, and where beneficial, previous ones have been updated and/or clarified. I am particularly fond of juxtaposing points to help make them salient. So, for example, in making the point in Chapter 14 about how the Sarbanes-Oxley Act has led to organizational change, I prepared a table (Table 14.2) to compare various business practices before and after passage of the act. Likewise, in Table 3.5, I describe what it takes for 360-degree feedback to be successful and juxtapose these points with the corresponding consequences of not following these suggestions. Many more such tables may be found in this book. This, I believe, highlights the point better than might be done in a paragraph or two in the text by making the core points salient.

Likewise, I am fond of using diagrams to illustrate (literally) my points, just as I might sketch them on a board for students. In this book, however, these can be more elaborate and are rendered far more artistically. For example, to clarify the nature of nature and nurture in the formation of personality, and the joint roles of personality and situations as determinants of behavior in Chapter 3, I illustrate these ideas graphically in Figures 3.1 and 3.2.

Also noteworthy among this book's graphics are figures using "*talking graphics.*" These are graphs summarizing the findings of OB studies in a manner that highlights the key conclusions to be drawn from them. By reinforcing the points made in both the figure captions and the body of the text itself, these diagrams are useful for helping the findings of OB research "pop out" before the reader, thus greatly facilitating interpretation. Of course, more visually oriented learners will find these especially beneficial.

Return of Popular Pedagogical Features

Back by popular demand are several of the most highly regarded pedagogical features from the previous edition of this book. These features, found in each chapter, are as follows:

➤ *Learning Objectives.*   At the beginning of each chapter, readers are provided a list of six specific things they should be able to do after reading that chapter. These all begin with action words such as "define," "describe," "identify," and "distinguish." These learning objectives highlight exactly what readers can expect to get out of each chapter.

➤ *Three Good Reasons Why You Should Care About. . . .*   Understandably, today's busy students may be prone to challenge the relevance of material, asking what value it has to them. Assuming that students are most receptive to learning about topics that have some recognizable benefits to themselves, these sections begin each chapter by indicating precisely why readers should care about the topic at hand.

➤ *You Be the Consultant.*   These brief sections describe a hypothetical organizational problem and then challenge readers to draw on the material to find ways of solving it. This simple exercise is designed to bring the material to life by getting students to think about how each chapter's material may be applied to practical organizational problems.

I also have retained in each chapter the two skills-based exercises that were so popular in earlier editions of this book. These are as follows:

➤ *Self-Assessment Exercise.*   These exercises are designed to provide readers insight into key aspects of their own individual attitudes and/or behavior relevant to the material covered.

➤ *Group Exercise.*   These are hands-on experiences requiring the joint efforts of small groups of students to help illustrate or to promote thinking about key phenomena described in the text.

These exercises can be an important part of students' learning experiences. They not only expose students to some of the phenomena described in the text on a first-hand basis, but they also stimulate critical thinking about those phenomena. Of equal importance, they offer fascinating insights into oneself and the OB phenomena under consideration.

TEACHING AND LEARNING AIDS

This book is accompanied by a very helpful set of materials to aid both students and instructors. These teaching aids and learning aids were prepared especially for this book.

Companion Website for Students

Students reading this book will benefit greatly by using special features found in its Companion Website: http://www.pearsonhighered.com/Greenberg/.

> ➤ *Learning Objectives*   Each chapter includes six specific learning objectives. These are things students should be able to do (e.g., key concepts to recognize and understand) after reading each chapter. Readers should find these useful both *before* studying a chapter, by cluing them to things to look for while reading, and *after* studying a chapter, by providing a checklist of key points covered.

> ➤ *Interactive Study Guide*   The book's Companion Website also includes a set of test questions based on the material appearing in each chapter. The questions are of three different types: multiple-choice, true-false, and essay. To make these effective as a study aid, feedback on these tests is provided instantly. Also, to stimulate thinking about each question, helpful "hints" are just a mouse-click away.

ACKNOWLEDGMENTS: SOME SINCERE WORDS OF THANKS

Writing a book such as this is an endeavor one cannot undertake alone. Acknowledging this, I welcome the opportunity to thank the many hard-working reviewers, publishing professionals, and colleagues whose efforts have made this book possible.

Insightful Reviewers

To begin, I thank my colleagues who have provided valuable suggestions and comments in response to various drafts of this and earlier editions of this book. These include:

> ➤ Richard Grover, *University of Southern Maine*
> ➤ Jeffrey Miles, *University of the Pacific*
> ➤ Michael Buckley, *University of Oklahoma*
> ➤ Suzyn Ornstein, *Suffolk University*
> ➤ Fabia Fernandes, *Boise State University*
> ➤ Pal A. Fadil, *Valdosta University*
> ➤ William A. Walker, *University of Houston*
> ➤ Henry Moon, *London Business School*
> ➤ Raymond T. LaManna, *New York Medical College*
> ➤ Charles Albano, *Farleigh Dickinson University*
> ➤ Leonard Glick, *Northeastern University*

Talented Publishing Professionals

Second, I wish to thank the editorial, production, and marketing teams at Prentice Hall. My editor, Jennifer Collins, and project manager, Claudia Fernandes, provided the steadfast support, along with the "gentle reminders," required to bring this book to fruition. Jennifer's contributions to shaping the form, tone, and direction of this book were immeasurable. I am indebted as well to Kelly Warsak and Angela Williams Urquhart for guiding this book through the production process. Their tireless efforts (not to mention their tolerance for my bouts of impatience) transformed my ramblings into the beautiful book you have before you. Nikki Jones also must be acknowledged for her insightful marketing advice that helped me make key decisions at various stages of this project. My efforts to acknowledge the dedicated folks at Pearson would not be complete without also thanking Editorial Director Sally Yagan for assembling the best management and organizational behavior publishing group in the business. I am truly indebted to these hard-working professionals for lending their talents to this project.

Generous Colleagues and Students

In conclusion, I wish to thank the many kind and dedicated professionals throughout the world who have supported my work in many ways over the past few years as I wrote this book—most importantly, by providing the intellectual environments that promoted my own learning about OB. This includes colleagues and students in the United States at the Ohio State University, and the RAND Corporation's Institute for Civil Justice; in Australia, at the University of Queensland; in New Zealand, at the University of Otago; and in Singapore, at the National University of Singapore. To have worked with students and colleagues at these fine institutions has been a privilege that has enriched me as a scholar, teaching me a great deal about OB both intellectually and experientially. To have the backing of such a generous cast of teachers, researchers, and practitioners is something I don't take for granted. I can only hope the scores of individuals involved are well aware of my gratitude.

Jerald Greenberg

Managing Behavior in Organizations

Chapter 1

The Field of Organizational Behavior

Learning Objectives

After reading this chapter, you will be able to:

1. **DEFINE** organizational behavior (OB).

2. **DESCRIBE** the major characteristics of the field of OB.

3. **DISTINGUISH** between the Theory X and Theory Y philosophies of management.

4. **IDENTIFY** the fundamental assumptions of the field of OB.

5. **DESCRIBE** the historical roots of the field of OB.

6. **CHARACTERIZE** the nature of the field of OB today.

3 GOOD REASONS why you should care about . . .

Organizational Behavior

You should care about organizational behavior because:

1. Understanding the dynamics of behavior in organizations is essential to achieving personal success as a manager, regardless of your area of specialization.

2. Principles of organizational behavior are involved in making people both productive on their jobs and satisfied with them.

3. To achieve success in today's rapidly changing environment, the individuals who run organizations must successfully address a wide variety of OB issues.

Making the Case for Organizational Behavior

Floyd's Barbershop: A Cut Above the Rest

In 2001, when the O'Brien brothers, Paul, Ron, and Bill, opened Floyd's 99 Barbershop in Denver, their only experience in the hair care business was as customers. Lacking tonsorial training, their particular skills, it seems, lay not in grooming hair but grooming loyal, creative, and hard-working employees.

(continued)

1

Floyd's, named after the iconic barber from television's classic, *The Andy Griffith Show,* was conceived to be a friendly, neighborhood place like the one owned by its namesake. But that's where the similarity ends. In the O'Briens' vision, Floyd's was not your father's traditional barbershop, nor was it a plush, unisex salon that smelled like hair chemicals. Instead, Floyd's was designed to be a hip and lively place for contemporary men. In many locations—there are now 27 Floyd's 99 Barbershops in 6 states—popular music is heard (played by live DJs on Saturdays), posters of rock stars adorn the walls, and sporting events are shown on plasma TV screens. The place is so hip that the Floyd's shop in Hollywood, California was a location for an episode of the HBO series, *Entourage.* It's no wonder that Bill O'Brien refers to Floyd's as "Hard Rock meets the barbershop."

Stylists at Floyd's know all the latest, contemporary cuts but also include old-fashioned services such as neck shaves with each haircut, and at reasonable prices ("less than twice the price of lunch" according to Rob O'Brien). Because it's impractical for today's highly mobile young men to commit to making appointments for haircuts, Floyd's doesn't take them. Yet, acknowledging the importance of timely service, customers can phone-in their place in line an hour or so ahead of arriving. But for anyone who does have to wait for his favorite barber (whose working hours can be checked online), it's not so bad because pool tables and computers with Internet access are available to help pass the time.

Not only are the O'Brien brothers attuned to what their customers want, they also are keenly sensitive to their employees. Illustrating this, consider how the O'Briens responded in March of 2003 when a blizzard struck Denver. When the nightclub next door collapsed onto their shop, managers pleaded with firefighters to rummage through the mounds of debris to retrieve their employees' tools and personal belongings. Unfortunately, the building housing Floyd's had to be demolished due to structural damage, leading to concerns about the business's future. Although the building was broken, the O'Briens' spirit was not broken—and employees came to appreciate this. Until a new shop could be built, complete with chrome and leather chairs and a barber pole out front, current employees were absorbed into other Floyd's locations and nobody lost a job. In fact, a billboard and the company's Web site made light of the events, adding to the belief that all would be well.

Although the O'Briens don't know how to cut hair, they surely know how to trim through layers of uncertainty to assuage their employees' fears. Employees and industry pundits would be hard pressed to challenge Bill's wife, Karen, who said of Floyd's that, "The founders' passion, personalities, and their constant desire to make a positive impact on people, along with the support of a qualified and professional management team, have poised the company for national and international expansion."

There can be no mistaking the uniqueness of Floyd's 99 Barbershops. The chain has filled a void between expensive salons and discount haircutters. It offers customers a place where they can be assured of getting a contemporary cut with old-school service in a comfortable, fun environment. This has been a successful business model for the O'Briens, but only part of it. The other key to Floyd's success has to do with its approach to employees. Company employees enjoy a friendly atmosphere. When you work at Floyd's, you get the feeling that you're part of a family that really cares about you. And this care, it's clear, has translated into care for customers. So when customers return—and that they do—they are likely to find their favorite barber still there to trim their locks. Although employee turnover runs high in the hair care business—about 40 percent in the United States' 80,000 salons—at Floyd's, customer loyalty has translated to employee loyalty.[1] And for this, both the company and its customers can be assured of not getting clipped.

Behind Floyd's success is a management team that, it's safe to say, recognizes the importance of the human side of work. There can be no organizations without people, of course. So, no matter how sophisticated a company's equipment may be, how talented its employees are, or how healthy its bottom line is, people problems can bring an organization down very quickly. Just imagine, for example, what would happen if all the barbers at Floyd's walked out in protest. On the other hand, organizations in which people work happily and effectively, such as Floyd's, can benefit greatly. Hence, it makes sense to realize that the human side of work is critical to the effective functioning—and basic existence—of organizations. It is this people-centered orientation that is taken in the field of *organizational behavior*—the topic of this book.

This chapter will introduce you to the field of organizational behavior—its characteristics, its history, and the tools it uses to learn about the behavior of people in organizations. We will begin by formally defining the field, describing exactly what it is and what it seeks to accomplish. Following this, we will summarize the history of the field of organizational behavior, tracing its roots from its origins to its emergence as a modern science. Finally, we will outline the methods scientists use to learn about the behavior of people in organizations.

WHAT IS ORGANIZATIONAL BEHAVIOR AND WHY DOES IT MATTER?

Before going any further, it is necessary for you to understand exactly what we mean by organizational behavior and why it is important to learn about it.

Organizational Behavior: A Definition

As we have been implying, the field of **organizational behavior** (or **OB,** as it is commonly called) deals with human behavior in organizations. Formally defined, organizational behavior is the multidisciplinary field that seeks knowledge of behavior in organizational settings by systematically studying individual, group, and organizational processes.[2] This knowledge is used both by scientists interested in understanding human behavior and by practitioners interested in enhancing organizational effectiveness and individual well-being. In this book we will highlight these dual purposes, focusing both on explaining the nature of this scientific knowledge as well as on how it has been—or may be—used for practical purposes. This dual focus is fundamental to the field of organizational behavior because it is considered an applied science.

Characteristics of the Field of OB

Our definition of OB highlights four central characteristics of the field that we now will examine more closely.

OB applies the scientific method to practical managerial problems

The definition of OB refers to seeking knowledge and to studying behavioral processes. Although it is neither as sophisticated as the study of physics or chemistry nor as mature as these disciplines, the orientation of the field of OB is still scientific in

Table 1.1   Research Methods Used in OB: A Summary

The field of OB is based on knowledge derived from scientific research. The major techniques used to conduct this research are summarized here.

Research Method	Description	Comments
Survey research	Questionnaires are developed and administered to people to measure how they feel about various aspects of themselves, their jobs, and their organizations. Responses to some questionnaires are compared to others, or to actual behaviors, to see how various concepts are interrelated.	This technique is the most popular one used in the field of OB.
Experimental research	Behavior is carefully studied—either in a controlled setting (a lab) or in an actual company (the field)—to see how a particular variable that is systematically varied affects other aspects of behavior.	This technique makes it possible to learn about cause–effect relationships.
Naturalistic observation	A nonempirical technique in which a scientist systematically records various events and behaviors observed in a work setting.	This technique is subject to the biases of the observer.
Case study	A thorough description of a series of events that occurred in a particular organization.	Findings from case studies may not be generalizable to other organizations.

nature. Thus, like other scientific fields, OB seeks to develop a base of knowledge by using an empirical, research-based approach. That is, it is based on the systematic development of theory and precise measurement of the phenomena of interest.[3] For an overview of some of the research techniques used in the field of OB, see Table 1.1. Although we might not always make it explicit, the points we make about OB in this book are all based on the findings of the latest research.

Why is it so important to learn about behavior in organizational settings? To social scientists, learning about human behavior on the job is valuable for its own sake. After all, scientists are interested in the generation of knowledge—in this case, insight into the effects of organizations on people and the effects of people on organizations. This is not to say, however, that such knowledge has no value outside scientific circles. Far from it! OB specialists also apply knowledge from scientific studies, putting it to practical use. As they seek to improve organizational functioning and the quality of life of people working in organizations, they rely heavily on knowledge derived from OB research.

Thus, there are both scientific and applied sides to the field of OB—facets that not only coexist but that complement each other as well. (Because we have all experienced OB phenomena, it sometimes seems commonsensical, leading us to wonder sometimes why the scientific approach is necessary. However, as you will see in the Group Exercise on pages 31–32, our common sense is not always a reliable guide to the complexities of human behavior at work.)

OB focuses on three levels of analysis: Individuals, groups, and organizations

To fully appreciate behavior in organizations, OB specialists do not focus exclusively on individuals acting alone. After all, in organizational settings people frequently work together in groups and teams. Furthermore, people—alone and in groups—both influence and are influenced by their work environments. Considering this, it should not be surprising to learn that the field of OB focuses on three interrelated levels of analysis—individuals, groups, and organizations.

The field of OB recognizes that all three levels of analysis must be considered to comprehend fully the complex dynamics of behavior in organizations. Careful attention to all three levels of analysis is a central theme in modern OB and will be reflected fully throughout this text (see Figure 1.1). Consider these particulars.

➤ We will describe how OB scientists are concerned with individual perceptions, attitudes, and motives. This orientation, focusing primarily on the behavior of individuals, is known as the **micro approach** to OB. As indicated in the lower left corner of Figure 1.1, we cover this approach in Chapters 2–6 of this book.

➤ At the other extreme, the field of OB also examines organizations as a whole—the way they are structured and operate in their environments and the effects of their operations on the individuals and groups within them. As shown in the upper-right corner of Figure 1.1, this so-called **macro approach** to OB is covered in Chapters 12–14.

➤ Between these two extremes, and sharing some characteristics of each, is the behavior of individuals in groups and of groups themselves. For example, in Chapters 7–11, we will describe such phenomena as how people communicate, make decisions, and lead others.

It is important to recognize that the lines between these approaches are not clear-cut, nor are they meant to be. Instead, they reflect the broad continuum of foci (indicated by the dashed line in Figure 1.1) that characterize the field of OB.

OB is multidisciplinary in nature

When you consider the broad range of issues and approaches taken by the field of OB, it is easy to appreciate that the field is multidisciplinary in nature. By this, we mean that it draws on a wide variety of social science disciplines. Rather than studying a topic from only one particular perspective, the field of OB is likely to consider a wide variety of approaches. These range from the highly individual-oriented approach of psychology, through the more group-oriented approach of sociology, to issues in organizational quality studied by management scientists.

For a summary of some of the key fields from which the field of OB draws, see Table 1.2. If, as you read this book, you recognize some particular theory or approach as familiar, chances are good that you already learned something about it in another class. What makes OB so special is that it combines these various orientations into a single—very broad and very exciting—field. After all, OB is a vast hybrid, a field that requires a multidisciplinary orientation.

OB seeks to improve organizational effectiveness and the quality of life at work

In the early part of the twentieth century, bosses treated employees like disposable machines, replacing those who quit or who died from accidents with others who

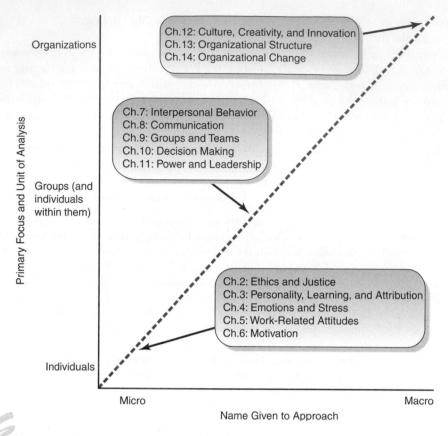

Figure 1.1   Levels of Analysis in the Field of Organizational Behavior

As indicated by the dashed line shown here, the topics studied in the field of OB (and, of course, that are covered in this book) vary along a continuum ranging from those focusing primarily on the behavior of individuals (known as the *micro approach*) to others focusing mainly on the behavior of organizations (known as the *macro approach*). Between these extremes, OB specialists also study the behavior of groups and the individuals within them. Because of the many interrelationships between these factors, the study of OB tends to be quite complex, making the lines between these orientations blurred in practice.

waited outside factory gates. Assuming that people were irresponsible, these managers held very negative views of employees, and they treated workers disrespectfully. This very negativistic approach, which has been with us for many years, reflects the traditional view of management called the **Theory X** orientation. This philosophy of management assumes that people are basically lazy, dislike work, need lots of direction, and will work hard only when they are pushed into performing.

Today, however, if you asked corporate officials to describe their views of human nature, you'd probably encounter more positive and optimistic beliefs. Although some of today's managers still think that people are basically lazy, many others would disagree, arguing that most individuals are just as capable of working hard as they are of "goofing off." If employees are recognized for their efforts (such as by being fairly paid) and are given an opportunity to succeed (such as by being well trained), they may be expected to work very hard without being pushed. Thus, employees may put forth a great deal of

Table 1.2   The Multidisciplinary Roots of OB

Specialists in OB derive knowledge from a wide variety of social science disciplines to create a unique multidisciplinary field. Some of the most important parent disciplines are listed here, along with some of the OB topics to which they are related (and the chapters in this book in which they are discussed).

Discipline	Relevant OB Topics
Psychology	Perception and learning (Chapter 3); personality (Chapter 3), emotion and stress (Chapter 4); attitudes (Chapter 5); motivation (Chapter 6); decision making (Chapter 10)
Sociology	Group dynamics (Chapter 9); communication (Chapter 8)
Anthropology	Leadership (Chapter 11); organizational culture (Chapter 12)
Political science	Interpersonal conflict (Chapter 7); organizational power and leadership (Chapter 11)
Economics	Negotiation (Chapter 7); decision making (Chapter 10); organizational power (Chapter 11)
Management science	Technology (Chapter 13); organizational change (Chapter 14)

effort simply because they want to. Management's job, then, is to create those conditions that make people want to perform as desired.

The approach that assumes that people are *not* intrinsically lazy but that they are willing to work hard when the right conditions prevail is known as the **Theory Y** orientation. This philosophy assumes that people have a psychological need to work and seek achievement and responsibility. In contrast to the Theory X philosophy, which essentially demonstrates distrust for people on the job, the Theory Y approach is strongly associated with improving the quality of people's work lives (for a summary of the differences, see Figure 1.2).

The Theory Y perspective prevails within the field of organizational behavior today. It assumes that people are highly responsive to their work environments and that the ways they are treated will influence the ways they will act. In fact, OB scientists are very interested in learning exactly what conditions will lead people to behave most positively—that is, what makes work both productive for organizations and enjoyable for the people working in them. (Do your own assumptions about people at work more closely match a Theory X or Theory Y perspective? To find out, complete the Self-Assessment Exercise on pages 30–31.)

After reading this section, you may find yourself wondering about productivity and profitability. After all, the primary reason why businesses exist is to make a profit. What does all this talk about people have to do with the bottom line? The answer is simple. Yes, OB is concerned about the profit of organizations. In fact, making organizations more profitable is one of the field's key objectives. However, the way it goes about doing this is different than in other areas of business. OB doesn't deal with the design of machines used in manufacturing; it doesn't address a company's accounting and marketing procedures; and it has nothing to say about the pricing strategies that help sell products and services. Instead, OB seeks to make organizations more

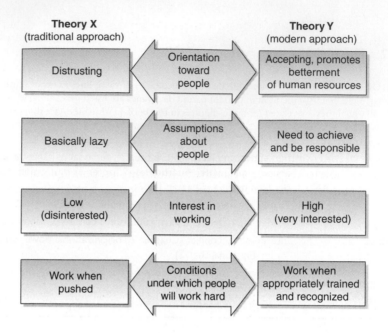

Figure 1.2   Theory X Versus Theory Y: A Summary

The traditional *Theory X* orientation toward people is far more negativistic than the contemporary *Theory Y* approach, which is widely accepted today. Some of the key differences between these management philosophies are summarized here.

profitable by focusing on people, such as by addressing how people are treated, how they get along with others, how they do their jobs, and so on. As you read this book, you will see exactly how vital this mission is and how the field goes about fulfilling it.

Why Does OB Matter?

Rather than keeping you in suspense about the importance of OB, allow us to whet your appetite for things to come by indicating just a few of the ways in which the field of OB matters to people and organizations.

> ➤ Companies whose managers accurately appraise the work of their subordinates enjoy lower costs and higher productivity than those that handle their appraisals less accurately.[4]

> ➤ People who are satisfied with the ways they are treated on the job are generally more pleasant to their co-workers and bosses and are less likely to quit than those who are dissatisfied with the ways others treat them.[5]

> ➤ People who are carefully trained to work together in teams tend to be happier and more productive than those who are simply brought together without any definite organizational support.[6]

> ➤ Employees who believe they have been treated unfairly on the job are likely to steal more from their employers and to reject the policies of their organizations than those who believe they have been fairly treated.[7]

> ➤ People who are mistreated by their supervisors on the job experience more mental and physical illnesses than those who are treated with kindness, dignity, and respect.[8]

> ➤ Organizations that treat employees well with respect to pay and benefits, opportunities, job security, friendliness, fairness, and pride in company are, on average, twice as profitable as the Standard & Poor's 500 companies.[9]

> ➤ Companies that offer good employee benefits and that have friendly working conditions are more profitable than those that are less people oriented.[10]

We could go on, but the point is clear: The issues studied in the field of OB make an enormous difference in organizations and the lives of the people working in them.

Although OB is a separate area of study, putting it into practice cuts across all areas of organizational functioning. Managers in all departments have to know how to motivate their employees, how to keep people satisfied with their jobs, how to communicate fairly, how to make teams function effectively, how to design jobs most effectively, and so on. In short, dealing with people at work is everybody's responsibility on the job. So, no matter what job you do in a company, knowing OB is sure to help you do it better.

WHAT ARE THE FIELD'S FUNDAMENTAL ASSUMPTIONS?

For you to get the most out of this book, it is essential to understand the two central tenets of the field of OB that we now will describe.

OB Recognizes the Dynamic Nature of Organizations

Thus far, our characterization of the field of OB has focused more on the behavior of individuals than on organizations themselves. Often, though, both are involved because, as you know, organizations are made up of people. So, to study how organizations operate, it helps to know about the behavior of people in them. And, to understand how these individuals think, feel, and act, you have to know how they are influenced by the organizations within which they work. Simply put, all the pieces of the puzzle are interconnected.

In the field of OB scientists and practitioners pay a great deal of attention to the nature of organizations themselves. Under what conditions will organizations change? How are organizations structured? How do organizations interact with their environments? Questions such as these are of major interest to specialists in OB. But before we can consider them (as we will do in Chapters 13 and 14), as well as how organizations influence and are influenced by individuals (as we do in Chapters 2–6) and groups (as we do in Chapters 7–12), we first must clarify exactly what we mean by an organization.

Formally, we define an **organization** as a structured social system consisting of groups and individuals working together to meet some agreed-upon objectives. In other words, organizations consist of structured social units, such as individuals and/or work groups, who strive to attain a common goal. Typically, we think of making a profit as the primary goal of an organization—and indeed, for many business organizations, it is. However, different organizations may be guided by different goals. For example, charitable organizations may focus on the objective of helping people in need, political parties may be interested in electing candidates with certain ideas, schools strive to educate students, and religious organizations may strive to save souls. Regardless of the specific goals sought, the structured social units working together toward them may be considered organizations.

OB scientists recognize that organizations are not static but rather dynamic and ever-changing entities. In other words, they recognize that organizations are

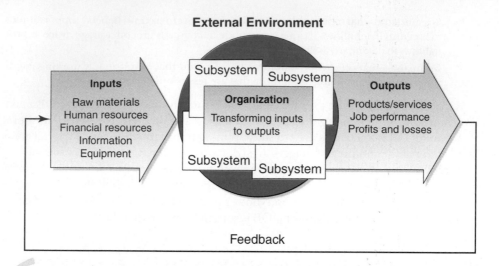

Figure 1.3   Organizations as Open Systems

The *open systems* approach is characteristic of modern-day thinking in the field of OB. It assumes that organizations are self-sustaining—that is, that they transform inputs to outputs in a continuous fashion.

(Source: Based on suggestions by Katz and Kahn, 1978; see Note 11.)

open systems—that is, self-sustaining systems that use energy to transform resources from the environment (such as raw materials) into some form of output (e.g., a finished product).[11] Figure 1.3 summarizes some of the key properties of open systems.

As this diagram suggests, organizations receive input from their environments and continuously transform it into output. This output then gets transformed back to input, and the cyclical operation continues. Consider, for example, how organizations may tap the human resources of the community by hiring and training people to do jobs. These individuals may work to provide a product in exchange for wages. They then spend these wages, putting money back into the community and allowing more people to afford the company's products. This, in turn, creates the need for still more employees, and so on. If you think about it this way, it's easy to realize that organizations are dynamic and constantly changing.

The dynamic nature of organizations can be likened to the operations of living things. As people breathe, they take in oxygen and transform it into carbon dioxide. This, in turn, sustains the life of green plants that emit oxygen for people to breathe. The continuous nature of the open system characterizes not only human life but the existence of organizations as well.

OB Assumes There Is No "One Best" Approach

What's the most effective way to motivate people? What style of leadership works best? Should groups of individuals be used to make important organizational decisions? Although these questions are reasonable, there is a problem with all of them.

Namely, they all assume that there is a simple, unitary answer—that is, one best way to motivate, to lead, and to make decisions.

Specialists in the field of OB today agree that there is no one best approach when it comes to such complex phenomena. To assume otherwise is not only overly simplistic and naive but, as you will see, also grossly inaccurate. When it comes to studying human behavior in organizations, there are no simple answers. Instead, OB scholars embrace a **contingency approach**—an orientation that recognizes that behavior in work settings is the complex result of many interacting forces. This orientation is a hallmark of modern OB.

In general, an individual's personal characteristics (e.g., personal attitudes and beliefs) in conjunction with various situational factors (e.g., an organization's culture, relations between co-workers) work together to influence how a particular individual is likely to behave on the job. As a result, explaining OB phenomena often requires saying, "it depends." Not surprisingly, as our knowledge of work-related behavior becomes increasingly complex, it is difficult to give "straight answers." Rather, it usually is necessary to say that people will do certain things "under some conditions." This phrase provides a clear indication that the contingency approach is being used. In other words, a certain behavior occurs "contingent upon" the existence of certain conditions. So, when we say, "it depends," we are not attempting to avoid a question, but rather, indicating the complexity of the answer.

OB Is Responsive to Changes in Social, Economic, and Technological Conditions

Since the industrial revolution in the early part of the twentieth century, people performed carefully prescribed sets of tasks—known as *jobs*—within large networks of people who answered to those above them—hierarchical arrangements known as *organizations*. This picture, although highly simplistic, characterizes the working arrangements that most people had during much of the last 100 years. Since the dawn of the new millennium, however, the essential nature of jobs and organizations as we have known them has been changing, and a major catalyst has been rapidly advancing computer technology, especially the use of the Internet and wireless technology.[12] As you might imagine, this state of affairs has important implications for the economy and the interrelationships between people on the job—and, hence, the field of OB.

After all, as more work is shifted to digital brains, some work that was once performed by human brains becomes obsolete. At the same time, new opportunities arise as people scurry to find their footing amidst the shifting terrain of the high-tech revolution. Consider, for example, that many of the routine tasks at your bank or utility company that once required a customer service representative (e.g., changing your address or checking your account balance) you now can perform by yourself directly online. In these cases, as often is seen today, people are being taken out of the mix. As you might imagine, the implications of this for OB are considerable. Most obvious, of course, is that many people have to be trained for new positions that require higher levels of technological sophistication.

We now consider some of the most prominent trends in the world of work that have been identified in recent years. Among other things, these involve when and how work is organized and performed, as well as the need for flexibility.

The compressed workweek

The 8-hour, 5-day workweek has been the traditional standard for many years. However, as employees have demanded more scheduling flexibility so as to have more personal time, companies have experimented with the **compressed workweek,** in which the time spent in a workweek is divided into fewer days. Three popular forms of the compressed workweek schedules have been used (for a summary, see Figure 1.4).[13]

➤ *Four-day workweek.* Employees work 10 hours per day for 4 consecutive days, Monday–Thursday. The company is closed from Friday through Sunday. This gives employees 3 days off each week.

➤ *Three-day workweek.* Two groups of employees are formed, each of which works for 3 days of 13 hours and 20 minutes per day. One group works Monday–Wednesday, the other works Thursday–Saturday. The company is closed on Sunday. This gives employees 4 days off each week.

➤ *5/4-9 compressed plan.* Two groups of employees are formed, each of which works 8 9-hour days one week and 1 8-hour day the next. The company is closed over traditional weekends, Saturday and Sunday. This arrangement gives employees 2 days off one week and 3 days off the next.

These alternative scheduling arrangements have been enjoyed by employees interested in improving the balance between their work lives and personal lives. They also have received a great deal of attention as a means of reducing the number of commutes to and from work. As gasoline prices have risen in recent years, many city and state governments in the United States have adopted the four-day workweek.[14] Not only does this reduce employees' travel expenses by 20 percent, but keeping buildings closed an extra day also saves energy costs within the facilities.

It is important to note, as you might imagine, that these alternative work schedules are not appropriate for all kinds of jobs. Obviously, such arrangements would not work when work must be performed only at certain times of day, such as when animals must be fed or when customers and suppliers are available to be contacted. Also, of course, we must consider fatigue. People may grow so tired working longer-than-usual days that their performance and safety may suffer. Under such conditions, lengthened days may not make good business sense. Finally, it's important to note that the assumed benefit of improving balance between work and life schedules assumed to come from compressed workweeks does not always occur. In particular, parents who have to pick up their children after school find it difficult to work late into the day.

All things considered, although compressed workweeks are useful in some cases, they certainly are not desirable in all. Still, it's clear that they are not only a viable possibility, but a reality, in many of today's organizations—and one that has keen implications for the study of behavior in organizations.

Leaner organizations: Automation and downsizing

Technology has made it possible for fewer people to do more work than ever before. **Automation,** the process of replacing people with machines, is not new, of course; it has gone on, slowly and steadily, for centuries. Unlike the gradual process of automation that occurred during the early 1900s, when mechanical machines were used to help people be more productive, today's advances in information technology are

Figure 1.4 The Compressed Workweek: Three Specific Schedules

The *compressed workweek* involves scheduling 5 standard days of work into 4 or fewer. Three particular schedules for accomplishing this, all used in various organizations, are summarized here.

FOUR – DAY WORKWEEK

MON	_____	
TUE	_____	} 10 hours / day ×
WED	_____	4 days =
THU	_____	40 hours / week
FRI	- - - - - - - -	off
SAT	- - - - - - - -	off
SUN	- - - - - - - -	off

THREE – DAY WORKWEEK

	GROUP A			GROUP B	
MON	_____	} 13 hrs 20 min / day		- - - - - - -	off
TUE	_____	× 3 days = 40 hrs / week		- - - - - - -	off
WED	_____	}		- - - - - - -	off
THU	- - - - - - -	off		_____	
FRI	- - - - - - -	off		_____	} 13 hrs 20 min / day ×
SAT	- - - - - - -	off		_____	} 3 days = 40 hrs / week
SUN	- - - - - - -	off		- - - - - - -	off

5/4 – 9 COMPRESSED PLAN

		WEEK 1			WEEK 2	
GROUP A	MON	_____	8hrs		- - - - - - -	off
	TUE	_____	9hrs		_____	9hrs
	WED	_____	9hrs		_____	9hrs
	THU	_____	9hrs		_____	9hrs
	FRI	_____	9hrs		_____	9hrs
	SAT	- - - - - - -	off		- - - - - - -	off
	SUN	- - - - - - -	off		- - - - - - -	off

44 hrs worked week 1   36 hrs worked week 2

80 hrs worked over 2 weeks

GROUP B	MON	- - - - - - -	off		_____	8hrs
	TUE	_____	9hrs		_____	9hrs
	WED	_____	9hrs		_____	9hrs
	THU	_____	9hrs		_____	9hrs
	FRI	_____	9hrs		_____	9hrs
	SAT	- - - - - - -	off		- - - - - - -	off
	SUN	- - - - - - -	off		- - - - - - -	off

36 hrs worked week 1   44 hrs worked week 2

80 hrs worked over 2 weeks

(Source: Adapted from U.S. Office of Personnel Management, 2008; see Note 13.)

occurring so rapidly that the very nature of work is changing as fast as we can keep up. With this, many jobs are disappearing, leaving organizations (at least the most successful ones!) smaller than before.[15] Not disappearing so rapidly, as a result, are jobs in the field of automation. In fact, industry leaders have noted that the worldwide market for automation products in factories was $30 billion in 2006 and is expected to swell to $47 billion by 2011.[16]

But it is not only blue-collar, manual-labor jobs that are eliminated due to automation but white-collar, mental-labor jobs as well. In many places, middle managers are no longer needed to make decisions that can now be made by computers (or by people with the aid of computers). It's little wonder that in the middle of 2008 alone, there were massive cuts among the managerial staffs of such notable companies as General Motors, Citibank, and the industrial giant, Siemens, to name just a few.[17]

Indeed, organizations have been rapidly reducing the number of employees needed to operate effectively—a process known as **downsizing.**[18] Sometimes, this involves more than laying off people just to save money. Rather, it is directed at adjusting the number of employees needed to work in newly designed organizations and is, therefore, also known as **rightsizing.**[19] Whatever you call it, the bottom line is clear: Many organizations need fewer people to operate today than in the past—sometimes far fewer.

Although poor economic conditions surely lead to layoffs, they do not tell the whole story. Some degree of downsizing has occurred in about half of all companies even during relatively strong economic periods—especially in the middle management and supervisory ranks (to see who's most likely and least likely to get laid off, see Table 1.3).[20] Experts agree that rapid changes in technology have been largely responsible for much of this. And as the world's economic crisis continues, companies are finding it more necessary than ever to rely on technology to do work that people used to do.

Table 1.3   Are You Likely to Become a Victim of Downsizing?

Based on prevailing patterns of downsizing, some people are more vulnerable to getting laid off, whereas others are generally safer. Here are some rough guidelines for assessing your own vulnerability to downsizing.

You Are Vulnerable to Getting Laid Off if . . .	You Are More Immune from Layoffs if . . .
You are paid over $150,000.	You have a good relationship with your boss.
You are inflexible and unwilling to transfer to a new job or to another city.	You have a midrange salary.
You work in retail, automotive, or manufacturing businesses.	You generate revenue for the company.
	You have expertise in a technical field.
You are a top executive of a division that is not performing up to expectations.	You have demonstrated willingness to work long hours whenever necessary.
You lack computer skills.	You are willing to relocate to another city or to transfer to another position in the company.
You do not have good leadership skills.	

(Source: Based on suggestions by McGinn & Naughton, 2001; see Note 20.)

Eliminating noncore aspects of business: Outsourcing

Another way organizations are restructuring is by completely eliminating those departments that focus on noncore sectors of the business (i.e., tasks that are peripheral to the organization) and hiring outside firms to perform these functions instead. This practice is known as **outsourcing.**[21] By outsourcing secondary activities an organization can focus on what it does best, its key capability—what is referred to as its **core competency.**

Companies like ServiceMaster, which provides janitorial services, and ADP, which provides payroll processing services, make it possible for their client organizations to concentrate on the business functions most central to their missions. So, for example, by outsourcing its maintenance work or its payroll processing, a manufacturing company may grow smaller and focus its resources on what it does best—manufacturing. An additional, and widespread, example can be seen in the field of information technology (referred to as IT). Many manufacturers of computer hardware and software have outsourced their customer service functions to companies that specialize in these services.

Because of the rapidly growing technological sophistication of people in many nations, it is not unusual for companies to relocate technologically oriented jobs to companies in foreign nations, a practice known as **offshoring.** This practice has been especially popular in some Asian nations, such as India and the Philippines, where people have both the language skills and technical knowhow to perform such jobs. By one recent estimate, India controls 44 percent of the global outsourcing market for software and related services, amounting to over $17 billion, and this figure is growing rapidly.[22]

Some critics fear that outsourcing represents a "hollowing out" of companies—a reduction of functions that weakens organizations by making them more dependent on others.[23] Others counter that outsourcing makes sense when the work that is outsourced is not highly critical to competitive success (e.g., janitorial services) or when it is so highly critical that it only can succeed by seeking outside assistance.[24] For example, it is a widespread practice for companies selling personal computers today to outsource the manufacturing of various components (e.g., hard drives, CD-ROMs, and chips) to other companies.[25] And because the labor rates are lower in many of the rapidly developing nations of the world (e.g., China), it is not unusual for such work to go to factories in such nations. This practice is more common than you might imagine. In fact, almost all companies in the *Fortune* 1000 outsource one or more of their functions.

The result of all this outsourcing, it's easy to see, is change (see Chapter 14). Some companies grow smaller by eliminating various units whereas other firms come into existence and grow larger by taking on the specialized functions dropped by their clients. As this goes on, the nature of work and the skills required by employees change considerably, providing rich opportunities for those interested in the study of behavior in organizations.[26]

The virtual corporation: A network of temporary organizations

As more companies are outsourcing various organizational functions and are paring down to their core competencies, they might not be able to perform all the tasks required to complete a project. However, they certainly can perform their own highly specialized part of it very well. Now, if you assemble several organizations whose competencies complement one another and have them work together on a special project, you'd have a very strong group of collaborators. This is the idea behind an organizational arrangement that is growing in popularity, known as the **virtual corporation.**

A virtual corporation is a highly flexible, temporary organization formed by a group of companies that join forces to exploit a specific opportunity.[27]

For example, various companies often come together to work on special projects in the entertainment industry (e.g., to produce a motion picture) and in the field of construction (e.g., to build a shopping center). After all, technologies are changing so rapidly and skills are becoming so specialized these days that no one company can do it all. And so, companies join forces temporarily to form virtual corporations—not permanent organizations, but temporary ones without their own offices or organization charts. Although virtual corporations are not yet common, they are becoming increasingly widespread whenever practical (for more on this phenomenon, see Chapter 14).[28]

Telecommuting: Going to work without leaving home

In recent years, the practice of **telecommuting** (also known as **teleworking**) has been growing in popularity. This is the practice of using communications technology to enable work to be performed from remote locations, such as the home or anyplace with e-mail access. Although telecommuting was somewhat experimental at the close of the twentieth century, it's safe to say that it's in full swing today. In fact, telecommuting currently is used by 23 percent of all American workers on a regular basis and by about two-thirds at least some of the time.[29]

This popularity is not surprising when you consider the benefits to both employers and employees. Workers stand to benefit by saving money that otherwise would have gone to the costs of commuting (e.g., fuel and parking) and purchasing clothing to wear on the worksite. Of course, they also enjoy the flexibility that such arrangements provide, which can improve their personal lives a great deal.

Companies also benefit in several ways. For example, telecommuting allows companies to comply with governmental regulations such as the Federal Clean Air Act of 1990, which requires them to reduce the number of trips made by their employees. And because telecommuting allows companies to reduce office space, it gives them an opportunity to enjoy considerable savings. In fact, the home appraisal unit of a large bank saved $166,000 per month by eliminating rental charges and cubicle occupancy costs for 225 of its teleworkers.[30] (For some examples of benefits enjoyed by companies using telecommuting, see the Winning Practices section on p. 17.)

Despite these benefits, as you might imagine, telecommuting is not for everyone; it also has limitations.[31] It works best on jobs that require concentration, have well-defined beginning and end points, are easily portable, call for minimal amounts of special equipment, and can be done with little supervision.[32] At least some aspects of most sales and professional jobs meet these standards. Even so, making telecommuting work requires careful adjustments in the way jobs are done. For a closer look at these considerations, see Figure 1.5 (p. 18).

OB Takes a Global Perspective

As our discussion of offshoring suggested, to understand behavior in organizations fully we must appreciate the fact that today's organizations operate within an economic system that is truly international in scope.[33] The nations of the world are not isolated from one another economically; what happens in one country affects other countries. For example, when the subprime mortgage market collapsed in the United States in 2007,

Winning Practices

Telecommuting: More a Matter of "When" Than "If"

Typically, telecommuting is not an all or nothing arrangement. It is more likely to be more of a part-time arrangement in which an individual spends some time in the office and some time working from a remote location. Such practices have worked well for many employees. Consider these examples, all from companies in the greater Seattle area.[34]

- The 50 people who work at the downtown Seattle office of Alliance Data Systems (ADS) are responsible for developing and supporting software for utility companies. Ten of these individuals work from home 1–2 days per week and over half do so on an occasional basis. Company officials like this arrangement because it allows system programmers to respond quickly to clients, who demand around-the-clock service. Programmers who work from home spend more time in front of their computers than those who work in the office during conventional business hours, resulting in less down time for clients.

- Productivity gains also have been enjoyed by the marketing agency DDB Seattle. The nature of marketing, advertising, and public relations work is such that flexibility in work location and start time can be allowed. And, to attract the most talented individuals to the firm, DDB Seattle offers this flexibility to interest the growing number of prospective employees who seek the lifestyle benefits flexibility offers. Additionally, flexibility has proven to enhance productivity in another important way—by lifting barriers to creativity that otherwise might be found in a highly rigid, traditional office setting. Also, when peace and quiet is required to do their jobs, creative personnel can stay at home to avoid the constant onslaught of interruptions found at the office. The choice is theirs.

- The ability to work without distraction also is cited as the basis for rises in productivity among telecommuters working as call-center agents in the Seattle office of the cruise ship firm Holland America Line (HAL). In the mid-1990s, HAL experienced dramatic improvements in both the number of calls taken and time spent on each call during a pilot telecommuting program that it is now cruising along, full speed ahead with 74 full-time agents (comprising half the staff) working from home. Although the company has considerable expense associated with setting up employees' home offices (e.g., installing ISDN lines), it continues to derive great returns on these investments. One surprise benefit: In the event of earthquakes, hurricanes, or crises on a ship, teleworkers make it easy for HAL to extend call-center hours required to deal with these emergencies.

These and many other examples make it clear that telecommuting can be a very effective nontraditional work arrangement for both employees and their companies. And considering the high costs of commuting, it seems safe to say that employees will be looking for even more opportunities to work productively from home.

---

it sent ripples throughout the economic markets of the world for years to come. This tendency for the world's countries to be influenced by one another is known as **globalization**—the process of interconnecting the world's people with respect to the cultural, economic, political, technological, and environmental aspects of their lives.[35]

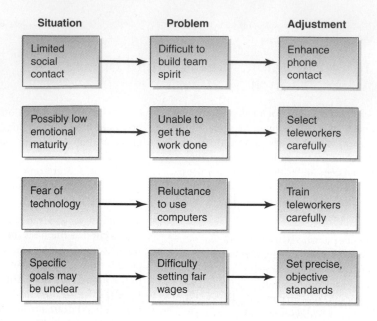

Situation	Problem	Adjustment
Limited social contact	Difficult to build team spirit	Enhance phone contact
Possibly low emotional maturity	Unable to get the work done	Select teleworkers carefully
Fear of technology	Reluctance to use computers	Train teleworkers carefully
Specific goals may be unclear	Difficulty setting fair wages	Set precise, objective standards

Figure 1.5   Adapting to Telecommuting

Jobs in which people engage in telecommuting often have to be adjusted in one way or another. Here are some of the major considerations.

While working abroad, people are exposed to different **cultures**—the set of values, customs, and beliefs that people have in common with other members of a social unit (e.g., a nation).[36] And, when people are faced with new cultures, it is not unusual for them to become confused and disoriented—a phenomenon known as **culture shock.**[37] People also experience culture shock when they return to their native cultures after spending time away from it—a process of readjustment known as **repatriation.**[38] In general, the phenomenon of culture shock results from people's recognition of the fact that others may be different from them in ways that they had never imagined, and this takes some getting used to.

Scientists have observed that the process of adjusting to a foreign culture generally follows a U-shaped curve (see Figure 1.6).[39] At first, people are optimistic and excited about learning a new culture. This usually lasts about a month or so. Then, for the next several months, they become frustrated and confused as they struggle to learn the new culture (i.e., culture shock occurs). Finally, after about six months, people adjust to their new culture and become more accepting of it and satisfied with it. These observations imply that feelings of culture shock are inevitable. Although some degree of frustration may be expected when you first enter a new country, the more time you spend learning its ways, the better you will come to understand and accept it.[40]

In general, culture shock results from the tendency for people to be highly *parochial* in their assumptions about others, taking a narrow view of the world by believing that there is one best way of doing things. They also tend to be highly *ethnocentric*, believing that their way of doing things is the best way. For example, many Americans tend to be highly parochial by speaking only English (whereas most Europeans speak

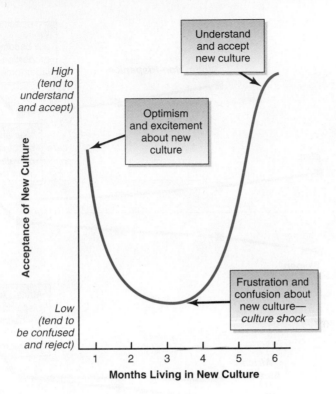

Figure 1.6   Adjusting to Foreign Culture: The General Stages

People's adjustment to new cultures generally follows the U-shaped curve illustrated here. After an initial period of excitement, *culture shock* often sets in. Then, after this period of adjustment (about six months), the more time spent in the new culture, the better it is accepted.

several languages) and ethnocentric by believing that everyone else in the world should learn their language. Such narrow and biased views about the management of people in organizations may severely limit our understanding of behavior in organizations.

With today's global economy, it is clear that an American-oriented approach may be highly misleading when it comes to understanding the practices that work best in various countries. After all, American culture is just one culture that dictates how people behave. In fact, there may be many possible ways to manage effectively, and these will depend greatly on the individual culture in which people live. Although the field of OB is still far from being completely international in its knowledge base, it rapidly is becoming far more global in its orientation to understanding human behavior in the workplace. By way of illustrating this, in various places throughout this book we will point out how scientists are becoming increasingly sensitive to the ways in which culture influences organizational behavior.

OB Embraces the Trend Toward Diversity

A broad range of people from both sexes, different races, ethnic groups, nationalities, and ages can be found throughout U.S. organizations, and as summarized in Figure 1.7, their proportions have been changing.[41] Modern organizations have taken steps to

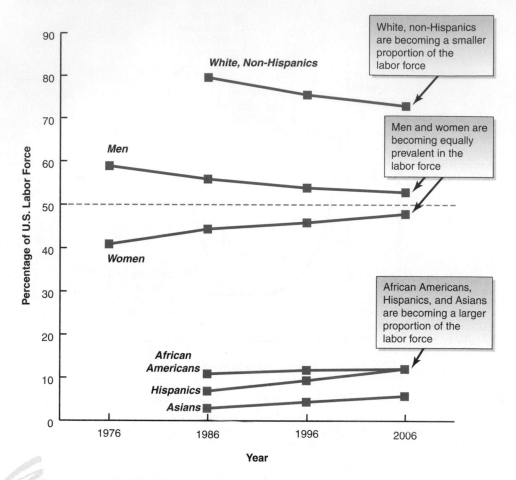

Figure 1.7   Changes in the U.S. Labor Force in the 20th Century:
More Women and Minorities

The U.S. Census has shown that whites, although still the largest percentage of the population, are becoming a smaller segment and that blacks and people of other races are growing in numbers. Additionally, although the numbers differ for various jobs, the overall percentage of women in the workforce (48%) now almost equals that of men (52%).

(Source: U.S. Department of Labor, 2009; see Note 41.)

accommodate—and capitalize on—growing levels of diversity within the workforce. This trend takes several forms, all of which have important implications for the field of OB.

More women are in the workforce than ever before

In the 1950s, the "typical American family" was characterized by a man who went to work and his wife who stayed at home and watched the children. Although this profile still may be found, it is far from typical. In fact, women comprise almost half of the workplace (48 percent in 2008), a figure that has risen steadily over the years (see Figure 1.7).[42]

This trend stems not only from economic necessity but also from the growing social acceptance of women working outside the home. As women, who traditionally

Table 1.4   Employee Support Policies

With increasing frequency, companies are taking proactive steps to help employees meet their personal needs and family obligations. In so doing, they make it possible for employees to satisfy the demands imposed by their nonwork lives. And this allows companies to draw on the talents of a diverse group of prospective employees who otherwise might not be able to lend their talents to the organization. The three practices listed here have proven especially useful in this regard.

Practice	Description	Example
Child-care facilities	Sites at or near company locations where parents can leave their children while they are working.	At Toyota's Georgetown, Kentucky, plant, a child-care center is open 24-hours a day, offering outstanding services at very reasonable fees.
Elder-care facilities	Centers where aged parents of employees can stay and be cared for while their adult children are working. Given the rapid aging of the population, this benefit is growing in popularity.	At its Armonk, New York, headquarters, IBM has been offering elder care to employees for over two decades. Recently, the company expanded this service by launching an online support group for individuals taking care of elderly parents.
Personal support policies	Widely varied practices that help employees meet the demands of their family lives, freeing them to concentrate on their work.	The Wilton Connor Packaging Co. in Charlotte, North Carolina, offers an on-site laundry, high school equivalency classes, door-to-door transportation, and a children's clothing swap center.

(until the 1960s) have worked inside the home, have moved to working outside the home, companies have found it beneficial—or even necessary, in some cases—to make accommodations that help make this possible. (For a look at some of the most popular practices in this regard, see Table 1.4.)

Racial and ethnic diversity is reality

Just as yesterday's workers were primarily males, they also were primarily white. However, just as growing numbers of women have made men less of a majority, so too has an influx of people from different racial and ethnic groups and differences in birth rates made white people a smaller majority. Specifically, the U.S. Census Bureau reported as follows:[43]

➤ Between 1980 and 2000, the population of minority group members grew 11 times as rapidly as the white non-Hispanic population.

➤ In 1900, about 1 in 8 Americans was of a race other than white but by 2000, this figure doubled to 1 in 4.

➤ In 2000, "races other than White or Black" in the U.S. Census consisted of American Indians and Alaskan Natives (0.9 percent), Asian and Pacific Islanders (3.8 percent), members of some other race (5.5 percent), and people of two or more races (2.4 percent).

The trend toward diversity is in full swing today, in the twenty-first century. In fact, "minority" group members, as a whole, currently outnumber traditional majority group members in two U.S. states, California and New Mexico.[44] And it has been estimated that by 2050, racial and ethnic minorities will comprise 47 percent of the entire U.S. population, making obsolete the current term *minority*.[45]

People are living—and working—longer than ever before

In the years after World War II the peacetime economy flourished in the United States. With it came a large increase in population as soldiers returned from war and began families. The generation of children born during this period is known as the **baby boom generation.** Today, this large wave of individuals is approaching retirement age. But, because retirement is no longer automatic at age 65, aged baby boomers will comprise a growing part of the population in the next few years. In fact, people over 85 years old are already the fastest-growing segment of the U.S. population.[46]

Two things occur as a result of this trend. First, older people in the workforce put more of a drain on the health care system. As healthy as they may be thanks to modern medicine, it's a simple truth that older bodies eventually wear out and require medical attention. And, of course, the physical prowess of older people surely isn't as great as it was when they were younger. This limits the physical nature of the work they can perform, which can be an issue for some manual labor jobs. But because technology has made physical labor less important than it was in years past, this is less of a problem today than it might have been a generation or so ago.[47]

Second—and the other side of the coin—because older people are more experienced on the job, they offer skills that only time can provide. In fact, as such individuals retire, it is not unusual for them to leave gaps in the workplace that are difficult to fill. In many organizations, this creates serious problems. When older top executives retire they take with them decades of experience that are almost impossible to replace. For this reason, many companies are instituting programs such as the following, which are designed to help keep older employees working a little longer before ceasing employment completely.

➤ *Phased-retirement plans.* These plans allow individuals who are approaching the usual retirement age of 65 to make a transition to full retirement by continuing to work, usually with a reduced workload, as a transition to full-time retirement. This arrangement, which presumably allows the best of both work and retirement, can take the form of permitting part-time or seasonal work (in which employees work only on occasion) or offering extended leaves of absence (in which employees can take off time but can return to work when ready to do so).

➤ *Deferred retirement option plan (DROP).* This arrangement allows a person who has reached retirement age to continue working while depositing his or her retirement benefit into a separate account that he or she can claim as a lump sum when formally retired, usually 1–5 years later. This provides a financial incentive for people who want to extend their working years a bit beyond the usual retirement age.

Such programs are important not only today, when there are many older individuals in the workplace, but they promise to be even more important when the next generation of workers approaches retirement age. We say this because there has been another recent wave of births: A record number of babies were born in the United

States in 2007, over 4.31 million, the most since the middle of the baby boom in 1957.[48] As such, we can expect not only record numbers of Americans entering the workplace in the 2020s, but another large wave of people approaching retirement in the 2060s.

Implications for OB

That more women, people of color, and older workers are in the workforce than ever before is not merely an idle sociological curiosity. It also has important implications for OB—ones that we will examine more closely in this book. After all, the more people differ from each other, the more challenges they are likely to face when interacting with one another.

How these interactions play out is likely to be seen on the job in important ways.[49] For example, as we will describe, differences in age, gender, and ethnic group membership are likely to bring with them differences in communication style that must be addressed for organizations to function effectively (see Chapter 8). It also is the case that people at different stages of their lives are likely to be motivated by different things (see Chapter 6) and to be satisfied with different aspects of their jobs (see Chapter 5). And, as workers adjust to a wider variety of people in the workplace, issues about their norms and values (see Chapter 9) are likely to come up, as well as their willingness to accept others who are different from themselves (see Chapter 5). This can have important implications for potential stress and conflict in the workplace (see Chapters 4 and 7), which may be expected to influence their capacity to work effectively as members of the same work teams (see Chapter 9).

OB THEN AND NOW: A CAPSULE HISTORY OF THE FIELD

The importance of understanding the behavior of people at work has not always been recognized as widely as it is today. In fact, it was not until the early part of the twentieth century that the idea first developed, and it was only during the last few decades that it gained widespread acceptance. Now, in the twenty-first century, it is clear that the field has blossomed and matured. So that we can appreciate how the field of OB got to where it is today, we will now briefly outline its history and describe some of the most influential forces in its development.

Scientific Management: The Roots of Organizational Behavior

The earliest attempts to study behavior in organizations came out of a desire by industrial efficiency experts to improve worker productivity. Their central question was straightforward: What could be done to get people do more work in less time? It's not particularly surprising that attempts to answer this question were made at the beginning of the twentieth century. After all, this was a period of rapid industrialization and technological change in the United States. As engineers attempted to make machines more efficient, it was a natural extension of their efforts to make people more productive too. Given this history, it should not be surprising that the earliest people we now credit for their contributions to OB were actually industrial engineers.

In the 1880s, while a foreman at Philadelphia's Midvale Steel Company, Frederick Winslow Taylor became aware of some of the inefficient practices of the employees.[50] Noticing, for example, that laborers wasted movements when shifting huge vats of molten iron, Taylor studied the individual components of this task and identified a set of the most efficient motions needed to perform it. A few years later, while at Pittsburgh's Bethlehem Steel, Taylor similarly redesigned the job of loading and unloading railcars so these tasks too could be done as efficiently as possible. On the heels of these experiences, in 1911 Taylor published his groundbreaking book, *The Principles of Scientific Management.* In this work, he argued that the objective of management is "to secure the maximum prosperity for the employer, coupled with the maximum prosperity of each employee."[51]

Beyond identifying ways in which manual labor jobs could be performed more efficiently, Taylor's **scientific management** approach was unique in its focus on the role of employees as individuals. Specifically, Taylor advocated two ideas that hardly seem special today but were quite new at the beginning of the twentieth century. First, he recommended that employees be carefully selected and trained to perform their jobs. Second, he believed that increasing workers' wages would raise their motivation and make them more productive. Although this idea is unsophisticated by today's standards—and not completely accurate (as we will see in Chapter 6)—Taylor may be credited with recognizing the important role of motivation in job performance.

It was contributions such as these that stimulated further study of behavior in organizations and created an intellectual climate that eventually paved the way for the development of the field of OB. Acknowledging these contributions, management theorist Peter Drucker has described Taylor as "the first man in history who did not take work for granted, but who looked at it and studied it."[52]

Taylor's work inspired other scientists to study people at work. Among the most strongly influenced were the industrial psychologists Frank and Lillian Gilbreth. This husband-and-wife team pioneered an approach known as **time-and-motion study,** a type of applied research designed to classify and streamline the individual movements needed to perform jobs with the intent of finding "the one best way" to perform them. Although this approach appears to be highly mechanical and dehumanizing, the Gilbreths, parents of 12 children, practiced "Taylorism" with a human face in their personal lives. (If this sounds at all familiar, it may be because it is depicted in the classic 1950 film and the 2003 remake, *Cheaper by the Dozen,* which tells the story of how the Gilbreths applied the principles of scientific management to their own rather large household.)

The Human Relations Movement and the Hawthorne Studies

Many experts rejected Taylorism, favoring instead an approach that focused on employees' own views and that emphasized respect for individuals. At the forefront of this orientation was Elton W. Mayo, an organizational scientist and consultant regarded as the founder of the **human relations movement.** This management philosophy rejects the primarily economic orientation of scientific management and focuses instead on the noneconomic, social factors operating in the workplace. Mayo and other proponents of the human relations movement recognized that task performance was greatly influenced by the social conditions that existed in organizations— that is, the way employees were treated by management and their relationships with one another. For a comparison between scientific management and the human relations movement, see Table 1.5.

In 1927 a series of studies was begun at Western Electric's Hawthorne Works outside Chicago. The researchers were interested in determining several things, including the effects of illumination on work productivity. In other words, they examined how brightly

Table 1.5 Scientific Management Versus the Human Relations Movement: A Summary

Although both are early approaches to the study of behavior in organizations, *scientific management* and the *human relations movement* are different in several key ways summarized here.

Scientific Management	Human Relations Movement
Emphasis on human efficiency on the job	Emphasis on social conditions in organizations
Sought to improve productivity by minimizing wasted movements	Sought to improve productivity by developing good working relationships
Major proponent was Frederick Winslow Taylor	Major proponent was Elton Mayo

or dimly lit the work environment should be for people to produce at their maximum levels. Two groups of female employees took part in the study. One group, the control room condition, did their jobs without any changes in lighting; the other group, the test room condition, worked while the lighting was varied systematically, sometimes getting brighter and sometimes getting dimmer. The results were puzzling: Productivity increased in both locations. Just as surprising, there was no clear connection between illumination and performance. In fact, output in the test room remained high even when the level of illumination was so low that workers could barely see what they were doing!

Before explaining these surprising results, consider another study conducted at the company's Bank Wiring Room. Here, men in various work groups were observed during regular working conditions and were interviewed at length after work. In this investigation, no attempts were made to alter the work environment. What Mayo found here also was surprising. Instead of improving their performance, employees deliberately restricted their output. Not only did the researchers actually see the men stopping work long before quitting time, but also in interviews the men admitted that they easily could have done more if they desired.

What accounts for these unexpected findings? Mayo and his associates recognized that the answer resided in the fact that organizations are social systems. How effectively people worked depended, in great part, not only on the physical aspects of the working conditions experienced but also on the social conditions encountered. In the Hawthorne studies, Mayo noted, productivity rose simply because people responded favorably to the special attention they received. Knowing they were being studied made them feel special and motivated them to do their best. (To this day, scientists refer to the **Hawthorne effect** when describing short-term improvements in work performance that result from observing workers' behavior.) Hence, it was these social factors more than the physical factors that had such profound effects on job performance.

The same explanation applied in the Bank Wiring Room study as well. Here, the employees feared that because they were being studied, the company would eventually raise the amount of work they were expected to do. So to guard against the imposition of unreasonable standards (and, hopefully, to keep their jobs!), the men agreed among themselves to keep output low. In other words, informal rules (known as norms, as we will discuss in Chapter 9) were established about what constituted acceptable levels of job performance. These social factors proved to be much more potent determinants of job performance than the physical factors studied.

This conclusion is important because it ushered in a whole new way of thinking about behavior at work. It suggests that to understand behavior on the job, we must appreciate fully people's attitudes and the processes they use to communicate with each other. This way of thinking, so fundamental to modern OB, may be traced back to Elton Mayo's pioneering studies. Although the research was flawed in some important ways (e.g., conditions in the study rooms were not carefully controlled), what they revealed about the importance of human needs, attitudes, motives, and relationships in the workplace was quite influential and novel for its time.

Classical Organizational Theory

While proponents of scientific management were getting scientists to begin thinking about the interrelationships between workers and their jobs, another approach to managing people was emerging as well. This perspective, known as **classical organizational theory,** focused on the efficient structuring of organizations. This is in contrast, of course, to scientific management, which sought to effectively organize the work of individuals.

Although several different theorists are identified with organizational theory, two of the best known are Henri Fayol and Max Weber. Fayol was a French industrialist who attributed his managerial success to various principles he developed. Among these are the following (which are described more fully in Chapter 13):

➤ A *division of labor* should be used because it allows people to specialize, doing only what they do best.

➤ Managers should have *authority* over their subordinates, the right to order them to do what's necessary for the organization.

➤ Lines of authority should be uninterrupted; that is, a clear *chain of command* should connect top management to the lowest-level employees.

➤ There should exist a clearly defined *unity of command,* such that employees receive directions from only one other person so as to avoid confusion.

➤ Subordinates should be allowed to *formulate and implement their own plans.*

Although many of these principles are still well accepted today, it is widely recognized that they should not always be applied in exactly the same way. For example, whereas some organizations thrive on being structured according to a unity of command, others require that some employees take directions from several different superiors. We will have more to say about this subject when we discuss various types of organizational designs in Chapter 13. For now, suffice it to say that current organizational theorists owe a debt of gratitude to Fayol for his pioneering and far-reaching ideas.

Probably the best-known classical organizational theorist is the German sociologist Max Weber. Among other things, Weber proposed a form of organizational structure well known today—the **bureaucracy.** Weber's idea was that the bureaucracy is the one best way to efficiently organize work in all organizations—much as proponents of scientific management searched for the ideal way to perform a job. The elements of an ideal bureaucracy are summarized in Table 1.6.

When you think about bureaucracies, negative images probably come to mind of lots of inflexible people getting bogged down in lots of red tape. Weber's "universal" view of bureaucratic structure lies in contrast to the more modern approaches to organizational design (see Chapter 13) in which it is recognized that different forms of

Table 1.6   Characteristics of an Ideal Bureaucracy

According to Max Weber, bureaucracies are the ideal organizational form. To function effectively, however, they must possess the characteristics identified here.

Characteristics	Description
Formal rules and regulations	Written guidelines are used to control all employees' behaviors.
Impersonal treatment	Favoritism is to be avoided, and all work relationships are to be based on objective standards.
Division of labor	All duties are divided into specialized tasks and are performed by individuals with the appropriate skills.
Hierarchical structure	Positions are ranked by authority level in clear fashion from lower-level to upper-level ones.
Authority structure	The making of decisions is determined by one's position in the hierarchy; higher-ranking people have authority over those in lower-ranking positions.
Lifelong career commitment	Employment is viewed as a permanent, lifelong obligation on the part of the organization and its employees.
Rationality	The organization is committed to achieving its ends (e.g., profitability) in the most efficient manner possible.

organizational structure may be more or less appropriate under different situations. Although the bureaucracy may not have proven to be the perfect structure for organizing all work, many of Weber's ideas are still considered viable today.

Despite differences between Fayol's and Weber's principles for organizing work, both approaches assume that there is a single most effective way to structure organizations. Although, as noted earlier, such approaches seem simplistic by modern standards, we are indebted to Fayol, Weber, and other classical management theorists for calling our attention to the important effects of organizational design (a topic to which we devote an entire chapter in this book; see Chapter 13).

The Modern Era of OB: Second Half of the Twentieth Century

The pioneering contributions noted thus far set the stage for the emergence of the modern science of organizational behavior, which began in the late 1950s and early 1960s. At that time, active programs of research were being conducted on such topics as motivation, leadership, and the impact of organizational structure on productivity.

In the 1960s, the Ford Foundation issued a report advocating that students being trained in business receive firm grounding in the social sciences. This stimulated growth in the field of OB as scientists began borrowing ideas from various disciplines. In fact, the field of OB as we know it today may be characterized as a hybrid science that draws from many social science fields (recall Table 1.2 on p. 7). This multifaceted and interdisciplinary quality of modern OB is reflected in advances in key topics covered in this book. We see these, for example, in studies on motivation (Chapter 6), attitudes (Chapter 5), group dynamics (Chapter 9), communication (Chapter 8), and other social science topics that characterized the field of OB in the second half of the twentieth century.

Organizational Behavior Today

Today, in the early part of the twenty-first century, the field of OB has added a few new characteristics worth noting. These reflect both changes that are occurring in the world as a whole and changes that have occurred as a result of scientific advances in the field over the years. Although there are too many new developments to mention them all, a few current trends deserve to be pointed out.

➤ In keeping with the ever-growing globalization of business, the field of OB has been paying more attention than ever to the *cross-cultural aspects of behavior,* acknowledging that our understanding of organizational phenomena may not be universal. Today, research that considers the international generalizability of OB phenomena is considered key to understanding organizational competitiveness in a global society. Acknowledging this trend, you will find multicultural examples of OB throughout this book.

➤ Ever since the Enron scandal of 2001, the study of *unethical behavior in organizations* has been considered more important than ever before. Indeed, OB scientists are fascinated by understanding the factors that lead people to make ethical or unethical decisions and by their willingness to engage in such antisocial behaviors as lying, cheating, stealing, and acting violently (see Chapter 7).[53] We will describe some of the factors that motivate people to behave unethically in Chapter 2.

➤ As energy costs rise and as technology makes it feasible to make operations more energy efficient, many of today's organizations are being proactive about conserving energy. And by using sustainable energy sources that help preserve the environment, organizations are also being good stewards of our planet. This trend has not escaped the attention of OB scientists, given that it may have implications for the way people do their jobs.[54]

➤ As noted earlier today's workforce is *more diverse* than ever before.[55] Fortunately, diverse employees help bring a wide variety of perspectives to the workplace that tend to improve the quality of organizational decisions. On the other hand, this benefit is too often threatened by prejudice and discrimination against such individuals, making it a major concern to today's OB specialists (see Chapter 5).

➤ The world's financial troubles resulted from leaders who made bad decisions. Either greedy or biased to the point of denying reality, some individuals' decisions proved to be tragically flawed. Scientists in the field of OB have been working to understand these dynamics and to prevent their recurrence in the future (see Chapters 2, 10, and 11).

➤ Traditionally, people either worked alone or in small groups in which they had clear-cut responsibilities. Today, however, because it is common for people to work as members of *teams,* it is not only individuals but also entire team products for which individuals are responsible. As a result, employees tend to have more responsibilities than ever before and are paid in ways that reflect their team's accomplishments. Naturally, such developments are important to the field of OB, and we will discuss them more fully in Chapter 9.

➤ Organizations are facing *unrelenting change*—a fact that is of great interest to OB scientists and practitioners. As you will see in Chapter 14, the field pays a great deal of attention to how people cope with change, and it seeks ways of encouraging people to accept change. After all, unless people adapt to change, their organizations will find it difficult to thrive—or even to survive. Today's global economic crisis makes this abundantly clear.

As you read this book, you will learn more about not only the traditional issues of concern in OB but also about these rapidly developing topics. One thing that makes the field of OB so interesting is that these trends, and many others, are all operating at once, making organizations highly concerned about a wide variety of OB principles and practices.

What Lies Ahead in This Book?

Now that you know what the field of OB is all about, you are in a good position to appreciate what to expect as you continue reading this book. In the chapters ahead, you will learn about a wide variety of organizational behavior phenomena. Our orientation will reflect the dual purposes of the field of OB—understanding and practical application. In other words, the focus will be on both basic processes as well as ways these can be applied to organizational practice. And, just to eliminate doubt about whether this material really matters in organizations, we will share lots of current examples to illustrate how OB principles have been followed within actual companies.

As indicated in Figure 1.1, the field of OB focuses on three units of analysis—individuals, groups, and organizations. Not surprisingly, this book is organized in this manner. Specifically, Part II consists of Chapters 2–6, focusing on individual behavior. Part III, consisting of Chapters 7–11, examines group behavior. And finally, in Part IV, with Chapters 12–14, attention will be paid to organization-level processes.

In a sense, these distinctions are artificial insofar as anything that happens in an organization is a blend of forces stemming from all three sources. With this in mind, you can expect to see several important connections between topics as you go through this book. These connections are indeed real and reflect the complexities of the field of OB as well as its multidisciplinary nature.

Rather than finding them frustrating, we think you will come to appreciate the fascination that they hold. After all, the field of OB can be no more straightforward than people themselves—and, as you know, we are not all that simple to understand! So with all this in mind, we hope you enjoy your tour of the field of OB presented in the next 13 chapters.

Back to the Case

Answer the following questions about this chapter's Making the Case (pp. 1–2) to illustrate the insights you have derived about the material in this chapter.

1. In running Floyd's 99 Barbershop, do the O'Brien brothers appear to adhere to a Theory X or Theory Y philosophy? On what do you base this answer?
2. In what ways has Floyd's 99 Barbershop relied on technology to enhance its business? How else might they do so?
3. What changes in society and economic conditions are likely to affect the behavior of people working at Floyd's 99 Barbershop? Specifically, what influences do you think these factors will have?

You Be the Consultant

Designing the Office Environment

A large publishing company hired you to help design a new suite of offices in which proofreaders will be working. Your task is to determine the levels of illumination that help proofreaders work most effectively. Answer the following questions relevant to this situation based on the material in this chapter.

1. What specific trends in the nature of the workforce do you think would make a difference in answering this? Explain your answer.

2. How would managers adopting the Theory X philosophy differ from those adopting the Theory Y philosophy in approaching this issue?

3. What would be the major approach of Taylor's scientific management orientation to this matter?

SELF-ASSESSMENT EXERCISE

Testing Your Assumptions About People at Work: Theory X or Theory Y?

What assumptions do you make about human nature? Are you inclined to think of people as primarily lazy and disinterested in working (a Theory X approach) or as willing to work hard under the right conditions (a Theory Y approach)? This exercise is designed to give you some insight into this question.

Directions

For each of the following eight pairs of statements, select the one that better reflects your feelings by marking the letter that corresponds to it.

1. (a) If you give people what they need to do their jobs, they will act very responsibly.
   (b) Giving people more information than they need will lead them to misuse it.
2. (c) People naturally want to get away with doing as little work as possible.
   (d) When people avoid working, it's probably because the work itself has been stripped of its meaning.
3. (e) It's not surprising to find that employees don't demonstrate much creativity on the job because people tend not to have much of it to begin with.
   (f) Although many people are, by nature, very creative, they don't show it on the job because they aren't given a chance.
4. (g) It doesn't pay to ask employees for their ideas because their perspective is generally too limited to be of value.
   (h) When you ask employees for ideas, you are likely to get some useful suggestions.
5. (i) The more information people have about their jobs, the more closely their supervisors have to keep them in line.
   (j) The more information people have about their jobs, the less closely they have to be supervised.
6. (k) Once people are paid enough, the less they tend to care about being recognized for a job well done.
   (l) The more interesting the work is that people do, the less likely they care about their pay.

7. (m) Supervisors lose prestige when they admit that their subordinates may have been right whereas they were wrong.
    (n) Supervisors gain prestige when they admit that their subordinates may have been right whereas they were wrong.
8. (o) When people are held accountable for their mistakes, they raise their standards.
    (p) Unless people are punished for their mistakes, they will lower their standards.

Scoring

1. Give yourself one point for selecting b, c, e, g, i, k, m, and p. The sum of these points is your Theory X score.
2. Give yourself one point for selecting a, d, f, h, j, l, n, and o. The sum of these points is your Theory Y score.

Discussion Questions

1. Which perspective did this questionnaire indicate that you more strongly endorse, Theory X or Theory Y? Is this consistent with your own intuitive conclusion?
2. Do you tend to manage others in ways consistent with Theory X or Theory Y ideas?
3. Can you recall any experiences that may have been crucial in defining or strengthening your Theory X or Theory Y philosophy?

GROUP EXERCISE

Putting Your Common Sense About OB to the Test

Even if you already have a good intuitive sense about behavior in organizations, some of what you think may be inconsistent with established research findings (many of which are noted in this book). So that you don't have to rely on your own judgments (which may be uniquely yours), working with others in this exercise will give you a good idea about collective common sense regarding behavior in organizations. You just may be enlightened.

Directions

Divide the class into groups of approximately five students. Then within these groups discuss the following statements, reaching a consensus as to whether each is true or false. Spend approximately 30 minutes on the entire discussion.

1. People who are satisfied with one job tend to be satisfied with other jobs too.
2. Because "two heads are better than one," groups make better decisions than individuals.
3. The best leaders always act the same, regardless of the situations they face.
4. Specific goals make people nervous; people work better when asked to do their best.
5. People get bored easily, leading them to welcome organizational change.
6. Money is the best motivator.
7. Interpersonal conflict is likely in a highly diverse workforce.
8. People generally shy away from challenges on the job.

Scoring

Give your group one point for each item you scored as follows: 1 = True, 2 = False, 3 = False, 4 = False, 5 = False, 6 = False, 7 = False, and 8 = False. (Should you have questions about these answers, information bearing on them appears in this book as follows: 1 = Chapter 5, 2 = Chapter 9, 3 = Chapter 11, 4 = Chapter 6, 5 = Chapter 14, 6 = Chapter 6, 7 = Chapter 7, 8 = Chapter 6.)

Discussion Questions

1. How well did your group do? Were you stumped on a few?
2. Comparing your experiences to those of other groups, did you find that there were some questions that proved trickier than others (i.e., ones where the scientific findings were more counterintuitive)? If you did poorly, don't be frustrated. These statements are a bit simplistic and need to be qualified to be fully understood. Ask your instructor to explain the statements that the class found most challenging.
3. Did this exercise give you a better understanding of the sometimes surprising (and complex) nature of behavior in organizations?

Organizational Justice, Ethics, and Corporate Social Responsibility

Learning Objectives

After reading this chapter, you will be able to:

1. **IDENTIFY** four different forms of organizational justice and the impact of each on individuals and organizations.
2. **DESCRIBE** things that can be done to promote organizational justice.
3. **EXPLAIN** what is meant by ethical behavior and why organizations should be concerned about ethics.
4. **DESCRIBE** the individual and situational factors responsible for unethical behavior in organizations and methods for minimizing such behavior.
5. **EXPLAIN** the idea of the pyramid of corporate social responsibility.
6. **DESCRIBE** the nature of the relationship between socially responsible behavior and financial profitability in organizations.

3 GOOD REASONS why you should care about . . .

Organizational Justice, Ethics, and Corporate Social Responsibility

You should care about organizational justice, ethics, and corporate social responsibility because:

1. Treating employees unfairly can adversely affect fundamental work attitudes and behaviors.
2. The public has become intolerant of unethical corporate behavior, but managers can take steps to promote ethical behavior in their organizations.
3. Consumers and investors tend to support socially responsible companies, enhancing their financial performance.

Making the Case for Organizational Justice, Ethics, and Corporate Social Responsibility

HP = Hidden Pretexting? What Did In Dunn?

On January 23, 2006, CNET News.com quoted an anonymous source describing strategic plans made at an allegedly private meeting of HP's board of directors. Because the meeting was held behind closed doors and similar media leaks had been occurring for about a year, HP's chair, Patricia Dunn, had enough. Frustrated, she wanted in the worst way to get to the bottom of this and root out the mole before serious damage could be done. Although one can hardly blame Dunn for wanting to protect the interests of her company, her tactics may be considered questionable, at best.

Dunn was so angry that she authorized a private investigation firm to uncover the source of the leaks. But the firm she hired to conduct the probe, the data-brokering company, Action Research Group, went a bit too far. Using a practice known as "pretexting," the investigators obtained the telephone records of over a dozen people—reporters, HP board members, and HP employees—by pretending to be them (i.e., contacting the telephone company under false pretexts). Because Dunn believed that the practice already had been going on and that it seemed to be an appropriate means of exposing the individuals who leaked vital information, it went on with Dunn's full consent and knowledge for about a year.

There was only one problem with the plan: It was illegal. Almost a year to the day that the CNET story broke, a California Superior Court found that HP willingly and knowingly accessed telephone account information without the account holder's permission and that it violated an identity theft statute by obtaining personally identifying information and then using it for unlawful purposes. A settlement was agreed upon in which HP admitted no liability and no civil actions would be taken against company officers. In exchange, HP's attorneys agreed to take steps that would help ensure the company's ethical behavior in the future. Specifically, for five years, HP was required: (1) to appoint a chief ethics and compliance officer, (2) to retain an expert in the field of investigations to assist this individual in conducting proper investigations, (3) to expand the role of the company's chief privacy officer to review HP's investigation practices, and (4) to expand the codes of conduct followed by the company's employees and vendors so that they covered appropriate investigation procedures.

To ensure that these practices would be followed, HP was required to set aside $13.5 million. Unlike Enron, whose officials took steps to hide their guilt, Dunn cooperated fully with authorities, although, of course, she stepped down as chair. Dunn explained that she was never aware that the tactics used in the probe were illegal, and that she regretted the use of "inappropriate techniques." Anxious to put this distasteful chapter behind them, Dunn's replacement, HP chair Mark Hurd, explained that he is "committed to ensuring that HP regains its standing as a global leader in corporate ethics and responsibility."

With the benefit of hindsight, it's now easy to see that Patricia Dunn's actions, well intentioned though they may have been, were misguided. At the time, however, blinded by anger and believing that pretexting is a legal gray area (with the exception of getting other people's financial records, this remains the case in most states), she felt she had a right—indeed, an obligation—to protect HP's interests by taking decisive measures. Although ultimately Patricia Dunn paid for her actions with her job and her company paid in cash and in damage to its reputation, it's not difficult to understand her motives. After all, is assuming another's identity for purposes of gathering information really so bad when compared to leaking information that could be financially damaging to a large company (including its thousands of stockholders and employees)?

We could debate this, of course, but the sides are likely to remain divided. Given that great philosophers over the years have not reached consensus about what constitutes "the right thing" to do, we shouldn't be surprised that distinguishing between right and wrong in the workplace is rarely a straightforward matter.[1] Yet, it's clear from many of the cases that were in the news at the beginning of the twenty-first century—Enron being the most visible—that many people have a good sense of wrongdoing when they see it.[2] Still, whether it's cheating among athletes and sports officials, illicit behavior among politicians, or unabashed greed among corporate officers, recent headlines make it clear that people in organizations seem to face an unending array of ethical obstacles.[3] Fortunately, as we will describe in this chapter, the field of OB provides a great deal of insight into why such unethical behavior occurs and can offer suggestions on how to curtail it.

As a natural outgrowth of the quest to behave ethically, many organizational leaders are going beyond merely doing what's right by proactively attempting to make things better in the communities in which they operate.[4] Indeed, many of today's organizations are demonstrating what is known as *corporate social responsibility*—not only attempting to meet prevailing legal and ethical standards but also exceeding them by embracing values that promote the greater welfare of society at large. Whether it involves donating money to charities, staffing community welfare projects, or taking steps to make our air and water clean, engaging in socially responsible behavior is of great concern to leaders of today's organizations. Here again, OB specialists have sought to explain this behavior, and their efforts will be outlined in this chapter.

Before describing the insight on ethics and corporate social responsibility offered by the field of OB later in this chapter, we begin by discussing a key concept that is central to understanding these themes—*justice*. Few topics are as controversial as what should be done in the name of justice—particularly in the workplace, where well-intentioned parties often disagree about what's fair. Although this may be unclear, it is very clear that people care dearly about matters of justice on the job. Just ask any worker who feels that the small pay raise he received does not adequately reflect his important contributions, or someone who suspects that the boss is playing favorites by giving one of her co-workers more desirable work assignments. Workers in these cases are bound to cry foul, claiming that they have been treated unfairly. Indeed, people are extremely sensitive to matters of justice and injustice in the workplace and are inclined to express their feelings in significant ways. Not surprisingly, OB specialists have studied these dynamics in the rapidly growing field of *organizational justice*, the topic to which we now turn our attention.

ORGANIZATIONAL JUSTICE: FAIRNESS MATTERS

Suppose you received a failing grade in a course (hypothetically, of course). Naturally, you don't like it, but can you say that the grade is unfair? Making such a judgment is one of the first things to enter your mind at this point. To answer this question, you would likely take several things into consideration. Does the grade reflect how well you performed in the course? Were your exam scores added accurately and were they computed in an unbiased fashion? Has the professor treated you in a courteous and professional manner? Finally, has the professor communicated the grading process to you adequately? In judging how fairly you have been treated, questions such as these are likely to be raised, and your answers will have a considerable impact on how you feel about your grade, the professor, and even the school as a whole. Moreover, your answers are likely to have a profound effect on how you respond, such as whether you quietly accept the grade, complain about it to someone, or even quit school entirely.

Although this example involves you as a student, the same kinds of considerations are likely to arise in the workplace. In that context, instead of talking about grades from professors, concerns about justice may take analogous forms. Does your salary reflect your work accomplishments? How was your performance evaluation determined? Were you treated in a respectful manner by your boss? And were you given important job information in a thorough and timely manner? Matters such as these are relevant to **organizational justice**—the study of people's perceptions of, and reactions to, fairness and unfairness in organizations.[5]

Two Important Points to Keep in Mind

Before we launch into our discussion of organizational justice, there are two important things about it you need to consider. First, unlike philosophers, who attempt to make objective statements about *what justice really is,* OB scientists generally adopt the approach of psychologists, which focuses on *how justice is perceived.* After all, people respond to how they perceive things, which may or may not be based on objective truths. You will come to appreciate this more fully as you venture further into this book (and as we will explain in more detail in Chapter 3). For now, though, it's important to recognize that we are talking about people's perceptions.

The second point to keep in mind has to do with the focus or target of those perceptions. When we speak about organizational justice, to whom or what are we making these judgments? We know that people consider the fairness of both individuals (e.g., specific managers) and larger units (e.g., their organizations as a whole), which may or may not be aligned. This orientation is known as the **multifoci approach to justice.**[6] Considering this, studies of organizational justice may examine one or more different sources. Likewise, efforts to promote fairness may focus on these various sources as well (i.e., making individuals or organizations fairer).

Now that we've made these points explicit, let's begin. Our discussion of organizational justice will focus on two important considerations—the major forms of organizational justice and suggestions for promoting justice in organizations.

Forms of Organizational Justice and Their Effects

The idea that justice is a multifaceted concept follows from the variety of questions just raised previously to everything from how much you get paid to how well you are treated by your boss. Acknowledging its complexity, OB scientists recognize that organizational justice takes four different forms. These are known as *distributive justice, procedural justice, interpersonal justice,* and *informational justice* (see Figure 2.1).[7]

Distributive justice

On the job, people are concerned with getting their "fair share" of resources. We all want to be paid fairly for the work we do and we want to be adequately recognized for our efforts and any special contributions we bring to the job. **Distributive justice** is the

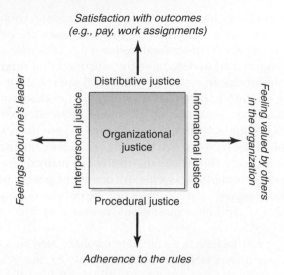

Figure 2.1   Forms of Organizational Justice and Their Effects

Organizational justice takes the four different forms identified here. Each of these forms of justice has been found to have different effects in organizations.

(Sources: Based on suggestions by Colquitt, 2001, and Greenberg, 1993; see Note 7.)

form of organizational justice that focuses on people's beliefs that they have received fair amounts of valued work-related outcomes (e.g., pay, recognition, etc.). For example, workers consider the formal appraisals of their performance to be fair to the extent that these ratings are based on their actual levels of performance.[8]

As shown in Figure 2.1, distributive justice affects workers' feelings of satisfaction with their work outcomes, such as pay and job assignments. Naturally, people will be dissatisfied with such important outcomes when these fall below expected standards. (Related to this, as you will see in the discussion of *equity theory* appearing in Chapter 6, feelings of distributive justice have a great impact on people's motivation to perform their jobs.)

To illustrate this, let's look at a study conducted in the tiny but economically thriving southeast Asian nation of Singapore.[9] In this investigation, researchers compared two groups of workers with respect to their feelings about distributive justice: a group of local workers from Singapore and a group of foreign workers, Chinese people who worked in Singapore to support the building boom there. In this setting, foreign workers tend to not be paid commensurate with their skills. Compared to the local Singaporeans, the foreign workers expressed higher levels of distributive injustice and, not surprisingly, they were less productive on their jobs. (By the way, in the United States and many other countries it would be illegal to pay people of different races and national origins different wages for the same work.)

Procedural justice

Assuming it's not too painful for you to do so, recall our earlier example regarding receipt of a failing grade. In assessing the fairness of this situation you would want to know precisely how your grade was determined. After all, if the professor made an error in calculating your grade, it would be unfair for you to be penalized. In other words, fairness involves consideration of not only *how much* of various outcomes you receive (i.e., distributive justice) but also the process by which those outcomes are determined—that is, *procedural justice.* In other words, **procedural justice** refers to people's perceptions of the fairness of the procedures used to determine the outcomes they receive.

Again, let's consider as an example the formal appraisals of their performance that workers receive on the job. Research has shown that workers consider these ratings to be fair to the extent that certain procedures were followed, such as when raters are believed to be familiar with their work and when they believe that the standards used to judge them are applied to everyone.[10] As you might imagine, matters of procedural justice take a variety of different forms and are involved in many different situations.

Maintaining procedural justice is a major concern of people in all types of institutions. In legal proceedings, for example, cases may be dismissed if unfair procedures are used to gather evidence. And in organizations, people also reject decisions based on unfair procedures.

A good example may be seen in an incident involving New York City taxicab drivers. Several years ago, these drivers went on strike to protest the mayor's imposition of new safety rules.[11] Interestingly, the drivers had little gripe with the rules themselves. Rather, they complained that it was unfair for the mayor to impose the rules without consulting with them. In their eyes, fairness demanded having a voice in the decision-making process. This too is an important consideration when it comes to judging procedural justice. For a more complete list of some of the major factors that people take into account when forming judgments about procedural justice, see Table 2.1.

Following unfair procedures not only makes people dissatisfied with their outcomes (as in the case of distributive justice) but also leads them to reject the entire system as unfair.[12] Not surprisingly, as shown in Figure 2.1, procedural justice affects people's tendencies to follow organizational rules: Workers are inclined not to follow an organization's rules when they have reason to believe that its procedures are inherently unfair. And, of course, when this occurs, serious problems are likely to arise. Accordingly, everyone in an organization—especially top officials—would be well advised to adhere to the criteria for promoting procedural justice summarized in Table 2.1.

Interpersonal justice

Imagine that you were just laid off from your job. You're not happy about it, of course, but suppose that your boss explains this situation to you in a manner that takes some of the sting out of it. Although your boss cannot do anything about this high-level corporate decision, he or she is very sensitive to the problems this causes you and expresses concern for you in a highly respectful and caring manner.

Research has shown that people experiencing situations such as this tend to accept their layoffs as being fair and hold positive feelings about their supervisors (see Figure 2.1). Importantly, such individuals are less inclined to sue their former employers on the grounds of wrongful termination than those who believe they were treated in an opposite manner—that is, in an insensitive and disrespectful fashion.[13]

The type of justice demonstrated in this example is known as **interpersonal justice.** This refers to people's perceptions of the fairness of the manner in which they are treated by other people, such as authority figures. You probably wouldn't find it surprising that people are extremely sensitive to violations of interpersonal justice. After all, we all expect to be treated with dignity and respect—especially when bad news is being communicated

Table 2.1   Procedural Justice Criteria

In forming judgments of procedural justice, people take different factors into consideration. Some of the major ones are identified here, along with descriptions and examples of each.

Criterion	Description	Example
Voice in the making of decisions	Perceptions of procedural justice are enhanced to the extent that people are given a say in the decisions affecting them.	Workers are given an opportunity to explain their feelings about their own work to a supervisor who is evaluating their performance.
Consistency in applying rules	To be fair, the rules used as the basis for making a decision about one person must be applied equally to making a decision about others.	A professor must use the same exact standards in evaluating the term papers of each student in the class.
Accuracy in use of information	Fair decisions must be based on information that is accurate.	A manager calculating the amount of overtime pay a worker is to receive must add the numbers accurately.
Opportunity to be heard	Fair procedures are ones in which people have a readily available opportunity to correct any mistakes that have been made.	Litigants have an opportunity to have a judge's decision reconsidered in the event that an error was made in legal proceedings.
Safeguards against bias	A person making a decision must not have any opportunity to bias the results.	Lottery drawings are held in such a manner that each number is selected in a completely random, unbiased fashion.

(Source: Based on Information in Greenberg, 1996; see Note 8.)

(such as announcements about layoffs, pay cuts, or undesirable changes in organizational policies). To be treated otherwise is not only rude, but unfair.

Informational justice

Imagine that you are a heavy smoker of cigarettes and you learn that your company has just imposed a smoking ban. Although you may recognize that it's the right thing to do, you are unhappy about it because the ruling forces you to change your behavior and break an addictive habit. Will you accept the smoking ban as fair and do your best to go along with it?

Research suggests that you will do so only under certain circumstances, such as if you are given clear and thorough information about the need for the smoking ban (e.g., the savings to the company and improvements to the health of employees).[14] The form of justice illustrated in this example is known as **informational justice.** This refers to people's perceptions of the fairness of the information used as the basis for making decisions. Because detailed information was provided about the basis for implementing the smoking ban, informational justice was high, leading people to accept the fairness of the smoking ban.

A key explanation for this phenomenon is identified in Figure 2.1—namely, that informational justice prompts feelings of being valued by others in an organization. In other words, people believe that they are considered an important part of the organization when an organizational official takes the time to explain thoroughly to them the rationale behind a decision. And people experiencing such feelings may be expected to believe that they are being treated in a fair manner. (By now, you may be thinking about the four types of fairness in the organization in which you work. To help you assess these feelings in a systematic manner, complete the Self-Assessment Exercise on pp. 63–64.)

Suggestions for Promoting Organizational Justice

The examples provided thus far make a compelling case for treating employees as fairly as possible. Indeed, workers who believe they are fairly treated are less inclined to respond negatively (such as by stealing from their employers or by suing them if laid off) and more inclined to respond positively (such as by adhering to organizational policies or by being more productive). And if these individual effects aren't sufficiently convincing, think about what it would be like if entire departments or work groups were composed of employees who felt unfairly treated. The cumulative impact would be dramatic.

This is precisely what was found by scientists conducting a study of hotel workers.[15] Analyzing 4,539 employees from 783 departments in 97 different hotels, they found that departments composed of employees who felt unfairly treated suffered significantly higher rates of turnover and lower levels of customer satisfaction than those composed of employees who felt fairly treated. And, of course, these factors have enormous impact on a hotel's success.

In view of these findings, there is good reason for managers to go out of their way to promote justice in the workplace. However, they often fail to do so.[16] Fortunately, what we know about organizational justice points to some useful suggestions for doing so.

Pay workers what they deserve

The practices of saving a little money by underpaying employees, or by informally discouraging them from taking vacation days they are due, are doomed to fail. Instead, paying the "going wage" in your community for work of a certain type and not cheating workers out of what they have coming to them are far wiser investments. Likewise, workers should be paid in proportion to how well they have performed (in Chapter 6, we address the complexities of doing so).

After all, workers who feel cheated are unmotivated to perform at high levels. Worse yet, those who feel they have been dealt a distributive injustice will be inclined to "even the score" by stealing from their companies or behaving in an uncivilized manner.[17] And, of course, a company paying below-market wages is likely to lose because the best workers will be disinclined to remain working there or even to accept jobs there in the first place. Not giving workers what they have coming to them clearly is "penny wise and pound foolish," as the saying goes.

Explain decisions thoroughly—and in a manner demonstrating dignity and respect

Suppose you've gone out of your way to pay workers what they deserve based on prevailing standards and according to the performance levels they've achieved. This isn't enough. Although you believe it's fair, the workers receiving the pay also must understand that their pay is fair. And this involves explaining it to them. If you used some elaborate formula for determining people's pay, that's a good beginning. Now, all you have to do is explain this to the workers so they can be assured of the fairness of your pay decision. After all, if they don't know anything about it, they are left to think otherwise.

Managers should not assume that their fair actions automatically will be recognized as such. To reap the maximum benefits of your fair actions, it helps to ensure that others in the organization are keenly aware that you are being fair. Blatantly touting the fairness of one's actions not only may be inappropriately immodest, of course, but it also may arouse suspicion about one's true motives ("why is she making such a big deal about how fair she is?"). At the same time, however, it is very useful to let people know that you are following fair procedures and to assure them of this by announcing all decisions publicly within the company and graciously explaining how they were made to anyone who wants to know. Making decisions in such an open fashion not only promotes perceptions of fairness but also demonstrates to workers precisely what they have to do to be recognized (see Chapter 10).

Also, of course, it is essential for managers to take great care in how they present decisions to their employees. Specifically, fairness demands giving employees lots of information about how decisions are made and explaining those decisions in a manner that demonstrates dignity and respect. This is especially important when the decisions made have a negative impact on workers. After all, it's bad enough to learn something negative (e.g., a pay cut or a layoff) without having a supervisor add insult to injury by not bothering to explain that decision thoroughly or by demonstrating a lack of concern for your feelings.

Illustrating this point, consider what it's like to have to live through a long pay freeze. Although it's bound to be painful, people may be more accepting of a pay freeze as fair if the procedure used to determine the need for the pay freeze is believed to be thorough and careful—that is, if "a fair explanation" for it can be provided. This was precisely what was found in an interesting study of manufacturing workers' reactions to a pay freeze.[18] Specifically, the researchers made comparisons between two groups of workers: those who received a thorough explanation of the procedures necessitating the pay freeze (e.g., information about the organization's economic problems), and those who received no such information. Although all workers were affected adversely by the freeze, those receiving the explanation better accepted it. In particular, the explanation reduced their interest in looking for a new job.

The practical lesson to be learned from this is important: Even if managers cannot do anything to eliminate distributive injustice (e.g., their "hands may be tied" by company policies), they may be able to reduce some of the sting by providing sensitive and respectful explanations as to why these unfortunate conditions are necessary. In fact, behaving in this manner can be one of the most effective cost-free things a manager can do.

Follow fair procedures

Sure, it's easy to say that you should use fair procedures, but what exactly does this mean? Fortunately, research consistent with Table 2.1 provides some useful rules to follow.[19]

> **Consistency rule.** To be fair, the procedures used as the basis for making a decision about one person must be applied equally to making a decision about others. For example, a manager should always use the same guidelines to judge the performance of all workers who perform the same job.

> **Accuracy rule.** Unless decisions are made on accurate information, those decisions cannot be considered fair. For example, a manager calculating the amount of overtime pay a worker is to receive must add the numbers accurately.

> **Correctability rule.** Procedures should be put into place that provide opportunities for mistakes to be corrected. The "instant replay rule" used in the National Football League is a good example because it allows officials to overturn erroneous calls that were made on the field.

> **Bias protection rule.** Fair procedures are ones that deny the people involved from having an opportunity to cheat or influence the results in some way. For example, lottery drawings are held in such a manner that each number is selected in a completely random, unbiased fashion.

Give employees a voice in decision making

In addition to following the procedural justice rules noted above, it also is important, whenever possible, to give employees some degree of **voice**—that is, a chance to share information and to have a say in how things are going to be done. Please note that we're not saying that managers should give employees complete choice in the way things are done, but rather give them a say in the decisions affecting them.

One of the best-established principles of procedural justice is that people will better accept outcomes when they have had some input into determining them than when they are not involved.[20] This is known as the **fair process effect.** Often promoting fairness in this manner is accomplished simply by conducting regular meetings with employees to hear what they have to say. The benefits of doing so result not only from making better-quality decisions (because it taps workers' expertise) but also from merely involving workers in the process. After all, workers whose input is solicited are inclined to feel better accepted as valued members of their organization than those who are ignored. As shown in Figure 2.2, this leads them to perceive both that the resulting outcome is fair and that the procedure used to determine it is fair. And, as noted earlier, perceptions of distributive justice and procedural justice are quite beneficial to organizations.

Train workers to be fair

Most people perceive themselves to be fair individuals. However, as is clear from this section of the chapter, being fair involves several very specific things. And, when facing the everyday pressure to get the job done, managers may not be taking into account as many of the principles of organizational justice as they should. With this in mind, it has been found useful to train practicing managers on how to be fair (we will discuss the topic of training more thoroughly in Chapter 3).[21] In general, these efforts have been quite successful. Managers who have been trained to treat their employees more fairly (i.e., by being trained in the various forms of justice and practice in bringing them about) reaped several key benefits compared to those who have not been trained to be

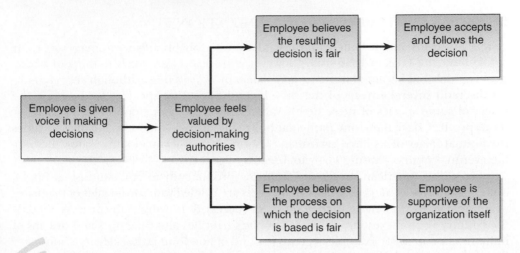

Figure 2.2   The Fair Process Effect: A Summary

According to the *fair process effect*, employees who are given a voice in the making of decisions affecting them will feel valued by the decision-making authorities (e.g., top company leaders). In turn, this leads employees to believe that both the decision-making procedure and the outcomes resulting from it are fair. As a result, employees will accept and follow the decision and be supportive of the organization itself.

fair. Not only are their employees less inclined to respond in a negative fashion (e.g., by stealing from the company), but the employees also are more inclined to pitch in and help others in the organization (a phenomenon known as *organizational citizenship behavior*, which we will describe in Chapter 7).

As an example of the effectiveness of training, consider a study that the author performed in several hospitals just a few years ago.[22] The results were so dramatic that they warrant describing the research here. Participants in the study were nurses at several hospitals and their immediate supervisors. The nurses in some of the hospitals experienced a change in their pay system that led them to suffer a pay cut of about 10 percent. Of course, they didn't like this distributive injustice. In fact, they suffered so much stress as a result (we will discuss this topic in detail in Chapter 4) that they reported symptoms of insomnia. In other words, they lost sleep over being treated unfairly.

As this was going on, the author trained the supervisors of the nurses in ways to enhance interpersonal justice and informational justice among their subordinates. Specifically, in two 4-hour classroom sessions we used case studies and role-playing exercises to train the supervisors specifically how to share information with employees in a manner that shows dignity and respect. An interesting thing happened: The nurses whose supervisors we trained in this manner reported significantly less insomnia after the training than before the training. However, the nurses whose supervisors were untrained failed to show any drops in insomnia during this same period. Bottom line: The training worked.

Training supervisors in interpersonal and informational justice (which managers generally have a chance to control on their own, unlike distributions and procedures, in many cases) helped buffer the negative effects of the distributive injustice. In other words, although managers who were trained to demonstrate high levels of informational and interpersonal justice toward their subordinates did not make their distributive injustices go away, they helped their employees to cope with them in a less stressful manner.

ETHICAL BEHAVIOR IN ORGANIZATIONS

When you think about Dutch tulips, your mind probably fills with images of their colorful beauty. Back in 1636–1637, however, Europeans were likely to think of a business scandal that became known as *tulip mania* or *tulipomania*. Although recent analyses discredit several aspects of the case, legend has it that speculators drove up the prices of some species of these highly valued flowers so they stood to make an enormous profit.[23] Back then, one particular bulb, the Viceroy, sold for as much as 28 times the annual salary of a skilled craftsman.[24] Soon, as they always do, the economic bubble eventually burst, causing many to lose lots of guilders.

Closer to American shores and featuring prominently in our own history books, accounts of the early days of American business are riddled with sordid tales of magnates who would go to any lengths in their quest for success, destroying in the process not only the country's natural resources and the public's trust but also the hopes and dreams of millions of people. For example, legends abound of how John D. Rockefeller, founder of Standard Oil, regularly bribed politicians and stepped all over people in his quest to monopolize the oil industry.

We do not mean to imply that unsavory business practices are only a relic of the past. Far from it! As you know, they are all too common today—so much so that one newspaper reporter referred to ethical scandals as having reached "epidemic levels."[25] Just consider some of the major headlines from recent years:

➤ After receiving billions of dollars from the U.S. government to keep it from failing, executives from the huge insurance company, A.I.G., were given multimillion-dollar bonuses.[26]

➤ Bernard Madoff, chairman of a large investment firm that bore his name, defrauded clients out of some $50 billion, making it the largest investment fraud ever committed by a single individual.[27]

➤ Preying on victims' desperation, a 42-year-old man was accused of felony home repair fraud for performing poor work or unfinished work on the homes of victims of Hurricane Katrina.[28]

➤ Illinois Governor, Rod Blagojevich, was impeached from office on the grounds that he attempted to sell a state senate seat vacated when Barack Obama was elected president of the United States.[29]

➤ In India, children are alleged to have been sold to owners of sweatshops, where they work for 16 hours a day making clothing for Gap stores.[30]

And, of course, who can forget the now-classic scandals that emerged at the dawn of the new millennium?

➤ Martha Stewart served time in prison after being charged with obstruction of justice and lying to federal investigators in connection with a government probe of her alleged insider trading of ImClone stock.[31]

➤ Enron officers were cited for "cooking the books" to make millions of dollars for themselves.[32]

➤ Sears was found to use fraudulent practices in its auto-repair business.[33]

➤ Adelphia Communications officials were charged with using corporate funds to make exorbitant personal purchases.[34]

Clearly, human greed has not faded from the business scene since tulip mania. However, something *has* changed—namely, the public's acceptance of unethical behavior on the part of organizations. Consider this statement by a leading expert on business ethics.

> Ethical standards, whether formal or informal, have changed tremendously in the last century. . . . Standards are considerably higher. Business-people themselves, as well as the public, expect more sensitive behavior in the conduct of economic enterprise. The issue is not just having the standards, however. It is living up to them.[35]

Not surprisingly—despite the spate of ethical crises that have captured the public's attention in recent years—growing intolerance of unethical business activity (and, cynically, fear of getting caught) has inspired business leaders to become more ethical than ever. According to a survey conducted a few years ago, workers report that top managers are more inclined to keep their promises, less inclined to engage in misconduct, less likely to feel pressure to be unethical, and perceive greater attention paid to practicing honesty and respect for others. At the same time, whatever ethical misdeeds they do witness are much more likely to be reported to organizational authorities.[36]

To the extent that people are increasingly intolerant of unethical business activity, it should not be surprising to learn that OB scientists are interested in understanding unethical practices and developing strategies for combating them. We will consider these issues in this section and the next section of this chapter. First, however, to help prepare you for understanding ethical behavior in organizations, we begin by addressing a fundamental question: What is ethics?

What Do We Mean by Ethics?

Because it's not always clear what people mean when they refer to ethics, let's define some key terms. First, we first must understand the concept of *moral values.* When social scientists speak of **moral values** they are referring to people's fundamental beliefs regarding what is right or wrong, good or bad. One of the most important sources of moral values is the religious background, beliefs, and training we receive. Although people's moral values may differ, several are widely accepted. For example, most people believe that helping someone in need (e.g., being charitable) is the right thing to do whereas harming someone (e.g., killing) is wrong.

Based on these beliefs, people are guided in ways that influence the decisions they make and the actions in which they engage. These standards are what we mean by *ethics.* Thus, **ethics** refers to standards of conduct that guide people's decisions and behavior (e.g., not stealing from others is one such ethical standard).[37] With this in mind, organizational scientists acknowledge that it is not a company's place to teach employees values. After all, these come with people as they enter the workplace. However, it *is* a company's responsibility to set clear standards of behavior and to train employees in recognizing and following them.[38] (For a summary of the distinction between moral values and ethics, see Figure 2.3.)

Just as organizations prescribe other behaviors that are expected in the workplace (e.g., when to arrive and leave), so too should they prescribe appropriate ethical behavior (e.g., indicating what precisely is considered a bribe). Not surprisingly, most top business leaders recognize that clearly prescribing ethical behavior is a fundamental part of good management. After all, says Kent Druyversteyn, former vice president of ethics at General Dynamics, "Ethics is about conduct."[39]

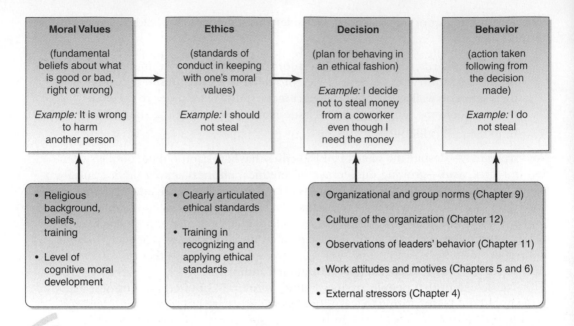

Figure 2.3   Moral Values Versus Ethics

As summarized here, *moral values* (which reside within an individual) provide the basis for *ethics* (which are standards of behavior that can be regulated by organizations). Ethical standards influence both decisions and behavior in the workplace, which also are affected by a host of other variables identified throughout this book.

In looking at Figure 2.3, please note the row of rounded boxes at the bottom. These identify some of the factors affecting moral values, ethics, decisions, and behavior. The ones corresponding to ethics and values are described in this section of the chapter. However, as indicated in the box in the lower right corner, the decisions people make and the behavior in which they engage are determined by a wide variety of considerations beyond ethics. Accordingly, these are discussed elsewhere throughout this book (note the references to other chapters).

Why Should Companies Care About Ethical Behavior?

It's obvious, of course, that companies *should* do things to promote ethical behavior among employees simply because they are morally appropriate. To some top executives, behaving ethically is an integral part of business. Take Levi Strauss & Co., for example, whose former chairman, Robert D. Haas, observed as follows:

> Levi has always treated people fairly and cared about their welfare. . . . In the past, however, that tradition was viewed as something separate from how we ran the business. We always talked about the "hard stuff" and the "soft stuff." The soft stuff was the company's commitment to our work force. And the hard stuff was what really mattered; getting pants out the door. What we've learned is that the soft stuff and the hard stuff are becoming increasingly intertwined. A company's values—what it stands for, what its people believe in—are crucial to its competitive success. Indeed, values drive the business. . . . Values are where the hard stuff and the soft stuff come together.[40]

All too often, as you know, forces sometimes deter even good people from doing the right thing. Pressure to meet "the bottom line" sometimes encourages people to do whatever it takes to make money, at least in the short run, even if it leads them to behave unethically. For example, some unscrupulous stockbrokers have been known to boost their own sales commissions by encouraging clients to make investments they know are questionable. Corporate leaders need to be concerned about this, if not for moral reasons, then out of recognition of two critical business realities—by being ethical, companies can (1) reap various financial benefits and (2) adhere to legal regulations.

Good ethics is good business

People promoting ethical behavior among businesses agree that good ethics is good business. In other words, the idea is that although one may benefit in the short run by behaving unethically (e.g., the stockbroker in our example), being ethical pays off in the long run. These benefits take several forms, including the following:[41]

- ➤ *Improved financial performance:*   Companies that make a clear commitment to ethics outperform those that make no such commitment on standard measures of financial success. In fact, one study reported that companies that made an explicit commitment to ethical behavior returned twice the value to shareholders than those that focused less on ethical issues.[42]

- ➤ *Reduced operating costs:*   Many efforts to reduce waste and to save energy, designed to protect the natural environment, also help save money.

- ➤ *Enhanced corporate reputation:*   Many customers are loyal to companies that demonstrate their commitment to social causes. For example, The Body Shop has benefited by promoting the things it does to help the poor people from third world nations from whom it buys raw materials. This attracts customers who share the company's values.

- ➤ *Increased ability to attract and retain employees:*   People generally like working at companies of which they can be proud and that treat them well. When talented employees are difficult to find, socially responsible companies have an easier job of getting people to work for them—and keeping them there.

If this evidence is not sufficiently convincing, then consider the other side of the coin. The evidence also is compelling that "bad ethics is bad business." Companies that survive ethical scandals do so under diminished capacity in large part because "the black eye" makes the public shy away from them—both as consumers and as stockholders—at least for a while.[43]

Good examples from years past include Dow Corning (whose breast implants were found to be unsafe), Exxon (whose ship, the *Valdez*, spilled oil off the coast of Alaska), and the United Way (whose top official was accused of misusing agency funds). These misdeeds have cost their respective organizations dearly, and regaining the public's trust has proven to be a slow process.

At the United Way, for example, although only one person, the president, was involved in the ethical scandal, completely independent and scrupulously ethical chapters of the esteemed philanthropic organization suffered severe reductions in donations (one-fifth of former donors stopped giving altogether and the remaining ones gave less) for at least five years.[44] The lesson is clear: Even if company executives do not recognize the benefits of behaving ethically, they surely cannot afford to ignore the costs of behaving unethically.

Legal regulations

Being ethical is not the same as following the law. In fact, a useful way to think of the law is as providing the minimum acceptable standard to which companies must adhere. Being ethical typically involves following a higher standard. Vin Sarni, former CEO of PPG, put this well when he said, "It is not enough simply to say that our conduct is lawful. The law is the floor. Compliance with it will be the absolute minimum with respect to the PPG associate, no matter where he or she works. Our ethics go beyond the legal code."[45]

At the same time, it must be noted that the law plays a large role in governing ethical behavior within organizations. Some of the major laws enacted in the United States that influence ethical behavior in organizations are as follows:

➤ *False Claims Act (1986):*   Provides procedures for reporting fraudulent behavior against U.S. government agencies and protects whistle-blowers (see Chapter 7) who do so.

➤ *Foreign Corrupt Practices Act (revised 1988):*   Prohibits organizations from paying bribes to foreign officials for purposes of getting business.

➤ *Federal Sentencing Guidelines for Organizations (1991):*   Provides guidelines for federal judges to follow when imposing fines on organizations whose employees engage in criminal acts.

➤ *Sarbanes-Oxley Act (2002):*   Enacted to guard against future accounting scandals (such as occurred at Enron), this law initiates reforms in the standards by which public companies report accounting data. (Because it is an impetus for organizational change, SOX is also described in some detail in Chapter 14.)

➤ *Federal Prosecution of Business Organizations (2003):*   To protect investors against unscrupulous acts by top executives (also in response to the Enron scandal), these revisions to the Federal Sentencing Guidelines for Organizations now focus on the role of boards of directors—the only parties in organizations with sufficient clout to prevent wrongdoing by high-ranking officials.[46]

Although all these laws are important when it comes to minimizing unethical behavior in organizations, two are particularly important. First, the Federal Sentencing Guidelines for Organizations have been the most explicit when it comes to specifying precisely what organizations should do to discourage unethical behavior. The underlying rationale is that the more proactively organizations discourage criminal behavior by employees, the less they will be penalized should such behavior occur. (After all, an organization cannot directly control everything every employee does!) Specifically, the Federal Sentencing Guidelines for Organizations identify several specific actions that, if taken, will be recognized as efforts to discourage illegal behavior.[47] Not surprisingly, these behaviors, which are listed and described in Table 2.2, are widely followed by companies in their efforts to promote ethical behavior.

The Sarbanes-Oxley Act, widely referred to as SOX, has been somewhat controversial in recent years in part because it has created an enormous reporting burden on organizations to stipulate that they are conforming to the law's various provisions.[48] Additionally, the law is very specific in places regarding precisely what must be done to avoid misreporting of financial information. For example, it has been stipulated that companies must do such things as the following (to name but a few):[49]

➤ Assess their risk for the occurrence of fraud.

➤ Evaluate controls designed to prevent or detect fraud.

➤ Evaluate controls over the safeguarding of assets.

Table 2.2 Practices Encouraged by the Federal Sentencing Guidelines for Organizations

According to the Federal Sentencing Guidelines for Organizations, companies following the practices listed here will be punished less severely should one of its employees engage in criminal conduct.

- Standards for complying with the law should be specified clearly and widely disseminated (e.g., in publications and training programs).
- A high-level official should be responsible for overseeing these standards (e.g., a vice president for ethics).
- A clear system for monitoring and auditing behavior should be in place so that criminal behavior can be detected when it occurs.
- Appropriate disciplinary action should be taken against employees who violate the standards.
- If an offense occurs, steps must be taken to prevent its recurrence.

(Source: Based on information reported by the Ethics and Policy Integration Centre, 2003; see Note 47.)

It's not too hard to realize that the complex and rapidly evolving nature of SOX has created a booming business in companies that specialize in helping organizations comply with it (much like the income tax code in this regard).[50] Make no mistake about it, complying with SOX is taken very seriously. If you have any doubts, consider the penalties stated in Section 802(a) of the law:

> Whoever knowingly alters, destroys, mutilates, conceals, covers up, falsifies, or makes a false entry in any record, document, or tangible object with the intent to impede, obstruct, or influence the investigation or proper administration of any matter within the jurisdiction of any department or agency of the United States or any case filed under title 11, or in relation to or contemplation of any such matter or case, shall be fined under this title, imprisoned not more than 20 years, or both.[51]

Why Do Some People Sometimes Behave Unethically—and What Can Be Done About It?

For many years, management experts have been interested in determining why some people behave unethically on at least some occasions. The main question is this: Is it a matter of essentially good people who are led to do bad things because of unethical external forces acting on them (i.e., "good apples in bad barrels") or is it that bad people behave inappropriately even if external forces encourage them to be ethical (i.e., "bad apples in good barrels")? Acknowledging the key role of leaders in determining the ethical climates of their organizations, some scientists have considered the possibility that because of their profound influence, some unethical leaders (so-called "bad apples") have made their companies unethical as well (turning "good barrels into bad"), or poisoning the whole barrel, so to speak.[52]

Although the relative importance of "apples" and "barrels" has yet to be firmly decided, it is clear that ethical and unethical behavior is determined by *both* of these classes of factors—that is, individual factors, the person (apples), and situational factors, the external forces people confront in the workplace (barrels). In this section of the chapter, we will consider both sets of factors.

Individual Differences in Cognitive Moral Development

As you know from experience, people appear to differ with respect to their adherence to moral considerations. Some individuals, for example, refrain from padding their expense accounts, even if they believe they will not get caught, solely because they believe it is the wrong thing to do. They strongly consider ethical factors when making decisions. However, others would not think twice about padding their expense accounts, often rationalizing that the amounts of money in question are small and that "the company expects me to do it." A key factor responsible for this difference is what psychologists refer to as **cognitive moral development**—that is, differences among people in their capacity to engage in the kind of reasoning that enables them to make moral judgments. (Scientists measure people's cognitive moral development by systematically analyzing how people say they would resolve various ethical dilemmas. For practice analyzing an ethical dilemma, complete the Group Exercise on p. 64.)

The most well-known theory of cognitive moral development was introduced over three decades ago by the psychologist Lawrence Kohlberg.[53] According to **Kohlberg's theory of cognitive moral development,** people develop over the years in their capacity to understand what is right. Specifically, the theory distinguishes among three levels of moral development (for a summary, see Figure 2.4). The first level is referred to as the *preconventional level of moral reasoning.* People at this level (children and about one-third of all adults) haven't developed the capacity to assume the perspective of others. Accordingly, they interpret what is right solely with respect to themselves: "It is wrong to do something if it leads me to be punished." Because their cognitive skills are not sufficiently advanced, such individuals generally cannot comprehend any argument you may make about something being wrong because it violates their social obligations to others.

As people interact with others over the years, most come to use higher-level cognitive processes to judge morality. In a more sophisticated fashion, they judge right and wrong in terms of what is good for the others around them and society as a whole. This second level is referred to as the *conventional level of moral reasoning.* Approximately two-thirds of adults fall into this category. What they do is governed strongly by what's expected of them by others, and they carefully scour the social environment for cues as to "what's right." People who engage in conventional moral reasoning obey the law not only because they fear the repercussions of not doing so, but also because they recognize that doing so is the right thing to do insofar as it promotes the safety and welfare of society as a whole.

Finally, Kohlberg's theory also identifies a third level of cognitive moral development, the *postconventional level.* At this level, people judge what is right and wrong not solely in terms of their interpersonal and societal obligations but also in terms of complex philosophical principles of duty, justice, and rights. Very few people ever attain this level. Those who do, however, follow their own "moral compass," doing what they are convinced is truly right, even if others don't agree.

Research has found that people behave in very different ways as a function of their level of cognitive moral development. For example, as you might expect, people

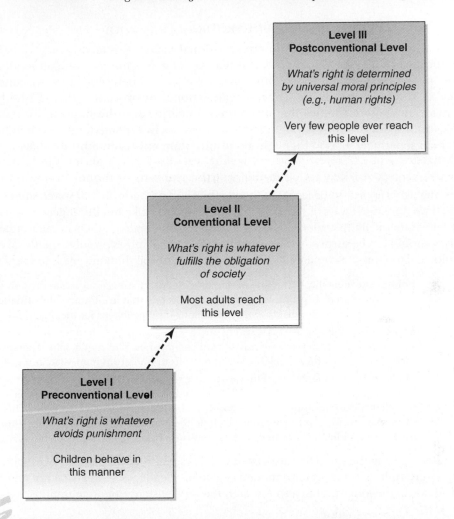

Figure 2.4   Kohlberg's Theory of Cognitive Moral Development: A Summary

According to *Kohlberg's theory of cognitive moral development,* people develop the capacity to make moral decisions as they develop over the years by interacting with others. The three major levels of cognitive moral development are identified here.

(Source: Based on information in Kohlberg, 1976; see Note 53.)

who are at higher levels of cognitive moral development (typically, conventional as opposed to preconventional) manifest their greater ethical behavior in several ways. Specifically, they are less inclined to harm others, less likely to misreport information even if it makes them look bad, and they steal less from their employers.[54] Although efforts to raise people's level of moral reasoning through training have been successful, few such efforts have been used in organizations.[55] This is in large part because most workers already function at the conventional level, making them sensitive to efforts to promote ethical behavior predicated on changing the social norms that exist within organizations. We now will consider some of the key social dynamics that influence ethical behavior.

Situational Determinants of Unethical Behavior

As you might imagine, many different situational factors can lead people to behave unethically on the job. Although the list may be long, it is not too difficult to identify some of the major organizational influences on unethical behavior. Here, we consider three of the most important ones—organizational norms encouraging unethical behavior, managerial values that discourage integrity, and the impact of unethical behavior by leaders. Although these factors surely are interrelated, it is worth identifying them separately so as to highlight their important effects on ethical behavior.

Some managerial values undermine integrity

Most managers appear to believe that "good ethics is good business." However, some managers have developed ways of thinking that lead them to make unethical decisions. Given how very influential top leaders are when it comes to influencing others in their organizations, it should not be surprising that unethical managerial values promote unethical organizational decisions.[56] Several well-known forms of unethical thinking are as follows.[57]

> **Bottom-line mentality**—This line of thinking supports financial success as the only value to be considered. It promotes short-term decisions that are immediately financially sound, despite the fact that they may cause long-term problems for the organization.

> **Exploitative mentality**—This view encourages "using" people in a way that promotes stereotypes and undermines empathy and compassion. This highly selfish perspective sacrifices concern for others in favor of benefits to one's own immediate interests.

> **Madison Avenue mentality**—This perspective suggests that anything is right if the public can be made to see it as right. The idea is that executives may be more concerned that their decisions appear to be right than about their legitimate morality. This kind of thinking leads some companies to hide their unethical behaviors (e.g., dumping toxic waste under cover of night) or to otherwise justify them as acceptable.

Recognizing the problems associated with these various orientations is not difficult. Their overemphasis on short-term monetary gain may lead to decisions that not only hurt individuals in the long run but also threaten the very existence of organizations.

Organizations sometimes encourage behavior that violates ethical standards

It is easy to understand that people may behave unethically on the job to the extent that they are encouraged to do so. Consider, for example, how some business executives are expected to say nothing about ethically dubious behavior they've witnessed in their companies. In fact, in many companies it is considered not only acceptable but also desirable to be secretive and deceitful. For example, the practice of **stonewalling**—willingly hiding relevant information—is quite common.

A major reason for this is that some organizations punish those who are too open and honest. As a classic case in point, in 1968 B.F. Goodrich allegedly rewarded employees who falsified and withheld data on the quality of aircraft brakes to win certification. This example illustrates how the *counternorms* of secrecy and deceitfulness were accepted and supported by the organization. By **counternorms** we are referring to accepted organizational practices that run contrary to society's prevailing ethical standards. For a summary of some of the most common counternorms found in organizations, see Figure 2.5.[58]

Figure 2.5   Ethical Norms Versus Organizational Counternorms

Although societal standards of ethics dictate the appropriateness of certain actions (i.e., *ethical norms*), *counternorms* that encourage and support opposite practices sometimes develop within organizations.

(Source: Based on suggestions by Jansen and Von Glinow, 1985; see Note 58.)

Workers emulate the unethical behavior of their superiors

Probably very few organizational leaders condone and actively promote unethical behavior. However, many organizational officials promote unethical behavior unwittingly by way of the examples they set for their employees. For example, suppose a manager submits an expense report to her administrative assistant to prepare for submission to the accounting office. Included on it are several items the assistant knows are not legitimate (e.g., lavish meals with clients). Although the manager might not be thinking about it, by padding her expense account she is sending a message to her administrative assistant that stealing from the company is an acceptable practice. Despite what she might say publicly about not stealing, her behind-the-scenes actions tell a different story. As a result, the administrative assistant might not think twice about taking a few dollars from the company's petty cash box to purchase her lunch. "After all," she may reason, "my boss takes a little extra money from the company, so it must be okay for me to do so too."

A survey of some 1,500 U.S. employees suggests that this is precisely what happens.[59] Specifically, employees who feel that the top managers in their organization act ethically themselves report seeing far less misconduct among their peers (15 percent) than those who feel that their top managers do not behave ethically themselves or who only talk about behaving ethically (56 percent). Obviously, when it comes to ethical conduct on the job, managers set an example by virtue of their own behavior, and their "actions speak louder than words." Putting it in the lingo of today's managers, to promote ethical behavior in their companies, it is essential for officials to "walk the talk."

Using Corporate Ethics Programs to Promote Ethical Behavior

Most companies today, particularly large ones, have in place some sort of formal, systematic mechanisms designed to promote ethics. These efforts, known as **corporate ethics programs,** are designed to create organizational cultures (see Chapter 12) that both make people sensitive to potentially unethical behavior and discourage them from engaging in them. If they didn't have such programs in place earlier, to comply with SOX regulations, they certainly do now.

Components of corporate ethics programs

Typically, corporate ethics programs consist of some combination of the following components.[60]

➤ *A code of ethics.*   A **code of ethics** is a document describing what an organization stands for and the general rules of conduct expected of employees (e.g., to avoid conflicts of interest, to be honest, and so on). In the mid-1990s, about 78 percent of all *Fortune* 1000 companies had codes of ethics in place, and that figure is considerably higher today.[61] Some codes are highly specific, stating, for example, the maximum size of gifts that can be accepted, whereas others are far more general.

➤ *Ethics training.*   Codes of ethics are especially effective when they are used in conjunction with training programs that reinforce a company's ethical values.[62] In the absence of such training, too many codes come across as merely "window dressing," and are ignored, if they are even read at all. Ethics training efforts range from lectures, videotapes, and case studies to more elaborate simulations. Citicorp, for example, has trained more than 40,000 employees in over 60 countries using an elaborate corporate ethics game, "The Work Ethic," that simulates ethical dilemmas that employees are likely to confront.[63]

➤ *Ethics audits.*   Just as companies regularly audit their books to check on irregularities in their finances, they also should assess the morality of their employees' behavior on a regular basis so as to identify irregularities in this realm. Such assessments are known as **ethics audits.** These require actively investigating and documenting incidents of dubious ethical value, discussing them in an open and honest fashion, and developing a concrete plan to avoid such actions in the future. Conducting an ethics audit can be quite revealing. For some useful guidelines on how to do so, see Table 2.3.[64]

➤ *An ethics committee.*   An **ethics committee** is a group of senior-level managers from various areas of the organization who assist an organization's CEO in making ethical decisions. Members of the committee develop and evaluate company-wide ethics policies.

➤ *An ethics officer.*   An **ethics officer** is a high-ranking organizational official (e.g., the general counsel or vice president of ethics) who is expected to provide strategies for ensuring ethical conduct throughout an organization. Because the Federal Sentencing Guidelines for Organizations specify that a specific, high-level corporate officer should be responsible for ethical behavior, many companies have such an individual in place.

➤ *A mechanism for communicating ethical standards.*   To be effective, ethics programs must clearly articulate and reinforce a company's ethical expectations to employees. With this in mind, growing numbers of companies are putting into place **ethics hot lines,** special phone lines that employees can call to ask questions about ethical behavior and to report any ethical misdeeds they may have observed.

Table 2.3   How to Conduct an Ethics Audit

A thorough ethics audit can reveal a great deal about a company's commitment to ethics and the extent to which its efforts to foster ethical behavior are effective. However, to recognize these benefits, it is crucial to conduct an ethics audit in an appropriate manner. The following guidelines will help.

1. Ensure that top executives, such as the CEO, are committed to the ethics audit and appoint a committee to guide it.
2. Create a diverse team of employees to write questions regarding the company's ethical performance. These should focus on existing practices (e.g., codes of ethics) as well as prevailing norms about company practices (e.g., people regularly padding their expense accounts).
3. Carefully analyze official documents, such as ethical mission statements and codes of ethics, to see how clear and thorough they are.
4. Ask people questions about why they think various unethical behaviors have occurred.
5. Compare your company's ethical practices to those of other companies in the same industry.
6. Write a formal report summarizing these findings and present it to all concerned parties.

(Source: Based on suggestions by Ferrell et al., 2002; see Note 64.)

The Effectiveness of Corporate Ethics Programs

By themselves, codes of ethics have only limited effectiveness in regulating ethical behavior in organizations.[65] However, an integrated ethics program that combines a code of ethics with additional components (e.g., an ethics officer, ethics training, etc.) can be quite effective. Specifically, it has been found that compared to companies that don't have ethics programs in place, within those that do, employees (a) are more likely to report ethical misconduct to company authorities, (b) are considered more accountable for ethics violations, and (c) face less pressure to compromise standards of business conduct.[66] Clearly, the effects of the ethics programs are being felt.

Additional evidence from a study the author conducted shows that an ethics program also may effectively reduce employee theft, one particularly costly form of unethical behavior.[67] This investigation compared the rate of petty theft between two groups of employees who worked for the same financial services company—one whose office had a corporate ethics program in place for the past six months, and one in a distant city that had no ethics program in place. The ethics program consisted of a code of ethics, an ethics committee, and 10 hours of training.

Prior to the study, employees were tested to identify their level of cognitive moral development. Some employees were found to be at the preconventional level whereas others were at the conventional level. The workers volunteered to complete a questionnaire sponsored by the company for one hour after work. They were told to expect "fair pay" for this task but were actually paid considerably less than their standard hourly wage ($2 as opposed to about $10). This motivated the workers to steal from the company in order to get even. In addition, workers were given an opportunity to steal by being allowed to take their own pay from a bowl of pennies in front of them while nobody watched. Because the researcher knew exactly how many pennies were

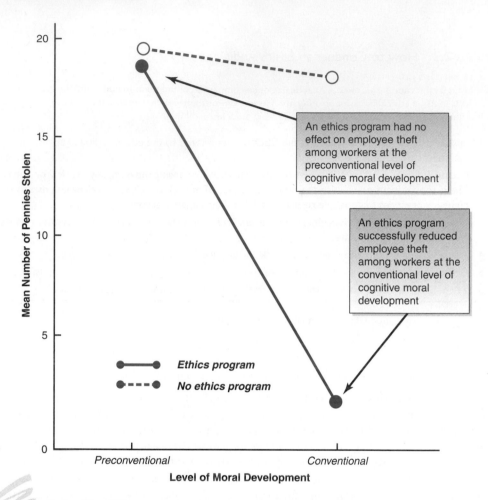

Figure 2.6   The Effectiveness of an Ethics Program Depends on Cognitive Moral Development: Summary of Research Findings

An experiment compared the amount that employees stole from their company as a function of whether or not their office had an ethics program in place and their level of cognitive moral development. It was found that an ethics program had no appreciable effect on employee theft among workers at the preconventional level, but that an ethics program successfully reduced employee theft among workers at the conventional level.

(Source: Based on data reported by Greenberg, 2002; see Note 67.)

in the bowl beforehand, he could determine precisely how much money was taken. Amounts in excess of $2 were considered by the researcher to constitute theft.

Did those workers who had a code of ethics in place at their office steal less from the company than those who did not? As shown in Figure 2.6, the answer depended on the workers' level of cognitive moral development. Workers whose office did not have an ethics program in place stole an average of just under 20 cents regardless of their level of cognitive moral development. Likewise, people from offices that had an ethics program stole about the same amount when they were at the preconventional level of moral development. However, hardly any theft occurred at all among workers at the conventional level who worked at an office that had an ethics program in place. In other words, the ethics program was effective in combating employee theft, but only among employees who had attained a sufficiently high level of moral development for the program to have an effect on them. By contrast, among workers at the preconventional level of moral development, the ethics program apparently had little, if any, impact. Given that such individuals are unlikely to fully comprehend and accept their ethics training, this makes perfect sense.

Although the amount of theft examined in this study was very small, the underlying conclusion to be drawn is straightforward. A corporate ethics program may have only limited effectiveness because it will influence only some workers—those who have reached a sufficiently high level of moral development. Fortunately, this constitutes about two-thirds of the population as a whole. Reaching the other one-third, those at the preconventional level, may well require other methods, such as emphasizing clear penalties for breaking the rules.

BEYOND ETHICS: CORPORATE SOCIAL RESPONSIBILITY

Usually, when we think of business organizations, we focus on their financial responsibilities to stockholders and investors—that is, to make money. Of course, this is not their only responsibility. As we have been discussing all along, organizations also are responsible for obeying the law and to answering to yet a higher standard, behaving ethically. In addition to these considerations, many of today's organizations are going beyond their ethical responsibilities by taking proactive steps to help society at large by virtue of their philanthropic contributions. Together, these four types of responsibilities, shown in Figure 2.7 in the form of a pyramid—thus called the pyramid of **corporate social responsibility**—comprise what we have in mind when we speak of *corporate social responsibility*.[68]

What Is Corporate Social Responsibility?

The term **corporate social responsibility** is used to describe business decision making linked to ethical values, compliance with legal requirements, and respect for individuals, the community at large, and the environment. It involves operating a business in a manner that meets or exceeds the ethical, legal, and public expectations that society has of business. Some examples of highly socially responsible actions from companies around the world are as follows:[69]

> ➤ *Whole Foods Market*—This nationwide chain specializing in organic foods developed an initiative to use solar energy for 25 percent of its power.
> ➤ *Stonyfield Farms*—This dairy company donates 10 percent of net profits to charities that help protect and restore the earth, and it pays farmers extra to not use synthetic bovine growth hormones in the milk it buys to make yogurt.
> ➤ *Royal Dutch Shell*—This large oil company has agreed not to engage in mining or oil exploration activities in areas of the world that have special biological or cultural significance.
> ➤ *Boise Cascade*—This paper and building materials company does not harvest timber from old-growth forests and endangered forests.

Figure 2.7   The Pyramid of Corporate Social Responsibility

To be socially responsible, companies must meet the four different types of responsibilities identified here. The most basic responsibilities, financial, are shown at the bottom because organizations would go out of business if they failed to meet their economic obligations.

(Source: Based on suggestions by Carroll, 1991; see Note 68.)

➤ *Natura Cosmeticos*—This Brazilian cosmetics firm promotes and supports local human rights initiatives (e.g., it does not use child labor), it promotes education, and it encourages its employees to volunteer for nonprofit organizations in their community.

➤ *Starbucks Coffee Co.*—Offering more than just a good cup of coffee, Starbucks has programs that benefit employees (e.g., retirement plans even for part-time workers), communities (e.g., promoting local charities), and the environment (e.g., developing reusable cups).

It's important to note that corporate social responsibility is not merely a collection of isolated practices or occasional gestures, nor does it involve initiatives motivated by marketing or public relations benefits. Instead, corporate social responsibility is a comprehensive set of policies, practices, and programs that are integrated throughout business operations and decision-making processes that are supported and rewarded by top management. Importantly, social responsibility involves more than simply making a few charitable donations; it must be a commitment to doing what's best for people and the community (as is the case with the companies spotlighted in these examples).

In recent years, many of the largest companies in the United States have been going out of their way to behave in a variety of socially responsible ways. For a summary of some of the world's most socially responsible companies, along with just a single noteworthy example of their commitment to social responsibility, see Table 2.4.[70] (As you might imagine, one of the most effective and dramatic ways that organizations can demonstrate socially responsible behavior is by taking steps to preserve the environment. For some examples, see the Winning Practices section on p. 60.)

Table 2.4   Top 10 Most Socially Responsible Companies in the World, 2008

In conjunction with two research firms, *Fortune* magazine ranked the world's largest companies in terms of their commitment to social and environmental goals. The top 10, listed here, excelled in different ways.

Rank	Company	Notable Socially Responsible Action
1	BP	Led the petroleum industry in the research and development of wind, solar, and carbon dioxide as alternative power sources.
2	Barclay's	This British bank refuses to invest in projects that cause people to be relocated or that disrupt the ecosystem.
3	ENI	Italys's large oil and gas producer uses high-tech equipment to shrink its carbon footprint and to reduce the energy used by its refineries.
4	HSBC Holdings	This global bank offers low-interest loans to companies investing in alternative energy sources and refuses to loan money to weapons manufacturers.
5	Vodaphone	Europe's largest cellular provider developed ways in which the developing nations of Africa can use mobile phones to expand access to financial markets.
6	Royal Dutch Shell	Built a plant in Australia that captures the natural gas produced from a coal power plant and uses that gas to produce more electricity.
7	Peugeot	To promote safety, the French automaker works with the government to make streets and traffic patterns safer and directly with drivers by teaching them defensive driving techniques.
8	HBOS	By driving mobile banking vans to rural areas, this UK consumer bank brings basic banking services directly to people who otherwise wouldn't have access to them.
9	Chevron	This oil company has worked with the Cawelo Water District in California's semi-arid San Joaquin Valley to export produced water from the Kern River oil field into a reservoir that irrigates thousands of acres of farmland.
10	Chrysler	This large automaker works with Mothers Against Drunk Driving to make the roads safer, and to make driving more fuel efficient, it is testing a fleet of hydrogen-fuel vehicles.

(Source: Based on information reported by Demos, 2008; see Note 69.)

Profitability and Social Responsibility: The Virtuous Circle

Do socially responsible companies perform better financially than those that are less socially responsible? The answer is not straightforward. Sometimes scientists find no clear connection, which is not surprising given the complexities of social responsibility and the fact that many different variables influence a company's financial performance. However, on many other occasions, they do find such a link. Consider, for example, that in the four decades from 1950 to 1990, highly socially responsible companies such as Johnson & Johnson, Coca-Cola, Gerber, IBM, Deere, Xerox, JCPenney, and Pitney Bowes grew at an annual rate of 11.3 percent compared to only 6.2 percent for other companies on the Dow Jones Industrials list over the same period.[71]

Winning Practices

Making a Difference with Green Power

These days, many companies are taking steps to preserve the environment by using energy sources that reduce the emission of greenhouse gases. Among the leaders in this regard are organizations recognized by the U.S. Environmental Protection Agency for using "green power," sources of electricity produced from solar, wind, geothermal, and other sources that avoid adverse environmental impact.[72]

- Intel Corporation, one of the world's leading information technology companies, uses a wide variety of practices designed to preserve the environment. These include: (a) using environmentally friendly materials in its products, factories, and offices, (b) reducing energy consumption in manufacturing plants and data centers, and (c) collecting and recycling wastewater, solid waste, and chemical waste.[73]

- PepsiCo, the huge food and beverage company, has long been regarded as a leader in its efforts to save energy. For example, its manufacturing plants rely on energy-efficient motors and energy-efficient windows and skylights are used to capitalize on natural lighting. Also, living up to its name, solar power is used in the factory that makes SunChips, the multigrain snack produced by PepsiCo's Frito-Lay division.[74]

- The U.S. Air Force is using wind power to generate electricity at many of its bases throughout the country—as much as 100 percent in some locations (e.g., Fairchild Air Force Base in Spokane, Washington). This is part of the Air Force's plan to reduce energy consumption in its facilities by 3 percent each year through 2015.[75]

- Wells Fargo, the huge financial institution, has taken an active role in promoting the environment by virtue of its investment practices. For example, it offers reduced mortgage interest rates to customers building energy-efficient, environmentally friendly houses (e.g., solar-powered homes) in low–moderate-income neighborhoods. The company also has a comprehensive recycling program in its 3,300 banking locations.[76]

Although they may involve quite a bit of expense, the initiatives outlined here are seriously worth considering by all organizations. Because they involve efforts to help preserve our planet they may be considered to be among the most socially responsible practices of all.

Although there are surely many different reasons for this, a key one, which we also mentioned in connection with ethics, is that people often support the socially responsible activities of organizations with their patronage and investments. With this in mind, there exist mutual funds that invest only in socially responsible companies and books that provide detailed information on the socially responsible (and irresponsible) behavior of companies that consumers and investors can use to guide their decisions.[77] Today, individuals who desire to support socially responsible companies by "voting with their dollars" can find it easy to get the information they need. That this may contribute to the financial well-being of a company is important, of course, since financial considerations are an organization's most basic responsibility (which is why they are at the base of the corporate social responsibility pyramid shown in Figure 2.8). Indeed, consider these recent research findings.

➤ Consumers indicated that they would be willing to pay $9.71/pound for coffee sold by a socially responsible company as compared to $8.31/pound from a company

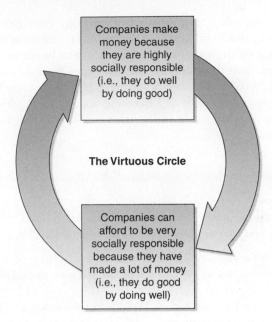

Figure 2.8   The Virtuous Circle

It is been suggested that socially responsible companies perform well financially because they are supported by customers and investors. As a result, they become wealthier, making it easier for them to become even more philanthropic. This is known as the *virtuous circle*.

(Source: Based on suggestions by Treviño and Nelson, 1999; see Note 39.)

whose social responsibility they don't know and only $5.89/pound for the same coffee sold by a socially irresponsible company.[78]

➤ Among current employees seeking new jobs, 48 percent indicate that they would be willing to work for lower pay if they could work for a socially responsible company.[79]

Despite these striking findings, it's important to keep in mind that most companies engage in socially responsible behavior for its own sake, not as a path to profitability.[80] However, profit often comes as a result.

Although profit may not be the primary objective for engaging in socially responsible behavior, it is clear that there is a strong link between the two. Moreover, this connection appears to be bidirectional in nature. The idea is straightforward: As noted earlier, companies that are highly socially responsible tend to perform well financially (i.e., they "do well by doing good"), and then because they have substantial resources, they can afford to allocate more resources (money, help from employees, etc.) to social causes (i.e., they "do good by doing well"). This relationship, which has been referred to as the **virtuous circle,** is summarized in Figure 2.8.[81]

With the virtuous circle in mind, it is not surprising to find that some of the world's most profitable organizations are also among the most philanthropic. For example, the highly profitable Microsoft Corporation regularly makes multimillion-dollar charitable contributions to worthwhile causes in the form of cash and software. In addition, a generous $24 million donation from its co-founder Bill Gates has made it possible for more good work to be accomplished around the world through the Bill and Melinda Gates Foundation. And with the $30 billion donation to this foundation by Warren Buffett in 2006 and Bill Gates's 2008 decision to leave Microsoft and begin working at the foundation full-time, it's clear that the Bill and Melinda Gates Foundation will be one of the world's most influential charitable organizations.[82] Although many big companies have been accused of exploiting people and harming society, examples like these make it clear that there is also another side to the story—and a very munificent and socially responsible one at that.[83]

Back to the Case

Answer the following questions about this chapter's Making the Case (pp. 33–34) to illustrate insights you have derived about the material in this chapter.

1. What forms of organizational justice did Patricia Dunn appear to violate? Specifically, what did she do that was unfair and what should she have done differently?

2. What forces may have led Patricia Dunn to behave as she did? What, if anything, do you think current HP officials might have learned from the pretexting scandal?

3. Over the years, HP has developed an excellent reputation for corporate social responsibility. Do you think that this reputation has been soiled as result of the pretexting scandal? What can the company do to put this incident behind it and enhance its reputation?

You Be the Consultant

Employee Theft in Convenience Stores

The district manager of a chain of 24-hour convenience stores is very concerned about her stores' rate of employee theft, which is currently about twice the industry average and rising rapidly. Because this problem has arisen suddenly, you and she suspect that it is in response to some recently introduced changes in the company's overtime policy. Managers who used to be paid time-and-a-half for each hour they worked over 40 are now paid a flat salary that typically results in lower total wages for the same amount of work. Answer the following questions based on the information in this chapter.

1. What form of justice appears to have been violated by the new pay policy? Explain your answer.

2. In this case, the new pay policy was implemented without first discussing it with store managers. Do you think that the theft rate might have been lower had this been done? What else could be done to reduce the growing theft rate?

3. The company's code of ethics expressly prohibits theft, but other than being handed a copy along with other company documents and forms upon being hired, hardly anyone pays attention to it. What do you think could be done to enhance the effectiveness of the code of ethics as a weapon for combating the theft problem?

SELF-ASSESSMENT EXERCISE

Assessing Organizational Justice Where You Work

To learn about how workers respond to various types of injustices they may experience in the workplace, scientists have found it useful to use rating scales like the one shown. By completing this scale, you will gain some useful insight into your own feelings about the fairness experienced in the organization in which you work.

Directions

1. Using the following scale, respond to each of the questionnaire items by selecting a number from 1 to 5 to indicate the extent to which it applies to you.

   1 = almost never

   2 = slightly

   3 = moderately

   4 = greatly

   5 = almost always

2. In responding to each item, think about a particular organization in which you work or, if you are a student, think about a particular class.

3. Where you see the word (*outcome*), substitute a specific outcome that is relevant to you (e.g., for a worker, pay; for a student, a grade).

4. Where you see the word (*superior*), substitute a specific authority figure that is relevant to you (e.g., for a worker, one's supervisor; for a student, one's teacher).

Scale

To what extent . . .

1. ____ Is it possible for you to express your views about your (outcome)?
2. ____ Are your (outcomes) generally based on accurate information?
3. ____ Do you have an opportunity to correct decisions made about your (outcome)?
4. ____ Are you rewarded appropriately for the effort you put into your work?
5. ____ Do the (outcomes) you receive reflect the quality of your work?
6. ____ Is your (outcome) in keeping with your performance?
7. ____ Are you treated politely by your (superior)?
8. ____ Does your (superior) treat you with dignity and respect?
9. ____ Does your (superior) refrain from making inappropriate comments?
10. ____ Does your (superior) communicate openly with you?
11. ____ Does your (superior) tell you things in a timely fashion?
12. ____ Does your (superior) explain decisions to you in a thorough fashion?

(Source: Adapted from Colquitt, 2001; see Note 7).

Scoring

1. Add your responses to questions 1, 2, and 3. This is your *distributive justice* score.
2. Add your responses to questions 4, 5, and 6. This is your *procedural justice* score.
3. Add your responses to questions 7, 8, and 9. This is your *interpersonal justice* score.
4. Add your responses to questions 10, 11, and 12. This is your *informational justice* score.
5. For each score, higher numbers (e.g., 12–15) reflect higher perceived amounts of the type of fairness in question, whereas lower scores (e.g., 3–6) reflect lower perceived amounts of that type of fairness.

Discussion Questions

1. With respect to what particular type of fairness did you score highest? What specific experiences contributed to this assessment?
2. With respect to what particular type of fairness did you score lowest? What specific experiences contributed to this assessment?
3. What kinds of problems resulted from any violations of any type of organizational justice you may have experienced? What could have been done to avoid these violations?

GROUP EXERCISE

Analyzing an Ethical Dilemma

More often than you might imagine, managers confront situations in which they have to decide the right thing to do. Such "ethical dilemmas," as they are known, are usually quite challenging. Discussing ethical dilemmas with others is often a useful way of shedding light on the ethical path by identifying ethical considerations that you may have overlooked on your own. This exercise will give you an opportunity to analyze an ethical dilemma.

Directions

1. Divide the class into multiple groups of three or four students.
2. Read the following ethical dilemma.
3. Working together with the others in your group, analyze the dilemma by answering the following questions:
   (a) As the vice president in this situation, what do you think you *would do?* What factors enter into your decision?
   (b) What do you think would be the *right thing* to do? Explain the basis for your answer.

Ethical Dilemma

You're the vice president of a medium-sized organization that uses chemicals in its production process. In good faith, you've hired a highly competent person to ensure that your company complies with all environmental laws and safety regulations. This individual informs you that a chemical the company now uses in some quantity is not yet on the approved EPA list. However, it's undergoing review and is scheduled to be placed on the approval list in about three months because it's been found to be safe. You can't produce your product without the chemical, yet you're not supposed to use the chemical until it's approved. Waiting for approval would require shutting down the plant for three months, putting hundreds of people out of work, and threatening the company's very survival.

Source: Managing Business Ethics (2nd ed.), by Linda K. Treviño and Katherine A. Nelson, p. 10. © 1999 John Wiley & Sons.

Discussion Questions

1. Did the members of your group generally agree or disagree about what they would do in the situation described? What new viewpoints, if any, did you learn from others in your group?
2. Did the members of your group generally agree or disagree about what they thought was the right thing to do? What were the major points of agreement and disagreement?
3. In judging the right thing to do, what factors were taken into account (e.g., the law, the layoffs, etc.) and in what manner were they considered?

Psychological Processes in Organizations: Personality, Perception, and Learning

Learning Objectives

After reading this chapter, you will be able to:

1. **DEFINE** personality and **EXPLAIN** the nature of its effects on behavior in the workplace.
2. **DESCRIBE** personality dimensions that are responsible for individual differences in organizational behavior.
3. **DEFINE** social perception and **EXPLAIN** the process of attribution.
4. **DESCRIBE** social identity theory and Kelley's theory of causal attribution and **EXPLAIN** the various biases that make the social perception process imperfect.
5. **DEFINE** learning and **DESCRIBE** the two basic kinds of learning that occur in organizations.
6. **EXPLAIN** various ways in which principles of learning are applied in organizations.

3 GOOD REASONS why you should care about . . .

Psychological Processes in Organizations

You should care about psychological processes in organizations because:

1. Understanding people's personalities helps us know what to expect of them, and understanding our own personalities provides valuable insight into our own behavior.
2. The process by which we perceive others is fundamental to a wide variety of organizational activities.
3. Effectively training, managing, and disciplining employees requires knowing the basic principles of learning.

Making the Case for Psychological Processes in Organizations

Kenneth Chenault: An American Success at American Express

Summer 2008 was a challenging time for American Express (AMEX). Faced with a slumping economy, cardholders cut their spending dramatically and record numbers of even the wealthiest clients had delinquent accounts. Despite this gloomy, recessionary profile, AMEX's chairman and CEO, Kenneth I. Chenault, vowed to turn things around—a proclamation that Wall Street would have dismissed as puffery had it come from an executive without a quarter-century of successes on his resumé.

Since joining AMEX in 1981, Chenault systematically worked his way to the top by masterminding a string of turnarounds in each unit he headed. In the mid-1980s, for example, he put himself on the map by reviving the once-struggling merchandise services unit. Partnering with Panasonic and Sharp (who were looking for markets for their new video recorders), he up-scaled the merchandise mix—which used to consist of only low-ticket items such as luggage tags and clocks—boosting annual sales from $100 million to $700 million in just a few years.

Basking in the glow of this accomplishment, Chenault earned a ticket to the company's more prestigious consumer-card division, where he transformed an admittedly uncompetitive niche company into a vast financial empire. One key to this success involved expanding the company's limited base of wealthy customers to less affluent people and signing up lower-level merchants who had never taken American Express cards, such as gas stations, discount stores, and supermarkets—eventually, even Wal-Mart. Aiding this effort, and in a move that raised more than a few eyebrows in New York headquarters, Chenault slashed the fees that merchants were charged for processing customers' purchases (which, traditionally, were much higher than those of competitors MasterCard and Visa). Despite reduced individual-transaction revenue, the company more than made up the difference in increased volume. In fact, as Chenault transformed AMEX into a card for the masses, the company's income skyrocketed each year he was at the helm.

Behind these accomplishments, and a long list of others, beats the heart of a man who, since high school, has demonstrated an insatiable quest for knowledge. One way Chenault likes to learn is by carefully analyzing his missteps (and there have been these as well) to ensure that they won't be repeated. Chenault also learns a little each day by encouraging his colleagues to question his ideas in a constructive manner. The more they challenge him, the more he thinks about the problem at hand. Given his highly analytical approach, it's not surprising that as a student at Bowdoin College and later at Harvard Law School, Chenault became known for debating important issues in a logical, fact-driven, and unemotional style.

A proud African American, Chenault never let race serve as a basis for choosing sides of an issue. A colleague once noted that, "Ken has the capacity to operate in the mainstream of both worlds" and is "never shunned by one group or the other." In fact, as Chenault rose through the ranks at AMEX based on his exceptional successes, people of all races were pulling for him—and were duly proud of him. Like Tiger Woods, whom he signed to a promotional contract with AMEX, Chenault is a leading figure in his field who just happens to be African American but whose winning appeal is universal.

Those who work with Ken Chenault know him to be never combative in style, but always honest and likeable, a true gentleman. Here, also like Tiger Woods, it would be a grievous error to take Chenault's quiet ways as a sign that he is anything less than a fierce competitor. Just as he wasn't afraid to take on the naysayers who were against the changes he brought about at AMEX, he also hasn't been

(continued)

afraid to take on competitors in the credit card business. In fact, over four years, Chenault ushered AMEX through a legal battle against Visa and MasterCard, claiming that these companies were guilty of restraint of trade by not allowing banks to issue American Express cards. In July 2008, just as bad financial news was released, AMEX won a $4 billion settlement—a tidy sum that will mitigate AMEX's financial losses during a difficult period. Chalk up another victory for Ken Chenault.

More than just a tale of financial successes, this case illustrates the importance of several basic psychological processes that are responsible for key aspects of people's behavior in organizations. These are processes within individuals that, strictly speaking, cannot be seen but whose existence can be inferred on the basis of people's behavior. In particular, our account of Kenneth Chenault at American Express highlights the three such individual processes discussed in this chapter, processes that explain a wide variety of forms of organizational behavior.

To begin, it is obvious that Ken Chenault is a very special individual. After all, it isn't everyone who, even without an advanced degree in business, works his way up to running a multibillion-dollar corporation. But then again, like Ken Chenault, we all have our own special combination of characteristics that makes us distinct from others. It is this unique pattern of traits that defines one's *personality*, the first topic we will examine in this chapter.

Clearly, one of Chenault's most special qualities is his capacity to approach issues in a clear-headed and unemotional fashion. Although this orientation has helped Chenault, it would be misleading to suggest that being this way is a road map to success for everyone. Different people take different paths. Indeed, many of the unique qualities that define who we are contribute to how we behave on the job. Understanding these, as you may suspect, is a key aspect of the study of organizational behavior.

Among the things that have contributed to Ken Chenault's success as an executive is the fact that people believe many positive things about him. As a result, they give him the freedom needed to succeed further. Chenault's colleagues, for example, judge him to be honest and likable—qualities that surely stand him well.

Although you probably never thought about it, this raises an important question: How do people come to make these judgments in the first place? To social scientists, this is a fundamental question, and one that has received quite a bit of attention. The term *social perception* is used to describe the process by which people come to make judgments of other individuals. This important process is the second topic we present in this chapter.

Finally, we cover another fundamental interpersonal process in this chapter—*learning*. Think about how Chenault came to know what to do, how to handle situations he faced. As described in the case, he carefully analyzed the effects of his actions, and he invited others to give him feedback as well. He learned a great deal in school and from his on-the-job experiences as he worked his way up in the company. In fact, if you asked him, he probably would admit that he never stopped learning.

As you will see from reading this chapter, the various individual processes touched on here are far broader in scope than this case suggests, and they account for a wide range of behavior in organizations. After reading this chapter, you will come away with a good understanding of some of the psychological processes that contributed to the success of Ken Chenault at American Express—and, more importantly to you, processes that also will contribute to your own personal success in the business world.

PERSONALITY: THE UNIQUE DIFFERENCES BETWEEN US

If our experience with other people tells us anything, it is that we are all in some way *unique,* and at least to a degree, we are *consistent* in this manner. That is, we each possess a distinct pattern of traits and characteristics not fully duplicated in any other person, and these are generally stable over time. Thus, if you know someone who is courteous and outgoing today, he or she probably showed these traits in the past and is likely to continue showing them in the future. Moreover, this person will tend to show them in many different situations over time.

Together, these two facts form the basis for a useful working definition of **personality**—the unique and relatively stable pattern of behavior, thoughts, and emotions shown by individuals. In short, personality refers to the lasting ways in which any one person is different from all others. And, as you might imagine, personality characteristics can be very important on the job.[1] With this in mind, we will review several key personality dimensions that are most relevant to OB. Before doing this, however, let's take a look at some basic aspects of personality.

The Nature of Personality: Some FAQs

To fully understand the nature of personality, we now address some fundamental questions about its nature.

How is personality determined?

Psychologists long have been interested in the source of people's most basic qualities, such as physical appearance, intelligence, and, of course, personality.[2] Are these qualities the result of *nature* (i.e., genetic predispositions we inherit from our parents) or *nurture* (i.e., our experiences in the world)? Over the years, many scientists have studied this question and have offered a variety of different opinions. However, to characterize current thinking on this complex question, the simple answer would have to be: *both.* In other words, our personalities are determined to some extent by genetic factors (i.e., biology) and to some extent by the conditions we experience as we grow up (i.e., the environment). For a graphic summary of this point, refer to Figure 3.1.

The main way scientists go about studying the nature-nurture controversy is by comparing the degree of similarity between sets of identical twins who were reared apart (i.e., people who share the same genetic makeups but who have been exposed to different conditions in their lives) and the degree of similarity between children whose siblings share the same natural parents and those who were adopted (i.e., people who have been exposed to similar conditions in their lives but who have different genetic makeups). Extensive research in this area has found that identical twins who have been

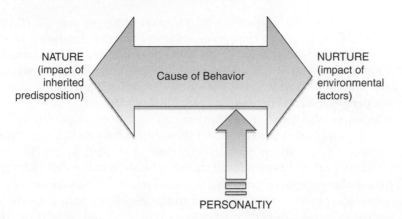

Figure 3.1   Is Personality the Result of Nature or Nurture?
Most scientists today believe that personality is the result of both the genetic qualities we inherit (i.e., *nature*) and the conditions we experience as we grow up (i.e., *nurture*), although the influence of nurture is considered greater.

reared apart have more personality traits in common than pairs of people selected at random. In addition, identical twins (who are genetically alike) have more similar personalities than fraternal twins (who have fewer genetic similatities).[3] Moreover, the personalities of biological siblings (i.e., ones who have the same parents) are more alike than the personalities of siblings who have been adopted. These findings make a clear case that, at least to a certain extent, personality is heritable.[4]

This is not to say, however, that our personalities are not also influenced by when, where, and how we grow up. Indeed, they are—and to a great extent. In fact, although both heritability and the environment are involved in determining personality, current evidence suggests that the environment plays a slightly greater role.[5] In other words, the conditions we face in formative years go a long way toward determining our personalities. These include, to a great extent, how we are treated by our parents and relatives, our experiences in school, and a wide variety of other environmental factors. For this reason, many scientists agree that for the most part, our personalities are pretty much set by the time we become adults.[6] Not surprisingly, then, understanding the exact nature of personality in the workplace can be quite important.

What role does personality play in the workplace?
If you think of personality as "who you are," then it makes sense that this would influence how you behave in the workplace. People who are shy would tend to say little, while those who are gregarious, for example, would be more talkative. However, it would be misleading to suggest that our personalities dictate entirely how we behave. After all, we also are influenced by the situations we're in, the contexts in which we live and work. Even the shy person, for example, may speak up in some circumstances (e.g., when badly mistreated) and even the gregarious person may keep quiet (e.g., showing respect while an important announcement is being made). The point is that although people possess stable traits and characteristics that predispose them to behave in certain ways, these qualities by themselves do not completely determine how someone will

behave in any given setting.[7] Situations also introduce forces that affect how one is likely to behave. Together, both the personal factors *and* the situational factors influence behavior. In other words, behavior usually is the result of both characteristics possessed by an individual (his or her knowledge, abilities, skills, and personality) and the nature of the situation in which that person operates. This approach, known as the **interactionist perspective,** is very popular in the field of OB today.[8]

As an example, the question of whether various aspects of personality affect job performance has long been of interest to OB scientists.[9] As we will note later in this chapter, certain aspects of personality are indeed related to job performance. Although this is important, it doesn't tell the whole story, however. The strength of the effects of personality depends on many situational factors. These may include such factors as *job demands* (i.e., the set of tasks and duties associated with a specific job that motivate people to behave in certain ways; see Chapter 6) and *social norms* (i.e., pressures to go along with others in one's group; see Chapter 9). Overall, both personality and situational factors can serve as *facilitators*—factors that encourage certain behaviors (e.g., make people work harder) or *constraints*—factors that discourage certain behaviors (e.g., hold people back from performing as well as possible).[10]

So, as you read about personality in this section of the chapter it's important to keep in mind that it alone is only one factor determinant of behavior in the workplace. To understand fully the factors that influence people we must take into account *both* their personalities and the nature of the situations they face (see Figure 3.2).

How is personality assessed?

Physical traits such as height and weight can be measured readily by means of simple tools. Various aspects of personality, however, cannot be assessed quite so simply. There are no rulers that we can put to the task. How, then, can we quantify differences

Figure 3.2   The Interactionist Perspective

According to the *interactionist perspective*, people's behavior is the result of the joint influences of both personality and the nature of the situations in which that behavior occurs.

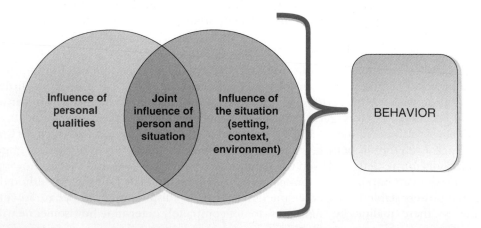

between individuals with respect to their various personality characteristics? Although several methods exist for accomplishing this task, far and away the most widely used technique in the field of OB is the *objective test*.

If you've ever completed a questionnaire in which you were asked to indicate whether each of a set of statements is true or false about yourself or the extent to which you agree or disagree with various statements, chances are good that you have completed an **objective test**—a paper-and-pencil inventory in which people are asked to respond to a series of questions designed to measure one or more aspects of their personality. The answers to the questions on objective tests are scored by means of special answer keys. The score obtained by a specific person is then compared with those obtained by many others who have taken the test previously and who are believed to have the personality characteristic in question. In this way, an individual's relative standing on the trait or ability being measured can be determined. Such tests are considered "objective" because they are scored by comparing individuals' answers to special scoring keys; subjective judgments by the test-givers do not play a role. (For two examples, refer to Table 3.1 and this chapter's Self-Assessment Exercise on pp. 97–98.)

Table 3.1 The Big Five Dimensions of Personality

The items listed here are similar to ones used to measure each of the *Big Five dimensions of personality*. Answering them may give you some insight into these key aspects of your personality.

Directions: Indicate the extent to which you agree or disagree with each item by entering a number in the space beside it. Enter 5 if you agree strongly with the item, 4 if you agree, 3 if you neither agree nor disagree, 2 if you disagree, and 1 if you disagree strongly.

Conscientiousness:

_____ I keep my room neat and clean.

_____ People generally find me to be extremely reliable.

Extraversion:

_____ I like lots of excitement in my life.

_____ I usually am very cheerful.

Agreeableness:

_____ I generally am quite courteous to other people.

_____ People never think I am cold and sly.

Emotional Stability:

_____ I often worry about things that are out of my control.

_____ I usually feel sad or "down."

Openness to Experience:

_____ I have a lot of curiosity.

_____ I enjoy the challenge of change.

Scoring: Add your scores for each item. Higher scores reflect greater degrees of the personality characteristic being measured.

Now that you're familiar with the basic nature of personality, let's consider some of the personality variables that are most strongly related to behavior in the workplace.

The "Big Five" Dimensions of Personality

Although many different dimensions of personality can be used to describe people, some are more important than others. One group of variables that scientists have found to be especially important is referred to as the **Big Five dimensions of personality.**[11] These are as follows:

➤ *Extraversion.*   A tendency to seek stimulation and to enjoy the company of other people. This reflects a dimension ranging from energetic, enthusiastic, sociable, and talkative at one end, to retiring, sober, reserved, silent, and cautious on the other.

➤ *Agreeableness.*   A tendency to be compassionate toward others. This dimension ranges from good-natured, cooperative, trusting, and helpful at one end, to irritable, suspicious, and uncooperative at the other.

➤ *Conscientiousness.*   A tendency to show self-discipline, to strive for competence and achievement. This dimension ranges from well-organized, careful, self-disciplined, responsible, and precise at one end, to disorganized, impulsive, careless, and undependable at the other.

➤ *Neuroticism.*   A tendency to experience unpleasant emotions easily. This dimension ranges from poised, calm, composed, and not hypochondriacal at one end, to nervous, anxious, high-strung, and hypochondriacal at the other.

➤ *Openness to experience.*   A tendency to enjoy new experiences and new ideas. This dimension ranges from imaginative, witty, and having broad interests at one end, to down-to-earth, simple, and having narrow interests at the other.

These five basic dimensions of personality are measured by means of questionnaires in which the people whose personalities are being assessed answer various questions about themselves. Some sample items similar to those on popular measures of the Big Five dimensions are shown in Table 3.1. By completing them, you can gain a rough idea of where *you* stand on each dimension.

The Big Five dimensions of personality are very important and they are related strongly to work performance.[12] For example, *conscientiousness* shows the strongest association with task performance: The higher individuals are on this dimension, the higher their performance.[13]

Another Big Five dimension, *emotional stability,* also is related to task performance, although not as strongly or consistently: To some extent, the more emotionally stable an individual is, the better his or her task performance is inclined to be.[14]

Other dimensions of the Big Five also are linked to task performance, but in more specific ways. For instance, *agreeableness* is related positively to various interpersonal aspects of work (e.g., getting along well with others). It also is related negatively to the tendency to be absent from work by choice: The more agreeable someone is, the less likely he or she is to stay home from work voluntarily.[15] And for some occupations—ones requiring individuals to interact with many other people during the course of the day (e.g., managers, police officers, salespeople)—*extraversion* is related positively to performance.

The Big Five dimensions also are related to team performance. Specifically, the higher the average scores of team members on conscientiousness, agreeableness, extraversion, and emotional stability, the better their teams perform.[16] Overall, the Big Five dimensions are indeed one determinant of job performance for teams as well as individuals.

Type A and Type B Behavior Patterns

Think about the people you know. Can you identify someone who always seems to be in a hurry, is extremely competitive, and is often irritable? Now name someone who shows the opposite pattern—a person who is relaxed, not very competitive, and easy-going. The people you have in mind represent extremes on one key dimension of personality. The first individual would be labeled *Type A* and the second *Type B*.

People categorized as **Type A** personalities show high levels of competitiveness, irritability, and time urgency (i.e., they are always in a hurry). In addition, they demonstrate certain stylistic patterns, such as loud and exaggerated speech, and a tendency to respond very quickly in many contexts. For example, during conversations they often begin speaking before others are finished. People classified as having a **Type B** personality show the opposite pattern; they are calmer and more relaxed.

Do people who are Type A's and Type B's differ with respect to job performance? Given their high level of competitiveness, it seems reasonable to expect that Type A's will work harder at various tasks than Type B's and, as a result, will perform at higher levels. In fact, however, the situation turns out to be more complex than this.[17] On the one hand, Type A's *do* tend to work faster on many tasks than Type B's, even when no pressure or deadline is involved. Similarly, they are able to get more done in the presence of distractions. In addition, Type A's often seek more challenges in their work than Type B's (e.g., given a choice, they tend to select more difficult tasks).

Despite these differences, Type A's do not always perform better than Type B's. For example, Type A's frequently do poorly on tasks requiring patience or careful, considered judgment. For the most part, they are simply in too much of a hurry to complete such work in an effective manner. A study comparing Type A and Type B nurses suggests why this may be so. Although Type A's were significantly more involved in their jobs and invested greater effort, they also were more overloaded (i.e., they took on too much to do) and experienced more conflict with respect to the various aspects of the job required of them. It is easy to understand how differences such as these may well interfere with any possible improvements in performance that may derive from effort alone.

These and other findings suggest that neither pattern has the overall edge when it comes to task performance. Their relative success depends on the nature of the task. Although Type A's may excel on tasks involving time pressure or solitary work, Type B's have the advantage when it comes to tasks involving complex judgments and accuracy as opposed to speed.

Positive and Negative Affectivity: Tendencies Toward Feeling Good or Bad

It is a basic fact of life that our moods fluctuate rapidly—and sometimes greatly—throughout the day (see Chapter 4). An e-mail message containing good news may leave us smiling, while an unpleasant conversation with a coworker may leave us feeling gloomy. Such temporary feelings, known as *mood states,* strongly affect anyone at almost any time. However, mood states are only part of the total picture when considering the effects of how our feelings and emotions can affect our behavior at work.

As you probably know from your own experience, people differ not just in terms of their current moods—which can be affected by many different events—but also with respect to more stable tendencies to experience positive or negative feelings.[18] Some people tend to be "up" most of the time whereas others tend to be more subdued or even depressed; and these tendencies are apparent in a wide range of contexts. In other words, at any given moment people's *affective states* (their current feelings) are based both on temporary conditions (i.e., ever-changing moods) *and* relatively stable differences in lasting dispositions to experience positive or negative feelings (i.e., stable traits).

These differences in predispositions toward positive and negative moods are an important aspect of personality. In fact, such differences are related to the ways in which individuals approach many events and experiences on their jobs and in their lives in general. People who are generally energetic, exhilarated, and have a real zest for life may be said to be high in positive affectivity. They are characterized as having an overall sense of well-being, seeing people and events in a positive light, and usually experiencing positive emotional states. By contrast, people who are low in positive affectivity are generally apathetic and listless.

Another dimension of mood is known as **negative affectivity.** It is characterized at the high end by people who are generally angry, nervous, and anxious, and at the low end by those who feel calm and relaxed most of the time.[19] As indicated in Figure 3.3, positive affectivity and negative affectivity are not the opposite of each other, but rather, two separate dimensions.

Figure 3.3   Positive and Negative Affectivity

Positive affectivity and *negative affectivity* are two independent dimensions. The mood states associated with high levels and low levels of each are shown here.

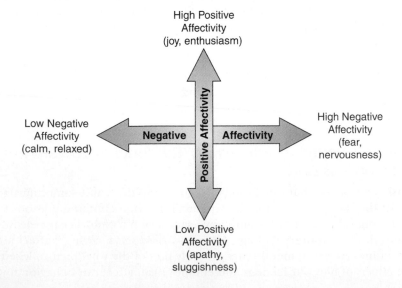

As you might suspect, people who are high in negative affectivity behave differently from those who are high in positive affectivity with respect to several key aspects of organizational behavior—and in undesirable ways. In fact, 42 percent of office workers responding to a survey indicated that they worked with people who could be described as "negative"—perpetual pessimists who think everything will turn out badly, criticizers who find fault with everything, and people who are just plain negative—they are simply "down" all the time.[20]

Not only do such individuals perform poorly themselves, but their negativity also interferes with the performance of others. In other words, they create an atmosphere that reduces productivity and that, of course, can be costly. Among the forms this takes are the following:

➤ *Decision making.*   People with high levels of positive affectivity make better decisions than those with high levels of negative affectivity.[21]

➤ *Team performance.*   Work groups that have a positive affective tone (those in which the average level of positive affectivity is high) function more effectively than groups that have a negative affective tone (those in which the average level of negative affectivity is high).[22]

➤ *Aggressive behavior.*   Because they tend to be very passive in nature, people who are high in negative affectivity are likely to be targets of aggression from others in their organizations.[23]

In view of these findings, it's little wonder that positive and negative affectivity are considered important personality traits when it comes to understanding organizational behavior.

Core Self-Evaluations: How Do We Think of Ourselves?

What is your image of yourself? To what extent is your self-concept positive or negative? Although most of us tend to view ourselves in positive terms, not everybody does so to the same degree. Moreover, the particular way in which we view ourselves is not indicative of a single personality variable, but rather, four distinct elements of personality known as **core self-evaluations.** These refer to people's fundamental evaluations of themselves, their bottom-line conclusions about themselves.[24]

People's core self-evaluations are based on four particular personality traits. These are as follows:

➤ *Self-esteem.*   The overall value one places on oneself as a person

➤ *Generalized self-efficacy.*   A person's beliefs about his or her capacity to perform specific tasks successfully

➤ *Locus of control.*   The extent to which individuals feel that they are able to control things in a manner that affects them

➤ *Emotional stability.*   The tendency to see oneself as confident, secure, and steady (the opposite of *neuroticism,* one of the Big Five personality variables)

Individually, each of the four dimensions of core self-evaluations has been researched extensively, and each is associated with beneficial organizational outcomes. For example, take self-esteem. Individuals with high levels of self-esteem tend to view opportunities to perform challenging jobs as valued opportunities and enjoy rising to the occasion. Not surprisingly, they also put forth a great deal of effort and perform at high levels. By comparison, people who have low self-esteem perceive difficult work situations as threats and dislike them. As a result, they either try to avoid such tasks or don't give it their full effort because they expect to fail, and as a result, they tend to perform poorly.[25]

Now, let's consider generalized self-efficacy. Individuals who have high amounts of this trait are confident that they can do well at whatever they do. (To measure yourself along this important dimension, see the Self-Assessment Exercise on pp. 97–98.) This, in turn, encourages them to take on such challenges, and because they believe they will succeed, they are unlikely to give up when things get rough. As a result, they tend to be successful at these jobs. Then, because they associate the work with success, they are inclined to be satisfied with the jobs themselves. In view of this, it's important to consider how to raise self-efficacy on the job. For some suggestions in this regard, see the Winning Practices section.

Locus of control also is related positively to job satisfaction and performance. Specifically, someone with a highly internal locus of control is likely to believe that he or she can do what it takes to influence any situation. He or she feels confident in being able to bring about change. As a result, individuals with a high internal locus of control tend to be satisfied with their jobs because they either make them better or seek new ones (not remaining in bad jobs because they believe their fates are sealed). And as a result of making situations better, they tend to perform at high levels as well.

Finally, emotional stability also makes a difference. As noted earlier, in conjunction with the Big Five dimensions of personality, emotional stability is the opposite of neuroticism (i.e., they are opposite ends of the same personality dimension). Somebody who is high on emotional stability is predisposed to have low levels of negative affect, which takes its toll on their general well-being. Also as we noted earlier, people with high levels of negative affect tend to experience low levels of job satisfaction and tend to perform their jobs poorly.

It's important to note that these individual effects are particularly strong when taken together. In the aggregate, core self-evaluations are "among the best dispositional predictors of job satisfaction and performance."[26] As a result, it's not surprising that OB scientists have paid a great deal of attention to core self-evaluations in recent years.[27]

Achievement Motivation: The Quest for Excellence

Can you recall the person in your high school class who was named "most likely to succeed"? If so, you probably are thinking of someone who was truly competitive, an individual who wanted to win in every situation—or, at least, in all the important ones. Now, in contrast, can you think of someone you have known who was not at all competitive—who couldn't care less about winning?

As you bring these people to mind, you are focusing on another important aspect of personality—one known as **achievement motivation** (also known as **need for achievement**). This refers to the strength of an individual's desire to excel at various tasks—to succeed and to do better than others.

Need for achievement and attraction to difficult tasks

One of the most interesting differences between persons who are high and low in the need for achievement involves their pattern of preferences for tasks of varying difficulty. As we will note, these differences have important effects on managerial success.

Winning Practices

Increasing Self-Efficacy Among Employees

When people believe that they can do a job and do it well, the chances that they really *can* succeed often increase. Why? Because heightened feelings of self-efficacy (belief in one's ability to accomplish a specific task) have important benefits. They increase both motivation and persistence ("Why give up? I know I can make it!") and encourage individuals to set challenging goals ("I know I can do much better than before"). So encouraging high levels of self-efficacy among employees is well worthwhile.

How can companies reach this objective? Here are some suggestions.

1. *Give Constructive—Not Destructive—Feedback:* Constructive feedback, information that focuses on how an employee can improve his or her performance (instead of information that tears down an individual's confidence) can promote self-efficacy because it helps reassure recipients that they *can* get there—that they have or can soon acquire the skills or strategies necessary for success. It is with this in mind that the luxury hotel chain, Ritz-Carlton, emphasizes the importance of using constructive feedback in training its employees.[28]

2. *Expose Employees to Models of Good Performance—and Success:* How do people learn to do their jobs effectively? From direct practice, of course; but in addition, they acquire many skills and strategies from others. And the more of these they possess, the more likely they are to perform well—and so to experience increased self-efficacy. This suggests that employees can learn a great deal from "shadowing" those with more experience. So effective is this approach that it is a regular part of the training of service personnel such as waiters and waitresses. In fact, Starbucks relies on this practice as a key method of helping budding baristas (people who make espresso drinks) build confidence in their skills.[29]

3. *Seek Continuous Improvement:* Another technique for enhancing self-efficacy involves the quest for continuous improvement. GE's "Six Sigma" program, for instance, rests on the basic idea that "we can do it better—always!"[30] The term "six sigma" refers to outstanding performance far above average (sigma is a statistical term relating to the normal distribution, and six sigma units above the mean is far above it!). Although some employees find this approach daunting at first, meetings and workshops soon convince them that they are part of a truly superb organization that will not settle for "average." The result? Employees come to view themselves as superior, and both self-efficacy and performance benefit.

For many organizations, these techniques involve some new ways of behaving, which can be challenging to bring about. However, the successes outlined here suggest that they indeed can be accomplished. And as self-esteem rises, individual performance is bound to follow, suggesting that the effort required to boost self-esteem is well worth the effort.

Because high need achievers so strongly desire success, they tend to steer away from performing certain kinds of tasks—those that are very easy and those that are very difficult. Very simple tasks are not challenging enough to attract high need achievers, and especially difficult ones are certain to result in failure, an unacceptable outcome. Not surprisingly, high need achievers are most strongly attracted to tasks that are moderately challenging, and thereby prefer tasks of intermediate difficulty.[31]

In contrast, the opposite pattern occurs among people who are low in achievement motivation. That is, they much prefer very easy and very difficult tasks to ones that are moderately difficult. The reason is that people who are low in achievement motivation like to perform easy tasks because success is virtually certain. At the same time, they also prefer tasks that are very difficult because if they fail, this can be attributed to external causes (i.e., it does not reflect on them) and does not threaten their self-esteem. In contrast, because failure on a moderately difficult task may make people feel bad about themselves, low need achievers prefer to avoid such tasks (see Figure 3.4). Let's now consider the implications of this pattern for the workplace.

Are high need achievers successful managers?

We have described people high in achievement motivation as having a highly task-oriented outlook. They are strongly concerned with getting things done, which encourages them to work hard and to strive for success. But do they always succeed, especially in managerial positions? The answer is far from simple.

Given their intense desire to excel, you might expect that people high in achievement motivation will be particularly successful in their careers. To some extent, research

Figure 3.4   Achievement Motivation and Attraction to Tasks

People who are high in achievement motivation are attracted to tasks of moderate difficulty, whereas people who are low in achievement motivation are attracted to tasks that are extremely easy or extremely difficult.

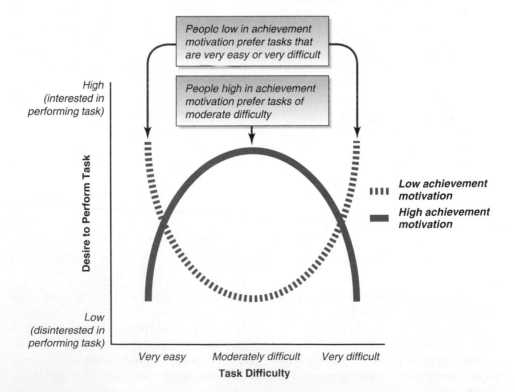

suggests that this is true: People with high amounts of achievement motivation gain promotions more rapidly than those who are low in achievement motivation, at least early in their careers.[32] Their focus on attaining success "jump starts" their careers. However, as their careers progress, their unwillingness to tackle difficult challenges becomes a problem that interferes with their success. Further, they tend to be so highly focused on their own success that they sometimes are reluctant to delegate authority to others, thereby failing to get the help they often need from subordinates. Research has shown that CEOs who are high in achievement motivation tend to keep organizational power in the hands of just a few people, failing to empower their team members as needed (see Chapter 11). This can prove disastrous from the point of view of being an effective manager.[33]

At the same time, people who are high in achievement motivation have an important advantage—namely, they have a strong desire for feedback about their performance. In other words, because they want to succeed so badly, they have a strong interest in knowing just how well they are doing at any given point in time. As a result, people who are high in need achievement have a strong preference for *merit-based pay systems*—ones in which pay and other rewards are based on performance. This is so because such systems recognize people's individual achievements. Conversely, persons high in need for achievement tend to dislike seniority-based pay systems (i.e., those in which pay is based on how long one has worked in the company) because these fail to focus on differences in employees' job-based achievements.[34]

SOCIAL PERCEPTION: UNDERSTANDING AND JUDGING OTHERS

What do the following organizational situations have in common? (1) You are interviewing a prospective employee for a new position in your company. (2) You apologize profusely after spilling a cup of coffee on your boss. (3) You complete a form asking you to rate the strengths and weaknesses of your subordinates.

If you don't immediately see the connection, it's probably because these situations all involve a phenomenon so automatic that you probably never thought about it before. The answer is that they all involve understanding and evaluating others—in other words, figuring out what they are like. In our example, you judge the applicant's qualifications, you make sure your boss's opinion of you is not negative, and you assess the extent to which your employees are doing their jobs properly.

In each of these instances, you are engaging in **social perception**—the process of integrating and interpreting information about others so as to understand them accurately. As these examples illustrate, social perception is a very important process in a wide variety of organizational situations.[35] To better understand social perception, we will examine several different approaches to how the process works.

Social Identity Theory: Answering the Question, "Who Are You?"

How would you answer if someone asked, "Who are you?" There are many things you could say. For example, you might focus on individual characteristics, such as your appearance, your personality, and your special skills and interests—that is, your **personal identity.** You also could answer in terms of the various groups to which you belong, saying, for example, that you are a student in a particular organizational behavior class, an employee of a certain company, or a citizen of a certain country—that is, your **social identity.**

The conceptualization known as **social identity theory** recognizes that the way we perceive others and ourselves is based on both our unique characteristics (i.e., personal identity) and our membership in various groups (i.e., social identity).[36] For an overview of this approach, see Figure 3.5.

Social identity theory claims that the way we identify ourselves is likely to be based on our uniqueness in a group. Say, for example, that you are the only business major in an English class. In this situation, you will be likely to identify yourself as "the business major," and so too will others come to recognize you as such. In other words, that will become your identity in this particular situation. Because we belong to many groups, we are likely to have several unique aspects of ourselves to use as the basis for establishing our identities (e.g., you may be the only left-handed person, the only one to have graduated college, or the only one to have grown up in another country).

How do we know which particular bases for defining their personal identities people will choose? Given the natural desire to perceive ourselves positively and to get others to see us positively as well, we are likely to identify ourselves with groups we

Figure 3.5   Social Identity Theory: An Overview

According to *social identity theory,* people identify themselves in terms of their individual characteristics and their group memberships. They then compare themselves to other individuals and groups to help define who they are, both to themselves and others.

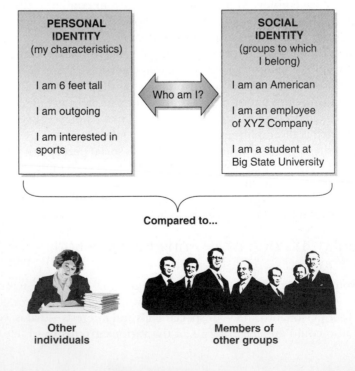

believe are perceived positively by others. We know, for example, that people in highly regarded professions, such as doctors, are more inclined to identify themselves with their professions than those who have lower-status jobs.[37] Likewise, people tend to identify themselves with winning sports teams by wearing the colors and logos of those teams. In fact, the tendency to wear clothing that identifies oneself as a fan of a certain team depends on how successful that team has been: The better a team has performed, the more likely its fans are to sport apparel that publicly identifies them with that team.[38]

In addition to explaining how we perceive ourselves, social identity theory also explains how we come to perceive others. Specifically, the theory explains that we focus on the differences between ourselves and other individuals as well as members of other groups (see the lower portion of Figure 3.5). In so doing, we tend to simplify things by assuming that people in different groups share certain qualities that make them different from ourselves—even if they really are not so different after all.

Not only do we perceive others as different from ourselves, but we also perceive them as different in negative ways. This is particularly so when we are competing against them (see Chapter 7). Take athletic competitions, for example. If you ever have heard the negative things that students from one college or university say about those from other schools whom they are competing against in various sports, then you know quite well the phenomenon we are describing here.

Although such perceptions tend to be groundless, most of us stick with them, nevertheless. The reason is simple. Making such categorizations helps bring order to the world. After all, distinguishing between "the good guys" and "the bad guys" makes otherwise complex judgments quite simple. And bringing simplicity to a complex world is what social perception is all about.

Attribution: Judging What People Are Like and Why They Do What They Do

A question we often ask about others is "why?" Why did the manager use the wrong data in his report? Why did the chief executive develop the policy she did? When we ask such questions, we're attempting to get at two different types of information: (1) What is someone really like? (2) What made the person behave as he or she did? People attempt to answer these questions in different ways.

Making correspondent inferences: Using acts to judge dispositions

Situations frequently arise in organizations in which we want to know what someone is like. Is your new boss likely to be tough or kind-hearted? Are your co-workers prone to be punctual or late? The more you know about what people are like, the better equipped you are to know what to expect and how to deal with them. How, then, do we go about identifying another's traits?

Generally speaking, the answer is that we infer others' traits based on what we are able to observe of their behavior. The judgments we make about what people are like based on what we have seen them do are known as **correspondent inferences.** Simply put, correspondent inferences are judgments about people's dispositions—their traits and characteristics—that correspond to what we have observed of their actions.

At first blush, this process seems deceptively simple. A person with a disorganized desk may be thought of as sloppy. Someone who slips on the shop floor may be considered clumsy. Such judgments might be accurate, but not necessarily! After all, the messy desk actually may be the result of a co-worker rummaging through it to find some important documents. Similarly, the person who slipped could have encountered oily conditions under which anyone, even the least clumsy individual, would have fallen. In other words, it is important to recognize that the judgments we may make about someone may be inaccurate because there are many possible causes of behavior. For this reason, correspondent inferences may not always be accurate.

Another reason why correspondent inferences may be misleading is that people frequently conceal some of their traits—especially when these may be viewed as negative. So, for example, a sloppy individual may work hard in public to appear to be organized. Likewise, the unprincipled person may talk a good show about the importance of being ethical. In other words, people often do their best to disguise some of their basic traits. Not surprisingly, this makes the business of forming correspondent inferences risky, at best.

Causal attribution of responsibility: Answering the question "why?"

Imagine finding out that your boss just fired one of your fellow employees. Naturally, you'd ask yourself, "Why did he do that?" Was it because your co-worker violated the company's code of conduct? Or was it because the boss is a cruel and heartless person? These two answers to the question "why?" represent two major classes of explanations for the causes of someone's behavior: *internal* causes, explanations based on actions for which the individual is responsible, and *external* causes, explanations based on situations over which the individual has no control. In this case, the internal cause would be the person's violation of the rules, and the external cause would be the boss's cruel and arbitrary behavior.

Generally speaking, it is very important to be able to determine whether an internal or an external cause was responsible for someone's behavior. Knowing why something happened to someone else might better help you prepare for what might happen to you. For example, in this case, if you believe that your colleague was fired because of something for which she was responsible herself, such as violating a company rule, then you might not feel as vulnerable as you would if you thought she was fired because of the arbitrary, spiteful nature of your boss. In the latter case, you might decide to take some precautionary actions, to do something to protect yourself from your boss, such as staying on his good side, or even giving up and finding a new job—before you are forced to.

The key question of interest to social scientists is: How do people go about judging whether someone's actions were caused by internal or external causes? An answer to this question is provided by **Kelley's theory of causal attribution.** According to this conceptualization, we base our judgments of internal and external causality on three types of information. These are as follows:

➤ *Consensus*—the extent to which other people behave in the same manner as the person we're judging. If others behave similarly, consensus is considered high; if they do not, consensus is considered low.

➤ *Consistency*—the extent to which the person we're judging acts the same way at other times. If the person acts the same at other times, consistency is high; if he or she does not, consistency is low.

➤ *Distinctiveness*—the extent to which this person behaves in the same manner in other contexts. If he or she behaves the same way in other situations, distinctiveness is low; if he or she behaves differently, distinctiveness is high.

According to the theory, after learning about these three factors, people combine this information to make attributions of causality. Here's how. If we judge that other people act like this one (consensus is high), that this person behaves in the same manner at other times (consistency is high), and that this person does not act in the same manner in other situations (distinctiveness is high), we are likely to conclude that this person's behavior stemmed from *external* causes. In contrast, imagine determining that other people do not act like this one (consensus is low), that this person behaves in the same manner at other times (consistency is high), and that this person acts in the same manner in other situations (distinctiveness is low). In this case, we will probably conclude that this person's behavior stemmed from *internal* causes.

Because this explanation is highly abstract, let's consider an example to illustrate how the process works. Imagine that you're at a business lunch with several of your company's sales representatives when the sales manager makes some critical remarks about the restaurant's food and service. Further imagine that no one else in your party acts this way (consensus is low), you have heard her say the same things during other visits to the restaurant (consistency is high), and you have seen her acting critically in other settings, such as the regional sales meeting (distinctiveness is low). What would you conclude in this situation? Probably that her behavior stems from internal causes. In other words, she is a "picky" person, someone who is difficult to please.

Now, imagine the same setting but with different observations. Suppose that several other members of your group also complain about the restaurant (consensus is high), that you have seen this person complain in the same restaurant at other times (consistency is high), but that you have never seen her complain about anything else before (distinctiveness is high). By contrast, in this case, you probably would conclude that the sales manager's behavior stems from external causes: The restaurant really *is* inferior. For a summary of these contrasting conclusions, see Figure 3.6.

Figure 3.6   Kelley's Theory of Causal Attribution: An Example
In determining whether another's behavior stems mainly from internal or external causes, we rely on the three types of information identified here.

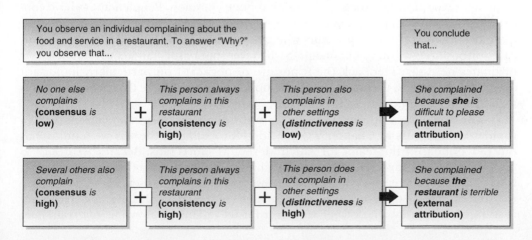

The Biased Nature of Social Perception

As you might imagine, people are far from perfect when it comes to making judgments of others. In fact, researchers have noted that there are several important types of biases that interfere with making completely accurate judgments of others.

The fundamental attribution error

Despite what Kelley's theory says, people are *not* equally predisposed to reach judgments regarding internal and external causality. Rather, they are more likely to explain one another's actions in terms of internal rather than external causes. In other words, we are prone to assume that others' behaviors are due to the way they are, their traits and dispositions (e.g., "she's that kind of person"). So, for example, we are more likely to assume that someone who shows up for work late does so because she is lazy rather than because she got caught in traffic. This tendency is so strong that it is known as the **fundamental attribution error.**

This phenomenon stems from the fact that it is far easier to explain someone's actions in terms of his or her traits than to recognize the complex pattern of situational factors that may have affected his or her actions. As you might imagine, this tendency can be quite damaging in organizations. Specifically, it leads us to assume prematurely that people are responsible for the negative things that happen to them (e.g., "he wrecked the company car because he is careless"), without considering external alternatives, ones that may be less damning (e.g., "another driver hit the car"). And this can lead to inaccurate judgments about people. And given that judging another's performance is a key part of managers' jobs, the consequences can be serious.

The halo effect

Imagine that you are a supervisor of a worker whom you generally like and who performs her job well. There is only one problem, however: She usually arrives to work late, causing others in her work team to have to cover for her. You are well aware of the problem, but despite this, when it comes to evaluating this employee's performance, you tend to give her high ratings, overlooking this one problem. Why?

The answer lies in what is called the **halo effect.** This refers to the tendency for a person's overall impression to bias his or her assessment of another on specific dimensions. This type of biased social perception is quite common. People want to have consistent perceptions of others, and so they overlook the one characteristic that doesn't quite fit with the others. This occurs whether that characteristic is negative (as in this case) or positive. As you might imagine, whenever supervisors fail to provide their subordinates necessary feedback (be it positive or negative) on particularly important aspects of their work, they are missing the opportunity to change that behavior (if it is negative) or to maintain it (if it is positive).

The halo effect applies not only to individuals but to work teams as well (a topic we will discuss in Chapter 9). Consider, for example, the way we tend to bias our perceptions of the teams for which we root as sports fans. Because we desire to see our team in a favorable light, we attribute positive characteristics to it when it wins ("This is the greatest team ever"). However, if our team loses, we tend to blame the loss on the mistakes or poor performance of one particular player ("The team is still good, but that one player ruined it for us"). This is known as the **team halo**

effect—the tendency for people to credit teams for their successes but not to hold them accountable for their failures.

Stereotypes: Fitting others into categories

Inaccurate judgments about people also can stem from the preconceived ideas we hold about certain groups. Here, we are referring to **stereotypes**—beliefs that all members of specific groups share similar traits and behaviors. Expressions of stereotypes usually take the form: "People from group *X* possess characteristic *Y*." For example, what comes to mind when you think about people who wear glasses? Are they studious? Eggheads? Although there is no evidence of such a connection, it is interesting that for many people such an image lingers in their minds.

Deep down inside many of us know, and can articulate, that not all people from a specific group possess the characteristics—either negative or positive—with which we associate them. In other words, most of us accept that the stereotypes we use are at least partially inaccurate. After all, not *all X*'s are *Y;* there are exceptions (maybe even quite a few!). If so, then why are stereotypes so prevalent? Why do we use them?

To a great extent, the answer lies in the fact that people tend to do as little cognitive work as possible when it comes to thinking about others. That is, we tend to rely on mental shortcuts. If assigning people to groups allows us to assume that we know what they are like and how they may act, then we can save the tedious work of having to learn about them as individuals. After all, we come into contact with so many people that it's impractical—if not impossible—to learn everything about them we need to know. So, we rely on readily available information—such as someone's age, race, gender, or job type—as the basis for organizing our perceptions in a coherent way. If you believe that members of group *X* tend to have trait *Y*, then simply observing that someone falls into category *X* becomes the basis for your believing something about that individual (in this case, that he or she possesses *Y*). To the extent that the stereotype applies in this case, then the perception will be accurate. But in that case we are just lucky. More likely than not, such mental shorthand will lead us to judgments about people that are inaccurate—the price we pay for using stereotypes.

It is easy to imagine how the use of stereotypes can have powerful effects on the kinds of judgments people make in organizations. For example, if a personnel officer believes that members of certain groups are lazy, then he purposely may avoid hiring anyone belonging to those groups. The personnel officer may firmly believe that he is using good judgment—gathering all the necessary information and listening to the candidate carefully. Still, without being aware of it, the stereotypes he holds may influence the way he judges people. The result, of course, is that the fate of the individual in question is sealed in advance—not necessarily because of anything he or she may have done or said, but because of the mere fact that he or she belongs to a certain group. In other words, even people who are not being intentionally bigoted still may be influenced by the stereotypes they hold. The effects of stereotypes may be quite subtle and unintentional.

Self-fulfilling prophecies: The Pygmalion effect and the Golem effect

In case it isn't already apparent just how important perceptions are in the workplace, consider the fact that the way we perceive others actually can dictate how effectively people will work. Put differently, perceptions can influence reality! This is the idea behind what is known as the **self-fulfilling prophecy**—the tendency for someone's expectations about another to cause that individual to behave in a manner consistent with those expectations.[39]

Self-fulfilling prophecies can take both positive and negative forms. In the positive case, holding high expectations of another tends to improve that individual's performance. This is known as the **Pygmalion effect.**[40] This effect was demonstrated in a study of Israeli soldiers who were taking a combat command course.[41] The four instructors who taught the course were told that certain trainees had high potential for success, whereas the others had either normal potential or an unknown amount of potential. In reality, the trainees identified as belonging to each of these categories were assigned to that condition at random. Despite this, trainees who were believed to have high potential were found at the end of the training session to be more successful (e.g., they had higher test scores). This demonstrates the Pygmalion effect: Trainees whose instructors expected them to do well actually did so.

Researchers also have found that the self-fulfilling prophecy works in the negative direction—that is, low expectations of success lead to poor performance. This is known as the **Golem effect.** Illustrating this phenomenon, researchers have found that paratroopers whose instructors expected them to perform poorly in their training class did, in fact, perform worse than those about whom instructors had no advance expectations.

The lesson to be learned from research on self-fulfilling prophecies is clear: Managers should make an effort to promote the Pygmalion effect and to discourage the Golem effect. When leaders display enthusiasm toward people and express optimism about each person's potential, such positive expectations become contagious and spread throughout the organization. Earlier, we noted that displaying optimism about a person's potential is a useful way to promote self-efficacy. Here, we add that these effects may spread as such optimism about good performance becomes self-fulfilling—that is, by actually promoting good performance.

Overcoming Bias in Social Perception: Some Guidelines

In most cases, people's biased perceptions of others are not the result of any malicious intent to inflict harm. Instead, biases in social perception occur because we, as perceivers, are imperfect processors of information. We assume that people are internally responsible for their behavior because we cannot be aware of all the possible situational factors that may be involved—hence, we make the fundamental attribution error. Furthermore, it is highly impractical to be able to learn everything about someone that may guide our reactions—hence, we use stereotypes. This does not mean, however, that we cannot minimize the impact of these biases. Indeed, there are several steps that can be taken to help promote the accurate perception of others in the workplace. For an overview of several such suggestions, see Table 3.2.

We recognize that many of these tactics are far easier to say than to do. However, to the extent that you conscientiously attempt to apply these suggestions to your everyday interaction with others in the workplace, you will stand a good chance of perceiving people more accurately. And this, of course, is a fundamental ingredient in the recipe for managerial success.

Table 3.2   Guidelines for Overcoming Perceptual Biases

Although perceptual biases are inevitable, the suggestions outlined here may be useful ways of reducing their impact.

Recommendation	Explanation
Do not overlook external causes of others' behavior.	Ask yourself if anyone else may have performed just as poorly under the same conditions. If the answer is yes, then you should not automatically assume that the poor performer is to blame. Good managers need to make such judgments accurately so that they can decide whether to focus their efforts on developing employees (when the cause is internal) or changing work conditions (when the cause is external).
Identify and confront your stereotypes.	Although it is natural to rely on stereotypes, erroneous perceptions are bound to result—and quite possibly at the expense of someone else. For this reason, it's good to identify the stereotypes you hold. Doing so will help you become more aware of them, taking a giant step toward minimizing their impact on your behavior.
Evaluate people based on objective factors.	The more objective the information you use to judge others (e.g., production or sales figures), the less your judgments will be subjected to perceptual distortion.
Avoid making rash judgments.	It is human nature to jump to conclusions about what people are like, even when we know very little about them. Take the time to get to know people better before convincing yourself that you already know all you need to know about them. What you learn may make a big difference in the opinions you form.

LEARNING: ADAPTING TO THE WORLD OF WORK

Question: What process is so broad and fundamental to human behavior that it may be said to occur in organizations—and throughout life, in general—continuously? The answer: *learning*. This process is so basic to our lives that you probably have a good sense of what learning is, but you may find it difficult to define. So, to make sure that we clarify exactly what it is, we formally define **learning** as a relatively permanent change in behavior occurring as a result of experience.

Several aspects of this definition bear pointing out. First, it's clear that learning requires that some kind of change occur. Second, this change must be more than temporary. Finally, it must be the result of experience—that is, continued contact with the world around us. Given this definition, we cannot say that short-lived performance changes on the job, such as those due to illness or fatigue, are the result of learning. Learning is a difficult concept for scientists to study because it cannot be directly observed. Instead, it must be inferred on the basis of relatively permanent changes in behavior.

We will now consider two of the most prevalent forms of learning that occur in organizations—*operant conditioning* and *observational learning*.

Operant Conditioning: Learning Through Rewards and Punishments

Imagine you are a chef working at a catering company where you are planning a special menu for a fussy client. If your dinner menu is accepted and the meal is a hit, the company stands a good chance of adding a huge new account. You work hard at doing the best job possible and present your culinary creation to the skeptical client.

Now, how does the story end? If the client loves your meal, your grateful boss gives you a huge raise and a promotion. However, if the client hates it, your boss asks you to turn in your chef's hat. Regardless of which of these outcomes occurs, one thing is certain: Whatever you did in this situation, you will be sure to do again *if* it succeeded, or you will avoid doing it again *if* it failed.

This situation nicely illustrates an important principle of **operant conditioning** (also known as **instrumental conditioning**), namely, that our behavior produces consequences and that how we behave in the future will depend on what those consequences are. If our actions have pleasant effects, then we will be more likely to repeat them in the future. If, however, our actions have unpleasant effects, we are less likely to repeat them in the future. This phenomenon, known as the **law of effect,** is fundamental to operant conditioning.

Our knowledge of this phenomenon comes from the work of the famous social scientist B. F. Skinner.[42] Skinner's pioneering research has shown us that it is through the connections between our actions and their consequences that we learn to behave in certain ways. We summarize this process in Figure 3.7.

The various relationships between a person's behavior and the consequences resulting from it are known collectively as **contingencies of reinforcement.** We may identify four different kinds of contingencies, each of which describes the conditions

Figure 3.7   The Operant Conditioning Process

The basic premise of *operant conditioning* is that people learn by associating the consequences of their behavior with the behavior itself. In this example, the manager's praise increases the subordinate's tendency to perform the job properly in the future.

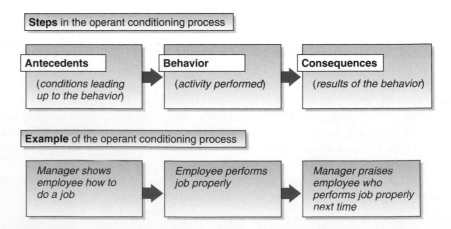

Table 3.3   Contingencies of Reinforcement

The four *contingencies of reinforcement* may be defined in terms of the presentation or withdrawal of a pleasant or unpleasant stimulus. Positively or negatively reinforced behaviors are strengthened; punished or extinguished behaviors are weakened.

Stimulus Presented or Withdrawn	Desirability of Stimulus	Name of Contingency	Strength of Response	Example
Presented	Pleasant	*Positive reinforcement*	Increases	Praise from a supervisor encourages continuing the praised behavior.
	Unpleasant	*Punishment*	Decreases	Criticism from a supervisor discourages enacting the punished behavior.
Withdrawn	Pleasant	*Extinction*	Decreases	Failing to praise a helpful act reduces the odds of helping in the future.
	Unpleasant	*Negative reinforcement*	Increases	Future criticism is avoided by doing whatever the supervisor wants.

under which rewards and punishments are either given or taken away. These are *positive reinforcement, negative reinforcement, punishment,* and *extinction*. As we discuss each of these next, you may find it useful to refer to the summary in Table 3.3.

Positive reinforcement

A great deal of behavior is learned because of the pleasurable outcomes that we associate with it. In organizations, for example, people usually find it pleasant and desirable to receive monetary bonuses, paid vacations, and various forms of recognition. The process by which people learn to perform acts leading to such desirable outcomes is known as **positive reinforcement.** Whatever behavior led to the positive outcomes is likely to occur again, thereby strengthening that behavior.

For a reward to serve as a positive reinforcer, it must be made contingent on the specific behavior sought. So, for example, if a sales representative is given a bonus after landing a huge account, the bonus will only reinforce the person's actions *if* he or she associates it with the landing of the account. When this occurs, the individual will be more inclined in the future to do whatever it was that helped get the account.

Negative reinforcement

Sometimes we also learn to perform acts because they permit us to avoid undesirable consequences. Unpleasant events, such as reprimands, rejection, probation, and termination, are some of the consequences faced for certain negative actions in the workplace. The process by which people learn to perform acts leading to the avoidance of such undesirable consequences is known as **negative reinforcement,** or **avoidance.** Whatever response led to the termination of these undesirable events is likely to occur again, thereby strengthening that response.

For example, you may stay late at the office one evening to revise a sales presentation because you believe that the boss will "chew you out" if it's not ready in the morning. You learned how to avoid this type of aversive situation and behave accordingly.

Punishment

Thus far, we have identified responses that are strengthened—either because they lead to the occurrence of positive consequences or the termination of negative consequences. However, the connection between a behavior and its consequences is not always strengthened; such links also may be weakened.

This is what happens in the case of *punishment*. **Punishment** involves presenting an undesirable or aversive consequence in response to an unwanted behavior. A behavior accompanied by an undesirable outcome is less likely to recur if the person associates the negative consequences with the behavior. For example, if you are chastised by your boss for taking excessively long coffee breaks, you are considered punished for this action. As a result, you will be less likely to take long breaks again in the future.

Extinction

The link between a behavior and its consequences also may be weakened by withholding reward—a process known as **extinction.** When a response that was once rewarded is no longer rewarded, it tends to weaken and eventually die out—or be *extinguished*.

Let's consider an example. Suppose for many months you brought boxes of donuts to your weekly staff meetings. Your colleagues always thanked you as they gobbled them down. You were positively reinforced by their approval, so you continued bringing the donuts. Now, after several months of eating donuts, your colleagues have begun dieting. So, although tempting, your donuts go uneaten. After several months of no longer being praised for your generosity, you will be unlikely to continue bringing donuts. Your once rewarded behavior will die out; it will be extinguished.

Observational Learning: Learning by Imitating Others

Although operant conditioning is based on the idea that we engage in behaviors for which we are directly reinforced, many of the things we learn on the job are *not* directly reinforced. Suppose, for example, on your new job you see many of your co-workers complimenting your boss on his attire. Each time someone says something flattering, the boss stops at his or her desk, smiles, and acts friendly. By complimenting the boss, they are reinforced by being granted his social approval.

Chances are, after observing this several times, you too will eventually learn to say something nice to the boss. Although you may not have directly experienced the boss's approval, you would expect to receive it based on what you have observed from others. This is an example of a kind of learning known as **observational learning,** or **modeling.** It occurs when someone acquires new knowledge *vicariously*—that is, by observing what happens to others.

A great deal of what is learned about how to behave in organizations can be explained as the result of the process of observational learning. On the job, observational learning is a key part of many formal job instruction training programs. As we will explain in the next section, trainees given a chance to observe experts doing their jobs, followed by an opportunity to practice the desired skills, and then given feedback on their work tend to learn new job skills quite effectively.

Observational learning also occurs in a very informal, uncalculated manner. For example, people who experience the norms and traditions of their organizations and who subsequently incorporate these into their own behavior may be recognized as having learned through observation.

Finally, it is important to note that people learn not only what to do by observing others but also what *not* to do. Specifically, people observing their co-workers getting punished for behaving inappropriately on the job tend to refrain from engaging in those same actions themselves. As you might imagine, this is a very effective way for people to learn how to behave without ever experiencing any displeasure themselves.

APPLICATIONS OF LEARNING IN ORGANIZATIONS

The principles of learning we have discussed thus far are used in organizations in many different ways. We now discuss three systematic approaches to incorporating learning in organizations: *training, organizational behavior management,* and *discipline.*

Training: Learning and Developing Job Skills

Probably the most obvious use to which principles of learning may be applied in organizations is **training**—that is, the process through which people systematically acquire and improve the skills and abilities needed to improve their job performance. Just as students learn basic educational skills in the classroom, employees must learn their job skills.

Training is used not only to prepare newly hired employees to meet the challenges of the jobs they will face but also to upgrade and refine the skills of existing employees. In fact, in 2007 American companies spent approximately $60 billion on training, much of which involved some type of training using Internet technology, known as *virtual training, online training,* or *e-training.*[43]

In view of this staggering investment, it is important to consider ways of enhancing the effectiveness of employee training.[44] Five major principles may be identified—*participation, repetition, active learning, transfer of training,* and *feedback.*

Promote participation

People not only learn more quickly but also retain the skills longer when they have participated actively in the learning process. This applies to the learning of both motor tasks (e.g., learning to ride a bicycle) as well as cognitive skills (e.g., learning a foreign language).

For example, when learning to swim, there's no substitute for "getting your feet wet," so to speak—that is, actually getting in the water and moving your arms and legs. In the classroom, students who listen attentively to lectures, think about the material, and get involved in discussions tend to learn more effectively than those who just sit passively.

Encourage repetition

If you know the old adage "practice makes perfect," you are already aware of the benefits of repetition on learning. Perhaps you learned the multiplication table, or a poem, or a foreign language phrase by going over it repeatedly. Scientists have not only established the benefits of repetition on learning but also have shown that these effects are even greater when practice is spread out over time rather than when it is lumped together. After all, when practice periods are too long, learning can suffer from fatigue, whereas learning a little bit at a time allows the material to sink in.

Use active learning techniques

For learning to be most effective, learners should be involved in an active manner (e.g., by completing some exercise), instead of a passive manner (e.g., by listening to lectures only). The term **active learning** is used to describe a collection of learner-centered techniques in which individuals are active participants in the learning process.

In this way, active learning is akin to "learning by doing" but goes beyond it in several key ways. Specifically, active learning techniques give people control over their learning experience. They also require learners to explore and experiment with a task so they can figure out how to perform it themselves. Typically these techniques require learners to think carefully about the subject matter and to have emotional reactions to it.

For an overview of the different techniques that fall into this category, see the summary in Table 3.4. Recent research has demonstrated that these techniques are quite effective in many different ways.[45]

Capitalize on transfer of training

As you might imagine, for training to be most effective, what is learned during training must be applied to the job. The term **transfer of training** refers to the process in which what you already know can be applied to learning something new. In general, the more closely a training program matches the demands of a job, the more effective the training will be.

A good example is the elaborate simulation devices used to train pilots and astronauts. At a more "down to earth" level is the equipment used in many technical schools for people to learn skilled trades such as welding, computer repair, and radiation technology.

Give feedback

It is extremely difficult for learning to occur in the absence of feedback—that is, knowledge of the results of one's actions. Feedback provides information about the effectiveness of one's training.[46] Of course, unless you learn what you already are doing well and what behaviors you need to correct, you will probably be unable to improve your skills.

Table 3.4   Active Learning Techniques

In contrast to traditional, passive learning, *active learning* gets people involved in the process of learning. The techniques summarized here are among the most widely used forms of active learning used today. As you can see, these differ with respect to the degree to which the trainer gets involved in guiding the trainee.

Technique	Description
Exploratory learning	Giving people opportunities to learn by exploring and experimenting with the task at hand so they can discover how to master it completely on their own
Guided exploration	Encouraging learners to explore things on their own but also helping by giving them directions to pursue that enable them to improve
Error framing	Instructing learners to make errors and to think about these as opportunities to learn
Mastery training	Encouraging learners to explore things on their own while also noting that errors are bound to occur and providing them with goals that help them master the skills involved

(Source: Based on information in Bell & Kozlowski, 2008; see Note 45.)

For example, it is critical for people being trained as word processing operators to know exactly how many words they correctly entered per minute if they are to be able to gauge their improvement (as we will note again in Chapter 5, this is a major source of motivation).

One type of feedback that has become popular in recent years is known as **360-degree feedback**—the process of using multiple sources from around an organization to evaluate the work of a single individual. This goes beyond simply collecting feedback from superiors, as is customary, but extends to the gathering of feedback from other sources, such as one's peers, direct reports (i.e., immediate subordinates), customers, and even oneself.[47]

About two-thirds of the largest companies in the United States now use 360-degree feedback in at least one organizational unit (e.g., a department), most focusing on the manager level and higher.[48] Some companies, such as General Electric, AT&T, Monsanto, DuPont, Westinghouse, Motorola, FedEx, Nabisco, and Warner-Lambert, have used 360-degree feedback for over a decade to give more complete performance information to their employees, greatly improving not only their own work but overall corporate productivity as well.[49]

Despite its popularity, it's important to caution that 360-degree feedback isn't always successful; indeed, it sometimes is misused, resulting in more harm than good. This suggests that as a tool, 360-degree feedback should not be thrown into an organization with the blind hope that it will do some good. Instead, it's important to use this technique only under certain circumstances. For a summary of these conditions, see Table 3.5.[50]

Organizational Behavior Management: Positively Reinforcing Desirable Organizational Behaviors

Earlier, in describing operant conditioning, we noted that the consequences of our behavior determine whether we repeat it or abandon it. Behaviors that are rewarded tend to be

Table 3.5   When Should 360-Degree Feedback Be Used?

For 360-degree feedback to be used successfully, it is essential that the following conditions be met. As outlined here, failing to adhere to these "four musts" may create problems that are likely to make the technique more of a liability than an asset.

For 360-degree feedback to be successful . . .	Or else, the following problem may occur . . .
Everyone involved must be trained carefully in how to give feedback.	People may be hurt by feedback that is destructive instead of constructive (see Chapter 8).
The consequences of engaging in poor performance must made perfectly clear.	People may lack motivation to perform at a high level (see Chapter 6).
The behavior being measured must be essential to business success.	People may focus on improving their performance in ways that don't really matter.
The information collected must be used only for appropriate purposes, such as to improve performance.	People may believe that the information shared about them constitutes a violation of their privacy.

strengthened and repeated in the future. With this in mind, it is possible to administer rewards selectively to help reinforce behaviors that we wish to be repeated in the future.

This is the basic principle behind **organizational behavior management** (also known as **organizational behavior modification,** or more simply, **OB Mod**). Organizational behavior management may be defined as the systematic application of positive reinforcement principles in organizational settings for the purpose of raising the incidence of desirable organizational behaviors.

Organizational behavior management programs have been used successfully to stimulate a variety of behaviors in many different organizations.[51] For example, B. F. Goodrich experienced a 300 percent increase in tire manufacturing by introducing a system that rewarded employees. However, few results of OB Mod plans are this extreme. More modest gains have been experienced in several companies, and with respect to modifying a wide variety of behaviors in the workplace, such as cleaning the workplace, greeting customers, and engaging in safe-driving practices.[52]

Discipline: Eliminating Undesirable Organizational Behaviors

Just as organizations systematically may use rewards to encourage desirable behavior, they also may use punishment to discourage undesirable behavior. Problems such as absenteeism, lateness, theft, and substance abuse cost companies vast sums of money, situations many companies attempt to manage by using **discipline**—the systematic administration of punishment.

By administering an unpleasant outcome (e.g., suspension without pay) in response to an undesirable behavior (e.g., excessive tardiness), companies seek to minimize the undesirable behavior. In one form or another, using discipline is a relatively common practice.

Survey research has shown, in fact, that 83 percent of companies use some form of discipline, or at least the threat of discipline, in response to undesirable behaviors. But, as you might imagine, disciplinary actions taken in organizations vary greatly. For a summary of commonly used disciplinary measures arranged in terms of severity, see Figure 3.8.[53]

The trick to disciplining effectively is to know how to administer punishment in a way that is considered fair and reasonable. Fortunately, research and theory have pointed to some effective principles that may be followed to maximize the effectiveness of discipline in organizations. We will now consider several of these.

➤ *Deliver punishment immediately after the undesirable response occurs.*   The less time that passes between the occurrence of an undesirable behavior and the administration of a negative consequence, the more strongly people will make the connection between them. When people make this association, the consequence is likely to serve as a punishment, thereby reducing the probability of the unwanted behavior. Thus, it is best for managers to talk to their subordinates about their undesirable behaviors immediately after they commit them. Expressing disapproval after several days or weeks have gone by will be less effective, because the passage of time will weaken the association between the behavior and its consequences.

➤ *Give moderate levels of punishment—neither too high nor too low.*   If the consequences for performing an undesirable action are not very severe (e.g., rolling one's eyes as a show of disapproval), then they are unlikely to serve as a punishment. After all, it is quite easy to live with such a mild response. In contrast, consequences that are overly severe might be perceived as unfair and inhumane. When this occurs, not

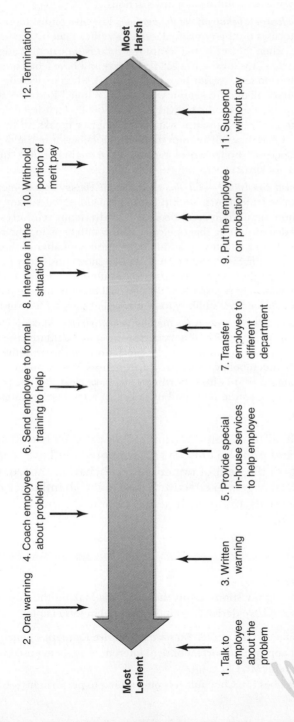

Figure 3.8 A Continuum of Disciplinary Measures

Ranked from mildest to most severe, these are the most common disciplinary tactics used by supervisors.

(Source: Based on findings reported by Trahan and Steiner, 1994; see Note 53.)

only might the individual resign, but also a strong signal will be sent to others about the unreasonableness of the company's actions.

➤ *Punish the undesirable behavior, not the person.*   Effective punishment is impersonal in nature and focuses on the individual's actions rather than his or her personality. So, for example, when addressing an employee who is repeatedly caught taking excessively long breaks, it is unwise to say, "You're lazy and have a bad attitude." Instead, it would be better to say, "By not being at your desk when expected, you're making it more difficult for all of us to get our work done on time." Responding in this manner will be less humiliating for the individual. Additionally, focusing on exactly what people can do to avoid such disapproval (taking shorter breaks, in this case) increases the likelihood that they will attempt to alter their behavior in the desired fashion. By contrast, the person who feels personally attacked might not only "tune out" the message but also not know exactly how to improve.

➤ *Use punishment consistently—all the time, for all employees.*   Sometimes managers attempting to be lenient turn a blind eye to infractions of company rules. Doing this may cause more harm than good because it inadvertently reinforces the undesirable behavior (by demonstrating that one can get away with breaking the rules). As a result, it is considered most effective to administer punishment after each occurrence of an undesirable behavior. Similarly, it is important to show consistency in the treatment of all employees. In other words, everyone who commits the same infraction should be punished the same way, regardless of the person administering the punishment. When this occurs, supervisors are unlikely to be accused of showing favoritism.

➤ *Clearly communicate the reasons for the punishment given.*   Making clear exactly what behaviors lead to what disciplinary actions greatly facilitates the effectiveness of punishment. Clearly communicated expectations help strengthen the perceived connection between behavior and its consequences. Wise managers use their opportunities to communicate with subordinates to make clear that the punishment being given does not constitute revenge but rather an attempt to eliminate an unwanted behavior.

If, after reading all this, you are thinking that it is truly difficult to properly administer rewards and punishments in organizations, you have reached the same conclusion as experts in the field of organizational behavior. Indeed, one of the key skills that make some managers so effective is their ability to influence others by properly administering rewards and punishments (to practice this skill, see the Group Exercise on pp. 98–99).

Back to the Case
Answer the following questions about this chapter's Making the Case (p. 66) to illustrate insights you have derived about the material in this chapter.

1. What personality traits would you say characterize Kenneth Chenault?
2. How does it appear that correspondent inferences are being used to make judgments about Mr. Chenault?
3. In what ways does Mr. Chenault rely on learning to perform his job successfully?

You Be the Consultant

Selecting, Training, and Appraising Employees

As human resources manager for a large information technology firm, you are responsible for three key functions—selecting prospective employees, training current employees, and appraising employees' job performance. Answer the following questions based on material in this chapter.

1. What personality characteristics would you recommend that the company try to find in its prospective employees? Which ones should it avoid? Explain your answers.

2. What types of biases and inaccuracies may be expected in the process of appraising employees' job performance? What can be done to minimize the impact of these factors?

3. Given that the company invests a great deal of money in its training program, you are interested in seeing that it works as effectively as possible. What specific steps can you take to ensure that learning of job skills occurs at a high level?

SELF-ASSESSMENT EXERCISE

Assessing Your Generalized Self-Efficacy

To objectively measure generalized self-efficacy (and most other personality variables), scientists rely on paper-and-pencil questionnaires. This scale, adapted from ones actually used by scientists to measure generalized self-efficacy, should give you some insight into this important aspect of your personality.

    Because this measure is brief and not scientifically validated, you shouldn't draw any definitive conclusions about yourself from it. Still, completing it will give you *some* insight into your own self-efficacy. Moreover, this exercise will give you a good feel for what these paper-and-pencil measures of personality are like in general.

Directions

For each of the six following items, indicate in the space provided whether you:

    strongly disagree (SD)
    disagree (D)
    agree (A)
    strongly agree (SA)

____ 1. Even if a problem is difficult, I usually find some way to solve it.
____ 2. Usually, if someone opposes me I still can find a way to get what I'm seeking.
____ 3. I usually can find a way to accomplish whatever goals I have.
____ 4. If something unexpected happens to me, I expect to be able to find a way to deal with it.
____ 5. If I put forth the effort, I can accomplish whatever I desire.
____ 6. When I confront a problem I don't worry too much because I believe I can handle it effectively.

Scoring

1. For each item, assign points as follows: $SD = 1$; $D = 2$; $A = 3$; $SA = 4$.
2. Add your points, which should range from 6 to 24. Higher scores reflect greater degrees of generalized self-efficacy.

Discussion Questions

1. Based on this questionnaire, how high or low is your generalized self-efficacy? Does your score make sense to you? In other words, does the questionnaire tell you something you already believed about yourself or did it provide new insight?
2. How do you think your score compares to the scores of others? Are you higher or lower than average on this characteristic?
3. Do you think the techniques outlined in the Winning Practices section on page 77 may help raise your self-efficacy? Which tactics do you will think will be most effective? Why?

GROUP EXERCISE

Disciplining a Generally Good Employee

Even the best employees sometimes behave inappropriately. When this occurs, managers confront a special challenge: How can they address the problem behavior without offending or turning off the employee in question? The following exercise will get you to think about handling this difficult, but not uncommon, type of dilemma.

Directions

1. Break into teams of two.
2. One member of each team should read the role of Michael M. The other individual should read the role of Michael's supervisor. Members of the class should read both roles.
3. After familiarizing themselves with their respective roles, the parties should discuss the situation as they would in a real organization.

Michael M.

You have been a laborer with a home construction company for almost four years, during which time you have developed an excellent record. You are an outstanding craftsman who always does meticulous work and completes his projects ahead of schedule. You have always gotten along well with your co-workers, and even customers have praised you for your kind and professional manner. You know that your boss likes you and is reluctant to fire you, so you have been taking advantage of him by showing up for work late—sometimes by as much as an hour. When your boss spoke to you about it, you admit to being late quite often but explain that this sometimes is necessary because you have to help send your children to school in the morning. Besides, you explain that because you work so quickly you make up for being late, so it shouldn't matter. However, you know that your company has a strict rule against being late ("three strikes and you're out"), and you are concerned about losing your job. You are worried about what your boss might say because you very much want to keep your job.

Michael M.'s Supervisor

Michael M. has been a laborer with your home construction company for almost four years, during which time he has developed an excellent record. He has been an outstanding craftsman who always does meticulous work and completes his projects ahead of schedule. Michael has always gotten along well with his co-workers, and even customers have praised him for his kind and professional manner. Employees like Michael are hard to find, making you very interested in keeping him happy so that he will continue to work for you. There has been one recurrent problem, however. Because he knows he is so good and that you are reluctant to fire him, Michael has been taking advantage of you by showing up for work late—sometimes by as much as an hour. When you have spoken to him about this, he admits to being late quite often but says that this sometimes is necessary because he has to help send his children to school in the morning. Besides, he claims that because he works so quickly he makes up for being late, so it shouldn't matter. However, your company has a strict rule against being late ("three strikes and you're out"), and you are concerned that by turning a blind eye to Michael, you are sending the message to the other employees that Michael is "above the law" and that you are "playing favorites" with him. You do not want to threaten your credibility by ignoring the problem, but you also don't want to risk making Michael quit.

Discussion Questions

1. Based on the guidelines for discipline described in this chapter, what specific steps should be taken to handle this situation?
2. As the roles were played out before you, what were the major strengths and weaknesses of the way Michael's supervisor handled the situation?
3. As Michael's supervisor, how would you be affected, if at all, by the fact that Michael's lateness resulted from the need to take care of his children? Did this matter? If so, how, and what would you do about it?

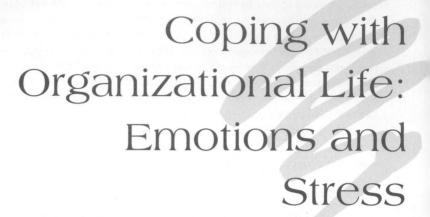

C h a p t e r 4

Coping with Organizational Life: Emotions and Stress

Learning Objectives

After reading this chapter, you should be able to:

1. **DISTINGUISH** between emotions and moods.

2. **EXPLAIN** how emotions and moods influence behavior in organizations.

3. **DESCRIBE** ways in which people manage their emotions in organizations.

4. **IDENTIFY** the major causes of organizational stress.

5. **DESCRIBE** the adverse effects of organizational stress.

6. **IDENTIFY** various ways of reducing stress in the workplace.

---

3 GOOD REASONS why you should care about . . .

Emotions and Stress

You should care about emotions and stress because . . .

1. People's everyday emotions can have dramatic effects on the way they feel and how they perform their jobs.

2. The effects of stress are often adverse, taking a serious toll on both individual health and organizational performance.

3. Managers are capable of doing many things to reduce the levels of stress experienced by their subordinates if they know how.

Making the Case for Emotions and Stress

A Basketball Court Judge Faces a Federal Court Judge

"I've brought shame on myself, my family and the profession," were the words of Tim Donaghy as a federal district judge sentenced him to 15 months behind bars in July 2008. Formally, the charges against him were conspiracy to engage in wire fraud and transmitting betting information through interstate commerce. In plain English, the 41-year-old Donaghy, a 13-year veteran National Basketball Association (NBA) referee, admitted to taking thousands of dollars in payoffs from a professional gambler in exchange for giving inside tips on games he officiated.

Upon sentencing Donaghy, U.S. District Judge Carol Amon gave him credit for cooperating with the court but explained that a jail term was justified because, "The NBA, the players and the fans relied upon him to perform his job in an honest, reliable and non-conflicted manner." Instead, she said, he was "compromised by a financial interest in the game he was refereeing." The contrite Donaghy stood with his arms folded and showed no emotion. When invited to speak, he told the judge, "I'm very sorry for the acts for which I stand before you."

Although sportswriters and NBA officials roundly criticized Donaghy for his actions, they also acknowledge the intensely stressful nature of the referee's job. Living out of a suitcase for over half a year, they log thousands of miles on the road during the season and face extreme pressure. Not only do they have to make split-second decisions, but they have to do it in the shadow of giant players and coaches who are not exactly reticent about sharing their opinions about the nature of their calls. Still, this does not justify Donaghy's actions.

Donaghy can serve his sentence and put the ordeal behind him but the problems for the NBA may be just beginning. In the course of defending himself, Donaghy revealed that NBA officials told referees to go easy on calling technical fouls against certain star players, whom fans wanted to see on the court, and to make calls that extended playoffs to seven games so as to boost income for the League. NBA Commissioner David Stern has repeatedly denied that corruption went beyond Donaghy, explaining that Donaghy fabricated the claims to create the appearance that he was sharing information in the hope of getting a lighter sentence. Although the court announced that Donaghy's claims of widespread game manipulation were unsubstantiated, the NBA recognizes the serious public relations nightmare it has on its hands.

Unless the game can be played with integrity on a level playing field (or court, in this case), it has no future. To ensure the quality of officiating from now on, Commissioner Stern created a new position, senior vice president of referee operations, staffed by retired U.S. Army General Ronald Johnson. If you think being a referee on the court is stressful, imagine what it's like to be in charge of all of them from behind a desk in a New York office.

If you're a basketball fan, you probably know this tale only too well. After all, it strikes at the heart of the game itself. Even if you're not a fan, it's easy to see how Donaghy's ordeal was a significant source of *stress* for both him and everyone involved. Understandably, with so much at stake, emotions ran high on both sides of the issue.

Although few of us face the kind of stress that Donaghy and NBA officials surely experienced—quite fortunately—spending any time in the workplace at all is bound to be stressful. Indeed, the workplace is the single greatest source of stress in people's lives. And its cost to American organizations is $200 to $300 billion annually.[1] Stress makes differences in how well people perform, the number of errors they make, and even whether or not they show up for work or remain on their jobs at all. Given that stress plays such an important role in the behavior of people in organizations, it clearly warrants the attention we devote to it in this chapter.

To understand stress fully, it helps to look more broadly at the wide range of emotions that people have in everyday work situations and their reactions to them. Whether your experiences are positive (e.g., getting a raise), negative (e.g., receiving a poor performance appraisal), or neutral (e.g., doing your job as usual), these every-day feelings—*emotions* and *moods*—play an important role in how we think and act. If emotions and moods seem to be trivial, it's simply because their effects are so wide-spread that we take them for granted. However, their impact on the way we work can be considerable.[2] Accordingly, we will examine them in this chapter as well.

We begin this chapter with an overview of emotions and mood in organizations, describing their basic nature and the important role they play in organizations. Following this, we examine the nature of stress on the job, focusing closely on specific steps that can be taken to minimize its often harmful effects.

UNDERSTANDING EMOTIONS AND MOOD

Imagine how you would feel if you were the character described in each of the following situations.

> ➤ After a gloomy winter, a beautiful, sunny day finally arrived, making James happy. He was inspired to come up with lots of new ideas for his clients.
> ➤ Kimberly was so upset about not making any progress on her sales report that she couldn't take it any more. She left the work piled up on her desk and went to the gym to work out.
> ➤ It was a special day for Ashley. She was so excited that Jason had asked her to marry him that she made her way through her delivery route with a lively spring in her step.

There's nothing special, here, right? James is happy, Kimberly is upset, and Ashley is excited. Although these are everyday reactions, you shouldn't be misled into thinking that they are unimportant, especially on the job. Indeed, scientists acknowledge that people's feelings at any given time are important. Specifically, two different kinds of feelings are involved—*emotions* and *mood*. These states, as we describe here, are far more important than you might imagine, and in highly complex ways.

Properties of Emotions

By definition, **emotions** are overt reactions that express feelings about events. You get angry when a colleague takes advantage of you. You become sad when your best friend leaves to take a new job. And you become afraid of what the future holds when the bank at which you've worked for 15 years merges with another financial institution. These are all examples of emotional reactions. To understand them, we now consider the various properties of emotions and the different forms they take.

> ➤ ***Emotions always have an object.***   Something or someone triggers emotions. For example, you may recognize that your boss made you angry when he falsely accused you of making a mistake or that your boyfriend surprised you with an engagement ring. In each case, there is someone who caused your emotional reaction.

➤ *The spread of emotions is contagious.*   If you've ever started laughing because others around you are cackling hysterically, then you probably recognize that people's emotions are often triggered by the emotions of others with whom they interact. This phenomenon, known as **emotional contagion,** is defined as the tendency of people to mimic the emotional expressions of others, converging with them emotionally.[3] Not surprisingly, emotional contagion is prevalent in organizations, where workers frequently display the same emotional responses of the higher-ranking others with whom they interact.[4]

➤ *Expression of emotions is universal.*   People throughout the world generally portray particular emotions by using the same facial expressions. In fact, even people living in remote parts of the world tend to express the same emotions in the same manner.[5] As a result, we can do a pretty good (but not perfect) job of recognizing the emotional states of others if we pay attention to their facial expressions. We have to be careful, however, because as we will point out later, people do not always express the emotions they really feel. When they do, however, we are fairly good at recognizing them.

➤ *Culture determines how and when people express emotions.*   Although people throughout the world generally express their emotions in the same manner, informal standards govern the degree to which it is acceptable for them to do so.[6] These expectations are known as **display rules.** For example, Italian cultural norms accept public displays of emotion (e.g., hugging good-bye at the airport, or yelling at one another in public), whereas cultural norms frown upon such public displays in Great Britain, encouraging people there to "tone down" their emotional displays. For some interesting national differences in willingness to express emotions, see Table 4.1.[7]

Table 4.1   National Differences in Expressivity

In a survey of over 5,000 people in 32 nations, researchers found that people in some countries are more inclined to express their emotions than those in other countries. Listed in order from most expressive (rank 1) to least expressive (rank 32), the findings are summarized here. The scores shown are an index created by the scientists to reflect each country's level of expressivity (higher scores reflect higher degrees of expressivity). Overall (but not always), Western cultures ranked higher than Eastern cultures.

Rank	Nation	Score	Rank	Nation	Score	Rank	Nation	Score
1	Zimbabwe	523	10 tied	India	495	23 tied	Italy	451
2	Canada	520	13	Mexico	485	23 tied	Croatia	451
3	United States	519	14	Georgia	478	25	South Korea	449
4	Australia	510	15 tied	Poland	477	26 tied	Switzerland	446
5	Nigeria	506	15 tied	Portugal	477	26 tied	Malaysia	446
6	Denmark	505	17	People's Republic of China	471	28	Israel	442
7	New Zealand	502	18	Czech Republic	468	29	Russia	432
8	Belgium	498	19	Turkey	467	30	Bangladesh	422
9	Netherlands	496	20	Japan	464	31	Indonesia	420
10 tied	Brazil	495	21	Germany	455	32	Hong Kong	399
10 tied	Hungary	495	22	Greece	452			

(Source: Based on data reported by Matsumoto et al., 2008; see Note 7.)

Types of Emotions

Despite what you might think, people do not have an infinite (or even a very large) number of unrelated emotions. Rather, people's emotions may be categorized in different ways. Depending on how you categorize them, different features of emotion are highlighted. We now describe three such ways of categorizing emotions.

Major emotions and their subcategories

Some scientists have noted that there are six major categories of emotions into which various subcategories may be classified. As shown in Figure 4.1, these major categories are anger, fear, joy, love, sadness, and surprise.[8] With the exception of surprise, each of these has associated with it various specific emotions that constitute subcategories of these major emotions. The underlying idea is that the six major groups of emotions are different from one another, but within each group, the various subcategories of emotions share similar characteristics (and, as a result, are difficult to distinguish from one another).

Figure 4.1   Major Categories of Emotion and Associated Subcategories

Scientists have found it useful to categorize people's emotions into the six major categories (and associated subcategories) identified here.

(Source: Based on information reported by Weiss & Cropanzano, 1996; see Note 8.)

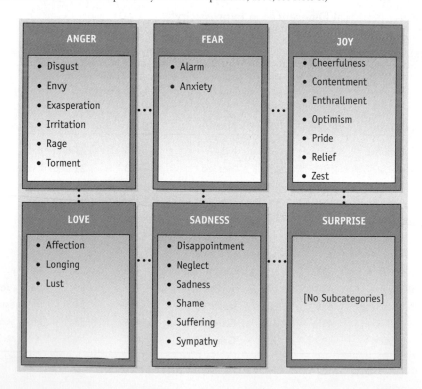

Self-conscious emotions vs. social emotions

Another useful way of distinguishing between emotions is by comparing those that come from internal sources and those that come from external sources. This is the essence of the distinction between so-called *self-conscious emotions* and *social emotions*.

Self-conscious emotions refer to feelings that stem from within. Examples include *shame, guilt, embarrassment,* and *pride.*[9] Scientists believe that self-conscious emotions developed within people to help them stay aware of and regulate their relationships with others. For example, we feel shame when we believe we have failed to meet expectations (as in the case of Tim Donaghy, described in the Making the Case section on p. 101), and in such cases we are likely to humble ourselves to others, allowing them to have the upper hand. So, if we have done something to harm a co-worker, we are likely to demonstrate—and express—feelings of embarrassment and shame, which help appease the relationship with that individual.[10]

In contrast, **social emotions** refer to people's feelings based on information external to themselves. Examples include *pity, envy, jealousy,* and *scorn*. For example, a worker may experience envy if she covets something that another has (e.g., a better work assignment) or pity if she feels sorry for someone else (e.g., someone who was hurt in an accident). All these emotions are likely to be experienced in the workplace.[11]

The circumplex model of affect

Another way scientists differentiate between emotions is by combining two different dimensions—the degree to which emotions are pleasant or unpleasant, and the degree to which they make one feel alert and engaged (a variable known as *activation*). This two-dimensional perspective is known as the **circumplex model of affect** (see Figure 4.2).[12] This diagram illustrates how various emotions are interrelated with respect to these two dimensions. Four major categories result.

To understand how to read this diagram (hence, to understand the circumplex model of affect), look, for example, at the upper right part of Figure 4.2. It shows that being elated is a pleasant emotion (because it makes us feel good) and that it also is a highly activated emotion (because it encourages us to take action). They fall into the activated positive affect category. The same applies to the two other emotions in that part of the diagram (enthusiastic and excited). Within the diagram, any emotions that lie directly opposite each other are characterized in the opposite manner. So, following through on our example, being bored, tired, and drowsy are emotions considered opposite to enthusiastic, elated, and excited. They are at the opposite ends of the two main dimensions—that is, they generate unactivated negative affect.

The Basic Nature of Mood

In contrast to emotions, which are highly specific and intense, we also have feelings that are more diffuse in scope, known as *moods*. Scientists define **mood** as an unfocused, relatively mild feeling that exists as background to our daily experiences. Whereas we are inclined to recognize the emotions we are feeling, moods are more subtle and difficult to detect. For example, you may say that you are in a good mood or a bad mood, but this isn't as specific as saying that you are experiencing a certain emotion, such as anger or sadness.

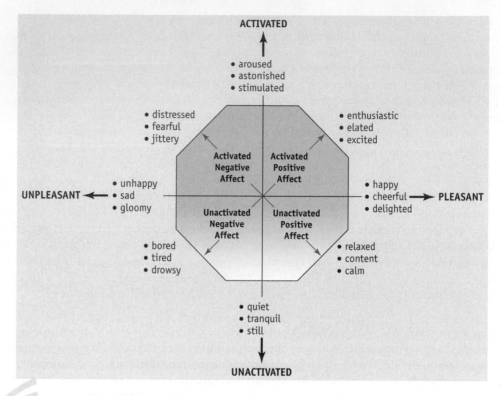

Figure 4.2   The Circumplex Model of Affect

This conceptualization summarizes emotions in terms of two key dimensions: activated-unactivated and pleasant-unpleasant. The emotions within each grouping are similar to one another. Those across from one another in this diagram are considered opposite emotions.

(Source: Based on Huelsman et al., 2003; see Note 12.)

Moods, as we all know, fluctuate rapidly, sometimes widely, during the course of a day. Favorable feedback from the boss may make us feel good, but harsh criticism may put us in a bad mood. Such temporary shifts in feeling *states*—short-term differences in the way we feel—are only partly responsible for the moods that people demonstrate.

Superimposed over these passing conditions are also more stable personality *traits*—consistent differences between people's predispositions toward experiencing positive or negative affect, as we discussed in Chapter 3. Mood, in other words, is a combination of both who we are—that is, a personality trait, and a response to conditions we face.[13]

THE ROLE OF EMOTIONS AND MOOD IN ORGANIZATIONS

Thus far, we've described emotions and mood in general terms, implying throughout that they are involved heavily in people's behavior. Indeed, it's safe to say that emotions and mood are strong determinants of behavior in organizations as well as important consequences of it.[14] Now, let's take a look at the specific role they play.

Are Happier People More Successful on Their Jobs?

Before answering this question, we should clarify what I mean by "happy." To social scientists, happy individuals are those who frequently experience positive emotions in their lives. Based on this definition, do people perform their jobs better when they are happy? Research shows that the answer is "yes"; happy workers enjoy two major advantages over their less happy peers.[15]

Job performance

Happier people tend to outperform less happy people in several ways. To begin with, they generally get better jobs—that is, ones that give them high levels of autonomy, meaning, and variety.[16] Then, once on their jobs, they perform their jobs more successfully.[17] This occurs among people in jobs ranging from dormitory resident advisors to cricket players.[18]

Interestingly, this same effect also occurs at the highest echelons of organizations. Happier CEOs of companies tend to have happier employees working for them. And, of course, happy employees are less inclined to resign (see Chapter 6).[19] In part because of this, their organizations tend to be more profitable.[20] Obviously, the importance of happiness cannot be overstated when it comes to job performance.

Income

Research has shown that happier people earn higher incomes—and this is the case in countries throughout the world. For example, high correlations between happiness and income have been found among people in Germany and Russia.[21] Fascinatingly, this same relationship was found even among indigenous Malaysian farmers, whose only income was the value of their property and belongings.[22]

In these cases, because the relationships are correlational in nature, it's unclear whether people make more money because they're happy or that people become happy because they make more money. Also, it's possible that this connection is related to the effect of job performance noted above: People earn more money (and are happy about it) because they perform well. Although research hasn't yet provided insight into these issues, it's clear that the connection between income and happiness is quite strong.

Affective Events Theory

In recent years, one of the guiding forces in the study of emotions in organizations has been **affective events theory (AET)**.[23] This theory identifies various factors that lead to people's emotional reactions on the job and how these reactions affect those individuals (see Figure 4.3).[24]

Beginning on the left side of Figure 4.3, AET recognizes that people's emotions are determined, in part, by various features of the work environment. For example, the way we feel is likely to be determined by various characteristics of the jobs we do (e.g., we are likely to feel good about jobs that are interesting and exciting), the demands we face (e.g., how pressured we are to meet deadlines), and by requirements for *emotional labor*.

The concept of **emotional labor** refers to the degree to which people have to work hard to display what they believe are appropriate emotions on their jobs. People in service professions (e.g., waitresses and flight attendants), for example, often have

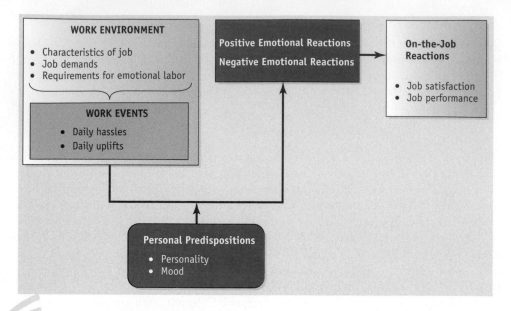

Figure 4.3   Affective Events Theory

According to *affective events theory*, people's job performance and job satisfaction are influenced by their positive and negative emotional reactions to events on the job. These events, in turn, are influenced by aspects of the work environment. People's emotional reactions to these events depend on such individual characteristics as their moods and aspects of their personalities.

(Source: Based on suggestions by Ashkanasy & Daus, 2002; see Note 24.)

to come across as being more pleasant than they really feel. As you might imagine, having to do this repeatedly can be very taxing (we will discuss this further later in this chapter).

These various features of the work environment are likely to lead to the occurrence of various events. These include confronting **daily hassles,** unpleasant or undesirable events that put people in bad moods (e.g., having to deal with difficult bosses or co-workers). They also include experiencing more positive events known as **daily uplifts.** These are the opposite—namely, pleasant or desirable events that put people in good moods (e.g., enjoying feelings of recognition for the work you do).

As Figure 4.3 shows, people react to these various work events by showing emotional reactions, both positive and negative. However, as the diagram also shows, the extent to which this occurs depends upon each of two types of personal predispositions: personality and mood. As noted in Chapter 3, personality predisposes us to respond in varying degrees of intensity to the events that occur. In keeping with our discussion, for example, a person who has a high degree of positive affectivity is likely to perceive events in a positive manner, whereas one who has a high degree of negative affectivity is likely to perceive those same events more negatively.

Mood also influences the relationship between work events and emotional reactions, as Figure 4.3 suggests. This is in keeping with the point we made earlier, that the mood we are in at any given time can exaggerate the nature of the emotions we experience in response to an event. So, for example, an event that leads a person to experience a negative emotional reaction (e.g., having a fight with a co-worker) is likely to make that individual feel even worse if he or she is in a bad mood at the time.

Finally, as the theory notes, these affective reactions have two important effects. First, they promote high levels of job performance. This should not be surprising, given that we already noted that happy people perform their jobs at high levels. Second, AET also notes that affective reactions are responsible for people's job performance and *job satisfaction*—that is, the extent to which they hold positive attitudes toward their jobs (we will discuss this in detail in Chapter 6). Indeed, research has established very strongly that people who are inclined to experience positive emotions are likely to be satisfied with their jobs.[25]

Besides being a useful scientific theory, AET sends a strong message to managers about the importance of not overlooking the emotional reactions of employees. In fact, when they accumulate over time, their impact can be considerable. Thus, it is clear that anyone in a supervisory capacity has to pay attention to managing emotions in the workplace. In view of this critical function, we now turn to this topic.

MANAGING EMOTIONS IN ORGANIZATIONS

Although emotions occur naturally, people do not always display the emotions they feel. After all, it's not always to our advantage to let our true emotions show—especially on the job. For example, you probably would be reluctant to display all the anger you feel toward your boss because you wouldn't want to jeopardize that relationship. With this in mind, let's now consider the various ways in which people manage their emotions.

Develop Emotional Intelligence

If you think about the people you've met in your life, you probably can recall some who are adept at recognizing and regulating their own emotions (e.g., holding their tempers in check) and who also are particularly good at recognizing and influencing the emotions of others (e.g., figuring out who's not excited about an idea and how to turn them around). Such individuals—and maybe you are one—may be said to be displaying a high amount of **emotional intelligence (EI)**.[26] Specifically, EI consists of the four components summarized in Figure 4.1.[27] To help make things clearer, this diagram also gives an example of a skill required to develop each of the elements of EI.

As you might expect, people who display high amounts of EI have an important edge over those who are not as adept. At the haircare and cosmetics company L'Oreal, for example, sales agents with the highest levels of EI significantly outsold their colleagues who had lower levels of EI by an average of $91,370 annually. In addition, among first-year employees, turnover was less than half as great among those with higher EIs (put differently, those with higher levels of EI were less likely to quit). Taken together, these benefits accounted for a net revenue increase of over $2.5 million in a single year.[28] These and many other research findings make it clear that having high levels of EI can make a big difference.

Not surprisingly, it's easy to make a strong business case for developing EI among employees. Fortunately, EI is not immutable and people are capable of changing in ways that boost their emotional intelligence.[29] Programs to develop EI, such as those offered by some universities and private consulting firms, typically use both group training activities and, with increasing popularity, one-on-one coaching. With respect

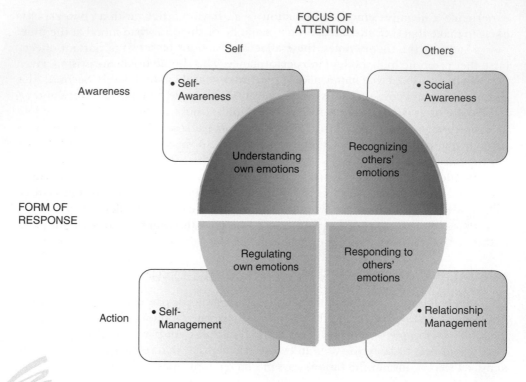

Figure 4.4   Components of Emotional Intelligence

EI consists of four components based on two distinct dimensions. These are summarized here along with a specific skill required to develop each of the components.

to content, these programs focus in varying degrees on the each of the four forms of EI summarized in Figure 4.4. For example, efforts to develop EI often focus on such skills as:

➤   Learning to be in touch with one's own emotions (building self-awareness)
➤   Learning to show empathy for others (social awareness)
➤   Learning to control one's own negative emotions (self-management)
➤   Learning to collaborate closely with others (relationhip management)

The best training programs incorporate case studies that are specific to the workplace, exercises in modeling appropriate behavior, and simulations and customized role-playing exercises. Such training programs have been effective in several ways, such as by improving both the health and performance levels of employees.[30] (To assess your own level of emotional intelligence, see the Self-Assessment Exercise on p. 131.)

Manage Emotional Displays

Imagine that you are a flight attendant for a major airline. After a long flight with rude passengers, you finally reach your destination. You're feeling tired and annoyed, but you do not have the option of expressing how you really feel. You don't even have the luxury of acting neutrally and expressing nothing at all. Instead, you are expected to act peppy and cheerful, smiling and thanking the passengers for choosing your airline and cheerfully saying goodbye (more like "b'bye") to them as they exit the plane.

The conflict between the emotion you feel (anger) and the emotion you are required to express (happiness) may take its toll on your well-being. This example illustrates a kind of situation that is all too typical—one in which you are required to display emotions on the job that are inconsistent with how you actually feel.

This phenomenon, known as **emotional dissonance,** can be a significant source of work-related stress (the major topic we discuss later in this chapter).[31] Emotional dissonance is likely to occur in situations in which there are strong expectations regarding the emotions one is expected to display by virtue of one's job requirements. Our flight attendant example illustrates this point. The same applies to sales clerks, bank tellers, entertainers—just about anyone who provides services to the public.

When emotional dissonance occurs, people have to try very hard to ensure that they display the appropriate emotions. As we noted earlier, the psychological effort involved in doing this is referred to as *emotional labor.* If you ever find yourself "biting your tongue"—that is, holding back from saying what you want to say—you are expending a great deal of emotional labor.

Not saying what you really think is only part of the situation. Emotional labor also is invested in saying things you don't really feel. For example, you would have to invest a great deal of emotional labor when confronting a co-worker who comes to you asking you how you feel about her new hairdo. You don't like it at all, but you struggle to keep your feelings to yourself. When pressed to say something, you engage in "a little white lie," by telling her how very flattering it is. Although this is a form of dishonesty, it is widely considered appropriate to keep from hurting people's feelings by saying the right thing .

This discussion underscores an important idea: The emotions people actually experience, known as **felt emotions,** may be discrepant from the emotions they show others, known as **displayed emotions.** This is not at all surprising. After all, our jobs do not always give us the luxury of expressing how we really feel. To do so, such as by expressing the anger you really feel toward a customer, is likely to lose the account. Social pressure compels people to conform to expectations about which particular emotions are appropriate to show in public and which are not.

As noted earlier, such *display rules* vary among cultures. But they also appear to differ as a function of people's occupational positions. It's an unspoken rule, for example, that an athletic coach is not supposed to be openly hostile and negative when speaking about an opponent (at least, when doing so in public).

It also is expected that people considered "professionals," such as doctors and lawyers, demonstrate appropriate decorum and seriousness when interacting with their patients and clients. Should your own doctor or lawyer respond to your difficult situation by saying, "Wow, I sure wouldn't want to be in your shoes," you may find yourself looking for someone else to help you. (Showing empathy is one thing but revulsion is quite another.)

Control Anger Before It Controls You

Quite often, behaving appropriately in business situations requires controlling negative emotions, particularly anger. After all, to be successful we cannot let the situations we face get the better of us. It's perfectly natural for anyone to get angry, particularly on the job, where there may be a great deal to anger us. We can be made angry, for example, by feeling unfairly treated (see Chapter 2), by believing that we are disrespected by others, by feeling that we are being attacked or threatened in some way, and the like.

Although we all know what *anger* is, and we have experienced it many times (perhaps too many), a precise definition is in order. To scientists, **anger** is a heightened state of emotional arousal (e.g., increased heart rate, rapid breathing, flushed face, sweaty palms, etc.) fueled by cognitive interpretations of situations. Anger reactions can run the gamut from irritation to outrage and fury.

Importantly, there are situations in which displaying anger can be purposeful and constructive. For example, to get a subordinate to take immediate action in a dangerous situation, a supervisor may express anger by raising her voice and looking that subordinate straight in the eye. This would be the case, for example, when a military officer displays her anger purposely to express urgency when ordering a soldier under her command to move immediately out of a combat zone. Because of its constructive and highly controlled nature, anger of this type is not problematic. In fact, it can be quite valuable. Where anger can be dangerous, however, is when it erupts violently and is out of control. We need to be concerned about this because aggression is a natural reaction to anger (see Chapter 7).

The challenge people face is to control their anger appropriately. This is the idea behind the practice of **anger management**—systematic efforts to reduce people's emotional feelings of anger and the physiological arousal it causes. Because you hardly ever can get rid of or avoid the things that anger you, nor can you alter them, it's important to learn to control your reactions. For some suggestions as to how to go about doing so, see Table 4.2.

Table 4.2   Managing Anger in the Workplace

Although it's widely believed that it's good to "let it all hang out" by expressing your anger fully, this is a dangerous myth. "Letting it rip" not only does little to alleviate the source of your anger, but it's likely to make things worse. Fortunately, however, we all can do various things to control our anger. Some of the most effective ones are described here.

Practice	Description
Practice relaxation	People who meditate are inclined to be affected less by events that anger others, so it's helpful to learn this technique. However, anyone beginning to feel anger can control his or her emotions by taking a deep breath and counting to 10.
Think logically	Angry people tend to think illogically about the sources of their anger. To avoid making problems worse, ask a friend to help you recognize more logical ways to behave.
Use humor	It's hard to be angry while being funny, so instead of focusing on the source of your anger, take the edge off your fury by being silly.
Leave the room	Changing your surroundings when angry can help you escape the source of your anger. The time spent moving elsewhere also can help by distracting you from the anger-inducing situation and keep you from saying something about which you will be sorry.

Show Compassion in Times of Trauma

In the last few years we've witnessed no end to traumatic events, both natural and man-made. Nobody will soon forget the September 11, 2001 terrorist attacks, or the devastation caused by Hurricane Katrina in 2005. Dramatic events such as these obviously have serious effects on the mood of people in the workplace, but so do tragic events that are known less widely because they involve fewer people.

Consider, for example, the tragic loss of three executives of Revel Entertainment, a gaming and entertainment company, who perished when the private plane carrying them went down in a Minnesota field in the summer of 2008. The effects on the employees of this firm were understandably traumatic.[32] Even when no lives are lost, as in the January 2009 emergency landing of U.S. Airways flight 1549 into New York's Hudson River, the emotional toll on victims, their families, and the flying public can be considerable.[33]

Although it's surely difficult or impossible to avoid many disasters, fortunately, there is something that leaders and managers can do to help everyone involved return to business as usual.[34] Specifically, company officials should create an environment in which people can express their emotions and in which they can do something to alleviate their own or others' suffering. In other words, they should express **organizational compassion.** For some suggestions on how to accomplish this, see Table 4.3.

Table 4.3   Coping with the Emotional Fallout of Disasters: How Can Companies Help?

Whether from terrorists or the wrath of Mother Nature, disasters leave people feeling vulnerable and unable to concentrate. This, of course, makes it difficult for them to focus on work, even if their workplaces still exist. Given the emotional fallout, companies find it necessary to cope in ways that they might never have considered earlier. Fortunately, there are several things companies can do to help.

Suggestion	Explanation
Provide accurate information.	It is not always clear what to do, but whatever is being done to promote workplace safety should be communicated clearly to all.
Encourage social interaction.	Social networks provide much-needed comfort and support. When disaster strikes, company social events should not be cancelled. They should be held because they are useful mechanisms for fostering social support.
Promote the use of health services.	It's easy for people to become ill when their emotions are running high. The company should encourage employees to take care of themselves, taking full advantage of the medical, counseling, and health club services that may be available.
Try to return to normalcy.	Routines are shattered during times of trauma. To help return to normal, it is useful to try to get back to "business as usual." This is not to ignore the emotions that people feel, because these need to be acknowledged. Still, it's useful to regain the security of one's regular routine.

(Source: Dutton et al., 2002; see Note 34.)

THE BASIC NATURE OF STRESS

Stress is an unavoidable fact of organizational life today, taking its toll on both individuals and organizations. According to one survey, 90 percent of American workers report feeling stressed at least once a week and 40 percent describe their jobs as very stressful most of the time.[35] What stresses them? Lots of things, but having too much work to do and fear of being laid off are among people's most common concerns.

As you might imagine, these sources of stress are both harmful to individual workers and costly to their organizations. In fact, about half of all American workers report that stress has adversely affected their health.[36] Not surprisingly, stress on the job has been linked to rises in accidents, lost productivity, and of course, enormous increases in medical insurance. Overall, work-related stress has been estimated to cost American companies $200 billion to $300 billion annually.[37]

In view of these sobering statistics, it is clearly important to understand the nature of organizational stress. Formally, scientists define **stress** as the pattern of emotional and physiological reactions occurring in response to demands from within or outside organizations. In this chapter, we will review the major causes and effects of stress and, importantly, various ways of effectively managing stress so as to reduce its negative impact. Before doing this, however, we describe the basic nature of stress in more detail.

Stressors in Organizations

What do each of the following situations have in common?

➤ You lose your job the day before you become eligible to receive your retirement pension.

➤ Your boss tells you that you will not be getting a raise this year.

➤ Your spouse is diagnosed with a serious illness.

The answer, besides that they are all awful, is that each situation involves external events (i.e., ones beyond your own control) that create extreme demands on you. Stimuli of this type are known as **stressors,** formally defined as any demands, either physical or psychological in nature, encountered during the course of living.

Scientists often find it useful to distinguish stressors in terms of how long lasting they are. This results in the following three major categories (see Figure 4.5):

➤ **Acute stressors** are those that bring some form of *sudden change* that threatens us either physically or psychologically, requiring people to make unwanted adjustments. For example, you may be assigned to a different shift at work, requiring you to get up earlier in the morning and to eat meals at different times. As your body's equilibrium is disrupted, you respond physiologically (e.g., by being tired) and emotionally (e.g., by being grouchy).

➤ **Episodic stressors** are the result of experiencing *lots of acute stressors* in a short period of time, such as when you "have one of those days" in which everything goes wrong. In other words, you are experiencing particularly stressful episodes in life. This would be the case, for example, if within the course of a week you have a serious disagreement with one of your subordinates, you lose a major sales account, and

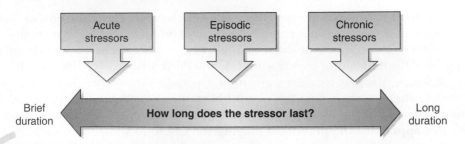

Figure 4.5   Different Types of Stressors

Whereas *acute stressors* tend to be of brief duration, *chronic stressors* are endured for long periods of time. *Episodic stressors* generally last for intermediate periods of time.

then, to top it off, the pipes burst in your office, causing water to ruin your important papers and your computer. For a list of some of the most common episodic stressors in the workplace, see Table 4.4.

➤ **Chronic stressors** are the most extreme type of stressor because they are constant and unrelenting in nature, having a long-term effect on the body, mind, and spirit. For example, a person experiences chronic stressors if he or she is in a long-term abusive relationship with a boss or spouse or has a debilitating disease (e.g., arthritis or migraine headaches) that adversely affects his or her ability to work. In recent years, in which layoffs have been common, people have suffered stress due to considerable uncertainties about their future.

The Cognitive Appraisal Process

The Roman emperor and philosopher Marcus Aurelius Antoninus (A.D. 121–180) is quoted as saying, "If you are distressed by anything external, the pain is not due to the thing itself, but to your estimate of it; and this you have the power to revoke at any moment." This observation is as true today as it was some 2,000 years ago, when first spoken.

Table 4.4   Common Episodic Stressors in the Workplace

Many of the most commonly encountered stressors in organizations are episodic in nature. If you think about these, it's not difficult to recognize how they actually are composed of several different acute stressors. For example, fear of losing one's job includes concerns over money, threats to self-esteem, embarrassment, and other acute stressors.

• Lack of involvement in making organizational decisions
• Unrelenting and unreasonable expectations for performance
• Poor communication with co-workers
• Fear of losing one's job
• Spending long amounts of time away from home
• Office politics and conflict
• Not being paid fairly given one's level of responsibility and performance

The basic idea is that the mere presence of potentially harmful events or conditions in the environment is not enough for them to be stressors. For an event to serve as a stressor to someone, he or she must think of it as a stressor and acknowledge the danger and the difficulty of coping with it. As you think about the events or conditions you encounter, you may consider some to be especially threatening (warranting your concern), whereas others pose less of a problem to you (and can be ignored safely). Your assessment of the dangers associated with any potential stressor is based on **cognitive appraisal**—the process of judging the extent to which an environmental event is a potential source of stress. Let's consider this process more closely.

On some occasions, people appraise conditions instantly. Suppose, for example, you are camping in the woods when a bear looks like it's going to attack. You immediately assess that you are in danger and run away as fast as you can. This is a natural reaction, which biologists call a **flight response.** Indeed, making a rapid escape from a dangerous situation occurs automatically. So, without giving the matter much thought, you immediately flee from a burning office building because you judge the situation to be life-threatening. The situation is extreme, so you appraised it as dangerous automatically. In the blink of an eye, you recognized the danger and sought to escape. Although you may not have deliberated all the pros and cons of the situation, you did engage in a cognitive appraisal process: You recognized the situation as dangerous and took action instantly.

Most of the situations managers face are neither as extreme nor as clear-cut. In fact, the vast majority of would-be stressors are stressors only if people perceive them as such. For example, if you are an expert at writing sales reports and really enjoy doing them, the prospect of having to work extra hours on preparing one is not likely to be a stressor for you. However, for someone else who finds the same task to be an obnoxious chore, confronting it may well be a stressor. Likewise, the deadline might not be a stressor if you perceive that it is highly flexible and that nobody takes it seriously, or if you believe you can get an extension simply by asking.

The point is simple: Whether or not an environmental event is a stressor depends on how it is perceived. What might be a stressor for you under some circumstances might not be a stressor at other times or even for someone else under the same conditions. Remember, it's all a matter of how things are appraised cognitively.

As you might imagine, it is important to appraise potential threats as accurately as possible. For example, to think that everyone in your department is happy when, in reality, they are all planning to rebel surely would be a serious mistake. Likewise, interpreting a small dip in sales as a sign of economic collapse would cause you needless worry and might spark panic in others. As such, it is important to recognize what you can do as a manager to ensure that you and those around you are assessing potential stressors accurately. For some recommendations in this regard, see Table 4.5.

Bodily Responses to Stressors

When we encounter stressors, our bodies (in particular, our sympathetic nervous systems and endocrine systems) are mobilized into action, such as through elevated heart rate, blood pressure, and respiration.[38] Arousal rises quickly to high levels, and many physiological changes take place. If the stressors persist, the body's resources eventually may become depleted, at which point people's ability to cope (at least physically) decreases

Table 4.5   Tips for Assessing Potential Stressors Accurately

It is important to recognize potential stressors and to take appropriate action. However, it can be very disruptive to mistakenly assume that something is a stressor when, in reality, nothing is wrong. With this in mind, here are some useful guidelines for appraising potential stressors accurately.

Suggestion	Explanation
Check with others.	Ask around. If others are not concerned about a situation, then maybe neither should you be concerned. Discussing the situation with people either may alleviate any feelings of stress you may have had or it may verify that something should, in fact, be done.
Look to the past.	Your best bet for deciding what to do may be to consider what has happened over the years. You may want to be concerned about something that has caused problems in the past, but worrying about conditions that haven't been problems before might only make things worse by distracting your attention from what really matters.
Gather all the facts.	It's too easy to jump to conclusions, seeing situations as problems that really aren't so bad. Instead of sensing a problem and assuming the worst, look for more objective information about the situation.
Avoid negative mental monologues.	Too often, people talk themselves into perceiving situations as being worse than they really are, thereby adding to stress levels. You should avoid such negative mental monologues, focusing instead on the positive aspects of the situations you confront.

sharply, and severe biological damage may result. It is these patterns of responses that we have in mind when we talk about stress.

To illustrate this, imagine that you are in an office building when you suddenly see a fire raging. How does your body react? As a natural, biological response, your body responds in several ways—both immediately after experiencing the stressor, a few minutes later, and after repeated exposure (see Figure 4.6). For example, certain chemicals are released that make it possible for us to respond. Adrenaline boosts our metabolism, causing us to breathe faster, taking in more oxygen to help us be stronger and run faster. Aiding in this process, blood flows more rapidly (up to four times faster than normal) to prime the muscles, and other fluids are diverted from less essential parts of the body. As a result, people experiencing stressful conditions tend to experience dry mouths as well as cool, clammy, and sweaty skin. Other chemicals are activated that suppress the parts of the brain that control concentration, inhibition, and rational thought. (By the way, this is why people in emergency situations don't always think rationally or act politely.) In short, when exposed to stressors the body kicks into a self-protective mode, marshalling all its resources to preserve life. However, when this happens frequently, the chronic responses can be dangerous.

To the extent that people appraise various situations as stressors, they are likely to have stress reactions. And often these can have damaging behavioral, psychological, and/or medical effects. Indeed, physiological and psychological stress reactions can be so great that eventually they take their toll on the body and mind,

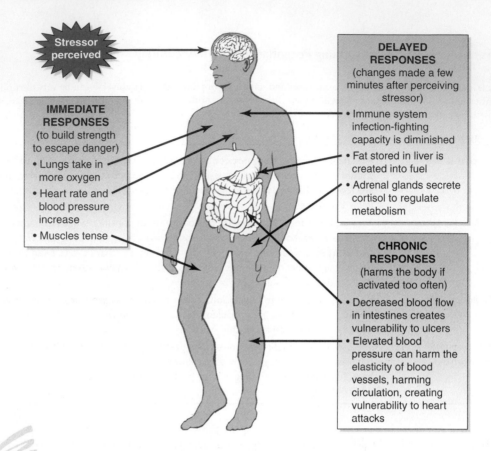

Figure 4.6   The Body's Reactions to Stress

As summarized here, the human body responds to stress in many different ways involving several different physiological mechanisms. These responses differ based on whether they occur immediately after perceiving a stressor a few minutes later, or after repeated exposure to stressors.

resulting in such maladies as insomnia, cardiovascular disease, and depression. Such reactions are referred to as **strain,** defined as deviations from normal states of human function resulting from exposure to stressful events. (As you probably have seen in dealing with different people in your own lives, some individuals are far tougher than others. That is, they have the mental toughness to focus their minds and manage their emotions under stressful conditions.[39] To see how well you and your fellow team members fare in this regard, complete the Group Exercise on pp. 131–132.)

Sometimes people find themselves worn down by chronic levels of stress. Such people are often described as suffering from **burnout**—a syndrome of emotional, physical, and mental exhaustion coupled with feelings of low self-esteem or low self-efficacy, resulting from prolonged exposure to intense stress and the strain reactions following from them.[40] Fortunately, some of the signs of burnout are clear if you know what to look for. The distinct characteristics of burnout are summarized in Table 4.6.[41]

Table 4.6   Symptoms of Burnout

Burnout is a serious condition resulting from exposure to chronic levels of stress. The symptoms of burnout, summarized here, are important to recognize so as to avoid making an already bad state of affairs even worse. Anyone experiencing these symptoms should seek medical attention.

Symptom	Description
Physical exhaustion	Victims of burnout have low energy and feel tired much of the time. They also report many symptoms of physical strain, such as frequent headaches, nausea, poor sleep, and changes in eating habits (e.g., loss of appetite).
Emotional exhaustion	Depression, feelings of helplessness, and feelings of being trapped in one's job are all part of burnout.
Depersonalization	People suffering from burnout often demonstrate a pattern of attitudinal exhaustion known as *depersonalization.* They become cynical, derogating others and themselves, including their jobs, their organizations, and even life in general.
Feelings of low personal accomplishment	People suffering from burnout conclude that they haven't been able to accomplish much in the past, and assume that they probably won't succeed in the future.

(Source: Based on information in Bakker et al., 2000; see Note 40.)

Let's summarize where we have been thus far. We have identified physical and psychological causes of stress known as stressors. Through the cognitive appraisal process, these lead to various physical and mental stress reactions. With prolonged exposure, physiological, behavioral, and psychological strain reactions result. Ultimately, in some cases, burnout occurs. For a graphic overview of this process, see Figure 4.7.

Figure 4.7   Stressors, Stress, Strain, and Burnout

Stimuli known as *stressors* lead to *stress* reactions when they are cognitively appraised as threatening and beyond one's control. The deviations from normal states resulting from stress are known as *strain.* Prolonged stressful experiences can lead to *burnout.*

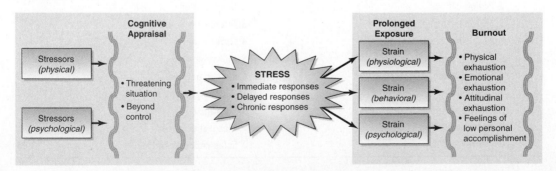

MAJOR CAUSES OF STRESS IN THE WORKPLACE

Stress is caused by many different factors. For example, stress may be caused by personal factors such as conflict with family members, financial problems, and illness. Stress also may be caused by societal factors, such as concerns over crime, terrorism, and downturns in the economy.

In this book, of course we are concerned mostly about job-related stress. What causes stress in work settings? Unfortunately, as you will see, many different factors play a role in creating stress in the workplace.

Occupational Demands

Some jobs, such as miner, police officer, and air traffic controller, expose the people who hold them to high levels of stress. Others, such as forester, bookbinder, and toolmaker, do not. This basic fact—that some jobs are much more stressful than others—has been confirmed by the results of a survey involving more than 130 different occupations.[42] For a listing of some of the most and least stressful jobs, see Table 4.7.

What, precisely, makes some jobs more stressful than others? Research has shown that several features of jobs determine the levels of stress they generate. Specifically, people experience greater stress the more their jobs require:

➤   Making decisions
➤   Constantly monitoring devices or materials
➤   Repeatedly exchanging information with others

Table 4.7   Top Ten Most Stressful and Least Stressful Jobs In America

Although very stressful situations can be found on just about any job, the ones shown here tend to have the highest and lowest overall levels of stress associated with them. As you review this list, you're likely to notice that the most stressful jobs contain high levels of the stress-inducing characteristics indicated. For example, air traffic controllers have to monitor devices, and police officers have to make decisions in unpleasant working conditions.

Top 10 Most Stressful Jobs	Top 10 Least Stressful Jobs
1. Inner city high school teacher	1. Forester
2. Police officer	2. Bookbinder
3. Miner	3. Telephone line worker
4. Air traffic controller	4. Toolmaker
5. Medical intern	5. Millwright
6. Stockbroker	6. Repair person
7. Journalist	7. Civil engineer
8. Customer service worker	8. Therapist
9. Secretary	9. Natural scientist
10. Waiter	10. Sales representative

(Source: Health Magazine.)

➤ Working in unpleasant physical conditions
➤ Performing unstructured rather than structured tasks

The greater the extent to which a job possesses these characteristics, the higher the level of stress that job produces among individuals holding it.

Nurses and long-distance bus drivers perform jobs that match this profile—and, not surprisingly, people doing these jobs tend to show many of the adverse signs of stress. This is not to imply that people do not experience stress in every job. In fact, as you can see from Table 4.8, many different causes of stress can be found in different types of jobs.[43]

Conflict Between Work and Nonwork

If you've ever faced the demands of working while at the same time trying to raise a family, you are probably well aware of how difficult this situation can be. Not only must you confront the usual pressures to spend time at work while concentrating on what you're doing, but you also must pay attention to the demands placed on you by members of your family (e.g., to spend time with them).

When people confront such incompatibilities in the various sets of obligations they have, they are said to experience **role conflict** (see Chapter 9). As you might expect, when we experience conflicts between our work and nonwork lives, something has to give. Not surprisingly, the more time people devote to their jobs, the more events in their nonwork lives (e.g., personal errands) adversely affect their jobs (e.g., not being able to get the work done on time).

Table 4.8   Sources of Stress in Everyday Jobs

Although some jobs are inherently more stressful than others, even people holding everyday jobs in all fields confront significant sources of stress. Here are some examples.

Field	Typical Jobs	Common Source of Stress
Financial	Accountants, stock market traders, bank tellers, mortgage consultants	Clients are concerned about money, so they put lots of pressure on people working in this field.
Media	Newspaper, magazine, radio, or television journalists, reporters, editors	These people experience calm times followed by frantic activity as deadlines approach and as major events unfold.
Sales	Sales and marketing managers, advertising executives	These jobs create pressure to meet certain target objectives. Salespeople always face pressure to make good impressions.
Medical	Doctors, nurses, pharmacists, physical therapists	When human lives are at stake, the pressure to make the right decision is great. Also, dealing with human distress is very difficult on people.
Technology	Computer programmers and technicians, systems analysts	Workers in the information technology (IT) field face considerable pressure to stay abreast of very rapid changes.

(Source: Based on information in Heller & Hindle, 1998; see Note 43.)

The stressful nature of role conflicts is particularly apparent among working parents, who often are expected to rapidly switch back and forth between the demands of work and family—a source of stress known as **role juggling.**[44] Indeed, the more people, such as working mothers and fathers, are forced to juggle the various roles in their lives, the less fulfilling they find those roles to be, and the more stress they suffer in their lives. The same also was found among student athletes: The more successfully they were able to separate their distinct roles as students and as athletes, the less stress and the more well-being they experienced.[45]

Sexual Harassment: A Pervasive Problem in Work Settings

There can be no doubt that a particularly troublesome source of stress in today's workplace is **sexual harassment**—unwanted contact or communication of a sexual nature, usually against women. The stressful effects of sexual harassment stem from both the direct affront to the victim's personal dignity and the harasser's interference with the victim's capacity to do the job. After all, it's certainly difficult to pay attention to what you're doing on your job when you have to concentrate on ways to ward off someone's unwanted attentions! Not surprisingly, sexual harassment has caused some people to experience many severe symptoms of illness, including various forms of physical illness, and voluntary turnover.[46]

Unfortunately, this particular source of work-related stress is shockingly commonplace. Indeed, when asked in a *New York Times*/CBS News poll whether they had ever been the object of sexual advances, propositions, or unwanted sexual discussions from men who supervise them, fully 30 percent of the women surveyed answered "yes." And this is not a one-sided perception: When asked if they had ever said or done something at work that could be construed by a female colleague as harassment, 50 percent of the men polled indicated that they had done so.[47]

There's good news, however. These days, many companies are training employees in ways to avoid sexual harassment. In fact, by California law (AB 1825), as of January 1, 2006, all employers must provide two hours of sexual harassment training and education to all supervisory employees. Efforts of this type (whether or not mandated by law) are helping people become aware of ways they are behaving that may be considered inappropriate.

This seems to be having a beneficial effect on the numbers of sexual harassment cases. U.S. government figures have shown a steady decline in the number of sexual harassment cases reported since 2000.[48] Although it surely is an encouraging sign that this important source of stress may be on the decline as today's employees become more enlightened, it's important to note that sexual harassment is far from gone. It remains a far too prevalent source of stress in today's workplace.

Role Ambiguity: Stress from Uncertainty

Even if individuals are able to avoid the stress associated with role conflict, they still may encounter an even more common source of job-related stress: **role ambiguity.** This occurs when people are uncertain about several aspects of their jobs (e.g., the scope of their responsibilities, what's expected of them, how to divide their time among various duties).

Most people dislike such uncertainty and find it quite stressful, but it is difficult to avoid. In fact, role ambiguity is quite common: 35 to 60 percent of employees surveyed report experiencing it to some degree.[49] Clearly, managers who are interested in promoting a stress-free workplace should go out of their way to help employees understand precisely what they are expected to do. As obvious as this may sound, such advice is all too frequently ignored in actual practice.

Overload and Underload

When the phrase "work-related stress" is mentioned, most people envision scenes in which employees are asked to do more work than they possibly can handle. Such an image is indeed quite legitimate, for such *overload* is an important cause of stress in many work settings. Findings of a recent study bear this out.[50] Half of the 1,300 Americans completing a survey about their work lives indicated that they routinely skip lunch to complete the day's work. And 52 percent reported that they often had to work more than 12 hours a day to get their jobs done.

If you think about it, this isn't particularly surprising. In today's business environment, where many companies are trimming staff size (the phenomenon known as *downsizing,* which we will discuss in Chapter 14), those employees who remain are required to do more work than ever before. Not only does this cause overload, but so too does the proliferation of information with which people are bombarded today as life involves communication via more sources than ever before. Scientists use the term **information anxiety** to refer to pressure to store and process great amounts of information in our heads and to keep up constantly with gathering it. This constitutes an all-too real source of overload today.

Overload is only part of the total picture when it comes to stress. Although being asked to do too much can be stressful, so too can being asked to do too little. In fact, there seems to be considerable truth in the following statement: "The hardest job in the world is doing nothing—you can't take a break." *Underload* leads to boredom and monotony. Because these reactions are quite unpleasant, underload, too, can be stressful.

Responsibility for Others: A Heavy Burden

By virtue of differences in their jobs, some people, such as managers, tend to deal more with people than others. And people, as you probably suspect, can be a major source of stress. In general, individuals who are responsible for other people experience higher levels of stress than those who have no such responsibility. Such individuals are more likely to report feelings of tension and anxiety and are more likely to show overt symptoms of stress, such as ulcers or hypertension, than their counterparts in nonsupervisory positions.

This probably isn't too surprising if you think about it. After all, managers are often caught between the need to satisfy their staff members (e.g., giving them raises) while simultaneously meeting the demands of their own superiors (e.g., maintaining budgets). They also are often faced with meeting a wide variety of demands, creating responsibilities that often weigh heavily on them. Not surprisingly, many managers think of stress as a normal, everyday part of their jobs.

Importantly, managers who deal with people ineffectively—such as those who fail to effectively organize work or who communicate poorly and who treat people unfairly—add stress to the lives of the people they supervise. As you surely know from your own experiences, a bad manager can be quite a significant source of stress. That said, it is clear that knowing and effectively practicing what you have learned about OB in this book can help alleviate stress among others in the workplace.

Lack of Social Support: The Costs of Isolation

According to an old saying, "misery loves company." With respect to stress, this statement implies that if we have to face stressful conditions, it's better to do so along with others (and with their support) rather than alone. Does this strategy actually work? In general, the answer is "yes."

Research has shown that when individuals believe they have the friendship and support of others at work—that is, when they have **social support**—their ability to resist the adverse effects of stress increases. For example, police officers who feel they can talk to their colleagues about their reactions to a traumatic event (such as a shooting) experience less stressful reactions than those who lack such support.[51] Clearly, social support can be an important buffer against the effects of stress.[52]

Social support can come from many different sources. One of these is cultural norms (e.g., caring for the elderly is valued among the Japanese, thereby reducing the social isolation many elderly people otherwise experience). Another source of social support comes from social institutions (e.g., counseling from the church or school officials, help from the Red Cross). And, of course, probably the most important and valuable source of support comes from one's own friends and family members.

These sources of support help in various ways.[53] These are as follows:

➤ *Boosting self-esteem.* Others can help make us feel better about ourselves.
➤ *Sharing information.* Talking to other people can help us learn about ways of coping with problems and give us a new perspective on things.
➤ *Providing diversion.* Spending time with others can be a friendly diversion from life's stressors, taking our minds off them.
➤ *Giving needed resources.* When we spend time with others, they may offer to help by giving money, advice, or other resources needed to alleviate stress.

As we have shown here, not only does misery love company, but also company can help alleviate misery. This is something worth remembering the next time you feel stressed. Remember, don't go it alone. Friends can help, so seek them out.

MAJOR EFFECTS OF ORGANIZATIONAL STRESS

By now, you probably are convinced that stress stems from many sources and that it exerts important effects on the people who experience it. What may not yet be apparent, though, is just how powerful and far-reaching such effects can be. In fact, so widespread are the detrimental effects of stress (i.e., strain) that it has been estimated that their annual costs exceed 10 percent of the U.S. gross national product![54] Let's now examine the some of the specific problems linked to stress.

Lowered Task Performance—But Only Sometimes

The most current evidence available suggests that stress exerts mainly negative effects on task performance. For the most part, the greater the stress people encounter on the job, the more adversely affected their job performance tends to be.[55] In some cases, this is particularly serious. For example, in a study, people who were experiencing higher levels of stress were found to have higher chances of having an auto accident than those experiencing lower levels of stress.[56]

It is important to note that the adverse relationship between stress and job performance does not always hold. For example, some individuals seem to "rise to the occasion" and turn in exceptional performances at times of potentially high stress. This may result from the fact that they are truly expert in the tasks being performed, making them so confident in what they are doing that they appraise a potentially stressful situation as a challenge rather than a threat. Thus, they might not experience the stress you'd expect.

However, even among individuals who experience stress, there are wide differences with respect to its impact on task performance. Whereas some people thrive on stress, finding it exhilarating and improving their performance, others avoid high levels of stress, finding it upsetting and a source of interference with job performance. Thus, the relationship between stress and job performance is more complex than meets the eye.

Stress and Health: The Silent Killer

How strong is the link between stress and personal health? The answer, say medical experts, is "very strong, indeed." In other words, physiological strain reactions can be quite severe. In fact, some authorities estimate that stress plays a role in anywhere from 50 to 70 percent of all forms of physical illness.[57] Included in these figures are some of the most serious and life-threatening ailments known to medical science. A list of some of the more common ones is shown in Table 4.9.

Even the most cursory look at this list must leave you with the conclusion that the health-related effects of stress are not only quite widespread but extremely serious. With this in mind, it's not surprising that today's companies are taking steps to keep these in check. (For a closer look at exactly what some companies are doing, see the Winning Practices section on p. 126.)

Table 4.9   Health-Related Consequences of Stress

Stress causes a variety of different health problems, including medical, behavioral, and psychological problems. Listed here are some of the major consequences within each category.

Medical Consequences	Behavioral Consequences	Psychological Consequences
Heart disease and stroke	Smoking	Family conflict
Backache and arthritis	Drug and alcohol abuse	Sleep disturbances
Ulcers	Accident proneness	Sexual dysfunction
Headaches	Violence	Depression
Cancer	Appetite disorders	
Diabetes		
Cirrhosis of the liver		
Lung disease		

(Sources: Based on material reported in various sources in Note 57.)

Winning Practices

The Rebirth of Onsite Medical Clinics

In the 1800s, it was not unusual for large companies to have doctors who worked on the premises to serve the healthcare needs of their employees. By the 1940s, however, most of these medical clinics began closing their doors in the wake of criticism that the doctors who worked there were more attuned to the financial needs of the companies that paid them than to the patients they saw.[58]

This was before stress reached epidemic levels and the cost of healthcare to contain it spiraled out of control, leading today's organizational officials to reconsider opening onsite medical facilities. As of 2009, about one-third of all companies with 1,000 or more employees have an onsite medical center for employees.[59]

Toyota's manufacturing plant in San Antonio, Texas is typical. Staffed by several doctors, dentists, physical therapists, and others, the clinic can take X-rays and treat most emergencies. For a mere $5 (compared to the $15 co-payment for outside doctors on the company's insurance plan), employees can see highly qualified general practitioners without ever leaving the factory. Employees like the service because not only is it inexpensive and convenient, but also the doctors give highly personalized service, spending over twice as much time with each patient (20 minutes

instead of 10) as primary-care physicians in the average medical practice.

Company officials like the service because it makes good business sense. Not only does it keep employees from having to take days off for doctor visits, but it also provides opportunities to treat maladies before they become serious and expensive to treat. For every dollar invested in the facility, it has been estimated that Toyota receives a $3–$5 return.

In addition to Toyota, its competitor, Nissan, has medical facilities for its employees as well. So too do Harrah's Entertainment and the Walt Disney Parks and Resort Group. The brand-new facility at Disney World in Orlando, Florida costs $6 million and is designed to serve over 40,000 employees and their dependents.

This is not to say that these companies are branching out into the medical business. Rather, they are outsourcing these facilities to specialized companies, such as Take Care Health (owned by Walgreens), that are qualified to design, staff, and run them. Importantly, this maintains a vital privacy buffer between companies and employees, preventing company officials from becoming prejudiced against employees based on information they might find out by peeking at their medical records.

REDUCING STRESS: WHAT CAN BE DONE?

Stress stems from so many different factors and conditions that to eliminate it entirely from our lives is impossible. However, there still are many things that both companies and individuals can do to reduce stress and to minimize its harmful effects.[60] To ensure that these tactics are followed, many companies have introduced systematic programs designed to help employees reduce and/or prevent stress. The underlying assumption of these programs is that by minimizing employees' adverse reactions to stress, they will be healthier, less likely to be absent, and, consequently, more productive on the job—which, in turn, has beneficial effects on the bottom line.

Employee Assistance Programs

About two-thirds of today's companies have some kind of formal program in place to help employees with various problems they may face in their personal lives (e.g., substance abuse, career planning, financial and legal problems).[61] Such efforts are known as **employee assistance programs (EAPs).** Sometimes, such programs supplement or take the place of similar programs sponsored by trade unions. In such cases, they are known as **member assistance programs (MAPs).**

Interest in offering systematic ways of promoting the welfare of employees has grown so great that many companies today are seeking the assistance of specialized organizations with whom they can contract to offer assistance programs for their employees. By outsourcing these services to firms that are expert in this area, companies are free to focus on their usual business while ensuring that they are taking care of their employees as needed.

Such efforts appear to be paying off. According to the Employee Assistance Professionals Association, a trade group for companies offering professional EAP services to organizations, employee work loss is avoided in 60 percent of the cases in which EAP services are provided.[62]

Stress Management Programs

Systematic efforts known as **stress management programs** involve training employees in a variety of techniques (e.g., meditation and relaxation) that they can use to become less adversely affected by stress. (We describe many of these techniques on pp. 128–130.) These are used by about a quarter of all large companies.

Among them is the Equitable Life Insurance Company. Its "Emotional Health Program" offers training in a variety of ways of learning to relax, including napping. Although some managers might not like the idea of seeing their employees asleep on the job, others recognize that brief naps can, in fact, help their employees recharge and combat the negative effects of stress.

Wellness Programs

About 56 percent of today's larger companies have **wellness programs** in place. These are systematic efforts to train employees in a variety of things they can do to promote healthy lifestyles. Very broad-based, wellness programs usually consist of workshops in which employees can learn how to reduce stress and maintain their health. Exercise, nutrition, and weight-management counseling are among the most popular areas covered.

As an interesting example, Blue Cross Blue Shield of Oklahoma built a financial incentive into the wellness program it uses for its 1,300 employees.[63] The company offers "Weight Watchers at Work" meetings. Employees have to pay to participate in the 16-week program—but as an incentive, if they attend at least 14 weekly sessions, they are reimbursed. In a recent five-year period, Blue Cross Blue Shield employees collectively have lost nearly 10 tons of excess weight. (This makes the company and its employees not "The Biggest Loser," like the TV show, but the biggest winners.)

As you might imagine, companies that have used such programs have found that they pay off handsomely. For example, at its industrial sites that offer wellness programs, DuPont has found that absenteeism is less than half of what it is at sites that do not offer such programs. Companies such as The Travelers Corporation and Union Pacific Railroad have enjoyed consistently high returns for each $1.00 they invest in employee wellness. And when it comes to saving money by promoting employee health, there is a lot at stake. Consider, for example, that the annual cost of health insurance in the United States due to obesity alone is $7.7 billion.[64]

As you might imagine, such programs help not only by reducing insurance costs, but also by reducing absenteeism due to illness. There's yet another way in which stress management efforts promise to help companies' bottom lines, and one of which most people are unaware. We are referring to the problem of **presentism**—the practice of showing up for work but being too sick to be able to work effectively. Paying workers who are not performing well is not only costly on its own, but also indirectly given that it may lower morale, and depending on the particular illness people have, it may spread disease throughout a workplace, compounding the problem. We tend to see this on an annual basis, for example, in places such as schools, where flu epidemics are so severe that it's sometimes necessary to close facilities for a while. Wellness programs promise to reduce this problem.

Managing Your Own Stress

Even if the organization at which you work does not have a formal program in place to manage stress, there still are several things you can do by yourself to help control the stress in your life. We now describe several such tactics.

Manage your time wisely

People who don't use their time effectively find themselves easily overwhelmed, falling behind, not getting important things done, and having to work longer hours as a result. Not surprisingly, **time management,** the practice of taking control over how we spend time, is a valuable skill for reducing one possible stressor. Some of the most effective time management practices are summarized in Table 4.10.

Eat a healthy diet and be physically fit

Growing evidence indicates that reduced intake of salt and saturated fats, and increased consumption of fiber- and vitamin-rich fruits and vegetables can greatly increase the body's ability to cope with the physiological effects of stress.[65] Regular exercise also helps. People who exercise regularly obtain many benefits that help resist the adverse effects of stress. For example, fitness reduces both the incidence of cardiovascular illness and the death rate from such diseases. Similarly, physical fitness lowers blood pressure, an important factor in many aspects of personal health.

With this in mind, it is not surprising that growing numbers of companies are taking steps to ensure that their employees maintain proper weight by eating properly and exercising regularly. Some even are offering monetary incentives for doing so.[66]

Relax and meditate

Many people find that it helps to relieve stress by engaging in **meditation,** the process of learning to clear one's mind of external thoughts, often by repeating a single syllable (known as a *mantra*) over and over again. Those who follow this

Table 4.10   Suggestions for Managing Your Time

Managing time well can be an effective means of reducing stress because it allows people to avoid last-minute crises, and because it permits work to flow in a regular manner. Although these three suggestions may be easier said than done, following them can be very helpful.

Tip	Explanation
Prioritize your activities.	Distinguish between tasks that are urgent (ones that must be performed right away) and important (ones that must be done, but can wait). When determining how to spend your time, assign the greatest priority to tasks that are both important and urgent, a lower priority to tasks that are important but less urgent, and the lowest priority of all to tasks that are neither important nor urgent.
Allocate your time realistically—do not overcommit.	When planning, accurately assess how much time needs to be spent on each of the various tasks you perform. Budgeting too much time can lead to underload and too little time can lead to overload. It also helps to build in buffers, some extra time to handle unexpected issues that might arise.
Take control of your time.	Make a "to do" list and carefully keep track of what you have to accomplish. Unless an urgent situation comes up, stay focused and don't allow others to derail you. The more you allow other people to interfere with your time, the less you will have accomplished at the end of the day.

systematic method of relaxing claim that it helps greatly to relieve the many sources of stress in their lives.

Get a good night's sleep

One of the most effective ways to alleviate stress-related problems is one of the simplest—if you can do it—sleeping. We all need a certain amount of sleep to allow our bodies to recharge and function effectively. Eight hours per day is average, although some need more and others can function just fine on less. Although a restful night's sleep can help people ward off the harmful effects of stress, the problem for many is that they are so stressed that they cannot get to sleep. For such individuals, meditation (as noted above) has proven to be a highly effective antidote.

Avoid inappropriate self-talk

This involves telling ourselves over and over how horrible and unbearable it will be if we fail, if we are not perfect, or if everyone we meet does not like us. Such thoughts seem ludicrous when spelled out in the pages of a book, but the fact is that most people entertain them at least occasionally.

Unfortunately, such thoughts can add to personal levels of stress, as individuals *awfulize* or *catastrophize* in their own minds the horrors of not being successful, perfect, or loved. Fortunately, such thinking can be readily modified. For many people, merely recognizing that they have implicitly accepted such irrational and self-defeating beliefs is sufficient to produce beneficial change and increased resistance to stress.

Take a time-out

When confronted with rising tension, people may find it useful to consciously choose to insert a brief period of delay known as a **time-out.** This can involve taking a short break, going to the nearest restroom to splash cold water on one's face, or any other action that yields a few moments of breathing space. Such actions interrupt the cycle of ever-rising tension that accompanies stress and can help to restore equilibrium and the feeling of being at least partly in control of ongoing events.

Back to the Case

Answer the following questions about this chapter's Making the Case (p. 101) to illustrate insights you have derived about the material in this chapter.

1. How would you characterize the difference between the felt emotions and the displayed emotions of Mr. Donaghy at the time of his sentencing? Do you think he experienced emotional dissonance? Was emotional labor involved? Explain.

2. Do you think that Commissioner Stern found the trial to be a stressful ordeal? If so, in what ways do you think it will affect his personal health and job performance?

3. Assuming that the Donaghy case impacts everyone who works at the NBA and its 30 teams, what might be done by these organizations to minimize any adverse effects?

You Be the Consultant

Stressed-Out Employees Are Resigning

As the managing director of a large e-tail sales company, you are becoming alarmed about the growing levels of turnover your company has been experiencing lately. It already has passed the industry average, and you are concerned about the company's capacity to staff the call center and the warehouse during the busy holiday period. In conducting exit interviews, you learned that the employees who are leaving generally like their work and the pay they are receiving. However, they are displeased with the way their managers are treating them, and this is creating stress in their lives. They are quitting so they can take less stressful positions in other companies. Answer the following questions based on material in this chapter.

1. Assuming that the employees' emotions and moods are negative, what problems would you expect to find in the way they are working?

2. How should the company's supervisors behave differently so as to get their subordinates to experience less stress on the job (or, at least, get them to react less negatively)?

3. What could the individual employees do to help manage their own stress more effectively?

SELF-ASSESSMENT EXERCISE

How Much Emotional Intelligence Do You Have?

People who are particularly good at recognizing and regulating their own emotions and who also are able to recognize and influence the emotions of others are said to have a high amount of emotional intelligence. Where do you stand in this respect? How high or low are you in terms of emotional intelligence? To find out, complete this brief questionnaire and the steps that follow.

Questionnaire

Using the following scale, indicate how true or untrue each of the following statements is as it applies to you.

   1 = totally untrue
   2 = slightly untrue
   3 = neither true nor untrue
   4 = slightly true
   5 = totally true

1. ____ I'm usually a good judge of how people are feeling.
2. ____ I often try to make people feel better when they are upset.
3. ____ I can usually read others well, able to tell how they are feeling in a given situation.
4. ____ I usually find it easy to work well with other people.
5. ____ I am usually pretty good at not revealing my negative emotions to others.
6. ____ I am almost always well aware of how I am feeling at any moment.
7. ____ I feel sad when I see that others seem to be sad.
8. ____ I am unlikely to display any emotions that might make someone else feel bad.

Scoring

Score the questionnaire by adding the points given on each item. The sum will range between 8 and 40. Higher scores reflect higher levels of emotional intelligence.

Questions for Discussion

1. How did your score compare to how you thought you might have scored before you completed this questionnaire? Were you surprised by scoring higher or lower than expected?
2. Do you think you are higher or lower than most other people when it comes to emotional intelligence?
3. What might you be able to do to raise your level of emotional intelligence? How effective do you think this might be?

GROUP EXERCISE

Are You Tough Enough to Endure Stress?

A questionnaire known as the Test of Attentional and Interpersonal Style (TAIS) has been used in recent years to identify the extent to which a person can stay focused and keep his or her emotions under control—the core elements of performing well under high-pressure conditions (see Note 42). Completing this exercise (which is based on questions similar to those actually used by such groups as Olympic athletes and U.S. Navy Seals) will help you understand your own strengths and limitations in this regard. And, by discussing these scores with your teammates, you will come away with a good feel for the extent to which those with whom you work differ along this dimension as well.

Directions

1. Gather in groups of three or four people whom you know fairly well. If you are part of an intact group, such as a work team or a team of students working on a class project, meet with your teammates.
2. Individually, complete the following questionnaire by responding to each question as follows: "never," "rarely," "sometimes," "frequently," or "always."
   1. ____ When time is running out on an important project, I am the person who should be called upon to take control of things.
   2. ____ When listening to a piece of music, I can pick out a specific voice or instrument.
   3. ____ The people who know me think of me as being "serious."
   4. ____ It is important to me to get a job completely right in every detail, even if it means being late.
   5. ____ When approaching a busy intersection, I easily get confused.
   6. ____ Just by looking at someone, I can figure out what he or she is like.
   7. ____ I am comfortable arguing with people.
   8. ____ At a cocktail party, I have no difficulty keeping track of several different conversations at once.
3. Discuss your answers with everyone else in your group. Item by item, consider what each person's response to each question indicates about his or her ability to focus and to remain in control.

Questions for Discussion

1. Which questions were easiest to interpret? Which were most difficult?
2. How did each individual's responses compare with the way you would assess his or her ability to focus under stress?
3. For what jobs is the ability to concentrate under stress particularly important? For what jobs is it not especially important? How important is this ability for the work you do?

Work-Related Attitudes: Prejudice, Job Satisfaction, and Organizational Commitment

Learning Objectives

After reading this chapter, you will be able to:

1. **DISTINGUISH** among the concepts of prejudice, stereotypes, and discrimination.
2. **EXPLAIN** how affirmative action plans and diversity management programs work.
3. **DESCRIBE** four theories of job satisfaction.
4. **IDENTIFY** the consequences of having dissatisfied employees and **DESCRIBE** ways of boosting job satisfaction.
5. **DISTINGUISH** among three fundamental forms of organizational commitment.
6. **IDENTIFY** the benefits of having a committed workforce and **DESCRIBE** ways of developing organizational commitment.

3 GOOD REASONS why you should care about . . .

Work-Related Attitudes

You should care about work-related attitudes because:

1. We are all potential victims of prejudice and discrimination on the job; nobody is immune.
2. The more people are satisfied with their jobs and committed to their organizations, the less likely they are to be absent and to resign voluntarily.
3. Changing attitudes is not impossible. There are specific things that practicing managers and their organizations can do to enhance the work-related attitudes of their employees.

Making the Case for Work-Related Attitudes

Madison Avenue Welcomes Disabled Athletes

When we watch TV, we're inundated with images of athletes, and with increasing frequency, it's not unusual to see people with disabilities. However, athletes with physical disabilities remain a rare sight in the media. Although this might suggest that there aren't many disabled athletes out there, Cheri Blauwet knows better.

Cheri and about 4,000 other athletes with disabilities from 145 different countries participated in the 2008 Paralympic Games in Beijing, China. These elite athletes competed in a variety of sports (e.g., rowing, sailing, wheelchair rugby, cycling, among many others) within categories based on their disability: spinal injury, amputee, visual impairment, cerebral palsy, and "les autres" (a category consisting of people with various locomotor conditions, such as multiple sclerosis and muscular dystrophy). A winner of several wheelchair races, Cheri also is an advanced medical student at Stanford University.

The thing that makes Cheri proudest, however, is the fact that she is the first female American Paralympian to be featured in a national television ad. First airing on May 29, 2008, the dramatic Visa spot shows her flying down a mountain road in her wheelchair as the rich voice of Morgan Freeman refers to her as a "heat-seeking, coming-through, get-out-of-the-way . . . world-class athlete." Visa officials like the fact that Cheri is "an incredible role model" and Cheri likes the fact that she paved the way for other athletes with disabilities to get endorsement deals.

Today, several disabled athletes are appearing in major media marketing efforts. A picture of Marlon Shirley, a below-the-knee amputee who is one of the world's fastest disabled sprinters, appears on McDonald's cups, for example. And Tatyana McFadden, a medal-winning wheelchair racer who was born with spina bifida, may be seen discussing her sport at the Hilton Hotel's Web site. Although these athletes aren't making Michael Phelps or Tiger Woods kind of money, the endorsements are helping to defray their costs of competing, which is greatly welcomed. While the money is nice, of course, most athletes with disabilities believe that the exposure helps send their message to the public: "Disabled does *not* mean unable."

It certainly must be gratifying for Cheri Blauwet and her fellow Paralympians to have an opportunity to participate in this event. The thrill of competing, let alone the medals and the celebrity, must be exciting. Still, once this special event is over, these talented athletes return to a world in which able-bodied people predominate and people with disabilities sometimes confront barriers that they, even with their athletic prowess, cannot readily overcome. We are referring here to our feelings about other people and things, known as *attitudes*.

As you might imagine, attitudes play key roles in people's lives, particularly on the job. Indeed, people tend to have definite feelings about everything related to their jobs, whether it's the work itself, superiors, co-workers, subordinates, or even such mundane things as the food in the company cafeteria. Feelings such as these are referred to as **work-related attitudes,** the topic of this chapter. As you might imagine, our attitudes toward our jobs or organizations have profound effects not only on the way we perform but also on the quality of life we experience while at work.[1] We will carefully examine these effects in this chapter. Specifically, this discussion of work-related attitudes will focus on three major targets—attitudes toward others (including a special kind of negative attitude known as *prejudice*), attitudes toward the job (known as *job satisfaction*), and attitudes toward the organization (known as *organizational commitment*).

PREJUDICE: NEGATIVE ATTITUDES TOWARD OTHERS

Because prejudicial attitudes can have devastating effects on both people and organizations, we will examine them closely in this section of the chapter. To give you a feel for how serious prejudices can be, we describe specific targets of prejudice in the workplace and the special nature of the problems they confront. We then will follow up on this by describing various strategies that have been used to overcome prejudice in the workplace. Before doing this, however, let's take a closer look at the concept of prejudice and distinguish it from related concepts.

Anatomy of Prejudice: Some Basic Distinctions

How do you feel about your colleague who works in the cubicle next to you? Or, how about your boss? Now, what about doctors, or lawyers, or accountants in general? Your feelings may be positive (e.g., "I like my boss") or negative (e.g., "I dislike members of *Group X*"). And when these feelings are negative, they are likely to be based on unflattering things you believe about them (e.g., "I believe that members of *Group X* are lazy or sneaky, etc.), even if they are unfounded.

As you might imagine, these feelings can make a big difference when it comes to how you treat the target in question. Negative feelings toward certain individuals or groups will predispose you to treat them in a negative fashion. For example, you may interfere with their job performance (e.g., sabotaging their work), say mean-spirited things (e.g., insulting them with your comments), be physically aggressive (e.g., shoving them into things, or perhaps even doing things that are more extreme).

What we are describing here is a type of attitude known as *prejudice*. Specifically, **prejudice** refers to negative feelings about people belonging to certain groups (see the left portion of Figure 5.1). For example, members of any particular group may become victims of prejudice to the extent that they are believed to be somehow inferior to others. Of course, prejudicial attitudes are of great concern in the field of OB because they can hold people back, creating barriers to their success.

Stereotypes

A key part of any prejudicial attitude (i.e., how positively or negatively you feel about a particular group) is the set of beliefs held about the group in question, what you think they are like (be they positive beliefs, such as being hard-working, or negative beliefs, such as being dishonest). In many cases, these beliefs are based not on what you personally have come to know about individuals on a first-hand basis, but instead, by relying on what you believe about people based on the groups to which they belong. Such beliefs are referred to as **stereotypes.**

For example, if a supervisor believes that her new assistant must be smart simply because he wears glasses, that supervisor is relying on a stereotype about people who wear glasses. Of course, because not everyone who wears glasses is intelligent, the stereotype is inaccurate, making the supervisor's judgment based on that stereotype highly questionable. If we knew more about someone than whatever we assumed based on his or her membership in various groups, we probably would make more accurate judgments. However, to the extent that we often find it difficult or inconvenient to learn

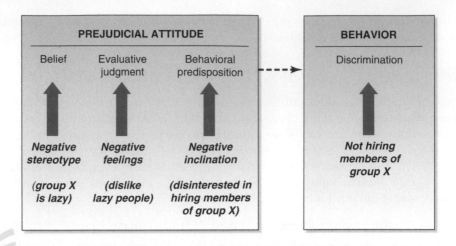

Figure 5.1 Prejudice Versus Discrimination: A Comparison

Prejudice is an *attitude* consisting of negative beliefs (known as *stereotypes*), negative feelings about those beliefs, and negative predispositions toward people described by those stereotypes. These attitudes sometimes (but not always) lead to behavior consistent with that attitude—that is, *discrimination*.

everything we need to know about someone, we frequently rely on stereotypes as a kind of mental shortcut.

Discrimination

Prejudicial attitudes are particularly harmful when they translate into actual behaviors. In such instances, people become the victims of others' prejudices—that is, **discrimination.** In other words, as summarized in Figure 5.1, prejudice is an attitude, whereas discrimination is a form of behavior consistent with that attitude.

So, if you believe that *Person A* comes from a group whose members are lazy and that being lazy would hinder his or her performance on a particular job, then you would be unlikely to hire *Person A* to perform that job. By acting this way, your behavior would be consistent with your attitude. Although this might be logical, it certainly is not in the best interest of the individual involved. After all, your behavior may be based on an attitude formed on the basis of inaccurate stereotypes.

For this reason, it is important to identify ways of overcoming the natural tendency to base our attitudes on stereotypes and to discriminate unfairly between people on this basis. Later in this chapter we will outline some strategies shown to be effective in this regard. Before doing so, however, it would be useful to give you a feel for the seriousness of prejudicial attitudes in organizations today.

Everybody Is a Victim of Prejudice!

Unfortunate as it may be, we are all potential victims of prejudicial attitudes. Indeed, no matter what personal characteristics we may have, there may very well be people out there who are prejudiced against us. This is not surprising if you consider that people hold stereotypes about many different things. Whatever you look like, wherever you're from, whatever your interests, chances are good that at least some people will approach you with predisposed beliefs about what you're like.

Sadly, for many groups of people, these beliefs have negative connotations, leading to discriminatory behavior. Here, we will describe some of the most prevalent targets of discrimination in American society today.

Prejudice based on age

As people are living longer and the birth rate is holding steady, the median age of Americans is rising all the time. Despite this trend—often referred to as the "graying of America"—prejudice against older people is all too common. Although U.S. laws (e.g., the Age Discrimination in Employment Act) have done much to counter employment discrimination against older workers, prejudices continue to exist.[2] Part of the problem resides in stereotypes that older workers are too set in their ways to train and that they will tend to be sick or accident-prone.

As in the case of many attitudes, these prejudices are not founded on accurate information. In fact, survey findings paint just the opposite picture: A Yankelovich poll of 400 companies found that older workers are considered very good or excellent, especially in such critical areas as punctuality, commitment to quality, and practical knowledge.

It is not just older workers who find themselves victims of prejudice but younger ones as well. For them, part of the problem is that as the average age of the workforce advances (from an average of 29 in 1976 to 39 today), there develops a gap in expectations between the more experienced older workers who are in charge and the younger employees just entering the workforce.[3]

Specifically, compared to older workers, who grew up in a different time, members of *Generation Y* (people born between 1979 and 1995), and *Millennials* (people born between 1982 and 2001) view the world differently. They are more prone to question the way things are done, to not see the government as an ally, and to not expect loyalty. They are likely to consider self-development to be their main interest and are willing to learn whatever skills are necessary to make them marketable. These differing perspectives may lead older employees, who are likely to be their superiors, to feel uncomfortable with their younger colleagues.

Prejudice based on physical condition

There are currently some 43 million Americans with disabilities, 14.6 million of whom are of working age, between 16 and 65. However, less than 30 percent of these individuals are working—and, among these, most work only part-time or irregularly. Clearly, there exist barriers that are keeping millions of potentially productive people from gainful employment (and we're not even talking about being Paralympians like the people featured in this chapter's Making the Case section on p. 134).

The most formidable barriers are not physical ones but attitudinal. Most people who are not physically challenged don't know how to treat and what to expect from those who are. Experts advise that people with disabilities don't want to be pitied; they want to be respected for the skills and commitment to work they bring to their jobs. That is, they wish to be recognized as whole people who just happen to have a disabling condition rather than a special class of "handicapped people."

Legal remedies have been enacted to help break down these barriers. For example, in the early 1990s, legislation known as the Americans with Disabilities Act (ADA) was enacted in the United States to protect the rights of people with physical and mental disabilities. Its rationale is straightforward: Simply because an employee is limited in some way does not mean that accommodations cannot be made to help the individual perform his or her job.[4] Companies that do not comply are subject to legal damages, and recent violators have paid dearly. However, probably the most important reason to refrain from discriminating against people with disabilities is not simply to avoid fines but to be able to tap into a pool of people who are capable of making valuable contributions if given an opportunity.

Prejudice against women

There can be no mistaking the widespread—and ever growing—presence of women in today's workforce. Several companies, in fact, are quite proactive in ensuring that women are actively involved in high-level positions. Consider the following examples:[5]

- ➤ *Johnson & Johnson.* This company runs a Woman's Leadership Initiative that helps develop female managers.
- ➤ *Kaiser Permanente.* A third of the board of directors and three-quarters of all managers are women.
- ➤ *American Express.* Two-thirds of the company's U.S. work force are women, and women comprise about half of its managers.

Unfortunately, however, these examples remain more the exception than the rule. For some data on the percentage of women holding top organizational positions, see Figure 5.2.[6] Equality for women in the workplace is improving, although it is a slow victory, to be sure.

Why is this the case? Although sufficient time may not have passed to allow more women to work their way into the top echelons of organizations, there appear to be more formidable barriers. Most notably, it is clear that powerful **sex role stereotypes** persist, narrow-minded beliefs about the kinds of tasks for which women and men are most appropriately suited. For example, 8 percent of the respondents to the

Figure 5.2   Women Are Still Not Prevalent at the Top

Although women and men are almost equally represented in today's workforce, very few women have worked their way up to top positions in large organizations. Today, the percentage of women executives holding the most powerful titles is still quite small.
(Source: CATALYST, 2009; see Note 6.)

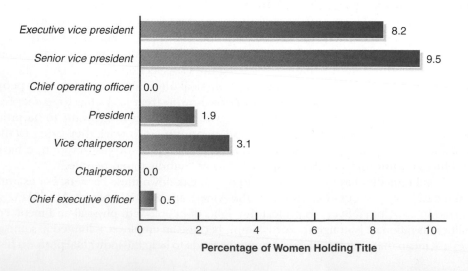

BusinessWeek/Harris poll indicated that females are not aggressive or determined enough to make it to the top. Although this number is small, it provides all-too-clear evidence of the persistence of a nagging—and highly limiting—stereotype.

Prejudice based on sexual orientation

Unlike people with physical disabilities, who are protected from discrimination by federal law, no such protection exists (yet, at least!) for another group whose members are frequently victims of prejudice—gay men, lesbian women, bisexuals, and transgendered people. (However, several states and over 100 municipalities have enacted laws to protect the rights of such individuals in the workplace.) Unfortunately, although more people than ever are tolerant of nontraditional sexual orientations, antihomosexual prejudice still exists in the workplace.[7] Indeed, about two-thirds of CEOs from major companies admit their reluctance to put a homosexual on a top management committee. Not surprisingly, without the law to protect them and with widespread prejudices against them, many gays and lesbians are reluctant to make their sexual orientations known openly (i.e., to "come out all of the closet").

This prejudice is not only hurtful to the individuals involved, causing them considerable stress, but it also is likely to be costly to organizations that reject many talented employees. Fortunately, many companies are taking steps to be less discriminatory toward people on the basis of their sexual orientations. Consider these recent statistics:[8]

➤ About 10,000 employers in the United States offer domestic partner health benefits for their employees. Of these, 95 percent offer the benefits to both same-sex and different-sex couples.

➤ Generally, the more successful the company, the greater the chance that it will offer domestic partner benefits. Fifty-one percent of *Fortune* 500 companies offer domestic partner health benefits, as do 80 percent of the *Fortune* 50.

Clearly, although some companies are passively discouraging diversity with respect to sexual orientation, others are encouraging it, much to their own—and their employees'—advantages.

Prejudice based on race and national origin

The history of the United States is marked by struggles over acceptance for people of various racial and ethnic groups. Although the American workplace is now more racially diverse than ever, it is clear that prejudice lingers on.

Not only do members of various minority groups believe they are the victims of prejudice and discrimination, but they are also taking action. For example, the number of complaints of discrimination based on national origin filed at the Equal Employment Opportunity Commission (EEOC) has been increasing steadily in recent years. Moreover, discrimination victims have been winning such cases. For example, the Supreme Court of the state of Washington upheld a $389,000 judgment against a Seattle bank brought by a Cambodian American employee who was fired because of his accent.

Outside the courtroom, companies that discriminate pay in other ways as well—notably, in lost talent and productivity. According to former EEOC Commissioner Joy Cherian, employees who feel victimized "may not take the initiative to introduce inventions and other innovations," adding, "every day, American employers are losing millions of dollars because these talents are frozen."[9]

Wisely, some companies are taking concrete steps to help minimize these problems. For example, AT&T Bell Labs in Murray Hill, New Jersey, is working with managers to find ways of helping the company's many ethnic minority employees get promoted more rapidly. Similarly, Hughes Aircraft Co. of Los Angeles has been assigning mentors to minority group employees to help teach them about the company's culture and the skills needed to succeed. Although both examples are only modest steps, they represent encouraging trends intended to help reduce a long-standing problem.

STRATEGIES FOR OVERCOMING WORKPLACE PREJUDICE: MANAGING A DIVERSE WORKFORCE

It's one thing to identify prejudicial attitudes and quite another to eliminate them. Two major approaches have been taken toward doing precisely this—*affirmative action plans* and *diversity management programs*.

Affirmative Action Plans

Traditionally, in the United States, **affirmative action plans** have been used to promote the ethical treatment of women and members of minority groups in organizations. Derived from civil rights initiatives of the 1960s, these generally involve efforts to give employment opportunities to qualified individuals belonging to groups that traditionally have been disadvantaged.

The rationale is straightforward: By encouraging the hiring of qualified women and minority group members into positions in which they traditionally have been underrepresented, more people will be exposed to them, forcing them to see that their negative stereotypes were misguided. Then, as these stereotypes begin to crumble, prejudice will be reduced, along with the discrimination on which it is based.

Despite the simplicity of the theory, there has been a fair amount of confusion with respect to practicing affirmative action, suggesting the need for clarification.[10] What the U.S. government had in mind may be referred to as **nonpreferential affirmative action:** efforts to get companies to conduct ongoing, conscious appraisal of their rules and procedures and to eliminate those that exclude women and members of minority groups without sufficient justification. Typically, this involves the following:

1. Take steps to ensure that there is a diverse pool of applicants.
2. Based on the racial composition of this pool, predict what the workforce would look like if selection of employees were nondiscriminatory (this is the so-called *affirmative-action goal*).
3. Compare results with goals and revise procedures and policies to alleviate any discrepancies.

Over the years, controversies emerged with respect to the ideal of affirmative action goals because the language of the law was misleading. Although a goal is something you aim at, this is not what the government intended. What they had in mind was not so much a finite number that had to be met (despite the language used) as much as an image of what things should be like.

Despite this, courts have interpreted the law literally and held companies to specific numeric goals. So if, say, 20 percent of a company's broad labor pool consisted of African Americans, then courts required it to hire this percentage of African Americans. This form of affirmative action, known as **preferential affirmative action,** is generally what the public has in mind. Today, although some people are enlightened, many well-intentioned people remain unaware of the spirit of the law.

After almost 40 years of experience with affirmative action programs, it is clear that there have been major gains in the opportunities that have become available to women and members of minority groups. Indeed, recent research has shown that most problems with affirmative action occur in the case of the preferential form.[11] However, nonpreferential affirmative action policies have been quite effective at increasing the attraction, selection, inclusion, and retention of underrepresented group members.

Yet, largely because of the misunderstanding about "goals," these programs are not always well accepted.[12] Not surprisingly, several myths about affirmative action programs have developed over the years.[13] For a summary of these and the facts that refute them, see Table 5.1.

Diversity Management Programs

In recent years, organizations have become increasingly proactive in their attempts to eliminate prejudice and have taken it upon themselves to go beyond affirmative action requirements. Their approach is not just to hire a broader group of people than usual but also to create an atmosphere in which diverse groups can flourish.[14] They are not merely trying to obey the law or attempting to be socially responsible (although they surely have these concerns), but they also recognize that diversity is a business issue. As one consultant put it, "A corporation's success will increasingly be determined by its managers' ability to naturally tap the full potential of a diverse workforce."[15]

Indeed, research has established that there is, in fact, an advantage to having a diverse workforce.[16] A study of the financial success of banks that actively pursued a growth strategy (i.e., those that were getting larger rather than smaller in size) found that the more highly diverse their workforce, the better they performed financially.[17] This, in turn, added value to these banks, giving them advantages over their competitors. Clearly, promoting diversity is a wise business strategy.

Table 5.1   Affirmative Action: Myth Versus Fact

Throughout the years, various myths about the ineffectiveness of affirmative action programs have become popular. However, as summarized here, these don't square with the facts.

Myth	Fact
Affirmative action has not led to increased representation of women and minorities in the workplace.	Gains have been substantial. Affirmative action programs have helped 5 million minority group members and 6 million white and minority women rise to higher positions.
Affirmative action programs reduce the self-esteem of women and racial minorities.	The opposite is true. By providing women and minority group members opportunities to succeed, their self-esteem actually increases.
Affirmative action plans bring unqualified people into the workplace.	Affirmative action programs specify that only qualified women and minority group members be hired.
The public no longer supports affirmative action programs.	This is overstated. Eighty percent of Americans currently believe that some sort of affirmative action is a good idea.
Although affirmative action programs may have been useful in the 1960s, they are less beneficial today.	The playing field is still far from level. For every dollar earned by men, women earn 74 cents, African American women earn 63 cents, and Hispanic women earn only 57 cents.

(Source: Based on information from Kravitz, 2008, see Note 11; Polus, 1996; see Note 13.)

It is with this in mind that three-quarters of American organizations are adopting **diversity management programs**—efforts to celebrate diversity by creating supportive, not just neutral, work environments for women and minorities. Simply put, the under-lying philosophy of diversity management programs is that women and minorities—anyone who may be different—should be not just tolerated but included and valued within the organization.

Diversity management programs consist of various efforts not only to create opportunities for diverse groups of people within organizations but also to train peo-ple to embrace differences between them. For example, Xerox's "Step-Up" program, in existence for some 40 years, has been one of the most thorough and sustained efforts to hire minority group members and train them to succeed.

Similarly, Hewlett-Packard (HP) has extended such initiatives in its "Valuing Differences" program, an approach that focuses on not just giving people opportuni-ties to succeed but valuing them *because* of their differences. HP officials rationalize that the broader the spectrum of differences in the workplace, the richer the depth of ideas on which the organization can draw—hopefully, leading it to be more produc-tive. Many different companies have been actively involved in a wide variety of diversity management activities.[18] For a small sampling of these, see Table 5.2, and for a close-up look at one particularly successful program, see the Winning Practices section.

Table 5.2   Diversity Management: Some Current Practices

Many of today's companies are taking proactive steps to celebrate the diverse backgrounds of their employees. Summarized here are just a few illustrative practices.

Organization	Name of Program	Description
Goodyear	Race Weekend Internships	Selects high school students who are members of minority groups to learn about careers by having them work at NASCAR races
Levi Strauss	Standing Up for What We Believe	The first company to extend full medical coverage to domestic partners of employees (since 1952)
Tellabs	You've Got ConneXions	Offers lavish rewards to employees for referring talented members of ethnic minorities
AT&T	Gay and Lesbian Awareness Week	Designates one week in which gay and lesbian issues are discussed and celebrated
Hewlett-Packard	Putting Our Differences to Work	An open-door policy is in effect through which employees can discuss concerns about diversity, discrimination, or anything
DuPont Corp.	Committee to Achieve Cultural Diversity	Holds focus groups that lead to career development programs for minority group members
City of Toronto	National Aboriginal Day	Showcases teaching circles, fashion shows, musicians, and traditional drummers and dancers to teach others about Aboriginal culture
NASA Glenn Research Center	Model Workplace Program	Offers multicultural training for all workers

(Source: Based on information from the Web sites of the companies listed.)

Although most companies have been pleased with the ways their diversity management efforts have promoted harmony between employees, such programs are not automatically successful. For diversity management activities to be successful, experts caution that they must focus on accepting a range of differences among people. That is, they should not treat someone as special because he or she is a member of a certain group, but because of the unique skills or abilities he or she brings to the job.

To the extent that managers are trained to seek, recognize, and develop the talents of their employees without regard to the groups to which they belong, they will weaken the stereotypes on which prejudices are based. This, in turn, will bring down the barriers that made diversity training necessary in the first place. (One of the most difficult steps in eliminating prejudicial attitudes involves recognizing the sometimes subtle ways that these have infiltrated the culture of an organization. The Group Exercise on pp. 158–159 presents a useful way of identifying these negative attitudes.)

Winning Practices

Allstate: Where Diversity is a Business Strategy

Although many companies have diversity management programs, the Allstate Insurance Co. uses its program as a strategic weapon. The idea is straightforward: By reflecting the racial and ethnic diversity of its customers, Allstate employees can do a better job of meeting the needs of its broad customer base (e.g., by speaking their languages and understanding their cultures). According to Ed Liddy, Allstate's chairman, president, and CEO, "Our competitive advantage is our people and our people are diverse. Nothing less than an integrated diversity strategy will allow the company to excel."[19]

Allstate's diversity management program takes a broad perspective. Not limited to only gender and ethnicity, it also pays attention to diversity with respect to ages, sexual orientation, and religion. Specifically, it promotes diversity along three major fronts.

- Allstate recruiters visit historically black colleges and universities to attract members of the African American community. It also recruits from schools in Puerto Rico in an effort to expand its Hispanic customer base. From the many awards it has received for its efforts in these areas (e.g., the "Best Companies for Hispanics to Work"), such initiatives appear to be work-

ing. And, the more such recognition the company receives, the easier it is to attract individuals from these groups.

- Attracting recruits is half the battle, but retaining them is far trickier. With this in mind, Allstate emphasizes to all its employees that they are expected to show no bias toward others. It also goes out of its way to encourage minority candidates by showing them the route to promotion within the company. In fact, minority candidates are considered seriously when it comes time to plan for succession up the ranks.

- Within their first six months on the job, all new Allstate employees receive diversity training (about three-quarters of a million person-hours have been spent thus far). This consists of classroom training that encourages people to recognize the way they see themselves and others as well as ways of sustaining a trusting environment among people who are different. Refresher courses also are given to managers from time to time.

At the helm of these efforts has been Anise Wiley-Little, Allstate's first chief diversity officer

(continued)

and assistant vice president, who is responsible for ensuring diversity not only within the company but also in its suppliers.

Thus far, it looks like she's been successful. About 45 percent of Allstate's external hires are ethnically diverse, and the company increased spending to minority-owned companies by $32 million within her first 6 months at the job. Importantly, Allstate also does a great job of satisfying and retaining its customers. In

fact, Allstate is the top insurer of lives and automobiles among African Americans and also ranks as the top insurer of homes and lives among Hispanic Americans.

Clearly, at Allstate, diversity is a highly successful business strategy. Not surprisingly, it has been a 7-time winner of the award for the Best Company for Diversity sponsored by *DiversityInc* magazine.[20] It looks like efforts to promote diversity at Allstate are "in good hands."

THEORIES OF JOB SATISFACTION: ATTITUDES TOWARD JOBS

Do people generally like their jobs? Although the numbers differ for various groups, a recent survey revealed that overall, 86 percent of Americans are satisfied or very satisfied with their jobs and only 4 percent are very dissatisfied.[21] These feelings, reflecting attitudes toward their jobs, are known as **job satisfaction.**

Because job satisfaction plays an important role in organizations, it makes sense to identify the factors that contribute to job satisfaction. As we will point out, a great deal of research, theory, and practice bears upon this question. Although there are many different approaches to understanding job satisfaction, four particular ones stand out as providing our best insight into this very important attitude—the *two-factor theory of job satisfaction, value theory,* the *social information processing model,* and the *dispositional model.*

Two-Factor Theory of Job Satisfaction

There is no more direct way to find out what causes people's satisfaction and dissatisfaction with their jobs than to ask them. Over 40 years ago, an organizational scientist assembled a group of accountants and engineers and asked them to recall incidents that made them feel especially satisfied and especially dissatisfied with their jobs.[22] His results were surprising: Different factors accounted for satisfaction and dissatisfaction.

Rather than finding that the presence of certain variables made people feel satisfied and that their absence made them feel dissatisfied, as you might expect, he found that satisfaction and dissatisfaction stemmed from two different sources. For this reason, his approach is widely referred to as the **two-factor theory of job satisfaction.** The two factors are as follows:

➤ *Motivators.*   In general, what satisfied people most were aspects of their jobs that had to do with the work itself or with outcomes directly resulting from it. These included things such as chances for promotion, opportunities for personal growth, recognition, responsibility, and achievement. These variables are referred to as *motivators* because they are associated with high levels of satisfaction.

➤ *Hygiene factors.*   What dissatisfied people most were conditions surrounding the job, such as working conditions, pay, security, relations with others, and so on, rather than the work itself. These variables are referred to as *hygiene factors* because they prevent dissatisfaction when present.

Rather than conceiving of job satisfaction as falling along a single continuum anchored at one end by satisfaction and at the other by dissatisfaction, this approach conceives of satisfaction and dissatisfaction as separate variables. Motivators, when present at high levels, contribute to job satisfaction but, when absent, do not lead to job dissatisfaction—just less satisfaction. Likewise, hygiene factors only contribute to dissatisfaction when absent but not to satisfaction when present. You may find the diagram in Figure 5.3 helpful in summarizing these ideas.

Two-factor theory has important implications for managing organizations. Specifically, it suggests that managers would be well advised to focus their attention on factors known to promote job satisfaction, such as opportunities for personal growth. Indeed, several of today's companies have realized that satisfaction within their work-forces is enhanced when they provide opportunities for their employees to develop their repertoire of professional skills on the job.

With this in mind, front-line service workers at Marriott Hotels, known as "guest services associates," are hired not to perform a single task but to perform a wide variety of tasks, including checking guests in and out, carrying their bags, and so on. Because they perform a variety of different tasks, Marriott employees get to call on and develop many of their talents, thereby adding to their level of job satisfaction. (This approach, known as *job enrichment,* will be described more fully in Chapter 6 as a way to promote motivation.)

Two-factor theory also implies that steps should be taken to create conditions that help avoid dissatisfaction—and it specifies the kinds of variables required to do so (i.e., hygiene factors). For example, creating pleasant working conditions may be quite helpful in getting people to avoid being dissatisfied with their jobs.

Specifically, research has shown that dissatisfaction is great under conditions that are highly overcrowded, dark, noisy, and that have extreme temperatures and poor air

Figure 5.3   Two-Factor Theory of Job Satisfaction

According to the *two-factor theory,* job satisfaction and job dissatisfaction are not opposite ends of the same continuum but two separate dimensions. Some examples of *hygiene factors,* which lead to dissatisfaction, and *motivators,* which lead to satisfaction, are presented here.

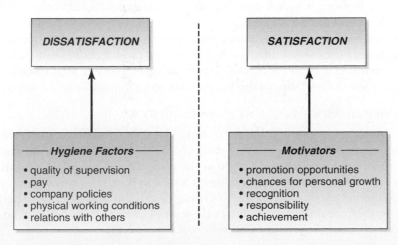

quality. These factors, associated with the conditions under which work is performed but not directly linked to the work itself, contribute much to the levels of job dissatisfaction encountered.

Value Theory

Another approach to job satisfaction, known as **value theory,** takes a broader look at the question of what makes people satisfied. This theory argues that almost any factor can be a source of job satisfaction so long as it is something that people value. The less people have of some highly valued aspect of the job (e.g., pay, learning opportunities) relative to the amount they want, the more dissatisfied they will be.

This approach to job satisfaction implies that an effective way to satisfy workers is to find out what they want and, to the extent possible, give it to them. Many organizations go to great lengths to find out how to satisfy their employees by systematically surveying them. For example, the U.S. Department of Homeland Security does this on an annual basis. Survey results are then carefully considered as the basis for making changes in ways that enhance employee satisfaction.[23]

Social Information Processing Model

Imagine the following scenario. It's your first day on a new job. You arrive at the office excited about what you will be doing, but you soon discover that your co-workers are far less enthusiastic. "This job stinks," they all say, and you hear all the gory details when you hang out with them during lunch. Soon your own satisfaction with the job begins to fade. What once seemed exciting now seems boring, and your boss, who once seemed so pleasant, now looks more like an ogre. Your attitudes changed not because of any objective changes in the job or your boss but because you changed your outlook based on the messages you received from your co-workers.

The idea that people's attitudes toward their jobs are based on information they get from other people is inherent in the **social information processing model.** This approach specifies that people adopt attitudes and behaviors in keeping with the cues provided by others with whom they come into contact.[24] The social information processing model is important because it suggests that job satisfaction can be affected by such subtle things as the offhand comments others make.

With this in mind, it makes sense for managers to pay careful attention to what workers are thinking and feeling about their jobs. These things can be as important as actual characteristics of the jobs themselves when it comes to how people feel about them. This approach also suggests that managers should be very careful about what they say. A few well-chosen remarks may go a long way toward raising employees' job satisfaction. By the same token, a few offhand slips of the tongue may go a long way toward lowering morale.

Dispositional Model of Job Satisfaction

Do you know some people who always seem to like their jobs, no matter what they are doing, and others who are always grumbling about their jobs? If so, you are aware of the basic premise underlying what is known as the **dispositional model of job satisfaction.** This approach claims that job satisfaction is a relatively stable characteristic that stays with people over various situations. According to this conceptualization, people who like the jobs they are doing at one time also tend to like the jobs they may be doing at another time, even if the jobs are different (see Figure 5.4).

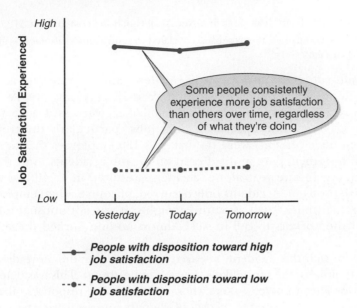

Figure 5.4   The Dispositional Model of Job Satisfaction

According to the *dispositional model of job satisfaction*, some people are consistently more satisfied with their jobs than others, even when they hold different jobs throughout their lives.

Supporting this approach, researchers have found that people are consistent in liking or disliking their jobs over as long as a 10-year period, although they have had several different jobs during that time.[25] Such evidence is in keeping with the idea that job satisfaction operates much like the stable dispositions toward positive and negative affect described in Chapter 3.

CONSEQUENCES OF JOB DISSATISFACTION—AND WAYS TO AVOID THEM

Thus far, we have been alluding to the negative effects of job dissatisfaction but without specifying exactly what these are. In other words, what consequences may be expected among workers who are dissatisfied with their jobs? Several effects have been well documented.

Employee Withdrawal: Voluntary Turnover and Absenteeism

As you might expect, people who are dissatisfied with their jobs want little to do with them—that is, they withdraw. An extreme form of employee withdrawal is quitting, formally referred to as **voluntary turnover.** Withdrawal also may take the form of *absenteeism.* As you might imagine, organizations are highly concerned about these behaviors because they are very costly. Consider these statistics:

➤ Coca-Cola determined that the cost of replacing a supermarket cashier who earns minimum wage runs over $4,000.[26]

➤ Replacing a front desk clerk at a New York City hotel costs almost $12,000.[27]

➤ For U.S. companies, the expenses associated with unplanned absences is about 9 percent of total salary costs.[28]

Although voluntary turnover is permanent, and absenteeism is a short-term reaction, both are ways employees withdraw from dissatisfying jobs. As an example, consider the reactions of the highly dissatisfied bakery workers at the Safeway market in Clackamas, Oregon. So upset with their jobs (particularly the treatment they received from management) were the bakery's 130 employees that they frequently were absent, quit their jobs, and suffered on-the-job accidents. And these were no minor problems. In one year alone, accidents resulted in 1,740 lost workdays—a very expensive problem. Accidents only occurred, of course, when employees showed up. At unpopular times, such as Saturday nights, it was not unusual for as many as 8 percent of the workers to call in sick. Almost no one worked there longer than one year.

Consistent with this incident, research has shown that the more dissatisfied people are with their jobs, the more likely they are to be absent. This was demonstrated in a study of British health care workers whose questionnaire responses on a measure of job satisfaction were compared to records of their absenteeism over a two-year period.[29] Specifically, as summarized in Figure 5.5, workers whose levels of job satisfaction deteriorated over the study period showed an increase in absenteeism, and those whose satisfaction increased over the study period showed a decrease in absenteeism.

The same general relationship has been found in the case of turnover, although the relationship is more complex. Whether or not people will quit their jobs depends on several factors. Among them is the availability of other jobs. So, if conditions are such that alternative positions are available, people may be expected to resign in response to dissatisfaction. However, when such options are limited, voluntary turnover is a less viable option. Not surprisingly, during the economic downturn at the end of the first decade of the twenty-first century, people who were fortunate enough to have jobs tended to stay in them. Hence, knowing that someone is dissatisfied with his or her job does not automatically suggest that he or she will quit. Indeed, many people stay on jobs that they dislike.

Job Performance: Are Dissatisfied Employees Poor Performers?

What about these dissatisfied employees who remain on their jobs? Does their performance suffer? The answer, as you might imagine, depends on the nature of the performance being considered.

Individual job performance

Suppose you're considering individual levels of performance, such as the number of units manufactured by a factory worker or sold by a salesperson. As in the case of withdrawal behaviors, the link between job performance and satisfaction also is quite modest. Indeed, several decades of research on this issue indicate that across many different jobs and organizations, the relationship between job satisfaction and work performance is relatively weak.[30] The strength of this relationship varies across

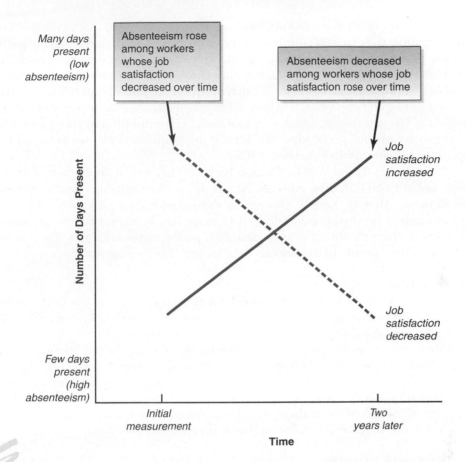

Figure 5.5   Job Satisfaction and Absence: Evidence of a Negative Relationship

A study tracing the levels of job satisfaction and absenteeism of health care workers over a two-year period found the relationship depicted here. Absenteeism dropped among those whose satisfaction rose, whereas absenteeism rose among those whose job satisfaction dropped.

(Source: Based on data reported by Hardy, Woods, and Wall, 2003; see Note 29.)

different occupations—for instance, the relationship is stronger for scientists and engineers than for nurses—but it is not very strong for any occupation studied.[31]

Although this weak association may seem odd at first, it's really not too surprising if you think about it more carefully. After all, people cannot always control all aspects of their job performance, making it impossible to do better even if they wanted to. For example, assembly-line employees are constrained by the speed at which the line moves. Similarly, people may perform poorly because they do not have access to the supplies and equipment needed to succeed. So, because people might not be able to control their job performance, they cannot adjust it (either upward or downward) in response to their attitudes. Furthermore, even someone who is inclined to lower his or her performance in response to negative job attitudes may refrain from doing so for fear of losing the job altogether (and even an undesirable job may help pay the bills better than no job at all).

Organization citizenship behavior

Our discussion thus far refers only to standard forms of work performance, such as quantity and quality of work. Although people may have little control over these aspects of job performance, they tend to have considerable control over the more discretionary, voluntary forms of behavior that occur on the job. We are referring here to such acts as helping one's co-workers or tolerating temporary inconveniences without complaint. These activities, which enhance social relationships and cooperation with the organization but go beyond the formal job requirements, are referred to as **organizational citizenship behaviors (OCB).**

Importantly, this form of behavior is highly related to job satisfaction: The more people are satisfied with their jobs, the greater the good citizenship contributions they tend to make. After all, people who are dissatisfied with their jobs are unlikely to go the extra mile to do anything they don't have to do. As you might imagine, these forms of behavior, although not reflected in standard performance measures (e.g., sales figures), contribute greatly to the smooth functioning of organizations.

Safety performance

Injuries at work are a serious matter—both for the employees who are hurt and their organizations. So anything that can reduce the risk of serious workplace accidents is, potentially, very valuable. Efforts to reduce workplace injuries often have focused on the design of equipment and jobs, and on restricting the number of hours employees can work so as to protect them from fatigue—all major factors in accidents.

Although these practices are indeed effective, evidence suggests that enhancing job satisfaction also can have beneficial effects.[32] When employees are satisfied with their jobs, they take pride in them and this translates into taking extra care, making them less prone to the errors associated with unsafe behavior.

Financial performance

Thus far, we have been discussing the relationship between job satisfaction and various individual-level measures of performance, but what about the financial performance of the companies in which those individuals work? Are they more profitable if their employees are more satisfied? Researchers examining this possibility revealed that the answer is yes.[33] Their study assessed the satisfaction of thousands of employees who worked in some of the largest and best-known companies in the United States over an eight-year period. The researchers also computed the financial performance levels of the organizations in which these individuals worked (two key indexes that are widely used by financial analysts: return on assets and earnings per share).

By conducting sophisticated statistical analyses, the scientists arrived at two fascinating conclusions. First, job satisfaction and financial performance were, in fact, associated with each other to a considerable degree. Second, and perhaps more interestingly, this was *not* the result of the tendency for highly satisfied workers to perform at higher levels (i.e., job satisfaction → financial performance), as you might expect, but the other way around: The good financial performance of the companies promoted high levels of job satisfaction (i.e., financial performance → job satisfaction).

To consider why this may be, imagine that because a company adopts policies that have been found to enhance employees' performance (e.g., involving them in key decisions, paying them for acquiring new skills), employees show high levels of performance. In turn, this good performance enhances the company's financial success. And, since it is successful, it can offer good benefits and increased pay, and enjoy a very positive reputation. The result? Employees feel well treated and are proud to work for their companies, and this leads them to experience high levels of job satisfaction. This is precisely what the research found.

Job Satisfaction and Life Outside Work

Do you think that what happens to people at work "spills over" into their lives outside work? For instance, if employees are satisfied with their jobs and generally feel happy at work, are they likely to take these positive reactions home with them at the end of the day? Conversely, if they are dissatisfied with their jobs and generally feel unhappy at work, will employees take these negative reactions home to their friends and families? The answer to both questions is yes.

We see this, for example, in a study in which employees at a large university were given questionnaires on which they were asked to rate their job satisfaction and their mood several times each day.[34] Participants did this on work days and nonwork days, so they rated their moods and job satisfaction both at work and at home. Results indicated that job satisfaction and mood were closely linked at work; in fact, each influenced the other. High job satisfaction was related to positive moods, and positive moods, in turn, were linked to experiencing high job satisfaction.

Perhaps even more interesting, job satisfaction at work also influenced the moods these employees experienced at home. High job satisfaction at work generated positive moods away from work, whereas low job satisfaction at work generated negative moods. Overall, job satisfaction spilled over into employees' moods at home. In other words, satisfaction with the work-related and nonwork-related aspects of people's lives are closely intertwined.

In summary, there is no doubt that job satisfaction is very important in organizations. Under some conditions, satisfied employees are more productive than dissatisfied ones; they also are less likely to quit their jobs or to experience serious accidents and are more likely to experience positive feelings and moods at home. In view of this, we now turn to a key question: How can managers promote job satisfaction?

Tips for Promoting Job Satisfaction

In view of the negative consequences of dissatisfaction, it makes sense to consider ways of raising satisfaction on the job. Although an employee's dissatisfaction might not account for all aspects of his or her performance, it is important to try to promote satisfaction if for no other reason than to make people happy. After all, satisfaction is a desirable end in itself. With this in mind, what can be done to promote job satisfaction? Drawing on available research, we offer several suggestions.

Pay people fairly

People who believe that their organizations' pay systems are inherently unfair tend to be dissatisfied with their jobs. (We discussed the importance of fairness in Chapter 2 and will revisit this topic again in Chapter 6.) This not only applies to salary and hourly pay but also to fringe benefits. In fact, when people are given opportunities to select the fringe benefits they most desire, their job satisfaction tends to rise. This idea is consistent with value theory. After all, given the opportunity to receive the fringe benefits they most desire, employees may have few discrepancies between those they want and those they actually have.

Improve the quality of supervision

It has been shown that satisfaction is highest among employees who believe that their supervisors are competent, treat them with respect, and have their best interests in mind. Similarly, job satisfaction is enhanced when employees believe that they have open lines of communication with their superiors.

For example, in response to the dissatisfaction problems that plagued the Safeway bakery employees described earlier, company officials responded by completely changing their management style. Traditionally, they were highly intimidating and controlling, leaving employees feeling powerless and discouraged. Realizing the problems caused by this iron-fisted style, they began loosening their highly autocratic ways, replacing them with a new openness and freedom. Employees were allowed to work together toward solving problems of sanitation and safety, and they were encouraged to make suggestions about ways to improve things. The results were dramatic: Workdays lost to accidents dropped from 1,740 a year down to 2, absenteeism fell from 8 percent to 0.2 percent, and voluntary turnover was reduced from almost 100 percent annually to less than 10 percent. Clearly, improving the quality of supervision went a long way toward reversing the negative effects of satisfaction in this organization.

Decentralize organizational power

Decentralization is the degree to which the capacity to make decisions resides in several people, as opposed to one or just a handful. (We will discuss this topic more thoroughly in Chapters 8 and 13.) When power is decentralized, people are allowed to participate freely in the process of decision making. This arrangement contributes to feelings of satisfaction because it leads people to believe that they can have some important effects on their organizations. By contrast, when the power to make decisions is concentrated in the hands of just a few, employees are likely to feel powerless and ineffective, thereby contributing to their feelings of dissatisfaction.

The changes in supervision made at the Safeway bakery provide a good illustration of moving from a highly centralized style to a highly decentralized style. The power to make certain important decisions was shifted into the hands of those who were most affected by them. Because decentralizing power gives people greater opportunities to control aspects of the workplace that affect them, it makes it possible for workers to receive the outcomes they most desire, thereby enhancing their satisfaction.

This dynamic also appears to be at work in many other organizations. For example, at Palms West Hospital (in Palm Beach County, Florida), a committee of employees meets monthly with the CEO to make important decisions concerning the hospital's operation. High job satisfaction in this organization can be traced in large part to the decentralized nature of decision-making power.

Match people to jobs that fit their interests

People have many interests, and these are only sometimes satisfied by what they do on the job. However, the more that people are able to fulfill their interests while on the job, the more satisfied they are with those jobs.

Research has shown, for example, that college graduates are more satisfied with their jobs when these are in line with their college majors than when their jobs fall outside their fields of interest. It is, no doubt, with this in mind that career counselors frequently find it useful to identify people's nonvocational interests. For example, several companies, such as AT&T, IBM, Ford Motor Company, Shell Oil, and Kodak, systematically test and counsel their employees so they can effectively match their skills and interests to the positions to which they are best suited. Some companies, including Coca-Cola and the Walt Disney Company, go so far as to offer individualized counseling to employees so that their personal and professional interests can be identified and matched.

ORGANIZATIONAL COMMITMENT: ATTITUDES TOWARD COMPANIES

Thus far, our discussion has centered around people's attitudes toward their jobs. However, to fully understand work-related attitudes we also must focus on people's attitudes toward the organizations in which they work—that is, their **organizational commitment.** The concept of organizational commitment is concerned with the degree to which people are involved with their organizations and are interested in remaining a part of them.

It is important to note that organizational commitment is generally independent of job satisfaction. Consider, for example, that a nurse may really like the kind of work she does but dislike the hospital in which she works, leading her to seek a similar job elsewhere. By the same token, a waiter may have positive feelings about the restaurant in which he works but may dislike waiting on tables. These complexities illustrate the importance of studying organizational commitment.

Our presentation of this topic will begin by examining the different dimensions of organizational commitment. We then will review the impact of organizational commitment on organizational functioning and conclude by presenting ways of enhancing commitment.

Varieties of Organizational Commitment

Being committed to an organization is not only a matter of "yes or no" or even "how much." Distinctions also can be made with respect to "what kind" of commitment. Specifically, scientists have distinguished among three distinct forms of commitment, which we review here (see summary in Figure 5.6).[35]

Continuance commitment

Have you ever stayed on a job because you just don't want to bother to find a new one (or believe that you cannot find a new one)? If so, you are already familiar with the concept of **continuance commitment.** This refers to the strength of a person's desire to remain working for an organization due to his or her belief that it may be costly to leave. The longer people remain in their organizations, the more they stand to lose

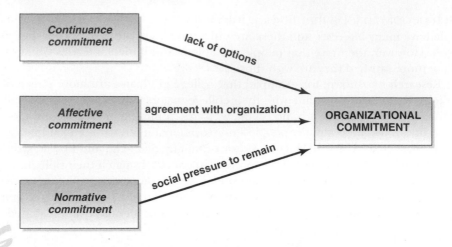

Figure 5.6 Three Types of Organizational Commitment

Scientists have distinguished among the three different types of organizational commitment summarized here.

what they have invested in the organization over the years (e.g., retirement plans, close friendships). Many people are committed to staying on their jobs simply because they are unwilling to risk losing these things. Such individuals may be said to have a high degree of continuance commitment.

A generation or two ago, most workers remained loyal to their companies throughout their working lives. Generally speaking, though, workers now are willing to move from job to job to advance their careers and gain new experience as desired. That is, if they can. In today's bad economy, however, many workers are staying put because they fear that as new employees in another company they may be the first to be let go when cuts are made.[36] For this reason, continuance commitment is particularly high today.

Affective commitment

A second type of organizational commitment is **affective commitment**—the strength of people's desires to continue working for an organization because they agree with its underlying goals and values. People feeling high degrees of affective commitment desire to remain in their organizations because they endorse what the organization stands for and are willing to support its mission. Sometimes, particularly when an organization is undergoing change, employees may wonder whether their personal values continue to be in line with those of the organization in which they continue to work. When this happens, they may question whether they still belong and, if they believe not, they may resign.

A few years ago, Ryder Truck Company successfully avoided losing employees on this basis by publicly reaffirming its corporate values. Ryder was facing a situation in which the company was not only expanding beyond its core truck leasing business but also facing changes due to deregulation (e.g., routes, tariffs, taxes). To help guide employees through the tumultuous time, chief executive Tony Burns went out of his way to reinforce the company's core values—support, trust, respect, and striving.

He spread the message far and wide throughout the company, using videotaped interviews, articles in the company magazine, plaques, posters, and even laminated wallet-size cards carrying the message of the company's core values. Along with other Ryder officials, Mr. Burns is convinced that reiterating the company's values was responsible for the high level of affective commitment that the company enjoyed during this turbulent period.

Normative commitment

A third type of organizational commitment is **normative commitment,** which refers to employees' feelings of obligation to stay with their organizations because of pressures from others. People who have high degrees of normative commitment are greatly concerned about what others would think of them for leaving. They would be reluctant to disappoint their employers and concerned that their fellow employees may think poorly of them for resigning.

Normative commitment, like the other two forms of commitment, is typically assessed using a paper-and-pencil questionnaire. (To see what questions measuring organizational commitment look like and to assess your own degree of organizational commitment, see the Self-Assessment Exercise on p. 158.)

Why Strive for a Committed Workforce?

As you might imagine, people who feel deeply committed to their organizations behave differently from those who do not. Specifically, several key aspects of work behavior have been linked to organizational commitment.[37]

Committed employees are disinclined to withdraw

The more highly committed employees are to their organizations, the less likely they are to resign and be absent (what we referred to as *withdrawal behavior* in the context of job satisfaction). Being committed leads people to stay on their jobs and to show up when they are expected to do so.[38]

This phenomenon has been demonstrated in a large-scale survey study in which dropout rates among U.S. Air Force cadets were traced over the four years required to get a degree. The more strongly committed to the service the cadets were upon entering the program, the less likely they were to drop out.[39] The finding that commitment levels could predict behavior so far into the future is a good indication of the importance of organizational commitment as a work-related attitude.

Committed employees are willing to make sacrifices for their organizations

Beyond remaining in their organizations, those who are highly committed to them demonstrate a great willingness to share and to make sacrifices required for those organizations to thrive. A good example is the annual pay of $1 that many top executives are taking while their companies are struggling to stay afloat during tough economic times (e.g., CEOs of Yahoo!, Apple, Google, and Detroit's "big 3" automakers).[40] Less committed executives would have little incentive to be so generous. This is not to imply that only highly magnanimous gestures result from commitment. In fact, small acts of good organizational citizenship are also likely to occur among people who are highly committed to their organizations.[41] This makes sense if you consider that it takes people who are highly committed to their organizations to be willing to make the investments needed to give of themselves for the good of the company.

Considering these benefits of organizational commitment, it makes sense for organizations to take the steps necessary to enhance commitment among their employees. We now describe several ways of doing this.

Ways to Develop Organizational Commitment

Some determinants of organizational commitment (e.g., economic conditions) fall outside of managers' spheres of control, giving them few opportunities to enhance these feelings. However, managers can do several things to encourage employees to want to keep working for their companies—that is, to enhance affective commitment.

Make jobs more interesting

It has been well established that people tend to be highly committed to their organizations when they have opportunities to take control over the way they do their jobs and are recognized for making important contributions. (This is a process known as *job enrichment,* a topic we will discuss in more detail in Chapter 6 because of its effectiveness in boosting motivation.)

As an example, Ford instituted its Employee Involvement program, a systematic way of involving employees in many aspects of corporate decision-making. Assembly-line workers not only got to perform a wide variety of tasks but also enjoyed considerable autonomy in doing them (e.g., freedom to schedule work, and to stop the assembly line if needed). A few years after the program was in place, Ford employees became more committed to their jobs—so much so, in fact, that the acrimony that usually resulted at contract renewal time had all but vanished. Although employee involvement may not be the cure for all commitment ills, it was clearly highly effective in this case.

Align the interests of the company with those of the employees

Whenever making something good for the company also makes something good for its employees, those employees are likely to be highly committed to those companies. Many organizations do this quite directly by introducing profit-sharing plans—that is, incentive plans in which employees receive bonuses in proportion to the company's profitability. Such plans are often quite effective in enhancing organizational commitment, especially when they are perceived to be administered fairly.

For example, workers at Allied Plywood Corporation (a wholesaler of building materials in Alexandria, Virginia) receive cash bonuses based on company profits, but these are distributed monthly as well as yearly. The monthly bonuses are the same size for all, whereas the annual bonuses are given in proportion to each employee's individual contributions to total profit, days worked, and performance. These plans are good examples of some of the things companies are doing to enhance commitment. Although the plans differ, their underlying rationale is the same: By letting employees share in the company's profitability, they are more likely to see their own interests as consistent with those of their company. And, when these interests are aligned, commitment is high.

Recruit and select new employees whose values closely match those of the organization

Recruiting new employees is important not only because it provides opportunities to find people whose values match those of the organization but also because of the dynamics of the recruitment process itself. Specifically, the more an organization invests in someone by working hard to lure him or her to the company, the more that individual is likely to return the same investment of energy by expressing commitment toward the organization. In other words, companies that show their employees they care enough to work hard to attract them are likely to find those individuals strongly committed to the company.

In conclusion, it is useful to think of organizational commitment as an attitude that may be influenced by managerial actions. Not only might people be selected who are predisposed to be committed to their organizations, but also various measures can be taken to enhance commitment in the face of indications that it is suffering.

Back to the Case

Answer the following questions about this chapter's Making the Case (p. 134) to illustrate insights you have derived about the material in this chapter.

1. Outside the Paralympic setting, what prejudicial attitudes and discriminatory behaviors are likely to be experienced by athletes with disabilities? What do you believe can be done to overcome these?
2. How do you think the athletes will be accepted relative to other individuals with disabilities who are not as athletic?
3. What steps can company officials take to enhance the job satisfaction and organizational commitment of people with disabilities?

You Be the Consultant

Addressing a Turnover Problem

The president of a small manufacturing firm comes to you with a problem: The company is spending a lot of money training new employees, but 75 percent of them quit after working less than a year. Worse, they take jobs at the company's biggest competitor. Answer the following questions relevant to this situation based on the material in this chapter.

1. Drawing on research and theory on job satisfaction, what would you suspect is the cause of the turnover? What advice can you offer about how to eliminate the problem?

2. Drawing on research and theory on organizational commitment, what would you suspect is the cause of the turnover? What advice can you offer about how to eliminate the problem?

3. Suppose you find out that the greatest levels of dissatisfaction exist among employees belonging to minority groups. What would you recommend doing to eliminate the prejudice that may be responsible for the turnover?

SELF-ASSESSMENT EXERCISE

How Strongly Are You Committed to Your Organization?

Questionnaires similar to the one presented here (which is based on established instruments) are used to assess three types of organizational commitment—continuance, affective, and normative.[42] Completing this scale will give you a good feel for your own level of organizational commitment and how this important construct is measured.

Directions

In the space to the left of each of the 12 statements that follow write the one number that reflects the extent to which you agree with it personally. Express your answers using the following scale: 1 = not at all, 2 = slightly, 3 = moderately, 4 = a great deal, 5 = extremely.

_____ 1. At this point, I stay at my organization more because I have to than because I want to.
_____ 2. I feel I strongly belong to my organization.
_____ 3. I am reluctant to leave a company once I have been working there.
_____ 4. Leaving my company would entail a great deal of personal sacrifice.
_____ 5. I feel emotionally connected to the company for which I work.
_____ 6. My employer would be very disappointed if I left my job.
_____ 7. I don't have any other choice but to stay on my present company.
_____ 8. I feel like I am part of the family at the company in which I work.
_____ 9. I feel a strong obligation to stay at my organization.
_____ 10. My life would be greatly disrupted if I left my present company.
_____ 11. I would be quite pleased to spend the rest of my life working for my current organization.
_____ 12. I stay on my job because people would think poorly of me for leaving.

Scoring

1. Add the scores for items 1, 4, 7, and 10. This reflects your degree of *continuance commitment*.
2. Add the scores for items 2, 5, 8, and 11. This reflects your degree of *affective commitment*.
3. Add the scores for items 3, 6, 9, and 12. This reflects your degree of *normative commitment*.

Discussion Questions

1. Which form of commitment does the scale reveal you have most? Which do you have least? Are these differences great or are they highly similar?
2. Did the scale tell you something you didn't already know about yourself, or did it merely reinforce your intuitive beliefs about your own organizational commitment?
3. To what extent is your organizational commitment, as reflected by this scale, related to your interest in quitting your job and taking a new position?

Group Exercise

Auditing Organizational Biases

Is your organization biased against certain groups of people? Even if you answer "no," chances are good that you may have missed some subtle and unintentional forms of prejudice lurking about. This exercise is designed to help you uncover some of these.

Directions

1. Reproduce the checklist that follows, making one copy for each member of the class.
2. Guided by this checklist, gather the information indicated for the organization in which you work (or, if you don't work, for any organization to which you have access) and check off all items that apply.
3. In answering, either use your existing knowledge of the company or ask those who might know. (If you do ask others, be sure to tell them that it's for a class project. Also, maintain the confidentiality of all responses by not identifying who completed the survey.)
4. Report back to the class after one week.

Does Your Organization . . .

____ have signs and manuals in English only although several employees speak other languages?

____ ignore important holidays celebrated by people of certain cultures, such as Martin Luther King Jr. Day, Yom Kippur, Cinco de Mayo, or Chinese New Year?

____ limit social events to married people?

____ restrict training opportunities available to women and people from minority groups?

____ emphasize male-oriented sporting events, such as football?

____ limit its recruitment efforts to colleges and universities that have predominately white students?

____ hire predominately females for secretarial positions?

____ discourage styles of dress that allow for the expression of varied cultural and ethnic backgrounds (e.g., the head scarves worn by Muslim women)?

Discussion Questions

1. How many of the eight items did you check off? How about other members of the class? What was the class average?
2. What items represented the biggest sources of bias? What are the potential consequences of these actions?
3. What steps could be taken to change these practices? Do you think the company would be willing to cooperate?

Chapter 6

What Motivates People to Work?

Learning Objectives

After reading this chapter, you will be able to:

1. **DEFINE** the concept of motivation.
2. **EXPLAIN** need hierarchy theory and how it applies in organizations.
3. **DESCRIBE** equity theory's approach to motivation in the workplace.
4. **OUTLINE** the basic assumptions of expectancy theory and its implications in organizations.
5. **EXPLAIN** how goals can be set to motivate high levels of job performance.
6. **DESCRIBE** ways in which jobs can be designed so as to enhance motivation.

3 GOOD REASONS why you should care about . . .

Motivation in Organizations

You should care about motivation in organizations because:

1. Managers typically have a variety of opportunities to motivate employees by virtue of how they treat them.
2. In many different ways, highly motivated employees tend to be the best performers.
3. Jobs can be designed so as to make them inherently interesting, which enhances their potential to motivate the people who perform them.

Making the Case for Motivation in Organizations

Costco: Doing Something Right

No doubt about it; customers love Costco. They like the broad product mix (from candy bars to automobiles), the generous return policy (almost anything can be returned at any time), and most of all, the low prices (no more than 15 percent over wholesale). It's no surprise, then, that Costco enjoys a larger share of the wholesale "club" market—some 54 percent—than its competitors Sam's Club and BJ's Wholesale Club. And although membership costs $50 annually, about 86 percent of the 51.8 million members renew each year.

But it's not only customers who like Costco; so too do employees. As evidence, consider the loyalty of its workforce. In the retail sector, it's generally considered good to keep about half your employees, but Costco retains about 94 percent. Obviously, they're doing something right, but what? What spurs Costco employees to give great customer service, to work hard, and to keep working?

Ask them and they'll tell you directly. A former schoolteacher who now works at a Costco lunch counter made it clear that opportunities for promotion abound, saying, "I know that sooner or later, I'll be given a bigger job—perhaps one with management responsibility, and that excites me." Although it may seem like quite a leap from selling hotdogs to being a manager, almost all promotions come from within, so it's not unrealistic for Costco employees to aspire to bigger things.

But internal promotions tell only part of the story when it comes to motivating Costco employees. Better-than-average wages also are key. Because wholesale clubs must keep costs down, wages are usually low. At Costco, however, the relatively high employee compensation—about $17/hour on average—is offset by savings from not having to select and train new employees, which runs about $2,500 per person. And because employees are well paid and know about the many bargains in the store, they tend to be among its most frequent shoppers, adding further revenue to the coffers.

Another key to Costco's success is its generally good customer service. Compared to many discount retail establishments whose surly clerks might bark one-word answers to your questions, if you can even find one in the first place, Costco employees are interested in helping. It's widely assumed that this is an extension of the company's demonstrated concern for them. As the lunch counter clerk put it, it's "because of the way I'm treated." And this is reflected at the cash register: The sales-per-square-foot of retail space at Costco is $795, compared to only $516 at Sam's Club. And with 554 stores averaging 141,000 square feet, the revenue is considerable.

Although none of this may be at the top of your mind when you visit your local Costco to stock up on a year's supply of paper towels or shaving cream, it just may give you a new appreciation of the experience.

Keeping Costco's 143,000 worldwide employees happy and working hard surely isn't easy, but it's clear that they're doing something—several things, in fact—right. For one, because Costco hires most managers and executives from within, employees have opportunities to work their way up the ladder to higher-level positions. Also, the company pays their associates fairly, keeping them from jumping ship whenever another potentially attractive opportunity comes along. In keeping with these things, employees feel that they're treated well, making them part of a large family. As you will see in this chapter, these are some of the key things it takes to motivate employees. We will discuss these and several other related ways of motivating employees in this chapter, identifying not only what you can do to motivate people but also precisely what makes various motivational techniques successful.

The question of exactly what it takes to motivate workers has received a great deal of attention by both practicing managers and organizational scientists.[1] In fact, it has been one of the most widely studied topics in the field of OB in the last 45 years.[2] We examine five different approaches to this question in this chapter. Specifically, we will focus on motivating by (1) meeting basic human needs, (2) treating people equitably, (3) enhancing beliefs that desired rewards can be attained, (4) setting goals, and (5) designing jobs to make them more desirable. Before turning attention to these specific orientations, let's first consider a very basic matter—the fundamental nature of *motivation.*

THE BASIC NATURE OF MOTIVATION

Motivation is a tricky concept. Everyone has some vague idea of what it means but for scientific analysis, we must be precise. So, with this in mind we launch this chapter by posing two fundamental questions: What is motivation? And, what motivates people to work?

What is motivation?

Scientists have defined **motivation** as the process of arousing, directing, and maintaining behavior toward a goal. As this definition suggests, motivation involves three components. The first component, *arousal,* has to do with the drive or energy behind our actions. For example, when we are hungry we are driven to seek food. The *direction* component involves the choice of behavior with respect to the arousal. A hungry person may make many different choices—eat an apple, have a pizza delivered, go out for a burger, and so on. The third component, *maintenance,* is concerned with people's persistence, their willingness to continue to exert effort until a goal is met. The longer you would continue to search for food when hungry, the more persistent you would be.

Putting it all together, it may help to think of motivation by using the analogy of driving a car. In this manner, arousal may be likened to the energy generated by the car's engine and fuel system. The direction it takes is dictated by the driver's manipulation of the steering wheel. Finally, maintenance may be thought of as the driver's determination to stay on course until the final destination is reached.

What motivates people to work?

This might seem like a silly question to you, thinking that the answer is money. However, that's not entirely correct. To shed light on this, suppose you struck it big in the lottery. Would you continue to go to work? Interestingly, most Americans say that they would, in fact, continue to work even if they didn't need the money.[3] Although money certainly is important to people, it's not the only thing that motivates us. In fact, research has shown that what motivates people most strongly is the prospect of performing jobs that are interesting and challenging. Getting paid was third on the list (see Figure 6.1).[4] As you will see in the rest of this chapter, the field of OB, not surprisingly, considers a wide variety of factors that motivate people, including those just described.

MOTIVATING BY MEETING BASIC HUMAN NEEDS

As our definition suggests, people are motivated to fulfill their needs—whether it's a need for food, as in our example, or other needs, such as the need for social approval. Companies that help their employees in this quest attract the best people and motivate them to perform at their highest levels.[5]

Some insight into how this may come about is provided by **need hierarchy theory.**[6] The basic idea is simple: People will not be healthy and well adjusted unless their needs are met. This idea applies whether we're talking about becoming a functioning member of society (the theory's original focus), or a productive employee of an organization,

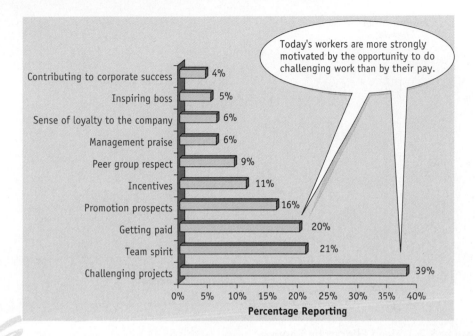

Figure 6.1   What Motivates People to Work?

People working in a wide variety of jobs in such fields as accounting, construction, insurance, and information technology were asked to indicate the job-related factors that motivated them most strongly. The top 10 things are shown here. Because people were allowed to select more than one, the figures exceed 100 percent.

(Source: Based on Robson, 2004; see Note 4.)

a later application. Specifically, need hierarchy theory identifies five different types of needs that are activated in a specific order. These start at the lowest, most basic needs and work upward to higher-level needs (which is what makes it a hierarchy). Furthermore, these needs are not aroused all at once nor are they triggered in random fashion. Rather, each need is activated only after the one beneath it in the hierarchy has been satisfied. The specific needs and the hierarchical order in which they are arranged are summarized in Figure 6.2.

Physiological Needs

The lowest-order needs involve satisfying fundamental biological drives, such as the need for air, food, water, and shelter. These **physiological needs,** as they are called, are surely the most basic needs, because unless they are met people will become ill and suffer. For this reason, they are depicted at the base of the triangle in Figure 6.2.

There are many things that companies do to help meet their employees' physiological needs. Probably the simplest involves paying a living wage, money that employees can exchange for food and shelter. But there's more to satisfying physiological needs than giving employees a paycheck. There also are coffee breaks and opportunities to rest. Staying physically healthy involves more than just resting, of course. It also requires exercise, something that the sedentary nature of many of today's

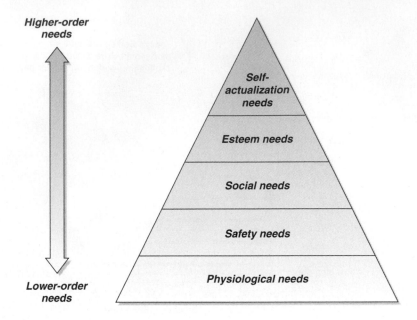

Figure 6.2   Need Hierarchy Theory

Need hierarchy theory specifies that the five needs shown here are activated in order, from lowest to highest. Each need is triggered after the one immediately below it in the hierarchy is satisfied.

technologically advanced jobs does not permit. In fact, the perk most desired by managers seeking new jobs is membership in a health club.[7]

 With this in mind, thousands of companies are providing exercise facilities for their employees. This makes perfectly good business sense. After all, by keeping the workforce healthy and fit companies are paving the way for people to become productive. One company that recognizes this is Georgia-Pacific Corp., whose 2,500 Atlanta employees are entitled to use a large state-of-the-art athletic club attached to the company parking garage.[8]

Safety Needs

After physiological needs have been satisfied, the next level of needs is triggered—**safety needs.** These are concerned with the need to operate in an environment that is physically and psychologically safe and secure, one free from threats of harm.

 Organizations help satisfy their employees' safety needs in several ways. For example, they protect shop workers from hazards in the environment by providing such basic services as security and fire prevention, and by fitting them with goggles and hard hats. Even seemingly safe work settings, such as offices, can be riddled with safety hazards. This is why efforts are made to spare office workers from eye strain, wrist injuries (such as the increasingly prevalent carpal tunnel syndrome), and back pain, by using ergonomically designed computer keyboards, desks, and chairs.

 Psychological safety is important as well. By offering health and disability insurance, companies are promoting their employees' psychological well-being by assuring them that they will not be harmed financially in the event of illness. Although almost all companies offer health insurance benefits, a select few have taken psychological security to the extreme by having no-layoff policies. Since 1948, Cleveland, Ohio's Lincoln Electric Company, for example, has not laid off a single worker who's been with the company at least three years.[9] When times are tough, they simply reassign their employees to other jobs. Knowing that your job will always be there regardless of economic conditions is surely a source of psychological reassurance.

Social Needs

Once people's physiological and safety needs have been satisfied, **social needs** are activated. These refer to the need to be liked and accepted by others. As social animals we want to be with others and to have them approve of us.

Organizations do much to satisfy these needs when they sponsor social events, such as office parties and company picnics. For example, by holding its annual "Family Day" picnic near its Armonk, New York, headquarters, IBM employees enjoy good opportunities to socialize with their co-workers and their families. Similarly, joining a company's bowling team or softball team also provides good opportunities to meet social needs within an organization. In discussing physiological needs we noted that many companies provide health club facilities for their employees. Besides keeping employees healthy, such opportunities also help satisfy social needs by bringing people together to socialize. "Playing hard" with those with whom we also "work hard" provides good opportunities to fulfill social needs on the job.

Esteem Needs

Not only do we need to be liked by others socially, but we also need to gain their respect and approval. In other words, we have a **need for self-esteem**—that is, to achieve success and have others recognize our accomplishments. Consider, for example, reserved parking spots or plaques honoring the "employee of the month." Both are ways of demonstrating esteem for employees. So too are awards banquets in which worthy staff members' contributions are recognized.[10]

The same thing is frequently done in print by recognizing one's organizational contributions on the pages of a corporate newsletter. For example, employees of the large pharmaceutical company Merck enjoyed the recognition they received for developing Proscar (a highly successful drug treatment for prostate enlargement) when they saw their pictures in the company newsletter. In fact, it meant more to Merck employees to have their colleagues learn of their success than it did to have their accomplishments touted widely to anonymous readers of the *New York Times*.

The practice of awarding bonuses to people making suggestions for improvement is another highly successful way to meet employees' esteem needs. Many companies use a variety of different small awards (e.g., gift cards, certificates) in this regard. However, few companies have taken the practice of rewarding contributions to the same high art as Mary Kay Cosmetics. Not only are lavish banquets staged to recognize modest contributions to this company's bottom line, but top performers are awarded the most coveted prize of all—a pink Cadillac. As the company's late founder Mary Kay Ash put it, "There are two things people want more than sex and money . . . recognition and praise."[11] Companies that cannot afford such lavish gifts needn't be concerned about failing to satisfy their employees' self-esteem needs.

After all, sometimes the best recognition is nothing more than a heartfelt "thank you." Or, as Mark Twain put it, "I can live for two months on a good compliment." This is good news for today's organizations, which have leaner budgets to use in getting employees to do more work.

Self-Actualization Needs

What happens after all an employee's lower-order needs are met? According to the theory, people will strive for **self-actualization**—that is, they will work to become all they are capable of being. When people are self-actualized, they perform at their maximum level of creativity and become extremely valuable assets to their organizations. For this reason, companies are interested in paving the way for their employees to self-actualize by meeting their lower-order needs.

As this discussion clearly suggests, need hierarchy theory provides excellent guidance with respect to the needs that workers are motivated to achieve. Indeed, many organizations have taken actions that are directly suggested by the theory and have found them to be successful. For this reason, the theory remains popular with organizational practitioners. Scientists, however, have noted that specific elements of the theory—notably, the assertion that there are only five needs and that they are activated in a specific order—have not been supported. Despite this shortcoming, the insight that need hierarchy theory provides into the importance of meeting human needs in the workplace makes it a valuable approach to motivation.

MOTIVATING BY BEING EQUITABLE

There can be little doubt about the importance of money as a motivator on the job. However, it would be overly simplistic and misleading to say that people only want to earn as much money as possible. Even the highest-paid executives, sports figures, and celebrities sometimes complain about their pay despite their multimillion-dollar salaries.[12] Are they being greedy? Not necessarily. Often the issue is not the actual amount of pay received, but rather, pay fairness. That is, how does the pay received compare to that of others who are doing similar work? Indeed, when it comes to judging the fairness of their pay, people are more inclined to compare themselves to others in their world than to general standards.[13]

As a case in point, consider the National Basketball Association's Houston Rockets. In recent years, low morale on this team was linked to the fact that it had three highly paid superstars who made multimillion-dollar salaries while the majority of the team's players made the league's minimum salary of $272,250.[14] Although you might not feel too sorry for someone who has to "rough it" on a quarter-million-dollar salary, many of these players felt underpaid because they thought that the stars who made eight or ten times more than them were not eight or ten times better.

Organizational scientists have been actively interested in explaining exactly what constitutes fairness on the job and how people respond when they believe they have been unfairly treated. The major approach to this issue is known as *equity theory*.

Equity Theory: Balancing Outcomes and Inputs

Equity theory proposes that people are motivated to maintain fair, or equitable, relationships between themselves and others and to avoid those relationships that are unfair or inequitable.[15] To make judgments about equity, people compare themselves to others by focusing on two variables: outcomes—what we perceive to get out of our jobs (e.g., pay, fringe benefits, prestige)—and inputs—the contributions we perceive to make (e.g., time worked, effort exerted, units produced). It helps to think of these judgments in the form of ratios—that is, the outcomes received relative to the inputs contributed (e.g., $1,000 per week in exchange for working 40 hours).

According to equity theory, people make equity judgments by comparing their own outcome/input ratios to the outcome/input ratios of others. This so-called "other" may be someone else in one's work group, another employee in the organization, an individual working in the same field, or even oneself at an earlier point in time—in short, almost anyone against whom we compare ourselves. As shown in Figure 6.3, these comparisons can result in any of three different states: *overpayment inequity, underpayment inequity,* or *equitable payment.*

Figure 6.3 Equity Theory: A Summary and Example

According to *equity theory,* people make judgments of equity or inequity by comparing the ratios of their own outcomes/inputs to the corresponding ratios of others. People are motivated to change inequitable relationships (such as the one shown on top) to equitable ones (such as the one shown on the bottom).

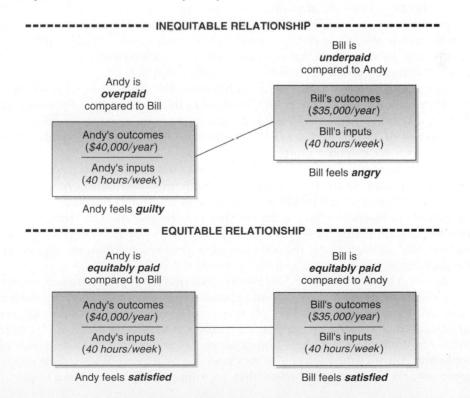

Let's consider an example. Imagine that Andy and Bill work together as copywriters in an advertising firm. Both men have equal amounts of experience, training, and education, and work equally long and hard at their jobs. In other words, their inputs are equivalent. But suppose Andy is paid an annual salary of $40,000 while Bill is paid only $35,000. In this case, Andy's ratio of outcomes/inputs is higher than Bill's, creating a state of *overpayment inequity* for Andy (because the ratio of his outcomes/inputs is higher) but *underpayment inequity* for Bill (because the ratio of his outcomes/inputs is lower).

According to equity theory, Andy, realizing that he is paid more than an equally qualified person doing the same work, will feel *guilty* in response to his *overpayment*. By contrast, Bill, realizing that he is paid less than an equally qualified person for doing the same work, will feel *angry* in response to his *underpayment*. Guilt and anger are negative emotional states that people are motivated to change. As a result, they will seek to create a state of *equitable payment* in which their outcome/input ratios are equal, leading them to feel *satisfied*.

Creating equity

How can inequitable states be turned into equitable ones? The answer lies in adjusting the balance of outcomes and/or inputs. Among people who are underpaid, equity can be created by raising one's outcomes and/or lowering one's inputs. Likewise, those who are overpaid may either raise their inputs or lower their outcomes. In both cases, either action would effectively make the two outcome/input ratios equivalent.

For example, the underpaid person, Bill, might lower his inputs, such as by slacking off, arriving at work late, leaving early, taking longer breaks, doing less work or lower-quality work—or, in an extreme case, quitting his job. (Indeed, an ESPN sideline reporter who was required to fly to events in coach airline seats recently quit her job because she felt underpaid relative to her colleagues, who flew first class.[16]) Bill also may attempt to raise his outcomes, such as by asking for a raise, or even taking home company property, such as tools or office supplies.

By contrast, the overpaid person, Andy, may do the opposite—raise his inputs or lower his outcomes. For example, he might put forth much more effort, work longer hours, and try to make a greater contribution to the company. He also might lower his outcomes, such as by working while on a paid vacation or not taking advantage of fringe benefits the company offers.

These are all specific *behavioral* reactions to inequitable conditions—that is, things people can *do* to turn inequitable states into equitable ones. However, people may be unable or unwilling to do some of the things necessary to respond behaviorally to inequities. In particular, they may be reluctant to steal from their employers or unwilling to restrict their productivity for fear of getting caught "goofing off." In such cases, people may attempt to resolve inequity *cognitively* by changing the way they think about the situation.

As noted earlier, because equity theory deals with perceptions, inequitable states may be redressed by altering one's thinking about their own and others' outcomes and inputs. For example, underpaid people may rationalize that others' inputs are really higher than their own (e.g., "I suppose she really *is* more qualified than me"), thereby convincing themselves that their higher outcomes are justified. Similarly, overpaid people may convince themselves that they really *are* better and deserve their relatively higher pay. So, by changing the way they see things, people can come to perceive inequitable situations as equitable, thereby effectively relieving their feelings of guilt and anger and transforming them into feelings of satisfaction.

Responding to inequities on the job

Research shows that people are motivated to redress inequities at work and that they respond much as equity theory suggests. Consider two examples from the world of sports. Professional basketball players who are underpaid (i.e., ones who are paid less than others who perform as well or better) score fewer points than those who are equitably paid.[17] Similarly, among baseball players, those paid less than others who play comparably well tend to change teams or even leave the sport when they are unsuccessful at negotiating higher pay. Cast in terms of equity theory, the underpaid players may be said to have lowered their inputs.

We also know that underpaid workers attempt to raise their outcomes. For example, in an organization studied by the author, workers at two manufacturing plants suffered an underpayment created by the introduction of a temporary pay cut of 15 percent.[18] During the 10-week period under which workers received lower pay, company officials noticed that theft of company property increased dramatically by approximately 250 percent. However, in another factory in which comparable work was done by workers paid at their normal rates, the theft rate remained low throughout the study period. This pattern suggests that employees may have stolen property from their company to compensate for their reduced pay. Interestingly, when the normal rate of pay was reinstated in the two factories, theft returned to its normal, low level. These findings suggest that companies that seek to save money by lowering pay may merely be encouraging their employees to find other ways of making up for what they believe is rightfully theirs.

Consider the examples given: Professional athletes performed worse (or quit) when they received salaries that were not commensurate with their performance, and factory workers stole from their employers while they received lower pay than usual. Together, these examples illustrate a key point explained by equity theory: People are highly motivated to seek equity and to redress the inequities they face on the job.

Managerial Implications of Equity Theory

Equity theory has important implications for ways of motivating people.[19] We highlight two key ones here.

Avoid underpayment

Companies that attempt to save money by reducing employees' salaries may find that employees respond in many different ways to even the score. For example, they may shave a few minutes off their workdays or otherwise withhold production.

In extreme cases, employees express their feelings of severe underpayment inequity by going on strike, stopping work and protesting their dissatisfaction. And as the following examples from just a single recent year suggest, this occurs all over the world.

> ➤ After the France-based cosmetics giant, L'Oreal, announced impressive profits, hundreds of the company's employees marched on picket lines to express their demand for their fair share in the form of pay raises.[20]

➤ In India, 100,000 film industry employees (e.g., actors, technicians) went on strike to protest the fact that they are paid less than others doing comparable work in other countries.[21]

➤ Workers at a Pakistani power plant went on strike, stopping the supply of electricity to some regions of the country, to demand regular payment of salaries that had not been paid for several months.[22]

Over the past few years, a particularly unsettling form of institutionalizing underpayment has come in the form of **two-tier wage structures**—payment systems in which newer employees are paid less than those hired to do the same work at an earlier point in time. Not surprisingly, proposals to introduce two-tier wage systems generally meet with considerable resistance among employees and, when applicable, the unions representing them. Unfortunately, however, such arrangements sometimes are necessary in response to troubled economic periods.

A good example may be seen at General Motors, which in 2007 agreed to a two-tier wage deal with officials of the United Auto Workers (UAW).[23] Ultimately, to equalize things among nonmanufacturing employees, the company agreed to offer initial payments of $3,000 followed by 3 years of bonuses of about 3 percent of annual wages. Before arriving at that figure, however, GM made an initial offer that UAW officials believed to be unfair, leading them to order 73,000 factory workers off their jobs.

This problem has been particularly severe among the growing legions of part-time or permanent-temporary workers who have been staffing offices and factories in recent years. Because these individuals often receive lower pay and fewer fringe benefits than their full-time counterparts performing the same work, they tend to feel underpaid. With this in mind, some organizations schedule such workers on different shifts or in different locations from full-time, permanent employees who are compensated more generously.[24] This practice—which amounts to attempting to hide an inequitable pay structure—cannot be condoned on ethical grounds. Moreover, making people feel underpaid is simply an unwise and ineffective managerial practice.

Avoid overpayment

You may think that because overpaid employees work hard to deserve their pay, it would be a useful motivational technique to pay people more than they merit. There are several reasons why this does not work. First, the increases in performance shown in response to overpayment inequity are only temporary. As time goes on, people begin to believe that they actually deserve the higher pay they're getting and bring their work level down to normal. A second reason why it is unwise to overpay employees is that when you overpay one employee, you are underpaying all the others. When the majority of the employees feel underpaid, they will lower their performance, resulting in a net *decrease* in productivity—and widespread dissatisfaction. Hence, the conclusion is clear: *Managers should strive to pay all employees equitably.*

We realize, of course, that this may be easier said than done. Part of the difficulty resides in the fact that feelings of equity and inequity are based on perceptions, and these aren't always easy to control. One approach that may help is to *be open and honest about outcomes and inputs.* People tend to overestimate how much their superiors are paid and, therefore, tend to feel that their own pay is not as high as it should be.[25] However, if information about pay is shared, inequitable feelings may not materialize.

EXPECTANCY THEORY: BELIEVING YOU CAN GET WHAT YOU WANT

Beyond seeking fair treatment on the job, people also are motivated by the belief that they can expect to achieve certain desired rewards by working hard to attain them. If you've ever put in long hours studying in the hopes of receiving an A in one of your classes, then you know what we mean. Believing that there may be a carrot dangling at the end of the stick and that it may be attained by putting forth the appropriate effort can be a very effective motivator.

This is one of the basic ideas behind the popularity of pay systems known as *merit pay plans,* or *pay-for-performance plans,* which formally establish links between job performance and rewards. Unfortunately, however, only 25 percent of employees see a clear link between good job performance and their pay raises. Clearly, companies are not doing all that they can to take advantage of this form of motivation. To better understand this process, let's take a look at a popular theory of motivation that addresses this issue—**expectancy theory.**

Three Components of Motivation

Expectancy theory claims that people will be motivated to exert effort on the job when they believe that doing so will help them achieve the things they want.[26] It assumes that people are rational beings who think about what they have to do to be rewarded and how much the reward means to them before they perform their jobs. Specifically, expectancy theory views motivation as the result of three different types of beliefs that people have. These are as follows:

➤ **Expectancy**—the belief that one's effort will affect performance
➤ **Instrumentality**—the belief that one's performance will be rewarded
➤ **Valence**—the perceived personal value of expected rewards

For a summary of these components and their role in the overall theory, see Figure 6.4. Let's now examine each more closely.

Expectancy

Sometimes people believe that putting forth a great deal of effort will help them get a lot accomplished. However, in other cases, people do not expect that their efforts will have much effect on how well they do. For example, an employee operating a faulty piece of equipment may have a very low *expectancy* that his or her efforts will lead to high levels of performance. Someone working under such conditions probably would not continue to exert much effort. After all, there is no good reason to go on trying to fill a bucket riddled with holes. Accordingly, good managers will do things that help their subordinates believe that their hard work will lead them to do their jobs better. With this in mind, training employees can be very effective in helping enhance expectancy beliefs (recall our discussion of training in Chapter 3). Indeed, a large part of working more effectively involves making sure that one's efforts will pay off.

Some companies have taken a more direct approach by soliciting and following their employees' suggestions about ways to improve their work efficiency. For example, United Electric Controls (a manufacturer of industrial temperature and pressure

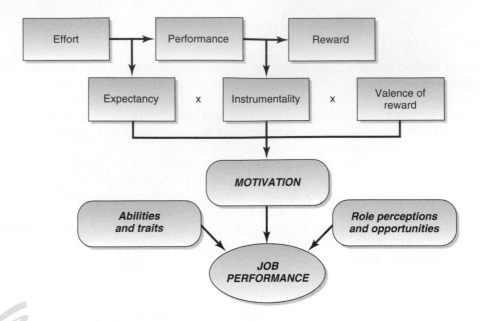

Figure 6.4 Overview of Expectancy Theory

Expectancy theory claims that motivation is the combined result of the three types of beliefs identified here—*expectancy, instrumentality,* and *valence of reward.* It also recognizes that motivation is only one of several determinants of job performance.

controls located in Watertown, Massachusetts) routinely asks its employees for ways to do their jobs more effectively. Since instituting this approach, the company's performance improved dramatically (e.g., on-time deliveries rose from 65 percent to 95 percent).

Instrumentality

Even if an employee performs at a high level, his or her motivation may suffer if that performance is not appropriately rewarded—that is, if the performance is not perceived as *instrumental* in bringing about the rewards. So, for example, an extremely productive employee may be poorly motivated if he or she has already reached the top level of pay given by the company. Recognizing this possibility, several organizations have crafted pay systems that explicitly link desired performance to rewards. These often are called **pay-for-performance** plans.

Consider, for example, the pay plan instituted for IBM's sales representatives. Previously, most of the pay these reps received was based on flat salary; their compensation was not linked to how well they did. Today, however, their pay is carefully tied to two factors that are essential to the company's success—profitability and customer satisfaction. So, instead of receiving commissions on the amount of the sale, as many salespeople do, 60 percent of IBMers' commissions are tied to the company's profit on that sale. As a result, the more money the company makes, the more the reps make. And, to make sure that the reps don't push only high-profit items that customers might not need, the remaining 40 percent of their commissions are based on customer satisfaction.

Checking on this, customers are regularly surveyed about the extent to which their sales representatives helped them meet their business objectives. The better the reps have done in this regard, the greater their commissions. Since introducing this plan a few years ago, IBM has been effective in reversing its unprofitable trend. Although there are certainly many factors responsible for this turnaround, experts are confident that this practice of clearly linking desired performance to individual rewards is a key factor.

Despite this success, it's important to note that not all pay-for-performance plans are equally successful. In fact, 83 percent of executives polled in a recent survey reported that their company's pay-for-performance plans were generally unsuccessful.[27] Generally, the problem in these cases lies not in the idea behind them, which is sound, but in the ways they are implemented.

These ineffective plans occur for several reasons. For example, tradition and political pressure dictate wages, which sometimes make them difficult to change. This is especially so among CEOs and other top-level executives. These individuals tend to be paid at very high levels, which some experts believe is unwarranted on the basis of their performance.[28] To give you an idea of just how high executive compensation may be, consider this: On average, it takes the CEO of an S&P 500 company only 3 hours to earn as much as a minimum-wage worker does in a whole year.[29]

Interestingly, CEOs' high levels of compensation, as you can see from Figure 6.5, are not always in keeping with the financial performance of their companies. Some CEOs who have led their companies to great success are paid far less than other CEOs whose companies are doing nowhere near as well. On the other hand, other executives arc (or now on Wall Street, wcre) paid lavishly despite their companies' poor financial performance. To avoid this in the U.S., a provision in the 2009 economic stimulus package (formally, the American Recovery and Reinvestment Act of 2009) prohibits cash bonuses and almost all other forms of incentive compensation to be given to the five most senior officers and the 20 highest-paid executives at large companies receiving federal bailout funds.[30]

Valence

Thus far, we have been assuming something that needs to be made explicit—namely, that the rewards the organization offers in exchange for attaining high levels of performance are desirable to the individuals receiving them. Using terminology from expectancy theory, they should have a positive *valence*. The **valence** of a reward refers to its degree of desirability in the eyes of the person receiving it.

This is no trivial point if you consider that the same so-called "rewards" are not likely to be equally desirable to everyone. For example, a $1,000 bonus may mean little to a multimillionaire CEO, although it's likely to be considered quite valuable to a minimum-wage employee struggling to make ends meet.

It's important to keep in mind that valence is not simply a matter of the amount of reward received but what that reward means to the person receiving it. And with the demographically diverse workforces found in many of today's organizations (see Chapter 5), it would be erroneous to assume that employees are equally attracted to the same rewards. For example, single, young employees might recognize the incentive value of a pay raise, whereas those taking care of families might prefer additional vacation days, improved insurance benefits, and day care or elder care facilities.

So, how can an organization find out what its employees want? Some companies have found a simple answer—ask them. For example, executives at PKF-Mark III

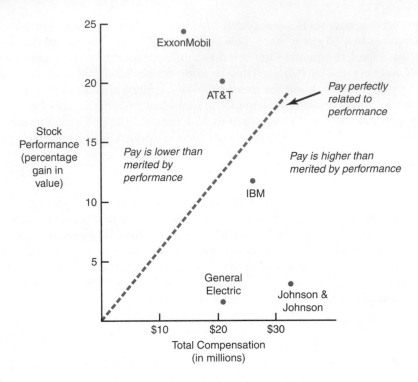

Figure 6.5   For Many CEOs, Pay Is *Not* Based on Performance

For CEOs of five of the largest U.S. corporations, the total compensation they received in 2007 was unrelated to the performance of their companies' stocks. Shown are companies whose CEOs were paid higher than (below the line) and lower than (above the line) what would have been merited by the financial performance of their companies.

(Source: Based on data reported by Kalwacki, 2008; see Note 29.)

(a construction company in Newton, Pennsylvania) have done just this. They put together a committee of employees representing a broad cross-section of the company and allowed them to select exactly what fringe benefits they wanted most. This led to a package of fringe benefits that was highly desirable to the employees.

Many more companies are taking a completely individualized approach, introducing **cafeteria-style benefit plans**—incentive systems allowing employees to select their fringe benefits from a menu of available alternatives.[31] Given that fringe benefits represent almost 40 percent of payroll costs, growing numbers of companies are recognizing the value of administering them flexibly. In fact, a survey found that such plans are in place in as many as half of all large companies (those employing over 5,000) and 22 percent of smaller companies (those with under 1,000 employees). For example, Primerica has had a flexible benefit plan in use since 1978—one that almost all of the employees believe is extremely beneficial to them. (Many of today's companies, large and small, are doing highly creative things to ensure that their employees can achieve rewards that have value to them. For a summary of some of these practices, see the Winning Practices section.)

Winning Practices

Going "Beyond the Fringe" in Benefits: Especially Creative Reward Practices

Traditionally, someone who gets a new job receives not only a salary but also a standard set of fringe benefits, such as health insurance, life insurance, a paid vacation, and a retirement plan. These days, however, these basic benefits are not enough to bring the best job prospects through the door. The incentives that motivate today's employees are far more varied and, in many cases, truly lavish.[32]

Suppose, for example, you work at the Framingham, Massachusetts, corporate headquarters of the office supply chain, Staples, and that you have children who need to be cared for while you are at work. No problem. You simply drop them off at the company's brand-new, $1.4 million, 8,000-square-foot child-care center near your office. Although there is a great need for onsite child-care facilities, only 11 percent of today's companies, like Staples, offer them. This benefit makes it possible for Staples employees to concentrate on their work without having to worry about who's taking care of their children.

If you work at Staples, you also have available to you a wonderful concierge service, which runs all kinds of errands for busy employees (e.g., picking up dry cleaning, washing cars), making their lives far easier. Staples isn't alone in offering concierge services. In fact, several companies have come into being in the past few years that offer concierge services to companies that seek them for their employees. For example, the San Francisco–based firm LesConcierges provides this service to employees of several well-known companies, including AOL (formerly America Online).

Some companies offer even more lavish benefits. For example, to attract employees to its out-of-the-way location in rural Wisconsin, Quad/Graphics, the printer, offers its employees rental apartments in its new $5 million complex. During its annual slow period, Rhino Foods (in Burlington, Vermont) helps its employees find jobs at other local businesses. Getting holidays off isn't so special; everyone gets them, right? Well, they might not be exactly the ones that you want to celebrate. This isn't a problem for employees of the Stamford, Connecticut, marketing firm Marquardt & Roche. This firm allows its employees to select any 11 out of 24 possible holidays.

Finally, some companies are even offering such benefits as pet insurance, auto financing, Internet access, home security systems, prepaid legal services, and even personal loans to their employees. If these examples are any indication, the days of finding so-called "standard" fringe benefits appear to be over. What passes for standard today is anybody's guess.

Emphasis on perception

It is important to emphasize that, like equity theory, expectancy theory focuses on people's perceptions of reality. It is *beliefs* about expectancy, instrumentality, and valence that matter as motivational forces. Of course, these beliefs are likely to be based at least in part on reality, but then again, people don't always perceive things accurately (a phenomenon discussed in Chapter 3). For example, a worker might not have an accurate view of how his or her pay is really determined. In the absence of a clear system for communicating information about pay, as well as the absence of any motivation to misperceive that information, it's likely that some employees might have inaccurate perceptions of the extent to which their performance is linked to the pay they receive.

The Role of Motivation in Performance

Thus far, we have discussed the three components of motivation identified by expectancy theory. However, expectancy theory views motivation as just one of several determinants of job performance. As shown at the bottom of Figure 6.4 (see p. 172), motivation combines with a person's skills and abilities, role perceptions, and opportunities to influence job performance.

It's no secret that the unique characteristics, special skills, and abilities of some people predispose them to perform their jobs better than others. For example, a tall, strong, well-coordinated person is likely to make a better professional basketball player than a very short, weak, uncoordinated one—even if that shorter person is highly motivated to succeed. Recognizing this, it would be a mistake to assume automatically that someone performing below par is poorly motivated. Instead, some poor performers may be very highly motivated but lack the knowledge or skills needed to succeed. With this in mind, companies often make big investments in training employees to ensure that they have what it takes to succeed (see Chapter 3), regardless of their levels of motivation. In other words, both motivation and abilities/skills contribute to task performance, and managers need to focus on both.

Expectancy theory also recognizes the role of *opportunities to perform* one's job. After all, even the best employees may perform at low levels if their opportunities are limited. This may occur, for example, if there is an economic downturn in a salesperson's territory or if the company's available inventory is insufficient to meet sales demand.

Finally, it is important to note that expectancy theory recognizes that job performance will be influenced by people's *role perceptions*—that is, what they believe is expected of them on the job. To the extent that there are uncertainties about what one's job duties may be, performance may suffer. For example, a shop foreman who believes his primary job duty is to teach new employees how to use the equipment may find that his performance is downgraded by a supervisor who believes he should be spending more time doing routine paperwork instead. In this case the foreman's performance wouldn't suffer due to any deficit in motivation but because of misunderstandings regarding what the job entails.

In conclusion, expectancy theory has done a good job of sensitizing managers to several key determinants of motivation, variables that frequently can be controlled. Beyond this, the theory clarifies the important—but not unique—role that motivation plays in determining job performance.

GOAL SETTING: TAKING AIM AT PERFORMANCE TARGETS

Just as people are motivated to satisfy their needs on the job, to be paid fairly, and to act in ways consistent with their beliefs about reality, they also are motivated to strive for and to attain goals. The process of setting goals is one of the most important motivational forces operating on people in organizations.[33] The term **goal setting** refers to the process of setting goals in a manner that motivates workers to raise their performance. In this section, we will describe a prominent theory of *goal setting* and then identify some practical suggestions for setting goals effectively.

Goal Setting Theory

Suppose that you are doing a task, such as word processing, when a performance goal is assigned. You are now expected, for example, to enter 70 words per minute (wpm) instead of the 60 wpm you've been doing all along. Would you work hard to meet this goal, or would you simply give up? Some insight into the question of how people respond to assigned goals is provided by a conceptualization known as **goal setting theory.**[34] This theory claims that an assigned goal influences people's beliefs about being able to perform the task in question (i.e., the personality variable of *self-efficacy*, described in Chapter 3) and their commitment to goals. Both of these factors, in turn, influence performance.

Goal setting theory has been called "quite easily the single most dominant theory in the field [of organizational behavior]."[35] The basic idea behind goal setting theory is that a goal serves as a motivator because it causes people to compare their present capacity to perform with that required to succeed at the goal (for an overview of the theory, see Figure 6.6). To the extent that people believe they will fall short of a goal, they will feel dissatisfied and will work harder to attain it so long as they believe it is possible for them to do so. When they succeed at meeting a goal, they feel competent and successful.[36] Having a goal enhances performance in large part because the goal makes clear exactly what type and level of performance is expected.

The theory also claims that assigned goals will lead to the acceptance of those goals as personal goals. In other words, they will be accepted as one's own. This is the idea of **goal commitment**—the extent to which people invest themselves in meeting a goal, their determination to reach a goal.[37] Indeed, it has been shown that people

Figure 6.6   Goal Setting Theory: An Overview

According to *goal setting theory*, when people are challenged to meet higher goals, several things happen. First, they assess their desire to attain the goal as well as their chances of attaining the goal. Together, these judgments affect their *goal commitment*. Second, they assess the extent to which meeting the goal will enhance their beliefs in their own *self-efficacy*. When levels of goal commitment and self-efficacy are high, people are motivated to perform at the goal level.

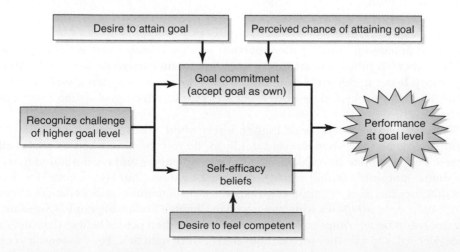

become more committed to a goal to the extent that they desire to attain that goal and believe they have a reasonable chance of doing so.[38] Likewise, the more strongly people believe they are capable of meeting a goal, the more strongly they will accept it as their own. By contrast, workers who perceive themselves as being physically incapable of meeting performance goals, for example, are generally not committed to meeting them and do not strive to do so.[39]

Research also has shown that goal commitment combines with goal difficulty to influence task performance.[40] In other words, as shown in Figure 6.6, people perform at the highest levels when they are striving to meet difficult goals to which they are highly committed. By contrast, people will not work hard to achieve difficult goals when they are not highly committed to them. For example, suppose you don't care about getting good grades in school (i.e., you are not committed to achieving academic success). In this case, you would not work very hard regardless of how easy or difficult the course may be (see the flat line at the bottom of Figure 6.7). By contrast, if you are highly committed to achieving success, then a difficult (but acceptable) goal (e.g., getting a good grade in a very challenging course) will have more meaning to you than an easy goal (e.g., getting a good grade in an easy course) because it enhances your self-efficacy. As a result, you will work harder to achieve it.

Finally, the model claims that beliefs about both self-efficacy and goal commitment influence task performance. This makes sense insofar as people are willing to exert greater effort when they believe they will succeed than when they believe their efforts will be in vain.[41] Moreover, goals that are not personally accepted will have little capacity to guide behavior. In fact, research has shown that the more strongly people are committed to meeting goals, the better they will perform.[42] In general, goal setting theory has been supported by several studies, suggesting that it is a valuable source of insight into how the goal setting process works.[43]

Guidelines for Setting Effective Performance Goals

Because researchers have been actively involved in studying the goal setting process for many years, it is possible to summarize their findings in the form of principles. These represent very practical suggestions that practicing managers can use to enhance motivation.

Assign specific goals

In our word processing example, the supervisor set a goal that was very specific (70 wpm) and also somewhat difficult to attain (10 wpm faster than current performance). Would you perform better under these conditions than if the supervisor merely said something general, like "do your best to improve"? Decades of research on goal setting suggest that the answer is "yes."

Indeed, people perform at higher levels when asked to meet specific high-performance goals than when directed simply to "do your best," or when no goal at all is assigned. People tend to find specific goals quite challenging and are motivated to try to meet them—not only to fulfill management's expectations, but also to convince themselves that they can do it. Scientists have explained that attaining goals enhances employees' beliefs in their *self-efficacy*, which we noted in Chapter 3 refers to people's assessments of themselves as being competent and successful. And, when people believe that they can, in fact, succeed at a task, they will be motivated to work hard at it. For this reason people

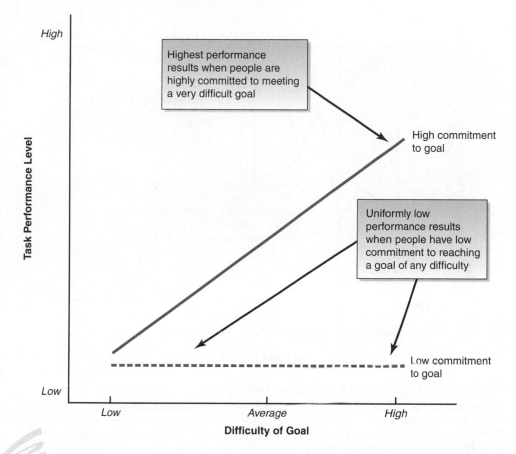

Figure 6.7   Effects of Goal Commitment and Goal Difficulty on Task Performance

Research has shown that task performance is influenced by goal commitment and goal difficulty in the manner summarized here. That is, performance is highest when people are highly committed to attaining a difficult goal. However, people who are not committed to meeting a goal perform poorly on tasks at all levels of difficulty.

(Source: Adapted from Klein et al., 1999; see Note 40.)

are motivated to pursue specific goals, ones that readily enable them to define their accomplishments, enhancing their self-efficacy beliefs.

To demonstrate this principle, let's consider a classic study conducted at an Oklahoma lumber camp owned by Weyerhauser, a major producer of paper products.[44] The initial step in the paper-making process involves cutting down trees and hauling them to the sawmill, where they are ground into pulp. For some time, loggers were loading the trucks to only about 60 percent of their maximum capacity, resulting in wasted trips that added considerable cost. To help solve this problem a goal setting program was introduced. A specific goal was set: The loggers were challenged to load the trucks to 94 percent of their capacity before returning to the mill.

How effective was this goal in raising performance? The results, summarized in Figure 6.8, show that the goal was extremely effective. In fact, not only was the specific

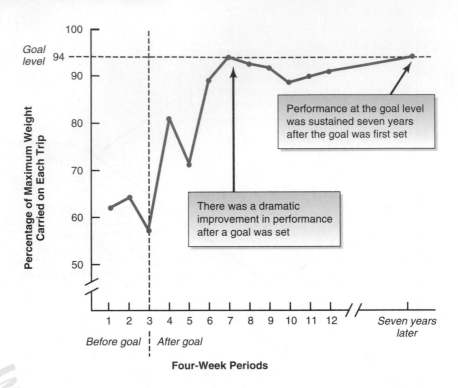

Figure 6.8   Goal Setting at a Logging Camp: An Impressive Demonstration

The performance of loggers loading timber onto trucks markedly improved after a specific, difficult goal was set. The percentage of the maximum possible weight loaded onto the trucks rose from approximately 60 percent before any goal was set to approximately 94 percent—the goal level—after the goal was set. Performance remained at this level as long as seven years.

(Source: Adapted from Latham & Baldes, 1975; see Note 33.)

goal effective in raising performance to the goal level in just a few weeks, but the effects were long-lasting as well. In fact, the loggers sustained this level of performance as long as seven years later! The resulting savings logged in by the company have been considerable, a classic goal setting success story.

Importantly, these dramatic effects are not unusual, nor are they limited to this special setting. Rather, this study is just one of many that highlight the effectiveness of setting specific, challenging performance goals in a variety of organizational contexts. For example, setting specific goals also has been used to help improve many other kinds of organizational behaviors, such as reducing absenteeism and lowering the occurrence of industrial accidents.

Assign difficult but acceptable performance goals

The goal set at the logging camp was successful not only because it was specific, but also because it pushed crew members to a higher standard. Obviously, a goal that is too easy to attain will *not* bring about the desired increments in performance. For example, if you already type at 60 wpm, a goal of 50 wpm, although specific, would probably *lower* your performance. The key point is that a goal must be difficult as well as specific for it to raise performance.

At the same time, however, people will work hard to reach challenging goals so long as these are within the limits of their capability. When goals become too difficult, performance suffers because people reject those goals as unrealistic and unattainable. As an illustration, let's pick up our earlier example about working to achieve success in school. The point is that you may work much harder as a student in a class that challenges your ability than in one that is very easy. In all likelihood, however, you would probably give up trying if the goal was far too difficult (such as if the only way of passing was to get perfect scores on all exams—a standard you would reject as being unacceptable). In short, specific goals are most effective if they are set neither so low as to make success automatic nor so high as to make success unattainable.

As you might imagine, this phenomenon occurs in organizations. For example, FedEx's customer service agents are expected to answer customers' questions within 140 seconds. Although this goal initially was considered difficult when it was imposed, employees eventually met—or exceeded—this goal and enjoyed the satisfaction of knowing they succeeded at this task.

How should goals be set in a manner that strengthens employees' commitment to them? One obvious way of enhancing goal acceptance is to involve employees in the goal setting process. Research on workers' participation in goal setting has demonstrated that people better accept goals that they have been involved in setting than goals that have been assigned by their supervisors—and they work harder as a result.[45] Most of today's executives generally agree that it is a good idea to let employees figure out the best way to meet new goals. According to Bob Freese, CEO of Alphatronix Inc., in Research Triangle Park, North Carolina, "We let employees tell us when they can accomplish a project and what resources they need. Virtually always they set higher goals than we would ever set for them."[46]

Participation in the goal setting process may have these beneficial effects for several reasons. First, people are more likely to better understand and appreciate goals they had a hand in setting themselves than those that are merely presented to them. Second, employees are likely to be committed to attaining goals they have set themselves because they must psychologically rationalize their decisions to set those goals.[47] (After all, one can hardly justify setting a specific goal and then not working to attain it.) Third, because workers often have more direct knowledge about what it takes to do a job than their supervisors, they are in a good position to come up with goals that are acceptably high but not unreasonable. For these various reasons, allowing people to participate in the setting of their own performance goals makes good sense.

Provide feedback concerning goal attainment

The final condition for setting effective goals appears to be glaringly obvious, although it is not followed in practice as often as you might expect: Provide feedback about the extent to which goals have been met. Just as golfers can improve their games when they learn where their tee shots have landed, so too do workers benefit by feedback about how closely they are approaching their performance goals.

A study of the performance of work crews in the U.S. Air Force illustrates the importance of using feedback in conjunction with goal setting.[48] A standardized index of job performance was used to measure five different groups repeatedly over a two-year period. During the first nine months, a baseline measure of effectiveness was taken that was used to compare the relative impact of feedback and goal setting. The groups then received feedback for five months (reports detailing how well they performed on various performance measures). Following this, the goal setting phase of the study was begun. During this period, the crew members set goals for themselves with respect to their performance on various measures. Then, for the final five months, in addition to the feedback and goal setting, an incentive (time off from work) was made available to crew members who met their goals.

It was found that feedback and goal setting dramatically increased group effectiveness. Group feedback improved performance approximately 50 percent over the baseline level. The addition of group goal setting improved it 75 percent over baseline. These findings show that the combination of goal setting and feedback helps raise the effectiveness of group performance. Groups that know how well they're doing and have a target goal to shoot for tend to perform very well. Providing incentives, however, improved performance only negligibly. The real incentive seemed to be meeting the challenge of performing up to the level specified by the goal.

In sum, goal setting is a very effective tool managers can use to motivate people. Setting a specific, acceptably difficult goal and providing feedback about progress toward that goal greatly enhance job performance. To demonstrate the effectiveness of goal setting in your own behavior, complete the Group Exercise on pages 189–190.

DESIGNING JOBS THAT MOTIVATE

As you may recall from Chapter 1, Frederick W. Taylor's approach to stimulating work performance was to design jobs so that people worked as efficiently as possible. No wasted movements and no wasted time added up to efficient performance, or so Taylor believed. However, Taylor failed to consider one important thing: The repetitive machine-like movements required of his workers were highly routine and monotonous. And, not surprisingly, people became bored with such jobs and frequently quit.

Fortunately, today's organizational scientists have found several ways of designing jobs that may not only be performed very efficiently but that are also highly pleasant and enjoyable. This is the basic principle behind **job design,** the process of creating jobs that people desire to perform because they are so inherently appealing.[49] We review several approaches to job design here.

Job Enlargement: Doing More of the Same Kind of Work

If you've ever purchased a greeting card, chances are good that you've picked up at least one made by American Greetings, one of the largest greeting card companies in the United States. What you might not know is that that this Cleveland, Ohio–based organization recently redesigned some 400 jobs in its creative division. Now, rather than always working exclusively on, say, Christmas cards, employees will be able to move back and forth between different teams, such as those working on birthday ribbons, humorous mugs, and Valentine's Day gift bags. These employees enjoy the variety, as do those at RJR Nabisco, Corning, and Eastman Kodak, other companies that allow some employees to make such lateral moves.

Scientists have referred to what these companies are doing as **job enlargement**—the practice of giving employees more tasks to perform at the same level. There's no higher responsibility involved or any greater skills, just a wider variety of the same types of tasks. Enlarged jobs are said to be changed *horizontally* because people's level of responsibility stays the same. The idea behind job enlargement is simple: You can decrease boredom by giving people a greater variety of jobs to do. (See the graph in the top right portion of Figure 6.9.)

Do job enlargement programs work? To answer this question, consider the results of a study comparing the job performance of people doing enlarged and unenlarged jobs.[50] In the unenlarged jobs different employees performed separate paperwork tasks such as preparing, sorting, coding, and keypunching various forms. The enlarged jobs combined these various functions into larger jobs performed by the same people. Although it was more difficult and expensive to train people to perform the enlarged jobs than the separate jobs, important benefits resulted. In particular, employees expressed greater job satisfaction and less boredom. And, because one person followed the whole job all the way through, greater opportunities to correct errors existed. Not surprisingly, customers were satisfied with the result.

In a follow-up investigation of the same company conducted two years later, however, it was found that not all the beneficial effects continued.[51] Notably, employee satisfaction leveled off, and the rate of errors went up, suggesting that as employees got used to their enlarged jobs they found them less interesting and stopped paying attention to all the details. Hence, although job enlargement may help improve job performance, its effects are only short-lived. It appears that the problem with enlarging jobs is that after a while people get bored with them, and they need to be enlarged still further. Because it is impractical to continue enlarging jobs all the time, the value of this approach is rather limited.

Job Enrichment: Increasing Required Skills and Responsibilities

As an alternative, consider another approach taken to redesign jobs. For many years, Procter & Gamble manufactured detergent by having large numbers of people perform a series of narrow tasks. Then, in the early 1960s, realizing that this rigid approach did little to utilize the full range of skills and abilities of employees, P&G executive David Swanson introduced a new way to make detergent in the company's Augusta, Georgia, plant. The technicians worked together in teams (see Chapter 9) to take control over large parts of the production process. They set production schedules, hired new co-workers, and took responsibility over evaluating each others' performance, including the process of deciding who was going to get raises. In short, they not only performed more tasks but also ones at higher levels of skill and responsibility. The general name given to this approach is **job enrichment.** Enriched jobs are said to be changed *vertically* because people's level of responsibility goes up. For a summary comparison between job enrichment and job enlargement, see Figure 6.9.

One of the best-known job enrichment programs was the one developed by Volvo, the Swedish auto manufacturer. In response to serious dissension within its workforce in the late 1960s, the company's president at the time, Pehr Gyllenhammar, introduced job enrichment in its Kalmar assembly plant. Cars were assembled by 25 groups of approximately 20 workers who were each responsible for one part of the car's assembly

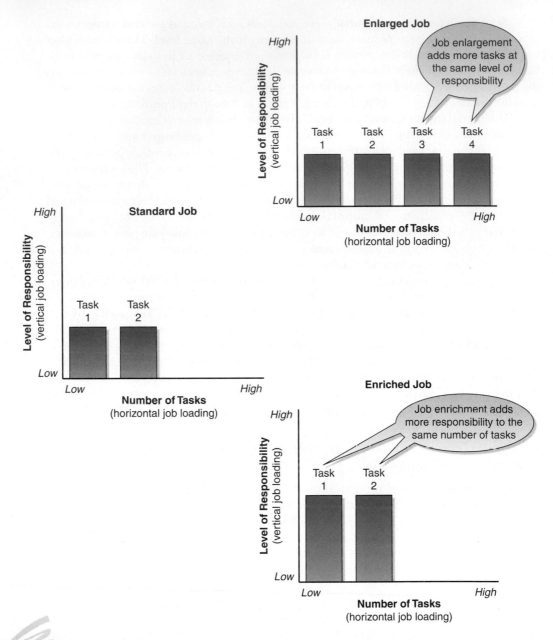

Figure 6.9   Job Enlargement and Job Enrichment: A Comparison

Redesigning jobs by increasing the number of tasks performed at the same level (*horizontal job loading*) is referred to as *job enlargement*. Redesigning jobs by increasing the employees' level of responsibility and control (*vertical job loading*) is referred to as *job enrichment*.

(e.g., engine, electrical system). In contrast to the traditional assembly-line method of manufacturing cars, Volvo's work teams are set up so they can freely plan, organize, and inspect their own work. In time, workers became more satisfied with their jobs and the plant experienced a significant reduction in turnover and absenteeism.

Although job enrichment programs also have been successful at other organizations, several factors limit their popularity. First, there is the difficulty of implementation. Redesigning existing facilities so that jobs can be enriched is often prohibitively expensive. Besides, the technology needed to perform certain jobs makes it impractical for them to be redesigned. Another impediment is the lack of universal employee acceptance. Although many relish it, job enrichment is not for everyone. Some people do *not* desire the additional responsibility associated with performing enriched jobs.

The Job Characteristics Model

Precisely *how* do you enrich a job? What elements of a job need to be enriched for it to be effective? An attempt to expand the idea of job enrichment, known as the **job characteristics model,** provides an answer to these important questions.[52]

Elements of the job characteristics model

This approach assumes that jobs can be designed to help people get enjoyment out of their jobs and care about the work they do. The model identifies how jobs can be designed to help people feel that they are doing meaningful and valuable work. In particular, it specifies that enriching certain elements of jobs alters people's psychological states in a manner that enhances their work effectiveness. Specifically, the model identifies five *core job dimensions* that help create three *critical psychological states,* leading, in turn, to several beneficial *personal and work outcomes* (see Figure 6.10).

The five critical job dimensions are *skill variety, task identity, task significance, autonomy,* and *feedback*. Let's take a closer look at these.

➤ **Skill variety** is the extent to which a job requires using several different skills and talents that an employee has. For example, a restaurant manager whose job has high skill variety will perform many different tasks (e.g., maintaining sales records, handling customer complaints, scheduling staff, supervising repair work, and the like).

➤ **Task identity** is the degree to which a job requires doing a whole task from beginning to end. For example, tailors will have high task identity if they do everything associated with making an entire suit (e.g., measuring the client, selecting the fabric, cutting and sewing it, and altering it to fit).

➤ **Task significance** is the amount of impact a job is believed to have on others. For example, medical researchers working on a cure for a deadly disease surely recognize the importance of their work to the world at large. Even more modest contributions can be recognized as being significant to the extent that employees understand the role of their jobs in the overall mission of their organizations.

➤ **Autonomy** is the extent to which employees have the freedom and discretion to plan, schedule, and carry out their jobs as desired. For example, a team of Procter & Gamble employees was put in charge of making all the arrangements necessary for the building of a new multi-million dollar facility for making concentrated Downy.

➤ **Feedback** is the extent to which people are given information about the effectiveness of their performance. For example, telemarketing representatives regularly receive information about how many calls they make per day and the monetary values of the sales made.

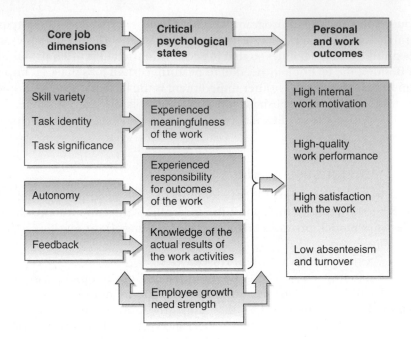

Figure 6.10   The Job Characteristics Model: Basic Components

The *job characteristics model* stipulates that certain *core job dimensions* lead to certain *critical psychological states*, which in turn lead to several beneficial *personal and work outcomes*. The model also recognizes that these relationships are strongest among individuals with high levels of *growth need strength*.

The job characteristics model specifies that these job dimensions have important effects on various critical psychological states. Specifically, skill variety, task identity, and task significance jointly contribute to a task's *experienced meaningfulness*. A task is considered meaningful insofar as it is experienced as being highly important, valuable, and worthwhile. Jobs that provide a great deal of autonomy are said to make people feel *personally responsible and accountable for their work*. When they are free to decide what to do and how to do it, they feel more responsible for the results, whether good or bad. Finally, effective feedback is said to give employees *knowledge of the results of their work*. When a job is designed to provide people with information about the effects of their actions, they are better able to develop an understanding of how effectively they have performed, and such knowledge improves their work.

The job characteristics model specifies that the three critical psychological states affect various personal and work outcomes—namely, people's feelings of motivation, the quality of work performed, satisfaction with work, absenteeism, and turnover. The higher the experienced meaningfulness of work, responsibility for the work performed, and knowledge of results, the more positive the personal and work benefits will be. When they perform jobs that incorporate high levels of the five core job dimensions, people should feel highly motivated, perform high-quality work, be highly satisfied with their jobs, be absent infrequently, and be unlikely to resign from their jobs.

We should also note that the model is theorized to be especially effective in describing the behavior of individuals who are high in *growth need strength*—that is, people who have a high need for personal growth and development. People not particularly interested in improving themselves on the job are not expected to experience the theorized psychological reactions to the core job dimensions, nor consequently, to enjoy the beneficial personal and work outcomes predicted by the model. By introducing this variable, the job characteristics model recognizes the important limitation of job enrichment noted earlier—not everyone wants enriched jobs or benefits from them.

Assessing the motivating potential of jobs

Based on the proposed relationship between the core job dimensions and their associated psychological reactions, the model claims that job motivation will be highest when the jobs performed rate high on the various dimensions. To assess this, a questionnaire known as the Job Diagnostic Survey (JDS) has been developed to measure the degree to which various job characteristics are present in a particular job. Based on responses to the JDS, we can make predictions about the degree to which a job has the potential to motivate people who perform it. Research has revealed that the higher a job's score on the JDS, the more highly motivated people are to perform it and the greater are the personal and work outcomes that result from performing it (shown on the right side of Figure 6.10).[53]

Suggestions for enhancing the motivating potential of jobs

The job characteristics model specifies several ways in which jobs can be designed to enhance their motivating potential. For example, instead of using several workers, each of whom performs a separate part of a whole job, it would be better to have each person perform the entire job. Doing so helps provide greater skill variety and task identity. For example, Corning Glass Works in Medford, Massachusetts, redesigned jobs so that people who assembled laboratory hot plates put together entire units instead of contributing a single part to the assembly process.

The job characteristics model also suggests that jobs should be set up so that the person performing a service (such as an auto mechanic) comes into contact with the recipient of the service (such as the car owner). Jobs designed in this manner will not only help the employee by providing feedback but also by enhancing skill variety (e.g., talking to customers in addition to fixing cars) and building autonomy (by giving people the freedom to manage their own relationships with clients). This suggestion has been implemented at Sea-Land Service, the large containerized ocean-shipping company. After this company's mechanics, clerks, and crane operators started meeting with customers, they became much more productive. Having faces to associate with the once abstract jobs they did clearly helped them take the jobs more seriously. After all, they didn't want to let down someone they knew.

Another implication of the job characteristics model is that jobs should be designed to give employees as much feedback as possible. The more people know how well they're doing (be it from customers, supervisors, or co-workers), the better equipped they are to take appropriate corrective action (see Chapter 3). As a case in point, Childress Buick, the Phoenix, Arizona, auto dealership, suffered serious customer dissatisfaction and employee retention problems before the owner, Rusty Childress, encouraged his employees to rely on feedback from customers and fellow employees to discover ways of doing their jobs better.

Back to the Case

Answer the following questions about this chapter's Making the Case (pp. 160–161) to illustrate insights you have derived about the material in this chapter.

1. What theories of motivation explain why Costco is so effective at motivating its employees? How so?
2. Of the various things done to keep members of Costco's workforce motivated, what tactics do you believe are most effective? What is the basis for this answer?
3. Based on the suggestions in this chapter, what additional steps might Costco take to motivate its employees?

You Be the Consultant

Boosting Low Morale Among Employees

Suppose you were just hired by executives of a large manufacturing company to help resolve problems of poor morale that have been plaguing the workforce. Turnover and absenteeism are high, and performance is at an all-time low. Answer the following questions relevant to this situation based on the material in this chapter.

1. Suppose, after interviewing the workers, you found that they believed that no one cared how well they were doing their jobs. What theories could help explain this problem? Applying these approaches, what would you recommend the company do to resolve this situation?

2. Company officials tell you that the employees are well paid, adding to their surprise about the low morale. However, your interviews reveal that the employees themselves feel otherwise. Theoretically, why is this a problem? What could be done to help?

3. "I'm bored with my job," an employee tells you, and you believe he speaks for many within the company. What could be done to make the jobs more interesting to those who perform them? What are the limitations of your plan? Would it work equally well for all employees?

SELF-ASSESSMENT EXERCISE

What Rewards Do You Value?

According to expectancy theory, one thing companies can do to motivate employees is to give rewards that have positive valence to them. What work-related rewards have the greatest value to you? Completing this questionnaire will help you answer this question.

Directions

Following are 10 work-related rewards. For each, circle the number that best describes the value that particular reward has for you personally. Use the following scale to express your feelings: 1 = no value at all, 2 = slight value, 3 = moderate value, 4 = great value, 5 = extremely great value.

Reward	Personal value				
Good pay	1	2	3	4	5
Prestigious title	1	2	3	4	5
Vacation time	1	2	3	4	5
Job security	1	2	3	4	5
Recognition	1	2	3	4	5
Interesting work	1	2	3	4	5
Pleasant conditions	1	2	3	4	5
Chances to advance	1	2	3	4	5
Flexible schedule	1	2	3	4	5
Friendly co-workers	1	2	3	4	5

Discussion Questions

1. Based on your answers, which rewards do you value most? Which do you value least? Do you think these preferences will change as you get older and perform different jobs? If so, how?
2. To what extent do you believe you will be able to attain each of these rewards on your job? Do you expect that the chances of receiving these rewards will improve in the future? Why or why not?
3. Do you believe that the rewards you value most are also the ones valued by other people? Are these reward preferences likely to be the same for all people everywhere or at least for all workers performing the same job in the same company?

GROUP EXERCISE

Demonstrating the Effectiveness of Goal Setting

The tendency for specific, difficult goals to enhance task performance is well established. The following exercise is designed to help you demonstrate this effect yourself. All you need is a class of students willing to participate and a few simple supplies.

Directions

1. Select a page of text from a book and make several photocopies. Then carefully count the words and number each word on one of the copies. This will be your score sheet.
2. Find another class of 30 or more students who don't know anything about goal setting. (We don't want their knowledge of the phenomenon to bias the results.) On a random basis, divide the students into three equal-size groups.
3. Ask the students in the first group ("baseline" group) to copy as much of the text as they can onto another piece of paper, giving them exactly one minute to do so. Direct them to work at a fast pace. Using the score sheet created in step 1, identify the highest number of words counted by any one of the students. Then multiply this number by 2. This will be the specific, difficult goal level.
4. Ask the students in another group ("specific goal" group) to copy the text on the same printed page for exactly one minute. Tell them to try to reach the specific goal number identified in step 3.

5. Repeat this process with the third group ("do your best" group) but instead of giving them a specific goal, direct them to "try to do your best at this task."

6. Compute the average number of words copied in the "specific goal" group and the "do your best" group. Have your instructor compute the appropriate statistical test (a *t*-test, in this case) to determine the statistical significance of the difference between the performance levels of the groups.

Discussion Questions

1. Was there, in fact, a statistically significant difference between the performance levels of the two groups? If so, did students in the "specific goal" group outperform those in the "do your best" group, as expected? What does this reveal about the effectiveness of goal setting?

2. If the predicted findings were not supported, why do you suppose this happened? What was it about the procedure that may have led to this failure? Was the specific goal (twice the fastest speed in the "baseline" group) too high, making the goal unreachable? Or was it too low, making the specific goal too easy?

3. What do you think would happen if the goal were lowered, making it easier, or raised, making it more difficult?

Interpersonal Behavior in the Workplace

Learning Objectives

After reading this chapter, you will be able to:

1. **DESCRIBE** two types of psychological contracts in work relationships and the types of trust associated with each.

2. **DESCRIBE** organizational citizenship behavior and **IDENTIFY** ways in which it may be promoted.

3. **IDENTIFY** ways in which cooperation can be promoted in the workplace.

4. **DESCRIBE** competition and why it is inevitable in organizations.

5. **DESCRIBE** the causes and effects of conflict in organizations.

6. **IDENTIFY** three forms of deviant organizational behavior and **EXPLAIN** how to minimize them.

3 GOOD REASONS why you should care about . . .

Interpersonal Behavior

You should care about interpersonal behavior at work because:

1. Cooperation between people can make life on the job not only more pleasant but more productive as well.
2. The effects of conflict can be beneficial in organizations, if managed properly, but harmful if mismanaged.
3. Managers can take several effective steps to reduce the likelihood of deviant organizational behavior, thereby avoiding its disruptive effects.

Making the Case for Interpersonal Relationships at Work

NASCAR: The Etiquette of Drafting

To the uninformed, there's really not much to it. A commentator once described a NASCAR race as simply a matter of "go straight, turn left, go straight, turn left," round and round again. Do this faster than anyone else 200 times and you've won NASCAR's biggest, richest, and most prestigious

(continued)

race, the Daytona 500, pocketing about $1.5 million for your trouble. Ask any of NASCAR's 75 million fans who are in the know, however, and they'll tell you that there's far more to the sport of racing high-performance stock cars than meets the untrained eye.

A great car, a talented crew, and drivers with nerves of steel can be taken for granted as keys to success, but to win races, drivers must know "how to compete by cooperating." And this, in a word, requires "drafting," the practice of following closely behind the car ahead of you so as to get sucked into its vacuum. Due to aerodynamics, drafting boosts the speed of both cars—not much, but enough to make all the difference in a long race, such as the annual 500-mile events at Daytona and Talladega. The more cars in a drafting line—at any given time, these typically range from a pair of cars to about 10—the more each benefits.

Knowing that if they don't draft, they lose, the best NASCAR drivers are adept at working multi-car draft lines and out-competing the others by out-cooperating them. Suppose a driver wants to pull ahead by swinging out of the pack, for example. He or she can do so, but unless another car pulls up behind, the absence of a draft will cause the car to lose momentum and fall back many places. In a draft line, both drivers benefit, but because each wants to win, these partnerships are fleeting. One moment, a driver may seek a nearby drafting partner to help move ahead, but inevitably, and just as quickly, he or she will defect in search of another. These fleeting partnerships between rivals at 190 mph may last a few seconds or a few laps, but in all cases they are essential.

Winning drivers know when to join draft lines (or to invite others to join theirs) and when to defect. This interplay between cooperating and competing requires trusting other drivers to know and abide by the unspoken rules of the game. For this reason, veteran racers are wary of having rookies as draft partners until they have earned the confidence of the other drivers on the track. Trust also is an issue for allies, members of the same racing team. Confident that cooperation will be forthcoming, other cars from the driver's racing team are inclined to be multi-lap draft partners. Still, because drivers seek individual glory, even members of their own teams become rivals when the end of the race is near and the driver of the second-place car wants to "slingshot" ahead of the lead car to cross the finish line at the last second.

As you might imagine, having drafting partners enter a line requires close communication. Drivers sometimes have pre-race arrangements to cooperate with one another, but most drafting partnerships emerge on the fly. To broker these deals, drivers may use hand gestures, but these might be difficult to see and, of course, removing one's hands from the steering wheel for even a fleeting second can spell disaster. Instead, most deals are made by drivers communicating by radio with spotters, diplomatic envoys in the stands who negotiate drafting deals with the spotters of other drivers. These partnerships may last only the 10 seconds required to pull ahead of another rival, but of course, the helping driver is expected to return the favor later in the race if needed. After all, on the racetrack, as in other things in life, "what goes around comes around."

Although you might be unaware of these dynamics as you watch a NASCAR race, they are potent illustrations that it involves far more than just driving around in circles. Being a winning NASCAR driver also requires good interpersonal relationships with other drivers. As one expert put it, "A driver's reputation as a trustworthy person may affect the outcome as much as his reputation as a driver."[1]

Of course, the same could be said of people in many other lines of work, including ones that are less glamorous and far safer. Indeed, the themes highlighted here—trust, negotiation, cooperation, and competition—play prominent roles in just about any job. These processes of working with others and against them, broadly referred to as **interpersonal behavior,** are the focus of this chapter. Specifically, we will summarize a wide array of interpersonal behaviors that occur in the workplace and describe how they influence the way people work and how they feel about their jobs and organizations.

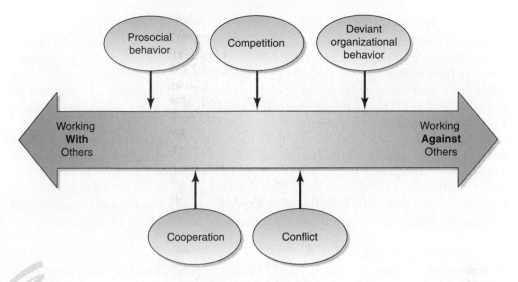

Figure 7.1   Varieties of Interpersonal Behavior

The five types of interpersonal behavior observed in organizations, and presented in this chapter, can be summarized as falling along a continuum ranging from those involving working with other people to those involving working against them.

Figure 7.1 identifies the major forms of interpersonal behavior in the workplace that we will examine. This diagram organizes interpersonal behaviors along a continuum ranging from those that involve working with others, shown on the left, to those that involve working against others, shown on the right. This forms a useful road map of how we will proceed in this chapter.

Beginning on the left, we first will examine *prosocial behavior*—the tendency for people to help others on the job, sometimes even when there doesn't appear to be anything in it for them. Following this, we will discuss situations in which people help each other and receive help from them—that is, the tendency to *cooperate*. In NASCAR races and elsewhere in the world of business, as you know, people and entire companies don't always work with each other; they also *compete* against each other—that is, as one tries to win, it forces the other to lose. Under such circumstances, it is not unusual for *conflict* to emerge, breeding ill-will. And, when taken to the extreme, this results in *deviant* behavior—extreme acts such as stealing from the company or even harming another person. Before examining these various forms of behavior, we begin by describing some of the basic dynamics that guide all forms of interpersonal behavior in the workplace.

THE DYNAMICS OF INTERPERSONAL RELATIONSHIPS

To appreciate interpersonal behavior in organizations you must understand the basic building blocks of social relationships in general. What factors influence the kinds of relationships people develop among them? Although the answer to this question is more complicated than we can address here, we can identify two important factors—*psychological contracts* and *trust*.

Psychological Contracts: Our Expectations of Others

Whenever people have relationships with each other, they are bound to have certain expectations about what things will be like and how each will behave. Leave a phone message for a friend, for example, and you expect him or her to return your call. Put in a fair day's work for your boss, and you expect to get paid in return. These examples illustrate what is known as the **psychological contract**—a person's beliefs about what is expected of another in a relationship.[2]

Although these are not legal contracts, they guide what we expect of others in much the same way. However, unlike legal contracts, in which the terms are made explicit, psychological contracts are perceptual in nature. Not surprisingly, there may well be differences of opinion regarding psychological contracts: What one person expects may not be exactly what the other expects. As you know from experience, such perceptual disagreements often make interpersonal relationships challenging.

Transactional contracts

As you might imagine, the nature of the psychological contracts we have with others depends on the kind of relationships we have with them. This is particularly clear in the workplace. Suppose, for example, that you are a temporary employee working in the order-fulfillment department of a large retail e-business during the busy holiday period. You know that your relationship with your employer will have a definite ending and that it is based on a clearly defined set of economic terms. You go to work each day as scheduled, you do your job as directed, you get your paycheck, and at the end of the season, it's over. In this case, you would be said to have a **transactional contract** with your employer.[3] This relationship is characterized by an exclusively economic focus, a brief time span, an unchanging nature, and is narrow and well defined in scope.

I-deals

Recently, scientists have begun studying a particular form of transactional contract that constitutes a special, nonstandard arrangement that may be of longer duration. Consider these examples.

➤ Lindsey is a claims adjustor for a major insurance company who usually works from 9:00 a.m. to 5:00 p.m. Now, she needs to leave the office at 4:00 so she can pick up her aging mother from an elder-care facility. After discussing it with her boss, they agree that she can do this, so long as she makes up the extra hours either by arriving an hour early each day or by working for 5 hours each Saturday. This is not a standard arrangement, but something arranged specially to accommodate Lindsey, who has been a valued employee.

➤ Mark is an especially talented computer programmer who has applied for a position at a large software development firm. The firm would love to hire him because it would enable the firm to move in new directions that would help it grow. The only problem is that the company is located in Silicon Valley, but Mark has custody of his children, which requires him to stay in Boston. Although the company has never done this before, they agree to hire Mark but let him work from home on a "virtual" basis, staying in touch with everyone via e-mail and videoconferences.

In both cases, the companies involved agreed to nonstandard employment terms: working different hours for Lindsey and working from afar for Mark. In addition to being nonstandard, these arrangements share something else in common: They benefit both parties. The insurance company would hate to lose Lindsey as a valued employee, so it worked out deal that allowed them both to be happy. Likewise, the software firm came up with an arrangement that allowed Mark to join the staff without having to move. Both companies worked out arrangements with a present employee or a potential employee that were nonstandard, or idiosyncratic, but that enabled all parties to benefit. Such arrangements are known as **idiosyncratic deals,** or simply **i-deals,** not just as an abbreviation, but also to imply that the arrangements are meant to be ideal for everyone concerned.[4]

In the case of Lindsey, who is an existing employee, the i-deal was made after she already was on the job. These arrangements are referred to as **ex-post i-deals.** However, because Mark negotiated the terms of his employment agreement before he was hired, his may be said to be an **ex-ante i-deal.** The key difference is timing, but in both cases the results are the same: Both employees and employers benefit as a result of this particular type of transactional contract. And unlike most transactional contracts, i-deals may be relatively long-term, or even permanent, in nature.

As you might imagine, competition among companies to attract and retain the best employees has led i-deals to grow in popularity.[5] Although the nonstandard has yet to become standard, it may be safe to say that flexibility in employment relationships certainly has grown in popularity.

Relational contracts

By contrast to transactional contracts, other relationships between employers and employees are much more personal and far more complex in nature. In fact, they operate more like marriages—long term in scope, ever changing, and not clearly defined. For example, if you have worked 20 years for the same boss in the same company, chances are good that your relationship is based not only on money but on friendship as well. You expect that relationship to last well into the future, and you recognize that it may well change over the years. In addition, your relationship with the boss has likely become quite complex and involves aspects of your lives that go beyond those of worker and supervisor. Such relationships are based on **relational contracts.** Compared to the transactional contracts that short-term employees are likely to have with their supervisors, long-term employees are likely to have relational contracts. For a summary of the defining characteristics of transactional and relational contracts, see Figure 7.2.

The Importance of Trust in Relationships

One thing that makes relationships based on transactional contracts so different from those based on relational contracts is the degree to which the parties trust each other. By **trust,** we are referring to a person's degree of confidence in the words and actions of another.[6] Suppose, for example, that your supervisor, the local sales manager, will be talking to his own boss, the district sales manager, about getting you transferred to a desirable new territory. You are counting on your boss to come through for you because he says he will. To the extent you believe that he will make a strong case on your behalf, you trust him. However, if you believe that his recommendation will not be too enthusiastic, or that he will recommend someone else, you will trust him less or not at all.

Two major types of trust

These examples illustrate two different types of trust, each of which is linked to different kinds of relationships we have with others. The first is known as **calculus-based trust,** a kind of trust based on deterrence.[7] Calculus-based trust exists whenever people

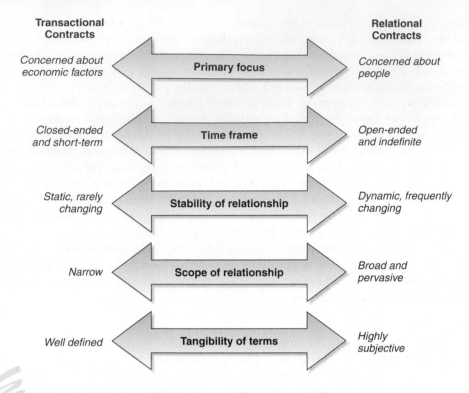

Figure 7.2   Two Kinds of Psychological Contracts: A Comparison

Psychological contracts may be considered either transactional or relational. The characteristics of each type are summarized here.

(Source: Based on suggestions by Rousseau & Parks, 1993; see Note 3.)

believe that another person will behave as promised out of fear of getting punished. We trust our employers to withhold the proper amount of taxes from our paychecks, for example, insofar as they risk fines and penalties from government agencies for failing to do so. People develop calculus-based trust slowly and incrementally: Each time they behave as promised, they build up the level of trust others have for them. This kind of trust is characteristic of professional relationships—the very kind in which people develop transactional contracts.

A second kind of trust, known as **identification-based trust,** is based on accepting and understanding the other person's wants and desires. Identification-based trust occurs when people know and understand each other so well that one is willing to allow the other to act on his or her behalf. For example, you might allow your spouse or a very good friend to select furniture for your house based on the belief that his or her judgment will be much like yours and that this person would not make any decisions of which you would disapprove. In short, you trust this person. The example described earlier in which you allow your boss to discuss your transfer with a higher-ranking official also illustrates identification-based trust. As you might imagine, identification-based trust is likely to be found in very close relationships, be they personal or professional in nature—those based on relational contracts.

How does trust develop?

Even when people first meet, chances are good that they already have some level of trust or distrust in one another based on what they know or believe about the other. What is responsible for this? In other words, what factors are responsible for the development of trust? Scientists have identified two important factors.

First, as you may already know from experience, some people tend to be more trusting than others. Indeed, the predisposition to be trusting of others is a personality variable (see Chapter 3). You probably know some people at the extremes in this regard: Whereas some individuals are cynical and hardly ever trust anyone, others are overly trusting of people, even when not warranted, to the point of being gullible.

Second, as you know, people develop reputations for being trustworthy or not trustworthy. That is, you may have learned by dealing with others directly that they will let you down and are not to be trusted. Importantly, based on their reputations, we also may judge people to be trustworthy or untrustworthy even if we have never met them. Because violating one's trust is such an affront, we are all very sensitive to this, making such information likely to be passed along to others—either by way of offering praise about never having been let down or by way of warning about the likelihood of getting let down (e.g., "Don't trust him!").

How to promote trust in working relationships

Obviously, it is important to be thought of as being a trustworthy individual. The success of your relationships with others depends on it. That said, the question arises as to what we can do to get others to trust us. Clearly, the key is to not let others down. But this is easier said than done. Fortunately, there are specific things we all can do to build others' trust in us. These are as follows:

1. ***Always meet deadlines.***   If you promise to get something done on time, it is essential to meet that deadline. Although one or two incidents of lateness may be overlooked, people who are chronically late in meeting deadlines rapidly gain a reputation for being untrustworthy. And, when others believe that you will not meet important deadlines, they are likely to overlook you when it comes to getting any important career-building assignments.

2. ***Follow through as promised.***   It is not only important to do things on time but also to perform those tasks in the manner that others expect. Suppose, for example, that the manager of your department often gives you incomplete figures needed to prepare important sales reports for which you are responsible. His inconsistency (i.e., not behaving as promised) will lead you to be distrusting of him. And as this individual develops a reputation within the company for not being trustworthy, he may come across some serious barriers to promotion.

3. ***Share personal values and goals.***   Remember, identification-based trust requires a keen understanding and appreciation of another person. And getting this understanding requires spending time together discussing common interests, common objectives, and the like. This has been the key to the success of Sir Adrian Cadbury, the former chairman of Cadbury, one of the largest confectionary companies in the world.[8] By taking time to get to know his employees and by sharing ideas with them, Cadbury got to know what his employees were like as individuals. And this is key to developing trust.

PROSOCIAL BEHAVIOR: HELPING OTHERS

At Starbucks, founder and CEO Howard Schultz goes out of his way to help his employees.[9] Not only is he polite and attentive, as you might imagine, but he also does things to help them get ahead in life. Indeed, helping others is essential to making work not only a pleasant experience but a productive one for both individuals and their organizations as well. Scientists refer to such acts that benefit others as **prosocial behavior.** We will now discuss two important forms of prosocial behavior.

Organizational Citizenship Behavior: Above and Beyond Job Requirements

Imagine the following scene. It's fast approaching 5:00 P.M. and you're wrapping up your work for the day. You're anxiously looking forward to getting home and relaxing. Meanwhile, at the next cubicle one of your colleagues has been working feverishly to complete an important report but appears to have hit a snag. She now has little hope of getting the report on the boss's desk before he leaves for the day—that is, without your help. Pitching in to help your colleague is something you don't have to do. After all, there's nothing in your formal job description that makes it necessary for you to do so. What's more, you're quite weary after your own long day's work. However, when you see the bind your colleague is in, you put aside your own feelings and offer to stay and help her out.

In this case, although you're probably not going to win any medals for your generosity, you are being helpful, and you have gone "above and beyond the call of duty." Actions such as these, which involve exceeding the formal requirements of one's job, are known as **organizational citizenship behavior** (or **OCB,** for short).[10] It is easy to imagine how such behaviors, although informal and sometimes minor in nature, can play a very important role when it comes to the smooth functioning of organizations.

The example we just gave of volunteering to help one of your co-workers is just one of five different forms that OCB can take. For a summary of all five, including examples of each, see Table 7.1.

Why does OCB occur?

As you know, people sometimes are selfish and do not engage in OCB. What, then, lies behind the tendency to be a good organizational citizen? Although there are several factors involved, evidence strongly suggests that people's beliefs that they are being treated fairly by their organization (especially their immediate supervisors) is a critical factor. The more people believe they are being treated fairly by the organization, the more they trust its management, and the more willing they are to go the extra mile to help out when needed.[11] By contrast, those who feel that their organizations are taking advantage of them are untrusting and not at all likely to engage in OCB.

Does OCB really matter?

As you might imagine, the effects of OCB are difficult to assess, largely because OCB is typically not included among the standard performance measures a company gathers about its employees. However, OCB does have important effects on organizational functioning. Specifically, people's willingness to engage in various types of OCB is related to such work-related measures as job satisfaction and organizational commitment, which, as described in Chapter 5, are related to organizational functioning in a number of complex ways.[12]

Table 7.1   Organizational Citizenship Behavior: Specific Forms and Examples

Organizational citizenship behavior (OCB) can take many different forms, most of which fall into the five major categories shown here.

Form of OCB	Examples
Altruism	• Helping a co-worker with a project
	• Switching vacation dates with another person
	• Volunteering
Conscientiousness	• Never missing a day of work
	• Coming to work early if needed
	• Not spending time on personal calls
Civic virtue	• Attending voluntary meetings and functions
	• Reading memos; keeping up with new information
Sportsmanship	• Making do without complaint ("Grin and bear it!")
	• Not finding fault with the organization
Courtesy	• "Turning the other cheek" to avoid problems
	• Not "blowing up" when provoked

In addition, being a good organizational citizen can have important effects on recruiting efforts. After all, the more positive statements current employees make about the companies where they are employed, the better those organizations will come to be regarded, and the more effectively those companies will be able to recruit the best new employees.[13] In conclusion, although the effects of OCB may be indirect and difficult to assess, they can be very profound.

Tips for promoting OCB

Given the importance of OCB, it makes sense to highlight some specific ways of bringing it about. Several potentially useful suggestions are as follows:

1. *Go out of your way to help others.*   The more you help your colleagues, the more likely they will be to help you. Soon, before you know it, with everyone helping everyone else, prosocial behavior will become the norm—that is, a widely accepted practice in the company.

2. *Be an example of conscientiousness.*   Employees are inclined to model the citizenship behavior of their supervisors. If, as a manager, you set a good example by coming to work on time and not making personal phone calls, your subordinates may be expected to follow your lead. Although it might not be this easy, at least you have some credibility when you do insist that your subordinates avoid these forms of poor citizenship.

3. *Fulfill psychological contracts.*   Research has found that employees tend to be better, more conscientious organizational citizens to the extent that they believe their employers have fulfilled their psychological contracts with them.[14] After all, employees who feel let down by company officials would have little incentive to go the extra mile for them, doing as little as possible to get by, but no more.

4. *Make voluntary functions fun.*   It only makes sense that employees will not be motivated to attend voluntary meetings or corporate functions of one kind or another

(e.g., picnics, award banquets) unless these are enjoyable. People are more likely to show the good citizenship associated with attending corporate functions when the company makes it worthwhile for them to do so. After all, the more desirable it is for someone to be prosocial, the more likely that individual will be a good organizational citizen.

5. ***Demonstrate courtesy and good sportsmanship.***   When something goes wrong, don't "make a stink;" rather, just "grin and bear it." Someone who "blows up" at the slightest provocation is not only a poor organizational citizen but also is one who may well discourage good citizenship among others.

Although these suggestions all seem like common sense, they certainly are not common practice. Even if you have only limited work experience you probably can tell a few tales about one or more individuals who behaved just the opposite of the manner outlined here. Keeping in mind how unpleasant these people made life in your organization may be just the incentive you need to follow these guidelines. Doing so will keep you from becoming a bad organizational citizen yourself—and from encouraging others to follow suit.

Whistle-Blowing: Helping Through Dissent

Sometimes employees face situations in which they recognize that their organization is behaving in an improper fashion. To right the wrong they reveal the improper or illegal practice to someone who may be able to correct it—an action known as **whistle-blowing.**[15] Formally, whistle-blowing is the disclosure by employees of illegal, immoral, or illegitimate practices by employers to people or organizations able to take action.

Is whistle-blowing a prosocial action? From the point of view of society, it usually is. In many instances, the actions of whistle-blowers can protect the health, safety, or security of the general public. For example, an employee of a large bank who reports risky or illegal practices to an appropriate regulatory agency may be protecting thousands of depositors from considerable delay in recovering their savings. Similarly, an individual who blows the whistle on illegal dumping of toxic chemicals by his or her company may save many people—and our planet—from serious harm. For a summary of some actual cases of whistle-blowing, see Table 7.2.[16]

As you might imagine, blowing the whistle on one's employer is likely to be a very costly act for employees, as they often find themselves facing a long, uphill battle attempting to prove the wrongdoing. They also frequently face ostracism and losing their jobs in response to their disloyalty. For example, a few years ago five agents from State Farm Insurance were fired after they accused the company of various consumer abuses.[17] Although various laws prevent employers from firing people directly because they blew the whistle, organizations frequently find alternative official grounds for dismissing "troublemakers."[18] It is not surprising, therefore, that six senior employees of the company that runs the 900-mile Trans-Alaskan pipeline chose to remain anonymous when voicing their complaints about safety violations to BP Amoco.[19] It is interesting to note that although whistle-blowing often involves considerable personal cost, the importance of the action motivates some people to go through with it.

Table 7.2   Whistle-Blowing: Some Examples

As the following examples illustrate, employees blow the whistle on many different types of organizations accused of committing a wide range of questionable activities.

Whistle-Blower	Incident
Coleen Rowley	This special agent wrote a letter to the FBI director (with copies to two key members of Congress) about the bureau's failure to take action that could have prevented the terrorist attacks of September 11, 2001.
Harry Markopolos	This Wall Street banker warned the U. S. Securities and Exchange Commission of his concerns about the suspicious activities of financial fraudster Bernard Madoff.
Sherron Watkins	She notified the press about her letter to her boss at Enron identifying the company's fictitious accounting practices.
Paul van Buitenen	Went public about fraud and corruption in the European Commission.
An unnamed U.S. Customs inspector	Alerted Congress of security problems at the Miami airport after management took no action.
Tonya Atchinson	This former internal auditor at Columbia-HCA Healthcare Corp. charged the company with illegal Medicare billing.
Daniel Shannon	An in-house attorney for Intelligent Electronics protested the company's alleged misuse of marketing funds from computer manufacturers.
Robert Young	This agent for Prudential Insurance accused other agents of boosting their commissions by encouraging customers to needlessly sell some policies and buy more expensive ones.
Bill Bush	This manager at the National Aeronautics and Space Administration (NASA) went public with the administration's policy of discouraging the promotion of employees older than 54 years of age.

(Sources: Based on various sources in Note 16.)

COOPERATION: PROVIDING MUTUAL ASSISTANCE

Thus far, our discussion has focused on one person's giving help to another. However, it is probably even more common in organizations to find situations in which assistance is mutual, with two or more individuals, teams, or organizations working together toward some common goal. Such efforts are known as acts of **cooperation.** As you know from experience, although cooperation is essential to organizational success, people do not always cooperate with one another. Unless individuals, teams, and entire organizations cooperate with each other, all are likely to fall short of their objectives. With this in mind, it makes sense to consider the factors that bring about cooperation, both within organizations and between them as well.

Cooperation Within Organizations

Several factors affect the tendency for people to cooperate with each other within organizations. We review some of the key ones here.

The reciprocity principle

We all know that "the golden rule" admonishes us to do unto others as we would have them do unto us. However, this doesn't describe exactly the way people behave. Instead of treating others as we would like to be treated, most people tend to treat others the way they have been treated in the past by them. In short, we are more inclined to follow a different principle: "an eye for an eye and a tooth for a tooth." Social scientists refer to this as the principle of **reciprocity**—the tendency to treat others as they have treated us.

To a great extent, the principle of reciprocity describes the way people behave when cooperating with others.[20] We already gave a perfect example of this in the opening case: When a driver calls upon another to draft, he or she is expected to do the same thing for that first driver. Don't do it, and you'd be ostracized—rejected by the other drivers, who will be unlikely to help you draft when needed. The key task in establishing cooperation in organizations is straightforward: getting it started. Once individuals or teams have begun to cooperate, the process may be largely self-sustaining. That is, one unit's cooperation encourages cooperation among the others. To encourage cooperation, therefore, managers should attempt to get the process under way by being as cooperative as possible.

Personal orientation

As you know from experience, by nature, some people tend to be more cooperative than others. In contrast, other people tend to be far more *competitive*—interested in doing better than others in one way or another. Not surprisingly, scientists have found that people can be reliably classified into four different categories in terms of their natural predispositions toward working with or against others.[21] These are as follows:

> **Competitors.**   People whose primary motive is doing better than others, besting them in open competition.

> **Individualists.**   People who care almost exclusively about maximizing their own gain and don't care whether others do better or worse than themselves.

> **Cooperators.**   People who are concerned with maximizing joint outcomes, getting as much as possible for everyone on their team.

> **Equalizers.**   People who are primarily interested in minimizing the differences between themselves and others—that is, equalizing each person's share of reward.

Although there are individual differences, men as a whole tend to favor a competitive orientation, attempting to exploit others around them. By contrast, women tend to favor a cooperative orientation, preferring to work with other people rather than against them, and they also tend to develop friendly ties with others.[22] Still, it would be a mistake for managers to assume that men and women automatically fall into certain categories. Instead, it is widely recommended that managers take the time to get to know their individual workers' personal orientations and then match these to the kinds of tasks to which they may be best suited. For example, competitors may be effective in negotiation situations, whereas cooperators may be most effective in teamwork situations. (To get a sense of which category best describes you, complete the Self-Assessment Exercise on p. 219.)

Organizational reward systems

It is not only differences between people that lead them to behave cooperatively but differences in the nature of organizational reward systems as well. Despite good intentions, companies all too often create reward systems that lead employees to compete against each other. This would be the case, for example, in a company in which various divisions sell similar product lines. Sales representatives who receive commissions for selling their division's products have little incentive to help the company by attempting to sell another division's products. In other words, the company's reward system discourages cooperative behavior.

With an eye toward eliminating such problems and fostering cooperation, many of today's companies are adopting **team-based rewards.**[23] These are organizational reward systems in which at least a portion of an individual's compensation is based on the performance of his or her work group. The rationale behind these incentive systems is straightforward (and follows from the principle of reinforcement described in Chapter 3): People who are rewarded for contributing to their group's performance will focus their energies on group performance. In other words, they will cooperate with each other. Although there are many difficult challenges associated with setting up team-based reward programs that are manageable (e.g., based on measurable rewards that really matter) and that people find acceptable (e.g., ones that are administered fairly), companies that have met these challenges have reaped benefits in terms of increased job satisfaction and productivity.

COMPETITION: THE OPPOSITE OF COOPERATION

If cooperation is so beneficial, why does it not always occur? In other words, why do people or organizations with similar goals not always join forces? To a large extent, the answer is that some goals cannot be shared. There can be only one winner of the Super Bowl and one winner of the World Series; the teams cannot share these prizes. Similarly, when several large companies court a takeover candidate, there can be only one winner as well. This was the case, for example, in the fall of 2008 when both Citibank and Wells Fargo were attempting to purchase the failed Wachovia Bank (ultimately, Wells Fargo prevailed). Such conditions breed **competition**—a pattern of behavior in which each person, group, or organization seeks to maximize its own gains, often at the expense of others. For a graphic summary of the differences between cooperation and competition, see Figure 7.3.

It is important to recognize that cooperation and competition may occur at the same time, as in NASCAR races. This is not the only context in which people have **mixed motives**—the motive to cooperate and the motive to compete operating simultaneously. Take the game of baseball, for example. Players may cooperate with each other, such as when it comes to getting a double play (where the shortstop might flip a ground ball to the second baseman, who then throws it to the first baseman). At the same time, these players also may be competing against each other for individual records. And, of course, they are working together to compete against the other team. Clearly, there are a lot of things going on in such situations: The motives to cooperate and to compete often coexist within the same situation.

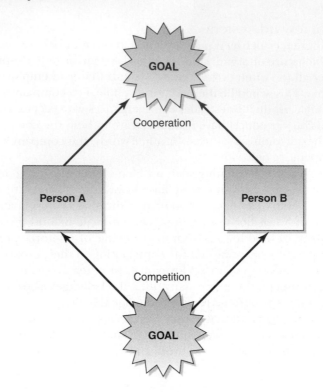

Figure 7.3 Cooperation Versus Competition: A Comparison

When *cooperating* with each other, people work together to attain the same goal that they share. However, when *competing* against one another, each person works to attain the same goal to the exclusion of the other.

In business, economists emphasize that competition is the natural order of things. Employees in the same company compete for a promotion, companies compete for the same government contract, and of course, retail businesses compete for the same customers. In recent years, for example, newer companies, such as Victory (which celebrated its tenth anniversary in 2009) introduced high-quality motorcycles that compete very favorably with cruisers from the legendary Harley-Davidson.[24] Victory has been trying to attract customers by offering more bike for the money, while Harley fans continue to be attracted to something less tangible—that company's reputation. Although only time will tell the outcome of this competition, it is clear that no matter what happens, there will always be companies competing against other companies.

CONFLICT: THE INEVITABLE RESULT OF INCOMPATIBLE INTERESTS

If we conceive of prosocial behavior and cooperation as being at one end of a continuum (as in Figure 7.1), then it makes sense to conceive of *conflict* as approaching the opposite end. In the context of organizations, **conflict** may be defined as a process in which one party perceives that another party has taken or will take actions that are incompatible with one's own interests. As you might imagine, conflict occurs quite commonly in organizations. In fact, it has been estimated that about 20 percent of managers' time is spent dealing with conflict and its effects.[25] Considering this, it makes sense to examine the types of conflict that exist, the causes and consequences of conflict, and ways to effectively manage conflict that occurs in the workplace.

Types of Conflict

As you might imagine, all conflict is not alike. In fact, scientists have identified three major types of conflict that commonly occur.[26] These are as follows:

> *Substantive conflict.*   It is not unusual for people to have different viewpoints and opinions with respect to a decision they are making with others. This variety of conflict is known as **substantive conflict.** In most cases, substantive conflict can be beneficial to helping groups make effective decisions because it forces the various sides to clearly articulate their ideas. (We will discuss group decision making more fully in Chapter 10.)

> *Affective conflict.*   When people experience clashes of personalities or interpersonal tension of some sort, the frustration and anger that result are signs of **affective conflict.** It is not unusual for affective conflict to result whenever people from different backgrounds are put together to perform tasks. Until they learn to accept one another, affective conflict is likely, resulting in disruption to group performance. After all, people who do not see the world in the same manner are likely to clash, and when they do, their joint performance tends to suffer.

> *Process conflict.*   In many work groups controversies arise about how they are going to operate—that is, how various duties and resources will be allocated and with whom various responsibilities will reside. This is known as **process conflict.** Generally, the more process conflict exists, the more group performance will suffer.[27]

As this discussion suggests, conflict takes several different forms and can have different effects—both positive and negative in nature. With this in mind, let's now turn to a discussion of the underlying causes of conflict.

Causes of Conflict

The conflicts we face in organizations may be viewed as stemming from a variety of causes, including both our interactions with other people and the organization itself. Here are just a few of the most important sources of organizational conflict.

Grudges

All too often, conflict is caused when people who have lost face in dealing with someone attempt to "get even" with that person by planning some form of revenge. Employees involved in this kind of activity are not only going out of their way to harm one of their co-workers, but by holding a grudge, they also are wasting energy that could be devoted to more productive organizational endeavors.

Malevolent attributions

Why did someone do something that hurt us? To the extent that we believe that the harm we suffer is due to an individual's malevolent motives (e.g., the desire to hurt us), conflict is inevitable. However, whenever we believe that we suffered harm because of factors outside someone's control (e.g., an accident), conflict is less likely to occur. (This is an example of the attribution process addressed in Chapter 3.) This causes problems in cases in which we falsely attribute the harm we suffer to another's negative intent when, in reality, the cause was externally based.

Destructive criticism

Communicating negative feedback in organizations is inevitable. All too often, however, this process arouses unnecessary conflict. The problem is that some people make the mistake of using **destructive criticism**—that is, negative feedback that angers the recipient rather than helps this person do a better job. The most effective managers attempt to avoid conflict by using **constructive criticism** instead—that is, criticism aimed at helping people improve. For some important comparisons between these two forms of criticism, see Table 7.3.

Distrust

The more strongly people suspect that some other individual or group is out to get them, the more likely they are to have a relationship with that person or group that is riddled with conflict. In general, companies that are considered great places in which to work are characterized by high levels of trust between people at all levels, and nobody believes that anyone in the company is out to get them.

Competition over scarce resources

Because organizations never have unlimited resources (such as space, money, equipment, or personnel), it is inevitable that conflicts will arise over the distribution of those resources. This occurs in large part because of a self-serving tendency in

Table 7.3   Constructive Versus Destructive Criticism: A Comparison

The factors listed here distinguish *constructive criticism* (negative feedback that may be accepted by the recipient to improve his or her performance) from *destructive criticism* (negative feedback likely to be rejected by the recipient and unlikely to improve his or her performance).

Constructive Criticism	Destructive Criticism
Considerate—protects the recipient's self-esteem	Inconsiderate—harsh, sarcastic, biting
Does not contain threats	Contains threats
Timely—occurs as soon as possible after the substandard performance	Not timely—occurs after an inappropriate delay
Does not attribute poor performance to internal causes	Attributes poor performance to internal causes (e.g., lack of effort, motivation, ability), even if they don't apply
Specific—focuses on aspects of performance that were inadequate	General—a sweeping condemnation of performance
Focuses on performance, not on the recipient himself or herself	Focuses on the recipient—his or her personal characteristics
Motivated by desire to help the recipient improve	Motivated by anger, desire to assert dominance over the recipient, desire for revenge
Offers concrete suggestions for improvement	Offers no concrete suggestions for improvement

people's perceptions (see Chapter 3); that is, people tend to overestimate their own contributions to their organizations. Believing that we make greater contributions leads us to feel more deserving of resources than others. Inevitably, conflict results when others do not see things this way.

Consequences of Conflict: Both Good and Bad

The word *conflict* doubtlessly brings to mind negative images—thoughts of anger and confrontation. Indeed, there is no denying the many negative effects of conflict. But, as we already noted (and as we will describe further), conflict has a positive side as well. With this in mind, we will now identify the many consequences of conflict in organizations, both positive and negative.

Negative consequences of conflict

The major problem with conflict, as you know from experience, is that it yields strong negative emotions. However, these emotional reactions mark only the beginning of a chain of reactions that can have harmful effects in organizations.

The negative reactions, besides being quite stressful, are problematic in that they may divert people's attention from the task at hand. For example, people who are focused on getting even with a co-worker and making him or her look bad in front of others are unlikely to be attending to the most important aspect of their jobs. In particular, communication between individuals or teams may be so adversely affected that any coordination of effort between them is compromised. Not surprisingly, such lowered coordination tends to lead to decrements in organizational functioning. In short, organizational conflict has costly effects on organizational performance. For some helpful suggestions on how to avoid many of these problems, see Table 7.4.[28]

Table 7.4 How to Manage Conflict Effectively

Although conflict is inevitable, there are concrete steps that managers can take to avoid the negative consequences that result from conflict between people in the workplace. Some of the key ones are listed here.

- Agree on a process for making decisions *before* a conflict arises. This way, when a conflict needs to be addressed, everyone knows how it is going to be handled.
- Make sure everyone knows his or her specific areas of responsibility, authority, and accountability. Clarifying these matters avoids potential conflicts when people either ignore their responsibilities or overstep their authority.
- Recognize conflicts stemming from faulty organizational systems, such as a pay system that rewards one department at the expense of another. In such cases, work to change the system rather than training employees.
- Recognize the emotional reactions to conflict. Conflicts will not go away until people's hurt feelings are addressed.
- Consider how to avoid problems rather than assign blame for them. Questions such as "Why did you do that?" only make things worse. It is more helpful to ask, "How can we make things better?"
- Conflicts will not go away by making believe they don't exist; doing so will only make them worse. Avoid the temptation not to speak to the other party and discuss your misunderstandings thoroughly.

(Source: Based on suggestions by Bragg, 1999; see Note 28.)

Positive consequences of conflict

Have you ever worked on a team project and found that you disagreed with someone on a key matter? If so, how did you react? Chances are good that you fell short of sabotaging that person's work or acting aggressively. In fact, the conflict may have even brought the two of you to the table to have a productive discussion about the matter at hand. As a result of this discussion you may have even improved relations between the two of you as well as the quality of the decisions that resulted from your joint efforts. If you can relate to this scenario, then you already recognize an important fact about organizational conflict—that some of its effects are positive.

When asked recently about his management philosophy, Starbucks' CEO and founder Howard Schultz touted the importance of conflict and debate, saying, "If there's no tension, I don't think you get the best result."[29] As this successful business leader suggests, organizational conflict can be the source of several benefits. Among these are the following:

> ➤ Conflict may improve the quality of organizational decisions (as in the preceding example).

> ➤ Conflict may bring out into the open problems that previously have been ignored.

> ➤ Conflict may motivate people to appreciate one another's positions more fully.

> ➤ Conflict may encourage people to consider new ideas, thereby facilitating needed change.

In view of these positive effects of conflict, the key is to make sure that more of these benefits occur as opposed to costs. It is with this goal in mind that managers work so diligently to effectively manage organizational conflict. We will now review some of the ways they go about doing this.

Reducing Conflict Through Negotiation

When conflicts arise between individuals, groups, or even entire organizations, the most common way to resolve them is to work together to find a solution that is acceptable to all the parties involved. This process is known as *negotiation* (or *bargaining*). Formally, we may define **negotiation** as the process in which two or more parties in dispute with each other exchange offers, counteroffers, and concessions in an attempt to find a mutually acceptable agreement.

Obviously, negotiation does not work when the parties rigidly adhere to their positions without budging—that is, when they "stick to their guns." For negotiation to be effective, the parties involved must be willing to adjust their stances on the issues at hand. And, for the people involved to be willing to make such adjustments, they must believe that they have found an acceptable outcome—one that allows them to claim victory in the negotiation process. For negotiation to be most effective in reducing conflict, this must be the case for all sides. That is, outcomes must be found for all sides that allow them to believe that they have "won" the negotiation process—results known as **win–win solutions.** In win–win solutions, everybody wins, precisely as the term implies.

Tips for negotiating win–win solutions

Several effective ways of finding such win–win solutions may be identified. (For practice in putting these techniques to use, see the Group Exercise on p. 220.)

1. ***Avoid making unreasonable offers.***   Imagine that a friend of yours is selling a used car with an asking price of $10,000—the car's established "book value." If you were to attempt to "lowball" the seller by offering only $1,000, your bad-faith offer might end the negotiations right there. A serious buyer would offer a more reasonable price, say $9,000—one that would allow both the buyer and the seller to come out ahead in the deal. In short, extreme offers tend to anger opponents, sometimes ending the negotiation process on a sour note, allowing none of the parties to get what they want.

2. ***Seek the common ground.***   All too often people in conflict with others assume that their interests and those of the other party are completely incompatible. When this occurs, they tend to overlook the fact that they actually might have several areas of interest in common. When parties focus on the areas of agreement between them, it helps bring them together on the areas of disagreement. So, for example, in negotiating the deal for purchasing the used car, you might establish the fact that you agree to the selling price of $9,000. This verifies that the interests of the buyer and the seller are not completely incompatible, thereby encouraging them to find a solution to the area in which they disagree, such as a payment schedule. By contrast, if either party believed that they were completely far apart on all aspects of the deal, they would be less likely to negotiate a win–win solution.

3. ***Broaden the scope of issues considered.***   It's not unusual for parties bargaining with each other to have several issues on the table. When this occurs, it is often useful to consider the various issues together as a total package. Labor unions often do this in negotiating contracts with company management whenever they give in on one issue in exchange for compensation on another issue. So, for example, in return for not freezing wages, a company may agree to concede to the union's other interests, such as gaining representation on key corporate committees. In other words, compared to bargaining over single issues (e.g., the price of the used car), when the parties get to bargaining across a wide array of issues, it often is easier to find solutions that are acceptable to all sides.

4. ***Uncover "the real" issues.***   Frequently, people focus on the conflicts between them in only a single area, although they may have multiple conflicts between them—some of which may be hidden. Suppose, for example, that your friend is being extremely stubborn when it comes to negotiating the price of the used car. He's sticking firmly to his asking price, refusing to budge despite your reasonable offer, possibly adding to the conflict between you. However, there may be other issues involved. For example, he may be trying to "get even" with you for harming him several years ago. In other words, what may appear to be a simple conflict between two people may actually have multiple sources. Finding long-lasting solutions requires identifying all the important issues—even the hidden ones—and bringing them to the table.

As you might imagine, it is almost always far easier to say these things than to do them. Indeed, when people cannot come to agreement about something, they sometimes become irrational, not seeking common ground and not taking

Winning Practices

Settling Disputes Quickly and Inexpensively Out of Court: Alternative Dispute Resolution

When a customer canceled a $60,000 wedding reception, Anthony Capetola, a caterer from Long Island, New York, was able to fill that time slot with an event bringing in only half as much.[30] Although Capetola was harmed by the customer's actions, as you might imagine, that customer was unwilling to cough up the lost revenue. Many business owners in Capetola's shoes would seek restitution by taking the customer to court, resulting in a delay of many months, or even years, and a huge bill for litigation, not to mention lots of adverse publicity. Fortunately, in their contract, Capetola and the customer agreed to settle any future disagreements using what is known as **alternative dispute resolution** (**ADR**). This refers to a set of procedures in which disputing parties work together with a neutral party who helps them settle their disagreements out of court.

There are two popular forms of ADR— *mediation* and *arbitration*. **Mediation** involves having a neutral party (the *mediator*) work together with both sides to reach a settlement. Typically, mediators meet together and separately with each side and try to find a common ground that will satisfy everyone's concerns. Mediators do not consider who's wrong and who's right but set the stage for finding a resolution. And that they do! In fact, by one recent estimate mediators help disputing parties find solutions about 85 percent of the time.

As you might imagine, however, for mediation to work the two sides must be willing to communicate with each other. When this doesn't happen, ADR may take the form of **arbitration.** This involves having a neutral third party listen to the facts presented by each side and then make a final, binding decision.

ADR is very popular these days because it helps disputants reach agreements rapidly (often in a matter of a day or two, compared to months or years for court trials) and inexpensively (usually for just a few thousand dollars split between the parties, compared to astronomical sums for attorney fees). Not surprisingly, more cases are settled in ADR than in regular court proceedings, thereby making alternative dispute resolution not so "alternative" at all.

Moreover, ADR keeps people who otherwise might end up in court out of the public eye, which could be damaging to their reputations— even the party in whose favor the judgment goes. Because it is low key and nonconfrontational, mediation is particularly valuable in cases in which the parties have an ongoing relationship (business or personal) that they do not want to go sour.[31] After all, the mediation process brings the parties together, helping them see each other's side—something that is usually lost for sure in the heat of a courtroom battle.

Not surprisingly, the popularity of ADR these days has led to the development of several companies specializing in rendering mediation and arbitration services. The largest of these, the American Arbitration Association, boasts offices in half the U.S. states, with a load pushing 80,000 cases per year. They maintain a file of some 18,000 arbitrators and mediators (typically lawyers, businesspeople, and former judges), enabling them to find a neutral party who is experienced in just about any kind of dispute that people are likely to have.

the other's perspective needed to find a win–win solution, but only thinking of themselves. In such circumstances, third parties can be useful to break the deadlock. For a description of a popular approach for doing this, see the Winning Practices section above.

DEVIANT ORGANIZATIONAL BEHAVIOR

In recent years, TV news reports have aired an alarming number of accounts of disgruntled employees who have returned to their past places of employment to exact revenge on their former bosses by holding them at gunpoint—and, tragically, sometimes pulling the trigger. This scenario became so prominent among employees of the U.S. Postal Service in the late 1990s that the phrase "going postal" entered into our everyday language to describe this form of violence. As news accounts chronicle, however, no one type of organization is immune from this extreme form of behavior. Clearly, this reflects the most negative end of the continuum of positive to negative behaviors we have been describing in this chapter.

Although acts of physical violence have been the subject of news stories, they represent just one very extreme form of what OB scientists call **deviant organizational behavior**.[32] This refers to actions on the part of employees that intentionally violate the norms of organizations and/or the formal rules of society, resulting in negative consequences. Some acts of deviance are considered relatively minor, such as leaving the workplace without permission or engaging in **incivility**—that is, showing a lack of regard for others, denying them the respect they are due (e.g., being rude). Others, however, are considered major, such as engaging in negligence that results in loss or damage to company property, tampering with attendance records, or even more extreme, physically attacking or even murdering another.

Many factors trigger deviant behavior, as we will see, but one of these we mentioned already—breaches of psychological contract. In fact, research has shown that the more employees believe that they have been victims of breach of psychological contract, the more motivated they are to seek revenge, which prompts deviant behavior. [33]

Varieties of Deviant Behavior

To understand such processes, it's important to get a handle on the variety of deviant behaviors that occur. With this in mind, scientists have devised a useful way of categorizing workplace deviance in a manner that helps us understand the various forms it takes. Specifically, the wide variety of behaviors that may be considered deviant can be categorized along two dimensions (see Figure 7.4).[34]

First, reading from left to right, deviant behavior may be distinguished in terms of the seriousness of its consequences. At the most serious extreme (shown on the right side of the diagram), we may find employees physically attacking and harming their past or present co-workers. Fortunately, physical violence doesn't occur all that often. Far more commonplace are acts that, although also considered deviant, are far less extreme (shown on the left side of the diagram), such as spreading malicious gossip about others, lying about your work, blaming others falsely, and the like.

Second, reading from top to bottom, scientists also categorize deviant organizational behavior with respect to the intended target. In this regard, we may distinguish between deviant acts designed to harm other individuals, such as one's bosses or co-workers (e.g., verbally abusing a co-worker), and deviant acts designed to harm the organization itself (e.g., sabotaging company equipment). By combining these two dimensions, we get the four categories of deviant behavior shown in Figure 7.4.

Looking at Figure 7.4, you will find a broad variety of deviant behaviors ranging from some benign acts directed at the company, such as taking long breaks, to extreme

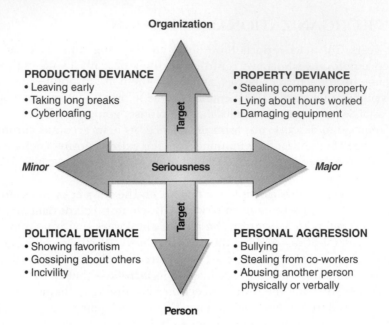

Figure 7.4   Dimensions and Categories of Deviant Organizational Behavior

Research has shown that deviant organizational behavior falls along the two dimensions shown here: seriousness (major or minor) and target of deviance (another person or the organization). Combining these two dimensions results in the four categories of behavior identified here, along with examples of each.

(Sources: Based on findings reported by Bennett & Robinson, 2000; Robinson & Bennett, 1995; see Note 34.)

acts aimed at other individuals, such as physical abuse. To give you a better feel for the nature of deviant organizational behavior, we now will take a closer look at two of the most prominent and widely studied forms of workplace deviance—*workplace aggression* and *employee theft*. To give you a feel for the wide variety of forms workplace deviance takes, our examples will draw from each of the four different categories we just described.

Workplace Aggression: Physical or Verbal Abuse and Bullying

Approximately 1.5 million Americans annually become victims of violence while on the job, costing some $4.2 billion.[35] Despite all the publicity given to workers going berserk and shooting up their offices, the good news is that such extreme acts of violence in the workplace occur very rarely. For example, only about 800 people are murdered at work each year in the United States (and even more in some other countries), and most of these crimes are committed by outsiders, such as customers.[36]

Despite their low occurrence, it is important to acknowledge such violent acts because they represent the visible "tip of the iceberg" of more prevalent forms of physical and verbal aggression that do occur. For example, even when guns are not involved, fistfights have been known to break out in offices and factories.

Still, deviant acts of the physical variety occur far less frequently than verbal forms of aggression, such as threatening physical harm or degrading or humiliating someone. If you've ever suffered verbal humiliation from another, you probably know only too well that such "sticks and stones," as the saying goes, can indeed be very harmful. Collectively, such acts of verbal and physical abuse are referred to as **workplace aggression**.[37]

Who engages in workplace aggression?

A study was conducted in which a group of employees were asked to report on the extent to which they behaved aggressively at work.[38] These individuals also completed various personality measures. Interestingly, the individuals who were most inclined to behave aggressively possessed characteristics that were associated with aggression. These were as follows:

➤ *High trait anger.*   The tendency to respond to situations in a predominantly angry manner

➤ *Positive attitude toward revenge.*   The belief that it is justifiable to get back at others who have caused one harm.

➤ *Past experience with aggression.*   A history that involves exposure to aggressive behavior.

These results are important because they suggest that some people are predisposed to behave more aggressively than others. In the future, as OB scientists come to understand this profile more fully, we will have a good chance of developing methods for screening those individuals who are most likely to behave aggressively on the job and keeping them out of jobs where they can do the most harm.

What job characteristics put people at risk for violence or aggression?

In addition to identifying individuals whose personal characteristics predispose them to behave aggressively, scientists also believe that aggressive behavior is triggered by the nature of the work people do. The possibility that people performing certain kinds of jobs are more likely to become victims of aggression than people performing other kinds of jobs surely is important to know in advance so that appropriate precautions can be taken.

With this in mind, scientists conducted a study in which they assessed the relationship between two variables in a broad sample of workers—characteristics of the work they performed (i.e., the extent to which their jobs put them in a position to do certain things, such as caring for other people, handling valuable goods, etc.) and the extent to which they experienced various forms of violence or aggression at work.[39] Their findings were quite interesting: People whose jobs led them to exercise control over others or to handle various weapons (e.g., police officers) or to have contact with people on medication or to take physical care of others (e.g., nurses) were among the most likely to experience violence on the job. Figure 7.5 identifies the seven job characteristics that were associated most strongly with violence on the job.

Workplace bullying

In recent years, OB scientists have become aware of a particularly widespread form of aggressive behavior known as **workplace bullying**.[40] This refers to the repeated mistreatment of individuals at work in a manner that endangers their physical or mental health.[41] Workplace bullying occurs by virtue of things people do intentionally to bring harm (e.g., chastising another) as well as things they don't do (e.g., withholding valuable information and training).

Unlike harassment based on race or gender, bullying is not strictly illegal (unless, of course, it results in harm), and it is quite widespread. According to a recent survey, one in six workers in the United States has been the victim of bullying in the past year.[42] Typically, bullies tend to be bosses (81 percent) who are abusing their power. Interestingly, bullies are equally likely to be women as men, but the vast majority of the

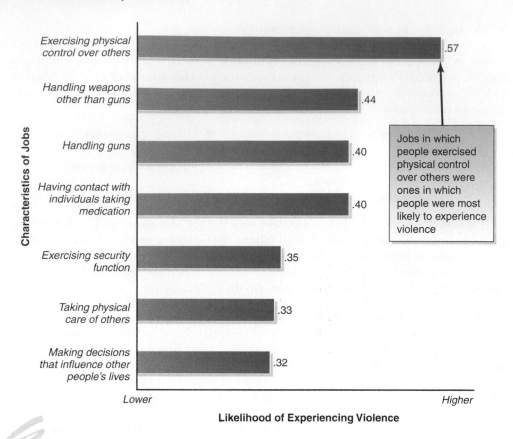

Figure 7.5　Job Characteristics That Put People at Risk for Violence

Research has found that the seven job characteristics listed here are strongly related to experiencing violence on the job. Insofar as these are characteristic of the work performed by police officers and nurses, it is not surprising that individuals performing these jobs also were found to suffer the highest occurrences of violence.

(Source: Based on data reported by LeBlanc & Kelloway, 2002; see Note 39.)

victims of bullying tend to be women (especially when the bullies are themselves women).[43] With widespread use of the Internet, it's becoming increasingly common for people to be bullied electronically, a phenomenon known as **cyberbullying**.[44] For a summary of the various forms of workplace bullying that exist, see Table 7.5.

The interesting thing about bullying is that it tends to repeat itself, thereby escalating its effects. For example, a bully's target is likely to complain to a higher-ranking organizational official. Typically, most higher-level managers will take some form of action (e.g., admonishing the bully) but will still leave the bully in place to strike again. This time, however, the bully is likely not only to strike again but also to retaliate with vengeance. Often, this results in high levels of fear that paralyze the workplace, causing people to seek new jobs and exposing employers to litigation. Part of the difficulty in dealing with this problem is that bullies often are so highly effective that they bring other employees into their webs, getting them either to join in on the abuse or to agree to keep silent about it. Soon what appears to be the inappropriate behavior of a lone individual becomes a serious problem for the entire organization.

Table 7.5   Forms of Workplace Bullying

Workplace bullying takes a variety of forms. Some of the most prevalent are summarized here.

Category	Description
Constant Critic	• Uses insulting and belittling comments, engages in name-calling
	• Constantly harangues the victim about his or her incompetence
	• Makes aggressive eye contact
Two-Headed Snake	• Denies victims the resources needed to work
	• Demands that co-workers provide damning evidence against the victim
	• Assigns meaningless work as punishment
Gatekeeper	• Isolates the victim; ignoring him or her with "the silent treatment"
	• Deliberately cuts the target out of the communication loop but still expects him or her to have the missing information
Screaming Mimi	• Yells, screams, and curses
	• Makes loud, angry outbursts and tantrums
	• Intimidates by slamming things and throwing objects

(Source: Based on information in Namie & Namie, 2000; see Note 43.)

Today's workplace bully is not simply a grown-up version of the same person as the schoolyard bully who threatened to beat you up after school back in second grade. Rather, workplace bullies are best understood from the same perspective as those who perpetrate domestic violence—they are individuals whose needs to control others are so extreme that they require psychological counseling. As you might imagine, the workplace bully, once rooted out, should be dealt with in a swift and effective manner. This might result in a leave of absence during which professional help is provided—or in many cases, termination. As you might imagine, of course, this is far easier said than done. After all, few among us would be willing to admit that we have a bully working in our midst, causing us to take only mild action, which, as we noted, can only make things worse. As in so many cases, the best offense here is likely to be "a good defense"—that is, to be on the lookout for bullies and to step in before they can get a foothold into the organization.

Although bullies are far too common in organizations, they still represent an extreme. Even the average worker who is not a bully or a "hothead" with a "short fuse" prone to "explode" may, if provoked, react strongly to adverse situations he or she has experienced. Frequent mergers and acquisitions make working conditions insecure for lots of people, causing almost anyone to behave aggressively from time to time.

Tips for avoiding workplace aggression

To keep such incidents from intensifying, it is important to recognize several things that managers can do to minimize the occurrence of aggression in the workplace. Here are three such tips:

1. *Establish clear disciplinary procedures.*   It is not unusual for people to curb aggressive reactions in organizations that have clearly understood disciplinary procedures in place.

Such programs not only send strong messages that inappropriate behavior will not be tolerated but also that it will be punished if it occurs (see Chapter 3). Such procedures go a long way toward deterring many forms of workplace aggression.[45]

2. *Treat people with dignity and respect.*   Managers who belittle their subordinates and who fail to show them the dignity and respect they deserve unknowingly may be promoting aggressive behavior. In some cases, this takes the form of people suing their former employers on the grounds of wrongful termination. Individuals who file such lawsuits are clearly striking back at their former employers, attempting to get even with them for harming them. Research has shown that the more unfairly people believe they have been treated on the job (i.e., the less dignity and respect they have been shown; interactional injustice, as described in Chapter 2), the more likely they are to file lawsuits against their former employers.[46] Obviously, this provides a strong lesson to managers about the importance of treating people fairly, something that is easily under their control.

3. *Train managers in ways to recognize and avoid aggression.*   Although we all recognize aggressive behavior when it occurs, too few of us know how to recognize potentially dangerous situations before they become serious. Managers should be trained in techniques for recognizing threats and be familiar with ways to defuse those threats. Probably the most significant tip in this regard is to take all threats seriously. Never assume that someone is merely making a joke. Talking calmly and rationally to someone who appears to be troubled can go a long way toward avoiding a potentially explosive situation.

Employee Theft

Retail stores are very concerned with problems of shoplifting, as you know. What you might not know, however, is that companies lose more money and goods from their own employees than from customers. Although estimates of costs of employee theft are quite varied, it is clear that the figures are staggering. For some recent figures on the costs and scope of employee theft in organizations, see Table 7.6.[47]

Table 7.6   Employee Theft: Facts and Figures

The following statistics paint a sobering picture of the scope and costliness of employee theft today.

- In the restaurant business, theft by employees costs between $15 billion and $25 billion per year.
- One out of every 28.2 employees is caught stealing from his or her employer.
- Most employees dislike the use of video surveillance cameras at work. At a Virginia restaurant, seven cashiers resigned the day before they believed closed-circuit surveillance cameras were going to be installed.
- Fraud cost American businesses about $400 billion a year.
- The average convenience store loses $20,000 per year due to employee theft.
- An employee who engages in theft takes an average of cash and/or merchandise valued at $808.09.
- Breaches of computer security are on the rise, but most of the people who break into corporate or government computers illegally are current employees rather than outsiders.

(Sources: See Note 47.)

To understand these statistics fully, we must consider an important fact: Almost everyone takes home some company property for personal purposes, but we are unlikely to consider this as theft. After all, you may say, "they expect it." Whether or not this is true, the taking of company property for nonbusiness uses constitutes **employee theft.** After all, who among us hasn't taken home a few pens or paper clips from the office at one time or another? Although these acts may seem innocent and innocuous enough, petty theft is so common that cumulatively it costs companies far more than the few acts of grand theft that grab newspaper headlines.[48]

Why do employees steal?

It's hardly surprising that many employees steal because they are troubled in some way (e.g., they are in serious debt or have a narcotics or gambling habit). Although this is undoubtedly true in some cases, it doesn't account for everyone.

Lots of people steal for a very simple reason—because *they see their co-workers doing it*. To the extent that everyone around you is taking home tools, office supplies, and even petty cash, it quickly seems not so inappropriate. After all, we rationalize that "everyone is doing it" and that "the company expects us to do it." Although this doesn't make it right, of course, and it clearly costs the company money, people are quick to convince themselves that petty theft is "no big deal" and not worth worrying about.

Similarly, many employees engage in theft because in some companies *not* stealing goes against the *informal norms* of the work group.[49] Unspoken rules go a long way toward determining how people behave on the job (as we will discuss in Chapter 9), and in some (probably small number of) companies an employee has to steal to feel accepted and to belong.

Finally, employees frequently also engage in theft because *they want to "even the score"* with employers who they believe have mistreated them. In fact, people who believe they have been underpaid frequently steal from their employers because in so doing they are righting a wrong by taking what they should have had all along (see Chapter 2's discussion of distributive justice).

Tips for reducing employee theft

Although you see security cameras just about everywhere, it's clear that they are not completely effective.[50] After all, many people keep on stealing. As a practicing manager, there are several things you can do to help chip away at the problem. Although you won't be able to stop theft completely, it's encouraging to know that you can make a difference by following these practical suggestions.

1.   *Involve employees in the creation of a theft policy.*   It is not always clear what constitutes theft. Does your company prohibit the use of personal phone calls or using the copy machine for personal purposes? If so, violating these policies constitutes theft of company resources, although chances are good that few will think of them as such. The trick is to develop very clear policies about employee theft and to involve employees in the process of doing so. The more involved they are, the more they will "buy into" the policies and follow them. Once such policies are developed, of course, it is critical to articulate them carefully in a formal document (such as a policy manual or code of ethics) and to carefully train all employees in them.

2. *Communicate the costs of stealing.*   Chances are good that someone in the accounting department of any company has a good idea of how much the company is losing each year due to employee theft. To the extent that this information is shared with other employees, along with a clear indication of how it costs them (e.g., through smaller raises and bonuses), many employees will think twice before they take company property for personal use.

3. *Treat people fairly.*   Many employees who steal from their employers are doing so because they are trying to strike back at employers who they believe have treated them unfairly in the past. Indeed, underpaid employees may steal company property in an effort to take for themselves what they are not being given by their company.

4. *Be a good role model.*   One of the most effective things managers can do to discourage theft is to not engage in theft themselves. After all, to the extent that employees see their managers making personal phone calls, padding their expense accounts, or taking home office supplies, they are left with the message that doing these kinds of things is perfectly acceptable. When it comes to discouraging employee theft, "walking the talk" is very important.

Back to the Case

Answer the following questions about this chapter's Making the Case (pp. 191–192) to illustrate insights you have derived from the material in this chapter.

1. What forms of trust appear to be at work in a NASCAR race?
2. What sources of conflict might exist in a NASCAR race? What problems, if any, are likely to result from them?
3. In addition to drafting on the track, where else in a NASCAR race is cooperation vitally important? Hint: It takes about 12–16 seconds.

You Be the Consultant

Sabotage in the Workplace

Life in your company has become tumultuous. Not only are people always on each other's backs, but also sometimes they get downright hostile to one another, sabotaging others' work. Even those who have not been involved are suffering the consequences—getting sick over the stress that's always in the air—and good employees are resigning. Answer the following questions using the material in this chapter.

1. What possible causes of the problem would you consider and why?

2. Assuming that these causes are real, what advice would you offer about how to eliminate them in the long run?

3. What steps would you advise taking to help minimize the immediate negative reactions—and what might these be?

SELF-ASSESSMENT EXERCISE

Assessing Your Personal Orientation Toward Others

On page 202, you read descriptions of four different personal orientations toward others—*competitors, individualists, cooperators,* and *equalizers.* As you read these, you probably developed some ideas as to which orientation best describes you. This exercise is designed to help you find out.

Directions

Use the following scale to indicate how well each of the following statements describes you.

1 = Does not describe me at all/never
2 = Describes me somewhat/some of the time
3 = Describes me moderately/half of the time
4 = Describes me greatly/much of the time
5 = Describes me perfectly/all of the time

_____1. I don't care how much money one of my co-workers earns, so long as I make as much as I can.
_____2. When playing a game with a close friend, I always try to keep the score close.
_____3. So long as I do better than the next guy, I'm happy.
_____4. I will gladly give up something for myself if it can help my team get ahead.
_____5. It's important to me to be the best in the class, even if I'm not doing my personal best.
_____6. I feel badly if I do much better than my friends on a class assignment.
_____7. I want to get an A in this class regardless of what grade others might get.
_____8. I enjoy it when the people in my work team all pitch in together to beat other teams.

Scoring

Insert the numbers corresponding to your answers to each of the questions in the spaces corresponding to those questions. Then add the numbers in each column (these can range from 2 to 10). The higher your score, the more accurately the personal orientation heading that column describes you.

Competitor	Individualist	Cooperator	Equalizer
3. _____	1. _____	4. _____	2. _____
5. _____	7. _____	8. _____	6. _____
Total = _____	Total = _____	Total = _____	Total = _____

Discussion Questions

1. What did this exercise reveal about you?
2. Were you surprised at what this exercise revealed, or was it something you already knew?
3. Do you tend to maintain the same orientation most of the time, or are there occasions in which you change from one orientation to another? What do you think this means?

GROUP EXERCISE

Negotiating the Price of a Used Car

This exercise is designed to help you put into practice some of the skills associated with being a good negotiator. In completing this exercise, follow the steps for negotiating a win–win solution found on page 209.

Steps

1. Find a thorough description of a recent-model used car online or from a newspaper.
2. Divide the class into groups of six. Within each group, assign three students to the role of buyer and three to the role of seller.
3. Each group of buyers and sellers should meet in advance to plan their strategies. Buyers should plan on getting the lowest possible price; sellers should seek the highest possible price.
4. Buyers and sellers should meet to negotiate the price of the car within the period of time specified by the instructor. Feel free to meet within your groups at any time to evaluate your strategy.
5. Write down the final agreed-upon price and any conditions that may be attached to it.

Discussion Questions

1. Did you reach an agreement? If so, how easy or difficult was this process?
2. Which side do you think "won" the negotiation? What might have changed the outcome?
3. How might the negotiation process or the outcome have been different had this been a real situation?

Organizational Communication

Learning Objectives

After reading this chapter, you will be able to:

1. **DEFINE** communication and **DESCRIBE** the various steps in the communication process.
2. **RECOGNIZE** the differences between formal and informal communication in organizations.
3. **DISTINGUISH** between verbal communication—both traditional and computer mediated—and nonverbal communication, and **IDENTIFY** the factors that make each effective.
4. **IDENTIFY** various inspirational techniques that can be used to enhance one's effectiveness as a communicator.
5. **DESCRIBE** what it takes to be a supportive communicator.
6. **EXPLAIN** how to meet the challenges associated with communicating with people from different cultures.

3 GOOD REASONS why you should care about . . .

Organizational Communication

You should care about organizational communication because:

1. Although managers spend a great deal of time communicating with others, they tend not to do so as effectively as possible.
2. Properly managing organizational communication is key to individual and organizational effectiveness.
3. Being a good communicator can help you advance to a higher-level organizational position.

Making the Case for Organizational Communication

Reducing Interruptions High-Tech Style at Microsoft and IBM

Human beings are predisposed to pay attention to distractions, psychologists tell us, because they signal changes in the environment of which we must be aware. The doorbell rings and we answer it. Someone calls our name and we look up. This fact of nature wasn't a problem before we were busily multi-tasking and faced with e-mails, phone calls, instant messages, and people stopping by to

(continued)

chat. Today, however, the sheer number of distractions takes its toll on productivity. In fact, a recent study found that most people "switch gears" every few minutes, and when this occurs it takes about a half hour to recover. Overall, people lose an average of 28 percent of their daily work hours due to disruptions, costing the U.S. economy some $650 billion.

As you might imagine, such an expensive problem has prompted a search for a solution. One fascinating fix comes from the company responsible for developing the technology that made possible many distractions in the first place, Microsoft. For over 10 years, Microsoft scientist Eric Horvitz has been working on an artificial-intelligence system that emulates the behavior of people at work. His computer program, Priorities, tracks everything that people do at their computers and handheld devices and then uses sophisticated statistical techniques to determine the costs and benefits of being interrupted by various e-mail messages. If the program computes that it's too costly to interrupt you with a particular message, it will keep it from you until such time as the interruption is less expensive. So, for example, word of a corporate shake-up is more likely to be presented to you than, say, a message about the day's cafeteria offerings. For better or worse, Microsoft is considering including some version of this technology in a forthcoming version of its Windows operating system.

Not to be outdone, IBM is taking a different approach to the problem of disruption. Their program, IMSavvy, is like an answering machine for instant messages. Based on the nature and extent of keyboard activity, the program senses when you're busy or away from your desk and tells people who are demanding your attention that you are unavailable. There's still something important that the program hasn't yet worked out: What if you're quiet because you are reading or thinking about something? Somehow, the silence or keyboard inactivity needs to be able to interpret this, but that's something for Version 2.0.

Probably the most fascinating feature of IMSavvy is the way it gives people the opportunity to determine if their message is sufficiently important to let the recipient decide if it warrants an interruption. The so-called "whisper" option is designed to emulate what might happen if someone knocks on your door while you're on the phone. You may wave the visitor away but listen to an important message whispered to you (e.g., "Hey, we closed the deal"). This way, people, rather than software, can determine the importance of any potential interruption. Of course, if this is abused, then we're back to the beginning by creating yet another (albeit softer) form of interruption.

Surely, few among us are unable to relate to the problem of interruptions. After all, they threaten to affect our productivity adversely at work and at home. Then again, what you may consider to be an interruption is simply a message you don't want to hear at a given moment. That message, in reality, may be quite important to you or to someone else, although it might better be attended to at some later time. Matters of this nature are involved in the vital and fundamental organizational process known as *communication*—the processes through which people send information to others and receive information from them.

Communication is a basic function of all managers' jobs, and performing it well is a key ingredient for organizational success. Everyone involved in organizations, from the lowest-level employee to the head of a large corporation, needs to be able to communicate effectively. Fortunately, improving communication skills, at least somewhat, is a manageable task. With this in mind, this chapter will focus on two key aspects of communication: how the communication process works and how to improve communication in organizations.

THE COMMUNICATION PROCESS

For organizations to function, individuals and teams must coordinate their efforts and activities carefully. Waiters must take their customers' orders and pass them along to the chef. Store managers must describe special promotions to their sales staffs. And a football coach must tell his team what plays to run. Clearly, communication is the key to these attempts at coordination. Without it, people would not know what to do, and groups and organizations would not be able to operate effectively—if at all!

It probably comes as no surprise that communication has been referred to as "the social glue . . . that continues to keep organizations tied together,"[1] and as "the essence of organizations."[2] Given the importance of communication in organizations, you may not be surprised to learn that managers spend as much as 80 percent of their time engaged in one form of communication or another (e.g., writing reports, sending e-mails, talking to others in person, etc.). We will begin discussing organizational communication by formally describing the communication process and then describing some of the forms it takes. Then, building on this foundation, we will describe several ways of improving organizational communication.

Steps in the Communication Process

Formally, **communication** is defined as the process by which a person, group, or organization (the *sender*) transmits some type of information (the *message*) to another person, group, or organization (the *receiver*). Figure 8.1 clarifies this definition and further elaborates on the process.

Figure 8.1   The Communication Process

Communication generally follows the steps outlined here. Senders *encode* messages and *transmit* them via one or more communication channels to receivers, who then *decode* these messages received. The process continues as the original receiver then sends *feedback* to the original sender. Factors distorting or limiting the flow of information—known collectively as *noise*—may enter into the process at any point.

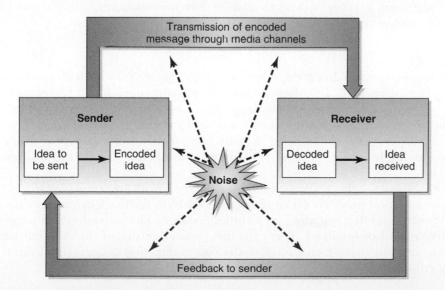

Encoding

The communication process begins when one party has a message it wishes to send another (either party may be an individual, a group, or an entire organization). It is the sender's mission to transform the idea into a form that can be sent to and understood by the receiver. This is what happens in the process of **encoding**—translating an idea into a form, such as written or spoken language, that can be recognized by a receiver. We encode information when we select the words we use to send an e-mail message or when we speak to someone in person.

Transmission via communication channels

After a message is encoded, it is ready to be transmitted over one or more **channels of communication** to reach the desired receiver. There are many different pathways over which information travels, including telephone lines, radio and television signals, fiber-optic cables, mail routes, and even the airwaves that carry the vibrations of our voices. Thanks to modern technology, people sending oral and visual messages have a wider variety of communication channels available to them than ever before for sending this information. Whatever channel is used, the goal is the same: to send the encoded message accurately to the desired receiver.

Decoding

Once a message is received, the recipient must begin the process of **decoding**—that is, converting that message back into the sender's original ideas. This can involve many different processes, such as comprehending spoken and written words, interpreting facial expressions, and the like. To the extent that a sender's message is decoded accurately by the receiver, the ideas understood will be the ones intended.

As you might imagine, our ability to comprehend and interpret information received from others is far from perfect. This would be the case, for example, if we were conducting business in a foreign country and lacked the language skills required to understand the speaker. However, even when it comes to understanding one's own native language, it's only too easy to imagine how we sometimes misunderstand what others intend to say.

Feedback

Once a message has been decoded, the process of communication may continue, but in reverse. In other words, the person receiving the message now becomes the sender of a new message. This new message is then encoded and transmitted along a communication channel to the intended recipient (the former sender), who then decodes it. This part of the communication process is known as **feedback**—providing information about the impact of messages on receivers.

Receiving feedback allows senders to determine whether their messages have been understood properly. Of course, once received, feedback can trigger another idea from the sender, initiating yet another cycle of communication and triggering another round of feedback. It is with this cyclical nature of the communication process in mind that we characterize the communication process in Figure 8.1 as being continuous.

Noise

Despite its apparent simplicity, the communication process rarely operates as flawlessly as we have described it here. As you will see, there are many potential barriers to effective communication. **Noise** is the name given to factors that distort the clarity of messages that are encoded, transmitted, or decoded in the communication process. Whether noise results from unclear writing (i.e., poorly encoded messages), a listener's inattentiveness (i.e., poorly decoded messages), or the dropping of a cell phone call (i.e., faulty communication media), ineffective communication is the inevitable result.

Formal Communication in Organizations

Imagine a CEO of a large conglomerate announcing plans for new products to a group of stockholders. Now, imagine a supervisor telling her subordinates what to do that day on the job. Both examples describe situations in which someone is sharing official information with others who need to know this information to do their jobs. This is referred to as **formal communication.**

The formally prescribed pattern of interrelationships existing between the various units of an organization is commonly described by using a diagram known as an **organization chart.** Such diagrams provide a graphic representation of an organization's structure, an outline of the planned, formal connections between its various units—that is, who is supposed to communicate with whom.

An organization chart revealing the structure of a small part of a fictitious organization, and an overview of the types of communication expected to occur within it, is shown in Figure 8.2. Each box represents a particular job, as indicated by the job titles

Figure 8.2   The Organization Chart: A Summary of Formal Communication Paths

Diagrams known as *organization charts* indicate the formal pattern of communication within an organization. They reveal which particular people, based on the jobs they hold, are required to communicate with each other. The types of messages generally communicated across different levels are identified here.

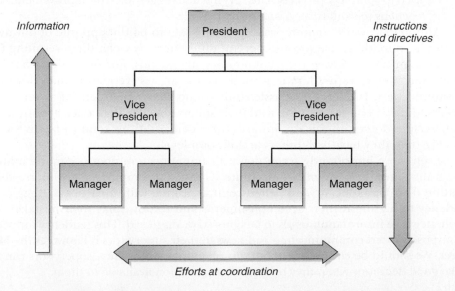

noted. The lines connecting the boxes show the formal lines of communication between the individuals performing those jobs—that is, who is supposed to communicate with whom. This particular organization chart is typical of most in that it shows that people communicate formally with those immediately above them and below them, as well as those at their own levels.

Downward communication

Formal communication differs according to people's positions in an organization chart. Suppose, for example, that you are a supervisor. How would you characterize the formal communication that occurs between you and your subordinates—that is, communication down the organization chart? Typically, **downward communication** consists of instructions, directions, and orders—that is, messages telling subordinates what they should be doing. We also would expect to find feedback on past performance flowing in a downward direction. A sales manager, for example, may tell the members of her sales force what products they now should be promoting based on the results of past sales campaigns.

As formal information slowly trickles down from one level of an organization to the next lowest level (as occurs when information is said to "go through channels"), it becomes less accurate. This is especially true when that information is spoken. In such cases, it is not unusual for at least part of the message to be distorted and/or omitted as it works its way down from one person to the next lowest-ranking person. (Anyone who has ever played the game of "telephone" has experienced this firsthand.) To avoid these problems, many companies have introduced programs in which they communicate formal information to large numbers of people at different levels all at one time.

Upward communication

When information flows from lower levels to higher levels within an organization, such as messages from subordinates to their supervisors, it is known as **upward communication.** Typically, such messages involve information that managers need to do their jobs, such as data required to complete projects. This may include suggestions for improvement, status reports, reactions to work-related issues, and new ideas.

Although upward communication would seem to be the opposite of downward communication, there are some important differences between them resulting from difference in status between the communicating parties. For example, it has been established that upward communication occurs far less frequently than downward communication. In fact, one classic study found that 70 percent of assembly-line workers initiated communication with their supervisors less than once a month. And, when people do communicate upward, their conversations tend to be far shorter than the ones they have with others at their own level.

Even more importantly, when upward communication does occur, the information transmitted is frequently inaccurate. Given that employees are interested in "putting their best foot forward" when communicating with their bosses, they have a tendency to highlight their accomplishments and to downplay their mistakes. As a result, negative information tends to be ignored or disguised. This tendency for people to purposely avoid communicating bad news to their supervisors is known as the **MUM effect.** We should be concerned about this phenomenon because supervisors can only make good decisions when they have good information available to them.

When subordinates are either withholding or distorting information so as to avoid looking bad, the accuracy of the information communicated is bound to suffer. As one executive put it, "All of us have our share of bonehead ideas. Having someone tell you it's a bonehead idea before you do something about it is really a great blessing."[3] Unfortunately, this does not occur as often as many executives would like. In fact, a survey found that although 95 percent of CEOs say that they have an open-door policy and will not harm those who communicate bad news, still, half of all employees believe that they will be jeopardizing their positions by sharing bad news, and frequently refrain from doing so as a result.[4]

Horizontal communication

Within organizations messages don't flow only up and down the organization chart, but sideways as well. **Horizontal communication** is the term used to identify messages that flow laterally, between people or units at the same organizational level. Messages of this type are characterized by efforts at coordination, attempts to work together. Consider, for example, how a vice president of marketing would have to coordinate her efforts with people in other departments when launching an advertising campaign for a new product. This would require the coordination of information with experts from manufacturing and production (to see when the products will be available) as well as those from research and development (to see what features people really want).

Unlike vertical communication, in which the parties are at different organizational levels, horizontal communication involves people at the same level. Therefore, it tends to be easier and friendlier. It also is more casual in tone given that there are fewer social barriers between the parties. This is not to say that horizontal communication is without its potential pitfalls. Indeed, people in different departments sometimes feel that they are competing against each other for valued organizational resources, leading them to show resentment toward one another. And when an antagonistic, competitive orientation replaces a friendly, cooperative one, work is bound to suffer (see Chapter 7).

Informal Communication: Beyond the Organization Chart

Imagine a group of workers standing around the coffee machine chatting about how tough the big boss is or who was dancing with whom at the company party. These too are examples of organizational communication, but because they involve the sharing of unofficial information, they are considered instances of **informal communication.** It's probably obvious to you that a great deal of information communicated in organizations goes far beyond sending formal messages up, down, or across organization charts. Such information is shared without any formally imposed obligations or restrictions.

Hearing it "through the grapevine"

When people communicate informally, they are not bound by their organizational positions. Anyone can tell anything to anyone else. Although it clearly would be inappropriate for a mail room clerk to share his thoughts with a vice president about matters of corporate policy, both parties may be perfectly at ease exchanging funny stories. The difference lies in the fact that the funny stories are unofficial in nature and are communicated informally—that is, without following the formal constraints imposed by an organization chart.

When anyone can tell something informally to anyone else, it results in a very rapid flow of information along what is commonly called **the grapevine.** This term refers to the pathways along which unofficial information travels. In contrast to formal organizational messages, which might take several days to reach their destinations, information travel-ing along the organizational grapevine tends to flow very rapidly. In fact, it is not unusual for some messages to reach everyone in a large organization in a matter of a few hours. This happens not only because informal communication crosses organizational bound-aries and is open to everyone, but also because it generally is transmitted orally, and oral messages not only reach more people but also do so more quickly than written messages.

As we noted earlier, however, oral messages run the risk of becoming inaccurate as they flow between people. Because of the possible confusion grapevines can cause, some people have sought to eliminate them. However, they are not necessarily bad. In fact, informally socializing with co-workers can help make work groups more cohesive, and it also may provide excellent opportunities for the pleasant social contacts that make life at work enjoyable. Moreover, the grapevine remains one of the most efficient channels of communication. Indeed, about 70 percent of what people learn about their companies they pick up by chatting with co-workers informally, such as in casual conversations at the coffee machine or in the corridors.[5]

Rumors: The downside of informal communication

Although the information communicated along the grapevine may be accurate in some respects, it may be inaccurate in others. In extreme cases information may be transmitted that is almost totally without any basis in fact and is unverifiable. Such mes-sages are known as **rumors.** Typically, rumors are based on speculation, someone's overactive imagination, and wishful thinking, rather than on facts.

Rumors race like wildfire through organizations because the information they contain is usually interesting and vague. This ambiguity leaves messages open to embellishment as they pass from one person to the next. And because such informa-tion tends to be shared orally between people at all levels, before you know it almost everyone in an organization may hear a rumor. When this occurs, its inaccurate mes-sage comes to be taken as fact ("Everyone knows it, so it must be true"). Even if there may have been some truth to a rumor at one point, the message quickly grows untrue.

If you've ever been the victim of a personal rumor, then you know how difficult they can be to crush, and how profound their effects can be. This is especially so when organizations are the victims of rumors. For example, rumors about the possibility of corporate takeovers may not only influence the value of a company's stock, but also are likely to threaten its employees' feelings of job security. Sometimes, rumors about company products can be very costly. To illustrate that rumors thrived long before the Internet, here are two classic examples:

➤ A rumor about the use of worms in McDonald's hamburgers circulated in the Chicago area in the late 1970s. Although the rumor was completely untrue, sales dropped as much as 30 percent in some restaurants.[6]

➤ The consumer products giant Procter & Gamble has been subject to consistent, nagging rumors linking it to Satanism.[7] Since 1980, rumors have swirled that the company's moon-and-stars trademark was linked to witchcraft. Although the company has emphatically denied the rumor and has won court judgments against various individuals spreading such rumors, the rumor has persisted. In an effort to quash the rumor once and for all, the company eventually changed its logo.

What can be done to counter the effects of rumors? One's immediate temptation is to refute the rumor, noting its implausibility and presenting information to the contrary. As an expert in information technology put it, "Rumors are analogous to wildfire. The longer they burn, the more they burn. If you are a manager, understand that the sooner you pour water onto a fire, the sooner it will extinguish. Companies are like forests that have not had rain for years: Fires will ignite no matter what."[8] This advice is not wasted on Coca-Cola. This company has been the victim of so many rumors that it has a page on its Web site at which it identifies and refutes rumors targeted against it (see Table 8.1).[9]

Unfortunately, however, directly refuting a rumor is not completely effective. As the P&G rumor illustrates, some rumors are difficult to disprove and do not die quickly. In such cases, directly refuting the rumors only fuels the fire. When you directly refute a rumor (e.g., "I didn't do it") you actually may help spread it among those who have not already heard about it ("Oh, I didn't know people thought that") and strengthen it among those who have already heard it ("If it weren't true, they wouldn't be protesting so much").

In the case of P&G, the problem is compounded by the allegation that some parties may be making a concerted effort to keep the rumor alive. In such cases, directing the public's attention away from the rumor may help minimize its adverse impact. For example, the company can focus its advertising on other positive things the public knows about it. In research studying the McDonald's rumor, for example, it was found that reminding people of other things they thought about McDonald's (e.g., that it is a clean, family-oriented place) helped counter the negative effects of the rumor.[10]

Table 8.1   Coca-Cola's Battle Against the Rumor Mill

Rumors involving Coca-Cola have been so extensive at times and have concerned so many issues that the company has been using its Web site to set the record straight. Here is just a small sampling of rumors that the company has denied. Remember, *these statements are false!*

Topic	Rumor
The Middle East	• People have been warned not to buy Coca-Cola because of possible contamination by terrorists. • The Coca-Cola trademark, when read backwards, reveals an anti-Muslim slogan.
Ingredients	• The acidity of cola drinks is strong enough to dissolve teeth and bones. • Phosphoric acid in Coca-Cola leads to osteoporosis.
Product and packaging	• Soft drinks can be used by farmers as pesticides for their crops. • Aluminum from soft drink cans leads to Alzheimer's disease.

(Source: Coca-Cola Web site, 2008; see Note 9.)

If you should ever become the victim of a rumor, try immediately to refute it with indisputable facts if you can. But, if it lingers, try directing people's attention to other positive things they already believe about you. Not surprisingly, advertising campaigns (including public relations efforts by politicians rumored to be involved in various scandals) frequently devote more time to redirecting the public's attention away from negative thoughts and toward positive ones that they already have. Although rumors may be difficult to stop, with some effort, and over time, their effects can be managed effectively.

COMMUNICATING WITH AND WITHOUT WORDS: VERBAL AND NONVERBAL COMMUNICATION

By virtue of the fact that you are reading this book, we know that you are familiar with **verbal communication**—transmitting and receiving ideas using words. Verbal communication can be either oral—that is, using spoken language, such as face-to-face talks or telephone conversations—or written, such as faxes, letters, or e-mail messages. It also can occur either with the assistance of computers (in which case it is known as *computer-mediated communication*) or without the assistance of computers (in which case it is known as *traditional communication*). Despite their differences, these forms of communication share a key feature: They all involve the use of words.

As you know, however, people also communicate a great deal without words, nonverbally—that is, by way of their facial gestures, body language, the clothes they wear, and even where at a table they choose to sit. This is referred to as **nonverbal communication.** In this section of the chapter, we will describe verbal communication media, both traditional and computer mediated, as well as nonverbal communication.

Traditional Verbal Media: Their Forms and Effectiveness

As you already know, organizations rely on a wide variety of verbal media. Some forms are considered *rich* because they are highly interactive and rely on a great deal of information. A face-to-face discussion is a good example. A telephone conversation may be considered a little less rich because it doesn't allow the parties to see each other. At the other end of the continuum are communications media that are considered *lean* because they are static (one-way) and involve much less information. Flyers and bulletins are good examples because they are broadly aimed and focus on a specific issue. Letters also are a relatively lean form of communication. However, because letters are aimed at a specific individual, they may be considered not as lean as bulletins. For a summary of this continuum, please refer to Figure 8.3.[11]

Forms of written communication

Although organizations rely on a wide variety of written media, two particular forms—*newsletters* and *employee handbooks*—deserve special mention because of the important roles they play. **Newsletters** are regularly published internal documents describing information of interest to employees regarding an array of business and nonbusiness issues. Traditionally, these are printed on paper, but today a great many company newsletters are published online, using the company's **intranet**—a Web site that can be accessed only by a company's employees. Many companies have found newsletters to

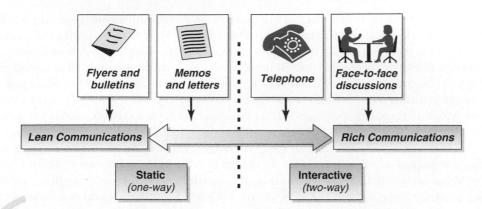

Figure 8.3   A Continuum of Traditional Verbal Communication Media

Traditional verbal communication media may be characterized along a continuum ranging from highly rich, interactive media (e.g., face-to-face discussions) to lean, static media (e.g., flyers and bulletins). (Source: Based on information in Lengel and Daft, 1988; see Note 11.)

be useful devices for explaining official policies and reminding everyone of important decisions made at group meetings.

At the public relations firm Widmeyer Communications, with offices in New York and Washington, DC, for example, employees use the company's intranet site to access an online newsletter that provides key information about what's going on in the company.[12] Particularly popular is a column called "The Buzz," which serves as a sort of electronic water cooler around which people gather (virtually) to share information about others in the company.

Employee handbooks also are important vehicles of internal organizational communication. These are formal documents describing basic information about the organization—its formal policies, mission, underlying philosophy, and its ethical requirements (see Chapter 2). Handbooks are widely used today. Not only do they do an effective job of socializing new employees into the company, but the explicit statements they provide also may help avoid serious misunderstandings and conflict between employees and their company's top management (see Chapter 7).

The effectiveness of verbal media: Matching the medium and the message

Given that people in organizations spend so much of their time using both oral and written communication, it makes sense to ask: Which is more effective? Although the answer is complex, we know that communication is most effective when it uses multiple channels—that is, *both* oral and written messages.[13] Oral messages help get people's immediate attention. Then written follow-ups are helpful because they provide permanent documents to which people later can refer. Oral messages also have the benefit of allowing for immediate two-way communication between parties, whereas written messages frequently are either one-way or take too long for a response. Not surprisingly, in organizations two-way communications (such as face-to-face discussions and telephone calls) occur more frequently than one-way communications (e.g., memos).

The matter of how effectively a particular communications medium works depends on the kind of message being sent. In general, managers prefer using oral media when communicating ambiguous messages (e.g., directions on how to solve a complex technical problem) but written media for communicating clear messages (e.g., sharing a price list). This makes sense if you think about it. After all, when a message is ambiguous, managers will find it easier to express themselves orally, especially given that spoken messages often provide immediate feedback, making it possible to tell how well the other person is getting the point (i.e., decoding the message).

However, when it comes to clear messages, putting them in writing is more effective insofar as it makes it easier for others to refer to them later on when needed. Not surprisingly, managers who follow this particular pattern of matching media with messages tend to be more effective on the job than those who do not do so. This suggests that demonstrating sensitivity to communicating in the most appropriate fashion is an important determinant of managerial success.

Computer-Mediated Communication

Today, a great deal of the verbal communication in organizations occurs with the assistance of computers, a process known as **computer-mediated communication.** Although people continue to talk to others in person, of course, various forms of online communication, such as e-mail messaging, Web conferencing, text messaging, and instant messaging, have become common in the workplace.[14] Not surprisingly, OB scientists have been involved in examining the nature and impact of this phenomenon.

Comparing face-to-face and online communication

In recent years, our understanding of communication media has expanded from distinguishing between oral and written media to communication that occurs orally in one of two ways—either face-to-face or online. Comparing these two forms of communication is particularly important given the growing popularity of online conferencing, the practice of communicating with others virtually, using online technology that makes it possible to communicate with others live via Internet connections. Because the price of computer-based telecommunications equipment has been dropping rapidly, businesses have found online conferencing to be a highly cost-effective alternative to getting people together to discuss things in person. This leads to an important question: How do online communications between people differ from in-person discussions?

A study examined this question by comparing groups of people who were brought together to have in-person discussions on a defined topic with an approximately equal number of people who were assembled to discuss the same topic via an online conference.[15] This particular conference did not provide visual contact with others using Web cameras (i.e., it was not a videoconference). Rather, participants merely shared their remarks with others by typing them on a computer keyboard. Although both groups discussed the topic for approximately the same amount of time, one hour, the groups differed significantly in several different ways.

As summarized in Figure 8.4, members of face-to-face groups made fewer comments than members of online groups, but the comments they made were longer and

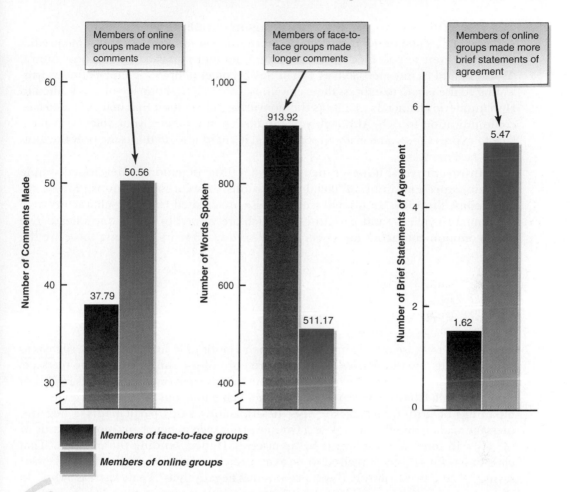

Figure 8.4   Face-to-Face Versus Online Communication: An Experimental Comparison

A recent study compared the way people communicate with one another in person versus when having live online discussions. It was found that although members of online groups made more comments, the comments made by members of face-to-face groups were longer and more detailed. Also, because online groups could not use non-verbal gestures to communicate their points, they relied more heavily on brief verbal statements to indicate their agreement with others.

(Source: Based on data reported by Schneider et al., 2002; see Note 15.)

more detailed. In other words, online participants were generally less likely to elaborate on the statements they made, failing to share equally deep insight into their ideas. Also, because members of online groups could not be seen, they were more inclined to rely on simple statements of agreement (e.g., "that's a good idea") in situations in which members of face-to-face groups would just nod. These findings suggest that face-to-face and online discussions may be used for different purposes. For example, market researchers may rely on online discussions to gather people's general and immediate reactions to new products. However, if they want to tap more detailed opinions, face-to-face discussions would appear to be a better choice.

Using "emoticons" to express emotions in e-mail

Today, e-mail is one of the most common forms of communication, and some predict that it will even surpass face-to-face communication in popularity in the near future. As useful and as indispensable as e-mail has become, people sometimes find it frustrating to use e-mail to express their emotions. After all, traditional e-mail is limited to alphanumeric characters and lacks the nonverbal information that makes face-to-face communication so rich. Although you can change the tone of your voice or make a face to express how you feel about something, it's harder to do this using only the tools of the keyboard.

In recent years, however, people have, rather ingeniously, developed simple graphic representations of facial expressions to express emotions. Known as **emoticons,** short for "emotional icons," these are created by typing characters such as commas, hyphens, and parentheses, which are viewed by tilting one's head. The most common emoticons have been in use for over 25 years.[16] Among these are the following:

> :-)   smile
> :-(frown
> ;-)   wink

People generally use emoticons to qualify their emotions in important ways, such as to communicate sarcasm. For example, the presence of the smiley face in the message, "He's really smart :-)" may be used to connote that the person in question is really not so smart at all. However, research has revealed that emoticons do *not* always qualify the meanings of written messages.[17] Specifically, among study participants, a negative message accompanied by a wink or a frown was not seen as being any more sarcastic or negative in tone than the words by themselves. Hence, sending the message "That class was awful ;-)" was perceived to be as sarcastic as "That class was awful." Likewise, saying "That class was awful :-(" was perceived as negatively as "That class was awful." In the case of positive statements, the effects were interesting. Saying "That class was great :-)" suggested that the speaker was happier than saying "That class was great," but it did not send the message that the class was any better. In other words, emoticons don't always have the effects that the communicator intended. One possible reason for this is that emoticons tend to be overused, and as a result, their impact has diminished over time.

Additional research has shown some interesting sex differences in the use of emoticons.[18] In general, women use emoticons more frequently than men. However, when men are communicating with women, they use emoticons more frequently than they do when they are communicating with other men. This is in keeping with research showing that in general men feel more comfortable expressing their emotions to women than to other men. Interestingly, men and women use emoticons differently. Whereas women use emoticons to be humorous, men use them to be teasing and sarcastic. Yeah, right ;-).

In conclusion, you should be careful using emoticons because they don't always do a good job of getting your message across. In fact, using emoticons is more likely to send a message about the gender of the communicator than it is to qualify the emotional meaning of the message itself.

Nonverbal Communication

It has been estimated that people communicate at least as much *nonverbally* (i.e., without words) as they do verbally.[19] Indeed, there can be no doubt that many of the messages we send others are transmitted without words. Here are just a few examples of how we communicate nonverbally in organizations:

➤ *Mode of dress.* Much of what we say about ourselves to others comes from the way we dress. For example, despite the general trend toward casual clothing in the workplace, higher-status people tend to dress more formally than lower-ranking employees.[20]

➤ *Waiting time.* Higher-status people, such as managers and executives at all ranks, tend to communicate their organizational positions nonverbally by keeping lower-ranking people waiting to see them—a gesture that sends the message that one's time is more important.[21]

➤ *Seating position.* Higher-ranking people also assert their higher status by sitting at the heads of rectangular tables, a position that not only has become associated with importance over the years but that also enables important people to maintain eye contact with those for whom they are responsible.[22]

As you read this, you may be asking yourself, "What can I do to present myself more favorably to those around me on the job?" Specifically, what can you do nonverbally to cultivate the impression that you have the qualities of a good leader and that you are worthy of promotion? Just as you can say certain things to enhance your image as a strong, effective employee, there also are several things you can do nonverbally that will enhance your image. For a summary of these, see Table 8.2.

IMPROVING YOUR COMMUNICATION SKILLS

There can be no doubt that successful employees at all levels, from the lowest-ranking person to the CEO, stand to benefit by improving their verbal communication skills. Although there are far too many ways of improving your verbal communication to review here, two general approaches are worthy of mention. These include using inspirational tactics and being a supportive communicator.

Table 8.2   How to Communicate Your Leadership Potential Nonverbally

People who are self-confident not only speak and write with assurance, but they also project their capacity to lead others in the various nonverbal ways summarized here.

- Stand and sit using an erect posture. Avoid slouching.
- When confronted, stand up straight. Do not cower.
- Nod your head to show that you are listening to someone talk.
- Maintain eye contact and smile at those with whom you are talking.
- Use hand gestures in a relaxed, nonmechanical way.
- Always be neat, well groomed, and wear clean, well-pressed clothes.

(Source: Based on suggestions by Dubrin, 2007; see Note 23.)

Use Inspirational Communication Tactics

Effective leaders know how to inspire others when they communicate with them. To become an effective leader, or even a more effective employee, it helps to consider several key ways of inspiring others when communicating with them.[23] These are as follows:

➤ *Project confidence and power with emotion-provoking words.*   The most persuasive communicators attempt to inspire others by sprinkling their speech with words that provoke emotion. For example, it helps to use phrases such as "bonding with customers" instead of the more benign "being friendly." Effective communicators also use words in ways that highlight their power in an organization. For some linguistic tips in this regard, see Table 8.3.[24]

➤ *Be credible.*   Communicators are most effective when they are perceived to be credible. Such perceptions are enhanced when one is considered trustworthy, intelligent, and knowledgeable. Bill Joy of Sun Microsystems (considered "the Thomas Edison of the Internet"), for example, has considerable credibility in the computer business because he is regarded as being highly intelligent. At the very least, credibility is enhanced by backing up your claims with clear data. People might not believe you unless you support your ideas with objective information.

➤ *Pitch your message to the listener.*   The most effective communicators go out of their way to send messages that are of interest to listeners. Assume that people will pay greatest attention when they are interested in answering the question "How is what you are saying important to me?" People will attend most carefully to messages that have value to them. John Stumpf, the CEO of Wells Fargo, appeared to have this rule in mind when he explained how his plan for combining its operations with those of the newly purchased Wachovia would benefit employees of both banks.

➤ *Avoid "junk words" that dilute your message.*   Nobody likes to listen to people who constantly use phrases such as "like," "know what I mean?" and "you know." Such phrases

Table 8.3   How to Project Confidence with Your Words

The most powerful and confident people tend to follow certain linguistic conventions. By emulating the way they speak, you, too, can enhance the confidence you project. Do you believe that the President of the United States does these things?

Rule	Explanation or Example
Always know exactly what you want.	The more committed you are to achieving a certain end, the more clearly and powerfully you will be able to sell your idea.
Use the pronoun "I" unless you are a part of a team.	This allows you to take individual credit for your ideas and to own up to them when they are faulty.
Downplay uncertainty.	If you are unsure of your opinion, make a broad but positive statement, such as "I am confident this new accounting procedure will make things more efficient."
Ask very few questions.	You may come across as being weak or unknowledgeable if you have to ask what something means or what's going on.
Don't display disappointment when your ideas are challenged.	It is better to act as though opposition is expected and to explain your viewpoint.
Make bold statements.	Be bold about ideas, but avoid attacking anyone personally.

(Source: Based on suggestions by Dubrin, 2007; see Note 23.)

send the message that the speaker is ill-prepared to express himself or herself clearly and precisely. Because many of us use such phrases in our everyday language, it's a good idea to make a concerted effort to stop saying these words, especially in business settings.

➤ *Use front-loaded messages.*   The most effective communicators come right out and say what they mean. They don't beat around the bush, and they don't embed their most important message in a long speech or letter. Instead, they begin by making the point they are attempting to communicate and then use the remainder of the message to illustrate it and flesh out the details.

➤ *Cut through the clutter.*   People are so busy these days that they easily become distracted by the many messages that come across their desks (see Figure 8.5).[25] The most effective communicators attempt to cut through the clutter, such as by making their messages interesting, important, and special. Dull and uninspiring messages are likely to get lost in the shuffle.

Be a Supportive Communicator

Thus far, we have been describing a way of being an effective communicator by being forceful and inspiring people. Good communicators, as you know, are also highly people oriented, requiring a low-key approach. To communicate effectively with others, we need to show that we are interested in what the other person has to say and respond in ways that strengthen the relationship between ourselves and the target of our

Figure 8.5   We Are Bombarded by Messages

The average U.S. office worker receives 189 messages per day—that's over 23 per hour. As summarized here, these come in many different forms.

(Source: Wurman, 2000; see Note 25.)

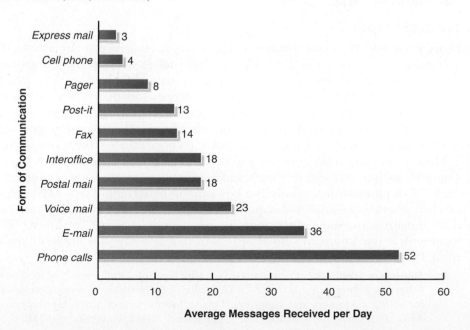

messages. In short, we need to demonstrate what is called **supportive communication.** Doing this requires adhering to the following rules:[26]

➤ *Focus on the problem instead of the person.*   Although people are generally receptive to ways of making things better, we all naturally resist suggestions that we somehow need to change ourselves. Saying, for example, "You need to be more creative," would lead most of us to become defensive and turn off the speaker. However, saying something more supportive, like "See if you can find more solutions to this problem," is bound to meet with a far better reaction.

➤ *Match your words and your body language.*   You can be a far more effective communicator when the things you say with your body match the words you use. For example, sending the message that you are excited about someone's idea is amplified by verbally explaining your satisfaction and nonverbally showing your excitement, such as by sitting up, looking alert, and opening your eyes widely. By contrast, crossing your arms, closing your eyes, and slumping while saying the same words would only detract from your message—if it even comes across at all.

➤ *Acknowledge the other person's ideas.*   Even if you disagree with what someone is saying, you don't want to make that individual feel badly about expressing his or her ideas. Not only is this rude, but also it is a good way of getting people to keep their ideas to themselves, which interferes with effective management. So, for example, if you have to reject someone's suggestion, don't make that person feel worse by suggesting that the idea is silly and devoid of merit. Instead, it would be far more supportive to highlight the good aspects of that person's ideas but explain precisely why it would be inappropriate to implement them right now.

➤ *Keep the conversation going.*   One sure way to block the exchange of ideas is to say or do things that stop conversations in their tracks. Long pauses may do this, as will saying things that change the topic. Effective communication requires keeping the conversation going, and this can be accomplished by listening carefully to what someone says and building on it when responding. (Suggestions as to how to do this are offered on pp. 241–242).

Encourage Open Feedback

In theory, it's simple: If accurate information is the key to effective communication, then organizations should encourage feedback since, after all, feedback is a prime source of information. However, we say "in theory" because it is natural for workers to be afraid of the repercussions they may face when being extremely open with their superiors. Likewise, high-ranking officials may be somewhat apprehensive about hearing what's really on their employees' minds. In other words, people in organizations may be reluctant to give and to receive feedback—a situation that can wreak havoc on organizational communication.

These problems would be unlikely to occur in an organization in which top officials openly and honestly seek feedback and in which lower-level workers believe they can speak their minds with impunity. But how can this be accomplished? Although this is not easy, several successful techniques for opening feedback channels have been used by organizations. Some of the more popular approaches are listed next. (For a close-up look at one company's novel approach to addressing this problem, see the Winning Practices section.)

➤ **360-degree feedback.**   Formal systems in which people at all levels give feedback to others at different levels and receive feedback from them, as well as outsiders—including customers and suppliers. This technique is used in such companies as Alcoa, BellSouth, General Mills, Hewlett-Packard, Merck, Motorola, and 3M.

➤ **Suggestion systems**.   Programs that invite employees to submit ideas about how something may be improved. Employees are generally rewarded when their ideas are implemented. For example, the state of Nebraska awards an employee who submits a suggestion that is adopted up to 10 percent of the money saved by implementing that suggestion (up to $6,000).[27]

➤ **Corporate hotlines**.   Telephone lines staffed by corporate officials ready to answer questions and listen to comments. These are particularly useful during times when employees are likely to be full of questions because their organizations are undergoing change. Today, for example, hotlines are being used to field questions from bank employees whose institutions are merging with others.

Winning Practices

Mistake of the Month

If your company has an important message to communicate to customers, the press, employees, financial analysts, or any such group, KDPaine & Partners can do research to help you find the most effective way of communicating with them. Given that this Portsmouth, New Hampshire–based company is in the communication research business, it probably comes as no surprise that it uses a particularly effective, yet counterintuitive, way of communicating within its ranks.[28]

It all started in 1989 when founder and CEO Katie Delahaye Paine made a serious mistake: She overslept, causing her to miss a flight to an important meeting with a client. Despite her obvious embarrassment, Paine learned from her big mistake a vital lesson about the importance of getting up on time.

But why, she thought, should this lesson be kept solely with her? After all, sharing it with others stood to benefit them as well. With this in mind, the next day Paine went to a staff meeting, where she put a $50 bill on the table and challenged her colleagues to tell a worse story about their own mistakes. That they did. One salesperson described how he went on a sales call without his business cards, and another admitted to having scheduled a presentation at Coca-Cola but left the presentation materials behind. Not only did they describe their embarrassing mistakes, but importantly, what they learned from them that others could learn as well.

So many people learned so many things about ways to mess things up—and how to avoid them—that the "Mistake of the Month" soon became a feature of staff meetings at KDPaine & Partners. It works like this. At each monthly staff meeting, a half-hour is devoted to identifying and discussing everyone's mistakes. Each is written on a board, and everyone gets to vote on two categories of mistakes—the one from which they learned the most and the one from which they learned the least. The person whose mistake is identified as helping the most is awarded a highly coveted downtown parking space for the next month. The person from whose mistake people learned the least is required to speak at the next meeting about what he or she is doing to ensure that it will never happen again. The time spent on this exercise is considered a wise investment insofar as it allows all employees to learn from everyone else's mistakes.

During the program's first 10 years, more than 2,000 mistakes have been identified—but few ever have been repeated, creating a positive effect on the company's work. Paine also notes that the program helps her identify steps she needs to take to improve things at the firm that bears her name. She also notes that sharing mistakes has been "a bonding ritual," adding "once you go through it, you're a member of the club." In 2007, the Small Business Administration named Ms. Paine New Hampshire Woman Business Owner of the Year, a decision that certainly does not appear to be a mistake.[29]

Use simple language

No matter what field you're in, chances are good that it has its own special language—its **jargon.** Although jargon may greatly help communication within specialized groups, it can severely interfere with communication among the uninitiated.

The trick to using jargon wisely is to know your audience. If the individuals with whom you are communicating understand the jargon, using it can help facilitate communication. However, when addressing audiences whose members are unfamiliar with specialized language, simple, straightforward language is bound to be most effective. In either case, the rationale is the same: Communicators should speak the language of their audiences. Although you may be tempted to try to impress your audience by using big words, you may have little impact on them if they don't understand you. My advice is clear: Follow the **K.I.S.S. principle**—that is, **k**eep **it** **s**hort and **s**weet.

Avoid overload

Imagine this scene: You're up late one night at the end of the term as you're writing a paper and studying for finals (or at least trying to) all at the same time. Your desk is piled high with books when your roommate comes in to explain what you should do to prepare for the end-of-semester party. If this sounds at all familiar to you, then you probably know only too well that it's unlikely that you'd be able to give everything you're doing your most careful attention. After all, when people are confronted with more information than they can process at any given time, their performance tends to suffer. This condition is known as **overload.**

As we noted earlier (recall both this chapter's opening case and Figure 8.5), these days we tend to be bombarded by messages so regularly that we take overload for granted. Staying competitive in today's hectic world often requires doing many things at once—but without threatening the performance that often results when communication channels are overloaded.

Part of the problem is that many people feel obligated to communicate with others because technology makes it possible for much of it to occur instantly. As a result, they fail to manage their own communication effectively, allowing themselves to become overloaded. We see this, for example, in the tendency for many people to use their BlackBerries so excessively that they are considered to be addicted to using them. For this reason, the slang term **crackberry** has emerged to describe a person who appears to be addicted to checking and/or sending messages on his or her BlackBerry or some other similar device.

Fortunately, several things can be done to avoid, or at least minimize, the problem of overload. These suggestions apply both to in-person communications and electronic communications. They are as follows:

➤ *Rely on gatekeepers.* People whose jobs require them to control the flow of information to potentially overloaded individuals, groups, or organizations are known as **gatekeepers.** In making appointments for top executives, administrative assistants provide a gatekeeping service for their bosses. For society at large, editors of newspapers and other media outlets serve as gatekeepers for the public by keeping us from being inundated with more stories than we possibly can handle. They decide what stories are allowed inside the gate and what other ones are kept out (i.e., by not publishing them).

➤ *Practice queuing.* A "queue" is a line. So, **queuing** involves lining up incoming information so that it can be attended to in an orderly fashion. Air traffic controllers do this when they "stack" incoming planes in a holding pattern so as to prevent them from tragically "overloading" the runway. Physicians rely on queuing by requiring their nonemergency patients to make appointments and then seeing them only in the appointed order. Busy supermarket deli clerks also use queuing when they ask you to "take a number" to ensure that customers are served in the order of arrival. Be it 747s, sick people, or customers wanting bologna, the practice of queuing can help avoid overload very effectively.

➤ *Screen phone calls.* The practice of screening phone calls is a good way to avoid overload because it allows you to take control over your time by taking the calls you want now and allowing the others to roll over into voice mail (which you can then answer at your convenience).

➤ *Filter your e-mail.* An easy way to become overloaded with information is by paying attention to unwanted e-mail messages—commonly called **spam,** but officially referred to as unsolicited commercial e-mail messages (UCE) by network administrators. In recent years, workers have been plagued by so much spam that it has been estimated that the average company loses about 10 days of productivity per year due to time lost by dealing with spam—even if employees spend as little as 5 seconds on each unwanted message.[30] Fortunately, free or very low-cost spam filters can be downloaded to help combat the problem. It is because spam is only one cause of overload that Microsoft and IBM are developing the technologies to help people filter the many legitimate messages that they also receive, as described in the Making the Case section on pages 221–222.

Walk the Talk

When it comes to effective communication, action definitely speaks louder than words. Too often, communication is hampered by the practice of saying one thing but meaning another. And, whenever implicit messages (e.g., "we may be cutting jobs") contradict official messages (e.g., "don't worry, the company is stable"), confusion is bound to result.

This is especially problematic when the inconsistency comes from the top. In fact, one of the most effective ways of fostering effective organizational communication is for CEOs to "walk the talk," that is, to match their deeds to their words. After all, a boss would lose credibility if she told her employees "My door is always open to you" but then was never available for consultation. Good communication demands consistency. And, for the words to be heard as loud as the actions, they must match up.

Be a Good Listener

Effective communication involves more than just presenting messages clearly. It also involves doing a good job of comprehending (i.e., decoding) others. Although most of us take listening for granted, effective listening is an important skill. In fact, given that managers spend about 40 percent of their time listening to others but are only 25 percent effective, listening is a skill that could stand to be developed in most of us. When we speak of *effective listening* we are not referring to the passive act of just taking in information that so often occurs. Rather, effective listening involves three important elements:

➤ Being nonjudgmental while taking in information from others.
➤ Acknowledging speakers in ways that encourage them to continue speaking.
➤ Attempting to advance a speaker's ideas to the next step.

Table 8.4   Tips for Improving Your Listening Skills

Being a good listener is an important skill that can enhance the effectiveness of communication in organizations. Although it may be difficult to follow the suggestions outlined here, the resulting benefits make it worthwhile to try to do so.

Suggestion	Description
Do not talk while being spoken to.	It is difficult, if not impossible, to listen to another while you are speaking to that person.
Make the speaker feel at ease.	Help the speaker feel that he or she is free to talk as desired.
Eliminate distractions.	Don't focus on other things: Pay attention only to the speaker.
Show empathy with the speaker.	Try to put yourself in the speaker's position, and make an effort to see his or her point of view.
Be as patient as possible.	Take the time needed to hear everything the speaker has to say.
Hold your arguments.	If you're busy forming your own arguments, you cannot focus on the speaker's points.
Ask questions.	By asking questions, you demonstrate that you are listening and make it possible to clarify areas of uncertainty.

(Source: Based on suggestions by Morrison, 1994; see Note 31.)

It is worthwhile to consider what we can do to improve our own effectiveness as listeners. Fortunately, experts have offered several good suggestions, some of which are summarized in Table 8.4.[31] Although it may require some effort, incorporating these suggestions into your own listening habits cannot help but make you a more effective listener.

Given its importance, it should not be surprising that many organizations are working hard to improve their employees' listening skills. For example, Unisys has long used seminars and self-training audiocassettes to train thousands of its employees in effective listening skills. Such systematic efforts at improving listening skills represent a wise investment insofar as good listening definitely pays off. Indeed, research has shown that the more effective one is as a listener, the more likely he or she is to get promoted to a management position—and to perform effectively in that role. (To practice your own listening skills, and to help others do the same, see the Group Exercise section on pp. 248–249.)

Be Sensitive to Cross-Cultural Communication

It's no secret that businesses operate in a global economy. Approximately two-thirds of large companies in Europe, Australia, and New Zealand have employees in six or more countries (compared to 56 percent of Asian companies, 43 percent of North American companies, and 33 percent of Latin American companies).[32] Keeping this economy going requires a keen understanding of the complexities of communicating with people from different countries. This is far easier said than done—and even the smallest mistakes may offend your hosts.

Imagine, for example, that you live in a large U.S. city, where you are entertaining a group of potential business partners from abroad. As you enter a restaurant, you find it odd that your guests are reluctant to check their coats, taking them to the table instead, although the inside temperature is quite comfortable. Upon prompting, your guests admit that they heard all about the crime problem in the United States and were advised against ever letting something of value out of their sight. If you are not immediately offended, you would feel at the very least uncomfortable about the message your visitors are sending about their trust of Americans—a potential problem given that you are considering partnering with them.

Clearly, when visiting abroad, it pays to not only learn the language spoken there (even if only somewhat, as a gesture of politeness) but also to familiarize yourself carefully with the local customs.[33] As a quick summary of some of the most easily recognized pitfalls of international communication, see Figure 8.6. (To see how familiar you are with the unique ways people from different cultures communicate, see the Self-Assessment Exercise on pp. 247–248.)

Figure 8.6   "When in Rome": Understanding National Customs

Understanding differences in local customs is essential when conducting business in today's global economy. A few important customs that might come as a surprise to American businesspeople are summarized here.

(Sources: Based on information in Marx, 2001, and Lewis, 2000; see Note 33.)

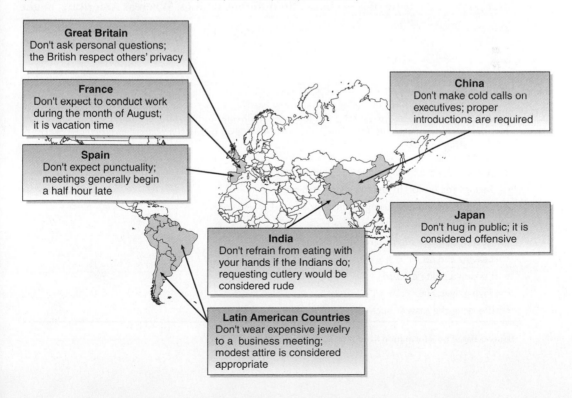

Great Britain
Don't ask personal questions; the British respect others' privacy

France
Don't expect to conduct work during the month of August; it is vacation time

Spain
Don't expect punctuality; meetings generally begin a half hour late

China
Don't make cold calls on executives; proper introductions are required

Japan
Don't hug in public; it is considered offensive

India
Don't refrain from eating with your hands if the Indians do; requesting cutlery would be considered rude

Latin American Countries
Don't wear expensive jewelry to a business meeting; modest attire is considered appropriate

Challenges of cross-cultural communication

Three key factors make communicating with people from different cultures a difficult task. First, different words may mean different things to different people. For example, as hard as it might be for people from countries with long-standing capitalist economies to realize, Russians have difficulty understanding words such as *efficiency* and *free market,* which have no direct translation in their own language. People who have never known a free-market economy while they were growing up under Communist rule may find it difficult to grasp the concept. It is, therefore, not surprising to find that communication barriers have been found to exist among American executives attempting to conduct business in Russia.[34]

Second, different cultures sometimes have very different cultural norms about using certain words. Take the simple word *no,* for example. Although the term exists in the Japanese language, the Japanese people are reluctant to say no directly to someone because doing so is considered insulting. For this reason, they often rely on other ways of saying no that can be quite difficult for foreigners to understand (see Table 8.5).[35] As such, it frequently is considered wise for foreign visitors to other countries to learn not only the language of that country but the customs about using language as well.

Third, cross-cultural communication is made difficult by the fact that in different languages even the same word can mean different things. Just imagine, for example, how confused an American executive might become when she speaks to her counterpart in Israel, where the same Hebrew word, *shalom,* means both "hello" and "good-bye" (as well as "peace"). Confusion is bound to arise. The same may be said for cultural differences in the tone of speech used in different settings. Whereas Americans might

---

Table 8.5   How to Say No in Japan

Although most Americans are not reluctant to come out directly and say "no" when necessary, doing so is frowned on by Japanese culture. As such, the Japanese rely on the following more indirect ways of communicating "no."

- Saying "no" in a highly vague and roundabout manner
- Saying "yes or no" in an ambiguous fashion
- Being silent and not saying anything at all
- Asking questions that change the topic
- Responding in a highly tangential manner
- Leaving the room
- Making a polite excuse
- Saying, "yes, but . . . "
- Delaying the answer, such as by promising a future letter

(Source: Based on information from various sources; see Note 35.)

feel free to say the word *you* in both formal and informal situations, the Spanish have different words in each (*tú* for informal speech and *usted* for formal speech). To confuse these may be tantamount to misinterpreting the nature of the social setting, a potentially costly blunder—and all because of a failure to recognize the subtleties of cross-cultural communication.

Guidelines for avoiding pitfalls in cross-cultural communications

Communication between people of different cultures can be promoted by taking into account several basic rules. To avoid misunderstandings that can strain or even ruin business relationships, it is especially important to follow these guidelines when conducting business with people from other countries.[36] These are as follows:

➤ *Learn local cultural rules.* By acknowledging that there are likely to be cultural differences between yourself and people from another country, learn what you can do to avoid embarrassing these people. Many Americans make this mistake, for example, when they publicly praise Asian visitors. Although this would be considered a very kind thing to do in American culture, Asians are likely to find it a source of discomfort inasmuch as their cultures value group performance more highly than individual performance. Pay special attention to rules of etiquette regarding how to address people (by first name, last name, or title). To avoid embarrassment, it's a good idea to check with local experts to ensure that you are doing this correctly.

➤ *Don't take anything for granted.* It is important when communicating with people from other nations to challenge your cultural assumptions. Don't assume, for example, that everyone values the same things that you do. Although it may come as a shock to many Americans, concepts such as equal achievement, autonomy, and individual accomplishment are not recognized as appropriate throughout the world.

➤ *Show respect for everyone.* We often find it funny when someone says or does something that runs counter to what we expect. However, giggling or telling someone that they have a funny accent is not only disrespectful, but also it imposes a tall barrier to effective communication. In this connection, it helps to focus on *what* people are saying rather than how they are saying it or how they look.

➤ *Speak slowly, clearly, and in straightforward language.* Even after you have studied a foreign language for a few years in high school or college, you may be surprised to find just how little you understand when you visit a country where that is the native language. "If they only spoke more slowly and clearly," you think to yourself, "I'd probably understand them." Indeed, you might. With this in mind, it's important for you to speak slowly and clearly (but not loudly!) when talking to people in languages that are not their native tongue. Moreover, it's important to avoid colloquial words or phrases that you take for granted but that they might not know.

➤ *Try to speak the local language—at least a little.* People always appreciate the effort you make to speak their language, so give it a try. It's a good way to show goodwill and to break the barrier between you. Whatever you do, however, check with a native speaker to make sure that your pronunciation is accurate and that you are not offending anyone by using the wrong words or gestures.

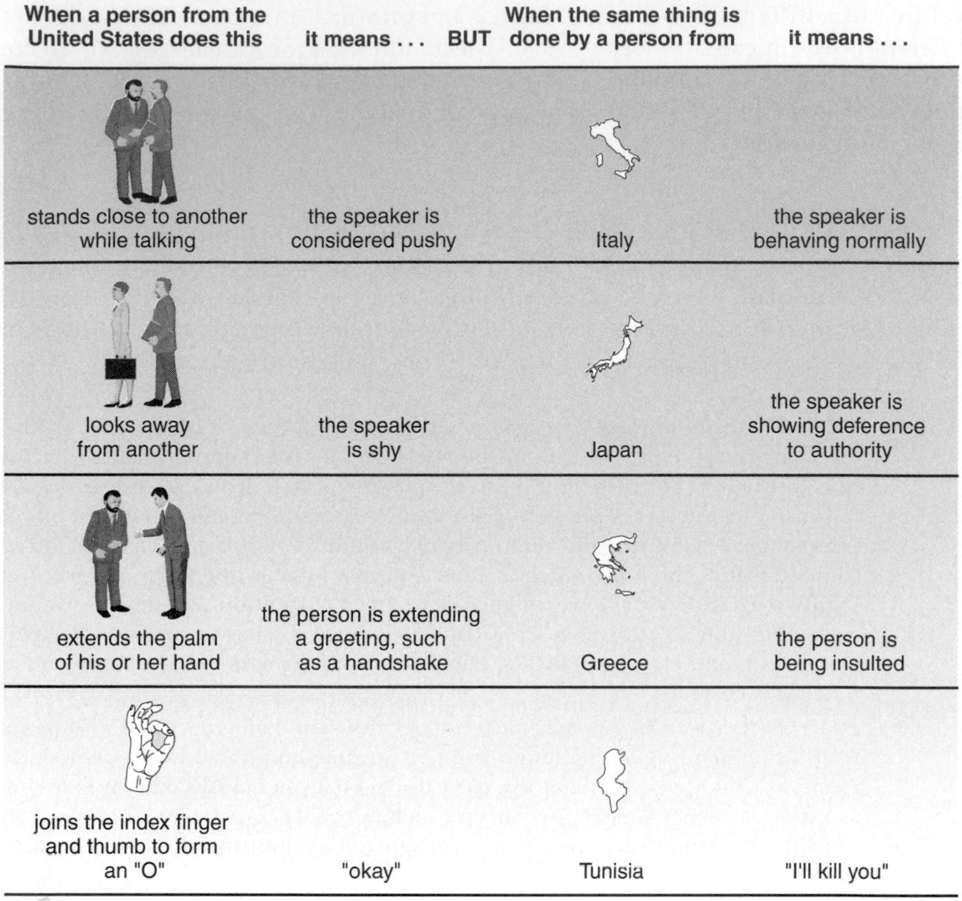

When a person from the United States does this	it means ...	BUT	When the same thing is done by a person from	it means ...
stands close to another while talking	the speaker is considered pushy		Italy	the speaker is behaving normally
looks away from another	the speaker is shy		Japan	the speaker is showing deference to authority
extends the palm of his or her hand	the person is extending a greeting, such as a handshake		Greece	the person is being insulted
joins the index finger and thumb to form an "O"	"okay"		Tunisia	"I'll kill you"

Figure 8.7   Beware of Nonverbal Miscommunication in Different Countries

Although people preparing to conduct business abroad may study their host country's language, they frequently fail to learn differences in the nonverbal language. As summarized here, this can lead to some serious miscommunication.

(Sources: Based on information from various sources; see Note 37.)

➤ *Beware of nonverbal differences.*   The same gestures that mean one thing in one country may mean quite another in another country. For example, an American may not think twice about hugging a colleague who has done well or touching another's arm to acknowledge him or her. However, these same acts would be considered not only inappropriate but also offensive to people from Korea. Bottom line: You have not completely learned a foreign language until you have learned its nonverbal language as well.[37] For some examples of cross-cultural differences in nonverbal behavior, see Figure 8.7.

Back to the Case

Answer the following questions about this chapter's Making the Case (pp. 221–222) to illustrate insights you have derived about the material in this chapter.

1. When it comes to reducing interruptions, how effective do you believe the solutions proposed by Microsoft and IBM will prove to be? Do you think they will make a noticeable difference in reducing overload? If so, under what conditions?
2. The techniques proposed by Microsoft and IBM address interruptions experienced while at the computer, but many people spend time elsewhere. What do you think can be done to reduce interruptions in other contexts, such as when reading reports or meeting with others?
3. Do you believe people would be pleased to use these technological "solutions" or might they be rejected? Explain the basis for your answer.

You Be the Consultant

A Crisis in Communicating Coordination

"Everyone is moving in different directions; no one seems to have any sense of what the company is and where it is going. Making things worse, people around here aren't paying any attention to each other, and everyone is doing his or her own thing." These are the words of an operations director of a large credit card processing center, who asks you to look into these problems in your capacity as manager of human resources. Answer the following questions relevant to this situation based on the material in this chapter.

1. Casting the problem as one of poor communication between company officials and lower-level employees, what steps could be taken to fill everyone in on the company's plans, goals, and activities?
2. What specific tactics would you advise the company's management to use to improve communication within? How effective do you believe these approaches will be?
3. In what ways might differences in nationality be responsible for this state of affairs, and what can be done to help improve communication despite these differences?

SELF-ASSESSMENT EXERCISE

How Familiar Are You with Foreign Communication Practices?

Expert communicators in today's global business world must have considerable familiarity with cultural differences in communication style around the world. This questionnaire is designed to assess your familiarity with many such communication practices. It is important to note that although people in any given country are not all alike, their cultural backgrounds lead them to share certain communication styles and practices.

Directions

Match the countries in the left-hand column to the communication characteristic that best describes its people, listed in the column on the right.

1. _____ Russia
2. _____ Brazil
3. _____ Germany
4. _____ Australia
5. _____ Japan
6. _____ Philippines
7. _____ Poland
8. _____ France
9. _____ Great Britain
10. _____ India

a. Chivalry and old-fashioned gallantry are important; first names are reserved for use only with close friends.
b. Show respect for speakers by being silent; tend to be shy and to refrain from open disagreement.
c. Women are deferent to men; good bargainers, who expect you to negotiate with them.
d. Raise their voice and use gestures when excited; formal dress and style are typical at meetings.
e. Punctuality is important; perfectionists, who demand lots of information from others.
f. Use humor a great deal, such as to break up tension; take time to make decisions.
g. Talk tough when they believe they have an advantage; tend to drink between meetings.
h. Being an hour or two late is not unusual; leadership is based on family name, age, and connections.
i. Very talkative and long-winded; tend to interrupt conversations with their own ideas.
j. Tend to be cynical and distrust people who praise them too enthusiastically.

(Source: Based on information in Rosen et al., 2000, see Note 32; and Lewis, 2000, see Note 33.)

Scoring

Using the following key, count how many correct matches you made.

   1 = g, 2 = i, 3 = e, 4 = j, 5 = b, 6 = h, 7 = a, 8 = d, 9 = f, 10 = c

Discussion Questions

1. How many correct matches did you make? How does this figure compare to how you expected to score before you began this exercise?
2. Based on your own experiences, to what extent do you believe these descriptions are generally accurate as opposed to merely stereotypic?
3. How would you characterize your own culture relative to those described in this exercise?

GROUP EXERCISE

Sharpening Your Listening Skills

Are you a good listener, a *really* good listener? Do you understand exactly what others are saying and get them to open up even more? Most of us tend to think that we are much better than we really are when it comes to this important skill. After all, we've been listening to people our whole lives—and, with that much practice, we must be at least reasonably acceptable. However, being a truly effective listener is an active skill, and it takes some practice to master. The following exercise will help you gain some insight into your own listening skills and those of others.

Directions

1. Divide the class into pairs of people who do not already know each other. Arrange the chairs so that the people within each pair are facing one another but are separated from the other pairs.

2. Within each pair, select one person as the speaker and the other as the listener. The speaker should tell the listener about a specific incident on the job in which he or she was somehow harmed (e.g., disappointed by not getting a raise, being embarrassed by another, getting fired, and so on), and how he or she felt about it. This discussion should last about 10 to 15 minutes.

3. Listeners should carefully attempt to follow the suggestions for good listening summarized in Table 8.4 (on p. 242). To help, the instructor should discuss these with the class.

4. After the conversations are over, review the suggestions with your partner. Discuss which ones the listener followed and which ones were ignored. Try to be as open and honest as possible about assessing your own and the other's strengths and weaknesses. Speakers should consider the extent to which they felt the listeners were really paying careful attention to them.

5. Now repeat steps 2 through 4 but change roles. Speakers now become listeners, and listeners now become speakers.

6. As a class, share your experiences as speakers and listeners.

Discussion Questions

1. What did this exercise teach you about your own skills as a listener? Are you as good as you thought? Do you think you can improve?

2. Was there general agreement or disagreement in the class about each listener's strengths and weaknesses? Explain.

3. Which particular listening skills were easiest and which were most difficult for you to put into practice? Do you think there may be certain conditions under which good listening skills may be especially difficult to implement? Explain.

Group Processes and Work Teams

Learning Objectives

After reading this chapter, you will be able to:

1. **DEFINE** what is meant by a group.
2. **DESCRIBE** the importance of norms, status, and cohesiveness within organizations.
3. **EXPLAIN** how individual performance in groups is affected by the presence of others (social facilitation) and the number of others with whom one is working (social loafing).
4. **DEFINE** what teams are and **DESCRIBE** the various types of teams that exist in organizations.
5. **DESCRIBE** the evidence regarding the effectiveness of teams in organizations.
6. **EXPLAIN** the factors responsible for the failure of some teams to operate as effectively as possible and steps that can be taken to build successful teams.

3 GOOD REASONS why you should care about . . .

Group Processes and Work Teams

You should care about group processes and work teams because:

1. The dynamics among people in groups are largely responsible for both the success and failure of many work units, as well as the satisfaction of the individuals working in them.
2. Groups and teams can be very effective if you know how to manage them properly.
3. Teams are the most popular way of coordinating the activities of people on the job. Knowing how to build effective teams is an essential competency among today's managers.

Making the Case for Group Processes and Work Teams

Making a "Better Place" One Electric Car at a Time

Can a five-person company change the world? Although it's unlikely, it's possible that if they work together in a carefully coordinated and focused fashion they just might make a difference. And this is precisely what Shai Agassi intends to do. As founder and CEO of Better Place, he works with governments and auto manufacturers to develop personal transportation systems that eliminate our dependence on oil and the environmental and economic damage that comes with it. His vehicle of choice to make the earth a "better place" is the electric car.

In operation since October 2007 and launched with $200 million in venture capital funds, Better Place's plan is straightforward: Pay for the transportation you need as a sustainable service. First, automakers have to replace their gasoline-guzzling engines with powerful, but quiet and smooth-running electric motors powered by batteries. Then, drivers pay a fee to access a network of charging spots and places where they can replace their batteries. Better Place operates the electric recharge grid that makes this possible.

To Idan Ofer, chairman of the board, this business plan benefits everyone. Drivers benefit by getting to enjoy their cars in cleaner environments. The auto industry benefits by getting to service a brand new market segment. The energy company also benefits by getting to introduce new technologies. The world's nations benefit by aligning economic and environmental interests. And, finally, of course, our planet benefits by being spared the pollution caused by the internal combustion engine.

Getting all this to work, as you might imagine, requires great teamwork, and it looks as if Better Place has this covered. Aliza Peleg, VP of operations, works carefully with Joe Paluska to bring the company's ideas to international auto companies, and hands these off to Agassi, who comes in to clench the deal. And deals have been rushing in, even within the company's first 6 months of existence. Soon after launch, Renault-Nissan signed on with Better Place to develop a line of battery-powered electric cars. Then, in January 2008, with the help of Moshe Kaplinsky, CEO of Better Place Israel, that nation became the first in the world to declare a plan for oil independence by 2020. As soon as 2011, in fact, Israel plans to have widespread deployment of an electric recharge grid to power electric vehicles—with all energy supplied by solar power. In March 2008, Denmark came onboard, working with Better Place to develop a recharge grid powered by energy from wind turbines.

If there's been any one problem with electric vehicles thus far, it's that they're actually too quiet. This makes the driving less than gratifying and takes away the auditory cues upon which blind pedestrians rely when crossing the street. Better Place has that covered as well. You know about ringtones for your phone? Well, Agassi is planning on "drivetones" that can be downloaded and controlled through a dashboard switch. So, even if you don't have a Ferrari, with a little digital wizardry, your electric car can at least sound like one.

To return to our opening question, it's hard to say if Better Place will ever change the world, but it's clear that Agassi and his team would be delighted to save it from pollution, thereby making it better. And this, after all, would make it a "better place" for all.

Sure, Mr. Agassi has a great idea and sound financial backing, but important as they are, these things alone don't guarantee success. In Better Place, he also has an essential third ingredient, a solid team whose members coordinate their efforts to make things happen. But this is hardly a secret ingredient. Today, work teams are extremely popular in many organizations. People in offices and factories everywhere are called on to coordinate their efforts toward achieving important organizational goals, and teams are often the mechanism for making this possible. Because doing this, however, is easier said than done, in this chapter we will examine the general effectiveness of teams and outline steps that can be taken to make them as productive as possible.

To understand the underlying factors that contribute to team success and failure, we first must consider the basic nature of *groups* in general. As you know, a great deal of the work performed in organizations is done by people working together in groups. In view of this, it makes sense to understand the types of groups that exist and the variables governing the interrelationships between them and individuals—commonly referred to as *group dynamics*. As a field of inquiry, **group dynamics** focuses on the nature of groups—the variables governing their formation and development, their structure, and their interrelationships with individuals, other groups, and the organizations within which they exist.[1] Because groups exist in all types of social settings, the study of group dynamics has a long history in the social sciences—including OB.[2]

In the first half of this chapter we draw on this work. Specifically, we describe the nature of groups by defining what groups are and outlining the dynamics of group interaction. Following this, we shift attention to how effectively groups operate, describing how people are affected by the presence of others and the tendency for individuals to withhold performance under certain group conditions.

WHAT IS A GROUP?

Imagine three people waiting in line at the cashier's lane at a supermarket. Now compare them to the board of directors of a large corporation. Which collection would you consider to be a "group"? Although in our everyday language we may refer to the people waiting in line as a group, they clearly are not a group in the same sense as the members of the board. Obviously, a group is more than simply a collection of people. But what exactly is it that makes a group a group?

Social scientists formally define a **group** as a collection of two or more interacting individuals with a stable pattern of relationships between them who share common goals and who perceive themselves as being a group.[3] To help understand this definition, let's take a closer look at its various elements.

➤ *Social interaction.*   One of the most obvious characteristics of groups is that they are composed of *two or more people in social interaction*. In other words, the members of a group have some influence on each other. The interaction between the parties may be either verbal (such as sharing strategies for a corporate takeover) or nonverbal (such as exchanging smiles in the hallway), but the parties must have some impact on one another to be considered a group.

➤ *Stability.*   Groups also must possess a *stable structure*. Although groups can change, and often do, there must be some stable relationships that keep group members together and functioning as a unit. A collection of individuals that constantly changes (e.g., the people inside an office waiting room at any given time) would not be considered a group. To be a group, a greater level of stability would be required.

➤ *Common interests or goals.*   A third characteristic of groups is that their *members share common interests or goals.* For example, members of a outdoor adventure club constitute a group that is sustained by the mutual interest of members. Some groups form because members with common interests help each other achieve a mutual goal. For example, the owners and employees of a community sewing shop constitute a group formed around a common interest in sewing and the common goal of making money.

➤ *Recognition as being a group.*   Finally, to be a group, the individuals involved must *perceive themselves as a group.* Groups are composed of people who recognize each other as members of their groups and can distinguish these individuals from non-members. The members of a corporate finance committee, for example, know who is in their group and who is not. In contrast, shoppers in a checkout line probably don't think of one another as being members of a group. Although they stand physically close to each other and may have passing conversations, they have little in common (except, perhaps, a shared interest in reaching the end of the line) and fail to identify with others in the line.

By defining groups in terms of these four characteristics, we have identified a group as a very special collection of individuals. As we shall see, these characteristics are responsible for the important effects groups have on organizational behavior.

THE BASIC BUILDING BLOCKS OF GROUP DYNAMICS

Now that you know what a group is, you are prepared to appreciate the basic elements that account for the dynamics of people in groups. Specifically, we will describe three basic building blocks of groups: the rules and expectations that develop within groups (*norms*), the prestige of group membership (*status*), and the members' senses of belonging (*cohesiveness*).

Norms: A Group's Unspoken Rules

One feature of groups that enhances their orderly functioning is the existence of group norms. **Norms** may be defined as generally agreed upon informal rules that guide group members' behavior.[4] They represent shared ways of viewing the world. Norms differ from organizational rules in that they are not formal and written. In fact, group members may not even be aware of the subtle group norms that exist and regulate their behavior. Yet, they have profound effects on behavior. Norms regulate the behavior of groups in such important ways as: fostering workers' honesty and loyalty to the company, establishing appropriate ways to dress, and dictating when it is acceptable to be late for or absent from work (so long as none of these things are specified formally in company rules).

If you recall the pressures placed on you by your peers as you grew up to dress or wear your hair in certain styles or to refrain from saying or doing certain things, you are well aware of the profound normative pressures exerted by groups. Some norms, known as **prescriptive norms,** dictate the behaviors that should be performed. Other norms, known as **proscriptive norms,** dictate specific behaviors that should be avoided. For example, groups may develop prescriptive norms to help a group member who needs assistance. They also may develop proscriptive norms to avoid telling each other's secrets to the boss.

Sometimes the pressure to conform to norms is subtle, as in the dirty looks given a manager by his peers for going to lunch with one of the assembly-line workers. At

Table 9.1   Group Norms: How Do They Develop?

Group norms develop in the four ways summarized here.

Basis of Norm Development	Example
1. Precedents set over time	Seating locations of each group member around a table tend to stabilize after several meetings
2. Carryovers from other situations	Informal professional standards influence how doctors talk to patients regardless of the hospital at which they work
3. Explicit statements from others	Working a certain way because you are told "that's how we do it around here"
4. Critical events in group history	After the organization suffers a loss due to one person's divulging company secrets, a norm develops to maintain secrecy

(Source: Based on Feldman, 1984; see Note 5.)

other times normative pressures may be quite severe, such as when one production worker sabotages another's work because he is performing at so high a level as to make his co-workers look bad.

Repeatedly saying something to employees about their inappropriate behavior is just one of several ways in which norms may develop. There are, in fact, several factors responsible for the formation of norms.[5] For a summary of these, see Table 9.1.

Status: The Prestige of Group Membership

Have you ever been attracted to a group because of the prestige accorded its members? You may have wanted to join a certain fraternity or sorority because it is highly regarded by the students. No doubt, members of championship-winning football teams proudly sport their Super Bowl rings to identify themselves as members of that highly regarded team.

Clearly, one potential reward of group membership is the status associated with being in that group. Even within social groups, different members are accorded different levels of prestige. Fraternity and sorority officers, and committee chairpersons, for example, may be recognized as more important members of their respective groups. This is the idea behind **status**—the relative social position or rank given to groups or group members by others.[6] Status may be recognized as both formal and informal in nature.

Formal and informal status

Formal status refers to attempts to differentiate between the degrees of formal authority given employees by an organization. This is typically accomplished through the use of **status symbols**—objects reflecting the position of an individual within an organization's hierarchy. Some examples of status symbols include job titles (e.g., director); perquisites, or perks, (e.g., country club membership); the opportunity to do desirable and highly regarded work (e.g., serving on important committees); and luxurious working conditions (e.g., having a large, private office that is lavishly decorated). Interestingly, having a corner office is another such example. Although they may have no inherent value of their own (except, perhaps, for extra windows), corner offices are rarer than others, signalling the special status of their occupants.

Interestingly, in this era of environmental consciousness, one of the greatest symbols of status for CEOs in California's Silicon Valley is not just a reserved parking space (traditionally, for a gas-guzzling luxury car), but one equipped with a station for recharging an electric car.[7] Until Mr. Agassi's dream comes true for automakers to manufacture electric vehicles, as described at the beginning of this chapter, other entrepreneurs are retrofitting existing hybrids into even more efficient electric cars. Because these conversions currently cost about $10,000 and require about 100,000 miles of driving to break even, they send strong messages about the drivers of these vehicles. In this case, that message is clear: I care about the environment and I am important enough for the company to support me in this.

Symbols of **informal status** within organizations are widespread. These refer to the prestige accorded individuals with certain characteristics that are not formally recognized by the organization. For example, employees who are older and more experienced may be perceived as higher in status by their co-workers. Those who have certain special skills (such as the home-run hitters on a baseball team) also may be regarded as having higher status than others. In some organizations, the lower value placed on the work of women and members of minority groups by some misguided individuals also can be considered an example of informal status in operation.[8]

Status and influence: A key relationship

One of the best-established findings in the study of group dynamics is that higher-status people tend to be more influential than lower-status people. (As will be described in Chapter 11, *influence* refers to the capacity to affect others in some fashion.) This phenomenon may be seen in a classic study of decision making in three-man bomber crews.[9] After the crews had difficulty solving a problem, the experimenter planted clues to the solution with either a low-status group member (the tail gunner) or a high-status group member (the pilot). It was found that the solutions offered by the pilots were far more likely to be adopted than the same solutions presented by the tail gunners. Apparently, the greater status accorded the pilots (because they tended to be more experienced and hold higher military ranks) was responsible for the greater influence they wielded.

Cohesiveness: Getting the Team Spirit

One obvious determinant of any group's structure is its **cohesiveness**—the strength of group members' desires to remain part of their groups. Highly cohesive work groups are ones in which the members are attracted to each other, accept the group's goals, and help work toward meeting them. In very uncohesive groups, the members dislike each other and may even work at cross-purposes.[10] In essence, cohesiveness refers to a *we-feeling*, an *esprit de corps*, a sense of belonging to a group.

Determinants of cohesiveness

Several important factors affect the extent to which group members tend to "stick together." These are as follows:

> ➤ *Severity of initiation.* The greater the difficulty people overcome to become a member of a group, the more cohesive the group will be.[11] The rigorous requirements for gaining entry into elite groups, such as the most prestigious medical schools and military training schools, are partly responsible for the high degree of camaraderie found in such groups. Having "passed the test" tends to keep individuals together and separates them from those who are unwilling or unable to "pay the price" of admission.

➤ *External threat.*   Group cohesion also is strengthened under conditions of high external threat or competition. When workers face a "common enemy," they tend to draw together. Such cohesion not only makes workers feel safer and better protected, but it also aids them by encouraging them to work closely together and coordinate their efforts toward the common enemy. A classic example of cohesion in response to shared external threat may be seen in the way employees of normally competing restaurants in New York City banded together to feed the hungry in the aftermath of the September 11, 2001 terrorist attacks.

➤ *Group size.*   As you might imagine, cohesiveness tends to be greater in smaller groups. Generally speaking, groups that are too large make it difficult for members to interact and, therefore, for cohesiveness to reach a high level.

➤ *History of success.*   "Nothing succeeds like success," as they say, and groups with a history of success tend to be highly cohesive. It is often said that "everyone loves a winner," and the success of a group tends to help unite its members as they rally around their success. For this reason, employees tend to be loyal to successful companies and sports fans tend to remain loyal to winning teams.

Beware—cohesiveness can be a double-edged sword

Thus far, our discussion has implied that cohesiveness is a positive thing. Indeed, it can be. For example, people are known to enjoy belonging to highly cohesive groups. Members of closely knit work groups participate more fully in their group's activities, more readily accept their group's goals, and are absent from their jobs less often than members of less cohesive groups.[12] Not surprisingly, cohesive groups tend to work together quite well and are sometimes exceptionally productive with low levels of voluntary turnover.[13]

However, highly cohesive groups also can be problematic. For example, if a highly cohesive group's goals are contrary to an organization's goals, that group is in a position to inflict a great deal of harm by working against the organization's interests.[14] Highly cohesive group members who conspire to sabotage their employers are a good example. With this in mind, it's important to recognize that when it comes to performance, group cohesiveness is a double-edged sword: Its effects can be both helpful and harmful to an organization.

INDIVIDUAL PERFORMANCE IN GROUPS

Now that we have reviewed the basic nature of groups, we will turn to an aspect of group dynamics most relevant to the field of organizational behavior—the effects of groups on individual performance. Specifically, we will examine two different issues in this connection: how people's work performance is affected by the presence of others and how performance is affected by group size.

Social Facilitation: Working in the Presence of Others

Imagine that you have been taking piano lessons for 10 years and you now are about to go on stage for your first major solo concert performance. You have been practicing diligently for several months, getting ready for the big night. Now, you are no longer alone in your living room but on stage in front of hundreds of people. Your name is announced and silence breaks the applause as you take your place in front of the concert grand. How will you perform now that you are in front of an audience? Will you freeze, forgetting parts of the piece you practiced, or will the audience spur you on to your best performance yet? In other words, what impact will the presence of the audience have on your behavior?

The social facilitation effect

After studying this question for over a century, using a wide variety of tasks and situations, social scientists found that the answer is not straightforward.[15] Sometimes people were found to perform better in the presence of others than when alone, and sometimes they performed better alone than in the presence of others. This tendency for the presence of others to enhance an individual's performance at times and to impair it at other times is known as **social facilitation.** (Although the word *facilitation* implies improvements in task performance, scientists use the term *social facilitation* to refer to both performance improvements and decrements stemming from the presence of others.)

The obvious question is this: Under what conditions will performance be helped by the presence of others and under what conditions will it be hindered? Research has shown that the answer depends on how well people know the task they are performing (for a summary, see Figure 9.1). When people are performing tasks they know quite well (e.g., a musical piece they have played for years), they generally perform better in front of an audience than alone. However, when people are performing tasks with which they are unfamiliar (e.g., a piece of music that is new to their repertoires), they generally perform better alone than in the presence of others.

Social facilitation and performance monitoring

It's easy to imagine how the social facilitation effect may have a profound influence on organizational behavior. For example, consider the effects it may have on people

Figure 9.1   The Social Facilitation Effect: A Summary

According to the phenomenon of *social facilitation*, a person's performance on a task will be influenced by the presence of others. Compared to performance when doing the task alone, performance in front of an audience will be enhanced if that task is well learned but impaired if it is not well learned.

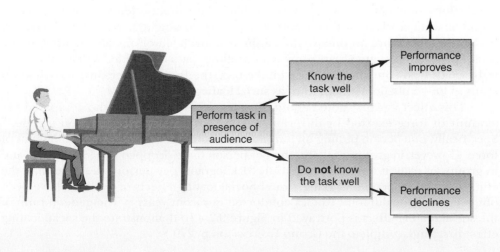

whose work is monitored, either by others who are physically present or by connections made via computer networks. The rationale behind *performance monitoring*—the practice of supervisors observing subordinates while working—is that it will encourage people to perform at their best. But does it really work this way?

The concept of social facilitation suggests that monitoring should improve task performance only if the people monitored know their tasks extremely well. However, if they are relatively new to the job, their performance would suffer when monitored. In fact, research suggests that this is precisely what happens.[16] For employees who are not well practiced at their jobs, performance monitoring does not have the intended effects. Accordingly, supervisors seeking to raise employees' performance levels by introducing performance monitoring should carefully consider the effects of social facilitation before doing so.

Social Loafing: "Free Riding" When Working with Others

Have you ever worked with several others helping a friend move into a new apartment, each carrying and transporting part of the load from the old place to the new one? Or how about joining forces with members of your family to shovel snow off your driveway? Although these tasks are different, they share a common characteristic: performing each requires only a single individual, but several people's work can be pooled to yield greater outcomes. Because each person's contributions can be added together with another's, such tasks are referred to as **additive tasks.**[17]

The social loafing effect

Over the years, many students have told me that they don't like working with their classmates on group projects because although they contribute their fair share, there's always someone who goofs off and just goes along for the ride. If this sounds familiar to you, there's a good reason. Research has found that when several people combine efforts on additive tasks, each individual contributes less than he or she would when performing the same task alone.[18] As suggested by the old saying "Many hands make light the work," a group of people would be expected to be more productive than any one individual. However, it doesn't always work this way. When several people combine their efforts on additive tasks, each individual's contribution tends to be less than it would be when working by themselves. Five people working together raking leaves will *not* be five times more productive than a single individual working alone; just as in the group project, there are always some who go along for a "free ride." In fact, the more individuals who contribute to an additive task, the less each person's contribution tends to be—a phenomenon known as **social loafing.**[19]

This effect was first noted about 70 years ago by a scientist who compared the amount of force exerted by different size groups of people pulling on a rope.[20] Specifically, one person pulling on a rope alone exerted an average of 63 kilograms of force. However, in groups of three, the per-person force dropped to 53 kilograms, and in groups of eight it was reduced to only 31 kilograms per person—less than half the effort exerted by people working alone! Social loafing effects of this type have been observed in many different studies conducted in recent years.[21] The general form of the social loafing effect is portrayed in Figure 9.2. (To demonstrate the social loafing effect firsthand, complete the Group Exercise on p. 279.)

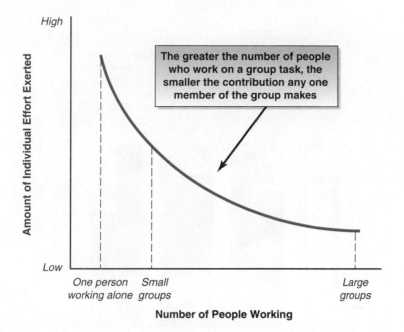

Figure 9.2   The Social Loafing Effect

When individuals work together on additive tasks, the greater the size of the group, the less effort each individual tends to exert. This phenomenon is known as *social loafing*.

Is social loafing a universal phenomenon?

A simple way of understanding social loafing is that it occurs because people are more interested in themselves (getting the most for themselves while doing the least) than their fellow group members (who are forced to do their work for them). But, are people like this all over the world? Is social loafing equally likely to occur in every country?

To begin considering this question, it probably isn't surprising that social loafing occurs in the United States because Americans tend to be to be highly *individualistic*. In **individualistic cultures** people highly value individual accomplishments and personal success. However, in other countries, such as Israel and the People's Republic of China, people place a high value on shared responsibility and the collective good of all. Such nations are referred to as having **collectivistic cultures.** In such cultures, people working in groups would not be expected to engage in social loafing because doing so would have them fail in their social responsibility to the group (a responsibility that does not prevail in individualistic cultures). In fact, to the extent that people in collectivistic cultures are strongly motivated to help their fellow group members, they would be expected to be more productive in groups than alone. In other words, not only wouldn't they loaf, but they would work especially hard!

These ideas were tested in an interesting experiment.[22] Managers from the United States, Israel, and the People's Republic of China were each asked to complete an exercise simulating the daily activities of managers, such as writing memos, filling out forms, and rating job applicants. They were all asked to perform this task as effectively as they could for a period of one hour but under one of two different conditions: either *alone* or

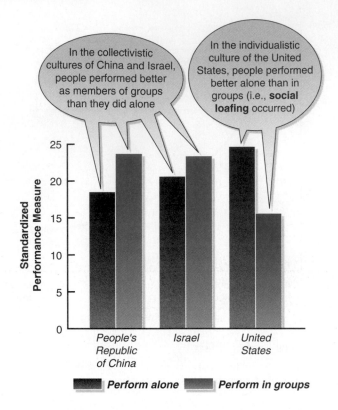

Figure 9.3   Social Loafing: Not a Universal Phenomenon

A researcher compared the performance of people from the United States, Israel, and the People's Republic of China who worked alone and in groups on a managerial task. Although individual performance alone was lower than performance as part of a group in the United States (i.e., *social loafing* occurred), the opposite was found in China and Israel. Compared to the more *individualistic* nature of American culture, the highly *collectivistic* nature of Chinese and Israeli cultures discouraged people in these nations from letting down their fellow group members.

(Source: Based on data reported by Earley, 1993; see Note 22.)

as part of a *group* of ten. Individual and group performance was then compared. Did social loafing occur, and in which countries? The results, summarized in Figure 9.3, show that social loafing occurred in the United States. That is, individual performance was significantly lower among people working in groups than those working alone. However, the opposite was found in each of the two highly collectivistic cultures, the People's Republic of China and Israel. In these nations, people not only failed to loaf in groups, but they worked *harder* than they did alone. Because they strongly identified with their group and were concerned about the welfare of its members, people from collectivistic cultures placed their group's interests ahead of their own.

This research suggests that culture plays an important part in determining people's tendencies to engage in social loafing. Although it may be tempting to think of social loafing as an inevitable aspect of human nature, the phenomenon is not as universal as you might think. Instead, loafing appears to be a manifestation of cultural values: Among cultural groups in which individualism is stressed, individual interests guide performance, but among groups in which collectivism is stressed, group interests guide performance.

Suggestions for overcoming social loafing

Obviously, the tendency for people to reduce their effort when working with others could be a serious problem in organizations. Fortunately, there are several ways in which social loafing can be overcome.

> ➤ *Make each performer identifiable.*   Social loafing may occur when people feel they can get away with "taking it easy"—namely, under conditions in which each individual's contributions cannot be determined. A variety of studies on the practice of *public posting* support this idea.[23] This research has found that when each individual's contribution to a task is displayed where it can be seen by others (e.g., weekly sales figures posted on a chart), people are less likely to slack off than when only overall group (or company-wide) performance is made available. In other words, when one's individual contribution to a group effort is highlighted, each person feels pressure to make a group contribution. Thus, social loafing can be overcome if one's contributions to an additive task are identified: Potential loafers are not likely to loaf if they fear getting caught.

> ➤ *Make work tasks more important and interesting.*   Research has revealed that people are unlikely to go along for a free ride when the task they are performing is believed to be vital to an organization.[24] For example, research has found that the less meaningful salespeople believe their jobs are, the more they engage in social loafing—especially when they think their supervisors know little about how they are performing.[25] To help in this regard, corporate officials should deliberately attempt to make jobs more intrinsically interesting to employees. To the extent that jobs are interesting, people may be less likely to loaf.

> ➤ *Reward individuals for contributing to their group's performance.*   Social loafing may be overcome by encouraging people's interest in their group's performance.[26] Doing this (e.g., giving all salespeople in a territory a bonus if they jointly exceed their sales goal) may help employees focus more on collective concerns and less on individualistic concerns, increasing their obligations to their fellow group members. This is important, of course, in that the success of an organization is more likely to be influenced by the collective efforts of groups than by the individual contributions of any one member.

> ➤ *Use punishment threats.*   Individuals generally are responsive to threats of punishment, suggesting that people would not loaf if they believed they would be punished for doing so. The author and one of his students demonstrated this in a experiment involving members of high school swim teams who swam either alone or in relay races during practice sessions.[27] Confirming the social loafing effect, we found that students swam faster alone than as part of relay teams when no punishment was threatened. However, when the coach threatened them with having to swim "penalty laps," the social loafing effect did not occur.

TEAMS: EMPOWERED WORK GROUPS

In recent years, as organizations have been striving to hone their competitive advantages, many have been organizing work around specific kinds of groups known as *teams*. Because the team movement frequently takes different forms, some confusion has arisen regarding exactly what teams are. In this section we will clarify the basic nature of teams by describing their key characteristics and then identifying the various types of teams that exist.

What Is a Team?

At the Miller Brewing Company in Trenton, Ohio, six to nineteen employees work together to perform all operations, including brewing, packaging, and distributing Miller Genuine Draft beer. They schedule their own work assignments and vacations, conduct assessments of their peers' performance, maintain the equipment, and perform other key functions. Each group is responsible for meeting prespecified targets for production, quality, and safety—and to help, data regarding costs and performance are made available to them.

Clearly, these groups are different in key respects from the ones we have been describing thus far, such as a company's budget committee. The Miller employees are all members of special kinds of groups known as *teams*. Formally defined, a **team** is a group whose members have complementary skills and are committed to a common purpose or set of performance goals for which they hold themselves mutually accountable. Applying this definition to our description of the way work is done at Miller's Trenton, Ohio plant, it's clear that teams are in use at this facility.

Given the complicated nature of teams, we will highlight some of their key characteristics and distinguish teams from the traditional ways in which work is structured.[28] As you read these descriptions, you might find it useful to refer to Table 9.2 as a summary.

Teams are organized around work processes rather than functions

Instead of having traditional departments focusing on a specialized function (such as engineering, planning, quality control, and so on), it is likely that team members have many different skills and come together to perform key processes, such as designing and launching new products, manufacturing, and distribution. As an example, Sterling Winthrop used to have 21 different departments working on various aspects of manufacturing medicine. Today, all facets of production (e.g., ordering supplies,

Table 9.2 Teams Versus Traditional Work Structures: Some Key Distinctions

Teams differ from traditional work structures with respect to the six key distinctions identified here.

Traditional Structure	Teams
Design around functions	Design around work processes
No sense of ownership over the work products	Ownership of products, services, or processes
Workers have single skills	Team members have many skills
Outside leaders govern workers	Team members govern themselves
Support staff and skills are found outside the group	Support staff and skills are built into teams
Organizational decisions are made by managers	Teams are involved in making organizational decisions for themselves

(Source: Adapted from Wellins et al., 1994; see Note 28.)

blending the formulation, scheduling work, etc.) are carried out by members of teams responsible for all aspects of the production process.

Teams "own" the product, service, or processes on which they work

By this, we mean that people feel part of something meaningful and understand how their work fits into the big picture (recall our discussion of the motivating properties of these kinds of beliefs described in Chapter 6). For example, employees at Florida's Cape Coral Hospital work in teams within four "minihospitals" (surgical, general, specialty medical, and outpatient)—not only to boost efficiency but also to help them feel more responsible for their patients. By working in small units, team members have greater contact with patients and are more aware of the effects of their efforts on patient care. This is in contrast to the traditionally more distant ways of organizing hospital work, in which employees tend to feel less connected to the results of their actions. And in hospitals, such feelings can lead medical professionals to make serious, or even tragic, mistakes.

Members of teams are trained in several different areas and have a variety of skills

At Milwaukee Insurance, policies are processed by team members who rate applications, underwrite policies, and enter them into the computer system. Before the switch to teams, these tasks were performed by specialists in three separate departments. In fact, this type of separation of tasks is typical within traditional work groups. Before the advent of work teams, it was usual for people to learn only single jobs and to perform them over and over again unless there was some specific need for retraining (or interest in doing so on the part of the employee). In work teams, however, this practice of learning to perform a variety of different tasks, known as **cross-training,** occurs regularly. Cross-training involves efforts to learn the jobs performed by one's team members.

An interesting experiment explains why cross-training is effective.[29] The participants in this study were college students who performed a military combat simulation game in a laboratory setting. Each person was carefully trained to perform a specific task (e.g., pilots learned how to fly, radar specialists learned how to interpret radar screens, and so on). In addition, some of the participants also were trained in how to perform the task of other group members. Researchers compared the performance of teams composed of members who were cross-trained to the performance of teams whose members were not cross-trained. (In this simulation game, good performance required "killing" enemy targets while keeping one's plane from being shot.) Overall, the cross-trained group performed significantly better.

By including additional questionnaire measures to assess *how* the teams operated, the researchers were able to determine precisely why this occurred. The process, summarized in Figure 9.4, appears to work as follows. When people are cross-trained, they develop what are called **shared mental models**—that is, a common understanding regarding how their team operates, including how people are expected to work together and who does what at particular points in time. These shared mental models, in turn, help people understand how to coordinate their efforts with others and, of course, how to assist others who may need help (i.e., how to back them up). And, as you might expect, these particular skills contribute to team success. By contrast, people who were not cross-trained failed to develop any shared mental models with their teammates, thereby lowering the degree of coordination and backup capacity that contributed to team success.

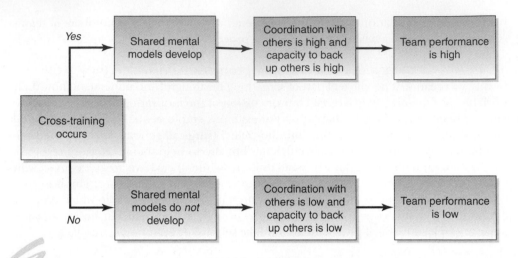

Figure 9.4   How Does Cross-Training Impact Team Effectiveness?

Research has established that cross-training promotes team effectiveness in the manner identified here. The process of cross-training helps create *shared mental models* (common views about how a team should operate), which in turn facilitate high levels of coordination within teams and the capacity for members to provide needed backup. These factors ultimately promote the success of cross-trained teams.

(Source: Based on suggestions by Marks et al., 2002; see Note 29.)

Teams govern themselves—at least to some extent

Because team members tend to be so highly trained and involved in a variety of organizational activities, it often is unnecessary for them to be governed closely in the traditional manner in which bosses supervise their subordinates. Instead, many team leaders serve as *coaches* who help team members achieve their goals rather than as traditional, more authoritarian leaders (see Chapter 11). In other words, teams are **empowered** to make decisions on their own behalf.

Here's a case in point. At Texas Instruments' defense electronics plant, teams appoint their own leaders, called "coordinators," who do exactly what the name implies—they work to ensure the smooth interaction between the efforts of team members. At other companies, such as Mine Safety Appliances, team members take turns as "captains," handling all the paperwork for a few weeks until the job is rotated to someone else. It is important to note, however, that not all teams enjoy such total self-regulatory freedom. As you might imagine, because many company officials are reluctant to give up power, complete self-governance by teams does not always occur. Still, at least some degree of self-governance tends to occur in today's work teams.

In teams, support staff and responsibilities are built in

Traditionally, such functions as maintenance, engineering, and human resources operate as separate departments that provide support to other groups requiring their services. Insofar as this may cause delays, teams often include members who have expertise in these crucial support areas. For example, at K Shoes, a British footwear manufacturing firm, there are no longer any quality inspectors. Instead, all team members are trained in matters of inspection and quality control techniques. Sometimes organizations hire people with highly advanced or specialized skills who are assigned to work as members of several teams at once. For example, this is done at Texas Instruments to give teams access to specialized engineering services. Regardless of how it's done, the point is that teams do not rely on outside support services to get their basic jobs done; they are relatively self-contained and self-sufficient.

Teams are involved in making company-wide decisions

Traditionally, high-level managers are used to make important organizational decisions. In work teams, however, this responsibility tends to fall on the shoulders of teams. For example, team members at Tennessee Eastman, a manufacturer of chemicals, fibers, and plastics, participate actively on company-level committees that develop policies and procedures affecting everyone. The underlying idea is that the people who are closest to the work performed should be the ones most involved in making the decisions. As noted earlier, the reluctance of some corporate leaders to completely empower teams may temper this process somewhat. In other words, although some companies may be reluctant to give teams total decision-making power, the granting of at least some decision-making authority is a hallmark of modern teams.

Team members back up one another

Suppose you are part of a team that is inundated with work. There's simply too much for you to do and it looks as if you won't complete the job as required. A potential benefit of working in teams is that one of your teammates may come to your rescue by putting down his or her own work and helping you. Known as **backing up,** this is a central feature of teams. If one team member has a much heavier workload than the other, backing up (by shifting some of the work to the person with the lighter load) can be an effective way to boost overall team performance. In such cases, of course, it is important to ensure that the teammate who's helping with backup does not do so at the expense of his or her own performance.[30]

Types of Teams

According to one expert, major U.S. companies are now either using some form of teams or are seriously considering them for the future. Although there has been a great amount of recent interest in teams, they have been around the workplace in one form or another for some time. In fact, many large corporations (e.g., Cummins Engine, General Motors, and Ford Motor Company) have been using them for quite a few years—with some, such as Procter & Gamble, for four decades.

In view of their widespread popularity, it should not be surprising that there are many different kinds of teams. We will summarize some of the major kinds of teams here in terms of some of the key ways they may be distinguished from one another.

Work teams and improvement teams

One way of distinguishing between teams has to do with their major *purpose* or *mission*. In this regard, some teams—known as **work teams**—are primarily concerned with the work done by the organization, such as developing and manufacturing new products, providing services for customers, and so on. Their principal focus is on using the organization's resources to create its products effectively (either goods or services). The examples I've given thus far fall into this category. Other teams—known as **improvement teams**—are oriented primarily toward the mission of increasing the effectiveness of the processes that are used by the organization. For example, Texas Instruments has relied on teams to help improve the quality of operations at its plant in Malaysia.

Temporary and permanent teams

A second way of distinguishing between types of teams has to do with how long-lasting they are. Specifically, some teams are only **temporary** and are established for a specific project with a finite life span. For example, a team set up to develop a new product would be considered temporary because as soon as its job is done, it disbands. However, other kinds of teams are **permanent** and remain intact as long as the organization is operating. For example, teams focusing on providing effective customer service tend to be permanent parts of many organizations.

Work groups and self-managed work teams

Teams also differ with respect to the degree of autonomy they have. Typically, this is reflected in terms of two key factors: the degree of responsibility people have and the degree to which they are held accountable for their own work outcomes. Along the resulting continuum we may identify three kinds of groups and teams (see Figure 9.5). These are as follows:

➤ At the low-autonomy extreme are **work groups,** in which leaders make decisions on behalf of group members, whose job it is to follow the leader's orders. This traditional form is becoming less popular, as more organizations are allowing employees to make their own key decisions.

➤ At the high-autonomy extreme are **self-managed work teams** (or **self-directed teams**). In such teams, small numbers (typically about 10) take on duties once performed by their supervisors, such as making work assignments, deciding on the pace of work, and so on.[31] About 20 percent of U.S. companies use self-managed work teams, and this figure is growing rapidly.

➤ Between these two extremes are **semiautonomous work groups.** These are groups whose members have some, but not complete, freedom to make decisions on their own behalf. Many companies making the move to self-managed work teams try using semiautonomous work groups along the way just to ensure that everyone involved is ready for the resulting freedom and responsibility that go with self-management.

Intact and cross-functional teams

Another way to distinguish teams is with respect to the team's connection to the organization's overall authority structure—that is, the connection between various formal job responsibilities. In some organizations, **intact teams** work together all the time and do not apply their special knowledge to a wide range of products. Teams in such organizations, such as Ralston-Purina, do not have to stray from their areas of expertise.

With growing frequency, however, teams are crossing over various functional units (e.g., marketing, finance, human resources, and so on). Such teams, referred to as **cross-functional teams,** are composed of employees at identical organizational levels

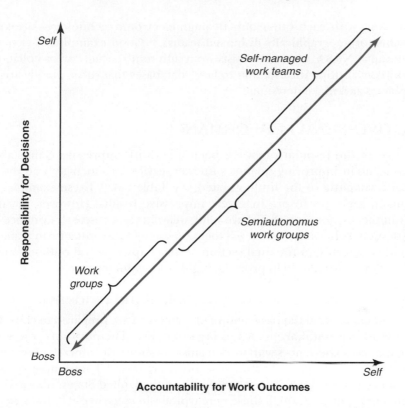

Figure 9.5   A Continuum of Autonomy

Work groups and teams differ with respect to the degree of autonomy they have. In *work groups,* bosses have responsibility over decisions and are accountable for work outcomes. The workers themselves have very little autonomy. By contrast, in *self-managed work groups,* the workers themselves have responsibility over decisions and are accountable for work outcomes. They are highly autonomous. *Semiautonomous work groups* fall between these two extremes.

but from different specialty areas. Cross-functional teams are an effective way of bringing people together from throughout the organization to cooperate on large projects. To function effectively, the boundaries between cross-functional teams must be permeable—that is, employees must be members of more than one team.

For example, members of an organization's manufacturing team must carefully coordinate their activities with members of its marketing team. To the extent that people are involved in several different kinds of teams, they may gain broader perspectives and make more contributions that are important to their various teams. As an example, Boeing used cross-functional teams to develop its latest, and largest, 777 aircraft.

Physical and virtual teams

The teams we have been describing thus far may be considered **physical teams** insofar as they involve people who physically meet to work together. Although teams have operated this way for many years, and will continue to do so, technology has made it possible for teams to exist without ever having their members get together physically. Teams of this sort—that operate across space, time, and organizational boundaries, communicating with each other only through electronic technology—are known as **virtual teams** (or **geographically disbursed teams**).[32] Good examples of virtual teams may be found at NASA, where scientists from different specialty areas collaborate on projects by contributing information to large databases that subsequently are used to solve problems and make decisions.

EFFECTIVE TEAM PERFORMANCE

In recent years, the popular press has been filled with impressive claims about the success of teams in improving quality, customer service, productivity, and the bottom line.[33] For a sampling of the findings cited, see Table 9.3.[34] These examples suggest that teams in general can produce very impressive results. However, because it is unclear whether or not such claims are valid, we will review research evidence bearing on this question. Following this, we will focus on some of the obstacles to team success. Then, building on this, in the final section of the chapter we will outline some of the things that can be done to help promote highly successful teams.

How Successful Are Teams? A Look at the Evidence

Now that you understand the basic nature of teams, you are prepared to consider a key question: How successful are teams in organizations? The most direct way to learn about companies' experiences with work teams is to survey the officials of organizations that use them. One large-scale study did precisely this.[35] The sample consisted of several hundred of the 1,000 largest companies in the United States. About 47 percent used some work teams, although these were typically in place in only a few selected sites as opposed to the entire organization. Where they were used, however, they were generally highly regarded. Moreover, teams were viewed as becoming increasingly popular over time.

Table 9.3 The Effectiveness of Teams: Some Impressive Results

Teams have helped many organizations enjoy dramatic gains in productivity. Here is a sampling of these impressive results.

Company	Result
Wilson Sporting Goods	Average annual cost savings of $5 million
Kodak Customer Assistance Center	Accuracy of responses increased 100 percent
Corning	Defects dropped from 1,800 ppm to 3 ppm
Sealed Air	Waste reduced by 50 percent
Exxon	$10 million saved in six months
Carrier	Unit turnaround reduced from two weeks to two days
Xerox	Productivity increased by 30 percent
Westinghouse	Product costs down 60 percent
Texas Instruments	Costs reduced by more than 50 percent

(Sources: Based on information in Redding, 2000; and Blanchard & Bowles, 2001; see Note 34.)

Case studies

These optimistic results are further supported by in-depth case studies of numerous teams in many different organizations.[36] Research of this type, although difficult to quantify and to compare across companies, provides some interesting insight into what makes teams successful and why.

Consider, for example, the work teams used in General Motors' battery plant in Fitzgerald, Georgia. The 320 employees at this facility operate in various teams, including managers working together in *support teams,* middle-level employees (such as foremen and technicians) working in *coordination teams,* and *employee teams,* natural work units of three to nineteen members performing specific tasks. Although the teams work closely together, coordinating their activities, they function almost as separate businesses.

Because employees must perform many different tasks in their team, they are not paid based on their positions but for their knowledge and competence. In fact, the highest-paid employees are individuals who have demonstrated their competence (usually in highly demanding tests) on all the jobs performed in at least two different teams. This is GM's way of rewarding people for broadening their perspectives, appreciating "the other guy's problems." By many measures, the Fitzgerald plant has been very effective. Its production costs are lower than comparable units in traditionally run plants. Employee satisfaction surveys also reveal that job satisfaction at this plant is among the highest found at any General Motors facility. Although this is only one example, many companies in a wide variety of businesses have reported successes using work teams.[37]

Empirical studies

Although case studies report successful experiences with teams, they are not entirely objective. After all, companies may be unwilling to broadcast their failures to the world. This is not to say that case studies cannot be trusted. Indeed, when the information is gathered by outside researchers (such as those on which we have reported here), the stories they tell about how teams are used, and the results of using them, can be quite revealing.[38] Still, there is a need for completely objective, empirical studies of team effectiveness.

Research objectively assessing the effectiveness of work teams has been performed in recent years. In one such investigation comparisons were made between various aspects of work performance and attitudes of two groups of employees at a railroad car repair facility in Australia: those who were assembled into teams that could freely decide how to do their jobs and those whose work was structured in the more traditional, nonautonomous fashion.[39] After the work teams had been in place for several months, it was found that they had significantly fewer accidents as well as lower rates of absenteeism and turnover.

Not all empirical studies, however, paint such an optimistic picture of the benefits of work teams. For example, in one study examining work teams in an English manufacturing plant it was found that employees were more satisfied with their jobs in teams than those who worked in conventional arrangements (in which individuals took orders from a supervisor), but they were individually no more productive.[40] However, because the use of teams made it possible for the organization to eliminate several supervisory positions, the company became more profitable.

Overall, what can we conclude? Are teams effective? Taken together, research suggests that teams are well received. Most people enjoy working in teams, at least after they have adjusted to them (which can take some work). Certainly, teams help enhance commitment among employees, and as we described in Chapter 5, there are benefits to be derived from this (e.g., reduced absenteeism and turnover). From an organizational perspective, teams appear to be an effective way of eliminating layers of management, thereby allowing more work to be done by fewer people, which also can be a valuable money-saving contribution. All of these benefits are tangible.

However, it is important to keep in mind that teams are not always responsible for making individuals and organizations any more productive. Cases of companies becoming wildly successful after adopting teams, although compelling, cannot always be generalized to all teams in all situations.

Potential Obstacles to Success: Why Do Some Teams Fail?

Although we have reported many success stories about teams, we also have hinted at several possible problems and difficulties in implementing them. After all, working in a team demands a great deal, and not everyone may be ready for one. (To see if you are predisposed to work as a member of a team, complete the Self-Assessment Exercise on pp. 278–279.) Fortunately, we can learn a great deal from the experiences of failed teams. Specifically, analyses of failed attempts at introducing teams into the workplace suggest several obstacles to team success, pitfalls that can be avoided if you know about them.[41] Here are some of the most common ones:

➤ *Lack of cooperation.* Some teams fail because their members are unwilling to cooperate with one another. This is what happened a few years ago at Dow Chemical Company's plastics group in Midland, Michigan, where a team was put into place to create a new plastic resin.[42] Some members (those in the research field) wanted to spend several months developing and testing new options, whereas others (those on the manufacturing end) wanted to alter existing products slightly and start up production right away. Neither side budged, and the project eventually stalled. By contrast, when team members share a common vision and are committed to attaining it, they are generally very cooperative with each other, leading to success.

➤ *Lack of support.* It is not unusual for teams to fail because they fail to receive the proper support needed by upper management. Consider, for example, the experience at the Lenexa, Kansas, plant of the Puritan-Bennett Corporation, a manufacturer of respiratory equipment.[43] After seven years of working to develop improved software for its respirators, product development teams did not get the job done, despite the fact that the industry average for such tasks is only three years. According to Roger J. Dolida, the company's director of research and development, the problem was that management never made the project a priority and refused to free up another key person needed to do the job. As he put it, "If top management doesn't buy into the idea . . . teams can go nowhere."[44]

➤ *Reluctance to relinquish control.* Traditional supervisors work their way up the corporate ladder by giving orders and having them followed. However, team leaders have to build consensus and must allow team members to make decisions together. As you might expect, letting go of control isn't always easy for some to do. This problem emerged at Bausch & Lomb's sunglasses plant in Rochester, New York, where some 1,400 employees were put into 38 teams.[45] Three years later, about half the supervisors had not adjusted to the change, despite receiving thorough training in how to work as part of a team. They argued bitterly with team members whenever their ideas were rejected, and eventually they were reassigned.

➤ *Failure to cooperate with other teams.*   Teams don't operate in a vacuum. To be successful, they must carefully coordinate their efforts with other teams. Not doing so is a recipe for failure. This problem occurred in General Electric's medical systems division when it assigned two teams of engineers, one in Waukesha, Wisconsin, and another in Hino, Japan, the task of creating software for two new ultrasound devices.[46] Not cooperating with each other, each team pushed features that made its products popular only in their own country and duplicated the other's efforts. When the teams met, language and cultural barriers separated them, further distancing the teams from one another. Without close cooperation between teams (as well as within them!), organizations are not likely to reap the benefits they sought when creating teams in the first place.[47]

HOW TO DEVELOP SUCCESSFUL TEAMS

Now that you know about the track record of teams and understand some of the factors that make them fallible, you are in a good position to understand the various steps that can be taken to develop successful work teams. As you might imagine, making teams work effectively is no easy task. Success is not automatic. Rather, teams need to be carefully nurtured and maintained for them to accomplish their missions.[48] As one expert expressed it, "Teams are the Ferraris of work design. They're high performance but high maintenance and expensive."[49] What, then, could be done to help make teams as effective as possible? Based on analyses of successful teams, several keys to success may be identified.[50]

Provide Training in Team Skills

To be effective, team members must have the right blend of skills needed for the team to contribute to the group's mission. Rather than simply putting teams together and hoping they will work, many companies are taking proactive steps to ensure that team members will get along and perform as they should. Formal efforts directed toward making teams effective are referred to as **team building.**

Team building is usually used when established teams are showing signs of trouble, such as when members lose sight of their objectives and when turnover is high. Workers having high degrees of freedom and anonymity require a depth of skills and knowledge that surpasses that of people performing narrower, traditional jobs. For this reason, successful teams are those in which investments are made in developing the skills of team members and leaders. In the words of one expert, "Good team members are trained, not born."[51]

Illustrating this maxim is Development Dimensions International (DDI), a human resource company, located in Pittsburgh, Pennsylvania. This small company has each of its 70 employees spend some 200 hours in training (in such areas as interaction skills, customer service skills, and various technical areas) during their first year—even more for new leaders. Then, after this initial period, all DDI employees receive a variety of training on an ongoing basis.

Key areas of team training
Two areas of emphasis are essential to the success of any team training effort—training in being a team member and training in self-management.

Table 9.4   Interpersonal Skills Required by Team Members

Experts have advocated that team members be trained in the various interpersonal skills summarized here (many of which are described elsewhere in this book).

Skill	Description
Advocating	Ways of persuading others to accept one's point of view (see Chapter 11)
Inquiring	Listening effectively to others and drawing information out of them (see Chapter 8)
Tension management	Managing the tension that stems from conflict with others (see Chapter 7)
Sharing responsibility	Learning to align personal and team objectives (see this chapter)
Leadership	Understanding one's role in guiding a team to success (see this chapter)
Valuing diversity	Acceptance—and taking advantage of—differences between members (see Chapter 5)
Self-awareness	Willingness to criticize others constructively and to accept constructive criticism from others (see Chapters 7 and 8)

(Source: Based on information in Caudron, 1994; see Note 51.)

➤ *Being a team member.* Linda Godwin, a mission specialist at NASA's Johnson Space Center in Houston, likens team success to the kind of interpersonal harmony that must exist within space shuttle crews. "We have to be willing to compromise and to make decisions that benefit everyone as a whole," says Godwin, a veteran of two successful shuttle missions.[52] In this regard, there are several key interpersonal skills in which training is most useful, and these are summarized in Table 9.4.

➤ *Self-management.* For teams to operate effectively, members must be able to manage themselves. However, most employees are used to being told what to do and don't know how to manage their own behavior. Specifically, this involves the various skills summarized in Figure 9.6.[53]

Figure 9.6   Self-Management Skills: A Key to Team Success

For teams to function successfully, it is essential for members to know how to manage themselves. Training in self-management focuses on the five skills summarized here.

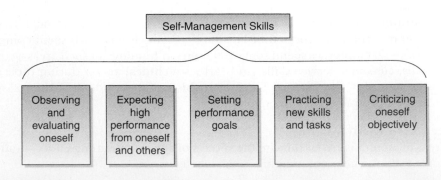

Team training exercises

Typically, team building involves having team members participate in various exercises designed to help employees learn how to function effectively as team members. Among the most widely used are the following:[54]

➤ *Role definition exercises.*   Are team members doing what others expect them to be doing? Teams whose members answer "no" are destined for trouble. To avoid such problems, some team-building exercises ask members to describe their own roles and the roles of others on their team. Members then systematically discuss these perceptions and highlight areas of disagreement so these can be worked on.

➤ *Goal-setting exercises.*   As described in Chapter 6, successful performance is enhanced by the setting of goals. As a team-building strategy, team members meet to clarify the various goals toward which they are working and to identify ways they can help achieve them.

➤ *Problem-solving exercises.*   Building successful teams requires ensuring that members are able to work together at solving important problems. To help in this regard, some team-building sessions require members to get together to systematically identify and discuss ways of solving problems more effectively.

➤ *Interpersonal process exercises.*   Some of the most popular team-building exercises involve activities that attempt to build trust and to open communication among members. The underlying idea is that those members who harbor hostility toward each other or who have hidden agendas are unlikely to work together well. There is usually a fun aspect to interpersonal process training as well. Black & Decker, for example, had members of its design team participate in a Spider Web activity requiring members to crawl through a large web of woven rope suspended between two trees without touching the rope. The underlying idea is that by helping each other through these exercises, team members can develop more positive relationships with each other and come to learn how they can influence each other's potential back on the job. In doing this, companies have used such diverse activities as trekking in the wilderness, going through obstacle courses, and having paintball wars. For a close-up example of one extreme form of building teams through interpersonal processes, see the accompanying Winning Practices section.

Is team building effective?

These various meetings and physical exercises may be fun, but do they have any value? In other words, are they worth the time and money invested in them? The answer is: *only sometimes.* For team-building exercises to be effective they must be applied correctly. Too often, however, exercises are used without first thoroughly analyzing precisely what the team needs. When it comes to team building, one size does not fit all! Another problem is that team-building exercises often are used as a one-time panacea. For them to be most effective, however, team-building exercises should be repeated regularly to keep the team in tip-top shape or, at least, at the very first sign of problems. And then, when on the job, everyone should be reminded of the lessons learned off-site.

Compensate Team Performance

Because the United States and Canada are highly individualistic cultures, most North American workers are used to highly individualistic compensation systems—ones that recognize individual performance. However, when it comes to teams, it also is very

Winning Practices

Altrec.com: Extreme Team Building in Action (and Lots of It!)

In the fast-paced, eat-or-be-eaten world of e-business, start-up companies have few options but to grow big overnight. Mike Morford, CEO of Altrec.com, which sells outdoor and travel gear online, was well aware of this as he planned a way to develop a senior team that could pull off the nearly impossible task of finding large investors while keeping at bay two equally hungry competitors.[55] Although his team of 10 star soloists looked good on paper, he realized that six were new to the company, and for things to gel, they had to learn to work together as a team.

Instead of bringing everyone together in the company's comfortable conference room, Morford opted for a more rugged venue—a 75-mile stretch of Idaho's lower Salmon River, one of the country's wildest waterways. There, in temperatures that reached 100 degrees, rode the fate of the company on an 18-foot rubber raft. The team had four days to come up with a six-month plan for the company. If they didn't become a cohesive team by the end of the run, they faced a threat more ominous than business failure—"the Slide," at high water, the largest rapids in North America. The rationale was simple enough: The lessons learned about teamwork in the course of navigating the minefield of unknown hazards on the trip could be taken back to the office, where the more conventional hazards of e-business confronted them.

Although the technical specialists looked forward to the adventure (some more than others), all were somewhat skeptical about whether the "touchy-feely" trip would be anything more than a fun adventure. The first three days were just plain scary, but on the fourth, the team faced a "sink-or-swim" challenge. Amidst what the guide called particularly "flippy" rapids, the raft rose straight up into the air and plummeted from a height of a story and a half, dumping everyone into the water. Fortunately, everyone came out okay—or even better than okay, as they learned how to help each other confront a force bigger than themselves.

The real challenge began immediately after the adventure, as Altrec.com's senior management team put its words into practice. Two particular strategies emerged. First, team members realized there was tension due to the fact that nobody knew exactly what one particular employee was supposed to be doing. Because this individual happened to be close friends with Morford, everyone just sidestepped the issue and resentment grew. During the trip, everyone agreed on a way to tackle the problem, and a plan was put in place to address it. Second, the team developed a strategy for development in four key areas: communication, feedback, decision making, and respect. After seeing his team in action, Morford, who welcomed a return to the dry and safe harbor of his office back in Redmond, Oregon, learned an important lesson himself: He had assembled a group of aggressive decision makers, and his job was to leverage, but not cripple, that strength.

Although everyone claimed to have enjoyed the adventure, back at the office, team members were no more than cautiously optimistic about what the future held for the company and the extent to which their river trip helped at all. If, after six months, the individuals begin working together as a team, none of the skeptical engineers is likely to bad-mouth the "touchy-feely" experience they had on—and in—the Salmon River.

important to recognize group performance. Teams are no places for hotshots who want to make their individual marks—rather, teams require "team players." And the more organizations reward employees for their teams' successes, the more strongly team spirit will be reinforced. Several companies in which teams are widely used—including the Hannaford Brothers retail food distribution company in New York—have plans in place that reward team members for reaching company-wide performance goals, allowing them to share in their companies' profits.

In view of the importance of team members having a variety of different skills, many companies, including Milwaukee Insurance, Colgate-Palmolive, and Sterling Winthrop, have taken to paying employees for their demonstrated skills as opposed to their job performance. Such a system is known as *skill-based pay*. A highly innovative skill-based pay system has been in use at Tennessee Eastman. This company's "pay-for-applied-skills-and-knowledge" plan—or *PASK*, as it is known—requires employees to demonstrate their skills in several key areas, including technical skills and interpersonal skills. The pay scale is carefully linked to the number of skills acquired and the level of proficiency attained. By encouraging the development of vital skills in this manner, the company is ensuring that it has the resources for its teams to function effectively.

Communicate the Urgency of the Team's Mission

Team members are prone to rally around challenges that compel them to meet high performance standards. As a result, the urgency of meeting those standards should be expressed. For example, a few years ago, employees at Ampex Corporation, once known in the broadcast industry as a manufacturer of videotape equipment, worked hard to make their teams successful when they recognized the changes necessitated by the shift to digital technology. Unless the company met these challenges, the plug surely would be pulled. Realizing that the company's very existence was at stake, work teams pushed to fast-forward Ampex into a position of prominence in its industry by ramping up development of digital recording technology. This was the right thing to do, and although the teams worked urgently to bring about the needed changes in direction, financial difficulties leave the company's ultimate future uncertain.

Promote Cooperation Within and Between Teams

Team success requires not only cooperation within teams but between teams as well. As one expert put it, "Time and time again, teams fall short of their promise because companies don't know how to make them work together with other teams. If you don't get your teams into right constellations, the whole organization can stall."[56] Boeing successfully avoided such problems in the course of developing its 777 passenger jet—a project involving some 200 teams.

As you might imagine, on such a large project coordination of effort between teams is essential. To help, regular meetings were held between various team leaders who disseminated information to members. And team members could go wherever needed within the organization to get the information required to succeed. As one Boeing team leader put it, "I can go the chief engineer. Before, it was unusual just to see the chief engineer."[57] Just as importantly, if after getting the information they need, team members find problems, they are empowered to take action without getting management's approval. According to Boeing engineer, Henry Shomber, "We have the no-messenger rule. Team members must make decisions on the spot. They can't run back to their functions [department heads] for permission."[58]

Select Team Members Based on Their Skills or Potential Skills

Insofar as the success of teams demands that they work together closely on a wide variety of tasks, it is essential for them to have a complementary set of skills. This includes not only job skills but also interpersonal skills (especially since getting along with one's teammates is very important). With this in mind, at Ampex (noted earlier) three-person subsets of teams were used to select their own new members because they have the best idea about what skills are needed and who would best fit into the teams. It also is important for teams frequently to project future skills that may be needed and to train team members in these skills. With this in mind, work teams at Colgate-Palmolive Company's liquid detergents plant in Cambridge, Ohio, initially receive 120 hours of training in such skills as quality management, problem solving, and team interaction, and subsequently receive advanced training in all these areas.

In an effort to keep team members' skills fresh, it is important to regularly confront members with new facts. Fresh approaches are likely to be prompted by fresh information, and introducing new facts may present the kind of challenges that teams need to say innovative. For example, when information about pending cutbacks in defense spending was introduced to teams at Florida's Harris Corporation (an electronics manufacturer), new technologies were developed that positioned the company to land large contracts in nonmilitary government organizations—including a $1.7 billion contract to upgrade the FAA's air traffic control system.

Back Up Teammates Selectively

Earlier in the chapter, we mentioned that a potential benefit of teams is that members may back up one another, thereby evening the workload. What makes this only a "potential" benefit, rather than a guaranteed one, is that redistributing the workload runs the risk of removing the helping member from his or her own work, causing it to suffer. And when this happens, one member's gain becomes the other's loss, thereby not ensuring a net gain to the team as a whole.

So, how can this problem be avoided? The key is for members to back up one another selectively—only when doing so does not overburden the helping member. This would be the case, for example, if the helping member has a particularly light workload. However, when workloads are evenly distributed to begin with, the practice of backing up teammates may come at a too high a cost. Thus, backing up is not something that should be done automatically. Instead, it should be decided upon on a case-by-case basis after carefully considering the costs and benefits of the workload redistribution.

A Cautionary Note: Developing Successful Teams Requires Patience

It is important to caution that, although these suggestions are important, they alone do not ensure the success of work teams. Many other factors, such as the economy, the existence of competitors, and the company's financial picture, also are important determinants of organizational success. Still, the fact that these practices are followed in many highly successful teams certainly makes them worthy of consideration.

However, developing effective teams is difficult, and the path to success is riddled with obstacles. It is also time-consuming. According to the late management expert Peter Drucker, "You can't rush teams. It takes five years just to learn to build a team and decide what kind you want."[59] And it may take most organizations over a decade to make a complete transition to teams. Clearly, teams are not an overnight route to success. But with patience and careful attention to the suggestions outlined here, teams have ushered many companies into extraordinary gains in productivity. For this reason, they must be considered a viable option for organizing work groups.[60]

Back to the Case

Answer the following questions about this chapter's Making the Case (p. 251) to illustrate insights you have derived about the material in this chapter.

1. What specific types of teams do you think Mr. Agassi might be using at Better Place?
2. Do you think these work groups are vulnerable to social loafing? Why or why not?
3. Better Place is planning to rewrite the history of the automobile by moving into uncharted territory. How do you think this may affect the nature of the teamwork required for success?

You Be the Consultant

Using Teams to Enhance Performance

A large manufacturing company has been doing quite well over the years but is now facing dramatic competition from overseas competitors that are undercutting its prices and improving on the quality of its goods. The company president has read a lot about teams in popular business magazines and has called on you as a consultant to help implement a transition to teams for the organization. Answer the following questions relevant to this situation based on the material in this chapter.

1. What would you tell the company president about the overall record of teams in being able to improve organizational performance?

2. The company president notes that the current employees tend to have relatively poor skills and are generally disinterested in acquiring new ones. Will this be a problem when it comes to using teams? Why or why not?

3. Several people in the company—including some top executives—are a bit concerned about relinquishing some of their power to teams. Is this likely to be a problem? If so, what can be done to help alleviate it?

SELF-ASSESSMENT EXERCISE

Are You a Team Player?

Let's face it, some people find it easier to work in teams than others. Are you already a "team player," or have you not yet developed the skills needed to work effectively with others in teams? Knowing where you stand along this dimension may come in handy when it comes to considering a new job or planning your next work assignment. The following questionnaire will give you insight into this question.

Directions

1. Read each of the following statements and carefully consider whether or not it accurately describes you on the job most of the time.

2. Then, on the line next to each statement, write "yes" if the statement describes you most of the time, or "no" if it does not describe you most of the time. If you are uncertain, write a question mark ("?").

3. Do your best to respond to all items as honestly as possible.

Most of the time, on the job, I . . .

_____ 1. demonstrate high ethical standards.
_____ 2. deliver on promises I make.
_____ 3. take initiative, doing what's needed without being told.
_____ 4. follow the norms and standards of the groups in which I work.
_____ 5. put team goals ahead of my own.
_____ 6. accurately describe my team to others in the organization.
_____ 7. pitch in to help others learn new skills.
_____ 8. do at least my share of the work.
_____ 9. coordinate the work I do with others.
_____ 10. try to attend all meetings and arrive on time for them.
_____ 11. come to meetings prepared to participate.
_____ 12. stay focused on the agenda during team meetings.
_____ 13. share with others new knowledge I may have about the job.
_____ 14. encourage others to raise questions about the way things are.
_____ 15. affirm positive things about others' ideas before noting concerns.
_____ 16. listen to others without interrupting them.
_____ 17. ask others questions to make certain I understand them.
_____ 18. make sure I attend to a speaker's nonverbal messages.
_____ 19. praise others who have performed well.
_____ 20. give constructive, nonjudgmental feedback to others.
_____ 21. receive constructive feedback without acting defensively.
_____ 22. communicate ideas without threats or ridicule.
_____ 23. explain the reasoning behind my opinions.
_____ 24. demonstrate my willingness to change my opinions.
_____ 25. speak up when I disagree with others.
_____ 26. show disagreement in a tactful, polite manner.
_____ 27. discuss possible areas of agreement with others with whom I am in conflict.

(Source: Based on material appearing in McDermott et al., 1998; see Note 60.)

Scoring

1. Count the number of times you responded by saying "yes."
2. Then count the number of times you responded by saying "no."
3. Add these two numbers together.
4. To compute your *team player score,* divide the number of times you said yes (step 1) by the total (step 3). Then multiply by 100. Your score will be between 0 and 100. Higher scores reflect greater readiness for working in teams.

Discussion Questions

1. What was your score, and how did it compare to those of others in your class?
2. What does this questionnaire reveal about the ways in which you are equipped to work in teams?
3. What does this questionnaire reveal about the ways in which you are deficient when it comes to working in teams? What do you think you could do to improve your readiness for working in teams?

GROUP EXERCISE

Demonstrating the Social Loafing Effect

The social loafing effect is quite strong and is likely to occur in many situations in which people make individual contributions to an additive group task. This exercise is designed to demonstrate the effect firsthand in your own class.

Directions

1. Divide the class into groups of different sizes. Between five and ten people should work alone. In addition, there should be a group of two, a group of three, a group of four, and so on, until all members of the class have been assigned to a group. (If the class is small, assign students to groups of vastly different sizes, such as two, seven, and fifteen.) Form the groups by putting people from the same group together at tables.
2. Each person should be given a page or two from a telephone directory and a stack of index cards. Then have the individuals and the members of each group perform the same additive task—copying entries from the telephone directory onto index cards. Allow exactly 10 minutes for the task to be performed, and encourage everyone to work as hard as they can.
3. After the time is up, count the number of entries copied.
4. For each group, and for all the individuals, compute the average per-person performance by dividing the total number of entries copied by the number of people in the group.
5. At the board, the instructor should graph the results. Along the vertical axis show the average number of entries copied per person. Along the horizontal axis show the size of the work groups—one, two, three, four, and so on. The graph should look like the one in Figure 9.2 (see p. 259).

Discussion Questions

1. Was the social loafing effect demonstrated? What is the basis for your conclusion?
2. Did members of smaller groups feel more responsible for their group's performance than members of larger groups?
3. What could have been done to counteract any "free riding" that may have occurred in this demonstration?

Making Individual
and Group Decisions
in Organizations

Learning Objectives

After reading this chapter, you will be able to:

1. **IDENTIFY** the steps in the decision-making process and **DESCRIBE** the effects of culture on decision making.

2. **DESCRIBE** the different varieties of decisions people make in organizations.

3. **EXPLAIN** the three major approaches to individual decision making (the rational-economic model, the administrative model, and image theory).

4. **IDENTIFY** various factors that contribute to imperfect decision making in organizations.

5. **DESCRIBE** the conditions under which individuals make better decisions than groups and groups make better decisions than individuals.

6. **EXPLAIN** how various structural techniques and computer-based techniques may be used to improve the quality of decisions made by groups.

3 GOOD REASONS why you should care about . . .

Decision Making in Organizations

You should care about decision making in organizations because:

1. Human decision making is inherently imperfect, although these imperfections can be overcome if you know what they are and how they operate.

2. Functioning effectively in today's business environment requires awareness of cultural differences in the way people make decisions.

3. Groups are widely used to make organizational decisions despite the fact they often are ineffective at dealing with the kinds of tasks they are likely to face.

Making the Case for Decision Making in Organizations

Coca-Cola: Deciding on the Look

What do Yao Ming and LeBron James have in common? They're professional basketball stars of the highest magnitude, of course, but you probably didn't know that each also designed his own Coke bottle. Now, before you start thinking that only celebrities get to do such cool things, you could have designed your own bottle too. In fact, in conjunction with the 2008 Olympics in Beijing, tens of thousands of people from around the world visited Coca-Cola's Web site, where, with the aid of a drawing application, they put stunningly beautiful finishing touches on classic Coke bottles.

Why did Coke bother with this? The answer is simple: Coca-Cola is deciding on a new bottle design and they stood to get great ideas from the submissions. And, because visitors to the site were asked to vote on the various designs submitted, company officials got a good sense of what consumers liked.

But in selecting a new look, designs by consumers were only one of the factors that Coke took into account, as you might imagine. David Butler, head of Coca-Cola's design team, was charged with creating a consistent new image for the company's products and he needed as much input as possible. With 450 different brands, over 300 different models of vending machines, and different design standards being used throughout the world, the task was enormous.

To make the job manageable, Butler needed clear criteria specifying precisely what he was trying to achieve. He and the members of his design team identified three considerations. The design had to identify the brand clearly, it must create a good experience for the user, and the container should be made from environmentally safe materials.

With these things in mind, Butler, with help from the design staff at the branding and packaging firm Turner Duckworth, created a new bottle design—an aluminum contour bottle in traditional Coke red with the white script logo wrapped prominently around the middle. It was considered a sexy, updated version of the classic Coke bottle—immediately recognizable but up-to-date. And being made of aluminum instead of glass, the beverage felt colder, it was lighter to ship, much less expensive to produce, and it was eco-friendly. In fact, the bottle is made of recycled aluminum that, itself, can be recycled. So highly regarded was the design that it won an award: the prestigious Grand Prix at the 2008 Cannes Lions advertising festival.

Although this bottle is in only limited use, such as in a few upscale clubs, its success has spurred Butler and his staff to redesign the remaining products in the company's vast portfolio. As overwhelming as this may seem, with a consistent look and design strategy to guide them, these decisions promise to be a little less challenging. Yet, when it comes to the iconic Coke brand, company officials are understandably cautious about making changes. In 1985, Coke decided to tweak the flavor of its flagship brand, yielding disastrous results. It was a classic marketing blunder. The public clamored for the return of their favorite beverage, and a few weeks later, they got it. With this legacy of fizzled decision making to haunt him, it's a safe bet that Butler is not making his design decisions casually.

Although the decisions you make as an individual may be less monumental than those of Coca-Cola's design team, they surely are very important to you. Personal decisions about what college to go to, what field to major in, and what job to accept can have a major impact on the direction your life takes. If you think about the difficulties involved in making decisions in your own life, you surely can appreciate how complicated—and important—the process of decision making can be in organizations, where the stakes are often considerable and the impact is widespread. In both cases, however, the essential nature of **decision making** is identical. Defined quite simply as the process of making choices from among several alternatives, the process of decision making is far from simple.

Management experts agree that decision making represents one of the most common and most crucial work roles of executives.[1] Every day people in organizations make decisions about a wide variety of topics ranging from the mundane to the monumental.[2] Understanding how these decisions are made and how they can be improved is an important goal of the field of organizational behavior. As such, we will devote a great deal of attention to these matters in this chapter. Before considering this, we begin by examining the general nature of the decision-making process and the wide variety of decisions made in organizations.

THE FUNDAMENTAL NATURE OF DECISION MAKING

To describe the fundamental nature of decision making we will focus on two things. First, we describe a general model of the decision-making process. Second, we will ask a fundamental question about decision making: How does culture affect the way we make decisions?

A General Model of Decision Making

Traditionally, scientists have found it useful to conceptualize the process of decision making as a series of steps that groups or individuals take to solve problems.[3] A general model of the decision-making process can help us understand the complex nature of organizational decision making (see Figure 10.1). This model highlights two important aspects of the decision-making process: *formulation,* the process of understanding a problem and making a decision about it, and *implementation,* the process of carrying out the decision made. As we outline this model, keep in mind that all decisions might not fully conform to the neat, eight-step pattern described (e.g., steps may be skipped and/or combined). However, for purposes of pointing out the general way the decision-making process operates, the model is quite useful.

1. *Identify the problem.*   To decide how to solve a problem, one must first recognize and identify it. For example, an executive may identify as a problem the fact that the company cannot meet its payroll obligations. This step isn't always as easy as it sounds. People frequently distort, omit, ignore, and/or discount information around them that provides important cues regarding the existence of problems (e.g., many people who suffer from alcoholism fail to acknowledge that they "have a problem"). This, of course, is problematic. After all, a problem cannot be solved if it is never recognized.

2. *Define objectives.*   After a problem is identified, the next step is to define the objectives to be met in solving it. It is important to conceive of problems in such a way that possible solutions can be identified. The problem identified in our example may be defined as "inadequate cash flow." By looking at the problem in this way, the objective is clear: Increase available cash reserves. Any possible solution to the problem should be evaluated relative to this objective.

3. *Make a predecision.*   A **predecision** is a decision about how to make a decision. By assessing the type of problem in question and other aspects of the situation, managers may opt to make a decision themselves, delegate the decision to another, or have a group (e.g., an executive committee) make the decision. Predecisions often are based on research that

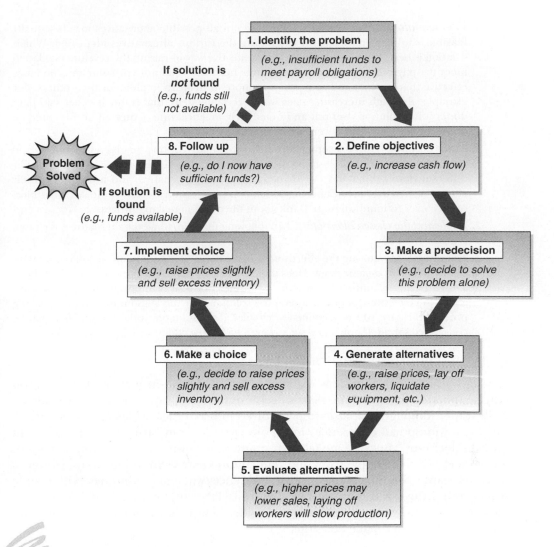

If solution is *not* found
(e.g., funds still not available)

1. Identify the problem
(e.g., insufficient funds to meet payroll obligations)

8. Follow up
(e.g., do I now have sufficient funds?)

2. Define objectives
(e.g., increase cash flow)

Problem Solved

If solution is found
(e.g., funds available)

7. Implement choice
(e.g., raise prices slightly and sell excess inventory)

3. Make a predecision
(e.g., decide to solve this problem alone)

6. Make a choice
(e.g., decide to raise prices slightly and sell excess inventory)

4. Generate alternatives
(e.g., raise prices, lay off workers, liquidate equipment, etc.)

5. Evaluate alternatives
(e.g., higher prices may lower sales, laying off workers will slow production)

Figure 10.1   The Decision-Making Process

The process of decision making tends to follow the eight steps outlined here. The running example illustrates how a particular problem—insufficient funds to meet payroll obligations—can be applied to each step.

(Source: Based on suggestions by Wedley & Field, 1983; see Note 3.)

tells us about the effectiveness of decisions made under different circumstances, much of which is reviewed in this chapter. Typically this information is summarized in computer programs known as **decision support systems (DSS).** These are complex databases of information about the success of past decisions that decision makers can use to help improve the quality of current decisions, particularly highly complex ones.

4. *Generate alternatives.*   Possible solutions to the problem are identified in this stage. Whenever possible in attempting to come up with solutions, people tend to rely on previously used approaches that may provide ready-made answers. In our example, some possible ways of solving the revenue shortage problem include reducing the workforce, liquidating unnecessary equipment, or increasing sales.

5. *Evaluate alternative solutions.* Because not all possible alternatives may be equally feasible, the fifth step calls for evaluating the various alternatives identified. Which solution is best? What would be the most effective way of raising the revenue needed to meet the payroll? The various alternatives need to be identified. Some may be more effective than others, and some may be more difficult to implement than others. For example, although increasing sales would certainly help, that is much easier said than done. It is a solution, but not an immediately practical one. (After all, if this could be done, the problem may never have arisen in the first place.)

6. *Make a choice.* After several alternatives are evaluated, one that is considered acceptable is chosen. As we will describe shortly, different approaches to decision making offer different views of how thoroughly people consider alternatives and how optimal their chosen alternatives are. Choosing which course of action to take is the step that most often comes to mind when we think about the decision-making process.

7. *Implement the chosen alternative.* In following this step, whatever alternative was chosen is now carried out.

8. *Follow-up.* Monitoring the effectiveness of the decisions they put into action is important to the success of organizations. Does the problem still exist? Have any new problems been caused by implementing the solution? In other words, it is important to seek feedback about the effectiveness of any attempted solution. For this reason, the decision-making process in Figure 10.1 is presented as circular. If the solution works, the problem may be considered solved. If not, a new solution will have to be attempted.

Cultural Differences in Decision Making

Having outlined the basic steps through which people go in making decisions, you may be thinking that everyone makes decisions the same way. However, this would be misleading. Although the basic steps involved in making decisions may be identical, there are widespread differences in the way people from various nations go about making decisions.[4] Because we take for granted our own ways of making decisions, differences between people from different cultures may seem strange to us. However, it is important to become aware of such differences when doing business with people from around the world (and with people from different countries within one's own nation). Accordingly, it makes sense to consider how people from different countries differ in the way they make decisions.

Recognizing problems

As we noted earlier, decision making begins by observing a problem. As obvious as this may seem, people from different countries do not always agree on what constitutes a problem. Suppose, for example, you are managing a large construction project and discover that your most important supplier will deliver some important materials several months late. If you are from the United States, Canada, or Western Europe, you may consider this unacceptable and decide to get another supplier. However, if you are from Thailand, Indonesia, or Malaysia, you would be likely to accept the situation as fate and allow the project to be delayed.

Preference for decision-making unit

In the United States, where people tend to have a highly **individualistic orientation** (i.e., their primary focus is on themselves as individuals), people tend to make decisions by themselves. However, in Asian countries, people have a more **collectivistic orientation** (i.e., their primary focus is on the groups to which they belong). As such, it would be inconceivable for a Japanese businessperson to make a decision without first checking with his or her colleagues. Individuals from such cultures are inclined to make group decisions rather than individual ones.

Who makes the decisions?

In Sweden, employees at all levels expect to be involved in making whatever decisions involve them. In fact, employees of the Scandinavian auto manufacturers Saab and Volvo routinely make decisions about how to do their jobs. In India, by contrast, the hierarchy of an organization matters a great deal. People there expect decisions to be made by others of higher rank. Empowered decision making (which we will describe more fully later in this chapter) is not well accepted.

Time taken to make decisions

In the United States, we generally respect people who make decisions quickly, referring to them as "decisive," a quality that is valued. In other cultures, however, time urgency is downplayed. For example, in the Middle East, quickly reaching a decision is seen as a sign of being overly hasty. In Egypt, the more important the matter, the more time one is expected to take when making a decision about it.

As these examples illustrate, there are some interesting and important differences in how people from various countries formulate and implement decisions. Understanding such differences is an important first step toward developing appropriate strategies for conducting business at a global level and within our multi-cultural society.[5]

VARIETIES OF ORGANIZATIONAL DECISIONS

Consider for a moment the variety of decisions likely to be made in organizations. Some decisions have consequences that don't matter much (e.g., what brand of paper clips to order for the company supply closet), whereas others are far-reaching (e.g., whether and how to count disputed ballots in a presidential election). People sometimes make decisions in situations in which the likely outcomes are relatively well known (e.g., the decision to underwrite life insurance on the basis of actuarial data), whereas at other times the outcomes are much more uncertain and difficult to predict (e.g., the decision to save the economy by investing billions of dollars in failing financial institutions). Finally, some decisions are issued from the top (e.g., an order from the department head that work will begin sharply at 8:00 A.M.) whereas other decisions are made by the very individuals who will be affected by them (e.g., a team whose members decide whom to hire).

These examples illustrate the three major characteristics of organizational decisions we now will describe: (1) how structured or unstructured the situation is, (2) the amount of certainty or risk the decision entails, and (3) the degree to which employees are involved in making the decisions affecting them.

Programmed Versus Nonprogrammed Decisions

Think of a decision that is made repeatedly, according to a preestablished set of guidelines. For example, a word processing operator may decide to make a backup disk of the day's work, or a manager of a fast-food restaurant may decide to order hamburger buns as the supply starts to dwindle. Decisions such as these are known as **programmed decisions**—routine decisions, made by lower-level personnel, that rely on predetermined courses of action.

In addition, people also make **nonprogrammed decisions**—ones for which there are no ready-made solutions. The decision maker confronts a unique situation in which the solutions are novel. The research scientist attempting to find a cure for a rare disease faces a problem that is poorly structured. Unlike the order clerk whose course of action is clear when the supply of paper clips runs low, the scientist in this example must rely on creativity rather than preexisting answers to solve the problem at hand.

Certain types of nonprogrammed decisions are known as *strategic decisions*. Typically, because these decisions have important long-term implications for the organization, they are made by coalitions of high-level executives.[6] **Strategic decisions** involve directing an organization in some specified fashion—that is, according to an underlying organizational philosophy or mission. For example, an organization may make a strategic decision to grow at a specified yearly rate or to be guided by a certain code of corporate ethics (see Chapter 2). Both of these decisions are likely to be considered "strategic" because they guide the future direction of the organization. Some examples of highly successful strategic decisions are summarized in Table 10.1.[7]

Table 10.1   Strategic Decisions: Some Highly Successful Examples

Decisions that guide the future directions of organizations are known as *strategic decisions*. Some of the best-known and most successful strategic decisions in business history are shown here.

Company	Decision Made
Toyota	In the aftermath of World War II, the company decided to emphasize high-quality manufacturing techniques.
Coca-Cola	During World War II, the company developed brand loyalty by selling bottles of Coke to members of the armed services.
IBM	In 1924, founder Thomas Watson, Sr., changed the company's name from the Computing-Tabulating-Recording Company to International Business Machines although it had no international operations at the time, boldly declaring its ambitions.
Microsoft	In 1981, Bill Gates decided to license MS-DOS to IBM, which relinquished control of the operating system for all non-IBM personal computers.
Apple	Steve Jobs decided to build his company around sales of a simple computer that could be used by individuals.
Sears	In 1905, the company decided on a way to bring its products to a wider audience by introducing a mail-order catalog.
Johnson & Johnson	In 1982, the company pulled all bottles of Tylenol capsules off store shelves after a few capsules were found to be poisoned.
Sony	In 1980, the company introduced the Walkman after officials noticed that young people like to have music with them wherever they go.
Hewlett-Packard	In 1984, the company decided to exploit an engineer's observation that metal heated in a certain way tended to splatter, resulting in the development of the ink-jet printer.

Certain Versus Uncertain Decisions

Think of how easy it would be to make decisions if we knew exactly what the future had in store. Making the best investments in the stock market would simply be a matter of looking up the changes in tomorrow's newspaper. Of course, we never know for sure what the future holds, but we can be more certain at some times than others. Certainty about the factors on which decisions are made is highly desired in organizational decision making.

Degrees of certainty and uncertainty are expressed as statements of risk. All organizational decisions involve some degree of risk—ranging from complete certainty (no risk) to complete uncertainty, "a stab in the dark" (high risk). To make the best possible decisions in organizations, people seek to "manage" the risks they take—that is, to minimize the riskiness of a decision by gaining access to information relevant to the decision.

What makes an outcome risky or not is the probability of obtaining the desired outcome. Decision makers attempt to obtain information about the probabilities, or odds, of certain events occurring given that other events have occurred. For example, a financial analyst may report that a certain stock has risen 80 percent of the time that the prime rate has dropped, or a meteorologist may report that the precipitation probability is 50 percent (i.e., in the past it rained or snowed half the time certain atmospheric conditions existed). These data may be considered reports of *objective probabilities* because they are based on concrete, verifiable data. Many decisions are also based on subjective probabilities—personal beliefs or hunches about what will happen. For example, a gambler who bets on a horse because it has a name similar to one of his children's, or a person who suspects it's going to rain because he just washed his car, is basing these judgments on *subjective probabilities.*

Obviously, uncertainty is an undesirable characteristic in decision-making situations. We may view much of what decision makers do in organizations as attempting to reduce uncertainty so they can make better decisions. In general, what reduces uncertainty in decision-making situations? The answer is *information.* Knowledge about the past and the present can be used to help make projections about the future. A modern executive's access to data needed to make important decisions may be as close as the nearest computer. A variety of online information services are designed to provide organizational decision makers with the latest information relevant to the decisions they are making.

Of course, not all information needed to make decisions comes from computers. Many managerial decisions also are based on the decision maker's experiences and intuition. This is not to say that top managers rely solely on subjective information in making decisions (although they might), but that their history of past decisions—both successes and failures—is often given great weight in the decision-making process. In other words, when it comes to making decisions, people often rely on what they believe has worked for them in the past. Some of this may be based on objective information and some of this may be purely subjective in nature.

Top-Down Versus Empowered Decisions

Traditionally, the job of making all but the most menial decisions has belonged to managers.[8] Subordinates collect information and give it to their superiors, who then use it to make decisions. Known as **top-down decision making,** this approach puts the power to make decisions in the hands of managers, leaving lower-level workers with only limited opportunity or no opportunity to make decisions.

Today, however, given the popularity of teams (see Chapter 9), another approach is in vogue. **Empowered decision making** allows employees to make the decisions required to do their jobs without seeking supervisory approval. As the name implies, this approach gives employees the power to do their jobs effectively. The rationale is straightforward: Allow the people who actually do certain jobs to make decisions about them. This practice is generally very useful because it is likely to lead to effective decisions. In addition, it helps build commitment to decisions. After all, people are more committed to the results of decisions they made themselves than those their bosses have made for them.

Empowered decision making occurs in many different organizations. For example, at Disney World, empowering employees to deal with customers is the rule rather than the exception.[9] Employees are given the authority to do whatever it takes (within reason, of course) to make hotel guests and park visitors happy on the spot. Management interference is discouraged. This is only one illustration of the great lengths to which companies are going to empower their employees to make decisions. It also highlights a key trend: Empowering workers is not a fad, but a practice that seems here to stay.[10]

HOW ARE INDIVIDUAL DECISIONS MADE?

Now that we have identified the types of decisions people make in organizations, we are prepared to consider how people go about making them. Perhaps you are thinking, "What do you mean, you just think things over and do whatever seems best?" Although this may appear to be true, you will see that there's a lot more to decision making than meets the eye. In fact, scientists have considered several different approaches to how individuals make decisions. Here, we will review three of the most important ones.

The Rational-Economic Model: In Search of the Ideal Decision

We all like to think that we are "rational" people who make the best possible decisions. But what exactly does it mean to make a *rational* decision? Organizational scientists view **rational decisions** as ones that maximize the attainment of goals, whether they are the goals of a person, a group, or an entire organization.[11] What would be the most rational way for an individual to go about making a decision? Economists interested in predicting market conditions and prices have relied on a **rational-economic model** of decision making, which assumes that decisions are optimal in every way. An economically rational decision maker will attempt to maximize his or her profits by searching systematically for the *optimum* solution to a problem. For this to occur, the decision maker must have complete and perfect information and be able to process all this information in an accurate and unbiased fashion.[12]

In many respects, rational-economic decisions follow the same steps outlined in our analytical model of decision making (see Figure 10.1). However, what makes the rational-economic approach special is that it calls for the decision maker to recognize *all* alternative courses of action (step 4) and to accurately and completely evaluate each one (step 5). It views decision makers as attempting to make *optimal* decisions.

Of course, the rational-economic approach to decision making does not fully appreciate the fallibility of the human decision maker. Based on the assumption that people have access to complete and perfect information and use it to make perfect decisions, the model can be considered a *normative* (also called *prescriptive*) approach—one that describes how decision makers ideally ought to behave so as to make the best possible decisions. It does not describe how decision makers actually behave in most circumstances. This task is undertaken by the next major approach to individual decision making, the *administrative model.*

The Administrative Model: The Limits of Human Rationality

You probably don't need too much convincing that people do not always act in a completely rational-economic manner. If they did, then many of the large investors who purchased securities backed by subprime mortgages would have thought twice about making these investments, precluding the financial crisis that began in 2008. But, they did, and for several reasons. In part, they made what proved to be improper assumptions about a rising real estate market. In part, they never fully understood the nature of their investment (presented in documents of about 450 pages). In part, they trusted the people selling the investments. And finally, in part, they simply were hopeful about making large amounts of money. These are the ways human beings behave, and it is a far cry from anything like the rational-economic decision maker.

Let's now focus on a far simpler example to illustrate the point that people generally fail to act in a rational-economic manner. Consider how employees of a company's personnel department might go about selecting a new receptionist. It's reasonable to expect that after interviewing several applicants for the job, the personnel manager then might choose the best candidate seen to that point and stop interviewing. Had the manager been following a rational-economic model, he or she would have had to interview all possible candidates before deciding on the best one. However, by ending the search after identifying the first candidate who is good enough to do the job, the manager is using a much simpler approach.

The process used in this example characterizes an orientation to decision making known as the **administrative model.**[13] This conceptualization recognizes that decision makers may have a limited view of the problems confronting them. The number of solutions that can be recognized or implemented is limited by the capabilities of the decision maker and the resources available to the organization. Also, because decision makers do not have perfect information about the consequences of their decisions, they cannot tell which one is best.

In most cases, people's imperfect decision making should not be taken as an indication that they do not want to behave rationally. Rather, innate limits in people's ability to make decisions as well as impediments in the work environment make it virtually impossible to make completely rational, perfect decisions. In fact, people tend to make irrational decisions so frequently (and sometimes predictably), that one scientist has referred to decisions as being "predictably irrational."[14]

In the next major section of this chapter we will examine some of the limitations of human decision making recognized by the administrative model. For now, however, suffice it to say that the administrative model does a better job than the rational-economic model of describing how decision makers actually behave. The approach is said to be *descriptive* (also called *proscriptive*) in nature. This interest in examining the actual, imperfect behavior of decision makers, rather than specifying the ideal, economically rational behaviors that decision makers ought to engage in, lies at the heart of the distinction between the administrative and rational-economic models. My point is not that decision makers do not want to behave rationally, but that restrictions posed by the innate capabilities of human decision makers preclude "perfect" decisions.

Image Theory: An Intuitive Approach to Decision Making

If you think about it, you'll probably realize that some, but certainly not all, decisions are made following the logical steps of our general model of decision making. Consider Elizabeth Barrett Browning's poetic question, "How do I love thee? Let me count the ways."[15] It's unlikely that anyone would ultimately answer the question by carefully counting what one loves about another (although many such characteristics can be enumerated). Instead, a more intuitive-based decision making is likely, not only for matters of the heart, but for a variety of important organizational decisions as well.[16]

The point is that selecting the best alternative by weighing all the options is not always a major concern when making a decision. People also consider how various decision alternatives fit with their personal standards as well as their personal goals and plans. The best decision for someone might not be the best for someone else. In other words, people may make decisions in a more automatic, *intuitive* fashion than is traditionally recognized. Representative of this approach is *image theory*, an approach to decision making summarized in Figure 10.2.[17]

Image theory deals primarily with decisions about adopting a certain course of action (e.g., should the company develop a new product line?) or changing a current course of action (e.g., should the company drop a present product line?). According to the theory, people make decisions on the basis of a simple two-step process. The first step is the *compatibility test,* a comparison of the degree to which a particular course of action is consistent with various images—particularly individual principles, current goals, and plans for the future. If any lack of compatibility exists with respect to these considerations, a rejection decision is made. If the compatibility test is passed, then the *profitability test* is carried out. That is, people consider the extent to which using various alternatives best fits their values, goals, and plans. The decision is then made to accept the best candidate. These tests are used within a certain *decision frame*—that is, with consideration of meaningful information about the decision context (such as past experiences). The basic idea is that we learn from the past and are guided by it when making decisions. The example shown in Figure 10.2 highlights this contemporary approach to decision making.

According to image theory, the decision-making process is very rapid and simple. The theory suggests that people do not ponder and reflect over decisions, but make them using a smooth, intuitive process with minimal cognitive processing. If you've ever found yourself saying that something "seemed like the right thing to do," or "something doesn't feel right," you're probably well aware of the kind of intuitive thinking that goes on in a great deal of decision making. Recent research suggests that when it comes to making relatively simple decisions, people tend to behave as suggested by image theory.[18] For example, people decide against various options when past evidence suggests that these decisions may be incompatible with their images of the future.[19]

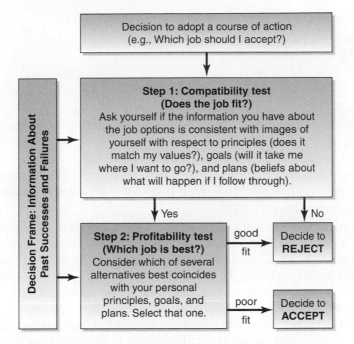

Figure 10.2   Image Theory: An Overview and Example

According to image theory, decisions are made in a relatively automatic, intuitive fashion following the two steps outlined here.

(Source: Adapted from Beach and Mitchell, 1990; see Note 17.)

To summarize, we have described three major approaches to individual decision making. The rational-economic approach represents the ideal way optimal decisions may be made. However, the administrative model and image theory represent ways that people actually go about making decisions. Both approaches have received support, and neither should be seen as a replacement for the other. Instead, several different processes may be involved in decision making. Not all decision making is carried out the same way: Sometimes decision making might be analytical, and sometimes it might be more intuitive. Modern organizational behavior scholars recognize the value of both approaches.

Something both approaches have in common is that they recognize the fallibility of the human decision maker. With this in mind, we now turn attention to the imperfect nature of human decisions.

THE IMPERFECT NATURE OF HUMAN DECISIONS

Although we may know better, most of us like to think of ourselves as "rational" people who make **rational decisions**—that is, decisions that maximize the attainment of individual, team, or organizational goals. However, as you know from experience and as we already noted, people do not always act in completely rational ways. So, how exactly can we characterize decision making in organizations?

Characteristics of Decisions in Organizations

As we have been suggesting, human decision making is far from perfect. Let's now examine the nature of some of these imperfections.

Decision makers have a limited view of the problems confronting them

The number of solutions that can be recognized or implemented is limited by the capabilities of the decision maker and by the resources available to the organization. Also, because decision makers do not have perfect information about the consequences of their decisions, they cannot tell which one is best. The idea is that people lack the cognitive skills required to formulate and solve highly complex business problems in a completely objective, rational way—what is known as **bounded rationality.**[20]

Decision makers consider solutions as they become available

Although it might be best to consider all possible solutions, making an **optimal decision,** people don't do so. Instead, they decide on the first alternative that meets their criteria for acceptability. Thus, the decision maker selects a solution that may be just good enough, although not optimal. Such decisions are referred to as **satisficing decisions.** In most situations satisficing decisions are acceptable and are more likely to be made than optimal ones. The following analogy has been used to compare the two types of decisions: Making an optimal decision is like searching a haystack for the sharpest needle, but making a satisficing decision is like searching a haystack for a needle just sharp enough to sew with.

Decision makers face time constraints

An unavoidable fact of life in contemporary organizations is that people often have only limited amounts of time to make important decisions. The rapid pace with which businesses operate these days results in severe pressures to make decisions almost immediately. Among firefighters, emergency room doctors, and fighter pilots, it's clear that time is of the essence. But in today's rapidly changing organizations, even those of us who toil in less dramatic settings also face the need to make good decisions quickly. The practice of thoroughly collecting information, carefully analyzing it, and then leisurely reviewing the alternatives is a luxury few modern decision makers can afford. In fact, three-quarters of managers believe that the number of decisions they are required to make each day has increased, and about half believe that they are able to devote less time to their decisions than in the past.[21] Often the result is that as people are rushed into action, bad—and inevitably, costly—decisions are made.

Decision makers are sensitive to political "face-saving" pressure

On some occasions, people make decisions that help them look good to others although the resulting decisions might not be in the best interest of their organizations. Consider, for example, how a junior executive may avoid risking his reputation as a highly regarded "team player" by refraining from challenging an unsuccessful policy advanced by the CEO. And when political conditions encourage decisions to be driven more by concerns about personal goodwill than by company success (i.e., when these objectives are misaligned), it's clear that something is amiss.

Systematic Biases in Individual Decisions

Beyond the fundamental limitations of people's capacity to process information, imperfect decisions also result from people's natural tendencies to bias decisions in systematic fashion.[22] We now describe some of the most prevalent biases in individual decision making.

Framing effects: "Half full or half empty?"

One well-established decision-making bias has to do with the tendency for people to make different decisions based on how the problem is presented to them—that is, the **framing** of a problem. Scientists have found that problems framed in a manner that emphasizes the positive gains to be received tend to encourage conservative decisions (i.e., decision makers are said to be *risk averse*), whereas problems framed in a manner that emphasizes the potential losses to be suffered lead to *risk-seeking* decisions. Consider the following example:

> The government is preparing to combat a rare disease expected to take 600 lives. Two alternative programs to combat the disease have been proposed, each of which, scientists believe, will have certain consequences. Program A will save 200 people, if adopted. Program B has a one-third chance of saving all 600 people, but a two-thirds chance of saving no one. Which program do you prefer?

When such a problem was presented to a group of people, 72 percent expressed a preference for Program A, and 28 percent for Program B. In other words, they preferred the "sure thing" of saving 200 people over the one-third possibility of saving them all. However, a curious thing happened when the description of the programs was framed in negative terms. Specifically:

> Program C will allow 400 people to die, if adopted. Program D allows a one-third probability that no one would die, and a two-thirds probability that all 600 would die. Now which program would you prefer?

If you compare these four programs, you will see that Program C is just another way of stating the outcomes of Program A, and Program D is just another way of stating the outcomes of Program B. However, Programs C and D are framed in negative terms, which led to opposite preferences: 22 percent favored Program C and 78 percent favored Program D. In other words, people tended to avoid risk when the problem was framed in terms of "lives saved" (i.e., in positive terms) but to seek risk when the problem was framed in terms of "lives lost" (i.e., in negative terms).

Why does this occur? According to **prospect theory,** such effects are due to the tendency for people to perceive equivalent situations framed differently as not really equivalent. Specifically, situations perceived in terms of losses are given greater weight than equivalent situations framed in terms of gains. In other words, focusing on the glass as "half full" leads people to think about it differently than when it is presented as being "half empty," although they might recognize intellectually that the two are really the same. Such findings illustrate that people are not completely rational decision makers but are systematically biased by the cognitive distortions created by simple differences in the way situations are framed.

Heuristics

Framing effects are not the only cognitive biases to which decision makers are subjected. It also has been established that people often attempt to simplify the complex decisions they face by using **heuristics**—simple rules of thumb that guide them through a complex array of decision alternatives. Although heuristics are potentially useful to decision makers, they may over-simplify complex situations so much that they represent potential impediments to decision making. Two common types of heuristics may be identified.

> ➤ **The availability heuristic.** This is the tendency for people to base their judgments on information that is readily available to them—although it may be inaccurate. Suppose, for example, that an executive needs to know the percentage of entering college freshmen who go on to graduate. There is not enough time to gather the appropriate statistics, so she bases her judgments on her own recollections of people she knew when she was a college student. If the percentage she recalls graduating, based on her own experiences, is higher or lower than the usual number, her estimate will be off accordingly.

> ➤ **The representativeness heuristic.** This is the tendency to perceive others in stereotypical ways if they appear to be typical representatives of the category to which they belong. For example, suppose you believe that accountants are bright, mild-mannered individuals, whereas salespeople are less intelligent but much more extroverted. Now imagine that there are twice as many salespeople as accountants at a party you are attending. You meet someone at the party who is bright and mild-mannered. Although mathematically the odds are two-to-one that this person is a salesperson rather than an accountant, chances are you will guess that the individual is an accountant because she possesses the traits you associate with accountants.

It is important to note that heuristics do not always deteriorate the quality of decisions made. In fact, they can be quite helpful. People often use rules of thumb to help simplify the complex decisions they face. For example, management scientists employ many useful heuristics to aid decisions regarding such matters as where to locate warehouses or how to compose an investment portfolio. We also use heuristics in our everyday lives, such as when we play chess ("control the center of the board") or blackjack ("hit on 16, stick on 17"). However, the representativeness heuristic and the availability heuristic may be recognized as impediments to superior decisions insofar as they discourage people from collecting and processing as much information as they should. Making judgments based on only readily available information or on stereotypical beliefs, although making things simple for the decision maker, does so at a potentially high cost—poor decisions. (Recall our discussion of the costs of stereotypes in Chapter 5.)

Escalation of commitment: Throwing good money after bad

It is inevitable that some organizational decisions will be unsuccessful. What would you say is the rational thing to do when a poor decision has been made? Intuitively, it makes sense for the ineffective action to be stopped or reversed, to "cut your losses and run." However, people don't always respond this way. In fact, it is not unusual to find that ineffective decisions are sometimes followed up with still further ineffective decisions.

Imagine, for example, that you have invested money in a company, but as time goes on, it appears to be failing. Rather than lose your initial investment, you may invest still more money in the hope of salvaging your first investment. The more you invest, the more you may be tempted to save those earlier investments by making later investments. That is to say, people sometimes may be found "throwing good money after bad" because they have "too much invested to quit." This phenomenon is known as **escalation of commitment**—the tendency for people to continue to support previously unsuccessful courses of action because they have sunk costs invested in them. For a summary of the escalation of commitment phenomenon, see Figure 10.3.

Although this might not seem like a rational thing to do, this strategy is frequently followed. For example, Motorola invested over $1.3 billion dollars in its Iridium Satellite System, a network of 60 low-orbiting communication satellites plus several "spares" (one of which was pressed into action after one of the main satellites collided with a defunct Russian satellite in February 2009). These satellites make it possible to initiate and receive wireless telephone calls from remote corners of earth where standard cellular service is unavailable. The initial satellites were launched in the late 1990s, and by 2000 it became clear that the system had serious technical limitations. And because of its high cost relative to the more widely available standard cellular service, Iridium service failed to attract enough subscribers to be profitable. Instead of accepting its losses and walking away from the project, as you might expect, Motorola officials continued to invest additional funds in the Iridium project, hoping that each successive dollar invested would be the one needed to turn the project around to make it profitable.[23]

Why do people do this? If you think about it, you may realize that the failure to back your own previous courses of action in an organization would be taken as an admission of failure—a politically difficult act to face in an organization. In other

Figure 10.3   Escalation of Commitment

According to the *escalation of commitment* phenomenon, people who have repeatedly made poor decisions will continue to support those failing courses of action in the future so that they may justify their original decisions.

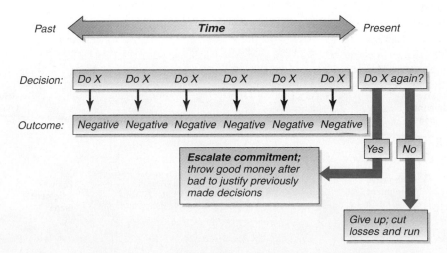

words, people may be very concerned about "saving face"—looking good in the eyes of others. Scientists believe that this tendency for self-justification is primarily responsible for people's inclination to protect their beliefs about themselves as rational, competent decision makers by convincing themselves and others that they made the right decision all along and are willing to back it up.

Person sensitivity bias

U.S. President George W. Bush first took office in January 2001, following a highly controversial election that some don't believe he won fairly and squarely. Many disapproved of his foreign policy, claiming that he was ill-suited to the position. Then, only eight months later, following the September 11 terrorist attacks, President Bush unified the country with impassioned speeches that sent his approval ratings into the stratosphere. His stance with respect to foreign policy was now widely praised. Then, years later when the war in Iraq faltered, his approval rating plummeted. The economy weakened seriously and his approval rating fell further, reaching historically low levels when he left office in January 2009.

This mini history lesson nicely illustrates an interesting aspect of human nature (beyond the fickle nature of politics, that is): When things are going poorly, nobody likes you, but when things are going well, everyone's your friend. Scientists refer to this as **person sensitivity bias.** Formally, this refers to the tendency for people to blame people too much when things are going poorly and to give them too much credit when things are going well (for a summary, see Figure 10.4).[24]

Figure 10.4   Person Sensitivity Bias: An Overview

According to the *person sensitivity bias,* we are likely to blame people too much when things are going poorly and to give them too much credit when things are going well. The same positive decision outcomes are perceived as being more positive when caused by people than by inanimate objects, such as computers. Likewise, equally negative decision outcomes are perceived as being more negative when caused by people than by objects.

(Source: Based on suggestions by Moon & Conlon, 2002; see Note 24.)

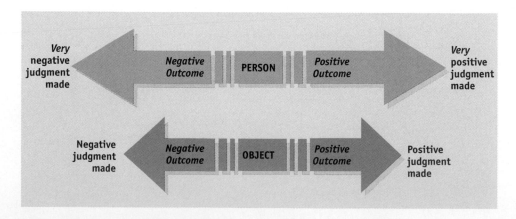

The person sensitivity bias is important insofar as it suggests that the decisions we make about others may not be completely objective. As people, we need to understand others (as we emphasized in Chapter 3), and it makes things easier for us if we keep our perceptions consistent: what's good is very good; what's bad is very bad. With such a bias underlying our judgments of others, it's little wonder that the decisions we make about them may be imperfect. After all, to the extent that effective decisions rely on accurate information, biases such as the person sensitivity bias predispose us to perceive others in less than objective ways.

Thus far in this chapter, we've focused only on decisions made by individuals. However, because many decisions are made by groups as well, we now turn to them.

GROUP DECISIONS: DO TOO MANY COOKS SPOIL THE BROTH?

Decision-making groups are a well-established fact of modern organizational life. Groups such as committees, study teams, task forces, or review panels are often charged with the responsibility for making important business decisions. They are so common, in fact, that it has been said that some administrators spend as much as 80 percent of their time in committee meetings. Given this, it is important to consider the strengths and weaknesses of using groups to make organizational decisions.

Group Decisions: A Double-Edged Sword

There is little doubt that there's much to be gained by using decision-making groups. Several potential benefits may be identified. First, bringing people together may increase the amount of knowledge and information available for making good decisions. In other words, there may be a *pooling of resources*. A related benefit is that in decision-making groups there can be a *specialization of labor*. With enough people around to share the workload, individuals can perform only those tasks at which they are best, thereby potentially improving the quality of the group's efforts. Another benefit is that group decisions are likely to enjoy *greater acceptance* than individual decisions. People involved in making decisions may be expected to understand those decisions better and be more committed to carrying them out than decisions made by someone else.

Of course, there also are problems associated with using decision-making groups. One obvious drawback is that groups are likely to *waste time*. The time spent socializing before getting down to business may be a drain on the group and be very costly to organizations. Another possible problem is that potential disagreement over important matters may breed ill will and *group conflict*. Although constructive disagreement can actually lead to better group outcomes, highly disruptive conflict may interfere with group decisions (see Chapter 7). Finally, we may expect groups to be ineffective sometimes because of members' *intimidation by group leaders*. A group composed of several "yes" men or women trying to please a dominant leader by always agreeing discourages open and honest discussion of solutions.

Given the several pros and cons of using groups to make decisions, we must conclude that *neither groups nor individuals are always superior.* Obviously, there are important trade-offs involved in using either one to make decisions.

Comparing Group and Individual Decisions: When Are Two (or More) Heads Better Than One?

Since there are advantages associated with both group and individual decision makers, a question arises as to when each should be used.[25] That is, under what conditions might individuals or groups be expected to make superior decisions?

When are groups superior to individuals?

Imagine a situation in which an important decision has to be made about a complex problem—such as whether one company should merge with another. This is not the kind of problem about which any one individual working alone would be expected to make a good decision. Its highly complex nature may overwhelm even an expert, thereby setting the stage for a group to do a better job.

Whether a group actually will do better than an individual depends on several important considerations. First, who is in the group? Successful groups are composed of heterogeneous group members with complementary skills.[26] So, for example, a group composed of lawyers, accountants, real estate agents, and other experts may make much better decisions on the merger problem than would a group composed of specialists in only one field. Indeed, the diversity of opinions offered by group members is one of the major advantages of using groups to make decisions.

Second, for a group to be successful, its members also must be able to communicate their ideas to each other freely in an open, nonhostile manner. Conditions under which one individual (or group) intimidates another from contributing his or her expertise can easily negate any potential gain associated with composing groups of heterogeneous experts. After all, having expertise and being able to make a contribution by using that expertise are two different things. Only when the contributions of the most qualified group members are given the greatest weight does the group derive any benefit from those members' presence. Thus, for groups to be superior to individuals, they must be composed of a heterogeneous collection of experts with complementary skills who can freely and openly contribute to their group's product.

In contrast to complex decision tasks, imagine a situation in which a judgment is required on a simple problem with a readily verifiable answer. For example, imagine that you are asked to translate a phrase from a relatively obscure language into English. Groups might do better than individuals on such a task only because the odds are increased that someone in the group knows the language and can perform the translation on behalf of the group. However, there is no reason to expect that even a large group will be able to perform such a task better than a single individual who has the required expertise. In fact, an expert working alone may do even better than a group because that expert may be distracted by others and may suffer from having to convince them of the correctness of his or her solution. For this reason, exceptional individuals tend to outperform entire committees on simple tasks. In such cases, for groups to benefit from a pooling of resources, there must be some resources to pool. The pooling of ignorance does not help. In other words, the question "Are two heads better than one?" can be answered this way: On simple tasks, two heads may be better than one *if* at least one of those heads has in it what's to succeed.

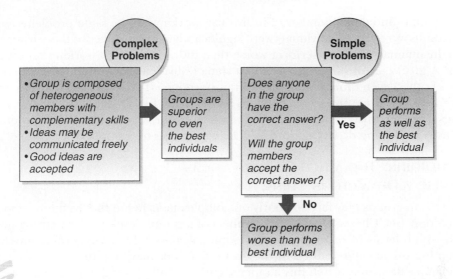

Figure 10.5   Comparing Group and Individual Decisions

As summarized here, groups make better decisions than individuals under some conditions, but individuals make better decisions than groups under others.

In summary, whether groups perform better than individuals depends on the nature of the task performed and the expertise of the people involved. For an overview of these key considerations, refer to Figure 10.5.

When are individuals superior to groups?

Most of the problems faced by organizations require a great deal of creative thinking (a topic that will be discussed in Chapter 12). For example, a company deciding how to use a newly developed adhesive in its consumer products is facing decisions about a poorly structured task. Although you would expect that the complexity of such creative problems would give groups a natural advantage, this is not the case. In fact, research has shown that on poorly structured, creative tasks, individuals perform better than groups.[27]

An approach to solving creative problems commonly used by groups is **brainstorming.** This technique was developed by an advertising executive as a tool for coming up with creative, new ideas.[28] The members of brainstorming groups are encouraged to present their ideas in an uncritical way and to discuss freely and openly all ideas on the floor. Specifically, members of brainstorming groups are required to follow four main rules: (1) avoid criticizing others' ideas, (2) share even far-out suggestions, (3) offer as many comments as possible, and (4) build on others' ideas to create your own.

Does brainstorming improve the quality of creative decisions? To answer this question, researchers conducted a study comparing the effectiveness of individuals and brainstorming groups working on creative problems.[29] Specifically, participants were given 35 minutes to consider the consequences of situations such as "What if everybody went blind?" or "What if everybody grew an extra thumb on each hand?" Clearly, the novel nature of such problems requires a great deal of creativity. Comparisons were made of the number of solutions generated by groups of four or seven people and a like number of individuals working on the same problems alone. The results were clear: Individuals were significantly more productive than groups.

In summary, groups perform worse than individuals when working on creative tasks. A great part of the problem is that some individuals feel inhibited by the presence of others even though one rule of brainstorming is that even far-out ideas may be shared. To the extent that people wish to avoid feeling foolish as a result of saying silly things, their creativity may be inhibited when in groups. Similarly, groups may inhibit creativity by slowing down the process of bringing ideas to fruition.

Groupthink: Too Much Cohesiveness Can Be a Dangerous Thing

One reason groups may fare so poorly on complex tasks lies in the dynamics of group interaction (see Chapter 9). When members of a group develop a very strong group spirit—high levels of *cohesiveness*—they sometimes become so concerned about not disrupting the like-mindedness of the group that they may be reluctant to challenge the group's decisions. When this happens, group members tend to isolate themselves from outside information, and the process of critical thinking deteriorates. This phenomenon is referred to as **groupthink.**

The concept of groupthink was proposed initially as an attempt to explain ineffective decisions made by U.S. government officials that led to fiascoes such as the Bay of Pigs invasion in Cuba and the Vietnam War.[30] Analyses of each of these cases have revealed that the president's advisers actually discouraged more effective decision making. An examination of the conditions under which the decision was made to launch the ill-fated space shuttles *Challenger* (in January 1986) and *Columbia* (in February 2003) revealed that they too resulted from groupthink.[31]

Subsequent analyses of conversations between *Challenger* mission personnel suggested that the team that made the decision to launch the shuttle under freezing conditions did so while insulating itself from the engineers who knew how the equipment should function. Given that NASA had such a successful history, the decision makers operated with a sense of invulnerability. They also worked so closely together and were under such intense pressure to launch the shuttle without further delay that they all collectively went along with the launch decision, creating the illusion of unanimous agreement. Tragically, things did not improve in the 16 years that followed.[32]

Groupthink occurs not only in governmental decision making, of course, but also in the private sector (although the failures may be less well publicized). It occurs when members of very cohesive groups have considerable confidence in their group's decisions, making them unlikely to raise doubts about these actions (i.e., "the group seems to know what it's doing"). As a result, they may suspend their own critical thinking in favor of conforming to the group.[33] When group members become fiercely loyal to each other, they may ignore potentially useful information from other sources that challenges the group's decisions. The result of this process is that the group's decisions may be completely uninformed, irrational, or even immoral.

Illustrating this, some suspect that groupthink may have been involved both in the decision making processes that led to 2008's catastrophic bank failures and in 2009's governmental efforts to address them.[34] (Fortunately, there are several strategies that can effectively combat groupthink. For a discussion of some of the most effective ones see the Winning Practices section.)

Winning Practices

Strategies for Avoiding Groupthink

Considering how serious the effects of group-think tend to be, it's not surprising that efforts have been made to avoid it by weakening the dynamics that trigger it. The following practices have proven to be especially useful in this regard.

1. *Promote open inquiry.* Remember, group-think arises in response to group members' reluctance to "rock the boat." Thus, group leaders should encourage members to be skeptical of all solutions and to avoid reaching premature agreements. It sometimes helps to play the role of *devil's advocate* by intentionally finding fault with a proposed solution.[35] Research has shown that when this is done, groups make higher-quality decisions.[36] In fact, some corporate executives use exercises in which conflict is intentionally generated just so the negative aspects of a decision can be identified before it's too late.[37] This is not to say that leaders should be argumentative. Rather, raising a nonthreatening question to force both sides of an issue can be very helpful in improving the quality of decisions.

2. *Use subgroups.* Because the decisions made by any one group may be the result of groupthink, basing decisions on the recommendations of two groups is a useful check. If the two groups disagree, a discussion of their differences is likely to raise important issues. However, if the two groups agree, you can be relatively confident that their conclusions are not *both* the result of groupthink.

3. *Admit shortcomings.* When groupthink occurs, group members feel very confident that they are doing the right thing. Such feelings of perfection discourage people from considering opposing information. However, if group members acknowledge some of the flaws and limitations of their decisions, they may open themselves to corrective influences. No decision is perfect, of course, so asking others to point out misgivings about a group's decisions may help avoid the illusion of perfection that contributes to groupthink.

4. *Hold second-chance meetings.* Before implementing a decision, it is a good idea to hold a *second-chance meeting* during which group members are asked to express any doubts and propose any new ideas they may have. Alfred P. Sloan, longtime president and chairman of General Motors during its growth period in the 1920s and 1930s, is known to have postponed acting on important matters until any group disagreement was resolved.[38] As people get tired of working on problems, they may hastily reach agreement on a solution. Second-chance meetings can be useful devices for seeing if a solution still seems good even after "sleeping on it."

Admittedly, these recommendations require additional work and may involve doing things that don't come naturally to many managers. However, considering the extremely adverse effects groupthink can have on organizations, managers would be wise to put these suggestions into practice.

STRUCTURAL APPROACHES FOR IMPROVING GROUP DECISIONS

As explained earlier, certain advantages can be gained from sometimes using individuals and sometimes using groups to make decisions. A decision-making technique that combines the best features of groups and individuals, while minimizing the disadvantages, would be ideal.[39] Here, we will describe two techniques that do so—the *Delphi technique,* and the *nominal group technique.* These reflect ways in which a group's activities may be specially structured so as to improve decision making.

The Delphi Technique

According to Greek mythology, people interested in seeing what fate the future held for them could seek the counsel of the Delphic oracle. Today's organizational decision makers sometimes consult experts to help them make the best decisions as well. A technique developed by the RAND Corporation, known as the **Delphi technique,** represents a systematic way of collecting and organizing the opinions of several experts into a single decision.[40] The steps in the process are summarized in Figure 10.6.

The Delphi process starts by enlisting the cooperation of experts and presenting the problem to them, usually in a letter. Each expert then proposes what he or she believes is the most appropriate solution. The group leader compiles all of these individual responses and reproduces them so they can be shared with all the other experts in a second mailing. At this point, each expert comments on the others' ideas and proposes another solution. These individual solutions are returned to the leader, who compiles them and looks for a consensus of opinions. If a consensus is reached, the decision is made. If not, the process of sharing reactions with others is repeated until a consensus is eventually obtained.

The obvious advantage of using the Delphi technique to make decisions is that it allows the collection of expert judgments without the great costs and logistical difficulties of bringing many experts together for a face-to-face meeting. However, the Delphi

Figure 10.6   Steps in the Delphi Technique

The *Delphi technique,* outlined here, allows decisions to be made by several experts without encountering many of the disadvantages of face-to-face groups.

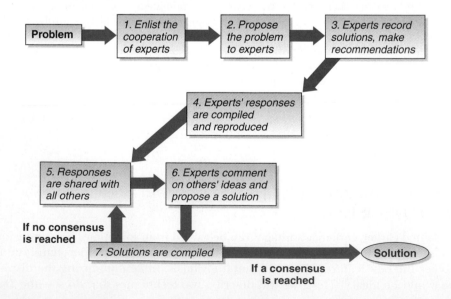

process can be very time-consuming. Sending out letters, waiting for everyone to respond, transcribing and disseminating the responses, and repeating the process until a consensus is reached can take quite a long time—often several months. Even using e-mail, the process may be slow because the experts involved may be exceptionally busy. Given this limitation, the Delphi approach would not be appropriate for making decisions in crisis situations or whenever else time is of the essence. However, the approach has been successfully employed to make decisions such as what items to put on a conference agenda and what the potential impact of implementing various new policies would be.

The Nominal Group Technique

When there are only a few hours available to make a decision, group discussion sessions can be held in which members interact with each other in an orderly, focused fashion aimed at solving problems. This is the idea behind the *nominal group technique*. The **nominal group technique (NGT)** brings together a small number of individuals (usually about seven to ten) who systematically offer their individual solutions to a problem and share their personal reactions to others' solutions. The technique is referred to as *nominal* because the individuals involved form a group in name only. Participants do not attempt to agree as a group on any solution but rather vote on all the solutions proposed. For an outline of the steps in the process, see Figure 10.7.

Figure 10.7   Steps in the Nominal Group Technique

The *nominal group technique*, whose steps are summarized here, structures face-to-face meetings in a way that allows for the open expression and evaluation of ideas.

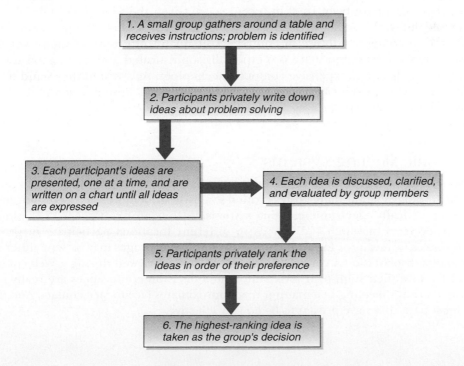

1. A small group gathers around a table and receives instructions; problem is identified

2. Participants privately write down ideas about problem solving

3. Each participant's ideas are presented, one at a time, and are written on a chart until all ideas are expressed

4. Each idea is discussed, clarified, and evaluated by group members

5. Participants privately rank the ideas in order of their preference

6. The highest-ranking idea is taken as the group's decision

As shown in Figure 10.7, the nominal group process begins by gathering group members together around a table and identifying the problem at hand. Members then write down their solutions. Next, one at a time, each member presents his or her solutions to the group as the leader records these on a chart. This process continues until all ideas have been expressed. Following this, each solution is discussed, clarified, and evaluated by the group members. Each member is given a chance to voice his or her reactions to each idea. After all the ideas have been evaluated, the group members privately rank-order their preferred solutions. The idea given the highest rank is taken as the group's decision.

The NGT has several advantages and disadvantages. We have noted already that it can be used to arrive at group decisions in only a few hours. Another benefit is that it discourages any pressure to conform to the wishes of a high-status group member because all ideas are evaluated and the preferences are expressed in private balloting. The technique must be considered limited, however, in that it requires the use of a trained group leader. In addition, using NGT successfully requires that only one narrowly defined problem be considered at a time. So, for very complex problems, many NGT sessions would have to be run—and only if the problem under consideration can be broken down into smaller parts.

COMPUTER-BASED APPROACHES TO PROMOTING EFFECTIVE DECISIONS

Now that we have reviewed traditional, structural techniques for improving decision-making effectiveness, we will move on to examining several new technology-based approaches that have been used in recent years. Given the widespread use of computers in the workplace, it probably comes as no surprise that attempts have been made to put computers to use in improving the quality of group decisions. For the most part, these techniques are not especially sophisticated and make good use of widely available and inexpensive computer technology. As a result, they stand to be widely used to the extent that they are effective. With this in mind, we will describe three such techniques: *electronic meeting systems, computer-assisted communication,* and *group decision support systems.*

Electronic Meeting Systems

Although nominal groups traditionally meet in face-to-face settings, advances in modern technology enable them to be formed even when members are in distant locations. Specifically, **electronic meeting systems,** as they are known, involve holding teleconferences in which individuals in different locations participate in group conferences by means of Internet connections.[41] The messages may be sent either via characters displayed on a computer monitor or images viewed during a Web conference. Despite their high-tech look, automated decision conferences are really just nominal groups meeting in a manner that approximates face-to-face contact. And, for the most part, they have proven to be equally effective.

Because electronic meetings allow for groups to assemble more conveniently than face-to-face meetings, they are growing in popularity. Presently, such companies as GE, Marriott Corp., and Sun Microsystems regularly rely on electronic meetings— and with the rapidly decreasing costs of communication technology (along with the costly nature of physical travel, both financially and time-wise), more organizations are hopping on the bandwagon all the time.

Computer-Assisted Communication

Another way of leveraging technology to facilitate group decision making involves using **computer-assisted communication,** which refers to the sharing of information, such as text messages and data relevant to the decision, over computer networks. (The term *computer-mediated communication,* identified in Chapter 8, means essentially the same thing.) The underlying idea of computer-assisted communication is that on-screen messages provide an effective means of sending some forms of information that can help groups make better decisions.

Does it work? The answer is "only sometimes" and this depends on the degree to which the people involved are highly open to new experiences.[42] Teams using computer-assisted communication make better decisions than teams using verbal communication only when they are composed of individuals who tend to have intellectual curiosity, who value learning, who have an active imagination, and who are intrigued by the use of technology. Because computer-assisted communication is still new to some people, its effectiveness is limited to those who are most accepting of new technology and who possess the creativity to use that technology properly. However, those who are not especially open to computer-assisted technology don't find it to render much "assistance" at all.

Group Decision Support Systems

Another approach to using technology to improve the effectiveness of decisions that has received attention in recent years is known as **group decision support systems (GDSS).** These are interactive computer-based systems that combine communication, computer, and decision technologies to improve the effectiveness of group problem-solving meetings. They often involve having people type their ideas into a computer program and discuss these ideas anonymously with others in chat rooms. A record of these discussions is then left for all to examine as needed. Their underlying rationale is straightforward: The quality of group decisions stands to be improved because this process removes some of the impediments to decision making. In this sense, just as decision support systems, described earlier in this chapter (see p. 283), can be used to identify effective ways of making decisions, so too can group decision support systems.

One of the reasons why face-to-face groups sometimes make poor decisions is that group members do not always share information they have available to them that might help the group. As we discussed earlier, in connection with the phenomenon of groupthink, this may occur because people sometimes censor unpopular ideas voluntarily, even if these are good ideas that can improve the quality of group decisions. This is where GDSS can be useful. Groups using GDSS may avoid this problem because the anonymous recording of ideas makes people less reluctant to share their thoughts and makes it easier than ever to have access to a complete set of ideas.[43]

For now, it seems that group decision support systems appear to be quite effective. However, because they are very new, we don't yet know all the conditions under which they will continue to be successful. As OB researchers conduct further research on this topic, we surely will learn more about this promising technique in the future.

Back to the Case

Answer the following questions about this chapter's Making the Case (p. 281) to illustrate insights you have derived about the material in this chapter.

1. What things did Coca-Cola's design team do that are in keeping with the rational-economic model of decision making?
2. Considering the imperfections of human decision making, what particular weaknesses or biases are especially likely to impact the way these design decisions are made at Coca-Cola? Explain your answer.
3. What structural or computer-based group decision making techniques might be especially effecctive in helping Coca-Cola's design team improve the quality of its decisions?

You Be the Consultant

Making Decisions Effectively

A business associate refers you to the president of a growing environmental management firm. The fact that the company is new and operates in a changing business environment makes all of its decisions especially crucial. As such, you are hired to assist in guiding the president in helping the company make decisions in the most effective possible way. Answer the following questions relevant to this situation based on the material in this chapter.

1. The president has been making decisions about how to deal with governmental regu-

lations all by himself. Should he consider delegating this task to a group instead? Why or why not?

2. What individual biases would be expected to interfere with the quality of the decisions made by individuals in this company?

3. In what ways might the group interaction limit the quality of decisions made? What steps can be taken to overcome these problems?

SELF-ASSESSMENT EXERCISE

Are You Risk Seeking or Risk Averse?

It's one thing to read about the effects of framing on riskiness but quite another to experience it firsthand. This exercise will help you demonstrate the effects of framing for yourself.

Directions

Read each of the following descriptions of hypothetical situations. Then, for each, answer the following question: *Which project will you select: Alpha or Beta?*

Situation 1: You are an executive whose policies have resulted in a $1 million loss for your company. Now you are considering two new projects. One of them, Alpha, will provide a definite return of $500,000. The other, Beta, will provide a 50-50 chance of obtaining either a $1 million return or a $0 return.

Situation 2: You are considering one of two new projects to conduct in your company. One of them, Alpha, will provide a definite return of $500,000. The other, Beta, will provide a 50-50 chance of obtaining either a $1 million return or a $0 return.

Discussion Questions

1. What choice did you make in Situation 1? Most people would select Beta in such a situation because it gives them a 50-50 chance of undoing the loss completely. Such a risk-seeking decision is likely in a situation in which people are focusing on undoing loss.
2. What choice did you make in Situation 2? Most people would select Alpha in such a situation because it gives them a sure thing, a "bird in the hand." Such a risk-averse decision is likely in a situation in which people are focusing on gains received.
3. Given that both situations are mathematically identical, why should people prefer one or the other?

GROUP EXERCISE

Running a Nominal Group: Try It Yourself

A great deal can be learned about nominal groups by running one—or, at least, by participating in one—yourself. Doing so will not only help illustrate the procedure but also demonstrate how effectively it works.

Directions

1. Select a topic suitable for discussion in a nominal group composed of students in your class. It should be a topic that is narrowly defined and on which people have many different opinions (these work best in nominal groups). Some possible examples include:
   - What should your school's student leaders be doing for you?
   - What can be done to improve the quality of instruction in your institution?
   - What can be done to improve the quality of jobs your school's students receive when graduating?

2. Divide the class into groups of seven to ten. Arrange each group in a circle, or around a table, if possible. In each group, select one person to serve as the group facilitator.

3. Following the steps outlined in Figure 10.7 (p. 303), facilitators should guide their groups in discussions regarding the focal question identified in step 1. (Remember to give all group members an equal opportunity to speak; don't allow any one person to dominate the discussion.) Allow approximately 45 minutes to one hour to complete this process.

4. If time allows, repeat the procedure using a different focal question and a different group leader.

Discussion Questions

1. Collectively, how did the group answer the question? Do you believe that this answer accurately reflected the feelings of the group? How do you think your group experiences would have differed had you used a totally unstructured, traditional face-to-face group to make the decision instead of the NGT?

2. How did the various groups' answers compare? Were they similar or different? Why?

3. What were the major problems, if any, associated with the nominal group experience? For example, were there any group members who were reluctant to wait their turn before speaking up?

The Quest for Leadership

Learning Objectives

After reading this chapter, you will be able to:

1. **DEFINE** leadership and **EXPLAIN** the major sources of power leaders have at their disposal.
2. **DESCRIBE** the trait approach to leadership and **IDENTIFY** the major characteristics of effective leaders.
3. **IDENTIFY** the types of behavior that have been most strongly associated with effective leadership.
4. **DESCRIBE** the basic tenets of three major contingency theories of leadership (LPC contingency theory, path-goal theory, and Situational Leadership® theory) and how they may be applied.
5. **IDENTIFY** the emerging trends and challenges in leadership practice.
6. **DESCRIBE** various approaches that can be taken to develop leaders in organizations.

3 GOOD REASONS why you should care about . . .

Leadership

You should care about leadership because:

1. An organization's success is greatly determined by the quality of its leadership.
2. There are steps that anyone can take to enhance his or her effectiveness as a leader.
3. Changing business practices, such as globalization and the use of the Internet, have important implications for the practice of leadership.

Making the Case for Leadership

Dave Yost: The Frugal CEO

Not too many CEOs answer their own phones, fly economy class (with 30-day advance fares, no less), decorate their offices with plastic plants, and lunch on sandwiches from a local deli—especially when they run a $66.1 billion company with 11,500 employees. But this is precisely the kind of frugality practiced by R. David Yost, the 62-year-old chief of AmerisourceBergen, one of the largest pharmaceutical services companies in the United States. Based in Valley Forge, Pennsylvania,

(continued)

the company is involved in distribution, which involves purchasing drugs from manufacturers, particularly makers of generic drugs, and selling them to retailers.

It would misleading to characterize Yost as an eccentric leader. Rather, his skinflint ways reflect a conscientious effort to set an example by doing whatever it takes to save money. "The leader is very important in controlling business costs," he says. And in an industry with razor-sharp margins—only about 1 percent—it seems to be paying off. Even in troubled financial times, AmerisourceBergen has grown twice as fast as the industry average and has enjoyed three times the profit of its competitors, McKesson and Cardinal Health.

Yost insists that the key to this success is not his penny-pinching ways per se, so much as his commitment to spending the company's money on exactly the right things. To Yost, this means investing in ways to grow the business. So, for example, AmerisourceBergen goes out of its way to attract the most talented prospective employees by paying competitive wages. On the technology side, the company has embarked on a 3–5-year plan to spend $100 million upgrading its customer service technology. And, although Yost's own office has a thrift shop appearance, his company's $400 million investment in distribution facilities promises to make it a state-of-the-art operation.

Yost's commitment to wise spending has inspired staffers to find their own ways to save, and in conjunction with the large investment in technology, he has done just that. Take the warehouse, for example. Instead of trying to keep track manually of packages picked up and unloaded, a task that is fraught with inaccuracy due to the fallible nature of human memory (not to mention the temptation to fudge the numbers a bit), this process has gone high tech. Warehouse workers now wear thimbles on their fingers equipped with infrared lasers that read the bar codes on every package touched. This technology not only facilitates the tracking of packages but also makes it possible to identify workers who are especially productive and to reward them with bonuses.

Dave Yost has expressed his commitment to creating a company that does the job better than any of its competitors. And his vehicle for making this happen has been ensuring that everyone buys into his vision of spending every penny wisely. By walking the talk (in inexpensive shoes, most likely) he has done precisely this, and the company's success suggests that he has done it quite well.

You probably wouldn't find Dave Yost hobnobbing with other CEOs at some tony country club, but writing him off as a penny-pinching eccentric would be a mistake. It makes better sense to think of him as committed to reinvesting his company's money on the business itself even if it means not partaking in the usual lavish indulgences of most CEOs. And with the thin profit margins he has to work with, this is probably wise. Also wise is the fact that his spending decisions send strong messages to lower-ranking employees that the company doesn't have money to waste. In this manner, he is encouraging employees to do the same, influencing and inspiring them to make sacrifices for the company. And with a recent increase in profits of 76.7 percent, there can be no doubt that it seems to be working.[1] As a leader, then, Mr. Yost seems to be quite successful.

Essentially, we are suggesting that effective *leadership* is a key ingredient for organizational success, and most experts would agree. This is not only a matter of opinion. Over a century's worth of research confirms that effective leadership is a major determinant of organizational outcomes (e.g., profitability, longevity, etc.).[2] In view of this, we will devote this chapter to describing various approaches to the study of leadership as well as their implications for managerial practice. Before launching into this discussion, however, we will begin by defining what we mean by leadership and distinguish it from some other terms with which it is frequently associated.

WHAT IS LEADERSHIP? SOME FUNDAMENTAL ISSUES

Although we all probably have a good intuitive sense of what leadership is and what leaders are like, to avoid confusion we begin this chapter with a formal definition of leadership and an overview of the ways in which leaders influence their followers.

A Definition

When you think of a leader, what image comes to mind? For many, a leader is an individual—often with a title reflecting a high rank in an organization (e.g., president, director, etc.)—who is influential in getting others to behave as required by the organization. Indeed, social scientists think of leaders as people who have a great deal of influence over others. Formally, **leadership** is defined as the process by which an individual influences others in ways that help attain group or organizational goals.[3]

From this definition, it may seem that *leaders* and *managers* are quite similar. Indeed, the two terms are often used interchangeably. However, this is misleading insofar as they are conceptually distinct (for a summary of key differences, see Table 11.1).[4] The primary function of a *leader* is to create the essential purpose or mission of an organization and the strategy for attaining it. As such, leaders are responsible for change. By contrast, it is the job of a *manager* to implement that vision. He or she is responsible for achieving that end and then taking the steps necessary to keep things running smoothly.

The reason for the confusion is that the distinction between establishing a mission and implementing it is often blurred in practice. After all, managers are often required to lead those who are subordinate to them while also carrying out their leaders' missions. Similarly, many leaders, such as top corporate executives, are frequently called on not only to create a vision but also to help implement it. With this in mind, it has been observed that too many so-called leaders get bogged down in the managerial aspects of their job, creating organizations that are "overmanaged and underled."[5]

Table 11.1   Leaders vs. Managers: What's the Difference?

Although in practice it's sometimes hard to distinguish between leaders and managers, the fundamental differences between them are many. Several of the key differences are summarized here.

Leaders	Managers
• Focus on innovating, changing things for the better	• Focus on administering, keeping things moving along on plan
• Set overall direction	• Make detailed plans
• Inspire people to work	• Tell people to work
• Take a long-term perspective	• Take a short-term perspective
• Willing to take risks	• Avoid taking risks

How Do Leaders Influence Others? Sources of Leadership Power

As our definition suggests, leaders influence others. To understand fully how leaders operate, it is necessary to identify how they come by the power to exert influence. The basis for a leader's power resides in his or her formal position as well as the way followers respond to his or her personal qualities.[6]

Position power

A great deal of the power that people have in organizations comes from the particular posts they hold in those organizations. In other words, they are able to influence others because of the formal power associated with their jobs. This is known as **position power.** For example, there are certain powers that the president of the United States has simply due to the authority given to this officeholder (e.g., signing bills into law, making treaties, and so on). These formal powers remain vested in the position and are available to anyone who holds that position. When the president's term is up, for example, his or her presidential powers transfer to the new officeholder. There are four bases of position power:

➤ **Legitimate power.**   The power that someone has because others recognize and accept the authority associated with his or her formal position. For example, students recognize that their instructors have the legitimate power (i.e., authority) to make class policies and to determine grades.

➤ **Reward power.**   The power to control the rewards others receive. For example, a supervisor has the power to reward one of her subordinates by recommending a large pay raise or a favorable assignment.

➤ **Coercive power.**   The capacity to control punishment. For example, a boss may tell a subordinate to do something "my way or else." Typically, dictators are inclined to use coercive power, whereas leaders avoid it whenever possible.

➤ **Information power.**   The power a person has by virtue of his or her access to valuable data or knowledge. Traditionally, people in top positions have available to them unique sources of information that are not available to others (e.g., knowledge of company performance, market trends, and so on). As they say, "knowledge is power," and such information greatly contributes to the power of people in many jobs.

As you read these descriptions of the different sources of position power, you may find yourself wondering what you could do to enhance your own position power where you are working. If so, don't feel self-conscious about being "power hungry." To the contrary, building a strong power base is an important step toward being an effective leader. With this in mind, you may find it interesting to review the various suggestions for enhancing position power summarized in Table 11.2.

Personal power

In addition to the power leaders derive from their formal positions in organizations, they also derive power from their own unique qualities or characteristics. This is known as **personal power.** There are four sources of personal power:

➤ **Rational persuasion.**   The power leaders have by virtue of the logical arguments and factual evidence they provide to support their positions on matters of interest. Rational persuasion is widely used by top executives, such as when they present detailed reports in making a case as to why certain organizational policies should be changed.

Table 11.2   Position Power: How to Get It

The following suggestions outline various ways of enhancing your position power in an organization.

Suggestion	Rationale
Expand your network of communication contacts.	The more contacts you have, the more information you will have, and the more others will count on you.
Make some of your job responsibilities unique.	People have power to the extent that they are the only ones who can perform certain tasks.
Perform more novel tasks and fewer routine ones.	People who perform routine tasks readily can be replaced by others, whereas those who perform novel tasks are more powerful because they are indispensable.
Increase the visibility of your job performance by joining task forces and making contact with senior people.	The more involved you are in organizational decisions, and the more important others consider your input to be, the more power you will have.
Become involved with activities that are central to the organization's top priorities.	People performing peripheral activities (e.g., sorting mail at a law firm) have far less power than those whose activities are in line with the organization's primary mission and its top priorities (e.g., winning clients' cases at a law firm).

➤ **Expert power.** The power leaders have to the extent that others recognize their expert knowledge on a topic. For example, athletes do what their coaches tell them in large part because they recognize and respect their coaches' expertise (i.e., athletes believe that doing what their coaches say can help them improve).

➤ **Referent power.** The power that individuals have because they are liked and admired by others. For example, senior managers who possess desirable qualities and good reputations may have referent power over younger managers who identify with them and wish to emulate them.

➤ **Charisma.** The power someone has over others because of his or her engaging and magnetic personality. As we will describe later in this chapter, leaders with this characteristic are highly influential and inspire their followers to do things.

As we have outlined here, leaders derive power from a variety of sources, some of which are based on the nature of the positions they hold and some of which are based on their individual characteristics. In the remainder of this chapter we will describe various approaches to understanding how leaders rely on these sources of power to achieve group and organizational success.

THE TRAIT APPROACH: ARE SOME PEOPLE "BORN LEADERS"?

Experience tells us that some people have more of "the right stuff" than others and are just naturally better leaders. And, if you look at some of the great leaders throughout history, such as Mahatma Gandhi, India's political and spiritual leader during the first half of the twentieth century; British Prime Minister during World War II, Sir Winston Churchill; and former U.S. President Abraham Lincoln, to name just a few, it is clear that such individuals certainly appear to be different from ordinary folks. The question is, "How are they different?" That is, what is it that makes great leaders so special?

Great Person Theory

For many years, scientists have devoted a great deal of attention to identifying the specific traits and characteristics that are associated with leadership success. In so doing, they have advanced what is known as the **great person theory**—the approach that recognizes that great leaders possess key traits that set them apart from most others. Furthermore, the theory contends that these traits remain stable over time and across different groups.

Most contemporary organizational scholars accept the idea that traits *do* matter—namely, that certain traits, together with other factors, contribute to leaders' success in business settings.[7] Specifically, as one team of scientists put it, "Leaders do not have to be great men or women by being intellectual geniuses or omniscient prophets to succeed, but they do need to have the 'right stuff' and this stuff is not equally present in all people."[8] (With this in mind, you may find it interesting to consider who the great leaders throughout the ages have been—a task that you will complete in the Group Exercise on p. 338.)

What are these traits? Table 11.3 lists and describes some of the key ones. But, because the meaning of some of these is not obvious, we describe these here.

Leadership motivation: The desire to lead

First, consider what has been termed **leadership motivation.** This refers to leaders' desires to influence others and, in essence, to lead.[9] Such motivation can take two distinct forms. On the one hand, it may cause leaders to seek power as an end in itself. Leaders who demonstrate such **personalized power motivation** wish to dominate others, and their desire to do so is often reflected in an excessive concern with status. In contrast, leadership motivation also can cause leaders to seek power as a means to achieve desired, shared goals. Leaders who evidence such **socialized power motivation**

Table 11.3   Characteristics of Successful Leaders

Research indicates that successful leaders demonstrate the traits listed here.

Trait or Characteristic	Description
Drive	Desire for achievement; ambition; high energy; tenacity; initiative
Honesty and integrity	Trustworthy; reliable; open
Leadership motivation	Desire to exercise influence over others to reach shared goals
Self-confidence	Trust in own abilities
Cognitive ability	Intelligence; ability to integrate and interpret large amounts of information
Knowledge of the business	Knowledge of industry and relevant technical matters
Creativity	Originality in approaching problems (see Chapter 12)
Flexibility	Ability to adapt to needs of followers and the requirements of situations

cooperate with others, develop networks and coalitions, and generally work with sub-ordinates rather than trying to dominate or control them. Needless to say, this type of leadership motivation is usually far more adaptive for organizations than personalized leadership motivation.

Flexibility

Another special characteristic of effective leaders is *flexibility*. This refers to their ability to recognize what actions are required in a given situation and then to act accordingly. Evidence suggests that the most effective leaders are not prone to behave in the same ways all the time, but to be adaptive, matching their style to the needs of followers and the demands of the situations they face.[10]

Focus on morality

Despite the considerable attention the press has paid to the dishonest dealings of some top business leaders in recent years (e.g., fraudulent investor Bernard Madoff), it's important to note that successful leaders do, in fact, emphasize ethical behavior (see Chapter 2). This orientation is in keeping with what has been called *authentic leadership*. **Authentic leaders** are highly moral individuals who are confident, hopeful, optimistic, and resilient, and who are strongly aware of the contexts in which they operate.[11] Because of their highly positive perspectives, authentic leaders play key roles in promoting the growth and development of their subordinates and, as a result, the sustained performance of their organizations.

Multiple domains of intelligence

Scientists have noted that leaders have to "be smart" in a variety of different ways. In other words, they have to demonstrate what is known as **multiple domains of intelligence**.[12] Specifically, leaders have to be intelligent in the following three special ways:

➤ *Cognitive intelligence.*   Of course, leaders must be capable of integrating and inter-preting large amounts of information. However, mental genius does not seem to be necessary for leadership. Although the best leaders are surely smart in the traditional sense, they tend not to be geniuses.[13] Moreover, research has shown that for people to become leaders, it's important for them to appear to be smart (i.e., they should give the impression of being intelligent).[14] After all, people are unlikely to accept leaders whose intellectual competence is questionable.

➤ *Emotional intelligence.*   In connection with the discussion of emotions in Chapter 4, we described *emotional intelligence* as people's abilities to be sensitive to their own and others' emotions. As you might imagine, successful leaders must have high levels of emotional intelligence. Indeed, effective leaders are keenly aware of people's emotional states and demonstrate their ability to connect with others.[15]

➤ *Cultural intelligence.*   Most of the research on leadership has focused on Americans working in companies based in the United States. However, the behavior of leaders is likely to be influenced by the cultures within which they operate, requiring different approaches to leadership in different countries. Sensitivity to this fact has been referred to as **cultural intelligence**.[16] In today's global economy, cultural intelligence is more important than ever. In the words of C. R. "Dick" Shoemate, former CEO of Best Foods, "It takes a special kind of leadership to deal with the differences of a multicountry, multicultural organization such as ours."[17]

Not surprisingly, most of the countries on *Fortune* magazine's list of the "Global Most Admired Companies" (including Apple, General Electric, Toyota, Procter & Gamble, and FedEx) pay considerable attention to training leaders to deal with the realities of the global economy.[18]

Transformational Leaders: Special People Who Make Things Happen

If you think about the great leaders throughout history, the names of Rev. Dr. Martin Luther King, Jr. and President John F. Kennedy are certain to come to mind. These individuals surely were effective at envisioning ways of changing society and then bringing these visions to reality. People who do things to revitalize and transform society or organizations are known as **transformational leaders.**[19] Rev. King's famous "I have a dream" speech inspired people to support the civil rights movement, and President Kennedy's shared vision of "landing a man on the moon and returning him safely to earth" before 1970 inspired the "space race" of the 1960s. For these reasons, they are considered transformational leaders.

Although these examples are useful, we must ask: Exactly what makes a leader transformational? The key characteristics of transformational leaders are as follows:

➤ *Charisma.*   Transformational leaders have a mission and inspire others to follow them, often in a highly emotional manner.

➤ *Self-confidence.*   Transformational leaders are highly confident in their ability and judgment, and others readily become aware of this.

➤ *Vision.*   Transformational leaders have ideas about how to improve the status quo and do what it takes to change things for the better, even if it means making personal sacrifices.

➤ *Environmental sensitivity.*   Transformational leaders are highly realistic about the constraints imposed on them and the resources needed to change things. They know what they can and cannot do.

➤ *Intellectual stimulation.*   Transformational leaders help followers recognize problems and identify ways of solving them.

➤ *Interpersonal consideration.*   Transformational leaders give followers the support, encouragement, and attention they need to perform their jobs well.

➤ *Inspiration.*   Transformational leaders clearly communicate the importance of their company's mission and rely on symbols (e.g., slogans) to help followers focus on them.

➤ *Morality.*   Transformational leaders tend to make decisions in a manner showing advanced levels of moral reasoning (recall this concept from Chapter 2). For a summary of some recent evidence in this regard, see Figure 11.1.[20]

In the world of business, a good example of a transformational leader is Jack Welch, the illustrious, now-retired CEO of General Electric (GE).[21] Under Welch's leadership, GE underwent a series of changes with respect to the way it did business.[22] At the individual level, GE abandoned its highly bureaucratic ways and began listening to its employees. Since that time, GE consistently ranked among the most admired companies in its industry in *Fortune* magazine's annual survey of corporate reputations (including a number-one ranking in several recent years!).[23] In the 1980s, Welch bought and sold many businesses for GE, using the guideline that GE would keep a

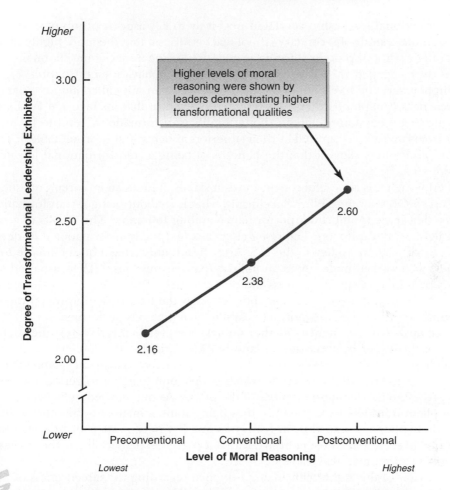

Figure 11.1 Transformational Leadership and Morality: Evidence of a Connection

In a sample of workers from Canada and the United Kingdom scientists assessed the degree to which leaders were judged by their subordinates as having the characteristics of transformational leaders. These leaders also were assessed in terms of the degree of moral reasoning they displayed on a paper-and-pencil test. The findings, summarized here, were clear: The more transformational qualities leaders demonstrated, the higher levels of moral reasoning they displayed.

(Source: Based on data reported by Turner et al., 2002; see Note 20.)

company only if it placed either number one or number two in market share. If this meant closing plants, selling assets, and laying off personnel, he did it and got others to follow suit, earning him the nickname "Neutron Jack." Did Welch transform and revitalize GE? Having added well over $100 billion of value to the company, there can be no doubt about it.[24]

What we know about the effectiveness of transformational leadership goes beyond anecdotal examples and is based on sound scientific research.[25] Overall, transformational leadership is related positively to key aspects of job performance. For example, a study of secondary school teachers found that the more highly transactional their schools' principals were (as measured using a special questionnaire), the more they engaged in organizational citizenship behavior (see Chapter 7), and the higher were the levels of job satisfaction and organizational commitment among the teachers (Chapter 5).[26] Further research has shown that managers at FedEx who are rated by their subordinates as being highly transformational tend to be higher performers and are recognized by their superiors as being highly promotable.[27] These studies and others suggest that the benefits of being a transformational leader are considerable.[28]

Although this is a useful conclusion as it stands, it raises an important question of interest to OB scientists: Why? Specifically, what is it about being a transformational leader that leads to improved performance among followers? The results of a study shed light on this question. The researchers assessed the transformational leadership behavior of platoon leaders in the U.S. Army by administering a questionnaire to the soldiers who worked under them on military exercise missions.[29] They also used judgments by military experts to assess the performance of these leaders' platoons as a whole. The findings were clear: The more strongly the leaders demonstrated transformational characteristics, the more successfully their platoons performed.

So far, this is consistent with other studies. However, in this research, the scientists went a step further by also assessing another key variable—the soldiers' perceptions of the degree of cohesiveness in their platoons (as you may recall from Chapter 9, cohesiveness has to do with the extent to which people pull together to get the job done). This proved to be an important piece of the puzzle. As summarized in Figure 11.2, the more platoon leaders were recognized as being transformational, the more cohesive were their platoons, and this, in turn, was one key determinant of how well those platoons performed. Thus, cohesiveness is a partial explanation for the successful impact of transformational leaders.

In view of this rather convincing evidence regarding the effectiveness of transformational leadership, you may be asking yourself how to become more of a transformational leader yourself. Although it isn't easy to take charge of transforming one's organization, you may find it worthwhile to consider the ways of developing your transformational qualities summarized in Table 11.4.

Figure 11.2 Transformational Leadership and Group Performance: The Important Role of Group Cohesiveness

A study found that transformational leadership among military platoon leaders led to improved performance among platoons. Group cohesiveness was found to play an important role in this process. Transformational leaders tended to raise the cohesiveness levels of their platoons, which in turn improved their effectiveness in military maneuvers.

(Source: Based on suggestions by Bass et al., 2003; see Note 29.)

Table 11.4   Guidelines for Becoming a Transformational Leader

Being a transformational leader is not easy, but following the suggestions outlined here may help leaders transform and revitalize their organizations.

Suggestion	Explanation
Develop a vision that is both clear and highly appealing to followers.	A clear and compelling vision will guide followers toward achieving organizational goals and make them feel good about doing so.
Articulate a strategy for bringing the vision to life.	Don't present an elaborate plan; rather, state the best path toward achieving the mission.
State your vision in ample detail and promote it to others.	Visions must not only be clear but also interesting, such as by using anecdotes.
Show confidence and optimism about your vision.	If a leader lacks confidence about success, followers will not try very hard to achieve that vision.
Express confidence in followers' capacity to carry out the strategy.	Followers must believe that they are capable of implementing a leader's vision. Leaders should build followers' self-confidence.
Build confidence by recognizing small accomplishments toward the goal.	If a group experiences early success, it will be motivated to continue working hard.
Celebrate successes and accomplishments.	Formal or informal ceremonies are useful for celebrating success, thereby building optimism and commitment.
Take dramatic action to symbolize key organizational values.	Visions are reinforced by things leaders do to symbolize them. For example, one leader demonstrated concern for quality by destroying work that was not up to standards.
Set an example; actions speak louder than words.	Leaders serve as role models. If they want followers to make sacrifices, for example, they should do so themselves.

(Sources: Based on suggestions by Bass & Bass, 2008; see Note 2, and Yukl, 2009; see Note 3)

THE BEHAVIOR APPROACH: WHAT DO LEADERS DO?

The great person theory paints a somewhat fatalistic picture, suggesting that some people are, by nature, more prone to being effective leaders than others. After all, some of us have more of "the right stuff" than others; that's just the way it is. However, other approaches to leadership—particularly, those focusing on what leaders do rather than who leaders are—paint a more encouraging picture for those of us who aspire to leadership positions. This orientation is known as the **behavior approach.** By emulating the behavior of successful leaders the possibility exists that anyone may become an effective leader.

Two Critical Leadership Behaviors

Precisely what behaviors hold the key to leadership success? Although the answer to this question is quite complex, evidence points to two particular leadership behaviors. The first is showing a *concern for people*, also known as **consideration.** In describing your boss, would you say that he or she cares about you as a person, is friendly, and listens to you when you want to talk? If so, he or she may be said to demonstrate a high amount of consideration.

The second main type of leadership behavior is showing a *concern for getting the job done*, also known as **initiating structure.** In describing your boss, would you say that he or she gives you advice, answers your questions, and lets you know exactly what is expected of you? If so, he or she may be said to demonstrate a high amount of initiating structure.

A large body of research suggests that leaders differ greatly along these two dimensions. In several classic investigations subordinates completed questionnaires in which they described their leaders' behavior. Those leaders scoring high on initiating structure were mainly concerned with production and focused primarily on getting the job done. They engaged in actions such as organizing work, inducing subordinates to follow rules, setting goals, and making expectations explicit. In contrast, leaders scoring lower on this dimension showed less of a tendency to engage in these actions.

Leaders at the high end of the consideration dimension were concerned primarily with establishing good relations with their subordinates and being liked by them. They engaged in actions such as doing favors for subordinates, explaining things to them, and assuring their welfare. People who scored low on this dimension didn't care much about how they got along with their subordinates.

It has been well established that leaders are likely to be most successful when they demonstrate high concern for both people (showing consideration) *and* production (initiating structure). Indeed, this is precisely what New York City's Mayor Rudolph Giuliani did in the aftermath of the September 11 terrorist attacks. He said things that inspired confidence in nerve-rattled Americans while also taking steps to ensure that the daily operations of New York City were returned to normal. Showing consideration is beneficial insofar as it leads to high levels of group morale and low levels of turnover and absenteeism. At the same time, high levels of initiating structure are useful in promoting high levels of efficiency and performance. Not surprisingly, highly skilled leaders combine both orientations into their overall styles to produce favorable results.

In a fascinating study, two top executive recruiters analyzed the specific behaviors that characterize the way America's 50 most successful business leaders behave.[30] Rather than being completely different in their approaches to leadership, they found that these individuals shared a commitment to behaving in certain ways, including the following:

1. Demonstrating the utmost integrity in whatever they did
2. Developing strategies for building on what the company does best
3. Building a skilled management team whose members shared their own values
4. Communicating so well that they inspired others to achieve greatness
5. Making it possible for their organizations to make changes rapidly
6. Developing compensation systems that reinforced the company's mission

Interestingly, this list is completely consistent with the well-established findings about the importance of paying attention to both people (items 1, 3, 4) and the work itself (items 2, 5, 6). It also offers a highly specific and very insightful list of some particular forms these behaviors take.

Developing Successful Leader Behaviors: Grid Training

How can one go about developing these two forms of leadership behavior—demonstrating concern for production and concern for people? A technique known as **grid training** proposes a multistep process designed to cultivate these two important skills.[31]

The initial step calls for conducting a *grid seminar*—a session in which an organization's managers (who have been previously trained in the appropriate theory and skills) help organization members analyze their own management styles. This is done using a specially designed questionnaire that allows managers to determine how they stand with respect to their *concern for production* and their *concern for people*. Each participant's approach on each dimension is scored using a number ranging from 1 (low) to 9 (high).

Managers who score low on both concern for production and concern for people are scored 1,1, showing evidence of *impoverished management.* A manager who is highly concerned about production but shows little interest in people scores 9,1, demonstrating the *task management* style. In contrast, those who show the opposite pattern—high concern with people but little concern with production—are described as having a *country club* style of management; they are scored 1,9. Managers scoring moderately on both dimensions, the 5,5 pattern, are said to follow a *middle-of-the-road* management style. Finally, there are individuals who are highly concerned with both production and people, those scoring 9,9. This is the most desirable pattern, representing what is known as *team management.* These various patterns are represented in a diagram like that shown in Figure 11.3, known as the *managerial grid®*.

After a manager's position along the grid is determined, training begins to improve concern over production (planning skills) and concern over people (communication

Figure 11.3   The Managerial Grid®

A manager's standing along two basic dimensions—concern for production and concern for people—can be illustrated by means of a diagram such as this, known as the managerial grid®. To promote effective leadership, managers are trained to demonstrate high amounts of both dimensions.

(Source: Based on suggestions by Blake & Mouton, 1969, 1982; see Note 31.)

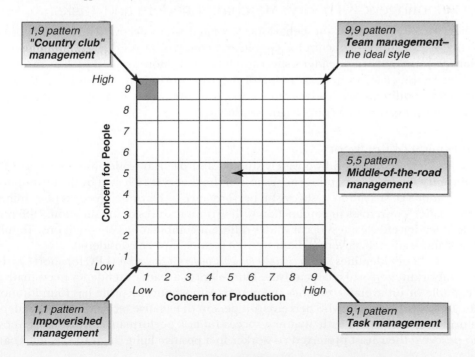

skills) to reach the ideal 9,9 state. This consists of organization-wide training aimed at helping people interact more effectively with each other. Then training is expanded to reducing conflict between groups that work with each other. Additional training includes efforts to identify the extent to which the organization is meeting its strategic goals and then comparing this performance to an ideal. Next, plans are made to meet these goals, and these are implemented. Finally, progress toward the goals is continuously assessed, and problem areas are identified.

Grid training is widely considered an effective way of improving the leadership behaviors of people in organizations. Indeed, for over 40 years, the grid approach has been used to train hundreds of thousands of people from over 40 countries in ways to develop the two key types of leadership behavior.[32]

CONTINGENCY THEORIES OF LEADER EFFECTIVENESS

By now, it should be clear that leadership is a complex process. It involves intricate social relationships and is affected by a wide range of variables. In general, it may be said that leadership is influenced by two main factors—the characteristics of the individuals involved and the nature of the situations they face. This basic point lies at the heart of several approaches to leadership known as **contingency theories** of leader effectiveness. According to this approach, there is no one best style of leadership. Instead, certain leadership styles are considered most effective under certain conditions. Contingency theories seek to identify the specific conditions and factors that determine whether, and to what degree, leaders will enhance the performance and satisfaction of their subordinates. We now describe three such approaches.

LPC Contingency Theory: Matching Leaders and Tasks

Earlier, we explained that the behaviors associated with effective leadership fall into two major categories—concern for people and concern for production. Both types of behavior contribute to a leader's success. However, a more refined look at this issue leads us to ask exactly when each type of behavior works better. That is, under what particular conditions are leaders more successful when they demonstrate a concern for people compared to a concern for production?

The basics of the theory

This question is addressed by a widely studied approach to leadership known as **LPC contingency theory.** The contingency aspect of the theory is reflected by the assumption that a leader's contribution to successful performance by his or her group is determined by the leader's own traits in conjunction with various features of the situation. Different levels of leader effectiveness occur under different combinations of conditions. To fully understand leader effectiveness, both types of factors must be considered.

The theory identifies *esteem (liking) for least preferred co-worker* (**LPC** for short) as the most important personal characteristic. This refers to a leader's tendency to evaluate in a favorable or unfavorable manner the person with whom she or he has found it most difficult to work. Leaders who perceive this person in negative terms (low LPC leaders) are primarily concerned with attaining successful task performance. In contrast, those who perceive their least preferred co-worker in a positive light (high LPC leaders) are concerned mainly with establishing good relations with subordinates. LPC is considered a leadership style that is relatively fixed and cannot be changed.

Which type of leader—one low in LPC or one high in LPC—is more effective? As suggested by the word *contingency* in the name, the answer is: "It depends." And what it depends on is the degree to which the situation is favorable to the leader—that is, how much it allows the leader to have control over subordinates. This, in turn, is determined largely by three factors: (1) the nature of the *leader's relations with group members* (the extent to which he or she enjoys their support and loyalty), (2) the *degree of structure* in the task being performed (the extent to which task goals and subordinates' roles are clearly defined), and (3) the leader's *position power* (as described on p. 312). Combining these three factors, the leader's situational control can range from very high (positive relations with group members, a highly structured task, and high position power) to very low (negative relations, an unstructured task, and low position power).

What types of leaders are most effective under these various conditions? According to the theory, low LPC leaders (ones who are task-oriented) are superior to high LPC leaders (ones who are people-oriented) when situational control is either very low or very high. In contrast, high LPC leaders have an edge when situational control falls within the moderate range (refer to Figure 11.4).

The rationale for these predictions is quite reasonable. Under conditions of low situational control, groups need considerable guidance to accomplish their tasks. Without such direction, nothing would get done. For example, imagine a military combat group led by an unpopular platoon leader. Any chance of effectiveness this person has would result from paying careful attention to the task at hand rather than hoping to establish better relations with the group. (In fact, in the military, it is often said that a leader in an emergency is better off giving wrong orders than no orders whatsoever.) Because low LPC leaders are more likely to provide structure than high LPC leaders, they usually are more effective in such cases.

Similarly, low LPC leaders are also superior under conditions that offer the leader a high degree of situational control. Indeed, when leaders are liked, their power is not challenged, and when the demands of the task make it clear what a leader should be doing, it is perfectly acceptable for them to focus on the task at hand. Subordinates expect their leaders to exercise control under such conditions and accept it when they do so. And this leads to task success. For example, an airline pilot leading a cockpit crew is expected to take charge and not to seek the consensus of others as she guides a plane onto the runway for a landing. Surely, she would be less effective if she didn't take charge but instead asked the copilot what he thought she should do.

Things are different, however, when situations offer leaders moderate situational control. Consider, for example, a situation in which a leader's relations with subordinates are good, but the task is unstructured, and the leader's power is somewhat restricted. This may be the case, for example, within a research and development team attempting to find creative new uses for a company's products. Here, it would be clearly inappropriate for a low LPC leader to impose directives. (You cannot order people to be creative.) Rather, a highly nurturing leader who is considerate of the feelings of others would likely be more effective—that is, a high LPC leader.

Applying LPC contingency theory

Practitioners have found LPC contingency theory to be quite useful when it comes to suggesting ways of enhancing leader effectiveness. Because the theory assumes that

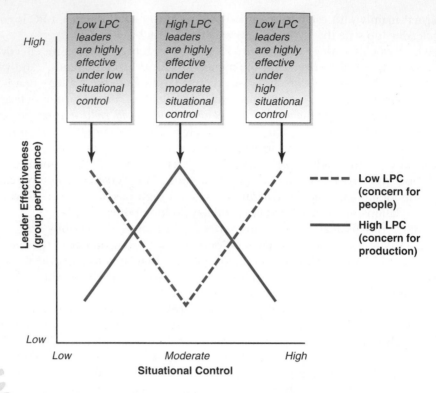

Figure 11.4   LPC Contingency Theory

According to *LPC contingency theory*, low LPC leaders (i.e., ones who are primarily task oriented) will be more effective than high LPC leaders (ones who are primarily people oriented) when situational control is either very low or very high. However, when situational control is moderate, high LPC leaders will be more effective than low LPC leaders.

certain kinds of leaders are most effective under certain kinds of situations and that leadership style is fixed, the best way to enhance effectiveness is to fit the right kind of leaders to the situations they face. This involves completing questionnaires that can be used to assess both the LPC score of the leader and the amount of situational control he or she faces in the situation. Then, using these indexes, a match can be made such that leaders are put into the situations that best suit their leadership styles—a technique known as **leader match.**

This approach also focuses on ways of changing the situational control variables—leader–member relations, task structure, and leader position power—when it is impractical to reassign leaders. For example, a low LPC leader should be moved to a job in which situational control is either extremely high or extremely low. Alternatively, the situation could be changed (such as by altering relations between leaders and group members or by raising or lowering his or her position power) to increase or decrease the amount of situational control encountered. Several companies, including Sears, have used the leader match approach with great success. In fact, research has found that this approach is a very effective way of improving group effectiveness.

Path-Goal Theory: Leaders as Guides to Valued Goals

In defining leadership, we indicated that leaders help their groups or organizations attain their goals. This basic idea plays a central role in the *path-goal theory* of leadership.[33] In general terms, **path-goal theory** contends that subordinates react favorably to leaders who are perceived as helping them make progress toward various goals by clarifying the paths to such rewards. Specifically, the theory claims that the things a leader does to help clarify the nature of tasks and to reduce or eliminate obstacles will increase subordinates' perceptions that working hard will lead to good performance and that good performance, in turn, will be recognized and rewarded. And, under such conditions (as you may recall from our discussion of expectancy theory in Chapter 6), motivation will be enhanced (which may help boost performance).

How, precisely, can leaders best accomplish these tasks? Again, as in the case of LPC contingency theory, the answer is: "It depends." (In fact, this answer is your best clue to identifying any contingency theory.) And what it depends on is a complex interaction between key aspects of *leader behavior* and certain *contingency* factors. Specifically, with respect to leader behavior, path-goal theory suggests that leaders can adopt four basic styles:

➤ **Instrumental** (directive).   An approach focused on providing specific guidance, establishing work schedules and rules

➤ **Supportive.**   A style focused on establishing good relations with subordinates and satisfying their needs

➤ **Participative.**   A pattern in which the leader consults with subordinates, permitting them to participate in decisions

➤ **Achievement oriented.**   An approach in which the leader sets challenging goals and seeks improvements in performance

According to the theory, these styles are not mutually exclusive; in fact, the same leader can adopt them at different times and in different situations. Indeed, as described earlier in this chapter, showing such flexibility is key to being an effective leader. (Recognizing that it is important to adopt these styles, many of today's leaders have adopted an approach to leadership known as *coaching*. For a look at this orientation to leadership, see the Winning Practices section.)

Which of these styles is best for maximizing subordinates' satisfaction and motivation? The answer depends on several characteristics of subordinates. For example, if followers are high in ability, an instrumental style of leadership may be unnecessary; instead, a less structured, supportive approach may be preferable. On the other hand, if subordinates are low in ability, they may need considerable guidance to help them attain their goals. Similarly, people high in need for affiliation (that is, those desiring close, friendly ties with others) may strongly prefer a supportive or participative style of leadership. Those high in the need for achievement may strongly prefer an achievement-oriented leader, one who can guide them to unprecedented levels of success.

The theory suggests that the most effective leadership style also depends on several aspects of the work environment. Specifically, path-goal theory predicts that when tasks are unstructured and nonroutine, an instrumental approach by the leader

Winning Practices

Leadership Lessons from Sports Coaches

If you ever played on a sports team, you've experienced firsthand the important leadership function of a coach. What did your coach do? Chances are that he or she was actively involved in helping you in the following ways:

- By analyzing ways of improving your performance and extending your capabilities so that you can reach your potential

- By creating a supportive climate, one in which barriers to development are eliminated

- By encouraging you to improve, no matter how poorly you perform or how good you already may be

Coaching has been around for a long time, but only recently has it emerged as a philosophy of leadership in organizations.[34]

In recent years, some of the most successful athletic coaches (such as the former Notre Dame football coach, Lou Holtz) and team executives (such as the Green Bay Packers' executive vice president and general manager, Ron Wolf) have written books describing what makes coaching a unique form of leadership.[35] The key, they explain, is the special trust that develops in relationships between coaches and players. Team members acknowledge the coach's expertise and trust the coach to have his or her own best interests, as well as the entire team's best interests, in mind. At the same time, coaches believe in their team members' capacities to profit from their advice. In other words, coaching is a partnership in which both the coach and the team member play an important part in achieving success.

Additional dimensions of the coach's leadership power have been described by basketball hall of famer and former U.S. Senator Bill Bradley.[36] A key to coaching, Bradley emphasizes, is to get players to commit to something bigger than themselves. In sports this may mean winning a championship, and in other

businesses it may mean landing a huge contract or surpassing a long-standing sales record. Focusing on the goal itself, and identifying how each individual may contribute to it, is key.

Bradley also advises that the best coaches don't do all the talking when someone gets out of line. Rather, they harness the power of team members to put pressure on the problem person. As a case in point, consider what happened when the Chicago Bulls' Scottie Pippin angrily took himself out of a 1994 semifinal championship game after Coach Phil Jackson called for teammate Toni Kukoc to make the final, game-deciding shot. Naturally, Coach Jackson came down hard on Pippin in his postgame interview, but that was mostly for show. The real work in getting Pippin to see the error of his ways came not from the coach but from his teammates. After the game, the coach left the locker room, announcing that the team had something to say to Pippin. Then, one by one, members of the Bulls expressed their disappointment in Pippin for letting down the team. Seeing the error of his ways, Pippin apologized on the spot and immediately went back to being the team player he had been all along. Had the coach not orchestrated this session, the effects would not have been as successful.

One way coaches can be supportive of their team members and earn their trust is to refrain from bad-mouthing team members to others. Athletic coaches who use the media to send critical messages to their players live to regret it, Bradley tells us. However, behind the closed doors of the locker room, it's quite a different story. In that setting, there's no such thing as being too frank. The same applies in the office or shop as well. A manager who complains to other managers what a poor job one of her employees has been doing is not only making herself look bad but also, more importantly, betraying that employee's trust. And, as noted earlier, trust is at the heart of the coaching game.

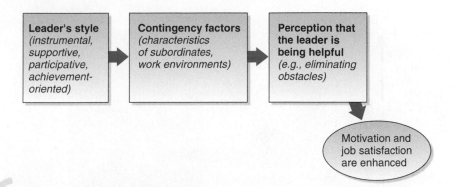

Figure 11.5   Path-Goal Theory

According to *path-goal theory*, perceptions among employees that leaders are helping them attain valued goals enhance their motivation and job satisfaction. Such perceptions are encouraged when a leader's style is consistent with the needs and characteristics of subordinates and various aspects of the work environment.

(Source: Based on suggestions by House, 1996; see Note 33.)

may be best; much clarification and guidance are needed. However, when tasks are structured and routine, such leadership may get in the way of good performance and may be resented by subordinates who think the leader is engaging in unnecessary meddling. (See Figure 11.5 for an overview of all these aspects of path-goal theory.)

Situational Leadership® Theory: Adjusting Leadership Style to the Situation

Another theory of leadership, **Situational Leadership® theory,** is considered a contingency theory because it focuses on the best leadership style for a given situation. The scientists who developed the theory argue that leaders are effective when they select the right leadership style for the situation they face.[37] Specifically, this depends on the maturity of followers—that is, their readiness to take responsibility for their own behavior. This, in turn, is based on two variables with which we are already familiar: (1) task behavior (the degree to which followers have the appropriate job knowledge and skills—that is, their need for guidance and direction), and (2) relationship behavior (the degree to which followers are willing to work without taking direction from others—that is, their need for emotional support).

As shown in Figure 11.6, by combining high and low levels of these independent dimensions, four different types of situations are identified (denoted by *S* in the diagram), each of which is associated with a leadership style that is most effective.

➤ *Lower-right corner of Figure 11.6 (S1).*   Situations in which followers need a great deal of direction from their leaders but don't need much emotional support from them. The practice of *telling* followers what to do is most useful in such situations. That is, giving followers specific instructions and closely supervising their work may be the best approach.

➤ *Upper-right corner of Figure 11.6 (S2).*   Situations in which followers still lack the skill to be able to succeed, although in this case, they require more emotional support.

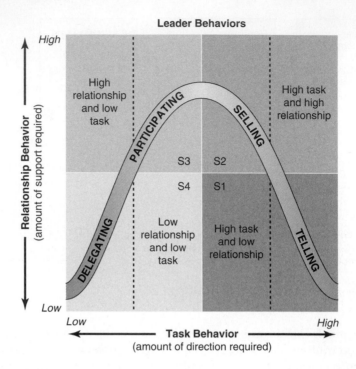

Figure 11.6 Situational Leadership® Theory

Situational Leadership® theory specifies that the most appropriate leadership style depends on the amount of emotional support followers require in conjunction with the amount of guidance they require to do their jobs.

(Source: © Copyright 2006. Reprinted with permission of the Center for Leadership Studies, Inc., Escondido, CA 92025. All rights reserved.)

Under these conditions, *selling* works best. Being very directive may make up for the followers' lack of ability, while being very supportive will help get them to go along with what the leader is asking of them.

➤ **Upper-left corner of Figure 11.6 (S3).**   Conditions in which followers need very little guidance with respect to how to do their jobs, but considerable emotional hand-holding and support to motivate them. That is, low levels of task behavior, but high levels of relationship (supportive) behavior are required. A *participating* style of leadership works well in such situations because it allows followers to share their expertise while enhancing their desire to perform.

➤ **Lower-left corner of Figure 11.6 (S4).**   Followers are both willing and able to do what is asked of them. In other words, low levels of task behavior and low levels of relationship behavior are required. Under such conditions, *delegating* is the best way to treat followers—that is, turning over to them the responsibility for making and implementing their own decisions.

According to Situational Leadership® theory, leaders must be able to (1) diagnose the situations they face, (2) identify the appropriate behavioral style, and then (3) implement that response. Because the situations leaders face may change all the time, leaders must constantly reassess them, paying special attention to their followers' needs for guidance and emotional support. To the extent that they do so, they are likely to be effective.

Specialized training in these skills has been found to be quite useful. In fact, the approach has been widely used to train leaders at such corporate giants as Xerox, ExxonMobil, and Caterpillar, as well as the U.S. military services. (Which style of leadership are you most prone to follow in your treatment of others? To give you some insight into this question, complete the Self-Assessment Exercise on pp. 337–338.)

EMERGING TRENDS AND CHALLENGES IN LEADERSHIP PRACTICE

Now that your understanding of the nature of leadership has a solid foundation, you are prepared to appreciate several emerging trends and challenges that leaders face in today's rapidly changing business environment. We will describe three such issues: the practice of co-leadership, as well as the implications for leadership associated with the use of teams and the digital economy.

Co-CEOs: The Buck Splits Here

Traditionally, companies have only one chief executive officer (CEO), a top leader in charge of the company. These days, however, many companies are finding several good reasons to have two talented leaders in charge—**co-CEOs,** who share power.[38] The major reasons are as follows:

➤ The sheer size, complexity, and geographic challenges of running today's mega-corporations makes having two CEOs somewhat of a necessity. This long has been recognized at Unilever, the world's second-largest consumer products company, which has had co-CEOs since 1930. In an unusual arrangement, instead of having two CEOs at once, Royal Dutch Shell has two executives who alternate turns as CEOs (one from Royal Dutch Petroleum and the other from Shell Transport and Trading).

➤ The wave of megamergers has led to the growth of co-CEOs as the newly created companies scramble to find places for the CEOs of the formerly individual firms.[39] Co-CEO arrangements frequently are well received following mergers and acquisitions because they are friendly in tone (in contrast to some of the hostile takeovers that occurred in the past). When the leaders of the two formerly separate companies work well together, they send a strong message to lower ranking employees that they are expected to do the same.

➤ Because of the considerable amount of work required of leaders of family-owned startup businesses, it's not unusual for them to have co-CEOs. In fact, about 13 percent of such businesses have more than one CEO and even more expect to have them in the future.[40]

➤ Having a co-CEO helps in succession planning because it ensures that an experienced CEO remains onboard when the older of the two retires. This was the reasoning behind the 2008 appointment of Leo Apotheker to serve alongside Henning Kagerman at the large German software company, SAP.[41] The two will divide the responsibilities until Kagerman retires, at which time Apotheker will be prepared to assume the duties on his own.

Unfortunately, as you might imagine, not all such "professional marriages" are successful. In fact, some experts say that companies with co-CEOs are unstable.[42] In the case of the proposed merger of pharmaceutical giants GlaxoWellcome and SmithKline Beecham, arguments about who would lead were so intense that the deal was canceled before it ever occurred. Attempts at installing co-CEOs failed in the mergers between Time-Life and Warner Brothers (forming Time Warner) and that between INA Corp. and Connecticut General (forming Cigna Corp). In both cases, after the two CEOs tore their companies apart with their acrimony, the power-sharing arrangements were disbanded. Both companies now have single CEOs.

At this time, the future of co-leadership is not clear. Although it works sometimes, it's just as likely to fail. The keys to its success seem to be (a) the willingness of each party to yield power to the other, and (b) the recognition by each party that the other makes a vital contribution to the company. When these criteria are met, co-CEOs have a chance at sharing leadership successfully. Otherwise, the relationship may be doomed.

The Challenge of Leading Teams

Traditionally, leaders make strategic decisions on behalf of followers, who are responsible for carrying them out. In many of today's organizations, however, where teams predominate (see Chapter 9), leaders are called upon to provide special resources to team members, who are empowered to implement their own missions in their own ways. Instead of "calling the shots," team leaders help subordinates take responsibility for their own work. As such, they are very different from the traditional, "command and control" leaders we have been discussing.[43] As Table 11.5 suggests, leading teams is very different from leading individuals in the traditional manner.

Table 11.5   Leading Groups Versus Leading Teams

The popularity of teams in today's organizations has important implications for how leaders go about fulfilling their roles. Some of the key differences between leading traditional work groups and leading teams are summarized here.

In Traditional Work Groups, Leaders . . .	But, in Teams, Leaders . . .
Tell people what to do.	Ask people what they think and share responsibility for organizing and doing the work.
Take all the credit.	Share the limelight with all their teammates.
Focus on training employees.	Concentrate on expanding their team's capabilities by functioning primarily as coaches who build confidence in team members, cultivating their untapped potential.
Relate to others individually.	Create a team identity by helping the team set goals, helping members meet them, and celebrating when they have been met.
Work at reducing conflict between individuals.	Make the most of team differences by building respect for diverse points of view and ensuring that all team members' views are expressed.
React to change.	Recognize that change is inevitable and foresee it, better preparing the organization to make appropriate adaptations.

Clearly, the special nature of teams makes the leader's job very different. Although appreciating these differences is easy, making the appropriate adjustments may be extremely challenging—especially for individuals who are well practiced in the traditional, "command and control" ways of leadership. However, given the prevalence of teams in today's work environment, the importance of making the adjustments cannot be overstated. With this in mind, here are a few guidelines that should be followed to achieve success as a team leader.

1. Instead of directing individuals, *team leaders work at building trust and inspiring teamwork.* One way this can be done is by encouraging interaction among all members of the team as well as among the team and its customers and suppliers. Another key ingredient is to take the initiative to make things better. Instead of taking a reactive, "if it ain't broke, don't fix it" approach, teams may be led to success by individuals who set a good example for improving the quality of their team's efforts.

2. Rather than focusing simply on training individuals, effective *team leaders concentrate on expanding team capabilities.* In this connection, team leaders function primarily as coaches, helping team members by providing all members with the skills needed to perform the task, removing barriers that might interfere with task success, and finding the resources required to get the job done. Likewise, team leaders work at building the confidence of team members, cultivating their untapped potential.

3. Instead of managing one-on-one, *team leaders attempt to create a team identity.* In other words, leaders must help teams understand their missions and recognize what they're doing to help fulfill them. In this connection, team leaders may help the group set goals— pointing out ways they may adjust their performance when they do not meet these goals and planning celebrations when team goals are attained.

4. Although traditional leaders have worked at preventing conflict between individuals, *team leaders are encouraged to make the most of team differences.* Without doubt, it is a considerable challenge to meld a diverse group of individuals into a highly committed and productive team, but doing so is important. This can be done by building respect for diverse points of view, making sure that all team members are encouraged to present their views, and to respect these ideas once they are expressed.

5. Unlike traditional leaders who simply react to change, *team leaders should foresee and influence change.* To the extent that leaders recognize that change is inevitable (a point we will emphasize in Chapter 14), they may be better prepared to make the various adaptations required. Effective team leaders continuously scan the business environment for clues to changes that appear to be forthcoming and help teams decide how to be responsive to them.

In conclusion, leading teams is a far cry from leading individuals in the traditional directive (or even a participative) manner. The special nature of teams makes the leader's job very different. Although appreciating these differences is easy, making the appropriate adjustments may be extremely challenging—especially for individuals who are well practiced in the ways of traditional leadership. However, given the prevalence of teams in today's work environment, the importance of making the adjustments cannot be overstated. Leading new teams using old methods is a surefire formula for failure.

Leading in the Digital Age

Most of what we know about leading people is derived from the era in which (a) there were clear hierarchies in organizations and everyone knew who was in charge, (b) changes were made slowly, and (c) people expected to follow their leaders' orders. Many of these characteristics do not apply to today's organizations, and none describe the high-tech world of Internet businesses. In today's digital economy, organizations are highly **decentralized**—that is, power to make decisions is spread out among many different people. What's more, the pace of change is so blindingly fast that leaders rarely have the luxury of making decisions with careful deliberation. Finally, unlike traditional workers, many of today's employees demand independence and autonomy. In short, they are reluctant to be led in the traditional sense of having someone tell them precisely what to do.

As you might imagine, these considerations have important implications for the way today's dot-com leaders are required to operate. Some of the most important implications of the Internet economy for leadership are as follows:[44]

> ➤ *Growth occurs so quickly that strategies have to be changed constantly.*   For example, Meg Whitman, former president and CEO of eBay, noted that because her company has grown so rapidly (in some previous years, a whopping 40 to 50 percent each quarter!), it becomes an entirely different company every few months.[45] Leaders cannot take anything for granted, except the fact that whatever they decided to do yesterday may need to be changed tomorrow.

> ➤ *Leaders of Internet companies are not expected to have all the answers.*   The highly technical nature of the business and the rapid pace of change make it impossible for just one or two people to make all the right decisions. According to Jonathan Buckeley, former CEO of Barnesandnoble.com, today's leaders "must be evangelists for changing the system, not preserving it."[46]

> ➤ *Showing restraint is critical.*   There are so many opportunities available to Internet companies today that executives can too easily enter into a bad deal. For example, Andrew Jarecki, cofounder of Moviefone, Inc., ignored the many suggestions he received to go into business with a big portal before agreeing to what proved to be the right deal—acquisition by AOL for $386 million in stock.

> ➤ *Hiring and retaining the right people is more important than ever.*   In the world of the Internet, the average tenure of a senior executive is only 18 months. Constant change means that the people who are hired for today's jobs must meet the demands of tomorrow's jobs as well. As Jay Walker, founder of Priceline.com, put it, "You've got to hire ahead of the curve," adding, "If you wait until you're actually doing [as much business as you expect] to hire the necessary talent, then you'll be too late."[47]

> ➤ *Today's leaders must not take anything for granted.*   When Mark Cuban and his partner founded Broadcast.com (before selling it to Yahoo! four years later for $5.7 billion), they made lots of incorrect decisions. Instead of sticking by them, they quickly adjusted their game plan to fit the realities they faced.

> ➤ *Internet leaders must focus on real-time decision making.*   Traditional leaders were trained to gather lots of data before making carefully researched decisions. According to Ruthann Quindlen, a successful venture capitalist, leaders can no longer afford to do so: "If your instinct is to wait, ponder, and perfect, then you're dead. . . . Leaders have to hit the undo key without flinching."[48]

As we have outlined here, many of the traditional ways of leading need to be adjusted to accommodate today's Internet economy. Before you think of ignoring everything you learned about leadership in this chapter, please note that the Internet world does *not* require us to rewrite all the rules about good leadership. For example, showing concern for people and concern for production have not gone out of style! In fact, to successfully accommodate the fast-paced, modern era, they may be considered more important than ever.

LEADERSHIP DEVELOPMENT: BRINGING OUT THE LEADER WITHIN YOU

In case it's not clear by now, being an effective leader isn't easy. If you happen to be fortunate enough to be born with "the right stuff," it helps. It also helps to find yourself in the kind of situation in which an opportunity exists to demonstrate your capacity as a leader. However, it is possible for anyone to develop the skills needed to become a more successful leader.

The systematic process of training people to expand their capacity to function effectively in leadership roles is known as **leadership development.** In recent years, many organizations have invested heavily in leadership development efforts, recognizing that effective leadership is a source of competitive advantage for an organization.[49]

All leadership development programs are based on two key assumptions: (1) Leadership makes a difference in an organization's performance, and (2) it is possible for leaders to grow and change to be more effective.[50] However, the various leadership development techniques go about the mission of promoting leadership skills in different ways. We now identify some of the most widely used techniques.[51]

360-Degree Feedback

In Chapter 3, we described *360-degree feedback*, which is the process of using multiple sources from around the organization to evaluate the work of a single individual. Here we note that this practice has proven to be an effective way for leaders to learn what key others, such as peers, direct reports, and supervisors, think about them.[52] This is a useful means of identifying aspects of an individual's leadership style that are in need of change. Its basic assumption is that a person's performance is likely to vary across different contexts, suggesting that different people will have different perspectives on someone's leadership.

The practice of collecting 360-degree feedback is extremely popular these days. In fact, nearly all of the *Fortune* 500 companies rely on this technique in one way or another.[53] However, collecting feedback and taking appropriate action based on it are two entirely different things. After all, many people are threatened by negative feedback and defend against it psychologically by dismissing it as invalid. Even those who agree with it might not be willing to change their behavior (a topic we will revisit in Chapter 14). Furthermore, even the most well-intentioned leaders may fail to take action on the feedback they receive if that information is too complex or inconsistent, which may well occur. To help in this regard, many companies have found that leaders who have face-to-face meetings with others in which they get to discuss the feedback they receive are particularly likely to follow up in an effective manner.[54]

Networking

Far too often, leaders find themselves isolated from things that are going on somewhere in their organizations. Accordingly, when they need help, they don't know where to look within them. As a leadership development tool, **networking** is designed to break down these barriers. Specifically, it is aimed at helping leaders learn to whom they should turn for information and to find out the problem-solving resources that are available to them. Networking is so important to Accenture, the worldwide consulting firm, for example, that it holds an annual five-day seminar designed to give its global partners a chance to meet one another and to exchange views. The goal is to allow partners to strengthen their personal networks, making it possible to address problems and take on projects that otherwise would have been overlooked.

Networking is beneficial to leadership development because it promotes peer relationships in work settings. These relationships are valuable insofar as they involve mutual obligations, thereby promoting cooperation. What's more, they tend to be long-lasting. In fact, it is not unusual for some peer relationships to span an entire career. Importantly, personal networks tend to be effective because they transcend organizational boundaries, thereby bringing together people from different parts of an organization who otherwise would not normally come into contact with one another.

Executive Coaching

A highly effective method of developing leaders involves custom-tailored, one-on-one learning aimed at improving an individual leader's performance known as **executive coaching**.[55] This can be either a one-time process aimed at addressing some specific issues, or it can be an ongoing, continuous process. In either case, executive coaching typically includes an integrative assessment of a leader's strengths and weaknesses along with a comprehensive plan for improvement. Executive coaching programs tend to follow the specific steps outlined in Figure 11.7.

In some organizations, being assigned a coach is seen as a remedial measure and a sign of weakness. In such cases, any benefits of coaching may be minimized because leaders fail to get involved in the process out of embarrassment. For this reason, organizations that use coaches are advised to provide these services to an entire executive group, thereby removing any stigma associated with coaching and putting all leaders on an equal footing. Executive coaching is particularly effective when it is used following a formal training program.[56]

Job Assignments

When it comes to leadership, the phrase "experience is the best teacher" holds true. Indeed, one of the most effective ways of training leaders is by assigning them to positions that promise to give them needed experience. With this in mind, several companies intentionally assign personnel to other countries so they can broaden their experiences. For example, Coca-Cola transferred over 300 professional and managerial employees from the United States to facilities in other countries for one year in an effort to develop their skills before returning them home to assume new positions of leadership. Gillette International does the same thing on a regular basis, assigning prospective leaders to positions at foreign affiliates for periods of one to three years. In many ways, this is akin to Major League Baseball's practice of developing players by having them play on minor league "farm teams."

For job assignments to serve their developmental function, it is necessary for the newly assigned positions to provide the kind of opportunities that make

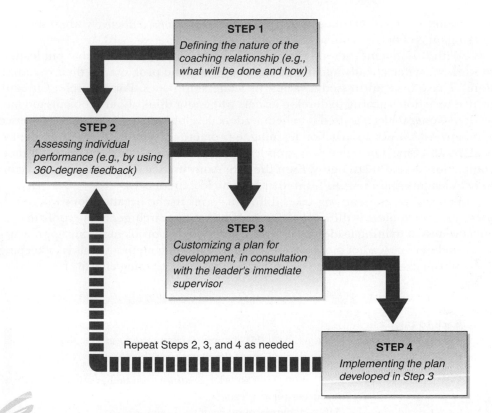

STEP 1

Defining the nature of the coaching relationship (e.g., what will be done and how)

STEP 2

Assessing individual performance (e.g., by using 360-degree feedback)

STEP 3

Customizing a plan for development, in consultation with the leader's immediate supervisor

STEP 4

Implementing the plan developed in Step 3

Repeat Steps 2, 3, and 4 as needed

Figure 11.7 Steps in the Executive Coaching Process

The process of executive coaching generally follows the four steps outlined here.

(Source: Based on information in Chapman et al., 2003; see Note 56.)

learning possible. Ideally, the new positions are ones that give developing leaders opportunities to try out different approaches to leadership so they can see what works for them. In other words, they should have the latitude to try different approaches, even if they fail. It is important to keep in mind that the purpose of the job assignment is to facilitate learning, in which case failure is inevitable. However, should an emphasis be placed on job performance instead, it's unlikely that the new assignment will have the intended benefits and is destined to be looked upon unfavorably.

Action Learning

Traditionally, much of the learning that takes place when people learn to lead occurs in the classroom. The problem with this approach, however, is that shortly after the formal training sessions are over, people revert to their old ways, resulting in little if any developmental progress. To combat this problem, many organizations have been turning to **action learning,** which is a continuous process of learning and reflection that is supported by colleagues and that emphasizes getting things done.[57] The underlying assumption of action learning is that leaders develop most effectively when they are working on real organizational problems.[58]

With this in mind, several companies have developed exercises that put leaders to work on systematically making plans to solve specific problems in their organizations. These have addressed a variety of leadership issues. For example, Citibank turned to action learning to develop leaders who won't think about problems too narrowly.[59] General Electric used it to help leaders develop new markets, the foodservice company ARAMARK used action learning to promote cross-cultural opportunities for leaders, and Shell Oil relied on action learning to alter leaders' perceptions of their companies' financial strengths. Even the U.S. Army used action learning as a means to help leaders share lessons from their battlefield experiences.[60]

Because action learning takes different forms in the organizations where it is used, its effectiveness is difficult to assess. However, research generally confirms the effectiveness of training leaders by using the kind of active problem-solving approaches suggested here instead of more passive, classroom training methods (this is in keeping with our discussion in Chapter 3 of the factors that make training effective).

Back to the Case
Answer the following questions about this chapter's Making the Case (pp. 309–310) to illustrate insights you have derived about the material in this chapter.

1. From what you can tell about Mr. Yost, what qualities does he have that appear to make him successful as a leader?
2. Considering the high-tech nature of many of the operations at AmerisourceBergen, what special considerations are there for its leaders?
3. Under what conditions might Mr. Yost be most effective as a leader? Base your answer on one or more of the contingency theories described in this chapter.

You Be the Consultant

A Controlling Leadership Style

The president and founder of a large office furniture manufacturer tells you, "Nobody around here has any respect for me. The only reason they listen to me is because this is my company." Company employees report that he is a highly controlling individual who does not let people do anything for themselves.

1. What behaviors should the president attempt to emulate to improve his leadership style? How may he go about doing so?

2. Under what conditions would you expect the president's leadership style to be most effective? Do you think that these conditions might exist in his company?

3. Would your advice be any different if he were in charge of a small Internet start-up firm instead of a large manufacturing company? If so, how?

SELF-ASSESSMENT EXERCISE

Determining Your Leadership Style

As noted on pages 327–329, *Situational Leadership® theory* identifies four basic leadership styles. To be able to identify and enact the most appropriate style of leadership in any given situation, it is first useful to understand the style to which you are most predisposed. This exercise will help you gain such insight into your own leadership style.

Directions

Following are eight hypothetical situations in which you have to make a decision affecting you and members of your work group. For each, indicate which of the following actions you are most likely to take by writing the letter corresponding to that action in the space provided.

- *Action A.* Let the members of the group decide themselves what to do.
- *Action B.* Ask the members of the group what to do but make the final decision yourself.
- *Action C.* Make the decision yourself but explain your reasons.
- *Action D.* Make the decision yourself, telling the group exactly what to do.

1. ____ In the face of financial pressures, you are forced to make budget cuts for your unit. Where do you cut?
2. ____ To meet an impending deadline, someone in your secretarial pool will have to work late one evening to finish assembling an important report. Who will it be?
3. ____ As coach of a company softball team, you are required to trim your squad to 25 players from 30 currently on the roster. Who goes?
4. ____ Employees in your department have to schedule their summer vacations so as to keep the office appropriately staffed. Who makes the first selection?
5. ____ As chair of the social committee, you are responsible for determining the theme for the company's annual ball. How do you do so?
6. ____ You have an opportunity to buy or rent an important piece of equipment for your company. After gathering all the facts, how do you make this choice?
7. ____ The office is being redecorated. How do you decide on the color scheme?
8. ____ Along with your associates you are taking a visiting dignitary to dinner. How do you decide what restaurant to go to?

Scoring

1. Count the number of situations to which you responded by marking *A*. This is your *delegating* score.
2. Count the number of situations to which you responded by marking *B*. This is your *participating* score.
3. Count the number of situations to which you responded by marking *C*. This is your *selling* score.
4. Count the number of situations to which you responded by marking *D*. This is your *telling* score.

Discussion Questions

1. Based on this questionnaire, what was your most predominant leadership style? Is this consistent with what you would have predicted in advance?

2. According to Situational Leadership® theory, in what kinds of situations would this style be most appropriate? Have you ever found yourself in such a situation, and if so, how well did you do?

3. Do you think that it would be possible for you to change this style if needed?

GROUP EXERCISE

Identifying Great Leaders in All Walks of Life

A useful way to understand the great person theory is to identify those individuals who may be considered great leaders and then to consider what it is that makes them so great. This exercise is designed to guide a class in this activity.

Directions

1. Divide the class into four equal-size groups, arranging each in a semicircle.

2. In the open part of the semicircle, one group member—the recorder—should stand at a flip chart, ready to write down the group's responses.

3. The members of each group should identify the 10 most effective leaders they can think of—living or dead, real or fictional—in one of the following fields: business, sports, politics/government, or humanitarian endeavors. One group should cover each of these domains. If more than 10 names come up, the group should vote on the 10 best answers. The recorder should write down the names as they are identified.

4. Examining the list, group members should identify the traits and characteristics that the people on the list have in common that distinguish them from others who are not on the list. In other words, what is it that makes these people so special? The recorder should write down the answers.

5. One person from each group should be selected to present his or her group's responses to members of the class. This should include both the names of the leaders identified and their special characteristics.

Discussion Questions

1. How did the traits identified in this exercise compare to the ones described in Table 11.3 (p. 314) as important determinants of leadership? Were they similar or different? Why?

2. To what extent were the traits identified in the various groups different or similar? In other words, were different characteristics associated with leadership success in different walks of life? Or were the ingredients for leadership success cut across various domains?

3. Were some of some traits identified surprising to you, or were they all what you would have expected?

C h a p t e r   1 2

Culture, Creativity, and Innovation

Learning Objectives

After reading this chapter, you will be able to:

1. **DEFINE** organizational culture and **IDENTIFY** the functions it serves in organizations.

2. **DESCRIBE** the major types of organizational culture identified in the competing values framework.

3. **IDENTIFY** the factors responsible for creating organizational culture, for transmitting it, and for getting it to change.

4. **DEFINE** creativity and **DESCRIBE** the basic components of individual and team creativity.

5. **DESCRIBE** various approaches to promoting creativity in organizations.

6. **IDENTIFY** the basic components of general innovation and organizational innovation, and the stages through which each progresses.

3 GOOD REASONS why you should care about . . .

Culture, Creativity, and Innovation

You should care about culture, creativity, and innovation because:

1. Organizational culture exerts profound influences on employees, both positive and negative.

2. Managers play an important role in creating, transmitting, and changing organizational culture.

3. Individual and team creativity is an important determinant of an organization's capacity to be innovative. This, in turn, is largely responsible for organizational success.

Making the Case for Culture, Creativity, and Innovation

Is Zipcar the Antidote to High Fuel Prices and Congested Roads?

When you own a car, how much time are you actually driving it? Many cars spend more time in the garage than on the road. But even when parked, vehicles rack up bills for insurance and loan interest while their values are depreciating. You can always go to one of the traditional car rental companies, but these tend to be very expensive and inconvenient. Still, you need wheels, so what's the alternative?

Antje Danielson had an answer inspired by something she saw while on vacation in Germany—a car-sharing service. Why not have fleets of cars stationed all around a city that you could rent on a short-term basis by phoning in a last-minute, no-hassle reservation? Just walk up to the parked vehicle, swipe a card, and drive away. When you're done, drop off the car at one of the many conveniently located lots, leave the keys, and walk away. You're billed a reasonable daily or hourly fee for a rental that includes everything—all insurance, fuel, and parking.

One day in 1999, in Cambridge, Massachusetts, Danielson approached Robin Chase with her "wheels when you want them" idea and Zipcar was born. Their plan was to introduce facilities into congested areas, such as downtowns of major cities and areas around the campuses of large universities, where people are inclined to need cars for short trips but where ownership is prohibitively expensive. It would work, they reasoned, if they could meet four requirements: (1) develop a phone and online reservation system that was blazingly fast and easy to use, (2) offer a variety of different kinds of vehicles for different occasions, (3) have pick-up and drop-off locations that are as easy to find as ATMs, and, of course, (4) keep rental fees reasonable.

This required considerable start-up funds, so Danielson and Chase partnered with major investors, including a company backed by AOL co-founder Steve Case and Staples founder Thomas G. Stemberg. With strong financial backing, Zipcar now operates in over 50 U.S. cities and has about a quarter-million members, making it the largest car-sharing company in the world. And with high fuel costs, this figure is rising fast. For an annual fee of $50, members can rent cars for $11 per hour (and up, depending on the vehicle and location), or $77 for a whole day, with a generous mileage allowance.

Zipcar has been so popular with customers that over 40 percent either put off buying a new car or sell their existing cars within their first year of membership. This has resulted in saving each member about $5,000. And as word of such sizable savings has spread, the number of subscribers has grown.

As it is for any good idea, Zipcar's success has spawned imitators. In 2008, Hertz began offering hourly rates for cars in New York and Boston, and Enterprise began testing a pilot program for hourly rentals in St. Louis. Potentially so beneficial to reducing traffic congestion is the car-sharing business that the city of Chicago and the U.S. Transportation Department have backed a nonprofit civic group in Chicago that is launching their own venture, I-Go Car Sharing.

With this competition, especially competitors with government backing, Zipcar's future, like the future of many relatively new startup firms, is uncertain. Although it's never easy to predict the future of any individual business venture, the Zipcar story strongly suggests that car-sharing is here to stay.

Zipcar's founders didn't invent the car rental business, of course, but they surely came up with an entirely new way of operating one. Its convenient new twist on picking up and returning short-term rental vehicles makes it the proverbial "better mousetrap" of this $50 billion industry. Behind it were founders who demonstrated considerable *creativity*. Of course, coming up with the kind of idea that makes you say,

"Why didn't I think of that?" and bringing it to fruition are two different things. And just as some individuals are more creative than others, some companies—3M, General Electric, and Rubbermaid, for example—are particularly adept at routinely doing the nonroutine. They take creative ideas and turn them into cutting-edge solutions, making them highly *innovative.* Considering the importance of creativity and innovation in today's rapidly changing, technologically oriented business environment, we focus on them in this chapter.

When thinking about why some organizations are more innovative than others, it's tempting to speculate that because people have different personalities, the organizations in which they work are likely to be different as well. However, when you consider that entire organizations are often so consistently different from one another, it's apparent that there's more involved than simply differences in the personalities of the employees. In fact, even in companies where employees are constantly changing, the organizations do not reinvent themselves. In fact, it is often the new employees who change rather than their organizations. In a sense, then, organizations have a stable existence of their own, apart from the unique combination of people of which they are composed at any given time. This is the idea behind *organizational culture*—the shared beliefs, expectations, and core values of people in an organization.[1]

Because it provides much of the foundation for individual creativity and an organization's tendency toward innovation, we begin this chapter by examining organizational culture. Specifically, we describe the basic nature of organizational culture, its major types, the processes through which it is formed and maintained, tools for transmitting culture, the effects of organizational culture on organizational functioning, and finally, how culture is subject to change. With this foundation in place, we then shift attention to the topics of creativity and innovation. This includes a discussion of not only their fundamental characteristics, but also specific tips and suggestions on how to bring out your own creativity and how to make your own organization more innovative.

ORGANIZATIONAL CULTURE: ITS BASIC NATURE

So that you can fully appreciate organizational culture, we begin by offering a formal definition and then point out several of its key features.

Organizational Culture: A Definition

Scientists define **organizational culture** as a cognitive framework consisting of assumptions and values shared by organization members.[2] For example, organizations tend to have *absence cultures* (i.e., shared understanding by employees of the appropriateness of taking off from work) and these may differ. At one organization, for example, healthy employees may feel that it's appropriate to call in sick if they have unused sick days available. However, at other companies, people wouldn't think of taking off unless they really are ill. In both of these companies, employees take for granted these various *assumptions* about sick leave. They are said to be ingrained into the organizational culture and are taken for granted.

As the definition indicates, organizational culture also reflects different *values* that are shared by members of the organization. By *values,* we are referring to stable, long-term beliefs about what is important. For example, some companies consider their employees as valuable only insofar as they contribute to production, much as they view machinery. Such organizations, where people do not feel valued, are considered to have *toxic organizational cultures*. In fact, about half of all working people believe their organizations have toxic cultures.[3] Not surprisingly, such organizations tend to lose good employees.

By contrast, organizations that treat people well—said to have *healthy organizational cultures*—tend to have very low turnover. Examples of companies with healthy cultures include Hewlett-Packard, the Men's Wearhouse, and Starbucks. Not only are such organizations pleasant places to work, but having a healthy organizational culture also can pay off handsomely on the bottom line.[4]

Despite widespread differences, cultures in all organizations serve the following three vital functions.

1. ***Provide a sense of identity for members.***   The more clearly an organization's shared perceptions and values are defined, the more strongly people can associate themselves with their organization's mission and feel a vital part of it. Being part of the organization is who they are.

2. ***Generate commitment to the organization's mission.***   Sometimes it's difficult for people to go beyond thinking of their own interests: How will this affect me? However, a strong, overarching culture reminds people of what their organization is all about.

3. ***Clarify and reinforce standards of behavior.***   Culture guides employees' words and deeds, making it clear what they should or shouldn't do or say in a given situation, thereby providing stability to behavior.

Cultures Within Organizations: One or Many?

Thus far, the discussion has implied that each organization has only a single, uniform culture—one set of shared values and expectations. In fact, this is rarely the case. Instead, organizations, particularly large ones, typically have *several* cultures operating within them.

In general, people tend to have more attitudes and values in common with others in their own fields of work or their own company units than they do with those in other fields or other parts of their organizations. These various groups may be said to have several different **subcultures**—cultures existing within parts of organizations rather than entirely through them. These typically are distinguished with respect to either functional differences (i.e., the type of work done) or geographic distances (i.e., the physical separation between people). Indeed, several subcultures based on occupational, professional, or functional divisions usually exist within any large organization. For example, the sales department of an insurance company in New York may have a subculture that differs from that of the sales department in Los Angeles, the underwriting department in Denver, or the culture of the company as a whole.

This is not to say, however, that there also may not be a **dominant culture,** a distinctive, overarching "personality" of an organization—the kind of culture to which we have been referring. An organization's dominant culture reflects its **core values,** dominant perceptions that are generally shared throughout the organization. Typically, although members of subcultures may share additional sets of values, they generally also accept the core values of their organizations as a whole. Thus, subcultures should not be thought of as a bunch of separate cultures but rather as "mini" cultures operating within a large, dominant culture.

Major Types of Organizational Culture: The Competing Values Framework

As you might imagine, just are there are many different organizations, there also are many different types of organizational culture. Although each organization may be unique in several ways, key similarities in underlying organizational cultures may be noted. Fortunately, organizational scientists have developed useful ways of organizing and identifying these cultures. One such approach is the *competing values framework*.[5] According to the **competing values framework,** the cultures of organizations differ with respect to two sets of opposite values: (1) the extent to which the organization values flexibility and discretion as opposed to stability, order, and control, and (2) the relative amount of attention paid to internal affairs as opposed to activities in the external environment. By combining both dimensions, as shown in Figure 12.1, scientists have been able to identify the following four unique types of organizational culture.

➤ *Hierarchy culture.*   Organizations described as having a **hierarchy culture** (shown in the lower left corner of Figure 12.1) have an internal focus and emphasize stability and control. Here the most effective leaders are good coordinators of projects and emphasize a smooth-running organization, often relying on formal rules and policies to do so. Governmental agencies and large corporations tend to fall into this category. At McDonald's, for example, key values center on maintaining efficient and reliable production, and to ensure this, both the equipment used and the procedures followed—described in a 350-page manual—are designed with this in mind.

Figure 12.1   The Competing Values Framework

According to the *competing values framework,* the cultures of organizations can be distinguished in terms of the two opposite dimensions identified here. Combining these two sets of competing values results in the four types of organizational cultures shown.

(Source: Adapted from Cameron & Quinn, 1999; see Note 5.)

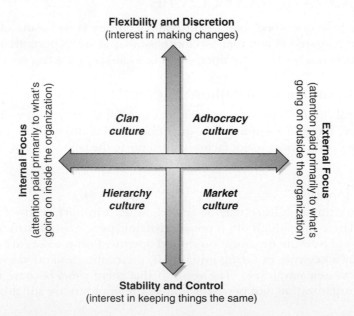

➤ *Market culture.*   The term **market culture** describes organizations that are concerned with stability and control but that are external in their orientation (see the lower-right corner of Figure 12.1). The core values of such organizations focus on competitiveness and productivity, emphasizing bottom-line results. They do this by carefully identifying the markets in which they are going to compete and then by taking a very hard-driving, results-oriented approach to getting things done. A prototypical example is General Electric under the guidance of former CEO Jack Welch, who made it clear that the company would sell any businesses in which it was not ranked number one or number two in its markets.

➤ *Clan culture.*   An organization is said to have a **clan culture** when it has a strong internal focus along with a high degree of flexibility and discretion (see the upper-left corner of Figure 12.1). With goals that are highly shared by members of the organization and high levels of cohesiveness (see Chapter 9), such organizations feel more like extended families than economic entities. This depicts the culture at many small high-tech startup companies, where management is highly informal and employees (who may own stock in the company) govern themselves.

➤ *Adhocracy culture.*   Organizations that have an *adhocracy culture* emphasize flexibility while also paying a great deal of attention to the external environment (see upper-right corner of Figure 12.1). Typical of contemporary organizations, which often have to make rapid changes in the way they operate (see Chapter 14), the adhocracy culture is characterized by recognizing that to succeed organizations need to be highly innovative (a concept we will describe later in this chapter) and to assess continuously what the future requires for them to survive, let alone grow. Adhocracy cultures are typical in the aerospace industry, software development firms, and film production companies, where highly innovative products and services are essential to success.

THE FORMATION AND MAINTENANCE OF ORGANIZATIONAL CULTURE

Now that we have described what organizational culture is and some of the forms it takes, we are prepared to consider two more issues that are important: how culture is created initially and how it is sustained—that is, what keeps it going once it is created.

How Is Organizational Culture Created?

Organizational culture is so prevalent that we often fail to consider how it is created in the first place. Yet, understanding how organizational culture is created is essential to managing its effects. Three major factors contribute to the emergence of organizational culture.

Company founders

First, organizational culture may be traced, at least in part, to the founders of a company.[6] These individuals often possess dynamic personalities, strong values, and a clear vision of how the organization should operate. Because they are on the scene first and play a key role in hiring initial staff, their attitudes and values are readily transmitted to new employees. The result is that these views become the accepted ones in the organization and persist as long as the founders are still around.

For example, the culture at Microsoft calls for working exceptionally long hours, in large part because that's what co-founder Bill Gates has always done (even though he is no longer involved in the day-to-day operations of the company). Sometimes the founder's values continue to drive an organization's culture even after that individual has passed away. For example, the late Ray Kroc founded the McDonald's restaurant chain on the values of good food at a good value served in clean, family-oriented surroundings—key cultural values that persist today.

Experience with the environment

Second, organizational culture often develops out of an organization's experience with the external environment. Every organization must find a niche for itself in its industry and in the marketplace. As it struggles to do so in its early days, it may find that some values and practices work better than others. For example, one company may determine that delivering defect-free products is its unique market niche; by doing so, it can build a core of customers who prefer its high quality orientation to those of competing businesses. As a result, the organization may gradually acquire a deep, shared commitment to high quality. In contrast, another company may find that selling products of moderate quality but at attractive prices works best. In this case, a dominant value centering on *price leadership* takes shape.

Contact with others

Third, organizational culture develops out of contact between groups of individuals within an organization. As this occurs, people's interpretations of events and actions are likely to be shared, promoting the development of organizational culture. In other words, organizational culture reflects the fact that people assign similar meaning to various events and actions so that they come to perceive the key aspects of the world, those relevant to the organization's work, in a similar manner (see Chapter 3).

Tools for Transmitting Culture

How are an organization's cultural values transmitted between employees? In other words, how do people come to learn about their organizations' cultures? Several key mechanisms are involved: *symbols, stories, jargon, ceremonies,* and *statements of principle*.

Symbols: Objects and statements that say more than meets the eye

One vehicle organizations use to transmit culture is *symbols*—words or objects that connote meanings that extend beyond their intrinsic content. For example, some companies use impressive buildings to symbolize their strength and significance, showing that they are large and stable. The Sears tower in Chicago, for example, was constructed in the late 1960s as the largest building in North America to reflect the company's status at the time as the largest retailer.

Organizations also communicate their cultures using symbols in the form of words—slogans that reflect organizations' core values. For example, Wal-Mart uses the slogan, "Save money. Live better" to expresses its commitment to helping people lead good lives that they can afford. Regardless of their form, symbols are potent tools for sending messages about organizational culture. (To demonstrate this phenomenon for yourself, complete the Group Exercise on pp. 367–368.)

Stories: "In the old days, we used to . . ."

Organizations also transmit information about culture by virtue of the *stories* that are told in them, both formally and informally. Stories illustrate key aspects of an organization's culture, and telling them can effectively introduce or reaffirm those values to employees.[7] For example, employees of Nike are told tales about how the company was founded in an effort to underscore the company's abiding commitment to athletes (for some examples, see Table 12.1).[8] It is important to note that stories need not involve some great event, such as someone who saved the company with a single wise decision, but they may be small tales that become legends because they so effectively communicate a message.

Jargon: Special language that defines a culture

Even without telling stories, the everyday language used in companies helps sustain culture. For example, the slang or *jargon* used in a company helps its employees define their identities as members of an organization. As a case in point, someone who works in a human resources department may be found talking about the FMCS (Federal Medication and Conciliation Service), ERISA (the Employee Retirement Income Security Act), BFOQs (bona fide occupational qualifications), RMs (elections to vote out a union), and other acronyms that sound odd to the uninitiated. Over time, as organizations—or departments within them—develop unique language to describe their work, their terms, although strange to newcomers, serve as a common factor that brings together individuals belonging to a corporate culture or subculture.

Ceremonies: Special events that commemorate corporate values

Organizations also do a great deal to sustain their cultures by conducting various types of *ceremonies*, celebrations of an organization's basic values and assumptions. Just as a wedding ceremony symbolizes a couple's mutual commitment and a presidential

---

Table 12.1   The Nike Story: Just Telling It—And Keeping It Alive

New employees at Nike are told stories that transmit their company's underlying cultural values. The themes of some of the most important Nike stories are summarized here along with several of the ways the company helps keep its heritage alive.

New employees are told the following stories . . .

- Founder Phil Knight was a middle-distance runner who started the business by selling shoes out of his car.
- Knight's running coach and company co-founder, Bill Bowerman, developed the famous "waffle sole" by pouring rubber into his family's waffle iron.
- The late Steve Prefontaine, coached by Bowerman, battled to make running a professional sport and was comitted to helping athletes.

To ensure that these tales of Nike's heritage are kept alive, the company . . .

- Takes new hires to the track where Bowerman coached and the site of Prefontaine's fatal car crash.
- Has created a "heritage wall" in its Eugene, Oregon, store.
- Requires salespeople to tell the Nike story to employees of the retail stores that sell its products.

(Source: Based on information in Ransdell, 2000; see Note 8.)

inauguration ceremony marks the beginning of a new presidential term, various organizational ceremonies also celebrate some important milestone. For example, one accounting firm celebrated its move to much better facilities by throwing a party, a celebration signifying that it "made it to the big time." Such ceremonies convey meaning to people inside and outside the organization. As one expert put it, "Ceremonies are to the culture what the movie is to the script . . . values that are difficult to express in any other way."[9]

Statements of principle: Defining culture in writing

A fifth way in which culture is transmitted is via the direct *statements of principle*. Some organizations have explicitly written their principles for all to see. Consider these examples:

➤ Forrest Mars, the founder of the 100-year-old candy company M&M Mars, developed his "Five Principles of Mars" that still guide his company today.[10] These are: quality (everyone is responsible for maintaining quality), responsibility (all employees are responsible for their own actions and decisions), mutuality (creating a situation in which everyone can win), efficiency (very few resources are wasted), and freedom (giving employees opportunities to shape their futures).

➤ For over 20 years, the design firm IDEO has developed a culture that promotes creativity—and it makes this clear in its statement of principle: "Our values are part mad scientist (curious, experimental), bear-tamer (gutsy, agile), reiki master (hands-on, empathetic), and midnight tax accountant (optimistic, savvy). These qualities are reflected in the smallest details to the biggest endeavors, composing the medium in which great ideas are born and flourish."[11]

ORGANIZATIONAL CULTURE: ITS EFFECTS AND CAPACITY TO CHANGE

By now, you probably are convinced that organizational culture plays an important role in the functioning of organizations. To make this point explicit, we now will examine the various ways in which organizational culture has been found to affect organizations and the behavior of individuals in them. Because some of these effects might be undesirable, organizations are sometimes interested in changing their cultures. Accordingly, we also will consider why and how organizational culture might be changed.

The Effects of Organizational Culture

Organizational culture exerts many effects on individuals and organizational processes—some dramatic, others subtle. Culture generates strong pressures on people to go along, to think and act in ways consistent with the existing culture. So, for example, customer service is very highly valued at Saks Fifth Avenue, often leading customers to praise this aspect of their shopping experience at this venerable high-end retail chain.[12] An organization's culture also can strongly affect everything from the way employees dress (e.g., very casual clothes are worn by most employees of software development firms to reflect the creative and casual atmosphere that prevails in them) and the amount of time allowed to elapse before meetings begin, to the speed with which people are promoted within the company.

Organizational performance

How does an organization's culture influence its financial performance? A link has been established between culture and performance but as you might imagine, its complex in nature.[13] We know, for example, that to influence performance, organizational culture must be strong. A **strong corporate culture** is one that because of the consistency of its message and widespread acceptance throughout the organization exerts major effect on employees. A **weak corporate culture,** by contrast, is one composed of inconsistent messages, limited acceptance, and as a result, far more limited effects. For an overview of these differences, see Table 12.2.

When corporate culture is strong, values are shared widely across the workforce, and everybody is moving in the same direction, making it possible for culture to influence performance. And this can have positive benefits. In fact, relative to other companies in their fields, those with strongest corporate cultures tend to have the best financial performance.[14] The main reason for this is clear: When values are strongly shared and the interests of employees and their companies are strongly aligned, everyone is moving in the same direction and this can enhance performance.

Importantly, this assumes that companies are operating in stable business environments, ones in which little is changing.[15] Under such conditions, the strong culture can fuel a "well-oiled machine" that points everyone in the same, appropriate direction. However, when the business environment is uncertain, things are turbulent and in need of rapid change, leading the same dynamic to have the opposite effect. Namely, the strong culture may interfere with organizational performance because it promotes existing ways of doing things that need to be chaged. The inertia resulting from strong culture in this case keeps things moving in directions that need to be altered, thereby

Table 12.2   Characteristics of Strong and Weak Organizational Cultures

Strong and weak organizational cultures differ in terms of the characteristics summarized here.

Characteristic	Strong culture	Weak culture
Clarity regarding the company's mission and philosophy	Clear	Unclear
Time spent communicating values and beliefs	Great deal of time	Little or no time
Written creed or statement of values	Exists and is adhered to	Does not exist
Norms and values shared throughout the organization	Highly shared norms and values	No consistent norms and values
Prospective employees screened for fit with values	Yes, screened carefully	Not considered
Traditions celebrated	Yes, regularly	Few, if any, exist
Existence of subcultures	Very few	Many
Sense of company identity	Strong	Weak

interfering with efforts to promote change (see Chapter 14). In summary, then, it makes sense to consider strong organizational culture a double-edged sword.

Why and How Does Organizational Culture Change?

My earlier comments about the relative stability of organizational culture may have left you wondering if and when organizational culture ever changes. Why isn't it simply passed from one generation of organizational members to the next in a totally static manner? The basic answer, of course, is that the world in which all organizations operate constantly changes (see Chapter 14). External events such as shifts in market conditions, new technology, altered government policies, and many other factors change over time, necessitating changes in an organization's mode of doing business—and, hence, its culture.

Composition of the workforce

Over time, the people entering an organization may differ in important ways from those already in it, and these differences may impinge on the existing culture of the organization. For example, people from different ethnic or cultural backgrounds may have contrasting views about various aspects of behavior at work. They may hold dissimilar views about style of dress, the importance of being on time (or even what constitutes "on time" behavior), the level of deference one should show to higher-status people, and even what foods should be served in the company cafeteria. In other words, as large numbers of people with different backgrounds and values enter the workplace, changes in organizational culture may be expected to follow.

Mergers and acquisitions

Another and even more dramatic source of cultural change is *mergers* and *acquisitions*, events in which one organization purchases or otherwise absorbs another.[16] When this occurs, there is likely to be a careful analysis of the financial and material assets of the acquired organization. However, it is rare that any consideration is given to the acquired organization's culture. This is unfortunate because there have been several cases in which the merger of two organizations with incompatible cultures has led to serious problems referred to as *culture clashes*. As you might imagine, life in companies with incompatible cultures tends to be conflict-ridden and highly disruptive, often resulting in arguments and considerable uncertainty about what to do. In some cases, organizations have even been known to disband because of extreme culture clashes. For several examples of culture clashes resulting from mergers and acquisitions over the years, see Table 12.3.[17]

Planned organizational change

Even if an organization doesn't change by acquiring another, cultural change still may result from other planned changes, such as conscious decisions to alter the internal structure or the basic operations of an organization (a topic we will describe in detail in Chapter 13). A good example may be found at Siemens, the giant, 160-year-old German electronics and engineering firm with operations in 190 countries. In 2006, only two years after Klaus Kleinfeld took over as CEO, the company's sales grew 16 percent and profits jumped 35 percent. He had transformed the company from one that was known for stodginess to one that was aggressive and fast-moving.[18] This was the result of drastic

Table 12.3 Organizational Culture Clashes: Four Examples

Four major examples of culture clashes in the past few decades are summarized here, along with the cast of characters. As you read about these, think about what it must have been like to work in these companies at the time the clashes were occurring.

Original Company and CEO at Time of Merger	Original Company and CEO at Time of Merger	New Company (Merger Date) and Original Officers	Nature of Culture Conflict
AOL Steve Case, CEO	**Time Warner** Gerald M. Levin, CEO	**AOL Time Warner** (2001), renamed **Time Warner** (2003), Steve Case, CEO	The first "bricks-and-clicks" media empire to be formed suffered as AOL officials spent money in reckless fashion (far more lavishly than accurate accounting methods suggest would have been prudent), whereas the more conservative Time Warner officials were not accustomed to such high-flying ways. Although AOL Time Warner was officially a business entity, from the perspective of organizational culture, no merger ever really occurred. It was with this in mind that the company dropped the AOL from its name in 2003, returning to Time Warner.
Chrysler Robert J. Eaton, CEO	**Daimler-Benz** Jürgen E. Schrempp, CEO	**DaimlerChrysler** (1998) Robert J. Eaton and Jürgen E. Schrempp, co-CEOs	The so-called "merger of equals" was decidedly unequal. Executives' lifestyles were in sharp contrast. Those who came from Chrysler traveled together to meetings in minivans and flew economy class. However, Daimler-Benz officials arrived in chauffeur-driven Mercedes-Benz sedans and flew first class. While spending six months working this out, executives ignored important corporate problems. In 2007, Daimler and Chrysler went their separate ways.
RJ Reynolds Tylee Wilson, CEO	**Nabisco** Ross Johnson, CEO	**RJR Nabisco** (1988) Ross Johnson, CEO	Nabisco executives had a fast-paced lifestyle with perks such as corporate jets, penthouse apartments, and lavish parties. RJ Reynolds was characterized by a strong work ethic, much less autonomy for employees, and a deep commitment to its local, North Carolina community. A bitter feud erupted and Johnson fired RJ Reynolds executives.
HFS (franchising company) Henry Silverman, CEO	**CUC International** (membership-club company) Walter Forbes, CEO	**Cendant** (1997) Henry Silverman, CEO; and Walter Forbes, chairman of the board	Silverman was a control freak who insisted on seeing and knowing everything. However, Forbes saw himself as a visionary and left the details to others. Power clashes grew, eventually leading someone to blow the whistle on CUC officials for creating phony profits. The resulting scandal harmed the company greatly.

(Source: Based on information from references cited in Note 17.)

changes in organizational structure (see Chapter 13) that made operations more efficient and his effort to push Siemens' 475,000 employees to make decisions faster and to focus new energy on customer service.

You might think that employees would be proud of these accomplishments, but the workforce did not respond positively. Siemens' culture values slow-and-steady movement and focus on technology instead of customers, leading employees to protest loudly outside Mr. Kleinfeld's office window. Unfortunately, creating a new culture in keeping with his vision proved challenging because Siemens is a sprawling company with 11 separate business units that operate somewhat independently. This made it hard for him to communicate the need for culture change, although it was essential, he believed, to save jobs by helping the company prosper. Because this situation is ongoing, it's too soon to tell how it will play out, so stay tuned. (Perhaps Mr. Kleinfeld can take some suggestions from other large organizations that have been successful in promoting culture change. For a good example, see this chapter's Winning Practices section.)

Winning Practices

Alberto-Culver Undergoes an Organizational Culture Makeover

In 1955 Leonard and Bernice Lavin purchased a beauty supply company that made hundreds of different products. Immediately they discontinued the entire line except for one product—a conditioning hairdressing. Taking the name "Culver" from the man from whom they bought the company and a chemist named "Alberto" who developed the original hairdressing formula for Hollywood movie studios, they came up with their new company name, Alberto-Culver. That name and the original product, Alberto VO5, remain to this day.

As the years went on, the company located in suburban Chicago, developed new products, and acquired other companies, eventually reaching $2 billion in sales today. Besides Alberto VO5, brands such as Mrs. Dash seasonings, Static Guard, Sugar Twin, and the St. Ives line of botanically based cosmetic products all are from Alberto-Culver.[19] In October 2008, the company acquired Noxzema, making it even larger.[20]

In the early 1990s turnover was high and sales were flat, prompting Carol Lavin Bernick, president of Alberto-Culver North America, to intervene. Confident that the company's products were not to blame, she turned attention to the company's culture. It was a cold and indifferent place in which to work. Employees were in the dark about company operations, and even the most productive people were highly dissatisfied, eventually leaving. Realizing that something had to be done, she took several concrete steps to humanize the culture at Alberto-Culver.[21] Her key moves were as follows.

- 1993: A program was launched in which certain individuals called "growth development leaders" (GDLs) were honored by being selected to mentor a dozen or so other employees in such matters as the company's family-friendly benefit policies and career development.

- 1995: Bernick attempted "to open" the culture by giving detailed annual speeches on "the state of the company."

- 1997: The first "Business Builders Awards" were given to individuals and teams who went beyond their job requirements in ways that had a great impact on the company's growth and profitability.

(continued)

- 1998: Brief statements describing how each employee contributes to the company's profitability, called "individual economic values" (IEVs), were developed to help employees recognize precisely how their work helps the business.
- 1998: A list of 10 core cultural values was formalized (honesty, ownership, trust, customer orientation, commitment, fun, innovation, risk taking, speed and urgency, and teamwork), which employees are expected to be able to recite by heart.

In only a few years, these efforts to transform the culture at Alberto-Culver North America had beneficial effects on the bottom line. Sales increased dramatically, allowing the company to declare dividends for its investors each quarter. The company also enjoyed dramatic reductions in turnover and newfound ease in acquiring other companies, benefits that Bernick attributes to changes in the corporate culture. In fact, the founder of one purchased company agreed to the acquisition not because Alberto-Culver was the highest bidder but because, as he said, he "had a good feeling about its culture."

To conclude, it is clear that although organizational culture is generally stable, it is not immutable. In fact, culture often evolves in response to outside forces (e.g., changes in workforce composition) as well as deliberate attempts to change the design of organizations (e.g., through mergers and corporate restructuring). An important aspect of culture that organizations frequently strive to change is the degree to which it approaches problems in creative and innovative ways. With this in mind, we review the topics of *creativity* and *innovation* in the remainder of this chapter.

CREATIVITY IN INDIVIDUALS AND TEAMS

Although you probably have no difficulty recognizing creativity when you see it, defining creativity can be a bit more challenging. Scientists define **creativity** as the process by which individuals or teams produce novel and useful ideas.[22] With this definition to guide us, we will explain how the process of creativity operates. Specifically, we will begin by describing the components of individual and team creativity and then outline several steps you can take to enhance your own creativity.

Components of Individual and Team Creativity

Creativity in individuals and teams has three basic components—domain-relevant skills, creativity-relevant skills, and intrinsic task motivation. We describe these here.

Domain-relevant skills

Whether it's the manual dexterity required to play the piano or to use a computer keyboard, or the sense of rhythm and knowledge of music needed to conduct an orchestra, specific skills and abilities are necessary to perform these tasks. In fact, any task you might undertake requires certain talents, knowledge, or skills. These abilities constitute the raw materials needed for creativity to occur. After all, without the capacity to perform a certain task at even a basic level, one has no hope of demonstrating creativity on that task. For example, before he can even begin to create stunning automotive stunts, a stunt driver must have the basic skills of dexterity and eye-hand coordination required to drive a car at a high level of proficiency.

Creativity-relevant skills

Beyond the basic skills, being creative also requires additional skills—special abilities that help people approach the things they do in novel ways. Specifically, when fostering creativity, it helps to do the following:

- ➤ ***Break mental sets and take new perspectives.***   Creativity is enhanced when people do not limit themselves to old ways of doing things. Restricting oneself to the past can inhibit creativity. Instead, take a fresh look at even the most familiar things. This involves what is known as *divergent thinking*—the process of reframing familiar problems in unique ways. Divergent thinking often is promoted by asking people to identify as many unusual uses for common objects as possible.

- ➤ ***Understand complexities.***   Instead of making things overly simplistic, don't be afraid to consider complex ways in which ideas may be interrelated.

- ➤ ***Keep options open and avoid premature judgments.***   Creative people are willing to consider all options. To do so, they consider all the angles and avoid reaching conclusions prematurely. People are particularly good at this when they are new to an organization and, therefore, don't yet know enough to accept everything the way it is. With this in mind, some companies actually prefer hiring executives from outside their industry.

- ➤ ***Follow creativity heuristics.***   People sometimes use techniques known as *creativity heuristics* to help them come up with creative new ideas. Doing this allows people to approach tasks and problems in novel ways. For some examples, see Table 12.4.[23]

- ➤ ***Use productive forgetting.***   Sometimes our creativity is inhibited when we become fixated on certain ideas that we just can't seem to get out of our heads. With this in mind, it helps to practice *productive forgetting*—the ability to abandon unproductive ideas and temporarily put aside stubborn problems until new approaches can be considered.

Table 12.4   Creativity Heuristics

The exercises described here, known as *creativity heuristics,* help people develop new ways of solving problems and coming up with new ideas.

Heuristic	Description
Feature list	Make a list of the various features of an object or problem. Then, one by one, consider how each may be changed. This helps people focus on aspects of the object or problem they otherwise might have ignored.
Analogy	Using analogies to analyze things helps us imagine new features. For example, by analyzing the features of sharks (e.g., their skin is smooth), designers were able to develop swimsuits that allow people to swim faster (e.g., made of smooth fabric).
Search	To solve a problem, it helps to search through a list of possible solutions. For example, in developing the light bulb, Thomas Edison knew he had to make filaments from a material that would emit light but not burn. This enabled him to generate a list of possible materials and then systematically eliminate ones that did not meet these criteria.
Perspective shift	A creative solution to resolving a conflict with another person may be found by taking the other person's perspective, trying to see things through his or her eyes. This helps us identify aspects of the problem that otherwise might not have been considered.

(Sources: Various sources in Note 23.)

To help individuals and groups become more creative, many organizations invite employees to participate in training exercises designed to promote some of these skills. (These may include exercises similar to the one in the Self-Assessment Exercise on pp. 366–367. Try the exercise described here to experience firsthand how it may help your own creative juices flow.)

Intrinsic task motivation

The first two components of creativity, domain-relevant skills and creativity-relevant skills, focus on what people are *capable* of doing. However, the third component, intrinsic task motivation, refers to what people are *willing* to do. The idea is simple: For someone to be creative, he or she must be interested in performing the task in question. In other words, there must be a high degree of *intrinsic task motivation*—the motivation to do work because it is interesting, engaging, or positively challenging. Someone who has the capacity to be creative but who isn't motivated to do what it takes to produce creative outcomes certainly wouldn't be considered creative. People are most likely to be highly creative when they are passionate about their work.[24]

Intrinsic task motivation tends to be high under several conditions. For example, when an individual has a *personal interest* in the task at hand, he or she will be motivated to perform it—and may go on to do so creatively. However, anyone who doesn't find a task interesting surely isn't going to perform it long enough to demonstrate any signs of creativity. Likewise, task motivation will be high whenever an individual perceives that he or she has internal reasons to be performing that task. People who come to believe that they are performing a task for some external reason—such as high pay or pressure from a boss—are unlikely to find the work inherently interesting and are unlikely to show much creativity when performing it.

Putting it all together

As you might imagine, the components of creativity are important because they can be used to paint a picture of when people will be creative. In this connection, scientists claim that people will be at their most creative when they have high amounts of all three of these components (see Figure 12.2).

Specifically, it has been claimed that there is a multiplicative relationship among these three components of creativity. Thus, people will not be creative at all if any one of these components is at zero (i.e., it is completely missing). This makes sense if you think about it. After all, you would be unlikely to be creative at a job if you didn't have the skills needed to do it, regardless of how motivated you were to be creative and how well practiced you were at coming up with new ideas. Likewise, creativity would be expected to be nonexistent if either creativity-relevant skills or motivation were zero. The practical implications are clear: To be as creative as possible, people must strive to attain high levels of all three components of creativity.

A Model of the Creative Process

Although it isn't always obvious to us how people come up with creative ideas, scientists have developed a model that outlines the various stages of the creative process.[25] This model specifies that the process of creativity occurs in the following four stages:

1. ***Prepare to be creative.*** Although we often believe that our most creative ideas come "out of thin air," people are at their most creative when they have made suitable preparations. This involves gathering the appropriate information and concentrating on the problem.

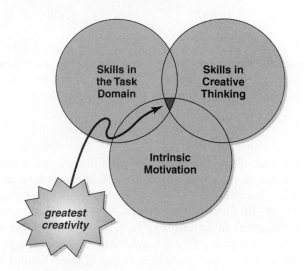

Figure 12.2 Components of Creativity

Scientists claim that people will be at their most creative when they exhibit high levels of the three factors shown here.

(Source: Adapted from Amabile, 1988; see Note 22.)

2. ***Allow ideas to incubate.***   Because ideas take time to develop, creativity can be enhanced by putting the problem out of our conscious minds and allowing it to incubate. If you've ever been successful at coming up with a fresh approach to a problem by putting it aside and working on something else, you know what we are describing. The phrase "sleep on it" captures this stage of the process.

3. ***Document insight.***   At some point during the first two stages, you are likely to come up with a unique idea. However, that idea may be lost if it's not documented. With this in mind, many people carry small digital voice recorders that allow them to capture their ideas before they become lost in the maze of other ideas. Likewise writers keep diaries, artists keep sketch pads, and song writers keep tape recorders handy to capture ideas whenever inspiration strikes.

4. ***Verify ideas.***   Coming up with an idea is one thing but verifying that it's any good is quite another. Assessing the usefulness of an idea requires consciously thinking about it and verifying it, such as by seeing what others have to say about it. In other words, you want to see if the ideas that came to you in a moment of inspiration in the middle of the night still are any good in the morning light.

Knowing about the creative process is particularly useful insofar as it can be applied to promoting individual and team productivity. We now turn to the process of doing so.

PROMOTING CREATIVITY IN ORGANIZATIONS

Highly creative people are an asset to any organization. But what exactly do organizations do to promote creativity within their ranks? In general terms, the answer lies in things that we can do as individuals and that organizations can do as a whole. Several specific approaches may be identified.

Train People to Be Creative

It is true that some people, by nature, are more creative than others. Such individuals are inclined to approach various situations in new ways and tend not to be encumbered by previous ways of doing things.[26] However, anyone can develop skills to become more creative. Generally, training people to become more creative involves three steps.[27]

Encourage openness to new ideas

Many good ideas go undeveloped because they are not in keeping with current ways of doing things. Becoming more creative requires allowing oneself to be open to new ideas or, as it is often described, *thinking outside the box*. Some companies do this by sending their employees on *thinking expeditions*—trips specifically designed to put people in challenging situations in an effort to help them think differently and become more creative. According to the CEO of a company that specializes in running such expeditions for clients, these trips "push people out of their 'stupid zone'—a place of mental and physical normalcy—so that they can start to think differently," adding that "it's an accelerated unlearning experience."[28]

Doing precisely this, General Mills recently did something novel to promote thinking outside the (cereal) box. To develop creative new ideas about how to improve efficiency in their Betty Crocker factories, General Mills officials went to an unlikely place—the pit of a NASCAR auto race track, where they carefully studied how pit crews changed tires on race cars in the midst of a race.[29] What they learned led them to creative new ways of making the changes necessary to swap factory configurations from one product to another, ultimately reducing the process from 4.5 hours to only 12 minutes. Clearly, General Mills' openness to new ideas led to some creative new ways of solving a problem.

Take the time to understand the problem

Meaningful ideas rarely come to those who don't fully understand the problem at hand. Only when time is taken to understand the many different facets of the issue can people be equipped to develop creative solutions. Consider, for example, BrightHouse, the Atlanta-based company calling itself "the world's first idea company."[30] This 15-year-old firm specializes in developing new ideas for its clients (among them have been Coca-Cola, Expedia.com, and Red Lobster).[31] For a fee of $500,000, the entire staff of BrightHouse devotes a full 10 weeks to the issues their clients have in mind (e.g., how to improve on billboard advertising at Turner Field, the home of baseball's Atlanta Braves).

Develop divergent thinking

As we noted earlier, divergent thinking involves taking new approaches to old problems. Teaching people various tactics for divergent thinking allows problems to incubate, setting the stage for creative new ideas to develop. One popular way of developing divergent thinking is known as *morphology*. A morphological analysis of a problem involves identifying its basic elements and combining them in systematically different ways. (For an example of this approach, and for a chance to practice it yourself, see the Self-Assessment Exercise on pp. 366–367.)

Developing Creative Work Environments

Thus far, we have identified ways of making people more creative as individuals. In conjunction with these approaches, it also is useful for organizations to take concrete steps to change work environments in ways that also bring out people's creativity. Several such approaches may be identified.[32]

Ensure autonomy

It has been established that people are especially creative when they are given the freedom to control their own behavior—that is, they have *autonomy* (see Chapter 6) and are *empowered* to make decisions (see Chapter 10). At the Japanese video game manufacturer, Nintendo, creativity is so important that no one considers it odd when designers leave work to go see a movie or a play. And if the runaway success of the company's Wii game console is any indication, this approach should be taken seriously.

Provide exposure to other creative people

It is widely assumed that workers are likely to be creative when they are surrounded by other creative individuals. After all, being around creative people inspires one to be creative oneself. Moreover, one can learn creativity-relevant skills from creative individuals. Although this is true under some circumstances, research suggests that the picture is not so simple. Specifically, the effect of having creative co-workers on a person's own creativity depends on the extent to which that individual is closely monitored by his or her supervisor.

A researcher studying this issue administered questionnaires to a group of employees to assess the extent to which they believed they were surrounded by creative co-workers as well as their beliefs about how closely they were monitored by their supervisors.[33] In addition, supervisors who were familiar with the work of each of these employees were asked to rate the degree of creativity they demonstrated in their work. The results summarized in Figure 12.3 show that the presence of creative co-workers promoted creativity when supervisory monitoring was low but that it actually discouraged creativity when supervisory monitoring was high.

These findings may be explained as follows. Workers who feel that they are constantly being watched, evaluated, and controlled by their bosses were reluctant to take the chances required to behave in a creative fashion for fear of doing something that is considered inappropriate. As a result, they tended to "play it safe" by simply imitating what others were doing, thereby demonstrating less creativity than they were capable of showing. By contrast, employees who were not closely monitored by their supervisors were more inclined to experiment with new ideas, thereby allowing them to reap the creative benefits of having creative co-workers around them.

Allow ideas to cross-pollinate

People who work on just one project run the risk of getting stale, whereas those who work on several are likely to come into contact with different people and have a chance of applying an idea they picked up on one project to another project. This is done all the time at the design firm IDEO (the firm behind several of Apple's most ingenious, award-winning product designs). For example, in coming up with an idea about how to develop a more comfortable handle for a scooter, designers

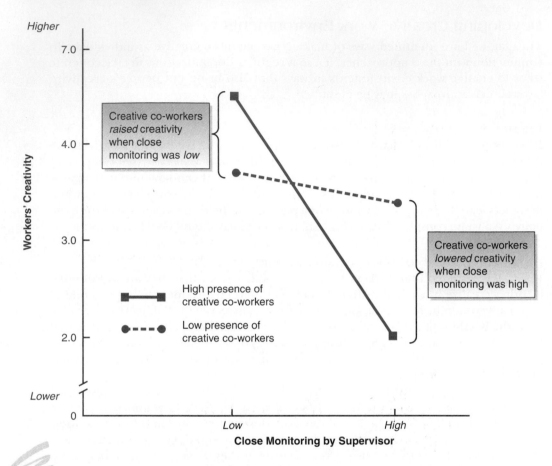

Figure 12.3   When Do Creative Co-Workers Boost Creativity? Research Findings

The effects of having creative co-workers present on a worker's level of creativity has been found to depend on the degree to which the worker is closely monitored by his or her supervisor. According to a recent study, having creative co-workers boosted creativity when close supervisory monitoring was low (because they provided encouragement and demonstrated creativity-relevant skills). However, having creative co-workers actually lowered creativity when close supervisory monitoring was high (because workers were so concerned about not doing anything out of the ordinary that they merely "played it safe" by imitating the behavior of others).

(Source: Based on data reported by Zhou, 2003; see Note 33.)

might use ideas they picked up while working on a project involving the design of a more comfortable computer mouse.

Make jobs intrinsically interesting

Research has shown that people are inclined to be creative when they are intrinsically interested in the work they do. After all, nobody will want to invest the effort it takes to be creative at a task that is uninteresting. With this in mind, creativity can be promoted by enhancing the degree to which tasks are intrinsically interesting to people. The essence of the idea is to turn work into play by making it interesting. For some specific suggestions on how to do this, see Table 12.5.

Table 12.5   Boosting Creativity by Making Jobs More Intrinsically Interesting

As summarized here, several specific features of the work environment can boost a job's intrinsic interest and, hence, the degree to which people are likely to demonstrate creativity.

Characteristic	Description
Challenge	People are likely to be creative at tasks they find interesting because they enjoy working to meet challenges.
Autonomy	People are likely to be interested their work and creative in performing it when they are free to determine how to do it.
Work group support	Intrinsic interest in a task is enhanced, as is creativity, when others share ideas about it and have the skills needed to perform it.
Supervisory and organizational encouragement	Workers are likely to be interested in performing a job, and to do it creatively, when they believe their immediate supervisor, or the organization as a whole, encourages their efforts.
Absence of organizational impediments	People will be interested in working and likely to be creative when key organizational impediments are eliminated, such as political pressures, negative criticism of new ideas, and pressure to maintain the status quo.

(Source: Based on suggestions from Amabile, 2000; see Note 24.)

This approach is used routinely at Play, a marketing agency in Richmond, Virginia. Instead of coming up with ideas by sitting in boring meetings, staff members are encouraged to play. For example, to aid the process of coming up with a new marketing campaign for the Weather Channel, employees spent time in a corner office developing costumes for superheroes. According to co-founder Andy Stefanovich, the idea is simple: "When you turn work into a place that encourages people to be themselves, have fun, and take risks, you fuel and unleash their creativity. The best ideas come from playful minds. And the way to tap into that playfulness is to play—together."[34]

Set your own creative goals

Being free to do as you wish does not necessarily imply goofing off. In fact, the freedom to make your own decisions pays off most handsomely when people set their own creative goals. For example, the famous inventor Thomas A. Edison set the goal of having a minor invention every 10 days and a major invention every six months. This kept Edison focused on being creative—and, with over 1,000 patents in his name, he clearly did an outstanding job of meeting his goals. It is important to underscore that I'm not talking about strict external pressure to be creative, which rarely results in anything positive. However, creativity is aided when people are encouraged to set their own goals about being creative.

Support creativity at high organizational levels

Nobody in an organization is going to go out of his or her way to be creative if it is not welcomed by the bosses. Supervisors, team leaders, and top executives must encourage employees to take risks if they are to have any chance of being creative. At the same time, this involves accepting any failures that result. This idea is embraced by Livio D. DeSimone, the former CEO of 3M, one of the most innovative companies in the world. "Failure is not fatal," he says, adding, "Innovations are simply chance break-throughs. And when you take a chance, there is always the possibility of a failure."[35]

Although most companies recognize their employees' accomplishments with some form of monetary reward, 3M takes things a step further by giving a variety of special, highly coveted awards to employees who have been among the most creative. For example, 3M has established an honorary society that recognizes extraordinary contributions to its science and technology. Members include individuals who have invented such ubiquitous products as Post-it Notes, Scotch Magic Transparent Tape, and Scotchgard fabric protector. Obviously, 3M goes out of its way to ensure that its employees are highly creative—and, to a large degree, this focus has been responsible for the company's century-long record of success.

THE PROCESS OF INNOVATION

Now that you know about the process of creativity, you are prepared to understand situations in which people implement their creative skills for the sake of improving their organizations. This is the process of **innovation**—the successful implementation of creative ideas within an organization. To understand this process we will review the various stages through which innovation progresses and then discuss ways of making the management process more innovative. Before doing this, however, we will begin by identifying the various components of innovation.

Components of Innovation: Basic Building Blocks

Earlier, we depicted individual creativity as having three components—motivation, resources, and skills. As it works out, these same components are involved in organizational innovation as well, albeit in somewhat different ways.

Motivation to innovate

Just as individual creativity requires that people are motivated to do what it takes to be creative, organizational innovation requires that organizations have the kinds of cultures that encourage innovation. When top executives fail to promote a vision of innovation and accept the status quo, change is unlikely. However, at companies such as Microsoft, where leaders envision innovation as being part of the natural order of things, it is not surprising that innovative efforts are constantly under way.

Resources to innovate

Again, a parallel to individual creativity is in order. Just as people must have certain basic skills to be creative, so too must organizations possess certain basic resources that make innovation possible. For example, to be innovative, at the very least, organizations must have what it takes in terms of human and financial resources. After all, unless the necessary skilled people and deep pockets are available to do what it takes to innovate, stagnation is likely to result.

At the large microchip maker AMD, for example, 35.9 percent of the dollars taken in on sales is spent on research and development.[36] Although this constitutes an incredibly large investment, its leaders consider it necessary to keep up with, or even pull ahead of, the market leader, Intel (for which the comparable figure is 16.4 percent). Further attempting to compete with Intel, in October 2008, AMD partnered with large investors to break the company into two separate companies, one focused on designing microprocessors and the other on the costly business of manufacturing them.[37] Although the effectiveness of this move is yet unknown, it's certainly clear that AMD is, in fact, investing the resources required to innovate.

Innovation management

Finally, just as individuals must hone special skills needed to be creative, so too must organizations develop special ways of managing people to encourage innovation—that is, *skills in innovation management*. Most notable in this regard is the matter of *balance*. Specifically, managers help promote innovation when they show balance with respect to three key matters: goals, reward systems, and time pressure (see Figure 12.4).

Figure 12.4   Skills in Innovation Management: A Careful Balancing Act

Managing innovation requires carefully balancing the three matters identified here.

(Source: Based on information reported by Amabile, 1988; see Note 22.)

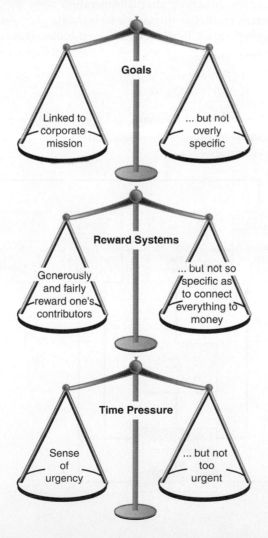

➤ Organizational innovation is promoted when *goals* are carefully linked to the corporate mission. However, they should not be so specific as to tie the hands of those who put them into practice. Innovation is unlikely when such restrictions are imposed.

➤ *Reward systems* should generously and fairly recognize individuals' contributions, but they should not be so specific as to connect literally every move to a bonus or some type of monetary reward. To do so discourages people from taking the kinds of risks that make innovation possible.

➤ Innovation management requires carefully balancing the *time pressures* under which employees are placed. If pressures are too great, people may be unimaginative and offer routine solutions. By the same token, if pressure is too weak, employees may have no sense of time urgency and believe that the project is too unimportant to warrant any creative attention on their part.

General Stages of the Organizational Innovation Process

Any CEO who snaps her fingers one day and expects her troops to be innovative on command will surely be in for disappointment. Innovation does not happen all at once. Rather, innovation occurs gradually, through a series of stages. Scientists have identified five specific stages through which the process of organizational innovation progresses.[38] We now will describe each of these five stages (see the summary in Figure 12.5).

Figure 12.5   The Process of Innovation

The innovation process consists of the various components and follows the steps shown here.
(Source: Adapted from Amabile, 1988; see Note 38.)

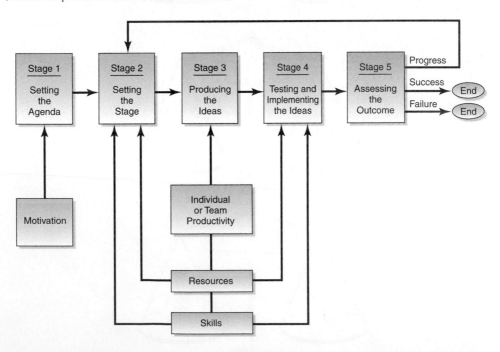

Stage 1: Setting the agenda

The first stage of the process of innovation begins by setting the agenda for innovation. This involves creating a *mission statement*—a document describing an organization's overall direction and general goals for accomplishing that movement. The component of innovation that is most involved here is motivation. After all, the highest-ranking officials of the organization must be highly committed to innovation before they will initiate a push toward it.

As a case in point, consider HP. Vyomesh Joshi, former head of the printer division, acknowledged that to keep printers from becoming commodities, his company must innovate. "Innovation is still important in this business," he said, putting up the $1 billion annual investment in research and development required to bring it to fruition.[39]

Stage 2: Setting the stage

Once an organization's mission has been established, it is prepared to set the stage for innovation. This consists of narrowing down certain broad goals into narrower, more specific tasks and gathering the resources to meet them. It also may involve assessing the environment, both outside and inside the organization, searching for anything that either may support or inhibit later efforts to "break the rules" by being creative. Effectively setting the stage for innovation requires using the skills necessary for innovation management as well as full use of the organization's human and financial resources.

Stage 3: Producing the ideas

This stage of the process calls for coming up with new ideas and testing them. It is in this third stage that individual and small group creativity enters the picture. As a result, all of the components of individual creativity mentioned earlier are involved. What's more, these may combine with various organizational factors. For example, an individual who has the skills and motivation to be highly creative might find his motivation waning as he attempts to introduce novel ideas in an organization that is not committed to innovation and that fails to make the necessary resources available. By contrast, the highly innovative nature of an organization may bring out the more creative side of an individual who may not have been especially creative.

Stage 4: Testing and implementing the ideas

This is the stage where implementation occurs. Now, after an initial group of individuals has developed an idea, other parts of the organization get involved. For example, a prototype product may be developed and tested, and market research may be conducted. In short, input from the many functional areas of the organization is provided.

We note in Figure 12.5 that skills in innovation management are important in this stage of the process. In large part, this is because for good ideas to survive it is necessary for them to be "nourished" and supported throughout the organization. Even the best ideas may be "killed off" if people in some parts of the organization are not supportive. Based on this same reasoning, resources in the task domain are another important component involved in this stage. After all, unless adequate amounts of money, personnel, material systems, and information are provided, the idea will be unlikely to survive.

Stage 5: Assessing the outcome

The final stage of the process involves assessing the new idea. What happens to that idea depends on the results of the assessment. Three outcomes are possible. If the resulting idea (e.g., a certain product or service) has been a total success, it will be accepted and carried out in the future. This ends the process. Likewise, the process is over if the idea has been a complete failure. In this case, there is no good reason to continue. However, if the new idea shows promise and makes some progress toward the organization's objectives but still has problems, the process starts all over again at stage 2.

Although this five-stage process does not account for all innovations you may find in organizations, this general model does a good job of identifying the major steps through which most innovations go as they travel along their path from a specific organizational need to a product or service that meets that need.

Management Innovation

Sometimes, the novel ideas introduced in organizations have to do not with new products or services, but with the process of management itself. This is referred to as **management innovation,** defined as the introduction of a new management of activities within an organization. (This builds upon the discussion on pp. 361–362 of how managers can promote and encourage innovation in their organizations.)

Traditional perspectives on management innovation

Scientists who study management innovation generally adopt one of the following four perspectives:[40]

➤ **Institutional perspective.**   Focuses on sociological trends (e.g., labor market trends) that promote progressive changes in management practice designed to promote more effective ways of working.

➤ **Fashion perspective.**   Focuses on the introduction of popular management trends that are hyped by some consultants and the disillusion that follows when they fail to work as desired.

➤ **Cultural perspective.**   Focuses on how management innovation shapes, and is shaped by, the organizational culture within which management operates.

➤ **Rational perspective.**   Assumes that innovation occurs as a result of people identifying problems and then introducing changes designed to improve their organizations.

Drawing on, but expanding, these approaches, and developing a new approach to the stages of innovation, theorists recently have developed an interesting conceptualization of management innovation.[41]

Management innovation as a four-step process

Theorists have described the process of management innovation as roughly following four steps. We say "roughly" because in reality, the process is not nearly as neat and simple as depicted. Sometimes, steps may be eliminated or combined. Still, it's useful to understand these steps because they paint an excellent picture of the complexities of management innovation.

1. *Motivation.*   To begin, someone from within the organization (e.g., a leader) will be motivated to introduce a new form of management. The degree to which he or she is motivated to do this is likely to depend on the existence of support from an external change agent (e.g., a consultant who believes it's a good idea) as well as appropriate organizational factors (e.g., clear evidence from company records that innovation is needed) and environmental factors (e.g., knowledge that economic conditions would not make such a change unwise).

2. *Invention.*   Next, someone from within the organization experiments with an innovative system on a limited, trial basis. This may be stimulated, for example, by reading ideas in books by management gurus (an external change agent), whose wisdom is then shared with others in support of the idea. For this innovative idea to advance, it will help to be supported by both the organizational context (e.g., such ideas have worked in the past) and the environmental context (e.g., there is no outside evidence that this approach has failed).

3. *Implementation.*   After a management innovation has been tried on an experimental basis, if it has succeeded, the internal change agent who promoted it is likely to push for it to be implemented more broadly and for it to be evaluated formally. Typically, this will require the assistance of external consultants who both implement the new plan and evaluate it using carefully developed questionnaires and financial measures. Once more, for this to occur both the organizational context and the environmental context would need to be supportive. For example, the plan might not be implemented until it gains complete support from top management and until there is assurance that it does not violate any legal regulations.

4. *Theorization and labeling.*   This fourth and final step in management innovation involves trying to figure out, after the fact, why a particular management innovation succeeded or failed. This often will involve having a management consultant work with company officials to make sense of what happened. These conclusions are likely to be incorporated into organizational culture, making it part of the organizational context to be considered on future occasions.

We conclude by noting that although this conceptualization seems quite reasonable, it is new, and as a result, untested. Until future research can lend support to the assertions underlying this approach, it must be regarded as inconclusive, yet promising.

Back to the Case

Answer the following questions about this chapter's Making the Case (p. 340) to illustrate insights you have derived about the material in this chapter.

1. Based on the nature of its operation, what do you believe the organizational culture of Zipcar would be like?
2. What might Zipcar's officers do to promote further creativity in its workforce?
3. What factors do you believe might hinder innovation at Zipcar? How might these be overcome? What conditions currently exist that help the company innovate?

You Be the Consultant

Promoting a Creative Organizational Culture

The president of your organization, a small manufacturing company, has been complaining that sales are stagnant. A key problem, you discover, is that the market for the products your firm makes is fully developed—and, frankly, the products themselves are not very exciting. No one seems to care about doing anything innovative. Instead, the employees seem more interested in doing things the way they always have done them. Answer the following questions based on the material in this chapter.

1. What factors do you suspect are responsible for the way the culture in this organization has developed over the years?

2. What do you recommend should be done to enhance the creativity of this company's employees?

3. What could be done to help make the company's products more innovative?

SELF-ASSESSMENT EXERCISE

Morphology in Action: Using the Idea Box

One day the marketing director of a company that makes laundry hampers was tinkering with ways of boosting sales in a stagnant, mature market.[42] To trigger his imagination, he thought explicitly about something that most of us take for granted—the basic parameters of laundry hampers. Specifically, he noted that they differ in four basic ways: the materials of which they are made, their shape, their finish, and how they are positioned. For each of these dimensions, he identified five different answers, resulting in the chart below, known as an *idea box*.

Then, by randomly combining one item from each column—net material, cylindrical shape, painted finish, and positioning on a door—the marketing director came up with a completely new idea. It was a laundry hamper made to look like a basketball net: about a yard of netting attached to a cylindrical hoop, hung from a backboard attached to the back of a door.

	Improve Design for Laundry Hamper			
	Material	Shape	Finish	Position
1	Wicker	Square	Painted	Sits on Floor
2	Plastic	Cylindrical	Painted	On Ceiling
3	Paper	Rectangle	Clear	On Wall
4	Metal	Hexagonal	Luminous	Chute to Basement
5	Net Material	Cube	Neon	On Door

(Source: Reprinted with permission from *Thinkertoys*, Second Edition, by Michael Michalko. Copyright 2006, 1991 by Michael Michalko, Ten Speed Press, Berkeley, CA. www.tenspeed.com.)

With some quick math, you can see that this particular idea box generates 600 different combinations. Given that this is a far greater number of ideas than you could probably generate without the aid of the idea box, it makes sense to practice generating idea boxes for situations you face in which creative new solutions are required. Nurture your own creativity by following the four simple steps identified by creativity expert Michael Michalko.[43]

Steps for Generating an Idea Box

1. *Specify the challenge you are facing.*   Although you may not be interested in developing exciting new laundry baskets, you must start at the same point indicated in our example—that is, by identifying exactly what you are attempting to do.
2. *Select the parameters of your challenge.*   Material, shape, finish, and position were the parameters of the laundry basket problem. What are yours? To help determine if the parameter you are considering is important enough to add, ask yourself if the challenge would still exist without that parameter.
3. *List variations.*   Our example shows five variations of each parameter, but feel free to list as many key ones as you can. After all, as your idea box grows larger, it gets increasingly difficult to spot new ideas. (For example, if your idea box had 10 parameters, each of which contained 10 variations, you'd face 10 billion potential combinations to consider—hardly a practical task!)
4. *Try different combinations.*   After your idea box is completed, work your way through the box to find some of the most promising combinations. Begin by examining the entire box and then eventually limit yourself to the most promising combinations.

Discussion Questions

1. Have you ever used the idea box, or something similar to it, before now? If so, how effectively has it worked?
2. For what kinds of challenges is the idea box most useful and least useful?
3. It has been said that generating an idea box is similar to writing a poem. How is this so?

GROUP EXERCISE

What Does Your Workspace Say About Your Organizational Culture?

Newcomers' impressions of an organization's culture depend greatly on the visual images of that organization they first see. Even without knowing anything about an organization, just seeing the workplace sends a message, intentional or unintentional, regarding what that organization is like. The following exercise is designed to demonstrate this phenomenon.

Directions

1. Each member of the class should take several photographs of his or her workplace and select the three that best capture, in his or her opinion, the essence of what that organization is like.
2. One member of the class should identify the company depicted in his or her photos, describe the type of work it does, and present the photos to the rest of the class.
3. Members of the class should then rate the organization shown in the photos using the following dimensions. Circle the number that comes closest to your feelings about the company shown.

unfamiliar	: 1 : 2 : 3 : 4 : 5 : 6 : 7 :	familiar
unsuccessful	: 1 : 2 : 3 : 4 : 5 : 6 : 7 :	successful
unfriendly	: 1 : 2 : 3 : 4 : 5 : 6 : 7 :	friendly
unproductive	: 1 : 2 : 3 : 4 : 5 : 6 : 7 :	productive
not innovative	: 1 : 2 : 3 : 4 : 5 : 6 : 7 :	innovative
uncaring	: 1 : 2 : 3 : 4 : 5 : 6 : 7 :	caring
conservative	: 1 : 2 : 3 : 4 : 5 : 6 : 7 :	risky
closed	: 1 : 2 : 3 : 4 : 5 : 6 : 7 :	open

4. Take turns sharing your individual reactions to each set of photos. Compare the responses of the student whose company pictures were examined with those of the students who were seeing the photos for the first time.

5. Repeat this process using the photos of other students' organizations.

Discussion Questions

1. For each set of photos examined, how much agreement or disagreement was there within the class about the companies rated?

2. For each set of photos examined, how close did the descriptions of members of the class come to the photographers' assessments of their own companies? In other words, how well did the photos capture the culture of the organization as perceived by an "insider"?

3. As a whole, were people more accurate in assessing the culture of companies with which they were already familiar than those they didn't already know? If so, why do you think this occurred?

Designing Effective Organizations

Learning Objectives

After reading this chapter, you will be able to:

1. **DEFINE** organizational structure and **DISTINGUISH** among five aspects of organizational structure represented in an organization chart.

2. **DISTINGUISH** among the three types of departmentalization: functional organizations, product organizations, and matrix organizations.

3. **DEFINE** organizational design and **DISTINGUISH** between classical and neoclassical approaches to organizational design.

4. **DESCRIBE** the contingency approach to organizational design.

5. **IDENTIFY** five emerging approaches to organizational design.

6. **DISTINGUISH** between conglomerates and strategic alliances as two types of interorganizational designs.

3 GOOD REASONS why you should care about . . .

Designing Effective Organizations

You should care about designing effective organizations because:

1. To understand how organizations function you must know about their structural elements, their basic building blocks.

2. The design of organizations has profound effects on organizational functioning.

3. The way organizations are designed has been changing recently (and will continue to change in the years ahead), making it important for savvy managers to keep abreast of the trends.

Making the Case for Designing Effective Organizations

NASA and Google Join Forces to Bring the Cosmos Down to Earth

You've probably used Google Earth to explore detailed overhead images of many places on earth. And you've probably also seen stunning photos taken from NASA's Hubble Space Telescope. But what do you get when you combine the two? The answer is Google Sky, an effort to map the sky just as Google Earth has mapped the earth.

A project this grand, as you might imagine, is likely to exceed the capabilities of any one organization. That's precisely why Google, with its mapping technology, joined forces with NASA, with its advanced imagery technology, to create Google Sky. And knitting these two technological giants together is the Space Telescope Science Institute (STSI), whose members have surveyed and categorized roughly 14 million stars in 69 galaxies.

Especially excited about this partnership is Carol Christian, an astronomer at STSI. "You have seen the Hubble images of objects such as the Eagle Nebula, the so-called pillars of creation," she says. "With Sky in Google Earth you can see where the objects are located in space, including the constellations in which they reside. Then you can discover other cool objects in nearby regions of the sky. And you don't have to know anything about astronomy to use the program." Making things even better for amateur astronomers (who now enjoy tools not imaginable to professional astronomers a few years ago), the database is constantly being updated, adding more stars and more photos to the program all the time.

For this to happen, it's clear that the partnership between NASA and Google (along with STSI) has to be ongoing. Not only has this relationship made Google Sky possible for everyone to enjoy for free, but their successful experience has led these two giant organizations to team up on another venture. In the summer of 2008, they announced that Google was going to develop a new, high-technology campus on 42.2 acres of NASA land in Mountain View, California. There, Google will build 1.2 million square feet of spaces for offices and facilities for research and development. Both organizations have expressed considerable enthusiasm about this project.

"With this new campus, we will establish a new era of expanded collaboration with Google that will further enhance our Silicon Valley connections," said Ames Director S. Pete Worden. "This major expansion of NASA Research Park supports NASA's mission to lead the nation in space exploration, scientific discovery, and aeronautics research."

And from Google's vice president of real estate and workplace services, David Ratcliffe: "This long-term lease agreement is a key component of Google's strategy for continued growth in Silicon Valley. We believe this collaboration between Google, NASA, and the city of Mountain View is emblematic of the mutually beneficial partnerships that can be created between the public and private sectors." Indeed, the collaboration is essential to get the venture not only off the ground but into the stars.

It's safe to say that Google Sky is not a product that either Google or NASA could have developed on its own. The close connections between them, each drawing on the strengths of the other, along with the services of STSI, made it possible. And, with the new research park venture under way, it seems that they will be joining forces again many times in the future. This raises an interesting question: Is it generally beneficial for companies to be working together? More broadly, within a given organization, how should units be organized to accomplish their objectives? These are venerable questions in the study of business organizations—and, as we explain in this chapter, very important ones.

OB researchers and theorists have provided considerable insight into the matter by studying what is called *organizational structure*—the way individuals and groups are arranged with respect to the tasks they perform—and *organizational design*—the process of coordinating these structural elements in the most effective manner.[1] As you may suspect, finding the best way to structure and design organizations is no simple matter. However, because understanding the structure and design of organizations is key to fully appreciating their functioning, organizational scientists have devoted considerable energy to this topic.

We will describe these efforts in this chapter. To begin, we will identify the basic structural dimensions of organizations. Following this, we will examine how these structural elements can be combined most effectively into productive organizational designs. In so doing, we will cover some of the traditional ways of designing organizations as well as some of the rapidly developing organizational forms emerging today.

STRUCTURAL DIMENSIONS OF ORGANIZATIONS

Think about how a simple house is constructed. It is composed of a wooden frame positioned atop a concrete slab covered by a roof and siding materials. Within this basic structure are separate systems operating to provide electricity, water, and telephone services. It is possible to extend this analogy to the structure of organizations. Let's use as an example an organization with which you are familiar—your college or university. It is probably composed of various departments working together to serve special functions. Individuals and groups are dedicated to tasks such as teaching, providing financial services, maintaining the physical facilities, and so on. Of course, within each group, even more distinctions can be made between the jobs people perform. For example, it's unlikely that the instructor for your OB course is also teaching seventeenth-century French literature.

This illustrates my main point: An organization is not a haphazard collection of people but a meaningful combination of groups and individuals working together purposefully to meet organizational goals. The term **organizational structure** refers to the formal configuration of individuals and groups with respect to the allocation of tasks, responsibilities, and authority within organizations.

Just as the internal structure of a house (e.g., its complete electrical and plumbing systems) is hidden, we also cannot see the structure of an organization (which is an abstract concept). However, in both cases, there are clear signs that these exist (water comes out the faucet and people in various departments throughout an organization work with one another). A wiring chart is a diagram showing the electrical connections in a house. Similarly, an **organization chart** is a diagram showing the connections between various clusters of functions of which an organization is composed. Accordingly, an organization chart may be considered a representation of an organization's internal structure. In other words, organization charts are useful for specifying how various organizational tasks or functions are interrelated.

As an example, look at the chart depicting part of a hypothetical manufacturing organization shown in Figure 13.1. Each box represents a specific job, and the lines connecting them reflect the formally prescribed lines of communication between the individuals performing those jobs (see Chapter 8). To specialists in organizational structure, as we now describe, such diagrams reveal a great deal more.

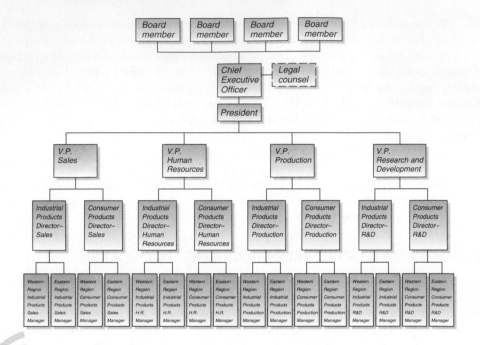

Figure 13.1   Organization Chart of a Hypothetical Manufacturing Firm

An *organization chart,* such as this one, identifies pictorially the various functions performed within an organization and the lines of authority between people performing those functions.

Division of Labor

The standard organization chart reflects the fact that the many tasks to be performed within an organization are divided into specialized jobs, a process known as the **division of labor.** The more that tasks are divided into separate jobs, the more those jobs are *specialized* and the narrower the range of activities job incumbents are required to perform. For example, the jobs performed by members of a pit crew for a race car are divided into highly specialized functions, such as refueling, changing tires, and so on. In theory, the fewer tasks a person performs, the better he or she may be expected to perform them, freeing others to work on the tasks that they perform best. (We say "in theory" because if specialization is too great, people may lose their motivation to work at a high level and performance may suffer; see Chapter 6.) Taken together, an organization is composed of people performing a collection of specialized jobs. This is probably the most obvious feature of an organization that can be observed from its organization chart.

As you might imagine, the degree to which employees perform specialized jobs is likely to depend on the size of the organization. Greater opportunities for specialization exist in larger organizations. For example, someone in the advertising department of a large agency is likely to specialize in a certain, narrowly defined task, such as writing radio jingles, whereas someone working at a smaller agency is likely to have to perform a much wider variety of tasks, including preparing copy for print ads, meeting with clients, and maybe even sending out the bills.

Hierarchy of Authority

Organization charts provide information about who reports to whom—what is known as **hierarchy of authority.** The diagram reveals which particular lower-level employees are required to report to which particular individuals immediately above them. In the hypothetical example in Figure 13.1, the various regional salespeople (at the bottom of the diagram) report to their respective regional sales directors, who report to the vice president of sales, who reports to the president, who reports to the chief executive officer, who reports to the members of the board of directors. As we trace these reporting relationships, we work our way up the organization's hierarchy. In this case, the organization has six levels. Organizations may have many levels, in which case their structure is considered *tall,* or only a few, in which case their structure is considered *flat* (see Figure 13.2).

In recent years, a great deal has appeared in the news about organizations restructuring their workforces by flattening them out. Although it has not been uncommon for large companies to lay off people in low-level jobs, in recent years, middle managers and executives, who long believed they were secure in their positions, have found themselves out of work as their companies made cuts. Whether the process is referred to, euphemistically, as "downsizing," "rightsizing," "delayering," "workforce optimization," "simplification" or "a reduction in force," it results in eliminating layers of organizations. This has occurred at the large pharmaceuticals firm, Pfizer, which has reorganized its marketing division into smaller, more focused units that enable it to provide better customer service.[2]

The underlying assumption behind this and other such moves is that fewer layers reduce waste and enable people to make better decisions (by moving them closer to the problems at hand), thereby leading to greater profitability. Although some layers of hierarchy are necessary, too many can be needlessly expensive. Moreover, as technology advances, fewer people are needed to carry out management roles. Painful as it may be, this is a fact of life in today's organizations.

Span of Control

Over how many individuals should a manager have responsibility? The earliest management theorists and practitioners alike (dating back to the Roman legions) addressed this question. When you look at an organization chart, the number of people formally required to report to each individual manager is immediately clear. This number constitutes what is known as a manager's **span of control.** Those responsible for many individuals are said to have a *wide* span of control, whereas those responsible for fewer individuals are said to have a *narrow* span of control. In our organization chart (top of Figure 13.2), the president is responsible for the actions of the three vice presidents, giving this individual a wider span of control than the vice presidents, who have a span of control of only one individual.

When a manager's span of control is wide, the organization itself has a flat hierarchy. In contrast, when a manager's span of control is narrow, the organization itself has a tall hierarchy. This is demonstrated in Figure 13.2. The diagram at the top shows a *tall* organization—one in which there are many layers in the hierarchy and the span of control is relatively narrow (i.e., the number of people supervised is low). By contrast, the diagram at the bottom of Figure 13.2 shows a *flat* organization—one in which

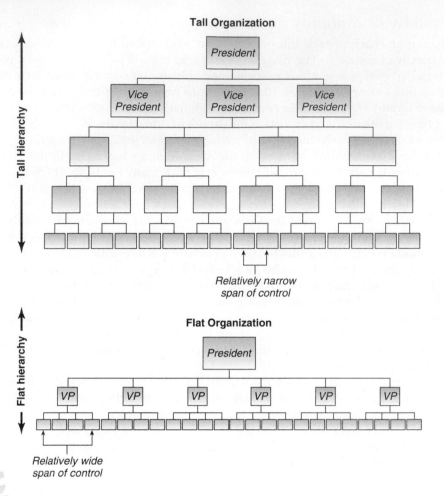

Figure 13.2   Span of Control in Tall Versus Flat Organizations

Each of the two organizations depicted here has 31 employees, but they are structured differently. In the *tall organization,* shown on top, the hierarchy has many layers and managers have a *narrow span of control.* However, in the *flat organization,* shown on the bottom, the hierarchy has fewer layers and managers have a *wide span of control.*

there are only a few levels in the hierarchy, and the span of control is relatively wide. Although both organizations depicted here have 31 positions, these are arranged differently.

It is not possible to specify the "ideal" span of control that should be sought. Instead, it makes better sense to consider what form of organization is best suited to various purposes. For example, because supervisors in a military unit must have tight control over subordinates and get them to respond quickly and precisely, a narrow span of control is likely to be effective. As a result, military organizations tend to be extremely tall. In contrast, people working in a research and development lab must have an open exchange of ideas and typically require little managerial guidance to be successful. Units of this type tend to have very flat structures. (As you might imagine, there may be widespread differences with respect to spans of control in different types of organizations. To learn about this possibility, complete the Group Exercise on p. 397.)

Line Versus Staff Positions

The organization chart shown in Figure 13.1 reveals an additional distinction that deserves to be highlighted—that between *line positions* and *staff positions*. People occupying **line positions** (e.g., the various vice presidents and managers) have decision-making power. However, the individual shown in the dotted box—the legal counsel—does not make formal organizational decisions but provides advice and recommendations to be used by the line managers. For example, such an individual may help corporate officials decide whether a certain product name can be used without infringing on copyright restrictions. This individual may be said to hold a **staff position.**

In many of today's organizations, human resources managers may be seen as occupying staff positions because they may provide specialized services regarding testing and interviewing procedures as well as information about the latest laws on personnel administration. Also holding staff positions are members of the IT (information technology) department, who keep computers and networks operating. They don't directly engage in the company's business, but make it possible for others to do so.

Differences between line and staff personnel are not unusual. Specifically, staff managers tend to be younger, better educated, and more committed to their fields than to their organizations. Line managers feel more committed to their organizations not only because of the greater opportunities they have to exercise decisions but also because they are more likely to perceive themselves as part of a company rather than as an independent specialist whose identity lies primarily within his or her professional specialty area.

Centralization Versus Decentralization

In the early 1900s, as companies grew larger, they shifted power and authority into the hands of a few upper-echelon administrators—executives whose decisions influenced the many people below them in the organizational hierarchy. In fact, during the 1920s Alfred P. Sloan, Jr., then president of General Motors, introduced the notion of a "central office," the place where a few individuals made policy decisions for the entire company.

Another part of Sloan's plan involved pushing lower and lower down the organizational hierarchy decisions regarding the day-to-day operation of the company, thereby allowing those individuals who were most affected to make the decisions. This process of delegating power from higher to lower levels within organizations is known as **decentralization.** It is the opposite of **centralization,** the tendency for just a few powerful individuals or groups to hold most of the decision-making power.

Trends

Recent years have seen a marked trend toward increasingly greater decentralization.[3] As a result, organization charts tend to show fewer staff positions, as decision-making authority is pushed farther down the hierarchy. Many organizations have moved toward decentralization to promote managerial efficiency and to improve employee satisfaction (the result of giving people greater opportunities to take responsibility for their own actions; see Chapter 5). For example, thousands of staff jobs were eliminated at companies such as 3M, AT&T, and GE as these companies decentralized.

People working in research and development positions are likely to enjoy the autonomy to make decisions that decentralization allows. With this in mind, many companies involved heavily in research and development—including parts of Hewlett-Packard, Intel Corporation, and Philips Electronics—have shifted to more decentralized (e.g., flatter) designs. By contrast, people working on production jobs are likely to be less interested in taking responsibility for decisions and may enjoy not having to take such responsibility. (As we noted in Chapter 5, this is a key reason why job enrichment is not always successful.)

Advantages and disadvantages

There are advantages of both centralization and decentralization. One top executive who seems to be well aware of this is William Weldon, the CEO of Johnson & Johnson (J&J), whose company long has favored a decentralized approach to operations. In a recent interview, he said as follows.

> I think there are pluses and minuses to [being] decentralized and centralized. I think J&J is probably the reference company for being decentralized. There are challenges to it, and that is you may not have as much control as you may have in a centralized company. But the good part of it is that you have wonderful leaders, you have great people that you have a lot of confidence and faith in and they run the businesses.[4]

Clearly, there are advantages and disadvantages of centralization. For a summary of these, see Table 13.1.

DEPARTMENTALIZATION: WAYS OF STRUCTURING ORGANIZATIONS

Thus far, we have been talking about "the" organization chart of an organization. Typically, such charts, like the one shown in Figure 13.1, distinguish an organization according to the various functions performed. However, this is only one option. Organizations can be divided not only by function but also by product or market, and by a combination of both. We will now take a closer look at these various ways of breaking up organizations into coherent units—that is, the process of **departmentalization.**

Table 13.1   Decentralization: Benefits When Low and When High

Various benefits are associated with low decentralization (high centralization) and high decentralization (low centralization) within organizations.

Low Decentralization (High Centralization)	High Decentralization (Low Centralization)
Eliminates the additional responsibility not desired by people performing routine jobs	Can eliminate levels of management, making a leaner organization
Permits crucial decisions to be made by individuals who have the "big picture"	Promotes greater opportunities for decisions to be made by people closest to problems

Functional Organizations: Departmentalization by Task

Because it is the form organizations usually take when they are first created, and because it is how we usually think of organizations, the *functional organization* can be considered the most basic approach to departmentalization. Essentially, **functional organizations** departmentalize individuals according to the functions they perform, with people who perform similar functions assigned to the same department. For example, a manufacturing company might consist of separate departments devoted to basic functions such as production, sales/marketing, research and development, and human resources (recall Figure 13.1).

Naturally, as organizations grow and become more complex, additional departments are added or deleted as the need arises. Consider, for example, something that has been happening at Johnson & Johnson (J&J). Although this company has long been highly decentralized, certain functions are now beginning to become centralized (e.g., the legal and human resources operations). New departments are being added, making it possible for resources to be saved by avoiding duplication of effort, resulting in a higher level of efficiency. Not only does this form of organizational structure take advantage of economies of scale (by allowing employees performing the same jobs to share facilities and not duplicating functions), but it also allows people to specialize, thereby performing only those tasks at which they are most expert. The result is a highly skilled workforce—a direct benefit to the organization.

Partly offsetting these advantages, however, are several potential limitations. The most important of these stems from the fact that functional organizational structures encourage separate units to develop their own narrow perspectives and to lose sight of overall organizational goals. For example, in a manufacturing company, an engineer might see the company's problems in terms of the reliability of its products and lose sight of other key considerations, such as market trends, overseas competition, and so on. Such narrow-mindedness is the inevitable result of functional specialization—the downside of people seeing the company's operations through a narrow lens.

Product Organizations: Departmentalization by Type of Output

Organizations—at least successful ones—do not stand still; they constantly change in size and scope. As they develop new products and seek new customers, they might find that a functional structure doesn't work as well as it once did. Manufacturing a wide range of products using a variety of different methods, for example, might put a strain on a manufacturing division of a functional organization. Similarly, keeping track of the varied tax requirements for different types of business (e.g., restaurants, farms, real estate, manufacturing) might pose quite a challenge for a single financial division of a company. In response to such strains, a **product organization** might be created. This type of departmentalization creates self-contained divisions, each of which is responsible for everything to do with a certain product or group of products. For a look at the structure of a hypothetical product organization, see Figure 13.3.

When organizations are departmentalized by products, separate divisions are established, each of which is devoted to a certain product or service or to groups of products or services. Each unit contains all the resources needed to develop, manufacture, and sell its products or services. The organization is composed of separate divisions, operating independently, the heads of which report to top management. Although

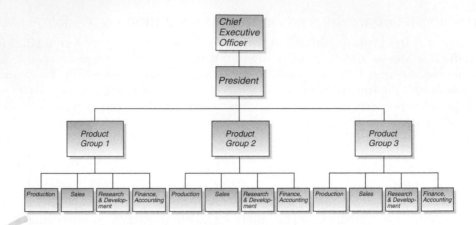

Figure 13.3   Structure of a Typical Product Organization

In a *product organization*, separate units are established to handle different product lines. Each of these divisions contains all the departments necessary for it to operate as an independent unit.

some functions might be centralized within the parent company (e.g., human resource management or legal staff), on a day-to-day basis each division operates autonomously as a separate company or, as accountants call them, "cost centers" of their own.

Consider, for example, how separate divisions of General Motors are devoted to manufacturing cars, trucks, locomotives, refrigerators, auto parts, and the like. The managers of each division can devote their energies to one particular business. Organizations may be beneficial from a marketing perspective as well. Consider, for example, the example of Honda's 1987 introduction of its line of luxury cars, Acura. By creating a separate division, manufactured in separate plants and sold by a separate network of dealers, the company made its higher-priced cars look special and avoided making its less expensive cars look less appealing by putting them together with superior products on the same showroom floors. Given Honda's success with this configuration, it is not surprising that Toyota and Nissan followed suit when they introduced their own luxury lines, Lexus and Infiniti, in 1989.

Product organizations also have several drawbacks. The most obvious of these is the loss of economies of scale stemming from the duplication of various departments within operating units. For example, if each unit carries out its own research and development functions, the need for costly equipment, facilities, and personnel may be multiplied. Another problem associated with product designs involves the organization's ability to attract and retain talented employees. Because each department within operating units is necessarily smaller than a single combined one would be, opportunities for advancement and career development may suffer. This, in turn, may pose a serious problem with respect to the long-term retention of talented employees. Finally, problems of coordination across product lines may arise. In fact, in extreme cases, actions taken by one operating division may have adverse effects on the outcomes of one or more others.

A clear example of such problems was provided by Hewlett-Packard, a major manufacturer of computers, printers, and scientific test equipment.[5] For most of its history, Hewlett-Packard adopted a product design. It consisted of scores of small, largely autonomous divisions, each concerned with producing and selling certain products. As it grew—merging with Compaq in 2002—the company found itself in an increasingly untenable situation in which sales representatives from different divisions sometimes attempted to sell different lines of equipment, often to be used for the same basic purposes, to the same customers!

To deal with such problems, top management at Hewlett-Packard decided to restructure the company into four sectors—what they call "business groups"—based on the markets they serve: the Enterprise Systems Group (which provides information technology hardware for businesses), the Imaging and Printing Group (which focuses on printers for businesses and consumers), the Personal Systems Group (which focuses on personal computers for home and office use), and HP Services (which offers information technology services).[6] In short, driven by market considerations, Hewlett-Packard switched from a traditional product-based structure to a market-based structure.

Matrix Organizations: Departmentalization by Both Function and Product

When the aerospace industry was first developing, the U.S. government demanded that a single manager in each company be assigned to each of its projects so that it was immediately clear who was responsible for their progress. In response to this requirement, the large contractor TRW established a "project leader" for each project, someone who shared authority with the leaders of the existing functional departments. This temporary arrangement later evolved into what is called a **matrix organization,** a type of organization in which an employee is required to report to both a functional (or division) manager and the manager of a specific project (or product). In essence, they developed a complex type of organizational structure that combined both the function and product forms of departmentalization. Subsequently, many other companies have adopted matrix designs for at least some parts of their organizations. Among these are Liberty Mutual Insurance and Citibank.

To better understand matrix organizations, let's take a closer look at the organization chart shown in Figure 13.4. This diagram shows that employees in matrix organizations have two bosses (or, more technically, they are under *dual authority*).[7] One line of authority, shown by the vertical axes in Figure 13.4, is *functional,* managed by vice presidents in charge of various functional areas. The other, shown by the horizontal axes, is *product* (or it may be a specific project or temporary business), managed by specific individuals in charge of certain products or projects. In matrix designs, we find the following three major supervisory roles:

➤ *Top leader.* the individual who has authority over both lines of authority (the one based on function and the one based on product or project). It is this individual's task to enhance coordination between functional and product managers and to maintain an appropriate balance of power between them. In Figure 13.4, the top leader is denoted in the rectangle.

➤ *Matrix bosses.* people who head functional departments or specific projects. Because neither functional managers nor project managers have complete authority over subordinates, they must work together to assure that their efforts mesh rather than conflict. In addition, they must agree on issues such as promotions and raises for specific people working under their joint authority. In Figure 13.4, matrix bosses are denoted in the hexagons.

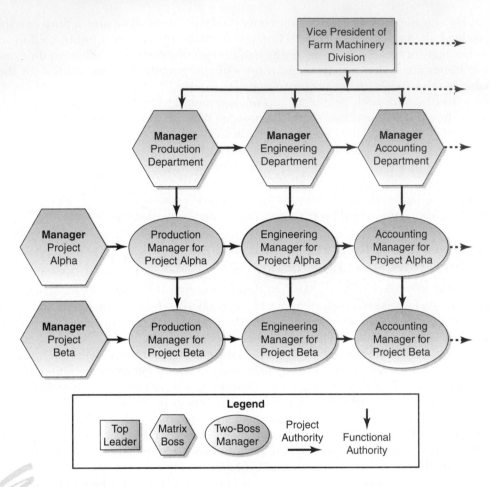

Figure 13.4   Structure of a Typical Matrix Organization

In a *matrix organization*, a product structure is superimposed on a functional structure. This results in a dual system of authority in which some managers report to two bosses—one for the specific product (or project) and one for the specific functional department involved.

➤   *Two-boss managers.*   people who must report to both product and functional managers and attempt to balance the demands of each. Because people working in this fashion have two bosses, they must have sufficient freedom to attain their objectives. As you might imagine, a fair amount of coordination, flexibility, openness, and trust is essential for this to work, suggesting that not everyone adapts well to such a system. In Figure 13.4, two-boss managers are denoted in the ovals.

Organizations are inclined to adopt matrix designs when they face complex and uncertain environments, ones in which there is frequent change and in which resources must be used wisely. Specifically, matrix designs frequently are adopted by medium-size organizations with several product lines that do not possess sufficient resources to establish fully self-contained operating units. Under such conditions, matrix designs are inclined to be effective.

Table 13.2   Advantages and Disadvantages of Matrix Organizations

Before adopting a matrix organizational form, it is important to appreciate their advantages and disadvantages. Some of the major ones are identified here.

Advantages	Disadvantages
• They permit flexible use of an organization's human resources. Individuals within functional departments can be assigned to specific products or projects as the need arises and then return to their regular duties when this task is completed.	• They can create frustration and stress in employees by requiring them to report to two different supervisors.
• They offer organizations (particularly medium-size ones) an efficient means of responding quickly to a changing, unstable environment.	• They result in ambiguity, conflict, and confusion caused by the absence of clear lines of authority. This makes the appraisal of job performance extremely difficult.
• They often enhance communication among managers by requiring bosses to discuss and agree on many matters.	• They require more administrative support than found in simpler organizational arrangements.

As you might imagine, however, the success of matrix designs cannot be assured. Like any other organizational form, there are advantages and disadvantages associated with using them, several of which are identified in Table 13.2. As you review these, it becomes clear that there are tradeoffs. In balance, however, increasing numbers of executives are adopting matrix organizations because they believe their benefits outweigh their problems. This is particularly so today, when organizations are scrambling to find ways of adapting to rapidly changing environments (see Chapter 14).[8]

TRADITIONAL ORGANIZATIONAL DESIGNS

We began this chapter by likening the structure of an organization to the structure of a house. Now we extend that analogy for purposes of introducing the concept of *organizational design*. Just as a house is designed in a particular fashion by combining its structural elements in various ways, so too can an organization be designed by combining its basic elements in certain ways. Accordingly, **organizational design** refers to the formal process of coordinating the structural elements of an organization in a manner that is most effective for meeting organizational objectives.[9]

Classical and Neoclassical Approaches: The Quest for the One Best Design

It is not difficult to realize that for organizations to function effectively, their designs must not be static but dynamic—changing in response to various conditions (e.g., governmental regulations, competition, and so on). As obvious as this may be to us today, the earliest theorists interested in organizational design paid little attention to the need for organizations to be flexible. Instead, they approached the task of designing organizations as a search for "the one best way," seeking to establish the ideal form for all organizations under all conditions—the universal design.

In Chapter 1, we described the efforts of organizational scholars such as Max Weber and Frederick Taylor. These theorists believed that effective organizations were ones that had a formal hierarchy, a clear set of rules, specialization of labor, highly routine tasks, and a highly impersonal working environment. You may recall that Weber referred to this organizational form as a *bureaucracy*. This **classical organizational theory,** which assumes that managers need to have close control over their subordinates, has fallen into disfavor because it is insensitive to human needs and is not suited to a changing environment. Unfortunately, the "ideal" form of an organization, according to Weber, did not take into account the realities of the world within which it operates. Apparently, what is ideal is not necessarily what is realistic.

In response to these conditions, and with inspiration from the Hawthorne studies, the classical approach to the bureaucratic model gave way to more of a human relations orientation (see Chapter 1). Several other organizational theorists attempted to improve upon the classical model—which is why their approach is labeled **neoclassical organizational theory**—by arguing that economic effectiveness is not the only goal of an industrial organization but that employee satisfaction is a goal as well. The key, they argued, was not rigidly controlling people's actions but actively promoting their feelings of self-worth and their importance to the organization. The neoclassical approach called for organizations to be designed with flat hierarchical structures (minimizing managerial control over subordinates) and a high degree of decentralization (encouraging employees to make their own decisions). Indeed, such design features may well serve the underlying neoclassical philosophy. (For a summary comparison between classical and neoclassical designs, see Figure 13.5.)

Figure 13.5   Classical Versus Neoclassical Designs: A Summary

The classical approach to designing organizations assumed that managers needed to have close control over their subordinates. As such, it called for designing organizations with tall hierarchies and a narrow span of control. In contrast, the neoclassical approach to designing organizations assumed that managers did not have to carefully monitor their subordinates. As such, it called for designing organizations with flat hierarchies and a wide span of control.

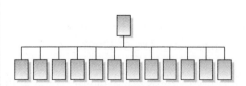

Classical Organizational Design

Neoclassical Organizational Design

- Tall hierarchy
- Narrow span of control
- Close control over subordinates

- Flat hierarchy
- Wide span of control
- Loose control over subordinates

Like the classical approach, the neoclassical approach also may be faulted on the grounds that it promoted a single best approach to organizational design. Although the benefits of flat, decentralized designs may be many, to claim that this represents the universal or ideal form for all organizations would be naive. In response to this criticism, more contemporary approaches to organizational design have given up on finding the one best way to design organizations in favor of finding different designs that are appropriate for the different circumstances and contexts within which organizations operate (see the "contingency approach," below).

The Vertically Integrated Organization

If you think about how the huge multinational oil companies operate, something very interesting is likely to strike you. Companies such as BP, ExxonMobil, and Royal Dutch Shell are involved in all aspects of the oil business associated with getting the gasoline into your vehicle's tank. This includes locating crude oil deposits, drilling and extracting those deposits from the earth, transporting oil, refining it into gasoline, distributing that gasoline to company-owned stations, and then selling it to you. Companies of this type, which own their own suppliers and purchase products from them internally, are said to be **vertically integrated.** For many years, Ford also has been a good model of vertical integration because it owned its own steel mills and its own financing arm for helping customers buy cars. (Because of problems in the auto industry in recent years, however, Ford may be selling-off some of its companies.) This kind of efficiency associated with having built-in markets is a hallmark of vertically integrated companies. After all, you don't have to worry about getting goods or services from a company if you own it.

Now, compare this approach to companies that are not vertically integrated. They buy parts from suppliers, assemble products from these parts, and then sell them to customers. Dell is a good example. It purchases microchips from Intel and AMD, video cards from nVidia or Radeon, and many other components from a wide host of suppliers and assembles them into PCs. For a comparison between vertically integrated companies and companies that are not vertically integrated, see Figure 13.6.

Despite the benefits of vertical integration, companies organized in this fashion often face special challenges.[10] For one, they tend to find it difficult to balance their resources in the most effective manner, providing exactly enough resources to be used in manufacturing and exactly the right number of finished products to be sold. A second drawback of vertical integration comes from the fact that because the company's suppliers are internal, they don't face competition to keep their prices down, potentially resulting in higher costs for the company. Third, because the various parts of the organization are so tightly interconnected, it is very difficult for the organization to respond to changes, such as developing new products. Because this would involve changes in supplies, manufacturing, and sales, the vertically integrated company faces more challenges than its nonvertically integrated counterpart when it comes to making such changes.

The Contingency Approach: Design Based on Environmental Conditions

Today, it is widely believed that the best design for an organization depends on the nature of the environment (e.g., the economy, geography, labor markets) in which the organization is operating. This is known as the **contingency approach** to organizational

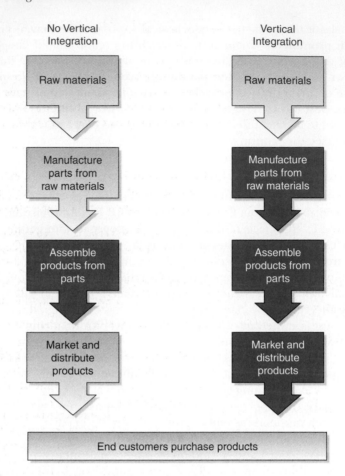

Figure 13.6   The Vertically Integrated Organization

A *vertically integrated organization,* like the one summarized on the right, owns the suppliers and/or the internal customers with whom it does business (the shaded portions of the diagram). Because it is involved only in the assembly business, the organization summarized on the left is not vertically integrated. The same would apply to an organization that focuses only on manufacturing or on marketing and distribution.

design. Although many features of the environment may be taken into account when considering how an organization should be designed, a key determinant appears to be how stable (unchanging) or unstable (turbulent) the environment is.

Mechanistic organizations under stable conditions

If you've ever worked at a McDonald's, you probably know how highly standardized each step of the most basic operations must be. Boxes of fries are to be stored 2 inches from the wall in stacks 1 inch apart. Making those fries is another matter—one that requires 19 distinct steps, each of which is clearly laid out in a training film shown to new employees. The process is the same, whether it's done in Melbourne, Florida or Melbourne, Australia. This is an example of a highly mechanistic task. Organizations can be highly mechanistic when conditions don't change. Although the fast-food industry has changed a great deal in recent years (with the introduction of healthier menu items and competitive pricing), making fries at McDonald's has not changed. The key to mechanization is lack of change. If the environment doesn't change, a highly **mechanistic form** of organization can be very efficient.

An environment is considered stable whenever there is little or no unexpected change in product, market demands, technology, and the like. These days, this characterizes very few organizations, but there are some. For example, have you ever seen an old-fashioned-looking bottle of E. E. Dickinson's witch hazel? Because the company has been making this product (which is an astringent used to cleanse the skin) following the same distillation process since 1866, it is certainly operating in a relatively stable manufacturing environment.[11] Without change, people can easily specialize. When change is inevitable, however, specialization is impractical because people have to learn to perform a variety of tasks.

Mechanistic organizations can be characterized in several additional ways (for a summary, see Table 13.3). Not only do mechanistic organizations allow for a high degree of specialization, but they also impose many rules. Authority is vested in a few people located at the top of a hierarchy who give direct orders to their subordinates. Mechanistic organizational designs tend to be most effective under conditions in which the external environment is stable and unchanging.

Organic organizations under changing conditions

Now, think about high-technology industries, such as those dedicated to computers, aerospace products, and biotechnology. Their environmental conditions are likely to be changing all the time. These industries are so prone to change that as soon as a new way of operating could be introduced into one of them, it would have to be altered.

It isn't only technology, however, that makes an environment turbulent. Turbulence also can be high in industries in which adherence to rapidly changing regulations is essential. For example, times were turbulent in the hospital industry when new Medicaid legislation was passed, and times were turbulent in the nuclear power industry when governmental regulations dictated the introduction of many new standards that had to be followed. In today's turbulent economy, the banking industry, which long has been stable, operates in a highly unstable environment (e.g., due to governmental intervention stemming from the subprime mortgage crisis).

Table 13.3 Mechanistic Versus Organic Designs

Mechanistic designs and *organic designs* differ along several key dimensions identified here. These represent extremes; many organizations fall in between.

	Structure	
Dimension	**Mechanistic**	**Organic**
Stability	Change unlikely	Change likely
Specialization	Many specialists	Many generalists
Formal rules	Rigid rules	Considerable flexibility
Authority	Centralized in a few top people	Decentralized, diffused throughout the organization

Since the 1970s, when foreign automobiles began dominating the United States, the once stable American auto industry has faced turbulent times. The traditionally highly mechanistic U.S. auto companies could not rapidly accommodate the changes needed to become more successful. By contrast, Japanese auto companies could make changes quickly because they have what's known as *organic* forms. The pure **organic form** of organization may be characterized in several different ways (see Table 13.3). In organic organizations, the degree of job specialization possible is very low; instead, a broad knowledge of many different jobs is required. Very little authority is exercised from the top. Rather, self-control is expected, and an emphasis is placed on coordination between peers. As a result, decisions tend to be made in a highly democratic, participative manner.

You should be aware that the mechanistic and organic types of organizational structure described here are ideal forms. The mechanistic–organic distinction should be thought of as opposite poles along a continuum rather than as completely distinct options for organization. Certainly, organizations can be relatively organic or relatively mechanistic compared with others but may not be located at either extreme. (Which particular form of organizational design do you prefer? The Self-Assessment Exercise on page 396 will give you some insight into your individual preferences for mechanistic and organic organizations.)

EMERGING ORGANIZATIONAL DESIGNS

Thus far, the organizational designs we have been describing have been around for a long time, and because they are so well known and often so effective, they are not likely to fade away any time soon. However, during the past decade, several emerging forms of organizational design have come onto the scene. Given how popular and promising these seem to be, we will describe them here.

The Horizontal Organization: Designing with Process in Mind

In today's "knowledge economy" (an economy based on information instead of production), a new organizational design has gained prominence, known as the **horizontal organization.** Many experts consider this to be "the first real, fundamentally different, robust alternative" to the functional organization.[12]

The essence of the idea is as follows.[13] Instead of organizing jobs in the traditional, vertical fashion by having a long chain of groups or individuals perform parts of a task (e.g., one group that sells the advertising job, another that plans the ad campaign, and yet another that produces the ads), horizontal organizations have flattened hierarchies. That is, they arrange autonomous work teams (see Chapter 9) in parallel, each performing many different steps in the process (e.g., members of an advertising team may bring different skills and expertise to a single team responsible for all aspects of advertising). Essentially, organizations are structured around *processes* instead of tasks. Performance objectives are based on customers' needs, such as lowered cost or improved service. Once the core processes that meet these needs (e.g., order generation, new product development) have been identified, they become the company's major components—instead of the traditional departments such as sales or manufacturing (for a summary, see Figure 13.7).

According to consultant Michael Hammer, "In the future, executive positions will not be defined in terms of collections of people, like head of the sales department,

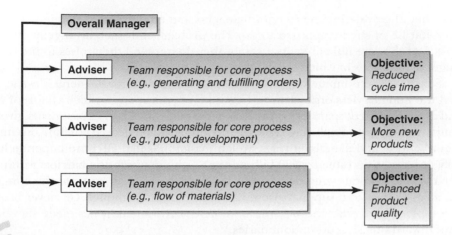

Figure 13.7   The Horizontal Organization

In a *horizontal organization,* teams of employees with diverse skills are created to meet objectives relating to various core processes that must be performed.

but in terms of processes, like senior-VP-of-getting-stuff-to-customers, which is sales, shipping, billing. You'll no longer have a box on an organization chart. You'll own part of a process map."[14] Envision it as a whole company lying on its side and organized by process. An ardent believer in this approach, Lawrence Bossidy, an award-winning executive at General Electric and Allied Signal, who came out of retirement to run Honeywell, says, "Every business has maybe six basic processes. We'll organize around them. The people who run them will be the leaders of the business."[15] In an industrial company, for example, these processes might include new product development, flow of materials, and the order-delivery-billing cycle. Individuals will constantly move into and out of various teams as needed, drawing from a directory of broadly skilled in-house corporate experts available to lend their expertise.

Although the horizontal organization is already a reality in at least parts of several of today's organizations—including AT&T (network systems division), Eastman Chemical (a division of Kodak), Hallmark Cards, and Xerox, carefully controlled studies have yet to assess the impact of this new approach. Still, those who have used it are convinced of its effectiveness. One top consultant, for example, claimed that this approach to organizational design can help companies cut their costs by at least one-third. Some of their clients, they boast, have done even better.

Will the horizontal organization replace the traditional pyramid of the hierarchical organization? Only time will tell. Meanwhile, those who have turned to horizontal organizational structures appear to be glad they did.

The Boundaryless Organization: Business Without Barriers

You hear it all the time: Someone is asked to do something but responds defiantly, saying, "It's not my job." As uncooperative as this may seem, such a comment may make a great deal of sense when it comes to the traditional kind of organizational structures we've been describing—ones with layers of carefully connected boxes neatly stacked atop each other in hierarchical fashion. The advantage of these types of organizations is that they clearly define the roles of managers and employees. Everyone knows precisely what he or she is supposed to do. The problem with such arrangements, however, is that they are inflexible. As a result, they do not lend themselves to the rapidly changing conditions in which today's organizations operate.

Sensitive to this limitation, Jack Welch, the former CEO of General Electric, proposed the **boundaryless organization.** This is an organization in which chains of command are eliminated, spans of control are unlimited, and rigid departments give way to empowered teams. Replacing rigid distinctions between people are fluid, intentionally ambiguous, and ill-defined roles. Welch's vision was that GE would operate like a family grocery store (albeit a $60 billion one)—one in which the barriers within the company that separate employees from each other and that separate the company from its customers and suppliers would be eliminated.[16] Although GE never became the completely boundaryless organization Welch envisioned, it has made significant strides toward breaking down boundaries.[17]

For boundaryless organizations to function effectively, they must meet many of the same requirements as successful teams. For example, there must be high levels of trust between all parties concerned. Also, everyone involved must have such high levels of skill that they can operate without much, if any, managerial guidance. Insofar as the elimination of boundaries weakens traditional managerial power bases, some executives may find it difficult to give up their authority, leading to political behavior. However, to the extent that the elimination of boundaries leverages the talents of all employees, such limitations are worth striving to overcome.

The boundaryless organizations we have been describing involve breaking down both internal and external barriers. As a result, they are sometimes referred to as *barrier-free organizations.* However, there are variations of the boundaryless organization involving only the elimination of external boundaries.[18] These include the *modular organization* (in which secondary aspects of the company's operations are outsourced) and the *virtual organization* (in which organizations combine forces with others on a temporary basis to form new organizations, usually only briefly). We will describe these next. Meanwhile, for a summary of these three related organizational designs, see Figure 13.8.

Modular Organizations

Many of today's organizations outsource noncore functions to other companies while retaining full strategic control over their core business. Such companies may be thought of as having a central hub surrounded by networks of outside specialists that can be added or subtracted as needed. As such, they are referred to as **modular organizations.**[19]

As a case in point, you surely recognize Nike and Reebok as major designers and marketers of athletic shoes. However, you probably didn't realize that Nike's production facilities are limited, and that Reebok doesn't have any plants of its own. Both organizations contract all their manufacturing to companies in countries such as Taiwan and South Korea where labor costs are low. In so doing, not only can they avoid making major investments in facilities, but also they can concentrate on what they do best—tapping the changing tastes of their customers. While doing this, their suppliers can focus on rapidly retooling to make the new products.[20]

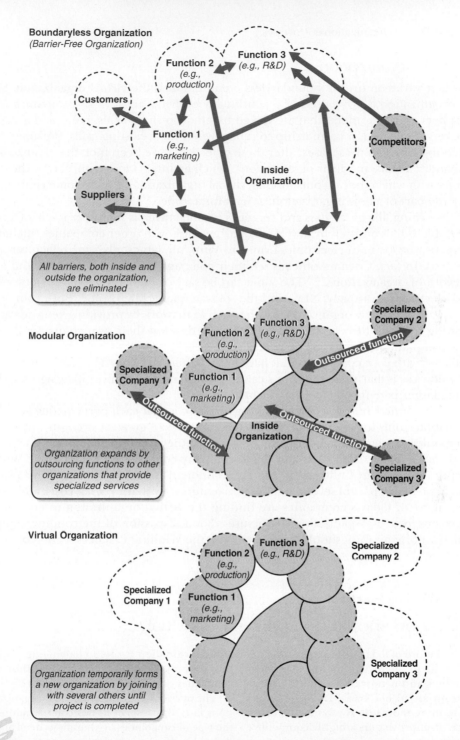

Figure 13.8 The Boundaryless Organization, the Modular Organization, and the Virtual Organization

The true *boundaryless organization* is free of both internal barriers and external barriers. Variants, such as the *modular organization* and the *virtual organization*, eliminate only external barriers.

Virtual Organizations

Another variation on the boundaryless organization is the **virtual organization.** Such an organization is composed of a continually evolving network of companies (e.g., suppliers and customers) that are linked together to share skills, costs, and access to markets. They form a partnership to capitalize on their existing skills, pursuing common objectives. In most cases, after these objectives have been met, the organizations disband.[21] Unlike modular organizations, which maintain close control over the companies with which they do outsourcing, virtual organizations give up some control and become part of a new organization, at least for a while.

Corning, the giant glass and ceramics manufacturer, is a good example of a company that builds on itself by developing partnerships with other companies (including Siemens, the German electronics firm, and Vitro, the largest glass manufacturer from Mexico). In fact, Corning officials see their company not as a single entity but as "a network of organizations."[22] The same can be said of the large Japanese networking and electronics company, NEC, and the software giant, Microsoft.[23] Both companies actively develop new organizations with which to network by providing venture capital funding for current research staff members to develop their own companies. These new companies are referred to as **affiliate networks**—satellite organizations that are affiliated with core companies that have helped them develop. The idea behind affiliate networks is that these new firms can work with, rather than compete against, their much larger parents on emerging technology.[24]

The underlying idea of a virtual organization is that each participating company contributes only its core competencies (i.e., its areas of greatest strength). By several companies mixing and matching the best of what they can offer, a joint product is created that is better than what any single company could have created alone. Virtual corporations are not unusual in the entertainment industry. Indeed, Time Warner also has become part of several multimedia ventures. By sharing risks, costs, and expertise, many of today's companies are finding the virtual organization to be a highly appealing type of organizational structure. (For a discussion of the conditions under which an organization should "go virtual," see the Winning Practices section below.)

Winning Practices

When Should Companies Go Virtual?

More and more of today's companies are finding it useful to "go virtual," downscaling their hierarchies and networking with other companies on an ad hoc basis. Doing so allows them to move more quickly, standing a better chance of improving in a highly competitive environment. However, virtual organizations are far from perfect. Because people from different companies do not share common values, interpersonal conflicts are likely to occur,

and coordination is often challenging. This raises an important question: When should companies organize in a virtual manner?

The answer depends on how the organizations fare with respect to two considerations: the type of capabilities organizations need and the type of change that will be made.[25] Specifically, organizational changes may be either *autonomous* or *systemic*. **Autonomous change** is one that is made independently of

(continued)

other changes. For an example, an auto company that develops a new type of upholstery may do so without revising the rest of the car. **Systemic change** is such that change in one part of an organization requires changes in another part of that same organization. For example, Sony's development of digital photography required changes in both memory storage and camera technologies.

A second key distinction involves the capabilities needed to complete the project. In some cases, outside capabilities are required. For example, in the early 1980s, IBM was able to develop its first personal computer in only 15 months because it went outside the company for expertise (e.g., buying chips from Intel and an operating system from Microsoft). Other times, capability can be found inside the company. For example, General Motors traditionally developed many of the components used in its cars, making it less dependent on other companies (although it now does far less of this than it used to).[26]

By combining these factors, it becomes clear when companies should "go virtual" and when they should work exclusively within their own walls. *Virtual organizations work best for companies considering autonomous changes and that rely on technologies that exist only outside their walls.* For example, Motorola has developed virtual organizations with several battery manufacturers for its cell phones and pagers. In so doing, it can focus on its core business—the delivery of wireless communication—while ensuring it has the battery power to make such devices work.

In contrast, *companies should keep their focus inward when changes are systemic in nature and involve capabilities the company either already has or can create.* Under such conditions, relying on outside help may be far too risky—and unnecessary. For example, these days Intel is making extensive investments to enhance its current and future capacities.

Finally, for conditions that fall between these extremes (i.e., when systemic changes are being made using capabilities that come only from outside the company, and when autonomous changes are being made using capabilities that must be created), virtual organizations should be created with extreme caution.

Clearly, the virtual organization has a key place in today's organizational world. The trick, however, lies in understanding precisely what that place is. These principles represent useful guidance in that respect.

INTERORGANIZATIONAL DESIGNS: GOING BEYOND THE SINGLE ORGANIZATION

All the organizational designs we described thus far have concentrated on the arrangement of units *within* an organization—what may be termed *intraorganizational designs.* However, sometimes at least some parts of different organizations must operate jointly. To coordinate their efforts on such projects, organizations must create *interorganizational designs,* plans by which two or more organizations come together.[27] Two such designs are commonly found: *conglomerates* and *strategic alliances.*

Conglomerates: Diversified "Megacorporations"

When an organization diversifies by adding an entirely unrelated business or product to its organizational design, it may be said to have formed a **conglomerate.** Some of the world's largest conglomerates may be found in Asia. For example, in Korea, companies such as Samsung and Hyundai produce home electronics, automobiles, textiles, and chemicals in large, unified conglomerates known as *chaebols.*[28] These are all separate companies overseen by the same parent company leadership.

Companies form conglomerates for several reasons. First, as an independent business, the parent company can enjoy the benefits of diversification. Thus, as one industry languishes, another may excel, allowing a stable economic outlook for the parent company. In addition, as in the case of vertically integrated organizations, conglomerates may provide built-in markets and access to supplies, since companies typically support other organizations within the conglomerate. For example, General Motors cars and trucks are fitted with Delco radios, and Ford cars and trucks have engines with Autolite spark plugs, separate companies that are owned by their respective parent companies. In this manner conglomerates can benefit by providing a network of organizations that are dependent on each other for products and services, thereby creating considerable advantages due to their built-in markets.

In recent years, however, many large conglomerates have been selling off parts of themselves in a move to concentrate on their core business.[29] For example, The Limited, the large women's clothing retailer, has closed or sold off some of its specialty stores (e.g., Cacique and Abercrombie & Fitch) so that it can focus on its core business.

Strategic Alliances: Joining Forces for Mutual Benefit

A **strategic alliance** is a type of organizational design in which two or more separate firms join their competitive capabilities to operate a new business. The goal of a strategic alliance is to provide benefits to each individual organization that could not be attained if they operated separately. They are low-risk ways of diversifying (adding new business operations) and entering new markets. Some companies, such as GE and Ford, have strategic alliances with many others. Although some alliances last only a short time, others have remained in existence for well over 30 years and are still going strong.[30]

A continuum of alliances

A study of 37 strategic alliances from throughout the world identified three types of cooperative arrangements between organizations.[31] These may be arranged along a continuum from those alliances that are weak and distant, at one end, to those that are strong and close, at the other end. As shown in Figure 13.9, at the weak end of the

Figure 13.9 Strategic Alliances: A Continuum of Interorganizational Relationships
The three types of *strategic alliances* identified here may be distinguished with respect to their location along a continuum ranging, at one end, from weak and distant, to strong and close at the other end.

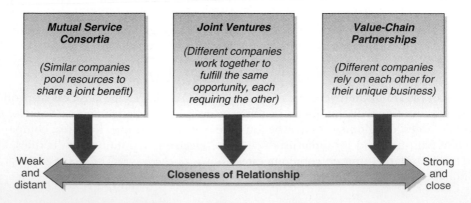

continuum are strategic alliances known as **mutual service consortia.** These are arrangements between two similar companies from the same or similar industries to pool their resources to receive a benefit that would be too difficult or expensive for either to obtain alone. Often the focus is some high-tech capacity, such as an expensive piece of diagnostic equipment (e.g., a magneto-resonance imaging or MRI unit) that might be shared by two or more small hospitals in a rural location.

At the opposite end of the scale are the strongest and closest type of collaborations, referred to as **value-chain partnerships.** These are alliances between companies in different industries that have complementary capabilities. Customer–supplier relationships are a prime example. In such arrangements one company buys necessary goods and services from another so that it can do business. Because each company greatly depends on the other, each party's commitment to their mutual relationship is high. As noted earlier, Toyota has a network of 230 suppliers with whom it regularly does business. The relationship between Toyota and these various companies represents value-chain partnerships.

Between these two extremes are **joint ventures.** These are arrangements in which companies work together to fulfill opportunities that require the capabilities of the other.[32] For example, two companies might enter into a joint venture if one has a valuable technology and the other has the marketing knowledge to help transform that technology into a viable commercial product. If this arrangement sounds familiar, it should. The way NASA, Google, and STSI joined forces to create Google Sky (as described in the Making the Case section on p. 370) is an example of a strategic alliance in action.

As information technology has flourished, many Internet-based organizations have developed joint ventures with newly forming companies (referred to as *start-ups*). Their mission: to facilitate the flow of knowledge and talent across companies in a manner that boosts their joint technical and marketing competence. This special kind of joint venture is known as a **networked incubator.**[33] These are partnerships between established companies (often Internet-based firms), which provide valued resources and experience, with start-ups, which are able to develop and market products quickly. When properly designed, networked incubators combine the best of both worlds—the scale and scope of large, established companies and the entrepreneurial spirit of small firms.

Strategic alliances in the global economy

Strategic alliances with companies in nations with transforming economies (such as China and eastern European countries) provide good opportunities for those nations' economies to develop. Given the rapid move toward globalization of the economy, we may expect to see many companies seeking strategic alliances in the future as a means for gaining or maintaining a competitive advantage. Frequently, companies form strategic alliances with foreign firms to gain entry into those firms' home markets.[34] Such arrangements also may allow for an exchange of technology and manufacturing services. For example, Korea's Daewoo receives technical information and is paid to manufacture automobiles for companies with which it has entered into alliances, such as General Motors, as well as Germany's Opel and Japan's Nissan.[35]

Direct managerial benefits also are associated with extending one company's organizational chart into another's. These benefits primarily come from improved technology and greater economies of scale (e.g., sharing functional operations across organizations). For these benefits to be derived, a high degree of coordination and fit must exist between the parties, each delivering on its promise to the other. Finally, it is noteworthy that strategic alliances with companies in nations with transforming economies provide good opportunities for those nations' economies to develop.[36] Given the rapid move toward globalization of the economy, we may expect to see many companies seeking strategic alliances in the future as a means for gaining or maintaining a competitive advantage.[37]

Strategic alliances can help minority-owned businesses

Although members of minority groups represent about 28 percent of the U.S. population, they control only 12 percent of the nation's businesses. In an effort to bring parity to this situation by boosting the number of minority-owned businesses, the U.S. government requires companies to meet specified targets for conducting business with minority-owned companies. The underlying rationale is that this practice is good for business. Jethro Joseph, Chrysler's head of special supplier relations, offers a simple explanation: "If we buy from minority suppliers, they will hire minority employees, who will have the wherewithal to buy our products. We look at it as a never-ending wheel."[38] To get this wheel moving, many large companies are finding it useful to form alliances with minority-owned companies, creating relationships from which both parties can benefit. For a sample of some of these alliances, see Table 13.4.

Table 13.4   Alliances Involving Minority-Owned Businesses

In recent years, many large companies have found it useful to enter into strategic alliances with small, minority-owned companies. Other companies have served as "matchmakers," bringing together firms with one or more minority group owners. Here are a few examples.

Large Company	Involvement with Small, Minority-Owned Company
Bank of America	Bank of America wanted to do business with R. J. Leeper, a black entrepreneur in the construction business. However, because he lacked experience, Bank of America helped him learn the business by getting him a job at a successful construction company and paying half his salary while he worked there. Leeper now has his own construction company, R. J. Leeper Construction, which is a supplier to Bank of America.
Procter & Gamble	Procter & Gamble purchases plastic bottles for Sunny Delight from a company that it helped create—a joint venture between Plastitec and minority-owned Madras Packaging.
Chrysler	Chrysler helped International Paper, one of its suppliers, form a joint venture with a black entrepreneur, Carlton Highsmith. His company, Specialized Packaging Group, now produces packaging for automotive parts made by Chrysler.
Ford Motor Company	Ford Motor Company officials wanted to buy conveyor systems from one of three minority-owned companies (Devon Contracting Services, Scion, and Gale & Associates), but they were too small. Ford helped these three firms merge, forming Tri-Tec, the larger and more stable company from which Ford now buys conveyor systems.
Johnson Controls	Johnson Controls purchases interior car parts from TKA Plastics. This company was the result of a partnership between two parties that Johnson Controls brought together: Del-Met, an injection molding company, and Michael Cherry, a black entrepreneur.

(Source: Based on information in Weisul, 2001; see Note 38, and the Web sites of the companies identified.)

Are strategic alliances successful?

As these descriptions of the various types of alliances illustrate, there are clear benefits to be derived from forming alliances. These primarily come in the form of improved technology, widened markets, and greater economies of scale (e.g., sharing functional operations across organizations). However, as you might imagine, for these benefits to be realized, a high degree of coordination and fit must exist between the parties, each delivering on its promise to the other.

In view of this, it probably comes as no surprise that not all strategic alliances are successful. For example, AT&T and the Italian firm, Olivetti, once tried to work together on manufacturing personal computers. The results were a disaster. Strong differences in management styles and organizational culture were cited as causes (recall the discussion of culture clashes in Chapter 12). Clearly, for strategic alliances to work, the companies must not only be able to offer each other something important, but they also must be able to work together to make it happen.

Back to the Case

Answer the following questions about this chapter's Making the Case (p. 370) to illustrate insights you have derived about the material in this chapter.

1. Besides forming a joint venture with NASA, how else might Google have gone about expanding Google Earth to Google Sky?
2. What problems do you envision might be faced down the road in the arrangement between Google and NASA?
3. How do you believe that the expenditure of resources on Google Sky might help or harm the other activities in which Google and NASA are involved?

You be the Consultant

Designing a Rapidly Growing Company

The president of a small but rapidly growing software company asks you to consult with him about an important matter. As the company expands, several options for designing the company's operations are being considered, and your job is to help him make a decision about which route to take. Answer the following questions relevant to this situation based on the material in this chapter.

1. What would you recommend with respect to the following structural variables: hierarchy of authority (tall or flat), division of labor (specialized or not), span of control (wide or narrow), and degree of centralization (highly centralized or highly decentralized)? Explain the reasons behind your recommendations.

2. How do you think the company should be departmentalized—by task (functional), by output (product), both task and output (matrix), or process (horizontal)? What are the reasons for these conclusions?

3. If the company were thinking about entering into a strategic alliance with another, what factors would have to be considered? What kind of company would be an effective partner in an alliance with this software firm?

SELF-ASSESSMENT EXERCISE

Which Do You Prefer—Mechanistic or Organic Organizations?

Because mechanistic and organic organizations are so different, it is reasonable to expect that people will tend to prefer one of these organizational forms over the other. This questionnaire is designed to help you identify your own preferences (and, in so doing, to help you learn about the different forms themselves).

Directions

Each of the following questions deals with your preferences for various conditions that may exist where you work. Answer each one by checking the one alternative that better describes your feelings.

1. When I have a job-related decision to make, I usually prefer to:
   ____ a. make the decision myself.
   ____ b. have my boss make it for me.
2. I usually find myself more interested in performing:
   ____ a. a highly narrow, specialized task.
   ____ b. many different types of tasks.
3. I prefer to work in places in which working conditions:
   ____ a. change a great deal.
   ____ b. generally remain the same.
4. When a lot of rules are imposed on me, I generally feel:
   ____ a. very comfortable.
   ____ b. very uncomfortable.
5. I believe that governmental regulation of industry is:
   ____ a. usually best for all.
   ____ b. rarely good for anyone.

Scoring

1. Give yourself one point each time you answered as follows: 1 = b; 2 = a; 3 = b; 4 = a; 5 = a. This score is your preference for *mechanistic organizations.*
2. Subtract this score from 5. This score is your preference for *organic organizations.*
3. Interpret your scores as follows: Higher scores (closer to 5) reflect stronger preferences and lower scores (closer to 0) reflect weaker preferences.

Discussion Questions

1. How did you score? That is, which organizational form do you prefer?
2. Think back over the jobs you've had. For the most part, have these been in organizations that were mechanistic or organic?
3. Do you think you were any more committed to organizations in which you worked whose designs matched your preferences as compared to those in which there was a mismatch?

GROUP EXERCISE

Comparing Span of Control in Organization Charts

One of the easiest things to determine about a company by looking at its organization chart is its span of control. This exercise will allow you to learn about and compare spans of control within different companies.

Directions

1. Divide the class into four equal-size groups.
2. Assign one of the following industry types to each group: (a) manufacturing companies, (b) financial institutions, (c) public utilities, and (d) charities.
3. Within the industry assigned to each group, identify one company per student. It helps to consider larger organizations inasmuch as these are more likely to have formal organization charts. For example, if there are five students in the "financial institutions" group, name five different banks or savings and loan institutions.
4. Each student should get a copy of the organization chart (or at least a portion of it) for the company assigned to him or her in step 3. You may be able to get this information from various companies' Web sites and/or by consulting their annual reports (which may be found in many libraries). If all else fails, you may have to ask someone you know who works at a given company to show you its organization chart.
5. Meet as a group to discuss the spans of control of the organizations in your sample.
6. Gather as a class to compare the findings of the various groups.

Discussion Questions

1. Were you successful in being able to collect the organization charts, or were the organizations reluctant to share them?
2. Did you find that there were differences with respect to span of control?
3. Were spans of control different at different organizational levels or for different industry groups? In what ways were they similar and different?

Managing Organizational Change: Strategic Planning and Organizational Development

Learning Objectives

After reading this chapter, you will be able to:

1. **IDENTIFY** the major external forces responsible for organizational change.
2. **DESCRIBE** what is meant by strategic planning and **IDENTIFY** the steps in the strategic planning process.
3. **EXPLAIN** why people are resistant to change in organizations and **DESCRIBE** ways in which such resistance may be overcome.
4. **DEFINE** organizational development (OD) and **DESCRIBE** three OD techniques.
5. **DESCRIBE** the conditions under which OD techniques are most effective.
6. **DESCRIBE** how OD is affected by national culture and **EXPLAIN** the ethical concerns that have been voiced about using OD techniques.

3 GOOD REASONS why you should care about . . .

Managing Organizational Change

You should care about managing organizational change and development because:

1. The success—even the mere survival—of companies depends on their ability to adapt to change.
2. For organizations to be effective, employees' resistance to change must be overcome.
3. Organizational development techniques can help people adapt to change.

Making the Case for Managing Organizational Change

Asustek Bets That for Laptops, Less Is More

Based in Taiwan, Asustek currently ranks sixth in sales of notebook computers. For CEO Jerry Shen and chairman Jonney Shih, that's not good enough. By 2013, they plan for the company to break into the top three, currently occupied by Hewlett-Packard, Dell, and Acer. While they surely are thinking big, their vehicle for riding to success is small—weighing in at only 2 pounds, in fact.

In an era in which computer makers are building faster and more powerful computers, Asustek moved in the opposite direction. Their "Eee" notebook has a 7-inch screen and just barely enough power to perform basic tasks, such as surfing the Web and checking e-mail. If it's gaming you want, forget it, but for routine communication uses, this mini-laptop suits most road warriors just fine. And at only $300 for the most basic model, it's not a drain on most budgets. Although the company's profit margin on these units is small, Shen and Shih plan to make it up on volume; they sold about 5 million units worldwide in 2008 alone.

Acknowledging that the Eee isn't for everybody, Shih put the Asustek design team, headed by Jimmy Chu, to work on another strategy for boosting sales—outshining the competition aesthetically. Going beyond the usual, dull-looking notebooks with their black or gray covers (the Eee is available in a line of jellybean colors), the company also makes a line of highly artistic models. Care for a notebook with a bamboo cover, or one boasting the same chrome and leather materials as a Lamborghini? They got it. Although there may be only a niche market for these products, it's clear that Asustek is distinguishing itself from the competition by moving in new directions. Not only are they changing the rules of the game in the notebook computer business, but they also have changed their own previously traditional product line.

As you might expect in view of its success (doubling in sales from 5 million units to 10 million units in a single year), the Eee has spawned imitators from the big boys. Hewlett-Packard, Dell, and Acer all have come out with similar "netbooks."

Meanwhile, when it comes to artful design and innovation, Asustek is the company to beat. That's the story now, but given how rapidly things change in the computer business, the only thing that's certain is that the future is up for grabs.

Clearly, Mr. Shen and Mr. Shih are striving to build new markets for Asustek computers and by using novel product lines as their vehicles, they are keeping their design team working overtime. The company has been growing dramatically, and if these two executives have their way, this is just the beginning of even more growth to come. The many changes they face in operations, organizational structure, and culture, among other things, in a market led by giants, promise to be considerable. Time will tell if they are prepared for the ride.

Of course, it's not only Asustek that is seeing dramatic changes. Just pick an industry. The major fast-food chains are clamoring to bring customers to their drive-through windows with $1 menu items. Many airlines struggling with soaring fuel prices have ended the long-standing practice of offering passengers free snacks. And even analog TV signals that once filled the airwaves transitioned to digital in 2009, bringing endless changes to the television industry. We could go on, but you get the point: The only thing not changing in today's organizations is that change is occurring.

Although the impact of *organizational change* can be found everywhere, especially these days, most people have difficulty accepting that they may have to alter their work methods. After all, if you're used to working a certain way, an abrupt change can be unsettling. Fortunately, social scientists have developed various methods, known collectively as *organizational development* techniques, which are designed to implement organizational change in a manner that is acceptable to employees while also enhancing the effectiveness of the organizations involved. We review these techniques in this chapter. Before doing so, however, we summarize different forces for change acting on organizations. We then will explore some major issues involved in the organizational change process, such as what is changed, when change will occur, why people are resistant to change, and importantly, how this resistance can be overcome (i.e., how people can become more comfortable with the inevitable changes they will face).

TODAY'S FIRST RULE OF BUSINESS: CHANGE OR DISAPPEAR!

A century ago, advances in machine technology made farming so highly efficient that fewer hands were needed to plant and reap the harvest. The displaced laborers fled to nearby cities, seeking jobs in newly opened factories, opportunities created by some of the same technologies that sent them from the farm. The economy shifted from agrarian to manufacturing, and the *industrial revolution* was under way. With it came drastic shifts in where people lived, how they worked, how they spent their leisure time, how much money they made, and how they spent it. Since the 1990s, we have been experiencing a second industrial revolution—one driven by a new wave of technological forces. As one observer put it, "This workplace revolution . . . may be remembered as a historic event, the Western equivalent of the collapse of communism."[1]

In recent years, just about all companies, large and small, have made adjustments in the ways they operate, some more pronounced than others. Citing just two examples, AT&T left and then reentered the cellular phone business; General Motors made mostly fuel-efficient vehicles, followed by gas-guzzling SUVs, then returned to ultra–fuel-efficient vehicles (and even ones that don't use fuel at all). These shifts have brought with them changes in the way these companies operate: their cultures, the technologies they use, their organizational structures, and the nature of their relations with customers and employees. With so many companies making such drastic changes, the message is clear: *either adapt to changing conditions or shut your doors.*

As technology and markets change, organizations face a formidable challenge to adapt. When they fail to do so, they are forced to close their doors forever. If you have any doubt about this, just consider what happened in the fall of 2008, when many venerable banks, brokerage firms, and mortgage companies folded as a result of having made bad loans (i.e., the so-called subprime mortgage crisis). The message that credit standards needed to be raised was heard loud and clear, leading lending institutions to tighten credit requirements to lenders (sometimes too much, causing additional problems).

Magnitude of Change: How Much Change Constitutes Change?

As you might imagine, not all organizational changes are equal in magnitude. Whereas some are minor and subtle (e.g., new locations for recycling bins), others are far more dramatic and far-reaching in scope and impact (e.g., new operating procedures required of American auto companies receiving "bailout" funds from the government).

First-order change

Change that is continuous in nature and that involves no major shifts in how an organization operates is known as **first-order change** (or **incremental change**). Changes of this type are apparent in the deliberate, incremental modifications Toyota has made in continuously improving the efficiency of its production process. Not surprisingly, employees are less threatened by incremental changes than by more monumental changes because they have time to adapt and to make appropriate adjustments.

Second-order change

Other types of organizational changes are far more complex. **Second-order change** (or **quantum change**) refers to radical change, involving major shifts in different levels of the organization and different aspects of the business.[2] For example, many large companies, such as General Electric, have radically altered the way they operate, their culture, the technology they use, their organizational structure, and the nature of their relations with employees. Not surprisingly, quantum change often is quite jarring and highly traumatic to employees, and as such, getting them to accept such changes is often difficult.

Regardless of their scope and magnitude, all organizational changes stem from two major forces: (1) reactions to external pressures and (2) internally inspired plans to introduce change deliberately, for strategic reasons. We will review these forces for change in the next two sections.

EXTERNAL FORCES FOR ORGANIZATIONAL CHANGE

What outside forces cause organizations to change? Although there are many different external drivers of organizational change, five particular forces are especially important: the introduction of information technology, changing employee demographics, performance gaps, government regulation, and global economic competition. We now describe these.

Advances in Technology

Probably the most potent impetus for organizational change was the introduction of the personal computer—the IBM Personal Computer and the Apple Macintosh—in the mid-1980s. In offices, word processing systems replaced typewriters; in factories, robots replaced people performing dangerous and repetitive jobs; and in recording studios, sophisticated synthesizer units housed in simple black boxes replaced orchestras full of musicians. Although office personnel, factory workers, and musicians surely have not become extinct, computer technology has changed the way they are doing their jobs. For an overview of ways in which the introduction of high-tech devices in the workplace has helped people to perform and to better serve the needs of customers and society at large, see Table 14.1.

Although some jobs have been eliminated because of automation, technology generally has helped those who have become displaced find more interesting and personally fulfilling jobs. The widespread fear that many people had about "being

Table 14.1 How Has Computer Technology Changed the Way We Work?

Advances in computer technology have revolutionized many of the ways we work. Some key ways in which this has been occurring are summarized here.

Area of Change	Old Way	New Technology Examples
Use of machines	Materials were moved by hand, with the aid of mechanical devices (e.g., pulleys and chains).	**Automation** is prevalent—the process of using machines to perform tasks that might otherwise be done by people. For example, computer-controlled machines manipulate materials and perform complex functions, a process known as **industrial robotics (IR)**.
Work by employees with disabilities	People with various physical or mental disabilities either were relegated to the most simple jobs, or they didn't work at all.	**Assistive technology** is widespread—devices and other solutions that help individuals with physical or mental disabilities perform the various actions needed to do their jobs. For example, **telephone handset amplifiers** make it possible for people with hearing impediments to use the telephone and **voice recognition systems** read to people with visual impairments.
Monitoring employees	Supervisors used to physically enter the offices of employees at work and observe them from afar.	**Computerized performance monitoring** systems are in widespread use, which allow supervisors to access their subordinates' computers for purposes of assessing how well they are performing their jobs.
Customer service	Individual service providers did things to help employees, customizing goods and services as time and skill allowed.	**Personalized service** is likely to take the form of greeting visitors to one's Web page with information customized to match the goods and services in which they expressed interest in their last visit (e.g., Amazon.com does this).
Environmental friendliness	Products at the end of their lives were buried in landfills, often polluting the earth.	**Design for disassembly (DFD)** is the process of designing and building products so that their parts can be reused several times and then disposed of at the end of the product's life without harming the environment.
Ease of communication	To communicate with others in distant locations, people were limited to talking on telephones that were connected by cords or by writing and mailing letters	Today's **cellular technology** makes it possible for people to talk by phone to others almost anywhere on earth. And the wide availability of high-speed Internet has made it possible to talk over computer lines (**VOIP technology**) and, of course, to use **e-mail**.

replaced by robots" has proven to be unfounded. More typically, people work along-side robots. For example, although robots play a large part in the production of auto-mobiles, the technology works only because of the people. Advanced technology alone won't build a successful car. In the words of the Japanese industrialist Jaruo Shimada, "Only people give wisdom to the machines."[3] The idea is that people and machines are complementary aspects of any organization.

Changing Employee Demographics

There can be no mistaking the fact that the composition of the workforce has changed in the past few years. As we noted in Chapters 1 and 5, the American workforce is now more racially and ethnically diverse than ever before. It also contains more women, more foreign nationals, and more elderly people.[4] These are not merely curious soci-ological trends but realities to which organizations must adapt.

For example, human resources specialists need to know if there will be a drop in the number of qualified applicants (suggesting the need to import employees from other locations, or even to relocate the company) as well as the specific skills future employees will be bringing to their jobs (suggesting the need to revise training pro-grams) and their special needs (such as child care or flexible working arrangements). In the words of a high-ranking executive at General Electric, the changes in workforce demographics "will turn the professional human-resources world upside down."[5]

Performance Gaps

A product line that isn't moving, a vanishing profit margin, a level of sales that isn't up to corporate expectations—these are examples of **performance gaps,** discrepancies between real and expected levels of organizational performance. Few things force change more than sudden and unexpected information about poor performance.

Good illustrations may be seen in General Motors' 2004 decision to phase out its Oldsmobile brand and its 2009 decision (as part of a government-based plan) to become leaner (and hopefully, profitable) by dropping additional lines (e.g., Pontiac, Saab, Volvo, and Hummer). Although the Oldsmobile was produced for over 100 years, and was popular during much of the 20th century, its failure to respond to changing demands (specifically, vehicles that were appealing to younger buyers) even-tually led to its demise.[6] Organizations that are well prepared to mobilize change in response to downturns are best equipped to succeed. Indeed, General Motors officials are hoping that these responses to performance gaps will help the company regain its prominence—indeed, its existence—in the auto industry.[7]

Government Regulation

One of the most commonly witnessed unplanned organizational changes results from government regulations. In recent years, restaurant owners in the United States had to alter the way they report the income of waiters and waitresses to the federal gov-ernment for purposes of collecting income taxes. And, of course, at the local level, restaurants are required to comply with a host of local government regulations regarding health and safety. Moreover, the U.S. federal government has been involved in imposing regulations in industries such as commercial airlines (e.g., man-dating inspection schedules), insurance (e.g., requiring companies to hold in reserve certain sums of money to ensure that they can cover customer's claims), and banking (e.g., requiring a license to operate that dictates, among many other things, how a bank must handle its capital in relation to its assets).

These examples illustrate the government's involvement in protecting consumers by ensuring that they don't fall prey to unscrupulous businesses. More recent examples may be seen in the financial services industry, where regulations are being instituted to safeguard consumers from *predatory lenders* (i.e., those who are dishonest in their practices) and issuers of *payday loans* (i.e., short-term loans secured by a customer's future paycheck, issued at very high interest rates). Such activities have greatly influenced the way business is conducted in these industries.

The Sarbanes-Oxley Act (SOX)

Probably the most sweeping legislation affecting business activities has been the **Sarbanes-Oxley Act** (commonly referred to as **SOX**). Enacted in 2002, this law is designed to protect the American public from the kind of questionable accounting practices used at Enron and other large companies that led investors and employees to lose vast sums of money at the turn of the twenty-first century. Because of the law's connection to the ethical practices of businesses, we already discussed SOX in Chapter 2. However, in view of its significance as a driver of many forms of organizational change, it bears describing further here.

SOX contains 11 titles, or sections, that, among other things, identify the responsibilities of members of corporate boards (and the penalties for failing to comply with these responsibilities) and require the Securities and Exchange Commission (SEC) to implement rulings assuring compliance with SOX regulations. To ensure that it may do so, funding for the SEC has doubled in recent years.[8] So, how exactly has SOX prompted changes in the way publicly owned organizations (i.e., those that sell stock) operate? For a summary, see Table 14.2.[9]

Global Economic Competition

Competition from the marketplace is a key driver of organizational change. Any company that fails to keep up with the competition (with respect to price, services, or other key features) doesn't stand a chance of surviving. Although competition always has been crucial to organizational success, competition today comes from all over the world. As it has become increasingly less expensive to transport materials around the world, the industrialized nations have found themselves competing with each other for shares of a marketplace that spans the globe.

This extensive globalization of the economy presents a strong need to change and be innovative.[10] No longer can companies of any serious size survive by serving only their own nations. In general, liberal trade laws and readily available transportation make it easy for companies from all countries to conduct business in other countries. For example, Toyota (a Japanese company) has design facilities in California, Volkswagen (a German company) has a plant in Tennessee, Honda (a Japanese company) has several factories in Ohio, BMW (a German company) has an assembly plant in South Carolina, and Mercedes Benz (a German company) has an assembly plant in Alabama. Additionally, most major auto companies have manufacturing plants in Mexico. Taking

Table 14.2　Changes Following Passage of the Sarbanes-Oxley Act

Since its passage in 2002, the Sarbanes-Oxey Act (SOX) has required people associated with publicly traded companies to make several important changes. Enacted in response to the irregularities that led to the collapse of Enron, these provisions are designed to safeguard employees and stockholders from corporate behavior that may cause them to lose money.

Before SOX	After SOX
Public accounting firms, which presumably were in place to serve as "watchdogs" for the public, were self-regulated. This allowed some to not perform their jobs as rigorously as necessary by "letting things slide."	SOX created the Public Company Accounting Oversight Board (PCAOB) to review independently the accuracy of the financial audits performed by public accounting firms. Essentially, they audit the auditors' audits.
Some external auditors reported problems so they could be hired as consultants to solve the problems they found. Because these contracts were lucrative, auditors had strong motives to misreport the findings of their audits.	SOX requires external auditors to be independent of the companies they audit.
Some executives didn't fully understand the complex financial reports filed by their Audit Committees but signed them anyway.	SOX makes senior executives individually responsible for the accuracy and completeness of their companies' financial reports. So, if they sign reports that contain inaccurate information, they will spend time in jail and face serious financial penalties.
Some securities analysts also were investment bankers who stood to benefit by offering lucrative services to their clients. This gave them strong financial incentives to make certain recommendations.	SOX requires securities analysts (individuals who make buy and sell recommendations on company stocks and bonds) to disclose conflicts of interest that may influence their judgments.
Before SOX, the temptation to tamper with records (and to threaten those who interfere with these actions) was, in many cases, extremely strong.	SOX requires criminal penalties for engaging in fraud by manipulating, destroying, or altering financial records. It also protects whistle-blowers (see Chapter 7) who report such behavior by fining and/or imprisoning individuals who take actions against them.

(Sources: Based on information in Shakespeare, 2008, and Kohn et al., 2004; see Note 9.)

only these examples, it's clear that today's autos are truly international in nature, making the phrase "foreign car" somewhat meaningless.

PLANNING STRATEGIC CHANGE

Thus far, we have described unplanned reactions to conditions requiring organizational change. However, organizations also make changes that are carefully planned and deliberate in nature. This is the idea of **strategic planning,** defined as the process of formulating, implementing, and evaluating organizational changes in ways that enable an organization to achieve its objectives.[11] In this section of the chapter, we will describe the strategic planning process.

Basic Assumptions About Strategic Planning

To understand the nature of strategic plans used in organizations today, it is important to identify three fundamental assumptions about them:[12]

1. *Strategic planning is deliberate.*   When organizations make strategic plans, they make conscious decisions to change fundamental aspects of themselves. These changes tend to be radical and second-order changes (e.g., changes in the nature of the business) as opposed to minor, first-order changes (e.g., changes in the color of the office walls).

2. *Strategic planning occurs when current objectives no longer can be met.*   Generally, when a company's present strategy is bringing about the desired results, change is unlikely. However, whenever it becomes clear that current objectives aren't being satisfied by existing plans, new strategies are formulated to turn things around.

3. *New organizational objectives require new strategic plans.*   Whenever a company takes steps to move in a completely new direction, it establishes new objectives, and it designs a strategic plan to meet them. Acknowledging that the various parts of an organization are interdependent, this new strategic plan is likely to involve all functions and levels of the organization.

In the sections that follow you will see several examples of strategic plans for change in a variety of organizations.

About What Do Companies Make Strategic Plans?

Organizations can make strategic plans to change just about anything. Most strategic planning today, however, involves changing either a company's products and services or its organizational structure.

Products and services

Over the past decade many well-known *bricks-and-mortar* retail establishments (ones with retail stores), such as Barnes & Noble and Toys "R" Us, jumped on the e-commerce bandwagon after it became apparent that doing so would expand their customer base by extending their well-known names to the Web. These so called *bricks-and-clicks* businesses (ones with retail stores and online sites) are making this strategic move as a hedge against losing business to companies with Web-only sites, such as Amazon.com, e-Toys, and CDW, whose online-only presence made serious inroads into their respective markets.

These are examples of strategic changes in the delivery of services. Many companies also have made strategic changes in their product offerings. We see this, for example, in the product offerings at fast-food restaurants. Several now serve wraps and healthy salads in response to consumer demands. In an interesting move, McDonald's began competing against Starbucks by offering premium coffee, mochas, lattes, and cappuccinos. These menu items were added as a strategic move to develop new segments of the market.

Organizational structure

In addition to making strategic plans about changes in products and services, companies also make strategic plans about their organizational structures (see Chapter 13). Consider, for example, PepsiCo's strategic decision to reorganize.[13] For many years, it had a separate international food service division, which included 62 foreign locations of its Pizza Hut and Taco Bell restaurants. Then, in 1990, because of the great profit potential from these foreign restaurants, PepsiCo officials decided to reorganize, putting these restaurants under direct control of the same executives responsible for the successful U.S. operations of Pizza Hut, Kentucky Fried Chicken, and Taco Bell. In 1997, however, PepsiCo made another strategic decision to get out of the restaurant business altogether. It spun off these three restaurants to form a separate, totally independent company, TRICON Global Restaurants. Then, in 2002, it changed its name to Yum! Brands, and added A&W Root Beer and Long John Silver's restaurants to its collection. Headquartered in Louisville, Kentucky, Yum! is the world's largest restaurant company, with over 35,000 restaurants in more than 110 countries.[14]

These days, organizations are making strategic changes regarding the nature of the work they do. Many, in fact, have completely eliminated units that focus on non-core sectors of their business and then have hired outside firms to perform these functions instead. This practice is known as **outsourcing.** For example, companies like ServiceMaster, which offers janitorial services, and ADP, which provides payroll-processing services, allow organizations to concentrate on the business functions most central to their missions, thereby freeing them from dealing with these functions that are important but peripheral to their core businesses.

Companies also institute strategic plans to outsource when the work they want to do is highly specialized. For example, many manufacturing companies have found it more cost-effective to outsource their manufacturing operations to specialized companies than to build the expensive plants and then find the trained workers required to build certain products. In fact, one industry analyst has estimated that 30 percent of the largest U.S. industrial firms outsource more than half their manufacturing.[15]

It's not only manufacturing that is outsourced, however, but also customer service for high-tech companies. If you find that you're having problems installing a computer peripheral you just bought, for example, you might call the tech support number. When you do, the person at the other end of the line may be talking to you from India, the Philippines, or any of several other nations. These may be employees of the companies whose products you are using, but more likely, they work for one of the hundreds of third-party companies that specialize in offering these services. Because this outsourcing takes place abroad, it is referred to as **offshoring.** Employing about 400,000 people, the offshoring of IT (information technology) is one of the most widely used forms of outsourcing and is an enormous business of its own.[16]

The Strategic Planning Process

The process of strategic planning typically follows 10 ordered steps, which we now describe.[17] These steps are not immutable, and they are not always followed in perfect order. However, they do a reasonably good job of describing how companies plan change strategically. As we describe these steps, you may find it useful to follow the summary in Figure 14.1.

1. ***Define goals.***   Strategic plans begin with clearly stated goals (the desirability of which we described in Chapter 6 as a motivational tool). Typically, these involve gaining a certain share of the market (e.g., market penetration of 40 percent) or achieving a certain financial standing (doubling the P/E ratio in five years). Organizational goals also can involve society (e.g., making $1 million in charitable donations) or organizational culture (e.g., making the workplace more pleasant for employees). It is important to note that overall organizational goals must be translated into corresponding goals to be achieved by various individual units. For example, if a company has the goal of achieving

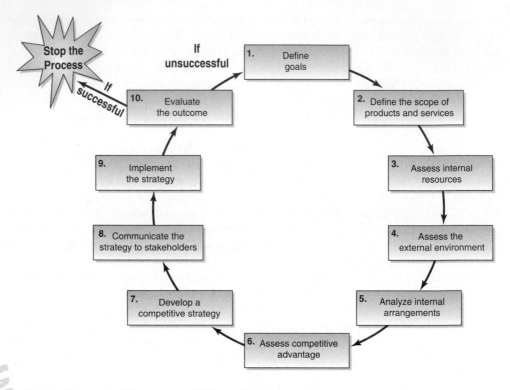

Figure 14.1 Strategic Planning: A 10-Step Process

Strategic planning—the process of formulating, implementing, and evaluating decisions that enable an organization to achieve its objectives—generally follows the 10 steps summarized here.

(Source: Based on suggestions by Christensen, 1994; see Note 17.)

10 percent penetration into a market, it is important to establish clear goals for the marketing department (e.g., how to advertise to reach the right customers) and the production department (e.g., producing finished products at the appropriate rate to meet market demands).

2. ***Define the scope of products or services.*** For a strategic plan to be effective, company officials must define their organization's scope—that is, the businesses in which it already operates and the new businesses in which it aims to participate. If a company's scope is defined too broadly, it will dilute its effectiveness; if scope is defined too narrowly, it will overlook opportunities. Beech-Nut faced this issue when confronted with the fact that lowered birthrates had shrunk the size of the market for baby foods. In an effort to rebuild its business, Beech-Nut executives made the strategic decision to broaden its scope by developing products to feed elderly people with digestive problems.[18]

3. ***Assess internal resources.*** Organizations must ask themselves: What resources does the company have available to plan and to implement its strategy? The resources in question may take the form of funds (e.g., cash to make purchases), physical assets (e.g., required space), and human assets (e.g., workers' knowledge and skills). The answers to these questions will help determine the nature and extent of changes that are possible.

4. ***Assess the external environment.*** As we have noted throughout this book, organizations do not operate in a vacuum. Rather, they function within environments that influence

their capacity to operate and to grow as desired. The extent to which the environment aids or hinders a company's growth—or even its existence—depends on several key factors. Specifically, a company has a favorable position in its environment under conditions in which: (1) its resources cannot easily be imitated by others, (2) its resources will not depreciate anytime soon, and (3) competitors do not have better resources.[19]

5. *Analyze internal arrangements.*   By "internal arrangements," we are referring to the nature of the organization itself. For example, are employees motivated to strive for corporate goals (see Chapter 6)? Does the organizational culture encourage people to be innovative and make changes (see Chapter 12)? Do people communicate with one another clearly enough to accomplish their goals (see Chapter 8)? These and other basic questions about the organization must be answered to formulate an effective strategic plan. After all, unless the organization is operating properly, even the best strategic plans are doomed to fail.

6. *Assess the competitive advantage.*   One company is said to have a competitive advantage over another to the extent that customers perceive its products or services as being superior to those of other companies. Superiority may be assessed in terms of factors such as quality, price, breadth of product line, reliability of performance, styling, service, and company image.

7. *Develop a competitive strategy.*   A competitive strategy is the means by which an organization achieves its goal. Based on careful assessment of the company's standing regarding the factors described earlier (e.g., available resources, competitive advantage, and so on), a decision is made about how to achieve its goal. Some possible strategies are described in Table 14.3.

8. *Communicate the strategy to stakeholders.*   The term **stakeholder** refers to an individual or group in whose interest the organization is run. The most important stakeholders include employees at all levels, boards of directors, and stockholders. It is essential to communicate a firm's strategy to stakeholders so they may contribute to its success, whether actively (e.g., employees who pitch in to help meet the goals) or passively (e.g., investors who pour money into the company to help meet goals). Unless stakeholders fully understand and accept a firm's strategy, that firm is unlikely to receive the full support needed to achieve its goals.

Table 14.3   Varieties of Competitive Strategies

Some of the most popular competitive strategies used by today's organizations are summarized here.

Strategy	Description
Market-share increasing strategies	Developing a broader share of an existing market, such as by widening the range of products, or by forming a joint venture (see Chapter 13) with another company that already has a presence in the market of interest
Profit strategies	Attempting to derive more profit from existing businesses, such as by training employees to work more efficiently or salespeople to sell more effectively
Market concentration strategies	Withdrawing from markets where the company is less effective and concentrating resources in markets where the company is likely to be more effective
Turnaround strategies	Attempting to reverse a decline in business by moving to a new product line or by radically restructuring operations
Exit strategies	Withdrawing from a market, such as by liquidating assets

9. *Implement the strategy.*   Once a strategy has been formulated and communicated, the time has come for it to be implemented. When this occurs, some fallout is inevitable as employees scramble to adjust to new ways of doing things. As we will explain later, people generally resist change, although steps can be taken to help individuals embrace the changes they need to make.

10. *Evaluate the outcome.*   Finally, after a strategy has been implemented, it is crucial to determine if the goals have been met. If so, new goals may be sought; if not, different goals may be defined or different strategies may be followed to achieve success next time.

If, after reading this, you are thinking that developing a strategic plan is very difficult and that carrying it out is even more challenging, you have reached the same conclusion as many top executives. For practice in creating your own strategic plan, see the Self-Assessment Exercise on pages 425–426.

READINESS FOR CHANGE: ACCEPTING AND RESISTING ORGANIZATIONAL CHANGE

As you might imagine, there are times when organizations are likely to change and times when change is less likely. In general, change is likely to occur when the people involved believe that the benefits associated with making a change outweigh the costs involved. The factors contributing to the benefits of making a change are as follows:

➤   The amount of dissatisfaction with current conditions
➤   The availability of a desirable alternative
➤   The existence of a plan for achieving that alternative

Theorists have claimed that these three factors combine multiplicatively to determine the benefits of making a change (see Figure 14.2). Thus, if any one of these factors is zero, the benefits of making a change and the likelihood of change itself will be zero. If you think about it, this makes sense. After all, people are unlikely to initiate

Figure 14.2   Organizational Change: When Will It Occur?

Whether or not an organizational change is made depends on people's beliefs regarding the relative benefits and costs of that change. The benefits are reflected by the three considerations reviewed here.

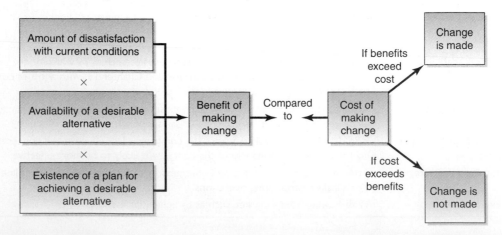

change if they are not at all dissatisfied or if they don't have any desirable alternative in mind (or any way of attaining that alternative, if they do have one in mind). Of course, for change to occur, the expected benefits must outweigh the likely costs involved (e.g., disruption, uncertainties).

Why Is Organizational Change Resisted?

Although people may be unhappy with the current state of affairs confronting them in organizations, they may be afraid that any changes will be potentially disruptive and will only make things worse.[20] Indeed, fear of new conditions is quite real and it creates unwillingness to accept change. Organizational scientists have recognized that **resistance to change** stems from both individual and organizational variables.

Individual barriers to change

Several factors that are threatening to individuals and that elicit their concerns are known to make people resistant to change in organizations.[21] Some of the key ones are as follows:

➤ *Economic insecurity.*   Because any changes on the job have the potential to threaten one's livelihood—by either loss of job or reduced pay—some resistance to change is inevitable.

➤ *Fear of the unknown.*   Employees derive a sense of security from doing things the same way, knowing whom their co-workers will be, and whom they're supposed to answer to from day to day. Disrupting these well-established, comfortable patterns creates unfamiliar conditions, a state of affairs that is often threatening, hence rejected.

➤ *Threats to social relationships.*   As people continue to work within organizations, they form strong bonds with their co-workers. Many organizational changes (e.g., the reassignment of job responsibilities) threaten the integrity of friendship groups that provide valuable social rewards.

➤ *Habit.*   Jobs that are well learned and become habitual are easy to perform. The prospect of changing the way jobs are done challenges people to develop new job skills. Doing this is usually more difficult than continuing to perform the job as it was learned originally. Although some may enjoy the challenge (see Chapter 6), many other people prefer the comfort of the routine.

➤ *Failure to recognize need for change.*   Unless employees can recognize and fully appreciate the need for changes in organizations, any vested interests they may have in keeping things the same may overpower their willingness to accept change. Until they acknowledge that things need to be improved, they will be content to accept the comfort of the status quo.

Organizational barriers to change

Resistance to organizational change also stems from conditions associated with organizations themselves.[22] Several such factors may be identified:

➤ *Structural inertia.*   Organizations are designed to promote stability. To the extent that employees are carefully selected and trained to perform certain jobs and are rewarded for doing them well, the forces acting on individuals to behave in certain ways are very powerfully determined—that is, jobs have *structural inertia*. And because jobs are designed to have stability, people are reluctant to shake things up.

➤ *Work group inertia.*   Inertia to continue performing jobs in a specified way comes not only from the jobs themselves but also from the social groups within which people work—*work group inertia*. Because of the development of strong social norms within groups (see Chapter 9), potent pressures exist to perform jobs in certain ways. Introducing change disrupts these established normative expectations, leading to formidable resistance.

➤ **Threats to the existing balance of power.**   If changes are made with respect to who is in charge, a shift in the balance of power between individuals and organizational sub-units is likely to occur. Those units that now control the resources, have the expertise, and wield the power may fear losing their advantageous positions resulting from any organizational changes.

➤ **Previously unsuccessful change efforts.**   Anyone who has lived through a past disaster understandably may be reluctant to endure another attempt at the same thing. Similarly, groups or entire organizations that have been unsuccessful in introducing change in the past may be cautious about accepting further attempts at introducing change into the system.

A classic case

During the 1980s and 1990s, General Electric (GE) underwent a widespread series of changes in its basic strategy, organizational structure, and relationship with employees. In this process, it experienced several of the barriers just identified. For example, GE managers had mastered a set of bureaucratic traditions that kept their habits strong and their inertia moving straight ahead. The prospect of doing things differently was scary for those who were so strongly entrenched in doing things the "GE way."

In particular, the company's interest in globalizing triggered many fears of the unknown. Resistance to change at GE also was strong because it threatened to strip organizational power from those units that traditionally possessed most of it (e.g., the Power Systems and Lighting division). Changes also were highly disruptive to GE's "social architecture"; friendship groups were broken up and scattered throughout the company. In all, GE has been a good example of many different barriers to change operating within a single company.

Factors Affecting Resistance to Change

To overcome resistance to change, it helps to discover the individual variables (e.g., personality) and aspects of the work setting to which such resistance is most closely linked. Doing this helps identify specific ways of changing people and/or changing situations so as to make employees more accepting of organizational change.

This approach was taken in a study of officials who worked for a large governmental agency.[23] Using questionnaires that assessed a variety of different individual differences and situational factors, the researchers sought to identify the factors that were linked most closely to an important concept—openness to change (i.e., the extent to which someone is willing to accept changes in their organization). The researchers found that three variables in particular were most strongly linked to openness to change: resilience (i.e., the extent to which they are capable of bouncing back from adversity; recall the discussion of this variable in conjunction with the material on stress in Chapter 4), information about change (i.e., specific facts about how things will be different), and change self-efficacy (i.e., beliefs in one's ability to function effectively despite the demands of change). As summarized at the top of Figure 14.3, the relationship between each of these variables and openness to change was positive—in other words, greater amounts of these variables were associated with greater openness to change.

Resilience, information about change, and change self-efficacy are associated with openness to change . . .

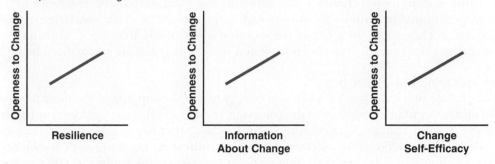

. . .and openness to change, in turn, is related to job satisfaction, work-related irritation, and intention to quit.

Figure 14.3 Variables Linked to Openness to Change: Research Findings

As summarized at the top of this diagram, three factors—resilience, information about change, and change self-efficacy—are positively associated with openness to change. And, as shown at the bottom, openness to change is in turn related to job satisfaction, work-related irritation, and intention to quit.

(Source: Based on findings reported by Wanberg & Banas, 2000; see Note 23.)

Of course, it's not only what people report on a questionnaire about their openness to change that matters but also how openness is related to key aspects of people's work attitudes and behavior. To learn about this, the researchers also assessed a number of variables in their questionnaire. What they found was interesting. Three particular variables were strongly associated with openness to change (see bottom portion of Figure 14.3). The first was job satisfaction (see Chapter 5). The more open to change employees were, the more satisfied they tended to be with their jobs, the less work-related irritation they showed (i.e., the less they tended to get angry or aggravated at work), and the less likely they were to consider quitting their jobs. Thus, openness to change can make a big difference when it comes to these important aspects of the job.

In view of this, an effort should be made to make employees more resilient to change, to increase the amount of information they have available about how their organizations will change, and to boost their beliefs that they will be able to respond positively to new work situations. As you will see in the next section, several of these suggestions are incorporated into specific approaches to overcoming resistance to organizational change.

How Can Resistance to Organizational Change Be Overcome?

Because organizational change is inevitable despite many employees' resistance to it, managers should be sensitive to ways in which resistance can be overcome. Helping people accept changes in their organizations often is easier said than done. Fortunately, several useful approaches have been suggested, and the key ones are summarized here.[24]

Shape political dynamics

For change to be accepted, it's often necessary to win the support of the most powerful and influential individuals in the company. Doing so builds a critical internal mass of support for change. Demonstrating convincingly that key organizational leaders endorse the change is an effective way to get others to go along with it—either because they share the leaders' vision or because they fear the leaders' retaliation for not going along with them. Hopefully, the shared vision will encourage compliance with change efforts because its effects will be more long-lasting and its impact on organizational culture (see Chapter 12) will be more positive, but either basis for support will facilitate acceptance of change.

Educate the workforce

Sometimes people are reluctant to change because they fear what the future has in store for them. To assuage these fears, they typically turn to experts. For example, to overcome financial concerns, investors may seek advice from financial advisors, experts who they trust (sometimes too much, as recent history has taught us) to lead them in the right direction (i.e., to make the right changes in their portfolios).

As part of educating employees about what organizational changes may mean for them, top management must show a considerable amount of emotional sensitivity. Doing so makes it possible for the people affected by change to help make it work. Some companies have found that simply answering the question, "What's in it for me?" can help allay a lot of fears.

"Sell" the need for change

For organizational change to occur, top management must accept the idea that change is required. And quite often, it's lower-level practicing managers, those who toil daily in the trenches, who offer the best ideas. For these ideas to be accepted and implemented, however, it's necessary for top officials to be convinced that the ideas are worthwhile.

How, then, do managers "sell" their bosses on the need for change? Scientists examined this question in an interesting study.[25] The researchers interviewed managers from various departments in a large hospital, inquiring as to how they went about presenting their ideas for change to top management. Carefully analyzing the responses led them to identify the following three major approaches, known as "issue selling" techniques (for a summary, see Figure 14.4).

➤ *Packaging moves.*   This involves combining several ideas into a coherent whole. It includes such approaches as presenting one's ideas in the form of a clear business plan and "bundling" those ideas together with other key organizational concerns (e.g., profitability).

➤ *Involvement moves.*   This has to do with involving other people in the selling of the idea, such as other top-level personnel, others at the same level, or even others outside the organization.

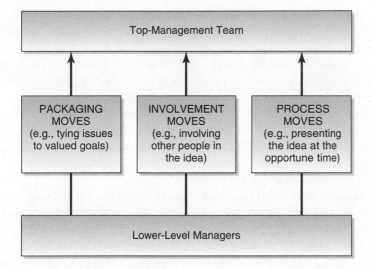

Figure 14.4   How Do Managers "Sell" Ideas About Change to Their Superiors?

Interviews with managers have revealed that to "sell" their superiors on ideas about organizational change, they rely on the three kinds of "moves" identified here.

(Source: Based on suggestions by Dutton et al., 2001; see Note 25.)

> ➤ *Process moves.*   This involves paying attention to matters of form and style, such as giving a thorough presentation with all the issues carefully thought out and presenting ideas at the most opportune time and in a persistent fashion.

Although one cannot guarantee that top leaders always will follow the advice of their lower level managers, for them to have any chance of doing so, they must be convinced of the merit of their ideas. And to increase the chances that managers' good ideas will come across, it may well help to follow these moves.

Involve employees in the change efforts

It is well established that people who participate in making a decision tend to be more committed to the outcomes of that decision than are those who are not involved. Accordingly, employees who are involved in responding to unplanned change, or who are made part of the team charged with planning a needed organizational change, may be expected to have very little resistance to change. Employees who are involved in the change process are better able to understand the need for change and are, therefore, less likely to resist it. In the words of a former general manager at Hewlett-Packard's microwave instruments division, "I don't think people really enjoy change, but if they can participate in it and understand it, it can become a positive [experience] for them."[26] In contrast, organizational changes that are "sprung" on the workforce with little or no warning might meet resistance simply as a knee-jerk reaction until employees have a chance to assess how the change affects them.

It's important to emphasize that involving employees in change efforts means more than simply giving them a voice in determining the organization's operations. It also means actively engaging employees at all levels in the problems the organization faces. Here's an example. For many years, officials from Shell Malaysia were unsuccessful in getting employees to work together to outsell the competition. They were highly complacent, and the competition was rapidly gaining market share as a result. In response to this, company officials called together all 260 managers for a $2\frac{1}{2}$-day session in which the problem of the rapidly encroaching competition was put before them. They emerged from this marathon session with a firm plan that was put into place. Back on the job, regular follow-up meetings were held to make sure the plan was implemented. Because the employees bought into the problem and met the challenge themselves, they rose to the occasion (as predicted by goal setting theory described in Chapter 6), making Shell Malaysia successful in changing the way it operated.

Reward constructive behaviors

One rather obvious and highly successful mechanism for facilitating organizational change involves rewarding people for behaving in the desired fashion (as based on principles of learning described in Chapter 3). Changing an organization's operations, for example, may necessitate changing the kinds of employee behaviors that need to be rewarded. This is especially critical when an organization is in the transition period of introducing the change. For example, employees who are required to learn to use new equipment should be praised for their successful efforts. Feedback on how well they are doing not only provides a great deal of useful assurance to uncertain employees but also helps shape the desired behavior (again, see Chapter 3).

Stress the urgency of change

It's not unusual for company officials to get in a rut, becoming lazy and complacent about the way they operate, even when it's necessary to take decisive action. This is *almost* what happened to Sears several years ago. The retailing giant was losing customers rapidly as officers sat by merely lowering sales goals. That's when Sears' CEO at the time, Arthur Martinez, lit a fire under everyone by stressing the importance of turning things around—or else! He generated a sense of urgency by setting very challenging goals (e.g., quadrupling market share, and increasing customer satisfaction by 15 percent). Although Martinez didn't have all the answers to Sears' problems, he provided something even more important—straightforward, honest talk about the company's problems, creating a sense of urgency that got everyone moving in the right direction (recall our discussion of the important role of feedback in the goal setting process discussed in Chapter 6).

Create relentless discomfort with the status quo

Following military maneuvers, the U.S. Army thoroughly debriefs all participants in what is called an "after action review." In these sessions, careful feedback is given about what soldiers did well and where they need to improve. By focusing in a relentless, detailed manner on work that needs to be done, officers eventually get soldiers to internalize the need for excellence. Soldiers return to their home bases asking themselves how they can do something better (faster, less expensively, more safely, or more accurately) or if there is a new and better approach that could be taken. In short, the status quo is the enemy; current performance levels are never accepted. Things can always be better. Army brass liken this commitment to continuous improvement to painting a bridge: The job is never over. Such an orientation also works well in other organizations.

Table 14.4   Ways to Become a Learning Organization

Learning organizations are successful at acquiring, cultivating, and applying knowledge that can be used to help them adapt to change. For an organization to become an effective learning organization, managers must follow the rules outlined here.

Rule	Description
Establish a commitment to change	Unless all employees clearly see top management as being strongly committed to changing and to improving the organization, they will be unlikely to invest in the changes necessary to bring about such improvements.
Adopt an informal organizational structure	Change is more readily accepted when organizational structures are flat (see Chapter 13), when cross-functional teams are created (see Chapter 9), and when formal boundaries between people are eliminated.
Develop an open organizational culture	As described in Chapter 12, managers play a key role in forming organizational culture. To adapt effectively to changes in their environments, organizations should have cultures that embrace risk taking, openness, and growth.

Create a "learning organization"

Although all organizations change, whether they want to or not, some do so more effectively than others. Those organizations that have developed the capacity to adapt and change continuously are known as **learning organizations.**[27] In learning organizations, people set aside old ways of thinking, freely share ideas with others, form a vision of the organization, and work together on a plan for achieving that vision. In many key respects, General Electric, Motorola, and Wal-Mart are good examples of learning organizations because within them the quest for improvement is ongoing.

As you might imagine, becoming a learning organization is no simple feat. In fact, it involves implementing many of the principles of organizational behavior described in this book. Specifically, for a firm to become a continual learner, management must follow the three steps outlined in Table 14.4. Although these suggestions may be easier to state than to implement, efforts at following them will be well rewarded. Given the many forces that make employees resistant to change, managers should keep these guidelines in mind. (For a chance to think more about resistance to organizational change and ways to overcome it, see the Group Exercise on p. 426.)

ORGANIZATIONAL DEVELOPMENT INTERVENTIONS: IMPLEMENTING PLANNED CHANGE

Now that you know the basic issues surrounding organizational change, we are prepared to examine systematic ways of implementing it—tactics collectively known as techniques of **organizational development (OD).** Formally, organizational development may be defined as a set of social science techniques designed to plan and implement change in work settings for purposes of enhancing the personal development of individuals and improving the effectiveness of organizational functioning. By planning organization-wide changes involving people, OD seeks to enhance organizational performance by improving the quality of the work environment and the attitudes and well-being of the employees within them.[28]

Over the years, many different strategies for implementing planned organizational change (referred to as **OD interventions**) have been used by specialists attempting to improve organizational functioning (referred to as **OD practitioners** or **change agents**). These individuals, usually from outside the organization, coordinate and facilitate an organization's change efforts. All the major methods of organizational development attempt to produce some kind of change in individual employees, work groups, and/or entire organizations.[29] This is the goal of all OD intervention techniques, including the three reviewed here.

Survey Feedback

For effective organizational change to occur, employees must understand their organization's current strengths and weaknesses. That's the underlying rationale behind the **survey feedback** method.[30] This technique, designed to get employees to take inventory of the state of their organizations, follows the three steps summarized in Figure 14.5.

1. Data are collected that provide information about matters of general concern to employees, such as organizational culture (see Chapter 12), leadership style (see Chapter 11), and job satisfaction (see Chapter 5). This may take the form of intensive interviews, structured questionnaires, or both. Because it is important that this information be as unbiased as possible, employees providing feedback should be assured that their responses will be kept confidential. For this reason, this process is usually conducted by outside consultants instead of company employees.

2. The information obtained is reported back to the employees during small group meetings. Typically, this consists of summarizing the average scores on the attitudes assessed in the survey. Profiles are created of feelings about the organization, its leadership, the work done, and related topics. Discussions also focus on why the scores are as they are and what problems are revealed by the feedback.

3. Problems dealing with communication (see Chapter 8), decision making (see Chapter 10), and other organizational processes are analyzed to make plans for dealing with them. Such discussions are usually most effective when they are carefully documented and a specific plan of implementation is made with someone put in charge of carrying it out.

Survey feedback is a widely used organizational development technique. This is not surprising in view of the advantages it offers. It is efficient, allowing a great deal of

Figure 14.5   Survey Feedback: An Overview

The *survey feedback* technique of OD follows the three steps outlined here: collecting data, giving feedback, and developing action plans.

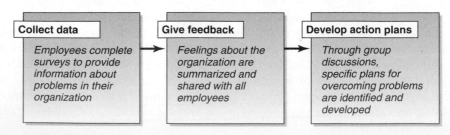

information to be collected relatively quickly. Also, it is very flexible and can be tailored to the needs of different organizations facing a variety of problems. However, the technique can be no better than the quality of the questionnaire used—it must measure the things that really matter to employees.

Of course, to derive the maximum benefit from survey feedback, it must have the support of top management. The plans developed by the small discussion groups must be capable of being implemented with the full approval of the organization. When these conditions are met, survey feedback can be a very effective OD technique. (The basic idea behind survey feedback is that employees receive information that guides them through the process of making changes. However, another source of information that may be used for this purpose comes from finding out what competitors are doing. For a closer look at this practice, see the Winning Practices section below.)

Winning Practices

Using Online Competitive Intelligence for Organizational Change

Only about 10 percent of American companies do it, and the other 90 percent probably should. What, you ask? Use **competitive intelligence (CI)**—the process of gathering information about competitors that can be used as the basis for planning organizational change.

CI is a search for clues about what competitors are doing or considering doing and then staying ahead of them by using this information as part of the strategic planning process. To stay competitive, some of the biggest companies—especially those in rapidly changing, high-tech fields, such as General Electric, Motorola, Microsoft, Hewlett-Packard, IBM, AT&T, and Intel—engage in CI all the time. In fact, Gary Costley, former president of Kellogg Co. North America, says that managers who don't engage in CI are "incompetent" insofar as it is "irresponsible to not understand your competitors."[31]

It's important not to dismiss CI on the grounds that it is unethical. CI is not industrial espionage (which involves illegally spying on competitors), and it is completely legal. CI efforts usually involve gathering readily available information, such as that contained in public records. In fact, it has been said that 90 percent of all the information a company needs to make critical decisions and to understand its market and its competitors is available in public data.[32]

For example, companies are required to disclose information on their finances, inventories, and compliance with various legal regulations. Documents containing this information are available to anyone online, and growing numbers of competitors are availing themselves of such information.

Research has found that the more a company uses the Internet for CI, the better is the quality of the competitive intelligence information it is able to collect. And, as the quality of competitive intelligence information improves, so too does a firm's capacity to make strategic decisions (see Chapter 10).[33] After all, companies that have competitive information not only recognize the need for change but also may find it possible to make the kinds of changes that are necessary to succeed. Not surprisingly, companies that use advanced systems to monitor their competitors' activities are more profitable than those that do not have such systems in place.[34]

Management by Objectives

In Chapter 6, we discussed the motivational benefits of setting specific goals. As you might imagine, not only individuals but also entire organizations stand to benefit from setting specific goals. For example, an organization may strive to "raise production" and to "improve the quality" of its manufactured goods. These goals, well-intentioned though they may be, will not be as useful to an organization as more specific goals, such as "increase production of widgets by 15 percent" or "lower the failure rate of widgets by 25 percent." After all, as the old saying goes, "It's usually easier to get somewhere if you know where you're going." The late Peter Drucker, consulting for General Electric during the early 1950s, was well aware of this idea and is credited with promoting the benefits of specifying clear organizational goals—a technique known as **management by objectives (MBO).**[35]

The MBO process, summarized in Figure 14.6, consists of three basic steps. These are as follows:

1. ***Goal selection.***   Goals are selected that employees will try to attain to best serve the needs of the organization. The goals should be selected by managers and their subordinates together. The goals must be set mutually by everyone involved, not simply imposed.

Figure 14.6   Management by Objectives: Developing Organizations Through Goal Setting

The OD technique of *management by objectives* requires managers and subordinates to work together on setting and trying to achieve important organizational goals. The basic steps in the process are outlined here.

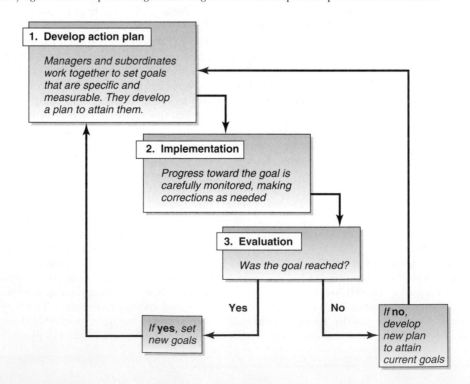

Furthermore, these goals should be directly measurable and have some time frame attached to them. Goals that cannot be measured (e.g., "make the company better") or that have no time limits are useless. It is also crucial that managers and their subordinates work together to plan ways of attaining the goals they have selected—developing what is known as an *action plan.*

2. *Implementation.*   Once goals are set and action plans have been developed, the second step calls for *implementation*—carrying out the plan and regularly assessing its progress. Is the plan working? Are the goals being approximated? Are any problems encountered in attempting to meet the goals? Such questions need to be considered while implementing an action plan. If the plan is failing, a midcourse correction may be in order—changing the plan, the way it's carried out, or even the goal itself.

3. *Evaluation.*   Finally, after monitoring progress toward the goal, the third step may be instituted: *evaluation*—assessing goal attainment. Were the organization's goals reached? If so, what new goals should be set to improve things still further? If not, what new plans can be initiated to help meet the goals? Because the ultimate assessment of the extent to which goals are met helps determine the selection of new goals, MBO is a continuous process.

MBO represents a potentially effective source of planning and implementing strategic change for organizations. Individual efforts designed to meet organizational goals get individual employees and their organizations working together toward common ends. Under the conditions, system-wide change results.[36] Of course, for MBO to work, everyone involved has to buy into it. Because MBO programs typically require a great deal of participation by lower-level employees, top managers must be willing to accept and support the cooperation and involvement of all.

Making MBO work also requires a great deal of time—anywhere from three to five years. Hence, MBO may be inappropriate for use in organizations that do not have the time to commit to making it work.

Despite these considerations, MBO has become one of the most widely used techniques for affecting organizational change in recent years. It not only is used on an ad hoc basis by many organizations but it also is an ingrained element of the organizational culture in several companies, such as Hewlett-Packard and IBM.

Appreciative Inquiry

Although survey feedback and MBO are highly regarded OD techniques, they focus on deficiencies, such as negative feedback and unmet goals. A relatively new approach to organizational development known as *appreciative inquiry* helps organizations break out of this focus on negative dynamics by emphasizing the positive and the possible.[37] Specifically, **appreciative inquiry** is an OD intervention that focuses attention away from an organization's shortcomings and toward its capabilities and its potential. It is based on the assumption that members of organizations already know the problems they face and that they stand to benefit more by focusing on what is possible.

As currently practiced, the process of appreciative inquiry follows four straight-forward steps. These are as follows:[38]

1. *Discovery.*   The discovery step involves identifying the positive aspects of the organization, the best of "what is." This frequently is accomplished by documenting the positive reactions of customers or people from other organizations.

2. *Dreaming.*   Through the process of discovering the organization's strengths, it is possible to begin dreaming by envisioning "what might be." By discussing dreams for a theoretically ideal organization, employees are free to reveal their ideal hopes and dreams.

3. *Designing.*   The designing stage involves having a dialogue in which participants discuss their ideas about "what should be." The underlying idea is that by listening to others in a highly receptive manner, it is possible to understand others' ideas and to come to a common understanding of what the future should look like.

4. *Delivering.*   After having jointly discussed the ideal state of affairs, members of the organization are ready to begin instituting a plan for delivering their ideas. This involves establishing specific objectives and directions regarding "what will be."

Because appreciative inquiry is an emerging approach to OD, it has not been used widely. However, officials of organizations in which it has been used have been quite satisfied with the results.[39]

KEY QUESTIONS ABOUT ORGANIZATIONAL DEVELOPMENT

No discussion of organizational development would be complete without addressing three important questions—do the techniques work, are their effects dependent on national culture, and are they ethical? We now turn to these questions.

The Effectiveness of Organizational Development: Does It Really Work?

Thus far, we have described some of the major techniques used by OD practitioners to improve organizational functioning. As is probably clear, carrying out these techniques requires a considerable amount of time, money, and effort. Accordingly, it is appropriate to ask if this investment is worthwhile. In other words, does OD really work? Given the popularity of OD in organizations, this question is quite important.

The answer is generally yes: Research has shown that OD interventions tend to be beneficial when it comes to improving organizational functioning.[40] We hasten to add that any conclusions about the effectiveness of OD should be qualified in several important ways. Specifically:

➤ OD interventions generally are more effective among blue-collar employees than among white-collar employees.

➤ The beneficial effects of OD can be enhanced by using a combination of several techniques instead of any single one.

➤ To be effective, OD techniques must have the support of top management; the more strongly OD programs are supported from the top, the more successful they are.

Despite the importance of attempting to evaluate the effectiveness of OD interventions, a great many of them go unevaluated. Although there are undoubtedly many reasons for this, one key factor is the difficulty of assessing change. Because many factors can cause people to behave differently in organizations, and because such behaviors may be difficult to measure, many OD practitioners avoid the problem of measuring change altogether. In a related vein, political pressures to justify OD programs may discourage some

OD professionals from honestly and accurately assessing their effectiveness. After all, in doing so, one runs the risk of scientifically demonstrating one's wasted time and money.

Is Organizational Development Dependent on National Culture?

For organizational development to be effective, people must be willing to share their ideas candidly with others, they must be willing to accept uncertainty, and they must be willing to show concern for others, especially members of their own teams. However, not all people are willing to do these things; this pattern better characterizes the people from some countries than others. For example, this profile perfectly describes people from Scandinavian countries, suggesting that OD may be especially effective in such nations. However, people from Latin American nations are much the opposite, suggesting that OD interventions will be not particularly successful when conducted there.[41] For a summary of the extent to which the basic assumptions of OD fit with the cultural styles of people from various nations, see Figure 14.7.

Although the predominant cultural values of people from the United States places it in the middle region of diagram in Figure 14.7, this is not to say that OD is doomed to be ineffective in American companies. Not all OD techniques are alike with respect to their underlying cultural values.[42] For example, MBO has become a very popular OD technique in the United States in large part because it promotes the American values of willingness to take risks and to work aggressively at attaining high performance. However, because MBO also encourages superiors and subordinates to negotiate freely with each other, the technique has been generally unsuccessful in France, where others' higher levels of authority are well accepted.[43] Reasoning similarly, one may expect survey feedback to be unsuccessful in the Southeast Asian nation of Brunei, where the prevailing cultural value is such that problems are unlikely to be confronted openly.[44]

These examples illustrate a key point: The effectiveness of OD techniques will depend, in part, on the extent to which the values of the technique match the underlying values of the national culture in which it is employed. As such, OD practitioners

Figure 14.7   Organizational Development: Its Fit with Cultural Values

Organizational development (OD) techniques tend to be more successful when the underlying values of the technique match the cultural values of the nation in which it is used. General OD values tend to conform more to the cultural values of some nations, shown on the right (where OD is more likely to be accepted) than to others, shown on the left (where OD is less likely to be accepted).

(Source: Based on suggestions by Jaeger, 1986; see Note 41.)

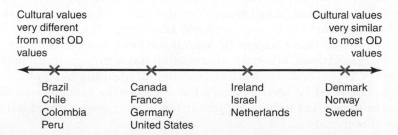

Cultural values very different from most OD values			Cultural values very similar to most OD values
Brazil	Canada	Ireland	Denmark
Chile	France	Israel	Norway
Colombia	Germany	Netherlands	Sweden
Peru	United States		

must fully appreciate the cultural norms of the nations in which they are operating. Failure to do so not only may make OD interventions unsuccessful, but they also may even have unintended negative consequences.

Is Organizational Development Inherently Unethical? A Debate

By its very nature, OD applies powerful social science techniques in an attempt to change attitudes and behavior. From the perspective of a manager attempting to accomplish various goals, such tools are immediately recognized as very useful. However, if you think about it from the perspective of the individual being affected, three key ethical issues arise:[45]

1. OD techniques impose the values of the organization on the individual without taking the individual's own attitudes into account. OD is a very one-sided approach, reflecting the imposition of the more powerful organization on the less powerful individual.

2. The OD process does not provide any free choice on the part of the employees. As a result, it may be seen as *coercive* and *manipulative*. When faced with a "do it, or else" situation, employees tend to have little free choice and are forced to allow themselves to be manipulated, a potentially degrading prospect.

3. The unequal power relationship between an organization and its employees makes it possible for the true intent of OD techniques to be misrepresented. As an example, imagine that an MBO technique is presented to employees as a means of allowing greater organizational participation, whereas in reality it is used as a means for holding individuals responsible for their poor performance and punishing them as a result. Although such an event might not happen, the potential for abuse of this type does exist, and the potential to misuse the technique—even if not originally intended—might later prove to be too great a temptation.

Despite these considerations, many professionals do *not* consider OD to be inherently unethical. Such a claim, it has been countered, is to say that the practice of management is itself unethical. After all, the very act of going to work for an organization requires one to submit to the organization's values and the overall values of society. One cannot help but face life situations in which others' values are imposed. This is not to say that organizations have the right to impose patently unethical values on people for making a profit (e.g., stealing from customers). Indeed, because they have the potential to abuse their power (such as in the MBO example), organizations have a special obligation to refrain from doing so.

Although abuses of organizational power sometimes occur, OD itself is not necessarily the culprit. Indeed, like any other tool (even a gun!), OD is not inherently good or evil. Instead, *whether the tool is used for good or evil will depend on the individual using it*. With this in mind, the ethical use of OD interventions will require that they be supervised by professionals in an organization that places a high value on ethics.

To the extent that top management officials embrace ethical values and behave ethically themselves (see Chapter 2), norms for behaving ethically are likely to develop in organizations. When an organization has a strong ethical culture, it is unlikely that OD practitioners would even think of misusing their power to harm individuals. The need to develop such a culture has been recognized as a way for organizations to take not only moral leadership in their communities but financial leadership as well.

Back to the Case

Answer the following questions about this chapter's Making the Case (p. 399) to illustrate insights you have derived from the material in this chapter.

1. What form of change is occurring at Asustek? What factors appear to be triggering these changes?
2. What forces for change is Asustek likely to experience in the years ahead?
3. To what degree would you suspect that Asustek employees will be resistant to the kinds of changes required for the company to succeed at its strategic plan? What can be done to overcome such resistance?

You Be the Consultant

Promoting Organizational Change

Things have been rough for the former employees at Small Town S&L ever since their institution was bought by First National Mega Bank. First National's procedures were more formal than those at Small Town. The CEO of First National is concerned about the employees' reacting negatively to the change and calls upon you for help. Answer the following questions relevant to this situation based on the material in this chapter.

1. Besides new operating procedures, what other planned and unplanned changes would you suspect are responsible for the employees' negative responses?
2. What barriers to change are likely to be encountered in this situation, and what steps would you propose to overcome them?
3. Do you think that an OD intervention would help in this case? If so, which one (or ones) do you propose, and why?

SELF-ASSESSMENT EXERCISE

Developing a Strategic Plan

Developing a strategic plan is not easy. In fact, doing it right requires a great deal of information—and a great deal of practice. This exercise will give you a feel for some of the challenges involved in developing such a plan.

Directions

1. Suppose you are the president of a small software-development firm that for years has sold a utility that added functionality to the operating system used in most computers. Now, you suddenly face a serious problem: Microsoft has introduced a new version of Windows that has made your product completely unnecessary.
2. Using the 10 steps outlined in Figure 14.1 (p. 408), develop a strategic plan to keep your company alive. Make any assumptions you need to develop your plan, but state these in the process of describing the plan.

Discussion Questions

1. How easy or difficult was it to develop this plan? What would have made the process easier?
2. What step do you imagine would be the easiest to implement? Which step do you think would be the most challenging?
3. What special challenges, if any, would the employees of your company face as they implemented this plan? How would you attempt to overcome these challenges?

GROUP EXERCISE

Recognizing and Overcoming Impediments to Change

When it comes to confronting the reality of organizational change, one of the most fundamental steps involves recognizing barriers to change. Then, once these impediments have been identified, consideration can be given to ways of overcoming them. This exercise is designed to help you practice thinking along these lines while working in groups.

Directions

1. Divide the class into groups of approximately six and arrange each group into a circle.
2. Each group should consider both of the following situations.
   - *Situation A:*   A large university is shifting from the quarter system to a semester system. The new scheduling will be introduced in one year and it will be university-wide.
   - *Situation B:*   A very popular employee who's been with the company for many years is retiring. He will be replaced by a completely new employee from the outside.
3. For each situation, discuss three major impediments to change.
4. Identify a way of overcoming each of these impediments.
5. Someone from the group should record the answers and present them to the class for a discussion session.

Discussion Questions

1. For each of the situations, were the impediments to change similar or different?
2. For each of the situations, were the ways of overcoming the impediments similar or different?
3. How might the nature of the situation confronted dictate the types of change barriers confronted and the ease with which these may be overcome?

Notes

Chapter 1

Case Notes

Forgrieve, J. (2008, May 23). Five questions for Rob O'Brien. *Rocky Mountain News*, p. 19. O'Brien, K. (2008). *The Floyd's story*. Online at floydsbarbershop.com. Cho, C. H. (2006, August 16). Male-themed salons: Barbershops with style. *Los Angeles Times*, pp. C1, C7. Kretikos, E. (2005, July 8–14). Forget Mayberry, this new Floyd's cuts a hip profile. *Washington Business Journal*, p. 7.

Chapter Notes

1. Hoover's. (2008). *Hair care services*. Austin, TX: Author. Beauty Salons Marketing Research (2008). Accessed online at http://www.researchwikis.com/Beauty_Salons_Market_Research
2. Miner, J. B. (2002). *Organizational behavior: Foundations, theories, analyses*. New York: Oxford University Press.
3. Colquitt, J. A., & Zapata-Phelan, C. P. (2008). Trends in theory building and theory testing: A five-decade study of the *Academy of Management Journal*. *Academy of Management Journal, 50*, 1281–1303. Rogelberg, S. G. (2002). *Handbook of research methods in industrial and organizational psychology*. Malden, MA: Blackwell.
4. Chingos, P. T., & Ferracone, R. (2008). *Implementing pay for performance*. New York: Wiley. Risher, H. (1999). *Aligning pay and results*. New York: AMACOM.
5. Judge, T. A., & Church, A. H. (2000). Job satisfaction: Research and practice. In C. A. Cooper & E. A. Locke (Eds.), *Industrial and organizational psychology: Linking theory to practice* (pp. 166–198). Malden, MA: Blackwell.
6. Hackman, J. R., Wageman, R., Ruddy, T. M., & Ray, C. L. (2000). Team effectiveness in theory and in practice. In C. A. Cooper & E. A. Locke (Eds.), *Industrial and organizational psychology: Linking theory to practice* (pp. 109–129). Malden, MA: Blackwell.
7. Greenberg, J. (2009). Promote procedural and interactional justice to enhance individual and organizational outcomes. In E. A. Locke (Ed.), *A handbook of principles of organizational behavior* (pp. 255–271). Malden, MA: Blackwell.
8. Benavides, F. G., Benach, J., Diez-Roux, A. V., & Roman, C. (2000). How do types of employment relate to health indicators? Findings from the Second European Survey on working conditions. *Journal of Epidemiology & Community Health, 54*, 494–501. Roberts, S. (2000, June 26). Integrating EAPs, work/life programs holds advantages. *Business Insurance, 34*(36), 3, 18–19. Vahtera, J., Kivimaeki, M., Pentti, J., & Theorell, T. (2000). Effect of change in the psychosocial work environment on sickness absence: A seven-year follow-up of initially healthy employees. *Journal of Epidemiology and Community Health, 54*, 484–493.
9. The Corporate Research Foundation UK. (2000). *Britain's best employers: A guide to the 100 most attractive companies to work for*. New York: McGraw-Hill.
10. Bollinger, D. (1996). *Aiming higher: 25 stories of how companies prosper by combining sound management and social vision*. New York: AMACOM.
11. Katz, D., & Kahn, R. (1978). *The social psychology of organizations*. New York: Wiley.
12. Werts, C. E. (2007, June). Technology as a catalyst for personal and organizational change. *Information Outlook, 11*(6), 54–57. It all depends where you sit. (2000, August 14). *BusinessWeek*, Frontier Section, p. F8.
13. U.S. Office of Personnel Management. (2008). *Handbook of alternative work schedules*. Washington, DC: Author.

14. Armour, S. (2008, June 2). Souring fuel prices drive some to try four-day workweeks. *USA Today,* p. A3.

15. Bridges, W. (1994). *Job shift: How to prosper in a workplace without jobs.* Reading, MA: Addison-Wesley.

16. Kiji International (2008). Necessity is the mother of invention. Accessed online at http://chennai.kijiji.in/c-Cars-Bikes-Spare-Parts-Accessories-Tools-NEW-PNEUMATIC-PRODUCTS-TAKES-INDUSTRIAL-AUTOMATION-BY-STORM-W0QQAdIdZ52734746

17. Stoll, J. D. (2008, July 7). GM plans layoffs, shakeout of brands. *Smart Money.* Accessed online at http://www.smartmoney.com/breaking-news/smw/index.cfm?story=20080707084335. Dash, E. (2008, June 22). Citi's investment bank braces for layoffs. *New York Times,* p. C1. Halper, M. (2008, July 8). It's official: Siemens axing 16,750 jobs. *Manufacturing Executive.* Accessed online at http://www.managingautomation.com/executive/news/read/Its_Official_Siemens_Axing_16750_Jobs_32115

18. Tomasko, R. M. (1990). *Downsizing: Reshaping the corporation for the future.* New York: AMACOM.

19. Hendricks, C. F. (1992). *The rightsizing remedy.* Homewood, IL: Business One Irwin.

20. McGinn, D., & Naughton, K. (2001, February 5). How safe is your job? *Newsweek,* pp. 36–43.

21. Tomasko, R. M. (1993). *Rethinking the corporation,* New York: AMACOM.

22. Statistics Related to Offshore Outsourcing. (2007, November 20). RTTS Software. Accessed online at http://www.rttsweb.com/outsourcing/statistics/

23. Bettis, R. A., Bradley, S. P., & Hamel, G. (1992). Outsourcing and industrial decline. *Academy of Management Review, 6,* 7–22.

24. Haapaniemi, P. (1993, Winter). Taking care of business. *Solutions,* pp. 6–8, 10–13.

25. See Note 20.

26. McIvor, R. (2008). What is the right outsourcing strategy for your process? *European Management Journal, 26,* 24–34. Doh, J. P. (2005). Offshore outsourcing: Implications for international business and strategic management theory and practice. *Journal of Management Studies, 43,* 695–704.

27. Goranson, H. T. (1999). *The agile virtual enterprise.* Greenwich, CT: Quorum.

28. Putnik, G. D., & Cunha, M. M. (2008). *Encyclopedia of networked and virtual organizations.* Hershey, PA: Information Science Reference.

29. Karnakas, C. (2007, November 27). Telecommuting: A quarter of U.S. workers do it regularly. *PC World.* Retrieved online from http://www.pcworld.com/article/140003/telecommuting _a_quarter_of_us_workers_do_it_regularly.html

30. Washington State University Cooperative Extension Energy Program. (2000). *Case study: Washington Mutual.* Pullman, WA: Author.

31. DuBrin, A. J. (1994). *Contemporary applied management: Skills for managers* (4th ed.). Burr Ridge, IL: Irwin.

32. Mariani, M. (2000, Fall). Telecommuters. *Occupational Outlook Quarterly,* pp. 10–17.

33. Cascio, W. E. (1995). Whither industrial and organizational in a changing world of work? *American Psychologist, 50,* 928–939. (quote, p. 928)

34. Commuter Challenge (2008). *Case studies: Telework.* Seattle, WA: Author. Retrieved from the Web at http://www.commuter challenge.org/cc/csintro2.html

35. Schelase, M. (2008). *Globalization, regionalization and business: Conflict, convergence and influence.* New York: Palgrave Macmillan. Lodge, G. C. (1995). *Managing globalization in the age of interdependence.* San Francisco: Pfeifer.

36. Rapaille, C. (2007). *The culture code.* New York: Broadway.

37. DeCieri, H., & Dowling, P. J. (1995). Cross-cultural issues in organizational behavior. In C. L. Cooper & D. M. Rousseau (Eds.), *Trends in organizational behavior* (Vol. 2, pp. 127–145). New York: John Wiley & Sons.

38. Perelstin, E., & Kristal, J. (2007). *Repatriation: A how-to guide for returning wisely.* White Plains, NY: Plain White Press.

39. Hesketh, B., & Bochner, S. (1994). Technological change in a multicultural context: Implications for training and career planning. In H. C. Triandis, M. D. Dunnette, & L. Hough (Eds.), *Handbook of industrial and organizational psychology*

(Vol. 4, pp. 190–240). Palo Alto, CA: Consulting Psychologists Press.

40. Janssens, M. (1995). Intercultural interaction: A burden on international managers? *Journal of Organizational Behavior, 16,* 155–167.

41. U.S. Department of Labor. (2009). *Women in the workplace.* Washington, DC: Author. Lerman, R. I., & Schmidt, S. R. (2002). *An overview of economic, social, and demographic trends affecting the labor market.* Report to the Urban Institute for U.S. Department of Labor (at www.dol.gov).

42. See Note 41.

43. Hobbs, F, & Stoops, N. (2008). *Demographic trends in the 20th century: Census 2000 special reports.* Washington, DC: U.S. Census Bureau.

44. See Note 43.

45. Carnevale, A. P., & Stone, S. C. (1995). *The American mosaic: An in-depth report on the future of diversity at work.* New York: McGraw Hill.

46. See Note 45.

47. Hawley, C. (2009). *Managing the older employee.* Cincinnati, OH: Adams Media.

48. Jayson, S. (2008, July 16). Is this the next baby boom? *USA Today,* pp. A1–A2.

49. Alsop, R. (2008). *The trophy kids grow up: How the millennial generation is shaking up the workplace.* San Francisco, CA: Wiley.

50. Kanigel, R. (1997). *The one best way.* New York: Viking.

51. Taylor, F. W. (1911). *The principles of scientific management.* New York: Harper Brothers.

52. Drucker, P. F. (1974). *Management: Tasks, responsibilities, practices.* New York: Harper & Row.

53. Verschoor, C. C. (1998). A study of the link between a corporation's financial performance and its commitment to ethics. *Journal of Business Ethics, 17,* 1509–1516.

54. Hoffman, A. J., & Ventresca, M. (2002). *Organizations, policy and the natural environment.* Palo Alto, CA: Stanford University Press.

55. Bureau of Labor Statistics (2009).www.bls.gov.

Chapter 2

Case Notes

AFX News Limited (2008, February 13). HP settles spying scandal claims. *Forbes.com.* From the Web at: http://www.forbes.com/ afxnewslimited/feeds/afx/2008/02/13/afx 4653525.html. Steffy, L. (2008, February 15). Privacy: Less and less is the trend. *Houston Chronicle.* From the Web at: http:// www.chron.com/disp/story.mpl/business/ steffy/5546747.html. Fried, I. (2006, December 8). HP settles with California in spy scandal. *CNET News.com.* From the Web at: http://www.zdnet.com.au/news/ business/soa/-HP-settles-with-California-in-spy-scandal/0,139023166,339272604, 00.htm?feed=pt_cnet. Ard, S., & Fried, I. (2006, September 12). Leak scandal costs HP's Dunn her chairman's job. *CNET News.com.* From the Web at: http://news.cnet.com/Leak-scandal-costs-HPs-Dunn-her-chairmans-job/2100-1014_ 3-6114655.html. Sandoval, G. (2006, October 5). Dunn to surrender Thursday. *ZD Net.* From the Web at: http://news .zdnet.com/2100-9584_22-6123054.html.

Chapter Notes

1. Painter-Morland, M. (2008). *Business ethics as practice.* New York: Cambridge University Press.

2. Schwartz, M., & Watkins, S. (2004). *Power failure: The inside story of the collapse of Enron.* New York: Doubleday Business.

3. Beck, H. (2008, July 6). For an Army general, a new rebuilding effort. *New York Times.* From the Web at http://www.nytimes.com/2008/ 07/06/sports/basketball/06nba.html?ref= sports. Hakim, D. & Rashbaum, W. K. (2008, March 10). Spitzer is linked to prostitution ring. *New York Times.* From the Web at http://www.nytimes.com/2008/03/10/ nyregion/10cnd-spitzer.html. Olson, G. (2008, June 27). "Energy drinks" crank up corporate greed. *Vancouver Courier.* From the Web at: http://www.canada.com/ vancouvercourier/news/opinion/ story.html?id=54db9478-33d4-4631-8653-dc09dde7ae39.

4. Harvard Business School Press. (2003). *Harvard Business Review on corporate responsibility.* Boston: Author.

5. Greenberg, J., & Colquitt, J. A. (2005). *Handbook of organizational justice.* Mahwah, NJ: Lawrence Erlbaum Associates.

6. Cropanzano, R., Byrne, Z. S., Bobocel, D. R., & Rupp, D. E. (2001). Moral virtues, fairness heuristics, social entities, and other denizens of organizational justice. *Journal of Vocational Behavior, 58,* 164–209.

7. Colquitt, J. A. (2001). On the dimensionality of organizational justice: A construct validation of a measure. *Journal of Applied Psychology, 86,* 386–400. Greenberg, J. (1993). The social side of fairness: Interpersonal and informational classes of organizational justice. In R. Cropanzano (Ed.), *Justice in the workplace: Approaching fairness in human resource management* (pp. 79–103). Hillsdale, NJ: Lawrence Erlbaum Associates.

8. Greenberg, J. (1996). *The quest for justice on the job: Essays and experiments.* Thousand Oaks, CA: Sage.

9. Ang, S., Van Dyne, L., & Begley, T. M. (2003). The employment relationships of foreign workers versus local employees: A field study of organizational justice, job satisfaction, performance, and OCB. *Journal of Organizational Behavior, 24,* 561–583.

10. Greenberg, J. (2009). Promote procedural and interactional justice to enhance acceptance of individual and organizational outcomes. In E. A. Locke (Ed.), *The Blackwell handbook of principles of organizational behavior* (pp. 255–271). Malden, MA: Blackwell.

11. Allen, M. (1998, May 15). Giuliani threatens action if cabbies fail to cancel a protest. *New York Times,* p. C1.

12. Greenberg, J., & Cropanzano, R. A. (2001). *Advances in organizational justice.* Stanford, CA: Stanford University Press.

13. Lind, E. A., Greenberg, J., Scott, K. S., & Welchans, T. D. (2000). The winding road from employee to complainant: Situational and psychological determinants of wrongful termination claims. *Administrative Science Quarterly, 45,* 557–590.

14. See Note 7.

15. Simons, T., & Roberson, Q. (2003). Why managers should care about fairness: The effects of aggregate justice perceptions on organizational outcomes. *Journal of Applied Psychology, 88,* 432–443.

16. Brockner, J. (2006, March). Why it's so hard to be fair. *Harvard Business Review,* pp. 44–50.

17. Cortina, L. M. (2008). Unseen injustice: Incivility as modern discrimination in organizations. *Academy of Management Review, 33,* 55–75.

18. Schaubroeck, J., May, D. R., & Brown, F. W. (1994). Procedural justice explanations and employee reactions to economic hardship: A field experiment. *Journal of Applied Psychology, 79,* 455–460.

19. Greenberg, J. (1986). Determinants of perceived fairness of performance evaluations. *Journal of Applied Psychology, 71,* 340–342. Leventhal, G. S. (1980). What should be done with equity theory? New approaches to the study of fairness in social relationships. In K. Gergen, M. Greenberg, & R. Willis (Eds.), *Social exchange: Advances in theory and research* (pp. 27–55). New York: Plenum Press.

20. See Note 7.

21. Skarlicki, D. P., & Latham, G. P. (2004). Can leaders be trained to be fair? In J. Greenberg & J. A. Colquitt (Eds.), *Handbook of organizational justice* (pp. 408–430). Mahwah, NJ: Lawrence Erlbaum Associates.

22. Greenberg, J. (2006). Losing sleep over organizational injustice: Attenuating insomniac reactions to underpayment inequity with supervisory training in interactional justice. *Journal of Applied Psychology, 81,* 58–69.

23. Goldgar, A. (2007). *Tulipmania: Money, honor, and knowledge in the Dutch golden age.* Chicago, IL: University of Chicago Press.

24. Mackay, C. (1852/2003). *Memoirs of extraordinary popular delusions and the madness of crowds.* Hampshire, UK: Harriman House.

25. McConahey, M. (2003, June 8). Ethics scandals reach epidemic level. *Press Democrat* (Santa Rosa, California), p. A8. (Also on the Web at www.jim-carroll.com/acrobat/publicity/pressdemocrat-1.pdf.)

26. Calmes, J., & Story, L. (2009, March 17). Outcry builds in Washington for recovery of AIG bonuses. *New York Times,* pp. A1–A6.

27. Reid, T. (2008, December 12). Wall Street legend Bernard Madoff arrested over "$50 billion Ponzi scheme." *New York Times: Times Online.* From the Web at http://www.times online.co.uk/tol/news/world/us_and_americas/article5331997.ece

28. Florida man arrested on Miss. Home repair fraud charges. (2008, February 21).

St. Cloud, FL Topix. From the Web at http://www.topix.com/city/st-cloud-fl/2008/02/florida-man-arrested-on-miss-home-repair-fraud-charges.

29. Governor says impeachment vote is politically driven. (2009, Janauary 9). *CNNPolitics.com.* From the Web at http://www.cnn.com/2009/POLITICS/01/09/blagojevich.impeachment/

30. Associated Press. (2007, October 28). Gap stores using child labor in Indian sweatshops, British newspaper reports. *Fox News.com.* From the Web at http://www.foxnews.com/story/0,2933,305703,00.html.

31. Weaver, J. (2003, June 4). Martha Stewart indicted on 9 counts. *MSNBC.* From the Web at stacks.msnbc.com/news/922014.asp.

32. Zellner, W., & Forest, S. A. (2001, December 17). The fall of Enron. *BusinessWeek*, pp. 30–34, 36.

33. Ferrell, O. C., Fraedrich, J., & Ferrell, L. (2002). *Business ethics: Ethical decision making and cases* (5th ed.). Boston: Houghton Mifflin.

34. The Corporate Library. (2002, July). Spotlight topic: Adelphia scandal. From the World Wide Web at www.thecorporatelibrary.com/spotlight/scandals/adelq.html.

35. Henderson, V. E. (1992). *What's ethical in business?* New York: McGraw-Hill.

36. Ethics Resources Center. (2003). *2003 National business ethics survey.* Washington, DC: Author.

37. Ethics Resource Center. (2003). *What is ethics?* From the World Wide Web at www.ethics.org/faq.html#eth_what.

38. Salopek, J. J. (2001, July). Do the right thing. *American Society for Training and Development.* From the World Wide Web at www.astd.org/CMS/templates/index.html?template_id=1&articleid=26983.

39. Treviño, L. K., & Nelson, K. A. (1999). *Managing business ethics* (2nd ed.). New York: John Wiley & Sons (quote, p. 14).

40. See Note 39 (quote, pp. 26–27).

41. MAALA Business for Social Responsibility. (2002). Corporate social responsibility. Tel Aviv, Israel: Author (also at www.maala.com). Verschoor, C. C. (1998). A study of the link between a corporation's financial performance and its commitment to ethics. *Journal of Business Ethics, 17,* 1509–1516. Embley, L. L.

(1993). *Doing well while doing good.* Upper Saddle River, NJ: Prentice Hall.

42. See Note 26.

43. See Note 30.

44. Johnson, D. C. (1997, November 9). United Way, faced with fewer donations, is giving away less. *New York Times,* p. A1.

45. See Note 30 (quote, pp. 30–31).

46. Kaplan, J. M. (2003, May/June). Justice Department revises corporate prosecution standards. *Ethikos, 16*(6), pp. 1–3, 13.

47. Ethics and Policy Integration Centre (2003). Toward an effective ethics and compliance program: The Federal Sentencing Guidelines for Organizations. Washington, DC: Author. Available on the World Wide Web at www.ethicaledge.com/appendix1.html.

48. Butler, H. N., & Ribstein, L. E. (2006). *The Sarbanes-Oxley debacle: What we've learned; how to fix it.* Washington, DC: AEI Press.

49. Public Company Accounting Oversight Board (2008, June 12). *Auditing standard number 5.* Washington, DC: Author.

50. Ramos, M. J. (2008*) How to comply with Sarbanes-Oxley Section 404: Assessing the effectiveness of internal control* (3rd ed.). New York: Wiley.

51. U.S.C. Sec. 1519.

52. Treviño, L. K., & Youngblood, S. A. (1990). Bad apples in bad barrels: A causal analysis of ethical decision-making behavior. *Journal of Applied Psychology, 75,* 378–385.

53. Kohlberg, L. (1976). Moral stages and moralization: The cognitive-developmental approach. In T. Lickona (Ed.), *Moral development and behavior: Theory, research, and social issues* (pp. 2–52). New York: Holt, Rinehart and Winston. Kohlberg, L. (1969). Stage and sequence: The cognitive-developmental approach to socialization. In D. A. Goslin (Ed.), *Handbook of socialization theory and research* (pp. 347–380). Chicago: Rand McNally.

54. Greenberg, J. (2002). Who stole the money, and when? Individual and situational determinants of employee theft. *Organizational Behavior and Human Decision Processes, 89,* 895–1003. Blass, T. (1999). *Obedience to authority: Current perspectives on the Milgram paradigm.* Mahwah, NJ: Lawrence Erlbaum Associates. Grover, S. L. (1993). Why

professionals lie: The impact of professional role conflict on reporting accuracy. *Organizational Behavior and Human Decision Processes, 55,* 251–272.

55. Treviño, L. K. (1992). Moral reasoning and business ethics. *Journal of Business Ethics, 11,* 445–459.

56. Brass, D. J., Butterfield, K. D., & Skaggs, B. C. (1998). Relationships and unethical behavior: A social-network perspective. *Academy of Management Review, 23,* 14–31.

57. Wolfe, D. M. (1988). Is there integrity in the bottom line: Managing obstacles to executive integrity. In S. Srivastava (Ed.), *Executive integrity: The search for high human values in organizational life* (pp. 140–171). San Francisco, CA: Jossey-Bass.

58. Jansen, E., & Von Glinow, M. A. (1985). Ethical ambivalence and organizational reward systems. *Academy of Management Review, 10,* 814–822.

59. See Note 27.

60. Cassell, C., Johnson, P., & Smith, K. (1997). Opening the black box: Corporate codes of ethics in their organizational context. *Journal of Business Ethics, 16,* 1077–1093.

61. Weaver, G. R., Treviño, L. K., & Cochran, P. L. (1996). Corporate ethics practices in the mid-1990s: An empirical study of the *Fortune* 1000. *Journal of Business Ethics, 18,* 283–294.

62. Ethics Resource Center. (1994). *Ethics in American business: Policies, programs and perceptions.* Washington, DC: Author.

63. See Note 29.

64. Ferrell, O. C., Fraedrich, J., & Ferrell, L. (2002). *Business ethics* (5th ed.). Boston: Houghton Mifflin. Waddock, S., & Smith, N. (2000, Winter). Corporate responsibility audits: Doing well by doing good. *Sloan Management Review,* pp. 66–83.

65. Singer, A. (2003, May/June). Excelon excels at reaching out. *Ethikos, 16*(6), pp. 7–9, 13.

66. From the World Wide Web at www.exelon corp.com/corporate/about/a_overview.shtml.

67. Greenberg, J. (2002). Who stole the money, and when? Individual and situational determinants of employee theft. *Organizational Behavior and Human Decision Processes, 89,* 985–1003.

68. Carroll, A. B. (1991). The pyramid of corporate social responsibility: Toward the moral management of organizational stakeholders. *Business Horizons, 34*(4), 39–48.

69. Demos, T. (2008). Accounting for accountability: 10 most "accountable" big companies. *Fortune.* From the Web at http://money.cnn.com/galleries/2007/fortune/0710/gallery.accountability.fortune/10.html.

70. Asmus, P. (2003, Spring). 2003 100 best corporate citizens. *Business Ethics,* pp. 6–10.

71. Margolis, J. D., & Walsh, J. P. (2001). *People and profits? The search for a link between a company's social and financial performance.* Mahwah, NJ: Lawrence Erlbaum Associates. Labich, K. (1992, April 20). The new crisis in business ethics. *Fortune,* pp. 167–170, 172, 174, 176.

72. U.S. Environmental Protection Agency. (2008, April). *Green power partnership.* From the Web at http://epa.gov/greenpower/.

73. Intel Corporation. (2008). *Environmental innovation, energy-efficient performance.* Accessed from the Web at http://www.intel.com/intel/environment/.

74. PepsiCo. (2009). *PepsiCo is committed to being an environmentally responsible corporate citizen.* Accessed from the Web at http://www.pepsico.com/PEP_Citizenship/EnvironmentalNews/index.cfm.

75. Memme, P. (2007). *Air Force facility energy center.* U.S. Air Force. Accessed from the Web at http://www.afcesa.af.mil/.

76. Wells Fargo. (2009). *Improving our environment.* Accessed from the Web at https://www.wellsfargo.com/about/csr/ea/.

77. McIntosh, M. (2003). *Raising a ladder to the moon: The complexities of corporate social and environmental responsibility.* New York: Palgrave Macmillan. Rayner, J. (2002). *Corporate social responsibility monitor.* London: Gee Publishing. Kinder, P. D., Lydenberg, S. D., & Domini, A. L. (1994). *Investing for good: Making money while being socially responsible.* New York: HarperCollins. Domini, A. L., Lydenberg, S. D., & Kinder, P. D. (1992). *The social investment almanac: A comprehensive guide to socially responsible investing.* New York: Henry Holt.

78. Trudel, R., & Cotte, J. (2008, May 12). Does being ethical pay? *Wall Street Journal,* p. B 1.

79. Care2.com (2006, August 2). Socially responsible companies rank high with job seekers. *CSR Wire.* From the Web at

http://www.csrwire.com/PressRelease
.php?id=6046.

80. Vogel, D. (2006). *The market for virtue: The potential and limits of corporate social responsibility.* Washington, DC: Brookings Institution.

81. See Note 30.

82. Romano, B. J. (2008, June 28). Microsoft says goodbye to Bill Gates. *Seattle Times.* From the Web at http://seattletimes .nwsource.com/html/microsoft/ 2008022508_gatesgoodbye28.html. Loomis, C. J. (2006, June 25). Warren Buffett gives away his fortune. *Fortune.com.* From the Web at http://money.cnn.com/2006/06/25/ magazines/fortune/charity1.fortune/.

83. Clark, J., & Driscoll, W. (2003). *Globalization and the poor: Exploitation or equalizer.* New York: International Debate Education Association. Steele, J. R. (2003). *"Is this my reward?" An employee's struggles for fairness in the corporate exploitation of his inventions.* New York: Pencraft Press.

Chapter 3

Case Notes

Wilchins, D. (2008, July 25). MasterCard settles lawsuit with American Express. *Reuters.* From the Web at http://uk.reuters .com/article/bankingfinancial-SP/ idUKN2542549620080625. Wilchins, D. (2008, July 22). American Express shares drop after gloomy earnings. *Reuters.* From the Web at http://uk.reuters .com/article/bankingfinancial-SP/ idUKN2227942820080722. Farrell, G. (2005, April 24). A CEO and a gentleman. *USA Today,* p. C. 1. Answers.Com (2007). Business biographies: Kenneth I. Chenault. From the Web at http://www.answers.com/ topic/kenneth-chenault. Colvin, G. (2007, September 19). Secrets of leadership from American Express. *Fortune,* pp. 15–16.

Chapter Notes

1. Furnham, A. (2008). *Personality and intelligence at work: Exploring and explaining individual differences at work.* New York: Psychology Press. Barrick, M., & Ryan, A. M. (2003). *Personality at work: Reconsidering the role of personality in organizations.* San Francisco: Jossey-Bass. Roberts, B. W., & Hogan, R. (2001). *Personality psychology in the workplace.* Washington, DC: American Psychological Association.

2. Ridley, M. (2003). *Nature vs. nurture: Genes, experience, and what makes us human.* New York: Harper Collins.

3. Zyphur, M. J., Narayanan, J., Arvey, R., & Alexander, G. J. (2008, August). *The genetics of risk preferences.* Paper presented at the annual meeting of the Academy of Management, Anaheim, CA.

4. Pinker, S. (2004, Fall). Why nature and nurture won't go away. *Daedalus,* pp. 7–20.

5. Plomin, R., DeFries, J. C., McClearn, G. E., & McGuffin, P. (2000). *Behavioral genetics* (4th ed.). New York: Worth.

6. McGue, M., Bouchard, T. J., Jr., Iacono, W. G., & Lykken, D. T. (1993). Behavioral genetics of cognitive ability: A life-span perspective. In R. Plomin & G. E. McClearn (Eds.), *Nature, nurture, and psychology.* Washington, DC: American Psychological Association.

7. See Note 1.

8. George, J. M., & Zhou, J. (2001). When openness to experience and conscientiousness are related to creative behavior: An interactional approach. *Journal of Applied Psychology, 86,* 513–524.

9. Chatman, J. A., Caldwell, D. F., & O'Reilly, C.A. (1999). Managerial personality and performance: A semi-idiographic approach. *Journal of Research in Personality, 33,* 534–545.

10. See Note 1.

11. Mount, M. K., & Barrick, M. R. (1998). Five reasons why the "Big Five" article has been frequently cited. *Personnel Psychology, 51,* 849–857.

12. Salgado, J. F. (1997). The five-factor model of personality and job performance in the European community. *Journal of Applied Psychology, 82,* 30–43.

13. Hurtz, G. M, & Donovan, J. J. (2000). Personality and job performance: The Big Five revisited. *Journal of Applied Psychology, 85,* 869–879.

14. Mount, M. K., & Barrick, M. R. (1995). The Big Five personality dimensions: Implications for research and practice in human resources management.

In K. M. Rowland & G. Ferris (Eds.), *Research in personnel and human resources management* (Vol. 13, pp. 153–200). Greenwich, CT: JAI Press.

15. Darvi, S. V., & Woods, S. A. (2006). Uncertified absence from work and the Big Five: An examination of absence records and future absence intentions. *Personality and Individual Differences, 41,* 359–369.

16. Barrick, M. R., Stewart, G. L., Neubert, M. J., & Mount, M. K. (1998). Relating member ability and personality to work-team processes and team effectiveness. *Journal of Applied Psychology, 83,* 377–391.

17. Kirkcaldy, B. D., Shephard, R. J., & Furnham, A. F. (2002). The influence of Type A behavior and locus of control upon job satisfaction and occupational health. *Personality & Individual Differences, 33,* 1361–1371.

18. George, J. M., & Brief, A. P. (1992). Feeling good—doing good: A conceptual analysis of the mood at work—organizational spontaneity relationships. *Psychological Bulletin, 112,* 310–329.

19. Isen, A. M., & Baron, R. A. (1992). Positive affect as a factor in organizational behavior. In B. M. Staw & L. L. Cummings (Eds.), *Research in organizational behavior* (Vol. 13, pp. 1–54). Greenwich, CT: JAI Press.

20. Magruder, J. (2004, August 5). Negative employees costing companies money. *The Arizona Republic,* p. B16.

21. Staw, B. M,, & Barsade, S. G. (1993). Affect and managerial performance: A test of the sadder-but-wiser vs. happier-and-smarter hypotheses. *Administrative Science Quarterly, 38,* 304–331.

22. George, J. M. (1990). Personality, affect, and behavior in groups. *Journal of Applied Psychology, 75,* 107–116.

23. Aquino, K., Grover, S. L., Bradfield, M., & Allen, D. G. (1999). The effects of negative affectivity, hierarchical status, and self-determination on workplace victimization. *Academy of Management Journal, 42,* 260–272.

24. Judge, T. A., Locke, E. A., & Durham, C. C. (1997). The dispositional causes of job satisfaction: A core evaluations approach. In L. L. Cummings & B. M. Staw (Eds.), *Research in organizational behavior* (Vol. 19, pp. 151–188). Greenwich, CT: JAI Press.

25. Judge, T. A., & Bono, J. E. (2001). Relationship of core self-evaluations traits—self-esteem, generalized self-efficacy, locus of control, and emotional stability—with job satisfaction and job performance: A meta-analysis. *Journal of Applied Psychology, 86,* 80–92.

26. See Note 25 (quote, p. 89).

27. Judge, T. A., Bono, J. E., Erez, A., & Locke, E. A. (2004). Core self-evaluations and job and life satisfaction: The role of self-concordance and goal attainment. *Journal of Applied Psychology, 90,* 257–268. Bono, J. E., & Judge, T. A. (2003). Core self-evaluations: A review of the trait and its role in job satisfaction and job performance. *European Journal of Personality, 17*(Supplement), S5–S18.

28. Mitchell, J. (2008). *The new gold standard: 5 leadership principles for creating a legendary customer experience courtesy of the Ritz-Carlton Hotel Company.* New York: McGraw-Hill.

29. Mitchell, J. (2008). *The Starbucks experience: 5 principles for turning ordinary into extraordinary.* New York: McGraw-Hill. Simmons, J. (2005). *My sister's a barista: How they made Starbucks a home away from home* (Rev. ed.). London: Cyan Communications.

30. Pandale, P. S., Neuman, R. P., & Cavanaugh, R. R. (2000). *The Six Sigma way: How GE, Motorola and other top companies are honing their performance.* New York: McGraw-Hill.

31. McClelland, D. C. (1985). *Human motivation.* Glenview, IL: Scott, Foresman.

32. McClelland, D. C. (1977). Entrepreneurship and management in the years ahead. In C. A. Bramletter (Ed.), *The individual and the future of organizations* (pp. 12–29). Atlanta, GA: Georgia State University.

33. Miller, D., & Droge, C. (1986). Psychological and traditional determinants of structure. *Administrative Science Quarterly, 31,* 539–560.

34. Turban, D. B., & Keon, T. L. (1993). Organizational attractiveness: An interactionist perspective. *Journal of Applied Psychology, 78,* 184–193.

35. Forgas, J. P. (2000). *Handbook of affect and social cognition.* Mahwah, NJ: Lawrence Erlbaum Associates.

36. Ashforth, B. E., & Mael, F. (1989). Social identity theory and the organization. *Academy of Management Review, 14,* 20–29.

37. LaTendresse, D. (2000). Social identity and intergroup relations within the hospital. *Journal of Social Distress and the Homeless, 9,* 51–69.

38. Cialdini, R. B., Borden, R. J., Thorne, A., Walker, M. R., Freeman, S., & Sloan, L. R. (1999). Basking in reflected glory: Three (football) field studies. In R. F. Baumeister (Ed.), *The self in social psychology* (pp. 436–445). Philadelphia: Psychology Press/Taylor & Francis.

39. Eden, D. (2003). Self-fulfilling prophecies in organizations. In J. Greenberg (Ed.), *Organizational behavior: State of the science* (2nd ed.) (pp. 91–122). Mahwah, NJ: Lawrence Erlbaum Associates.

40. Reynolds, D. (2007). Restraining Golem and harnessing Pygmalion in the classroom: A laboratory study of managerial expectations and task design. *Academy of Management Learning & Education, 6,* 475-483.

41. Eden, D., & Shani, A. B. (1982). Pygmalion goes to boot camp: Expectancy, leadership, and trainee performance. *Journal of Applied Psychology, 67,* 194–199.

42. Nye, R. D. (1992). *The legacy of B. F. Skinner: Concepts and perspectives, controversies and misunderstandings.* Belmont, CA: Brooks/Cole.

43. O'Leonard, K. (2008). *The corporate learning factbook, 2008: Statistics, benchmarks, and analysis of the U.S. corporate training market.* Oakland, CA: Bersin and Associates.

44. Arthur, W., Jr., Bennett, W., Jr., Edens, P. S., & Bell, S. T. (2003). Effectiveness of training in organizations: A meta-analysis of design and evaluation features. *Journal of Applied Psychology, 88,* 234–245. Kraiger, K. (2001). *Creating, implementing, and managing effective training and development: State-of-the-art lessons for practice.* San Francisco: Jossey-Bass.

45. Bell, B. S., & Kozlowski, S. W. J., (2008). Active learning: Effects of core training design elements on self-regulatory processes, learning and adaptability. *Journal of Applied Psychology, 93,* 296-316.

46. Ilgen, D. R., & Moore, C. F. (1987). Types and choices of performance feedback. *Journal of Applied Psychology, 72,* 401–406.

47. Hoffman, R. (1995, April). Ten reasons you should be using 360-degree feedback. *HR Magazine,* pp. 82–85.

48. Mercer Research. (2008). *360-degree feedback.* Washington, DC: Author.

49. Bailey, C., & Fletcher, C. (2002). The impact of multiple source feedback on management development: Findings from a longitudinal study. *Journal of Organizational Behavior, 23,* 853–867. Edwards, M. R., & Ewen, A. J. (1996). *360° feedback: The powerful new model for employee assessment and performance improvement.* New York: AMACOM.

50. Pfau, B., & Kay, I. (2002, June). Does 360-degree feedback negatively affect company performance? *HR Magazine,* pp. 20–27.

51. Stajkovic, A. D., & Luthans, F. (2003). Behavioral management and task performance in organizations: Conceptual background, meta-analysis, and test of alternative models. *Personnel Psychology, 56,* 155–194.

52. Clayton, M. & Myers, E. (2008). Increasing turn signal use by drivers exiting a university parking garage: A comparison of passive and mediated prompting. *Journal of Organizational Behavior Management 27*(4), 53–61. Doll, J., Livesey, J., McHaffie, E., & Ludwig, T. W. (2007). Keeping an uphill edge: Managing cleaning behaviors at a ski shop. *Journal of Organizational Behavior Management, 27*(3), 41–60. Squires, J., Wilder, D. A., Fixsen, A., Hess, E. Rost, K., Curran, R., & Zonneveld, K. (2007). The effects of task clarification, visual prompts, and graphic feedback on customer greeting and up-selling in a restaurant. *Journal of Organizational Behavior Management, 27*(3), 1–13.

53. Trahan, W. A., & Steiner, D. D. (1994). Factors affecting supervisors' use of disciplinary actions following poor performance. *Journal of Organizational Behavior, 15,* 129–139.

Chapter 4

Case Notes

Newsday.com. (2008, July 30). Tim Donaghy timeline. From the Web at http://www.newsday.com/sports/basketball/ny-sprefbox305782382jul30,0,6452591.story.

Fortado, L., & Hurtado, P. (2008, July 29). Ex-NBA referee Donaghy gets 15-month term for betting. Bloomberg.com. From the Web at http://www.bloomberg.com/apps/news?pid=newsarchive&sid=arILgbEs3O_4. Hays, T. (2008, July 30). BBA scandal: Corrupt ref gets 15-month sentence. From the Web at http://www.bloomberg.com/apps/news?pid=newsarchive&sid=arILgbEs3O_4. Price, J., & Wolfers, J. (2007, June). *Racial discrimination among NBA referees* (NBER working paper no. 13206). Cambridge, MA: National Bureau of Economic Research.

Chapter Notes

1. American Institute of Stress. (2009). *Job stress.* From the Web at http://www.stress.org/job.htm.
2. Kanfer, R., & Klimoski, R. J. (2002). Affect and work: Looking back into the future. In R. G. Lord, R. J. Klimoski, & R. Kanfer (Eds.), *Emotions in the workplace: Understanding the structure and role of emotions in organizational behavior.* San Francisco, CA: Jossey-Bass.
3. Hatfield, E., Cacioppo, J. T., & Rhapson, R. L. (1994). *Emotional contagion.* New York: Cambridge University Press.
4. Cherulnik, P. K., Donley, K. A., Wiewel, T. S. R., & Miller, S. R. (2001). Charisma is contagious: The effects of leaders' charisma on observers' affect. *Journal of Applied Social Psychology, 31,* 2149–2159.
5. Ekman, P., Friesen, W. V., & Ancoli, S. (2001). Facial signs of emotional experience. In W. G. Parrott (Ed.), *Emotions in social psychology* (pp. 255–264). Philadelphia, PA: Psychology Press.
6. Nakamura, N. (2000). Facial expression and communication of emotion: An analysis of display rules and a model of facial expression of emotion. *Japanese Psychological Review, 43,* 307–319.
7. Matsumoto, D., Yoo, S. H., & Fontaine, J. (2008). Mapping expressive differences around the world: The relationship between emotional display rules and individualism versus collectivism. *Journal of Cross-Cultural Psychology, 39,* 55–74.
8. Weiss, H. M., & Cropanzano, R. (1996). Affective events theory: A theoretical discussion of the structure, causes, and consequences of affective experiences at work. In B. M. Staw & L. L. Cummings (Eds.), *Research in organizational behavior* (Vol. 18, pp. 1–74). Greenwich, CT: JAI Press.
9. Tangney, J. P., & Fischer, K. W. (Eds.). (1995). *Self-conscious emotions: The psychology of shame, guilt, embarrassment, and pride.* New York: Guilford Press. Tracy, J. L., & Robins, R. W. (2004). Putting the self into self-conscious emotions: A theoretical model. *Psychological Inquiry, 15,* 103–125.
10. Keltner, D., & Anderson, C. (2000). Saving face for Darwin: The functions and uses of embarrassment. *Current Directions in Psychological Science, 9,* 187–192.
11. Poulson, C. F. II. (2000). Shame and work. In N. M. Ashkanasy, W. Zerbe, & C. E. J. Härtel. (2007). *Emotions in the workplace: Research, theory, and practice* (pp. 490–541). Westport, CT: Quorum Books. Vecchio, R. P. (2005). Explorations of employee envy: Feeling envious and feeling envied. *Cognition and Emotion, 19,* 69–81.
12. Huelsman, T. J., Furr, R. M., & Memanick, R. C., Jr. (2003). Measurement of dispositional affect: Construct validity and convergence with a circumplex model of affect. *Educational and Psychological Measurement, 63,* 655–673. Larsen, J., Diener, E., & Lucas, R. E. (2002). Emotion: Moods, measures, and differences. In R. G. Lord, R. J. Klimiski, & R. Kanfer (Eds.), *Emotions in the workplace* (pp. 64–113). San Francisco, CA: Jossey-Bass.
13. George, J. M., & Brief, A. P. (1996). Motivational agendas in the workplace: The effects of feelings on focus of attention and work motivation. In B. M. Staw & L. L. Cummings (Eds.), *Research in organizational behavior* (Vol. 18, pp. 75–109). Greenwich, CT: JAI Press.
14. Ashkanasy, N. M. (2008). *Research companion to emotion in organizations.* Northampton, MA: Edward Elgar.
15. Lyubomirsky, S., King, L., & Diener, E. (2005). The benefits of frequent positive affect: Does happiness lead to success? *Psychological Bulletin, 131,* 803–855.

16. Staw, B. M., Sutton, R. I., & Pelled, L. H. (1994). Employee positive emotion and favorable outcomes in the workplace. *Organization Science, 5,* 51–71.

17. Cropanzano, R., & Wright, T. A. (1999). A five-year study of change in the relationship between well-being and job performance. *Consulting Psychology Journal, 51,* 252–265. Wright, T. A., & Staw, B. M. (1999). Affect and favorable work outcomes: Two longitudinal tests of the happy-productive worker thesis. *Journal of Organizational Behavior, 20,* 1–23.

18. DeLuga, R. J., & Manson, S. (2000). Relationship of resident assistant conscientiousness, extraversion, and positive affect with rated performance. *Journal of Research in Personality, 34,* 225–235. Totterdell, P. (2000). Catching moods and hitting runs: Mood linkage and subjective performance in professional sports teams. *Journal of Applied Psychology, 83,* 848–859.

19. See Note 18.

20. Foster, J. B., Hebl, M. R., West, M., & Dawson, J. (2004, April). *Setting the tone for organizational success: The impact of CEO affect on organizational climate and firm-level outcomes.* Paper presented at the annual meeting of the Society for Industrial and Organizational Psychology, Toronto, Ontario, Canada. Pritzker, M. A. (2002). The relationship among CEO dispositional attributes, transformational leadership behavior and performance effectiveness. *Dissertation Abstracts International, 62*(12-B), 6008. (UMI No. AA13035464.)

21. Lucas, R. E., Clark, A. E., Georgellis, Y., & Deiner, E. (2004). Unemployment alters the set points for life satisfaction. *Psychological Science, 15,* 8–13. Graham, C., Eggers, A., & Sukhtanar, S. (2004). Does happiness pay: An exploration based on panel data from Russia. *Journal of Economic Behavior and Organization, 55,* 319–342.

22. Howell, C. J., Howell, R. T., & Schwabe, K. A. (2008). Does wealth enhance life satisfaction for people who are materially deprived? Exploring the association among the Orang Asli of Peninsular Malaysia. *Social Indicators Research, 27,* 22–33.

23. Weiss, H. M., & Cropanzano, R. (1996). An affective events approach to job satisfaction. In B. M. Staw & L. L. Cummings (Eds.), *Research in organizational behavior* (Vol. 18, pp. 1–74). Greenwich, CT: JAI Press.

24. Ashkanasy, N. M., & Daus, C. S. (2002). Emotion in the workplace: New challenges for managers. *Academy of Management Executive, 16,* 76–86.

25. See Note 14.

26. Goleman, D. (1995). *Emotional intelligence.* New York: Bantam Books.

27. See Note 26.

28. Spencer, L. M., Jr. , & Spencer, S. (1993). *Competence at work: Models for superior performance.* New York: John Wiley and Sons. Spencer, L. M. J., McClelland, D. C., & Kelner, S. (1997). *Competency assessment methods: History and state of the art.* Boston, MA: Hay/McBer.

29. Groves, K. S., McEnrue, M. P., & Shen, W. (2008). Developing and measuring the emotional intelligence of leaders. *Journal of Management Development, 27,* 225–250. Boyatzis, R. E., & Saatcioglu, A. (2008). A twenty-year view of trying to develop emotional, social and cognitive intelligence competencies in graduate management education. *Journal of Management Development, 27,* 92–108.

30. Kouzes, J. M., & Posner, B. Z., (2008). *The leadership challenge* (4th ed.). San Francisco, CA: Jossey-Bass. Goleman, D., Boyatzis, R. E., & McKee, A. (2004). *Primal leadership: Learning to lead with emotional intelligence,* Boston, MA: Harvard Business School. Salski, M., & Cartwright, S. (2003). Emotional intelligence training and its implications for stress, health and performance. *Stress and Health, 19,* 233–239.

31. Morris, J. A., & Feldman, D. C. (1997). Managing emotions in the workplace. *Journal of Managerial Issues, 9,* 257–274.

32. Revel Entertainment press release, August 1, 2008. From the company's Web site at http://www.revelentertainment.com/media.html.

33. Zagaroli, L. (2009, January 16). Hudson River crash: Three tales of fear and salvation. McClatchy Newspapers. From the Web at http://www.mcclatchydc.com/200/story/59914.html

34. Dutton, J. E., Frost, P. J., Workline, M. C., Lilius, J. M., & Kanov, J. M. (2002, January). Leading in times of trauma. *Harvard Business Review,* pp. 54–61.

35. Bolles, R. N. (2009). *What color is your parachute?* (2009 edition). Berkeley, CA: Ten Speed Press.

36. Northwestern National Life Insurance Company. (1999). *Employee burnout: America's newest epidemic.* Minneapolis, MN: Author.

37. Quick, J. C., Murphy, L. R., & Hurrell, J. J., Jr. (1992). *Stress and well-being at work.* Washington, DC: American Psychological Association.

38. Selye, H. (1976). *Stress in health and disease.* Boston: Butterworths.

39. Kane, K. (1997, October–November). Can you perform under pressure? *Fast Company,* pp. 54, 56. Enhanced Performance Web site: www.enhanced-performance.com.

40. Bakker, A. B., Schaufeli, W. B., Sixma, H. J., Bosveld, W., & Van Dierendonck, D. (2000). Patient demands, lack of reciprocity, and burnout: A five-year longitudinal study among general practitioners. *Journal of Organizational Behavior, 21,* 425–441.

41. See Note 40.

42. Stress at work (1997, April 15). *Wall Street Journal,* p. A12.

43. Heller, R., & Hindle, T. (1998). *Essential manager's manual.* New York: DK Publishing.

44. Major, V. S., Klein, K. J., & Erhart, M. G. Work time, work interference with family, and psychological distress. *Journal of Applied Psychology, 87,* 427–436.

45. Settles, I. H., Sellers, R. M., & Damas, A., Jr. (2002). One role or two? The function of psychological separation in role conflict. *Journal of Applied Psychology, 87,* 574–582.

46. Fisher, A. B. (1993, August 23). Sexual harassment: What to do. *Fortune,* pp. 84–86, 88.

47. Kolbert, E. (1991, October 10). Sexual harassment at work is pervasive. *New York Times,* pp. A1, A17.

48. Office of Research, Information, and Planning. (2006). Sexual harassment charges: EEOC and FEPAs combined: FY 1992–FY 2005. From: http://www.eeoc.gov/stats/harass.html.

49. McGrath, J. E. (1976). Stress and behavior in organizations. In M. D. Dunnette (Ed.), *Handbook of industrial and organizational psychology* (pp. 1351–1398). Chicago, IL: Rand McNally.

50. Niessen, B. (2000, November 15). Last straw survey—overworked, overwrought: "Desk rage" at work. CNN.com. From: http://archives.cnn.com/2000/CAREER/trends/11/15/rage/.

51. Stephens, C., & Long, N. (2000). Communication with police supervisors and peers as a buffer of work-related traumatic stress. *Journal of Organizational Behavior, 21,* 407–424.

52. Beehr, T. A., Jex, S. M., Stacy, B. A., & Murray, M. A. (2000). Work stressors and coworker support as predictors of individual strain and job performance. *Journal of Organizational Behavior, 21,* 391–405.

53. Treharne, G. J., Lyons, A. C., & Tupling, R. E. (2001). The effects of optimism, pessimism, social support, and mood on the lagged relationship between stress and symptoms. *Current Research in Social Psychology, 7*(5), 60–81.

54. Sullivan, S. E., & Bhagat, R. S. (1992). Organizational stress, job satisfaction, and job performance: Where do we go from here? *Journal of Management, 18,* 353–374.

55. Cropanzano, R., Rupp, D. E., & Byrne, Z. S. (2003). The interrelationship of emotional exhaustion to work attitudes, job performance, and organizational citizenship behaviors. *Journal of Applied Psychology, 88,* 160–169. Motowidlo, S. J., Packard, J. S., & Manning, M. R. (1986). Occupational stress: Its causes and consequences for job performance. *Journal of Applied Psychology, 71,* 618–629.

56. Legree, P. J., Heffner, T. S., Psotka, J., Martin, D. E., & Medsker, G. J. (2003). Traffic crash involvement: Experiential driving knowledge and stressful contextual antecedents. *Journal of Applied Psychology, 88,* 5–26.

57. Frese, M. (1985). Stress at work and psychosomatic complaints: A causal interpretation. *Journal of Applied Psychology, 70,* 314–328. Quick, J. C., & Quick, J. D. (1984). *Organizational stress and preventive management.* New York: McGraw-Hill.

58. Krajicinovic, I. (1997). *From company doctors to managed care: The United Mine Workers' noble experiment.* Ithaca, NY: Cornell University Press.

59. Welch, D. (2008, August 11). The company doctor is back. *BusinessWeek,* pp. 48-49.

60. Latack, J. C., & Havlovic, S. J. (1992). Coping with job stress: A conceptual evaluation framework for coping measures. *Journal of Organizational Behavior, 13,* 479–508.

61. Society for Human Resource Management. (2006). *Annual benefits survey.* Alexandria, VA: SHRM.

62. Employee Assistance Professionals Association. (2006). Recent EAP cost/benefit statistics research: 2000–present. From: http://www.eapassn.org/ public/ articles/ EAPcostbenefitstats.pdf.

63. Flora, C. (2004, January/February). Keeping workers and companies fit. *Psychology Today,* pp. 36–40. Also available online at http://www.psychologytoday.com/articles/pto-3285.html.

64. See Note 63.

65. See Note 63.

66. Singer, T. (2007, October 17). The balance of power. *Inc. 500,* pp. 105–108, 110.

Chapter 5

Case Notes

Hyman, M. (2008, September 8). Paralympians break the ad barrier. *BusinessWeek,* p. 70. International Paralympic Committee. (2008). Paralympic games: Facts and figures. From the Web at www.paralympic.org/release/Main_Sections_Menu/Media/Infosheets/2008_07_Paralympic_Games_Facts_and_Figures.pdf. Prosthetics by Ossur (2008). Marlon Shirley. From the Web at www.ossur.com/pages/3361. Cheri Blauwet (2008). From the Web at www.cheriblauwet.com/. Group Benefits from the Hartford. (2008). Cheri Blauwet. From the Web at http://groupbenefits.thehartford.com/usp/bios/blauwet.html

Chapter Notes

1. Harrison, D. A., Newman, D. A., & Roth, P. L. 2006. How important are job attitudes? Meta-analytic comparisons for integrative behavioral outcomes and time sequences. *Academy of Management Journal, 49,* 305–326.

2. Gregory, R. F. (2001). *Age discrimination in the American workplace: Old at a young age.* New Brunswick, NJ: Rutgers University Press.

3. See Note 2.

4. U.S. Department of Justice. (2009). Americans with Disabilities Act. From the Web at www.ada.gov.

5. Editors of Diversity Inc. (2008, May 12). The top 10 companies for executive women. *Diversity Magazine.* From the Web at http://www.diversityinc.com/public/3499.cfm

6. CATALYST (2000). *The glass ceiling in 2000.* New York: Author (from the Web at www.catalystwomen.org/press/factslabor00.html. Bureau of Labor Statistics, 1999; Catalyst, 1999 Census of Women Corporate Officers and Top Earners; 1999 Census of Women Board Directors of the *Fortune* 1000).

7. Hereck, G. M. (1998). *Stigma and sexual orientation: Understanding prejudice against lesbians, gay men, and bisexuals.* Newbury Park, CA: Sage.

8. Alternatives to Marriage Project. (2008). From the Web at http://www.unmarried.org/statistics.html.

9. Yang, C. (1993, June 21). In any language, it's unfair: More immigrants are bringing bias charges against employers. *BusinessWeek,* pp. 110–112 (quote, p. 111).

10. Philosophy and Public Policy. (2008). Civil rights and racial preferences: A legal history of affirmative action. From the Web at www.puaf.umd.edu/IPPP/2QQ.HTM

11. Kravitz, D. A. (2008). The diversity-validity dilemma: Beyond selection—the role of affirmative action. *Personnel Psychology, 61,* 173-193.

12. Kravitz, D. A., & Klineberg, S. L. (2000). Reactions to two versions of affirmative action among whites, blacks, and Hispanics. *Journal of Applied Psychology, 85,* 597–611.

13. Polus, S. (1996). Ten myths about affirmative action. *Journal of Social Issues, 52,* 25–31.

14. Ragins, B. R., & Gonzales, J. A. (2003). Understanding diversity in organizations: Getting a grip on a slippery construct. In J. Greenberg (Ed.), *Organizational behavior:*

The state of the science (2nd ed.) (pp. 125–163). Mahwah, NJ: Lawrence Erlbaum Associates.

15. Thomas, R. R., Jr. (1992). Managing diversity: A conceptual framework. In S. E. Jackson (Ed.), *Diversity in the workplace* (pp. 306–317). New York: Guilford Press.

16. Klein, K. J., & Harrison, D. A. (2007). On the diversity of diversity: Tidy logic, messier realities. *Academic of Management Perspectives, 21,* 26–33. Harrison, D. A. & Klein, K. J. 2007. What's the difference? Diversity constructs as separation, variety, or disparity in organizations. *Academy of Management Review, 32,* 1199–1228.

17. Richard, O. C. (2000). Racial diversity, business strategy, and firm performance: A resource-based view. *Academy of Management Journal, 43,* 164–177.

18. Gingold, D. (2000, July 26). Diversity today. *Fortune,* special section.

19. What's it like to work at Allstate? Diversity. (2009). From the Web at www.allstate.com/ Careers/PageRender.asp?Page=diversity.htm. Nance-Nash, C. (2008, Summer). Top 100 under 50 diverse executives. *Diversity MBA,* pp. 16–59.

20. Allstate. (2008). Awards and recognition. From the Web at http://media.allstate.com/ categories/18/releases/4025

21. University of Chicago, National Opinion Center (2007, August 31). HRM Guide: Job Satisfaction. Most Americans Satisfied with their Jobs. From the Web at http:// www.hrmguide.com/commitment/ job-satisfaction-positive.htm

22. Herzberg, F. (1966). *Work and the nature of man.* Cleveland, OH: World.

23. Department of Homeland Security: 2008 Federal Human Capital Survey Results. From the Web at http://www.dhs.gov/ xlibrary/assets/dhs_annual_employee_ survey_summary_2008.pdf

24. Salancik, G. R., & Pfeffer, J. R. (1978). A social information processing approach to job attitudes. *Administrative Science Quarterly, 23,* 224–252. Zalesny, M. D., & Ford, J. K. (1990). Extending the social information processing perspective: New links to attitudes, behaviors, and perceptions. *Organizational Behavior and Human Decision Processes, 47,* 205–246.

25. Judge, T. A. (1992). Dispositional perspective in human resources research. In G. R. Ferris & K. M. Rowland (Eds.), *Research in personality and human resources management* (Vol. 10, pp. 31–72). Greenwich, CT: JAI Press.

26. Coca-Cola Research Council. (2009, January). *New ideas for retaining store-level employees.* Atlanta, GA: Author.

27. Cornell University Hotel School. (2008). Compilation of turnover cost studies. *SASHA Corporation.* From the Web at http://www.sashacorp.com/ turnframe.html

28. Nichols, M. (2008, October 30). How can employers limit the cost of absenteeism? An international look. *Citizen Economists.* From the Web at http://www.citizeneconomists .com/view_articles_detail.php?aid=135

29. Hardy, G. E., Woods, D., & Wall, T. D. (2003). The impact of psychological distress on absence from work. *Journal of Applied Psychology, 88,* 306–314.

30. Judge, T. A., Heller, D., & Mount, M. K. (2002). Five-factor model of personality and job satisfaction. *Journal of Applied Psychology, 87,* 530–541.

31. Judge, T. A., Bono, J. E., & Patton, G. K. (2001). The job satisfaction–performance relationship: A qualitative and quantitative review. *Psychological Bulletin, 127,* 376–407.

32. Barling, J., Kelloway, E. K., & Iverson, R. D. (2003). High-quality work, job satisfaction, and occupational injuries. *Journal of Applied Psychology, 88,* 276–283.

33. Schneider, B., Hanges, P. J., Smith, D. B., & Salvaggio, A. N. (2004). Which comes first: Employee attitudes or organizational financial and market performance? *Journal of Applied Psychology, 88,* 836–851.

34. Judge, T. A., & Illies, R. (2004). Affect and job satisfaction: A study of their relationship at work and at home. *Journal of Applied Psychology, 89,* 661–673.

35. Snape, E., & Redman, T. (2003). An evaluation of a three-component model of occupational commitment: Dimensionality and consequences among United Kingdom human resource management specialists. *Journal of Applied Psychology, 88,* 152–159. Meyer, J. P., Allen, N. J., & Smith, C. A.

(1993). Commitment to organizations and occupations: Extension and test of a three-component conceptualization. *Journal of Applied Psychology, 78,* 538–551.

36. Dicker, J. (2008, December 17). Workers saying no to new jobs. CNNMoney.com. From the Web at http://money.cnn.com/2008/12/16/news/economy/job_hopping/index.htm

37. Lee, K., Carswell, J. J., & Allen, N. J. (2000). A meta-analytic review of occupational commitment: Relations with person- and work-related variables. *Journal of Applied Psychology, 85,* 799–811.

38. Clugston, M. (2000). The mediating effects of multidimensional commitment on job satisfaction and intent to leave. *Journal of Organizational Behavior, 21,* 477–486.

39. Lee, T. W., Ashford, S. J., Walsh, J. P., & Mowday, R. T. (1992). Commitment propensity, organizational commitment, and voluntary turnover: A longitudinal study of organizational entry processes. *Journal of Management, 18,* 15–32.

40. The Editorial Board. (2008, December 3). The auto CEOs in the $1-a-year club. *New York Times.* From the Web at http://theboard.blogs.nytimes.com/2008/12/03/the-auto-ceos-join-the-1-a-year-club/?hp.

41. Hui, C., Lam, S. S. K., & Law, K. K. S. (2000). Instrumental values of organizational citizenship behavior for promotion: A field quasi-experiment. *Journal of Applied Psychology, 85,* 822–828.

42. Meyer, J. P., & Allen, N. J. (1991). A three-component conceptualization of organizational commitment. *Human Resource Management Review, 1,* 61–89.

Chapter 6

Case Notes

Costco Wholesale. (2008). Member relations. From the Web at http://phx.corporate-ir.net/phoenix.zhtml?c=83830&p=irol-homeprofile. Costco Wholesale. (2008). *Wikinvest.* From the Web at http://www.wikinvest.com/stock/. Costco_Wholesale_(COST). Yukl, G., & Lepsinger, R. (2005). Why integrating the leading and managing roles is essential

for organizational effectiveness. *Organizational Dynamics,* 34(4), 361–375. Holmes, S., & Zellner, W. (2004, April 12). The Costco way: Higher wages mean higher profits; but try telling Wall Street. *BusinessWeek,* pp. 76–77. Kiel, F. (2008, October 6). Flaws in the selfish-worker theory. *BusinessWeek,* p. 78.

Chapter Notes

1. Locke, E. A., & Latham, G. P. (2008). Employee motivation. In J. Barling & C. Cooper (Eds.), *Sage handbook of organizational behavior* (Vol. 1, pp. 318–333). Thousand Oaks, CA: Sage.

2. Cascio, W. F., & Aguinis, H. (2008). Research in industrial and organizational psychology from 1963 to 2007: Changes, choices and trends. *Journal of Applied Psychology, 93,* 1062–1081.

3. The Gallup Poll. (2006). From the Web at: jttp://poll.gallup.com/.

4. Robson, C. (2004). What motivates workers today? London: Hays Office Support. From the Web at http://www.hays.com/uk/index.jsp?Channel=office&Content=/uk/jobseekers/office/what-motivates-office-workers-today.htm.

5. Pfeffer, J. (1998). *The human equation.* Boston: Harvard Business School Press.

6. Maslow, A. H. (1987). *Motivation and personality* (3rd ed.). Boston: Addison-Wesley.

7. Where's my Stairmaster? (1999, October). *Across the Board,* p. 5.

8. Cool Running. (2008). Employee health, fitness on companies' agendas. From the Web at http://www.coolrunning.com/major/97/training/news/0823976.htm

9. Lincoln Electric. (2008). Jobs/careers at Lincoln. From the Web at http://www.lincolnelectric.com/corporate/career/openings.asp. Against the grain. (1999, May). *Across the Board,* p. 1.

10. Klubnik, J. P. (1995). *Rewarding and recognizing employees.* Chicago: Richard D. Irwin. Leverence, J. (1997). *And the winner is . . .* Santa Monica, CA: Merritt.

11. Shepherd, M. D. (1993, February). Staff motivation. *U.S. Pharmacist,* pp. 82, 85, 89–93 (quote, p. 91).

12. Langley, M. (2003, June 9). Big companies get low marks for lavish executive pay. *Wall Street Journal*, p. C1.

13. Greenberg, J., Ashon-James, C. E., & Ashkanasy, N. M. (2007). Social comparison processes in organizations. *Organizational Behavior and Human Decision Processes, 102,* 22–41.

14. Friedman, T. L. (1999). *The Lexus and the olive tree.* New York: Anchor Books.

15. Colquitt, J. A., & Greenberg, J. (2003). Organizational justice: A fair assessment of the state of the literature. In J. Greenberg (Ed.), *Organizational behavior: The state of the science* (2nd ed.) (pp. 165–210). Mahwah, NJ: Lawrence Erlbaum Associates. Adams, J. S. (1965). Inequity in social exchange. In L. Berkowitz (Ed.), *Advances in experimental social psychology* (Vol. 2, pp. 267–299). New York: Academic Press.

16. Brinson, W. (2009, February 13). Stacey Dale quits ESPN over airline tix. *Fanhouse Back Porch.* From the Web at: http://backporch.fanhouse.com/2009/02/13/stacey-dales-quit-espn-over-airline-tix/.

17. Harder, J. W. (1992). Play for pay: Effects of inequity in a pay-for-performance context. *Administrative Science Quarterly, 37,* 321–335.

18. Greenberg, J. (1993). Stealing in the name of justice: Informational and interpersonal moderators of theft reactions to underpayment inequity. *Organizational Behavior and Human Decision Processes, 54,* 81–103.

19. Mowday, R. T., & Colwell, K. A. (2003). Employee reactions to unfair outcomes in the workplace: The contributions of Adams's equity theory to understanding work motivation. In L. W. Porter, G. A. Bigley, & R. M. Steers (Eds.), *Motivation and work behavior* (7th ed.). (pp. 65–82). Burr Ridge, IL: McGraw-Hill/Irwin.

20. Bird, K. (2008, February 19). Strike at L'Oreal over low wages. *Cosmetics Design Europe.* From the Web at http://www.cosmeticsdesign-europe.com/ Financial/Strike-at-L-Oreal-over-low-wages

21. Bhushan, N. (2008, October 2). Bollywood workers strike for better wages. *Reuters UK:* From the Web at http://uk.reuters.com/article/entertainmentNews/idUKTRE49100920081002?sp=true

22. Kahn, Z. A. (2008, August 27). Low wage staff of NAPWD end strike after two days. *Parmir News.* From the Web at http://pamirtimes.wordpress.com/2008/08/27/ low-wage-staff-of-napwd-end-strike-after-two-days/

23. Terlep, S, & Vlasic, B. (2007, September 26). Sides hammer out two-tier wage deal. *Detroit News.* From the Web at http://www.detroitnews.com/apps/pbcs.dll/article?AID=/20070926/AUTO01/709260398/1148

24. Baron, J., & Kreps, D. M. (1999). *Strategic human resource management.* New York: John Wiley & Sons.

25. Lawler, E. E., III. (1967). Secrecy about management compensation: Are there hidden costs? *Organizational Behavior and Human Performance, 2,* 182–189.

26. Porter, L. W., & Lawler, E. E., III. (1968). *Managerial attitudes and performance.* Homewood, IL: Irwin.

27. Chu, K. (2004, June 15). Firms report lackluster results from pay-for-performance plans. *Wall Street Journal*, p. D1.

28. Bogle, J. (2008). Reflections on CEO compensation. *Academy of Management Perspectives, 22,* 21–25. Kaplan, S. N. (2008). Are U. S. CEOs overpaid? *Academy of Management Perspectives, 22,* 5–20.

29. Kalwarski, T. (2008, September 8). Extravagant executive pay shows signs of moderation. *BusinessWeek*, p. 9.

30. Andrews, E. L., & Dash, E. (2009, February 13). Stimulus plan places new limits on Wall St. bonuses. *New York Times.* From the Web at: http://www.nytimes.com/2009/02/14/business/economy/14pay.html?_r=1&partner=rss&emc=rss&src=igw.

31. Schrage, M. (2000, April 3). Cafeteria benefits? Ha, you deserve a richer banquet. *Fortune*, p. 276.

32. Boreman, A. M. (1999, October 19). Clean my house, and I'm yours forever. *Inc.,* p. 216. Emerging optional benefits. (1998, December), p. 8. Hickins, M. (1999, April). Creative "get-a-life" benefits. *Management Review*, p. 7. Nelson, B. (1994). *1001 ways to reward employees.* New York: Waterman. Palmer, A. T. (1999, April 26). Who's minding the baby? The company. *BusinessWeek*, p. 32.

33. Locke, E. A., & Latham, G. (2009). Set goals to enhance task performance. In E. A. Locke (Ed.), *Handbook of principles of organizational behavior* (2nd ed.). Malden, MA: Blackwell.

34. Locke, E. A., & Latham, G. P. (1990). *A theory of goal setting and task performance.* Upper Saddle River, NJ: Prentice Hall.

35. Mitchell, T. R., & Daniels, D. (2003). Observations and commentary on recent research in work motivation. In L. W. Porter, G. A. Bigley, & R. M. Steers (Eds.), *Motivation and work behavior* (7th ed) (pp. 26–44). Burr Ridge, IL: McGraw-Hill/Irwin (quote, p. 29).

36. Mento, A. J., Locke, E. A., & Klein, H. J. (1992). Relationship of goal level to valence and instrumentality. *Journal of Applied Psychology, 77,* 395–406.

37. Wright, P. M., O'Leary-Kelly, A. M., Cortinak, J. M., Klein, H. J., & Hollenbeck, J. R. (1994). On the meaning and measurement of goal commitment. *Journal of Applied Psychology, 79,* 795–803.

38. Klein, H. J. (1991). Further evidence on the relationship between goal setting and expectancy theories. *Organizational Behavior and Human Decision Processes, 49,* 230–257.

39. Harrison, D. A., & Liska, L. Z. (1994). Promoting regular exercise in organizational fitness programs: Health-related differences in motivational building blocks. *Personnel Psychology, 47,* 47–71.

40. Klein, H. J., Wesson, M. J., Hollenbeck, J. R., & Alge, B. J. (1999). Goal commitment and the goal-setting process: Conceptual clarification and empirical synthesis. *Journal of Applied Psychology, 84,* 885–896.

41. Gellatly, I. R., & Meyer, J. P. (1992). The effects of goal difficulty on physiological arousal, cognition, and task performance. *Journal of Applied Psychology, 77,* 696–704.

42. Wright, P. M. (1992). An examination of the relationships among monetary incentives, goal level, goal commitment, and performance. *Journal of Management, 18,* 677–693.

43. Earley, P. C., & Litucy, T. R. (1991). Delineating goal and efficacy effects: A test of three models. *Journal of Applied Psychology, 76,* 81–98.

44. Latham, G., & Baldes, J. (1975). The practical significance of Locke's theory of goal setting. *Journal of Applied Psychology, 60,* 122–126.

45. Latham, G. P., Erez, M., & Locke, E. A. (1988). Resolving scientific disputes by the joint design of crucial experiments by the antagonists: Application to the Erez-Latham dispute regarding participation in goal setting. *Journal of Applied Psychology, 73,* 756–772.

46. Finegan, J. (1993, July). People power. *Inc.,* pp. 62–63 (quote, p. 63).

47. Donovan, J. J., & Williams, K. J. (2003). Missing the mark: Effects of time and causal attributions on goal revision in response to goal-performance discrepancies. *Journal of Applied Psychology, 88,* 379–390.

48. Pritchard, R. D., Jones, S. D., Roth, P. L., Stuebing, K. K., & Ekberg, S. E. (1988). Effects of group feedback, goal setting, and incentives on organizational productivity. *Journal of Applied Psychology, 73,* 337–358.

49. Morgenson, F. P., & Campion, M. A. (2003). Work design. In W. C. Borman, D. R. Ilgen, & R. J. Klimoski (Eds.), *Handbook of psychology, Vol. 12: Industrial and organizational psychology* (pp. 423–452). New York: John Wiley & Sons.

50. Campion, M. A., & McClelland, C. L. (1991). Interdisciplinary examination of the costs and benefits of enlarged jobs: A job design quasi-experiment. *Journal of Applied Psychology, 76,* 186–198.

51. Campion, M. A., & McClelland, C. L. (1993). Follow-up and extension of the interdisciplinary costs and benefits of enlarged jobs. *Journal of Applied Psychology, 78,* 339–351.

52. Hackman, J. R., & Oldham, G. R. (1980). *Work redesign.* Reading, MA: Addison-Wesley.

53. De Varo, J., Li, R. & Brookshire, D. (2007). Analysing the job characteristics model: New support from a cross-section of establishments. *International Journal of Human Resource Management, 18*(6), 986–1003.

Chapter 7

Case Notes

Leslie-Pelecky, D. (2008). *The physics of NASCAR: How to make steel + gas + rubber = speed.* New York: Dutton/Penguin. Clarke, L.

(2008). *One helluva ride: How NASCAR swept the nation.* New York: Villard/Random House. NASCAR.com (2008, July 17). History of NASCAR, http://www.nascar.com/news/features/history/. Ronfeldt, D. (2000, February). Social science at 190 mph on NASCAR's biggest speedways. First Monday, 5(2), firstmonday.org/issues/issue5_2/ronfeldt/index.html. Daytona International Speedway. (2008). Brief history of the 500. Daytona 500, http://www.daytona500.com/content-display.cfm/cat/Brief-History-of-the-500.

Chapter Notes

1. Ronfeldt, D. (2000, February). Social science at 190 mph on NASCAR's biggest speedways. *First Monday, 5*(2), from the Web at firstmonday.org/issues/issue5_2/ronfeldt/index.html.

2. Chen, Z. X., Tsui, A. S., & Zhong, L. (2008). Reactions to psychological contract breach: A dual perspective. *Journal of Organizational Behavior, 29,* 527–548. Rousseau, D. M. (2001). Schema, promise, and mutuality: The building blocks of the psychological contract. *Journal of Occupational and Organizational Psychology, 74,* 511–541. Robinson, S. L., & Morrison, E. W. (2000). The development of psychological contract breach violation: A longitudinal study. *Journal of Organizational Behavior, 21,* 525–546.

3. Guerrero, S., & Herrbach, O. (2008). The affective underpinnings of psychological contract fulfillment. *Journal of Managerial Psychology, 23,* 4–17. Rousseau, D. M., & Parks, J. M. (1993). The contracts of individuals and organizations. In L. L. Cummings & B. M. Staw (Eds.), *Research in organizational behavior* (Vol. 15, pp. 1–43). Greenwich, CT: JAI Press. Turnley, W. H., & Feldman, D. C. (2000). Re-examining the effects of psychological contract violations: Unmet expectations and job dissatisfaction as mediators. *Journal of Organizational Behavior, 21,* 25–42.

4. Rousseau, D. M., Ho, V. T., & Greenberg, J. (2006). I-deals: Idiosyncratic terms in employment relationships. *Academy of Management Review, 31,* 977–994.

5. Rousseau, D. M. (2005). *I-deals: Idiosyncratic deals employees bargain for themselves.* New York: M. E. Sharpe.

6. Lewicki, R. J., McAllister, D. J., & Bies, R. J. (1998). Trust and distrust: New relationships and realities. *Academy of Management Review, 23,* 438–458.

7. Lau, D. C., Liden, R. C. (2008). Antecedents of coworker trust: Leaders' blessings. *Journal of Applied Psychology, 93,* 1130–1138. Lewicki, R. J., & Wiethoff, C. (2000). Trust, trust development, and trust repair. In M. Deutsch & P. T. Coleman (Eds.), *The handbook of conflict resolution* (pp. 86–107). San Francisco, CA: Jossey-Bass.

8. Chapman, C. (2002, September/October). The human side of business. *BizEd,* pp. 20–25.

9. Schultz, H., & Yang, D. J. (1999). *Pour your heart into it: How Starbucks built a company one cup at a time.* New York: Hyperion.

10. Bommer, W., Dierdorff, E. C., & Rubin, R. S. (2007). Does prevalence mitigate relevance? The moderating effect of group-level OCB on employee performance. *Academy of Management Journal, 50,* 1481–1494. Podsakoff, P. M., MacKenzie, S. B., Paine, J. B., & Bachrach, D. G. (2000). Organizational citizenship behaviors: A critical review of the theoretical and empirical literature and suggestions for future research. *Journal of Management, 26,* 513–563.

11. Zellars, K. L., Tepper, B. J., & Duffy, M. K. (2002). Abusive supervision and subordinates' organizational citizenship behavior. *Journal of Applied Psychology, 87,* 1068–1076.

12. See Note 2.

13. Fomburn, C. J. (1996). *Reputation.* Boston: Harvard Business School Press.

14. Turley, W. H., Bolino, M. C., Lester, S. W., & Bloodgood, J. M. (2003). The impact of psychological contract fulfillment on the performance of in-role and organizational citizenship behaviors. *Journal of Management, 29,* 187–206. Coyle-Shapiro, J. A-M. (2002). A psychological contract perspective on organizational citizenship behavior. *Journal of Organizational Behavior, 23,* 927–946.

15. Miceli, M., Near, J., & Dworkin, T. (2008). *Whistle-blowing in organizations.* Mahwah, NJ: Lawrence Erlbaum Associates. Gundlach, M. J., Scott, D. S., & Martinko, M. J. (2003).

The decision to blow the whistle: A social information processing framework. *Academy of Management Review, 28,* 107–123.

16. Quinn, J. (2009, February 3). Bernard Madoff whistleblower Harry Markopolos to testify today. *Telegragph.co.uk.* From the Web at: http://www.telegraph.co.uk/finance/financetopics/bernard-madoff/4443217/Bernard-Madoff-whistleblower-Harry-Markopolos-to-testify-today.html. Fricker, D. G. (2002, March 27). Enron whistle-blower honored in Dearborn. From the World Wide Web at www.freep.com/money/business/htm. Anonymous. (2000, April). Paul van Buitenen: Paying the price of accountability. *Accountancy, 125*(1), 280. Taylor, M. (1999, September 13). Another Columbia suit unsealed. *Modern Healthcare, 29*(37), 10. Ettore, B. (1994, May). Whistleblowers: Who's the real bad guy? *Management Review,* pp. 18–23.

17. Gjersten, L. A. (1999). Five State Farm agents fired after accusing company of consumer abuse. *National Underwriter, 103*(51), 1, 23.

18. Martucci, W. C., & Smith, E. W. (2000). Recent state legislative development concerning employment discrimination and whistle-blower protections. *Employment Relations Today, 27*(2), 89–99.

19. Jones, M., & Rowell, A. (1999). Safety whistleblowers intimidated. *Safety and Health Practitioner, 17*(8), 3.

20. Falk, A., Gachter, S., & Kovacs, J. (1999). Intrinsic motivation and extrinsic incentives in a repeated game with incomplete contracts. *Journal of Economic Psychology, 20,* 251–284.

21. Knight, G. P., Dubro, A. F., & Chao, C. (1985). Information processing and the development of cooperative, competitive, and individualistic social values. *Developmental Psychology, 21,* 37–45.

22. Knight, G. P., & Dubro, A. F. (1984). Cooperative, competitive, and individualistic social values: An individualized regression and clustering approach. *Journal of Personality and Social Psychology, 46,* 98–105.

23. Kirkman, B. L., & Shapiro, D. L. (2000). Understanding why team members won't share: An examination of factors related to employee receptivity to team-based rewards. *Small Group Research, 31,* 175–209.

DeMatteo, J. S., Eby, L. T., & Sundstrom, E. (1998). Team-based rewards: Current empirical evidence and directions for future research. In B. M. Staw & L. L. Cummings (Eds.), *Research in organizational behavior* (Vol. 20, pp. 141–183). Greenwich, CT: JAI. Heneman, R.L. (2000). *Business-driven compensation policies.* New York: AMACOM.

24. Teerlink, R., & Ozley, L. (2000). *More than a motorcycle: The leadership journey at Harley-Davidson.* Boston: Harvard Business School Press.

25. Thomas, K. W., & Schmidt, W. H. (1976). A survey of managerial interests with respect to conflict. *Academy of Management Journal, 10,* 315–318.

26. Dirks, K. T., & McLean Parks, J. (2003). Conflicting stories: The state of the science of conflict. In J. Greenberg (Ed.), *Organizational behavior: The state of the science* (2nd ed.). (pp. 283–324). Mahwah, NJ: Lawrence Erlbaum Associates.

27. Jehn, K., & Mannix, E. (2001). The dynamic nature of conflict: A longitudinal study of intragroup conflict and performance. *Academy of Management Journal, 44,* 238–251.

28. Bragg, T. (1999, October). Ten ways to deal with conflict. *IIE Solutions,* pp. 36–37.

29. Resume: Howard Schultz (2002, September 9). *BusinessWeek Online.* From the Web at www.businessweek.com/magazine/content/02_36/b3798005.htm.

30. Bordwin, M. (1999). Do-it-yourself justice. *Management Review,* pp. 56–58.

31. Greenberg, J. (2004). Deviance. In N. Nicholson, P. Audia, & M. Pillutla (Eds.), *Blackwell encyclopedia of organizational behavior,* (2nd ed.). Malden, MA: Blackwell. Bennett, R. J., & Robinson, S. L. (2003). The past, present, and future of workplace deviance research. In J. Greenberg (Ed.), *Organizational behavior: The state of the science* (2nd ed.). (pp. 247–282). Mahwah, NJ: Lawrence Erlbaum Associates. Vardi, Y., & Weitz, E. (2003). *Misbehavior in organizations: Theory, research, management.* Mahwah, NJ: Lawrence Erlbaum Associates.

32. Lee, M. (1998, October 12). "See you in court—er, mediation." *BusinessWeek Enterprise,* pp. ENT22, ENT24.

33. Bordia, P., Restubog, S. L. D., & Tang, R. L. (2008). When employees strike back: Investigating mediating mechanisms between psychological contract breach and workplace deviance. *Journal of Applied Psychology, 93,* 1104–1117.

34. Bennett, R. J., & Robinson, S. L. (2000). The development of a measure of workplace deviance. *Journal of Applied Psychology, 85,* 349–360. Robinson, S. L., & Bennett, R. J. (1995). A typology of deviant workplace behaviors: A multidimensional scaling study. *Academy of Management Journal, 38,* 555–572.

35. See Note 29.

36. National Institute for Occupational Safety and Health, Centers for Disease Control and Prevention. (1993). *Homicide in the workplace.* [Document # 705003]. Atlanta, GA: Author.

37. Jockin, V., Arvey, R. D., & McGue, M. (2001). Perceived victimization moderates self-reports of workplace aggression and conflict. *Journal of Applied Psychology, 86,* 1262–1269.

38. Douglas, S. C., & Martinko, M. J. (2001). Exploring the role of individual differences in the prediction of workplace aggression. *Journal of Applied Psychology, 86,* 547–559.

39. LeBlanc, M. M., & Kelloway, E. K. (2002). Predictors and outcomes of workplace violence and aggression. *Journal of Applied Psychology, 87,* 444–453.

40. Varita, M., & Jari, R. (2002). Gender differences in workplace bullying among prison officers. *European Journal of Work and Occupational Psychology, 11,* 113–126.

41. Cowie, H., Naylor, P., Rivers, I., Smith, P. K., & Pereira, B. (2002). Measuring workplace bullying. *Aggression and Violent Behavior, 7,* 33–51.

42. Namie, G. (2000). *U.S. hostile workplace survey, 2000.* Benicia, CA: Campaign Against Workplace Bullying.

43. Namie, G., & Namie, R. (2001). *The bully at work.* Naperville, IL: Sourcebooks.

44. Kowalski, R. M., Limber, S. P., & Agatston, P. W. (2008). *Cyber bullying: Bullying in the digital age.* New York: Wiley Blackwell.

45. Trevino, L. K., & Weaver, G. R. (1998). Punishment in organizations: Descriptive and normative perspectives. In M. Schminke (Ed.), *Managerial ethics: Moral management of people and processes* (pp. 99–114). Mahwah, NJ: Erlbaum.

46. Lind, E. A., Greenberg, J., Scott, K. S., & Welchans, T. D. (2000). The winding road from employee to complainant: Situational and psychological determinants of wrongful-termination claims. *Administrative Science Quarterly, 45,* 557–590.

47. Jack L. Hayes International. (2008). Employee theft, From the Web at: http://www.hayesinternational.com/thft_srvys.html. Kooker, N. R. (2000, May 22). Taking aim at crime—stealing the profits: Tighter controls, higher morale may safeguard bottom line. *Nation's Restaurant News, 34*(21), 114–118. Young, D. (2000, May 1). Inside jobs. *Wireless Review, 17*(9), 14–20. Rosner, B. (1999, October). How do you feel about video surveillance at work? *Workforce, 78*(10), 26–27. Anonymous. (1999, May). As new CCTV system goes live, cashiers quit. *Security, 36*(5), 40. Wells, J. T. (1999, August). A fistful of dollars. *Security Management, 43*(8), 70–75. Vara, B. (1999, June). The "steal trap." *National Petroleum News, 91*(6), 28–31. Wimmer, N. (1999, June). Fingers in the till. *Asian Business, 35*(6), 59–60. Golden, P. (1999, May). Dangers without, dangers within. *Electronic Business, 25*(5), 65–70.

48. Jabbkerm, A. (2000, March 29). Agrium seeks $30 million in damages in embezzlement case. *Chemical Week, 162*(13), 22.

49. Greenberg, J. (1998). The cognitive geometry of employee theft: Negotiating "the line" between taking and stealing. In R. W. Griffin, A. O'Leary-Kelly, & J. M. Collins (Eds.), *Dysfunctional behavior in organizations: Non-violent dysfunctional behavior* (pp. 147–194). Stamford, CT: JAI Press.

50. Greenberg, J., & Tomlinson, E. (2006). Methodological issues in the study of employee theft. In R. Griffin & A. O'Leary-Kelley (Eds.), *The dark side of organizational behavior* (pp. 422–444). San Francisco, CA: Jossey-Bass.

Chapter 8

Case Notes

Jackson, M. (2008). *Distraction.* New York: Prometheus Books. Jackson, M. (2008, June 23). May we have your attention, please?

BusinessWeek, pp. 55–56. Marcus, G. (2008). *Kluge: The haphazard construction of the human mind.* New York: Houghton Mifflin. Eric Horvitz homepage. (2008), From the Web at http://research.microsoft.com/~horvitz/.

Chapter Notes

1. Roberts, K. H. (1984). *Communicating in organizations.* Chicago: Science Research Associates (quote, p. 4).
2. Gillis, T. (2008). *The IABC handbook of organizational communication.* San Francisco, CA: Jossey-Bass. Weick, K. E. (1987). Theorizing about organizational communication. In F. M. Jablin, L. L. Putnam, K. H. Roberts, & L. W. Porter (Eds.), *Handbook of organizational communication* (pp. 97–122). Newbury Park, CA: Sage.
3. Daft, R. L., Lengel, R. H., & Trevino, L. K. (1987). Message equivocality, media selection, and manager performance: Implications for information systems. *MIS Quarterly, 11,* 355–366.
4. Stromberg, R. M. (1998, September). No, it couldn't happen here. *American Management Association International,* p. 70.
5. Poe, R., & Courter, C. L. (1998, September). The great coffee grapevine. *Across the Board,* p. 7.
6. Thibaut, A. M., Calder, B. J., & Sternthal, B. (1981). Using information processing theory to design marketing strategies. *Journal of Marketing Research, 18,* 73–79.
7. Schiller, Z. (1995, September 11). P&G is still having a devil of a time. *BusinessWeek,* p. 46.
8. Voas, J. M. (2002). Corporate rumors and conspiracy theories. *IT Professional, 4*(2), 63–64. (quote, p. 63).
9. The Coca-Cola Company. (2008), From the Web at http://www2.coca-cola.com/contactus/myths_rumors/.
10. Solove, J. (2008). *The future of reputation: Gossip, rumor, and privacy on the Internet.* New Haven, CT: Yale University Press. McCarthy, E. (2003, May 1). Jousting with rumor mills. *Washington Post,* p. E1.
11. Lengel, R. H., & Daft, R. L. (1988). The selection of communication media as an executive skill. *Academy of Management Executive, 2,* 225–232.
12. Widmeyer Communications. (2008). Who we are, From the Web at http://www.widmeyer.com/contact/. Esterson, E. (1998). Inner beauties. *Inc. Tech,* pp. 78–80, 84, 86, 88, 90.
13. Jablin, F. M., & Putnam, L. L. (2006). *The new handbook of organizational communication: Advances in theory, research, and methods.* Thousand Oaks, CA: Sage.
14. Thurlow, C., Lengel, L., & Tomic, A. (2004). *Computer-mediated communication.* Thousand Oaks, CA: Sage.
15. Schneider, S. J., Kerwin, J., Frechtling, J., & Vivari, B. A. (2002). Characteristics of the discussion in online and face-to-face focus groups. *Social Science Computer Review, 20,* 31–42.
16. 25 years of the smiley face. (2007). From the Web at http://www.itpro.co.uk/news/125581.
17. Walther, J. B., & Addario, K. P. (2001). The impacts of emoticons on message interpretation in computer-mediated communication. *Social Science Computer Review, 19,* 324–347.
18. Wolf, A. (2000). Emotional expression online: Gender differences in emoticon use. *CyberPsychology & Behavior, 3,* 827–833.
19. Hickson, M. L., Stacks, D. W., & Moore, N-J. (2003). *Nonverbal communication: Studies and applications* (4th ed.). Los Angeles, CA: Roxbury Publishing.
20. Rafaeli, A., Dutton, J. Harquail, C., & Mackie-Lewis, S. (1997). Navigating by attire: The use of dress by female administrative employees. *Academy of Management Journal, 40,* 9–45.
21. Greenberg, J. (1989). The organizational waiting game: Time as a status-asserting or status-neutralizing tactic. *Basic and Applied Social Psychology, 10,* 13–26.
22. Zweigenhaft, R. L. (1976). Personal space in the faculty office: Desk placement and student–faculty interaction. *Journal of Applied Psychology, 61,* 628–632.
23. Dubrin, A. J. (2007). *Leadership* (5th ed.). Boston: Houghton Mifflin.
24. Tannen, D. (1998, February 2). How you speak shows where you rank. *Fortune,* p. 156.
25. Wurman, R. S. (2000). *Understanding.* Newport, RI: TED Conferences.
26. Whetten, D. E., & Cameron, K. S. (2002). *Developing management skills* (5th ed.). Upper Saddle River, NJ: Prentice Hall.

27. Castillo, C., Jr. (2008, April). Employee suggestion system improves efficiencies. *Statehouse Observer, 35*(8), p. 1.

28. Labarre, P. (1998, November). Screw up, and get smart. *Fast Company,* p. 58.

29. KDPaine & Partners. (2008). Who we are, From the Web at http://www.measuresof success.com/About+Us/Who+we+are/ default.aspx.

30. Computer Mail Services. (2003). *Spam calculator.* From the Web at http:// www.cmsconnect.com.

31. Morrison, K. E. (1994). *Leadership skills.* Tucson, AZ: Fisher Books.

32. Rosen, R., Digh, P., Singer, M., & Phillips, C. (2000). *Global literacies.* New York: Simon & Schuster.

33. Marx, E. (2001). *Breaking through culture shock.* London: Nicholas Brealey Publishing. Lewis, R. D. (2000). *When cultures collide* (Rev. ed.). London: Nicholas Brealey Publishing.

34. Mellow, C. (1995, August 17). Russia: Making cash from chaos. *Fortune,* pp. 145–146, 148, 150–151.

35. Alston, J. (2007). *Japanese business culture and practices: A guide to twenty-first century Japanese business.* Bloomington, IN: IUniverse. Hodgson, J. D., Sango, Y., & Graham, J. L. (2000). *Doing business with the new Japan.* Oxford, England: Rowman & Littlefield. Ueda, K. (1974). Sixteen ways to avoid saying no in Japan. In J. C. Condon & M. Saito (Eds.), *International encounters with Japan,* pp. 185–192. Tokyo: Simul Press.

36. See Notes 25 and 26.

37. Cohen, D. (2007) *Body language: What you need to know.* London: Sheldon Press. Hossell, K. P. (2003). *Body language.* Oxford, England: Heinemann Library. Knapp, M. L., & Hall, J. A. (2001). *Nonverbal communication in human interaction.* Belmont, CA: Wadsworth. Axtell, R. E. (1997). *Gestures: The do's and taboos of body language around the world.* New York: Wiley.

Chapter 9

Case Notes

Roth, D. (2008, August 18). Driven: Shai Agassi's audacious plan to put electric cars on the road. *Wired Magazine:* 16.09, From the Web at http://www.wired.com/cars/ futuretransport/magazine/16-09/ff_agassi. Ewing, J. (2008, September 1). My other car sounds like a Ferrari. *BusinessWeek,* p. 12. Better Place. (2008). From the Web at http://www.betterplace.com. Agassi, S. (2008, July 26). Tom Friedman's column. *The long tailpipe,* From the Web at http://shaiagassi.typepad.com/.

Chapter Notes

1. Turner, M. E. (2000). *Groups at work: Theory and research.* Mahwah, NJ: Lawrence Erlbaum Associates. Cartwright, D., & Zander, A. (1968). Origins of group dynamics. In D. Cartwright & A. Zander (Eds.), *Group dynamics: Research and theory* (pp. 3–21). New York: Harper & Row.

2. Toothman, J. (2000). *Conducting the experiential group: An introduction to group dynamics.* New York: John Wiley. Bettenhausen, K. L. (1991). Fifty years of groups research: What we have learned and what needs to be addressed. *Journal of Management, 17,* 345–381.

3. Nowak, A., Vallacher, R. R., & Miller, N. E. (2003). Social influence and group dynamics. In T. Millon & M. J. Lerner (Eds.), *Handbook of psychology: Vol. 5, Personality and social psychology* (pp. 383–418). New York: John Wiley & Sons. Forsyth, D. L. (1999). *Group dynamics* (3rd ed.). Belmont, CA: Wadsworth.

4. Hackman, J. R. (1992). Group influences on individuals in organizations. In M. D. Dunnette & L. M. Hough (Eds.), *Handbook of industrial and organizational psychology* (2nd ed.) (Vol. 3, pp. 199–268). Palo Alto, CA: Consulting Psychologists Press.

5. Janicik, G. A., & Bartel, C. A. (2003). Talking about time: Effects of temporal planning and time awareness norms on group coordination and performance. *Group Dynamics, 7,* 122–134. Feldman, D. C. (1984). The development and enforcement of group norms. *Academy of Management Review, 9,* 48–53.

6. Wilson, S. (1978). *Informal groups: An introduction.* Englewood Cliffs, NJ: Prentice Hall.

7. Kanellos, M. (2008, February 11). Latest Silicon Valley status symbol: The plug-in hybid. *CNet News,* From the Web at http://news.cnet.com/8301-11128_3-9869592-54.html.

8. Jackson, L. A., & Grabski, S. V. (1988). Perceptions of fair pay and the gender wage gap. *Journal of Applied Social Psychology, 18,* 606–625.

9. Torrance, E. P. (1954). Some consequences of power differences on decision making in permanent and temporary three-man groups. *Research Studies: Washington State College, 22,* 130–140.

10. Hare, A. P. (1976). *Handbook of small group research* (2nd ed). New York: Free Press.

11. Aronson, E., & Mills, J. (1959). The effects of severity of initiation on liking for a group. *Journal of Abnormal and Social Psychology, 59,* 178–181.

12. Cartwright, D. (1968). The nature of group cohesiveness. In D. Cartwright & A. Zander (Eds.), *Group dynamics: Research and theory* (3rd ed.), (pp. 91–109). New York: Harper & Row.

13. George, J. M., & Bettenhausen, K. (1990). Understanding prosocial behavior, sales performance, and turnover: A group-level analysis in a service context. *Journal of Applied Psychology, 75,* 698–709.

14. Douglas, T. (1983). *Groups: Understanding people gathered together.* New York: Tavistock.

15. Aiello, J. R., & Douthirt, E. A. (2001). Social facilitation from Triplett to electronic performance monitoring. *Group Dynamics, 5,* 163–180.

16. Aiello, J. R., & Svec, C. M. (1993). Computer monitoring of work performance: Extending the social facilitation framework to electronic presence. *Journal of Applied Social Psychology, 23,* 537–548.

17. Steiner, I. D. (1972). *Group processes and productivity.* New York: Academic Press.

18. Shepperd, J. A. (1993). Productivity loss in performance groups: A motivation analysis. *Psychological Bulletin, 113,* 68–81.

19. Latané, B., Williams, K., & Harkins, S. (1979). Many hands make light the work: The causes and consequences of social loafing. *Journal of Personality and Social Psychology, 37,* 822–832.

20. Kravitz, D. A., & Martin, B. (1986). Ringelmann rediscovered: The original article. *Journal of Personality and Social Psychology, 50,* 936–941.

21. Karau, S. J., & Williams, K. D. (1993). Social loafing: A meta-analytic review and theoretical integration. *Journal of Personality and Social Psychology, 65,* 681–706.

22. Earley, P. C. (1993). East meets West meets Mideast: Further explorations of collectivistic and individualistic work groups. *Academy of Management Journal, 36,* 319–348.

23. Nordstrom, R., Lorenzi, P., & Hall, R. V. (1990). A review of public posting of performance feedback in work settings. *Journal of Organizational Behavior Management, 11,* 101–123.

24. Bricker, M. A., Harkins, S. G., & Ostrom, T. M. (1986). Effects of personal involvement: Thought-provoking implications for social loafing. *Journal of Personality and Social Psychology, 51,* 763–769.

25. George, J. M. (1992). Extrinsic and intrinsic origins of perceived social loafing in organizations. *Academy of Management Journal, 35,* 191–202.

26. Albanese, R., & Van Fleet, D. D. (1985). Rational behavior in groups: The free-riding tendency. *Academy of Management Review, 10,* 244–255.

27. Miles, J. A., & Greenberg, J. (1993). Using punishment threats to attenuate social loafing effects among swimmers. *Organizational Behavior and Human Decision Processes, 56,* 246–265.

28. Wellins, R. S., Byham, W. C., & Dixon, G. R. (1994). *Inside teams.* San Francisco: Jossey-Bass.

29. Marks, M. A., Sabella, M. J., Burke, C. S., & Zaccaro, S. J. (2002). The impact of cross-training on team effectiveness. *Journal of Applied Psychology, 87,* 3–13.

30. Barnes, C. M., Hollenbeck, J. R., Wagner, D. T., DeRue, D. S., Nahrang, J. D., & Schwind, K. M. (2008). Harmful help: The costs of backing-up behavior in teams. *Journal of Applied Psychology, 93,* 529–539.

31. Robbins, H., & Finley, M. (2000). *The new why teams don't work.* San Francisco, CA: Barrett-Koehler.

32. Walvoord, A. A. G., Redden, E. R., Elliott, L. R., & Coovert, M. D. (2008). Empowering followers in virtual teams: Guiding principles from theory and practice. *Computers in Human Behavior, 24,* 1884–1906. Duarte, D. L., & Snyder, N. T. (2006). *Mastering virtual teams* (3rd ed.). San Francisco, CA: Jossey-Bass. Hertel, G., Geister, S., & Konradt, U. (2005). Managing virtual teams: A review of current empirical research. *Human Resource Management Review, 15,* 69–95. Willmore, J. (2003). *Managing virtual teams.* London: Spiro Press. Hoefling, T. (2003). *Working virtually: Managing people for successful virtual teams and organizations.* London: Stylus Publications.

33. Sheridan, J. H. (1990, October 15). America's best plants. *Industry Week,* pp. 28–64.

34. Blanchard, K. H., & Bowles, S. M. (2001). *High five: The magic of working together.* New York: William Morrow. Redding, J. C. (2000). *The radical team handbook.* New York: John Wiley & Sons. Fisher, K. (1993). *Leading self-directed work teams.* New York: McGraw-Hill.

35. Lawler, E. E., III., Mohrman, S. A., & Ledford, G. E., Jr. (1992). *Employee involvement and total quality management.* San Francisco: Jossey-Bass.

36. Hackman, J. R. (Ed.) (1990). *Groups that work (and those that don't).* San Francisco, CA: Jossey-Bass.

37. Wellins, R. S., Byham, W. C., & Wilson, J. M. (1991). *Empowered teams.* San Francisco: Jossey-Bass.

38. Blanchard, K. H., & Bowles, S. M. (2001). *High five: The magic of working together.* New York: William Morrow.

39. Pearson, C. A. L. (1992). Autonomous workgroups: An evaluation at an industrial site. *Human Relations, 45,* 905–936.

40. Wall, T. D., Kemp, N. J., Jackson, P. R., & Clegg, C. W. (1986). Outcomes of autonomous workgroups: A long-term field experiment. *Academy of Management Journal, 29,* 280–304.

41. Robbins, H., & Finley, M. (1995). *Why teams don't work.* Princeton, NJ: Peterson's/Pacesetters Books.

42. Stern, A. (1993, July 18). Managing by team is not always as easy as it looks. *New York Times,* p. B14.

43. See Note 42.

44. See Note 42.

45. See Note 42.

46. See Note 42.

47. West, M. A. (2004). *Effective teamwork.* Oxford, England: Blackwell. Maginn, M. D. (1994). *Effective teamwork.* Burr Ridge, IL: Business One Irwin.

48. Salas, E., Edens, E., & Nowers, C. A. (2000). *Improving teamwork in organizations.* Mahwah, NJ: Lawrence Erlbaum Associates.

49. Dumaine, B. (1994, September 5). The trouble with teams. *Fortune,* pp. 86–88, 90, 92 (quote, p. 86).

50. Barner, R. W. (2001). *Team troubleshooter.* Palo Alto, CA: Davies Black. Maruca, R. F. (2000, November). Unit of one. *Fast Company,* pp. 109–140.

51. LeStorti, A. (2003). *When you're asked to do the impossible: Principles of business teamwork and leadership from the U.S. Army's elite rangers.* Guilford, CT: Lyons Press. Caudron, S. (1994, February). Teamwork takes work. *Personnel Journal,* pp. 41–46, 49 (quote, p. 43).

52. Caudron, 1994; see Note 51 (quote, p. 42).

53. Stewart, G. L., & Manz, C. C. (1997). Leadership for self-managing work teams: A typology and integrative model. In. R. P. Vecchio (Ed.), *Leadership: Understanding the dynamics of power and influence in organizations* (pp. 396–410). Notre Dame, IN: University of Notre Dame Press.

54. Sundstrom, E., DeMeuse, K. P., & Futrell, D. (1990). Work teams: Applications and effectiveness. *American Psychologist, 45,* 128–137.

55. Altrec.com. (2008). About Altrec.com, From the Web at http://www.altrec.com/aboutus/index/static.htm. Balf, T. (1999, November). Extreme off-site. *Fast Company,* pp. 384–388, 390, 396, 398.

56. See Note 49 (quote, p. 88).

57. See Note 49 (quote, p. 90).

58. See Note 49 (quote, p. 88).

59. Anonymous. (1994, December). The facts of life for teambuilding. *Human Resources Forum,* p. 3.

Chapter 10

Case Notes

Scanlon, J. (2008, September 8). The shape of a new Coke. *BusinessWeek,* p. 72. Coca-Cola,

From the Web at http://www.coke.com/. Hays, C. (2004). *The real thing: Truth and power at the Coca-Cola Company.* New York: Random House. Prendergast, M. (1994). *For God, country and Coca-Cola: The definitive history of the great American soft drink and the company that makes it.* New York: Basic Books.

Chapter Notes

1. Mintzberg, H. J. (1988). *Mintzberg on management: Inside our strange world of organizations.* New York: Free Press.
2. Allison, S. T., Jordan, A. M. R., & Yeatts, C. E. (1992). A cluster-analytic approach toward identifying the structure and content of human decision making. *Human Relations, 45,* 411–422.
3. Wedley, W. C., & Field, R. H. (1984). A pre-decision support system. *Academy of Management Review, 9,* 696–703.
4. Brett, J. (2001). *Negotiating globally. How to negotiate deals, resolve disputes, and make decisions across cultural boundaries.* San Francisco, CA: Jossey-Bass. Adler, N. J. (1991). *International dimensions of organizational behavior.* Boston, MA: PWS Kent.
5. Roth, K. (1992). Implementing international strategy at the business unit level: The role of managerial decision-making characteristics. *Journal of Management, 18,* 769–789.
6. Greenhalgh, L. (2007). *Managing strategic relationships: The key to business success.* New York: Free Press.
7. Crainer, S. (2007, November). The 75 greatest management decisions ever made. *Management Review,* pp. 16–23.
8. Simon, H. (1977). *The new science of management decisions* (2nd ed.). Upper Saddle River, NJ: Prentice Hall.
9. Tschohl, J. (2006). Empowerment: The key to customer service. *M&T Bank Business Resource Center,* From the Web at http://www.mandtbank.com/smallbusiness/brc_humanresources_empowerment.cfm.
10. Sifonis, J. (2002, November–December). Empowering employees. *IQ Magazine: Cisco Systems,* From the Web at http://www.cisco.com/web/about/ac123/iqmagazine/archives/2001 _2002/empowering_employees.html.
11. Linstone, H. A. (1984). *Multiple perspectives for decision making.* New York: North-Holland.
12. Simon, H. A. (1979). Rational decision making in organizations. *American Economic Review, 69,* 493–513.
13. March, J. G., & Simon, H. A. (1958). *Organizations.* New York: Wiley.
14. Ariely, D. (2008). *Predictably irrational: The hidden forces that shape our decisions.* New York: HarperCollins.
15. Browning, E. B. (1850/1950). *Sonnets from the Portuguese.* New York: Ratchford and Fulton.
16. Mitchell, T. R., & Beach, L. R. (1990). " . . . Do I love thee? Let me count . . . " Toward an understanding of intuitive and automatic decision making. *Organizational Behavior and Human Decision Processes, 47,* 1–20.
17. Beach, L. R., & Mitchell, T. R. (1990). Image theory: A behavioral theory of image making in organizations. In B. Staw and L. L. Cummings (Eds.), *Research in organizational behavior* (Vol. 12, pp. 1–41). Greenwich, CT: JAI Press.
18. Dunegan, K. J. (1995). Image theory: Testing the role of image compatibility in progress decisions. *Organizational Behavior and Human Decision Processes, 62,* 710–786.
19. Dunegan, K. J. (1993). Framing, cognitive modes, and image theory: Toward an understanding of a glass half full. *Journal of Applied Psychology, 78,* 491–503.
20. Gigerenzer, G., & Selten, R. (2001). *Bounded rationality: The adaptive toolbox.* Cambridge, MA: MIT Press.
21. Hurry up and decide (2001, May 14). *BusinessWeek,* p. 16.
22. Brownstein, A. L. (2003). Biased predecision processing. *Psychological Bulletin, 129,* 545–568.
23. Crockett, R. L., & Yang, C. (1999, Aug. 30). Why Motorola should hang up on Iridium. *BusinessWeek,* p. 46.
24. Moon, H., & Conlon, D. E. (2002). From acclaim to blame: Evidence of a person sensitivity decision bias. *Journal of Applied Psychology, 87,* 33–42.
25. Forman, E., H., & Selly, M. A. (2001). *Decision by objectives: How to convince others that you are right.* London: World Scientific.

26. Salas, E., & Klein, G. (2007). *Linking expertise and naturalistic decision making.* Mahwah, NJ: Erlbaum.

27. Hill, G. W. (1982). Group versus individual performance: Are $N + 1$ heads better than one? *Psychological Bulletin, 91,* 517–539.

28. Osborn, A. F. (1957). *Applied imagination.* New York: Scribner's.

29. Bouchard, T. J., Jr., Barsaloux, J., & Drauden, G. (1974). Brainstorming procedure, group size, and sex as determinants of the problem-solving effectiveness of groups and individuals. *Journal of Applied Psychology, 59,* 135–138.

30. Janis, I. L. (2007). *Groupthink.* In R. P. Vecchio (Ed.), *Leadership: Understanding the dynamics of power and influence in organizations* (2nd ed.) (pp. 157–169). Notre Dame, IN: University of Notre Dame Press. Janis, I. L. (1982). *Groupthink: Psychological studies of policy decisions and fiascoes* (2nd ed.). Boston, MA: Houghton Mifflin.

31. Morehead, G., Ference, R., & Neck, C. P. (1991). Group decision fiascoes continue: Space shuttle *Challenger* and a revised groupthink framework. *Human Relations, 44,* 539–550.

32. Cabbage, M., & Harwood, W. (2004). *Comm check: The final flight of Shuttle Columbia.* New York: Free Press.

33. Kray, L. J., & Galinsky, A. D. (2003). The debiasing effect of counterfactual mind-sets: Increasing the search for disconfirmatory information in group decisions. *Organizational Behavior and Human Decision Processes, 91,* 69–81.

34. John McManus. (2009, February 16). Radical action needed, not "groupthink." Irishtimes. From the Web at: http://www.irishtimes.com/newspaper/finance/2009/0216/1233867938577.html

35. Schweiger, D. M., Sandberg, W. R., & Ragan, J. W. (1986). Group approaches for improving strategic decision making: A comparative analysis of dialectical inquiry, devil's advocacy, and consensus. *Academy of Management Journal, 29,* 51–71.

36. See Note 33.

37. Cosier, R. A., & Schwenk, C. R. (1990). Agreement and thinking alike: Ingredients for poor decisions. *Academy of Management Executive, 4,* 610–74.

38. Sloan, A. P., Jr. (1964). *My years with General Motors.* New York: Doubleday.

39. Nutt, P. C. (2002). *Why decisions fail.* San Francisco, CA: Berrett-Koehler.

40. Bäck-Pettersson, S., Hermansson, E., Sernert, N., & Björkelund, C. (2008). Research priorities in nursing: A Delphi study among Swedish nurses. *Journal of Clinical Nursing, 17,* 2517–2518. Dalkey, N. (1969). *The Delphi method: An experimental study of group decisions.* Santa Monica, CA: RAND Corporation.

41. Harmon, J., Schneer, J. A., & Hoffman, L. R. (1995). Electronic meetings and established decision groups: Audioconferencing effects on performance and structural stability. *Organizational Behavior and Human Decision Processes, 61,* 138–147.

42. Alge, B. J., Wiethoff, C., & Klein, H. J. (2003). When does the medium matter? Knowledge-building experiences and opportunities in decision-making teams. *Organizational Behavior and Human Decision Processes, 91,* 26–37.

43. Huang, W. W., Wei, K-K., Watson, R. T., & Tan, B. C. Y. (2003). Supporting virtual team-building with a GSS: An empirical investigation. *Decision Support Systems, 34,* 359–367. Lam, S. S. K., & Shaubroeck, J. (2000). Improving group decisions by better pooling information: A comparative advantage of group decision support systems. *Journal of Applied Psychology, 85,* 564–573.

Chapter 11

Case Notes

AmerisourceBergen. (2008). Corporate profile. From the Web at http://www.amerisourcebergen.com/investor/phoenix.zhtml?c=61181&p=irol-irhome. McConon, A. (2008, October 6). Lessons from a skinflint CEO. *BusinessWeek,* pp. 54–55. CEO portrait: David Yost. (2000, April 28). *Philadelphia Business Journal,* p. 16. Moukheiber, Z. (2001, October 29). Easy pill to swallow. *Forbes,* p. 74. Teosoriero, H. W. (2003, October 7). Big drug wholesaler fights charges of fakes, price fixing. *Wall Street Journal,* p. 87.

Chapter Notes

1. AmerisourceBergen. (2008). Fortune 500. From the Web at http://money.cnn.com/magazines/fortune/fortune500/2007/snapshots/95.html.

2. Bass, B. M., & Bass, R. (2008). *The Bass handbook of leadership: Theory, research, and managerial applications* (4th ed.). New York: Simon & Schuster.

3. Yukl, G. (2009). *Leadership in organizations* (7th ed.). Upper Saddle River, NJ: Prentice Hall.

4. Weathersby, G. B. (1999, March). Leadership vs. management. *Management Review*, p. 5.

5. See Note 3.

6. Yukl, G. (2009). Use power effectively. In E. A. Locke (Ed.), *The Blackwell handbook of principles of organizational behavior* (2nd ed.). (pp. 241–256). Malden, MA: Blackwell.

7. Kirkpatrick, S. A., & Locke, E. A. (1991). Leadership: Do traits matter? *Academy of Management Executive, 5,* 41–60.

8. See Note 7 (quote, p. 58).

9. Chan, K-Y., & Drasgow, F. (2001). Toward a theory of individual differences and leadership: Understanding the motivation to lead. *Journal of Applied Psychology, 86,* 481–498.

10. Zaccaro, S. J., Foti, R. J., & Kenny, D. A. (1991). Self-monitoring and trait-based variance in leadership: An investigation of leader flexibility across multiple group situations. *Journal of Applied Psychology, 76,* 308–315.

11. Avolio, B. J., & Walumbwa, F. O. (2006). Authentic leadership: Moving HR leaders to a higher level. In J. Martoccio (Ed.), *Research in personnel and human resources management* (Vol. 25, pp. 273–304). San Diego, CA: Elsevier.

12. Chemers, M. M. (2001). Efficacy and effectiveness: Integrating models of leadership and intelligence. In R. E. Riggio & S. E. Murphy (Eds.), *Multiple intelligences and leadership* (pp. 139–160). Mahwah, NJ: Erlbaum.

13. Lord, R. G., DeVader, C. L., & Alliger, G. M. (1986). A meta-analysis of the relation between personality traits and leadership perceptions: An application of validity generalization procedures. *Journal of Applied Psychology, 61,* 402–410.

14. Rubin, R. S., Bartels, L, L, & Bommer, W. J. (2002). Are leaders smarter or do they just seem that way? Exploring perceived intellectual competence and leadership emergence. *Social Behavior and Personality, 30,* 105–118.

15. Goleman, D., Boyzatis, R., & McKee, A. (2002). *Primal leadership: Realizing the power of emotional intelligence.* Boston, MA: Harvard Business School. George, J. M. (2000). Emotions and leadership: The role of emotional intelligence. *Human Relations, 53,* 1027–1055. Aditya, R., & House, R. J. (2001). Interpersonal acumen and leadership across cultures: Pointers from the GLOBE study. In R. E. Riggio & S. E. Murphy (Eds.), *Multiple intelligences and leadership* (pp. 215–240). Mahwah, NJ: Erlbaum. Caurso, D. R., Mayer, J. D., & Salovey, P. (2001). Emotional intelligence and emotional leadership. In R. E. Riggio & S. E. Murphy (Eds.), *Multiple intelligences and leadership* (pp. 55–74). Mahwah, NJ: Erlbaum.

16. Offerman, L. R., & Phan, L. U. (2001). Culturally intelligent leadership for a diverse world. In R. E. Riggio & S. E. Murphy (Eds.), *Multiple intelligences and leadership* (pp. 187–214). Mahwah, NJ: Erlbaum.

17. Anonymous. (1999, October 11). Molding global leaders. *Fortune*, p. 270.

18. Stein, N. (2000, October 2). Global most admired companies: Measuring people power. *Fortune*, pp. 273–288.

19. Bass, B. M. (1998). *Transformational leadership: Industry, military, and educational impact.* Mahwah, NJ: Erlbaum.

20. Turner, N., Barling, J., Epitropaki, O., Butcher, V., & Milner, C. (2002). Transformational leadership and moral reasoning. *Journal of Applied Psychology, 87,* 304–311.

21. Colvin, G. (1999, November 22). The ultimate manager. *Fortune*, pp. 185–187. Slater, R. (1999). *Jack Welch and the GE way.* New York: McGraw-Hill.

22. Tichy, N. M. (1993). *Control your destiny or someone else will.* New York: Doubleday Currency.

23. America's Most Admired Companies. (2008, March 3). *Fortune.* From the Web at http://money.cnn.com/magazines/fortune/mostadmired/2008/index.html

24. Welch, J., & Welch, S. (2005). *Winning.* New York: Collins Business. Krames, J. A. (2005). *Jack Welch and the 4 E's of Leadership.* New York: McGraw Hill.

25. Judge, T. A., & Bono, J. E. (2000). Five-factor model of personality and transformational leadership. *Journal of Applied Psychology, 85,* 751–765.

26. Koh, W. L., Steers, R. M. & Terborg, J. R. (1995). The effects of transformational leadership on teacher attitudes and student performance in Singapore. *Journal of Organizational Behavior, 16,* 319–333.

27. Hater, J. J., & Bass, B. M. (1988). Superiors' evaluations and subordinates' perceptions of transformational and trans-actional leadership. *Journal of Applied Psychology, 73,* 695–702.

28. Hauser, M., & House, R. J. (2000). Lead through vision and values. In E. A. Locke (Ed.), *The Blackwell handbook of principles of organizational behavior* (pp. 257–273). Malden, MA: Blackwell.

29. Bass, B. M., Avolio, B. J., Jung, D. I., & Berson, Y. (2003). Predicting unit performance by assessing transformational and transactional leadership. *Journal of Applied Psychology, 88,* 207–218.

30. Neff, T. J., & Citrin, J. W. (1999). *Lessons from the top.* New York: Doubleday.

31. Blake, R. R., & Mouton, J. S. (1982). Management by grid principles or situationalism: Which? *Group and Organization Studies, 7,* 207–210. Blake, R. R., & Mouton, J. S. (1969). *Building a dynamic corporation through grid organizational development.* Reading, MA: Addison-Wesley. Blake, R. R., & McCanse, A. A. (1991). *Leadership dilemmas—grid solutions.* Houston, TX: Gulf Publishing. Copyright 1991 by Scientific Methods, Inc. Reproduced by permission of the owners.

32. Grid: The Power to Change. (2008). *Grid International, Inc.* From the Web at http://www.gridinternational.com/index.html

33. House, R. J. (1996). Path-goal theory of leadership: Lessons, legacy, and a reformulated theory. *Leadership Quarterly, 7,* 323–352.

34. Whitworth, L., House, H., Sandahl, P., & Kimsey-House, H. (1998). *Co-active coaching:*

New skills for coaching people toward success in work and life. Palo Alto, CA: Davies-Black.

35. Holtz, L. (1998). *Winning every day.* New York: Harper Business. Wolfe, R. (1998). *The Packer way.* New York: St. Martin's.

36. Bradley, Bill. (1998). *Values of the game.* New York: Artisan.

37. Hersey, P., & Blanchard, K. H. (1988). *Management of organizational behavior.* Upper Saddle River, NJ: Prentice Hall.

38. Bennis, W., & Heenan, D. A. (1999). *Co-leaders: The power of great partnerships.* New York: Wiley.

39. Troiano, P. (1999, February). Sharing the throne. *Management Review,* pp. 39–43.

40. Chmura, M. (2004, March 12). Family biz Trend: Co-CEOs. *Babson College.* From the Web at http://www3.babson.edu/Newsroom/Releases/coceos.cfm

41. Co-CEOs now running software giant SAP. (2008, April 2). *Philadelphia Business Journal.* From the Web at http://www.bizjournals.com/gen/company.html?gcode=2019C51A36E947B68D47F58EE801E1B8

42. Sirower, M. (2000). *The synergy trap: How companies lose the acquisition game.* New York: Free Press.

43. Sheard, A. G., & Kakabadse, A. P. (2001). Key roles of the leadership landscape. *Journal of Managerial Psychology, 17,* 129–144. Zenger, J. H., Musselwhite, E., Hurson, K., & Perrin, C. (1994). *Leading teams: Mastering the new role.* Homewood, IL: Business One Irwin.

44. Labarre, P. (1999, June). Unit of one: Leaders.com. *Fast Company,* pp. 95–98, 100, 102, 104, 108, 110, 112.

45. Lashinsky, A. (2003, September 1). Meg and the machine. *Fortune,* pp. 68–72, 76, 78.

46. See Note 44 (quote, p. 96). Quindlen, R. (2000). *Confessions of a venture capitalist.* New York: Warner Business.

47. See Note 44 (quote, p. 100).

48. See Note 44 (quote, p. 104).

49. Fulmer, R. M. & Bleak, J. L. (2007). *The leadership advantage: How the best companies are developing their talent to pave the way for future success.* New York: AMACOM.

50. Pernick, R. (2001). Creating a leadership development program: Nine essential tasks. *Public Personnel Management, 30,* 429–444.

51. Day, D. V. (2001). Leadership development: A review in context. *Leadership Quarterly, 11,* 581–613.

52. Atwater, L. E., Ostroff, C., Yammarino, F. J., & Fleenor, J. W. (1998). Self–other agreement: Does it really matter? *Personnel Psychology, 51,* 577–598.

53. London, M., & Smither, J. W. (1995). Can multi-source feedback change perceptions of goal accomplishments, self-evaluations, and performance related outcomes? Theory-based applications and directions for research. *Personnel Psychology, 48,* 803–839.

54. Walker, A. G., & Smither, J. W. (1999). A five-year study of upward feedback: What managers do with their results matters. *Personnel Psychology, 52,* 393–423.

55. O'Neill, M. B. A. (2007). *Executive coaching with backbone and heart* (2nd ed.). San Francisco, CA: Jossey-Bass.

56. Chapman, T., Best, B., & Van Casteren, P. (2003). *Executive coaching: Exploding the myths.* New York: Palgrave Macmillan. Olivero, G., Bane, D. K., & Kopellman, R. E. (1997). Executive coaching as a transfer of training tool: Effects of productivity in a public agency. *Public Personnel Management, 26,* 461–469.

57. Brobank, A., & McGill, I. (2003). *The action learning handbook.* London: Kogan Page. Marquardt, M. J., & Revans, R. (1999). *Action learning in action.* Palo Alto, CA: Davies-Black.

58. Edmonstone, J. (2003). *The action learner's toolkit.* Hampshire, England: Gower Publishing. Pedler, M. (1997). Interpreting action learning. In J. Burgoyne & M. Reynolds (Eds.), *Management learning: Integrating perspectives in theory and practice* (pp. 248–264). London: Sage.

59. Dotlich, D. L., & Noel, J. L. (1998). *Action learning: How the world's top companies are recreating their leaders and themselves.* San Francisco, CA: Jossey-Bass.

60. See Note 59.

Chapter 12

Case Notes

Aston, A. (2008, September 8). Growth galore, but profits are zip. *BusinessWeek,* p. 62. Frankel, A. (2008, April 15). Zipcar drives toward the future. *MSNBC.* From the Web at http://www.msnbc.msn.com/id/23747341/. Block, D. (2008, April 22). Green car service zipping into the Bronx. *New York Daily News,* p. 22.

Chapter Notes

1. Schneider, B. (1990). *Organizational climate and culture.* San Francisco, CA: Jossey-Bass.

2. Schein, E. H. (1999). *The corporate culture survival guide.* San Francisco, CA: Jossey-Bass. Schein, E. H. (1985). *Organizational culture and leadership.* San Francisco, CA: Jossey-Bass.

3. Anonymous. (1999, April). Toxic shock? *Fast Company,* p. 38.

4. Webber, A. M. (1998, November). Danger: Toxic company. *Fast Company,* pp. 152–159.

5. Cameron, K. S., & Quinn, R. E. (1999). *Diagnosing and changing organizational culture: Based on the competing values framework.* Reading, MA: Addison-Wesley. Berrio, A. A. (2003). Organizational culture assessment using the competing values framework: A profile of Ohio State University extension. *Journal of Extension, 41*(2). From the Web at www.joe.org/joe/2003april/a3.shtml.

6. Martin, J., Sitkin, S. B., & Boehm, M. (1985). Founders and the elusiveness of a cultural legacy. In P. J. Frost, L. F. Moore, M. R. Louis, C. C. Lundberg, & J. Martin (Eds.), *Organizational culture* (pp. 99–124). Beverly Hills, CA: Sage.

7. Martin, J. (2001). *Organizational culture: Mapping the terrain.* Newbury Park, CA: Sage. Martin, J. (1982). Stories and scripts in organizational settings. In A. Hastorf & A. Isen (Eds.), *Cognitive social psychology* (pp. 255–306). New York: Elsevier.

8. Ransdell, E. (2000, January–February). The Nike story? Just tell it. *Fast Company,* pp. 44, 46.

9. Neuhauser, P. C. (1993). *Corporate legends and lore: The power of storytelling as a management tool.* New York: McGraw-Hill (quote, p. 63).

10. Mars. (2008). The 5 principles of Mars. From the Web at http://www.mars.com/global/Who+We+Are/The+5+Principles.htm. Brenner, J. G. (1999). *The emperors of chocolate: Inside the secret world of Hershey and Mars.* New York: Random House.

11. IDEO. (2008). Culture: Looking in. From the Web at http://www.ideo.com/culture/.

12. Crews, B. (2008, January 3). Amazing customer service at Saks Fifth Avenue. *About.com.* From the Web at http://collectibles.about.com/b/2008/01/03/amazing-customer-service-saks-fifth-avenue.htm

13. Weiner, Y. (1988). Forms of value systems: A focus on organizational effectiveness and cultural change and maintenance. *Academy of Management Review, 13,* 534–545.

14. McFarlin, D. (2002, October 11). Strong culture can be "double-edged sword." *Dayton Business Journal.* From the Web at http://www.bizjournals.com/dayton/stories/2002/10/14/smallb3.html.

15. See Note 13.

16. Walter, G. A. (1985). Culture collisions in mergers and acquisitions. In P. J. Frost, L. F. Moore, M. R. Louis, C. C. Lundberg, & J. Martin (Eds.), *Organizational culture* (pp. 301–314). Beverly Hills, CA: Sage.

17. Klein, A. (2003). *Stealing time.* New York: Simon & Schuster. Vlasic, B., & Stertz, B. A. (2001). *Taken for a ride: How Daimler-Benz drove off with Chrysler.* New York: Harper Business. Naughton, K. (2000, December 11). A mess of a merger. *Newsweek,* pp. 54–57. Elkind, P. (1998, November 9). A merger made in hell. *Fortune,* pp. 134–138, 140, 142, 144, 146, 149, 150. Burrough, B., & Helyar, J. (1990). *Barbarians at the gate.* New York: Harper Collins. Muller, J. (1999, November 29). Lessons from a casualty of the culture wars. *BusinessWeek,* p. 198. Muller, J. (1999, November 15). The one-year itch at DaimlerChrysler. *BusinessWeek,* p. 42.

18. Ewing, J. (2007, January 29). Siemens' culture clash. *BusinessWeek.* From the Web at http://www.businessweek.com/magazine/content/07_05/b4019058.htm.

19. Alberto-Culver: Our story. From the Web at http://www.alberto.com/ACCorpWeb/Pages/OurStory/OurStory.html#.

20. Alberto Culver Co. (2008, October 1). Press release: Alberto Culver announces the completion of Noxzema acquisition. From the Web at http://www.alberto.com/investing/index.aspx

21. Bernick, C. L. (2001). When your culture needs a makeover. *Harvard Business Review, 79*(6), 53–56, 58, 60–61.

22. Amabile, T. M. (1988). A model of creativity and innovation in organizations. In B. M. Staw & L. L. Cummings (Eds.), *Research in organizational behavior* (Vol. 10, pp. 123–167). Greenwich, CT: JAI Press.

23. McGuire, W. F. (1997). Creative hypothesis generating in psychology: Some useful heuristics. *Annual review of psychology* (Vol. 48, pp. 211–245). Palo Alto, CA: Annual Reviews. Spector, B. I. (1995). Creativity heuristics for impasse resolution: Reframing intractable negotiations. *ANNALS of the American Academy of Political and Social Science, 542*(1). 81–99. Open Courseware. (2008). Heuristics for creative thinking. From the Web at http://philosophy.hku.hk/think/creative/heuristics.php

24. Amabile, T. M. (2000). Stimulate creativity by fueling passion. In E. A. Locke (Ed). *The Blackwell handbook of principles of organizational behavior* (pp. 331–341). Oxford, England: Blackwell.

25. Kabanoff, B., & Rossiter, J. R. (1994). Recent developments in applied creativity. In C. Cooper & I. T. Robertson (Eds.), *International review of industrial and organizational psychology* (Vol. 9, pp. 283–324). London: Wiley.

26. Michalko, M. (1998, May). Thinking like a genius: Eight strategies used by the super-creative, from Aristotle and Einstein and Edison. *The Futurist,* pp. 21–25.

27. Kabanoff, B., & Bottiger, P. (1991). Effectiveness of creativity training and its reaction to selected personality factors. *Journal of Organizational Behavior, 12,* 235–248.

28. Muoio, A. (2000, January–February). Idea summit. *Fast Company,* pp. 151–156, 160, 162, 164 (quote, p. 152).
29. Gogoi, P. (2003). Thinking outside the cereal box. *BusinessWeek,* pp. 74–75.
30. BrightHouse. (2008). Who we are: Milestones. From the Web at http://www.thinkbrighthouse.com/.
31. Sittenfeld, C. (1999, July–August). This old house is a home for new ideas. *Fast Company,* pp. 58, 60.
32. Oldham, G. R., & Cummings, A. (1996). Employee creativity: Personal and contextual factors at work. *Academy of Management Journal, 39,* 607–634.
33. Zhou, J. (2003). When the presence of creative coworkers is related to creativity: The role of supervisor close monitoring, developmental feedback, and creative personality. *Journal of Applied Psychology, 88,* 413–422.
34. Dahle, C. (2000, January–February). Mind games. *Fast Company,* pp. 169–173, 176, 178–179.
35. Sutton, R. I., & Hargadon, A. (1996). Brainstorming groups in context: Effectiveness in a product design firm. *Administrative Science Quarterly, 41,* 685–718. (quote, p. 702).
36. Semicondoctor R&D spending growth to show 8% rise in 2008, IC Insight forecasts. (2008). *Electronics Design Strategy News.* From the Web at http://www.edn.com/index.asp?layout=article&articleid=CA6577202.
37. Vance, A. (2008, October 6). A.M.D. to split into two operations. *New York Times.* From the Web at http://www.nytimes.com/2008/10/07/technology/07chip.html?_r=1&ref=technology&oref=slogin.
38. See Note 37.
39. See Note 31.
40. Birkinshaw, J., Hamel, G, & Mol, M. J. (2008), Management innovation. *Academy of Management Review, 33,* 825–845.
41. See Note 40.
42. Michalko, M. (1991). *Thinkertoys.* Berkeley, CA: Ten Speed Press.
43. See Note 42.

Chapter 13

Case Notes

Hubble Site. (2007, August 22). Hubble teams with Google to bring the cosmos down to earth. *Press Release* from HubbleSite.org from the Web at http://hubblesite.org/newscenter/archive/releases/2007/22/full/. NASA. (2008, June 4). NASA and Google announce lease at Ames Research Center. *Press Release* from Ames Research Center. From the Web at http://www.nasa.gov/centers/ames/news/releases/2008/08_51AR.html.

Chapter Notes

1. Daft, R. L. (2003). *Essentials of organization theory and design* (8th ed.). Cincinnati, OH: South-Western.
2. Koroneos, G. (2008, October 8). Pfizer refocuses marketing division with new restructuring strategy. *Pharmexec.com.* From the Web at http://pharmexec.findpharma.com/pharmexec/News/Pfizer-Refocuses-Marketing-Division-with-New-Restr/ArticleStandard/Article/detail/556977?contextCategoryId=43753.
3. Kaufman, L. H. (2000). Centralized or decentralized management. *Railway Age, 201*(8), 47–52.
4. Knowledge@Wharton. (2008, June 25). Johnson & Johnson CEO William Weldon: Leadership in a decentralized company. From the Web at http://knowledge.wharton.upenn.edu/article.cfm;jsessionid=9a30400ae758397d28b2?articleid=2003.
5. Anders, G. (2003). *Perfect enough: Carly Fiorina and the reinvention of Hewlett-Packard.* Middlesex, England: Portfolio.
6. Hewlett Packard: About us. (2008). From the Web at http://www.hp.com/hpinfo/abouthp.
7. Hymowitz, C. (2003, August 12). Managers suddenly have to answer to a crowd of bosses. *Wall Street Journal,* p. B1.
8. Gottleib, M. R. (2007). *The matrix organization reloaded: Adventures in team and project management.* New York: Praeger.
9. Tushman, M. L., Nadler, N. B., & Nadler, D. A. (1997). *Competing by design: The power of*

organizational architecture. New York: Oxford University Press.

10. Harrigan, K. R. (2003). *Vertical integration, outsourcing, and corporate strategy.* Frederick, MD: Beard Group.

11. Pearce, D. (2005). *E E. Dickinson company records.* Storrs, CT: University of Connecticut.

12. Stewart, T. A. (1992, May 18). The search for the organization of tomorrow. *Fortune,* pp. 93–98 (quote p. 93).

13. Ostroff, F. (1999). *The horizontal organization.* New York: Oxford University Press.

14. Byrne, J. A. (1993, December 20). The horizontal corporation. *BusinessWeek,* pp. 76–81 (quote, p. 76).

15. Bossidy, L., & Charan, R. (2002). *Execution: The discipline of getting things done.* New York: Crown (quote, p. 44).

16. GE: Just your average everyday $60 billion family grocery store. (1994, May 2). *Industry Week,* pp. 13–18.

17. Ashkenas, R., Ulrich, D., Jick, T., & Kerr, S. (1998). *The boundaryless organization: Breaking the chains of organizational structure.* San Francisco, CA: Jossey-Bass.

18. Dees, G. D., Rasheed, A. M. A., McLaughlin, K. J., & Priem, R. L. (1995). The new corporate architecture. *Academy of Management Executive, 9,* 7–18.

19. See Note 13.

20. Tully, S. (1993, February 3). The modular corporation. *Fortune,* pp. 106–108, 110.

21. Byrne, J. (1993, February 8). The virtual corporation. *BusinessWeek,* pp. 99–103.

22. Sherman, S. (1992, September 21). Are strategic alliances working? *Fortune,* pp. 77–78 (quote, p. 78).

23. Nathan, R. (1998, July–August). NEC organizing for creativity, nimbleness. *Research Technology Management,* pp. 4–6.

24. Moore, J. F. (1998, Winter). The rise of a new corporate form. *Washington Quarterly,* pp. 167–181.

25. See Note 24.

26. Nooteboom, B. (2004). *Inter-firm collaboration, networks and strategy: An integrated approach.* London: Routeledge

27. Chesborough, H. W., & Teece, D. J. (1996, January–February). When is virtual virtuous? Organizing for innovation. *Harvard Business Review, 96,* 65–73.

28. Chang, S-J. (2003). *Financial crisis and transformation of Korean business groups: The rise and fall of chaebols.* London: Cambridge University Press.

29. Lubove, S. (1992, December 7). How to grow big yet stay small. *Forbes,* pp. 64–66.

30. Kanter, R. M. (1994, July–August). Collaborative advantage: The art of alliances. *Harvard Business Review,* pp. 96–108.

31. See Note 30.

32. Harrigan, K. R. (2003). *Joint ventures, alliances, and corporate strategy.* Frederick, MD: Beard Group.

33. Hansen, M. T., Chesbrough, H. W., Nohria, N., & Sull, D. N. (2000, September–October). Networked incubators: Hothouses of new economy. *Harvard Business Review,* pp. 74–84.

34. Fletcher, N. (1988, December 10). U.S., China form joint venture to manufacture helicopters. *Journal of Commerce,* p. 58.

35. Bransi, B. (1987, January 3). South Korea's carmakers count their blessings. *The Economist,* p. 45.

36. Newman, W. H. (1992). Focused joint ventures in transforming economies. *Academy of Management Executive, 6,* 67–75.

37. Reuer, J. J. (2003). *Strategic alliances: Theory and evidence.* New York: Oxford University Press.

38. Weisul, K. (2001, March 6). Minority mergers. *BusinessWeek,* Frontier section, pp. F14–F19.

Chapter 14

Case Notes

Lee, S. (2008, June 2). UPDATE 1-Asustek sees sales of low-cost Eee PC doubling in 2009. Reuters *Business and Finance.* From the Web at http://www.reuters.com/article/marketsNews/idUSTP15771220080602. Einhorn, B. (2008, June 15). The mini-laptop changing the game. *BusinessWeek,* p. 32. Asus unveils ultra-low-cost Linux laptop. (2007, June 6). From the Web at http://www.LinuxDevices.com. Chen, S. J. (2007, June 7). $199 laptop is no child's play. *Forbes,* p. 23. Asus. (2007, June 8).

Enter the "e" Era with ASUS Eee PC. Press release, From the Web at http://www.asus.com/press.

Chapter Notes

1. Sherman, S. (1993, December 13). How will we live with the tumult? *Fortune,* pp. 123–125.

2. Chaize, J. (2000). *Quantum leap: Tools for managing companies in the new economy.* New York: St. Martin's Press.

3. Neff, R. (1987, April 20). Getting man and machine to live happily ever after. *BusinessWeek,* pp. 61–63.

4. Society for Human Resource Management. (2008). *2007 workplace demographic trends survey.* Alexandria, VA: Author.

5. Stewart, T. A. (1993, December 13). Welcome to the revolution. *Fortune,* pp. 66–68, 70, 72, 76, 78.

6. Kiley, D. (2000, December 13). GM waves goodbye to its Oldsmobile brand. *USA Today,* pp. 1B, 3B.

7. Freeland, R. F. (2001). *The struggle for control of the modern corporation: Organizational change at General Motors.* New York: Cambridge University Press.

8. U.S. Securities and Exchange Commission. (2008). Frequently requested FOIA document: Budget history—BA vs. actual obligations. From the Web at http://www.sec.gov/foia/docs/budgetact.htm.

9. Shakespeare, C. (2008). Sarbanes-Oxley Act of 2002 five years on: What have we learned? *Journal of Business & Technology Law, 22,* 333–345. Kohn, S. M., Kohn, M. D., & Colapinto, D. K. (2004). *Whistleblower law: A guide to legal protections for corporate employees.* New York: Praeger.

10. Guillen, M. F. (2001). *The limits of convergence: Globalization and organizational change in Argentina, South Korea, and Spain.* Princeton, NJ: Princeton University Press.

11. Pitts, A. C. (2003). *Strategic planning for sustainability and profit.* Burlington, MA: Butterworth-Heinemann. Dudik, E. M. (2000). *Strategic renaissance: New thinking and innovative tools to create great corporate strategies using insights from history and science.* New York: AMACOM.

12. Meade, R. (1998). *International management* (2nd ed.). Malden, MA: Blackwell.

13. McCarty, M. (1990, October 30). PepsiCo to consolidate its restaurants, combining U.S. and foreign operations. *Wall Street Journal,* p. A4.

14. About Yum! Brands. (2008). Yum! Brands. From the Web at http://www.yum.com/about/default.asp.

15. See Note 4.

16. Gupta, A. (2008). *Outsourcing and offshoring of professional services: Business optimization in a global economy.* Hershey, PA: IGI Global.

17. Christensen, H. K. (1994). Corporate strategy: Managing a set of businesses. In I. L. Flahey & R. M. Randall (Eds.), *The portable MBA in strategy* (pp. 53–83). New York: Wiley.

18. Markides, C. (1997, Spring). Strategic innovation. *Sloan Management Review,* pp. 9–23.

19. Collis, D. J., & Montgomery, C. A. (1995, July–August). Competing on resources: Strategy in the 1990s. *Harvard Business Review, 73,* 118–128.

20. Marci, D. M., Tagliaventi, M. R., & Fabiola, B. (2002). A grounded theory for resistance to change in small organizations. *Journal of Organizational Change Management, 15,* 292–310. Duck, J. D. (2001). *The change monster: The human forces that fuel or foil corporate transformation and change.* New York: Crown.

21. Nadler, D. A. (1987). The effective management of organizational change. In J. W. Lorsch (Ed.), *Handbook of organizational behavior* (pp. 358–369). Upper Saddle River, NJ: Prentice Hall.

22. Katz, D., & Kahn, R. L. (1978). *The social psychology of organizations* (2nd ed.). New York: Wiley.

23. Wanberg, C., & Banas, J. T. (2000). Predictors and outcomes of openness to change in a reorganizing workplace. *Journal of Applied Psychology, 85,* 132–142.

24. Pascale, R., Millemann, M., & Gioja, L. (1997, November–December). Changing the way we change. *Harvard Business Review,* pp. 127–139. Nadler, D. A. (1987). The effective management of organizational change. In J. W. Lorsch (Ed.), *Handbook of organizational behavior* (pp. 358–369). Upper Saddle River, NJ: Prentice Hall.

25. Dutton, J. E., Ashford, S. J., O'Neill, R. M., & Lawrence, K. A. (2001). Moves that matter:

Issue selling and organizational change. *Academy of Management Journal, 44,* 716–736.

26. Huey, J. (1993, April 5). Managing in the midst of chaos. *Fortune,* pp. 38–41, 44, 46, 48.

27. Gard, G., Lindstroem, K., & Dallner, M. (2003). Towards a learning organization: The introduction of a client-centered team-based organization in administrative surveying work. *Applied Ergonomics, 34,* 97–105. Senge, P. M. (1990). *The fifth discipline.* New York: Doubleday.

28. Austin, J. R., & Bartunek, J. M. (2003). Theories and practices of organizational development. In W. C. Borman, D. R. Ilgen, & R. J. Klimoski (Eds.), *Handbook of psychology: Industrial and organizational psychology* (Vol. 12, pp. 309–332). New York: John Wiley & Sons.

29. Harigopal, K. (2001). *Management of organizational change: Leveraging transformation.* Newbury Park, CA: Sage.

30. Joens, I. (2000). Supervisors as moderators of survey feedback and change processes in teams. In M. Vartiainen & F. Avallone (Eds.), *Innovative theories, tools, and practices in work and organizational psychology* (pp. 155–171). Cambridge, MA: Hogrefe & Huber.

31. Ettorre, B. (1995, October). Managing competitive intelligence. *Management Review,* pp. 15–19.

32. Teo, T. S. H., & Choo, W. Y. (2001). Assessing the impact of using the Internet for competitive intelligence. *Information & Management, 39,* 67–83.

33. See Note 32.

34. Subramanian, R., & Ishak, S. T. (1998). Computer analysis practices of U.S. companies: An empirical investigation. *Management International Review, 38,* 7–24.

35. Drucker, P. F. (1976). What results should you expect? A user's guide to MBO. *Public Administration Review, 36,* 12–19.

36. Rodgers, R., & Hunter, J. E. (1991). Impact of management by objectives on organization productivity. *Journal of Applied Psychology, 76,* 322–336.

37. Cooperrider, D. L., Stavros, J. M., & Whitney, D. K. (2003). *The appreciative inquiry handbook.* San Francisco, CA: Berrett-Koehler. Watkins, J. M., & Mohr, B. J. (2001). *Appreciative inquiry: Change at the speed of imagination.* New York: John Wiley & Sons.

38. Ludema, J. D., Whitney, D., Bohr, B. J., & Griffin, T. J. (2003). *The appreciative inquiry summit: A practitioner's guide for leading large-group change.* San Francisco, CA: Berrett-Koehler. Whitney, D., & Sachau, C. (1998, Spring). Appreciative inquiry: An innovative process for organization change. *Employment Relations Today, 25,* pp. 11–21.

39. Bushe, G. R., & Coetzer, G. (1995). Appreciative inquiry as a team-developed intervention: A controlled experiment. *Journal of Applied Behavioral Science, 31,* 13–30.

40. Porras, J. I., & Robertson, P. J. (1992). Organization development: Theory, practice, and research. In M. D. Dunnette & L. Hough (Eds.), *Handbook of industrial and organizational psychology* (2nd ed., Vol. 3, pp. 719–822). Palo Alto, CA: Consulting Psychologists Press.

41. Jaeger, A. M. (1986). Organizational development and national culture: Where's the fit? *Academy of Management Review, 11,* 178–190.

42. Kedia, B. L., & Bhagat, R. S. (1998). Cultural constraints on transfer of technology across nations: Implications for research in international and comparative management. *Academy of Management Review, 13,* 559–571.

43. Trepo, G. (1973, Autumn). Management style *a la française. European Business, 39,* 71–79.

44. Blunt, P. (91988). Cultural consequences for organization change in a Southeast Asian state: Brunei. *Academy of Management Executive, 2,* 235–240.

45. Patching, K. (2001). *Management and organization development: Beyond arrows, boxes and circles.* New York: Macmillan. White, L. P., & Wotten, K. C. (1983). Ethical dilemmas in various stages of organizational development. *Academy of Management Review, 8,* 690–697.

Company Index

Page numbers followed by an *f* indicate figure.
Page numbers followed by a *t* indicate table.

Name Index

Page numbers followed by an *f* indicate figure.
Page numbers followed by a *t* indicate table.

Subject Index

Page numbers followed by an *f* indicate figure.
Page numbers followed by a *t* indicate table.